CADOGANguides

NORTHERN
SPAIN

*'In any bar or café you could see an old sailor delicately
sipping his camomile tea next to a young mother, baby under
her arm, stopping in for a beer break during her shopping;
walking into any of them can be an adventure.'*

Dana Facaros & Michael Pauls

About the Guide

The **full-colour introduction** gives the authors' overview of the country, together with suggested **itineraries** and a regional **'where to go' map** and **feature** to help you plan your trip.

Illuminating and entertaining **cultural chapters** on local history, culture, food, wine and everyday life give you a rich flavour of the country.

Planning Your Trip starts with the basics of when to go, getting there and getting around, coupled with other useful information, including a section for disabled travellers. The **Practical A–Z** deals with all the **essential information** and **contact details** that you may need while you are away.

The **regional chapters** are arranged in a loose touring order, with plenty of public transport and driving information. The author's top **'Don't Miss'** ✪ sights are highlighted at the start of each chapter.

A **language and pronunciation guide**, a **glossary** of cultural terms, ideas for **further reading** and a comprehensive **index** can be found at the end of the book.

Although everything we list in this guide is **personally recommended**, our authors inevitably have their own favourite places to eat and stay. Whenever you see this **Author's Choice** ⭐ icon beside a listing, you will know that it is a little bit out of the ordinary.

Hotel Price Guide (*see also* p.69)

Luxury	€€€€€	€180 and above
Very Expensive	€€€€	€130–180
Expensive	€€€	€80–130
Moderate	€€	€50–80
Inexpensive	€	under €50

Restaurant Price Guide (*see also* p.75)

Expensive	€€€€	over €40
Moderate	€€	€20–40
Inexpensive	€	under €20

About the Authors

Dana Facaros and Michael Pauls have written over 30 books for Cadogan Guides. They have lived all over Europe with their son and daughter, and are currently ensconced in a old farmhouse in southwestern France with a large collection of tame and wild animals.

6th Edition published 2008

01 INTRODUCING NORTHERN SPAIN

The north is the alternative Spain, the 'Green Spain', where all national stereotypes collapse, or at least those stereotypes we acquire on the Med. Northern landscapes can be just as spectacular, and beaches just as plentiful, with blue and emerald colours in the ocean and along the estuaries that bite into the coast; and the mountains – the western Pyrenees, the Cordillera Cantábrica and the Picos de Europa – are endearingly lovely and inviting to linger and walk in, unlike much of the austere, dry *meseta* to the south. Here are sheep in the meadows, cows in the corn and storks on every spire – the biggest colony of these, over a hundred, live atop Calahorra cathedral.

The northwest of the country is as rich and lush as the rest of Spain is traditionally hard and dry; here you'll find Spain's finest cheer: Galician seafood, La Rioja wine, Asturian cider, Cantabrian cheese, Navarrese garden vegetables, Castilian suckling pig and roast lamb, and the chefs with the best reputation for putting it all together – the Basques. Of course much of the north's luxuriance comes from the fact that no matter how Eliza Doolittle pronounces it, the rain in Spain does not fall mainly in the plain, but rather right on its head.

Northern Spain has the knack of acquiring a plethora of 'firsts' and then discreetly retiring into the background. The earliest settlers in Iberia found it convivial and left one of the world's great Palaeolithic masterpieces, at Altamira; the Basques, the oldest race in Europe, found it just as cosy and have called it home almost since the beginning of time. After the conquest of the Moors, the embryo of modern Spain, its architecture and language – Castilian – were formed in the mountains of Asturias and crystallized in

Above, from top:
Wooden burrow, Cantabria;
farmhouse, Galicia

Above: Cabo Finisterre, p.338

Opposite page: Farmhouse, Galicia

Burgos. With the discovery of the relics of St James in Galicia, the northwest became the forerunner of European tourism, inventing the pilgrimage to Santiago de Compostela, now in its second millennium.

Even though Spain's centre of gravity gradually moved south to Madrid, the cities and countryside of the north have been adorned with a generous helping of magnificent architectural treasures, from the Visigothic to the most florid Baroque, not to mention a few works by the great Catalan Modernista master Antoni Gaudí.

The Spaniards, especially the Madrileños, have in the past few decades guarded the northwest as a secret for themselves, although they only come in July and August, when it rains less. But even then you have to look hard to find beaches blighted by Benidormish excess (Laredo and Zarautz are the only ones that come close); tourism in northern Spain is more low-key, and by the nature of its short 'season' is probably destined to remain so.

To let the threat of a shower or two keep you away would be to miss out on the best preserved and most idiosyncratic corners of old Europe, a place that has kept a sense of place in the face of creeping homogeneity, one full of unexpected pleasures: a Roman bridge over a brook or a medieval one over a river, the fishmarket in A Coruña, a tableland in northern Castile abruptly cut away by a canyon filled with eagles, a spontaneous party that lasts until dawn in an outdoor *sidrería*, old women herding their cows home by twilight, the walls of stained glass in León, a Basque tug-of-war match, and a sunset at Finisterre, the end of the world.

Below: Vineyards, La Rioja Alavesa, p.182

Opposite page: Cathedral, Burgos, pp.256–9

Where to Go

From the Pyrenees to Galicia's Atlantic seaboard, our guide covers the northern sliver of Spain, broadly tracking the westward progress of the ancient pilgrimage route to Santiago de Compostela.

Navarra, where we begin, spills down from the Pyrenees in lush valleys of pine and beech forest. It is here that we pick up the pilgrimage trail down towards Pamplona, a city speared with narrow lanes through which bulls charge and crowds jeer during the world-famous madness of the *Los Sanfermines* festival. Beyond the barren plains south of Pamplona are the fertile banks of the River Ebro in La Rioja, a region pinstriped with vineyards.

The Basque Lands (Euskadi) are home to the oldest and proudest race in Europe. Among its features are the remote, unpronounceable villages of the Pyrenean lowlands, the golden bay of San Sebastián and Bilbao's dazzling Guggenheim museum – worldwide symbol of urban regeneration. Inland is stylish Vitoria, an industrial town that hosts the six-day *Fiesta de la Virgen Blanca*, with parties till dawn.

In the following chapter, we move from the rural idyll of **Cantabria**, where a common sight is a clog-clad farmer's wife driving home an ox-cart piled high with grass – Cantabria has the highest density of cows in Europe – to the peak-packed **Picos de Europa**, a haven for hikers and the most beautiful mountains in Spain. Cantabria is also home to the caves of Altamira, decorated in prehistoric times with exuberant works of artistic genius.

Then there is the rugged beauty of **Asturias**, its coastline studded with beaches, its tumbling mountain rapids and gentle lowland streams teeming with trout, salmon and eel; if you're lucky you might just catch a glimpse of the elusive Cantabrian bear. Inland, around Oviedo, you'll find a scattering of unusual pre-Romanesque churches, which have stood proud since the 9th century and are now protected by UNESCO.

Old Castile and León comprise the rolling scrub-pocked plains of the *meseta*, a land of hamlets and the most tortuous stretch of the Camino de Santiago. We track down ancient hermitages in the Valley of Silence, and describe the diaphanous beauty of Gothic cathedrals in Burgos and León, built half of stone, half of light and air.

Galicia, Spain's sea-battered northwest corner, is a place of its own, for many years removed from the mainstream of Spanish life and history. Its estuaries (*rías*) offer up a feast of sea creatures, which Galician cooks whip up in a thousand different ways, while its jagged shoreline (the 'coast of death') presents coves, cliffs and sandy beaches to explore. Moss-stained Santiago de Compostela, the original European tourist destination, is the culmination of the pilgrim's journey, and the tail end of our guide.

Chapter Divisions

FRANCE

Santander

San Sebastián (Donostia)   Hondarribia

09 CANTABRIA

Picos de Europa   **CANTABRIA & THE**
PICOS DE EUROPA
p.183

VIZCAYA

Bilbao (Bilbo)   EUSKADI

08
THE BASQUE LANDS
(EUSKADI)
p.127

Pamplona (Iruña)

ALA   Vitoria (Gasteiz)

NAVARRA

11
OLD CASTILE & LEÓN
p.243

BURGOS

Burgos

07
NAVARRA &
LA RIOJA
p.79

PALENCIA

LA RIOJA

ZARAGOZA

VALLADOLID   SORIA

SEGOVIA

Coasting Along

This is Spain, so the coasts all have names – from the Costa Vasca along the Bay of Biscay, to the Costa Verde of Asturias, to the wild Costa de la Muerte in the far west of Galicia. But the names only begin to hint at the extraordinary beauty, variety and sheer lushness of these Atlantic shores.

Unlike on Spain's Mediterranean *costas*, which were almost deserted until the mid-20th century when Europe en masse discovered an uncontrollable longing to bake by the sea, the towns here have plenty of history and little room for dense crops of tower blocks. In northern Spain, you can instead swan around gilded Belle Epoque resorts, beginning with San Sebastián and Santander. You can indulge in a dazzling array of exotic seafood in colourful fishing ports tucked along the jigsaw estuaries. You can laze on golden crescents of sand in Asturias and Cantabria – the season is short, but you'll have mostly Spaniards for company. Or you can take long walks along Galicia's savage Rías Altas, where wild horses roam the 2,000ft cliffs of San Andrés de Teixido and the ocean crashes against the world's end of Finisterre.

*Above, from top:
Shoreline, Cudillero,
Asturias, p.240;
Playa de La Concha,
San Sebastián, p.139*

Surf and Turf, *Viño* and *Sidra*

The seafood in Northern Spain is the stuff of legend, served as tapas or *pintxos* in a corner bar, or exquisitely prepared by one of several Michelin-starred chefs in San Sebastián. There are people who visit Galicia just for the shellfish – not only its fat and justly famous scallops, but also delicacies such as *santiaguiños* and *zamburiñas* that are found only in the *rías*. Inland, look for lamb, dried hams, sausages, rich stews and soups, tasty green peppers and the mighty cheeses from the mountains.

La Rioja, of course, produces Northern Spain's best-known red wine, while the white *txakoli* from the Basque lands and Galicia's Ribeiro are the

Above, from top: Mountain cheeses, Picos de Europa, pp.206–16; La Rioja wine bottles; seafood, Galicia

perfect accompaniment to all that seafood. And in Asturias, don't miss the *sidra*: cider poured with effervescent panache at arm's length. It's an acquired taste – give it a chance and don't give up after the first swallow.

Above: Picos de Europa, pp.206–16

Opposite page: Forest of Irati, p.83

Attitudes to Altitudes

Northern Spain's spinal ridge of mountains that rise to the high plains of Castile may not be the country's highest peaks, but they would win any Iberian mountain beauty contest hands down, and they are bursting with variety. Start with the Pyrenees of Navarra, where the pass at Roncesvalles is the classic entry point of pilgrims wending their way to Compostela and where numinous mountain sanctuaries, lost in deep forests, have a fairytale quality. The arid Bárdenas Reales near Tudela look like something out of the Wild West, and look nothing like the rolling vine-clad hills of La Rioja. In Euskadi and Cantabria, the hills are emerald-green, while heart-stoppingly sheer gorges mark the frontiers of Old Castile, including the majestic eagle-haunted canyons of the Ebro. West of Léon, ancient Roman gold mines, orchards and medieval hermitages await in the isolated mountains of El Bierzo.

Last but hardly least, Asturias and Cantabria share the fabled Picos de Europa, with their stunning cluster of limestone peaks that were designated Spain's very first national park – a top destination for trekking, canyoning, mountain-biking, rock-climbing, canoeing, and sighting rare flora and fauna (including brown bears).

Above, from top: Café, Burgos, p.263; Real Colegiata de San Isidora de León, p.288

Opposite page: Glassed-in solanas, León, pp.283–91

Urban Legends

Spaniards are among the most urbane people on earth, and Northern Spain's cities count among its greatest attractions, packed full of character and unique sights, and citizens intent on getting the most out of life. Some towns, such as the lovely granite Santiago de Compostela, have hosted visitors for over a thousand years, while once-industrial, hardworking Bilbao with its titanium-clad Guggenheim Museum has recently taken its place in the vanguard of 21st-century city-break chic. Burgos and Léon hold dazzling concentrations of architecture and art, and slightly dour Pamplona is synonymous with one of Europe's wildest parties in its July running of the bulls. A Coruña, nicknamed 'Crystal City' for its seafront façade of glass galleries, is a lively, salty mix of pleasure and business. But lesser-known cities such as Oviedo, Pontevedra and Vitoria throw up more than their share of surprises, too, and, being in Spain, concentrate more bustle and fun in their cores than many much larger cities in Northern Europe.

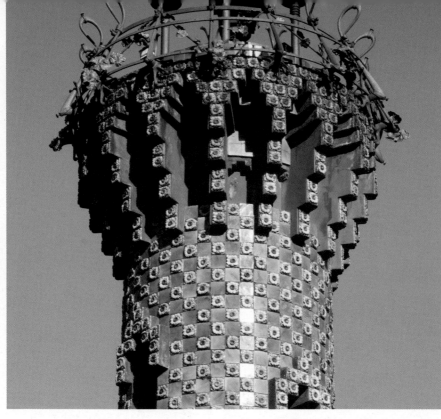

Above: Gaudí's El Capricho, Comillas, p.202

Opposite page, from top: Bullfight poster, Pamplona, pp.90–97; medieval bridge, Estella (Lizarra), pp.107–109; turret of Gaudí's Los Botines, León, p.287

Green Spain, Surprising Spain

It does rain in Spain, but unlike the song it's along the Atlantic coast rather than mainly on the plain – parts of the region are so green that they could be in Ireland (traditionally compared to Galicia) or Wales (traditionally compared to Asturias).

But northern Spain also has attractions you'll find nowhere else, attractions that go back beyond the night of time. It was a favourite dinosaur stomping ground – La Rioja Baja has Europe's greatest collection of fossilized footprints – and our ancestors found it congenial enough, leaving the oldest humanoid fossils yet found in Western Europe in Atapuerca near Burgos; over a million years later their descendants decorated the beautiful Palaeolithic caves at Altamira and the Cueva de Santimamiñe. The world's oldest continuous working lighthouse, the 2nd-century Torre de Hércules, still guides ships at A Coruña. Then there's the Virgin Mary's stone boat at Muxía, the Emir's emerald at Roncesvalles and some modern surprises: Gaudí's green and gold tower house at Comillas and his Bishop's Palace at Astorga, Frank Gehry's Guggenheim Museum in Bilbao, and the flash new designer *bodegas* in Rioja Alavesa around Laguardia built by Gehry and other leading architects – plus one in Haro by Zaha Hadid.

Itineraries

The Road to Compostela: Two Weeks by Car

Day 1 Crossing the traditional Valcarlos Pass in the Pyrenees, visit **Roncesvalles** and its Colegiata then continue to **Pamplona** to visit the cathedral complex and the Museo de Navarra.

Day 2 Drive west to the medieval villages of **Puente la Reina**, **Cirauqui** and **Estella**, the latter famous for its lovely churches, its medieval bridge, the 12th-century Palace of the Kings of Navarre and the monastery of Irache. Stay overnight in Estella.

Day 3 Pop into the churches of **Viana** and La Rioja's capital **Logroño**, and visit at least one *bodega*, before continuing west to **Navarrete** and **Nájera**; take in the monastery of Santa María la Real and its royal pantheon. Sleep in Nájera.

Day 4 Detour south to visit **San Millán de la Cogolla** and the 9th-century Monasterio de Suso. Then go west to **Santo Domingo de la Calzada** (the famous 'chicken church') and **San Juan de Ortega**. Overnight in Burgos.

Day 5 In **Burgos**, see the cathedral, the Monasterio de Las Huelgas and the Cartuja de Miraflores. Stay a second night here.

Day 6 The villages on the plain each have something to see: **Sasamón**, **Hornillos del Camino**, **Castrojerez**, **Boadillo del Camino**. Overnight in **Frómista**, home to the 'perfect Romanesque church'.

Day 7 Today you will head for the Templar town of **Villalcázar de Sirga**, the curious churches of Carrión de los Condes, and for a change, a 3rd-century Roman villa at **Quintanilla de la Cueza**. Overnight in Sahagún.

Day 8 See the *mudéjar* masterpieces of **Sahagún**; the 10th-century San Miguel de Escalada, then head for Léon to sleep.

Day 9 Spend the day in **Léon**, especially the cathedral and the Real Colegiata de San Isidoro, which has the finest Romanesque frescoes in Spain.

Day 10 Drive west to **Astorga** to see the cathedral and Gaudí's Bishop's Palace, and the pretty villages of **Castrillo de los Polvarares** and **Rabanal del Camino**. Overnight in **Ponferrada**.

Day 11 Visit charming **Villafranca del Bierzo** and enter Galicia at mountaintop **O Cebreiro** with its 9th-century church of Santa María; visit **Samos** and the Benedictine Abadía de San Xulián. **Sarriá** is a good place to stay overnight.

Day 12 **Portmarín**, **Vilar de Donas**, and **Melide** are the final stops on the way to Santiago de Compostela.

Days 13–14 **Santiago de Compostela**: the end of the journey for pilgrims and for you.

*Above: Balcony,
Santillana del Mar,
pp.199–200*

*Below: Mountain
village, Pyrenees,
pp.81–9; fishing boats*

The Scenic Route: Two Weeks of Coast and Mountains

Day 1 Start near the French border in **San Sebastián**, with beaches, walks, the Museum of San Telmo and the works of Eduardo Chillida.

Day 2 Continue west to the fishing port of **Getaria** and visit its tilted church, then take in the lovely sea cliffs between **Zumaia** and **Deba**, go for a swim in Lekeitio and spend the night there or in Gernika (Guernica).

Day 3 Visit **Gernika**, its Museo de La Paz and the decorated Palaeolithic **Cueva de Santimamiñe** before heading to Bilbao.

Day 4 See **Bilbao's** Guggenheim Museum, the Museo Maritimo Ría de Bilbao, and the Casco Viejo.

Day 5 Drive west into Cantabria to the resort/fishing port of **Castro Urdiales**, then carry on to **Santander** and spend the night, with a possible visit to the caves of **Puente Viesgo**.

Day 6 West to **Santillana del Mar**, 'the most beautiful village in Spain', and the Altamira Caves museum, then to **Comillas** to see Gaudi's El Capricho and spend the night.

Days 7–9 Head for **San Vicente de la Barquera** and **Unquera**, then turn south through the Desfiladero de la Hermida into the **Picos de Europa**. From **Potes** take the spectacular cable car from **Fuente Dé** up to the Mirador del Cable; go hiking; buy cheese in **Arenas de Cabrales**; visit the lakes of **La Ercina** and **Enol**, and squeeze into the narrow **Desfiladero de los Beyos**.

Day 10 Now you are on the **Costa Verde**, with golden beaches at **Llanes** and **Ribadesella**. Sup away an evening in a *chigre* (cider bar) and sleep overnight in **Villaviciosa**.

Day 11 Dip inland to **Oviedo** to see its cathedral and famous pre-Romanesque churches; in the afternoon continue west into Galicia, to the wild cliffs and beaches of **As Mariñas de Lugo**. Overnight in **Viveiro**.

Day 12 Continue west to the pretty fishing village of **O Barqueiro** and the gorgeous beach at **Bares**, and the cliffs and dunes, beaches and lagoons along the coast to **Ferrol**; visit medieval **Pontedeume** and then spend the night in **A Coruña**.

Day 13 Head south along the Costa da Morte, visiting its dolmens and **Finisterre**, and admire the strange Celtic souvenirs along the Ría de Muros y Noia. Eat peppers in **Padrón**, and spend the night in the pretty granite town of **Pontevedra**.

Day 14 Head to **Vigo** for a seafood lunch, or take a picnic out for a lazy day on the **Islas Cíes**.

CONTENTS

18

Contents

History

02

25,000 BC–AD 409

In which a cultural early bird slows down and gets carved up for lunch by Romans and Carthaginians

Along with southwestern France, this corner of Spain can claim itself as home to the world's oldest known culture. About 25,000 BC, in the Palaeolithic age, the peninsula's many caves began to fill up with Palaeospaniards (or perhaps the ancestors of the Basques, *see* p.129), living well enough off herds of bison and deer to create impressive works of art on cave walls from Cantabria to the western Pyrenees and Périgord. Scholars generally divide these people into the earlier Aurignacian and later Magdalenian cultures. The latter reached their height around 15,000 BC and created some of the Stone Age's finest art, notably in the caves of Altamira near Santander.

It's a long dull stretch from the Palaeolithic masters to the next interesting period in Europe, the Neolithic age. Neolithic culture, with settled farming, trade and megalithic building, may have come to Spain as early as 5500 BC, and it enjoyed a long and relatively peaceful reign over the peninsula, lasting until roughly 2000 BC. This culture, extending from Spain to Scandinavia, distinguished itself by creating Europe's first architecture, with its dolmens, other burial chambers, standing stones and stone circles. Neolithic peoples, though probably a matriarchal society, were sailors and traders, and liked to live near the coasts, including the northern coasts; large concentrations of megalithic monuments are found in the Basque country and Galicia. The latter seems to have been unusually prosperous; dolmen burials here included plenty of gold jewellery, rare for the time.

About 2000 BC, many of the peoples of Iberia learned the use of bronze and started using it to make weapons, while spending their spare time building fortresses to protect the bronze. In an Iberia increasingly turned towards the Mediterranean, the northern coast seems to have been spared most of this progress, and people carried on in their sweet old Neolithic way. About 800 BC, the native Iberians were joined by other peoples, notably the Celts from over the Pyrenees. These got along well enough with the Iberians; in many cases they gradually merged with some tribes, creating a new people, the Celtiberians, who occupied much of the centre and north of the peninsula. The heritage of the Celts everywhere is the *castro*, or, as it is called in France and sometimes here too, the *oppidum*. Astérix's lot didn't care much for towns, but wherever there was some trade to be conducted, or treasure to be guarded, the Celts would have a sort of tiny urban centre, perched on a hilltop and surrounded by walls – more a castle than a town.

Meanwhile, the Phoenicians were making their presence felt in the south. Their traders and colonists began taking over parts of coastal Andalucía *c.* 1200 BC, but evidence is lacking and it remains an open question just how much time the Phoenicians spent in the north. Several of the port towns have a height called *Atalaya*, believed to be a Phoenician word meaning 'tower', while *Spain* is another Phoenician word, meaning 'land of rabbits'. We can imagine that the northern coast was part of a fairly busy trade route, monopolized by Phoenician ships, bringing tin from Cornwall to make bronze in the Mediterranean – the Phoenicians were understandably secretive about the world they discovered outside the Pillars of Hercules, and they probably made up all the stories of sea monsters and such to scare off potential competitors.

Overlordship of Iberia fell to Rome in 202 BC, the big prize for the victory over Hannibal and Carthage in the Second Punic War. But, just as the Carthaginians had never really controlled the wild northwest, Roman rule here was mostly a vain boast for another two centuries. The Romans found the region inhabited by a people they called the *Vascones*, the Basques, and further west the Celtiberian *Cantabri*, *Asturi* and *Gallæci*. Unlike the Carthaginians, the Romans couldn't bear a messy map, and they spent those two centuries methodically grinding down Celtiberians and Basques alike. One highlight of the endless campaigns was the epic siege of Numancia, a Celtiberian stronghold in what is now northern Castile (near Soria). After beating off Roman attacks for 19 years, the Numancians escaped the dishonour of final defeat by burning the town with themselves inside it. To subdue Spain, Rome had to send its best – Cato, Pompey, Caesar and Augustus were all commanders in the Spanish conquest – and the job was not finished in some isolated areas until 20 BC.

The rest of Spain had metal ores to make it worth the trouble, and even in the far northwest Rome probably broke even, thanks to the gold mines of El Bierzo. Only a few towns were founded: *Pallantia* (Palencia) was probably the biggest, followed by *Clunia* (an abandoned site near Aranda de Duero), *Pompaelo* (Pamplona), *Asturica Augusta* (Astorga), *Brigantium* (A Coruña), and *Lucus Augusti* (Lugo). Nor did the Romans break the bank building roads here, although the most important one, linking Zaragoza to León, would one day become the pilgrimage route of the *camino de Santiago*. No town ever managed a population of more than about five thousand. So while the rest of Spain got a good washing and a Latin grammar to study, the peoples of the north were pretty much left alone. Compared to the rest of the western Empire, relatively few wealthy villas have been discovered here, a sign that the Roman élite barely penetrated the region.

Throughout most of the imperial era, the north was a forgotten corner of the province of *Tarracona*, with its capital on the Mediterranean, modern Tarragona. In one of the reforms of Diocletian, this sprawling province was split up, the far western part gaining the name of *Gallaecia* after its Gaulish inhabitants – the future Galicia. Christianity spread quickly in Spain, at least among the officials and landlords in the south, so much so that the peninsula held its first Church council in 313. The only representative from the north was the bishop of a little town called *Lanobriga* (León).

409–711

In which the northwest dozes fitfully through a depressing parade of barbarian hordes

The first Germans had found their way into Iberia during the great barbarian raid of the 260s, though the legions gradually recovered and threw them out again. When the Rhine frontier collapsed in 407, some of the Germans storming westwards were probably already thinking of Spain. Vandals, Alans and Suevi all made it over the pass at Roncesvalles by 409, and they separately ranged the peninsula looking for land and swag. To try and restore order, what was left of the Empire sent in another horde, the Visigoths, as allies to sort their cousins out. They smashed the Alans and Vandals, but let the Suevi keep the remote northwest. Rome, now worrying that the cure might be worse than the disease, talked the Visigoths into crossing the Pyrenees again to have some fun in southern Gaul. In the resulting vacuum, a new horde of Vandals (the Siling Vandals) broke in in 422. They did what Vandals will do, seven years of it, before crossing the Straits of Gibraltar in search of richer lands and towns in Africa.

That left the field clear for the Suevi (or Swabians – their stay-at-home relations gave the name to a region of southwestern Germany). Under their chief Rechila, they made a little kingdom for themselves, centred at Astorga, and by 448 controlled much of the peninsula. In 456, however, the Visigoths came back and defeated them near Astorga, bottling the remnant up in remote Galicia. The Visigoths thought they were just adding some Iberian possessions to their kingdom of southern Gaul – but when the Franks in turn defeated them at the great Battle of Vouillé in 507 and chased them over the Pyrenees, they found themselves in a position they would have to be content with – as rulers of Spain.

As Teutonic barbarians go, the Visigoths were a cut above the rest. They did not drink out of skulls, like the Lombards, or smear bear grease all over their bodies, like the Franks. The line of their kings went back to Alaric I, the Goth who had sacked Rome. For the next two centuries, the Visigoths ruled their Spanish kingdom from Toledo, building churches and inventing a rather blunt code of laws in vulgar Latin; in the northwest, they engaged in endless desultory fighting with the Suevi until 585, when the great King Leovigild finally put an end to their kingdom.

Meanwhile, up in their mountains, the Basques lapsed into *de facto* independence, meeting in democratic assembly around the oak of Gernika to make their own laws. They were expanding in all directions, and especially present in what is now Navarra – peacefully colonizing lands wasted by too many hard times and too many armies. The kings sent frequent expeditions north to try and squeeze some tribute money out of them, with occasional success. Asturias and Galicia proved just as hard to control, and the Visigothic kingdom probably had no more influence here than the Romans had.

711–800

In the middle of the Dark Ages, Spanish history records one of its most frantic centuries ever

At the dawn of the 8th century, it seemed that the Visigothic kingdom had truly established itself: a stable state, by the standards of the time, with a strong Church and some modest cultural achievements (in architecture and literature especially, Spain was more than holding its own). In fact, riven with clan feuds and religious bigotry, the kingdom was a plum waiting to be picked. Of all the luck, this happened to be the first century of Islam, with the explosive bursts of the Arab armies across the Middle East and North Africa. After they had digested North Africa, Spain was the only place to go on Islam's western front, and the first small force under Tariq ibn-Ziyad landed at Gibraltar in 711. The last Visigothic king, Roderick, was defeated and killed in a great battle near Toledo, and within three years the Muslims were in control of the entire peninsula – except, as you might have guessed by now, parts of the north.

The Arabs surged across the Pyrenees, only to be defeated and driven back by the Franks at Poitiers in 732, but what really kept them from consolidating their hold over northwest Spain was a short but intense revolt of the Muslim Berber troops in 740 against their Arab leaders. To hear the Spaniards tell the story, though, the turning of the tide came with a legendary prince of Asturias named Pelayo, who defeated the Moors at the 'Battle of Covadonga' in 718 and kept Asturias free and Christian. Now, there seems to have really been a historic Pelayo, a Visigothic baron, but no reliable record of such a battle is preserved anywhere, and Asturias like the rest of the region was still largely pagan. Spanish history and national mythology are becoming inextricably intertwined; a little inconsequential skirmish in the mountains that Iberia's new masters didn't even notice would some day, in retrospect, appear as the beginning of a national history. Nearly 40 years after the Battle of Covadonga, the *Chronicle of 754*, written by a Christian in al-Andalus, does not mention either the battle or the new Christian 'kingdom' in the north.

Later legends in Cantabria and Asturias spoke of the 'Foramontanos', who fled into the mountains from the Moors and 'returned to repopulate Castile'. And it seems likely that a number of die-hard Visigothic nobles took refuge up in the more inaccessible parts of Asturias. But the romantic legend of the last few defenders of the faith, heroically holed up in the Asturian mountains – the seed from which Spain would grow – is only partially true.

The records say that, only four years after the invasion began, the Moors were pretty much in control of Asturias and most of the rest of the northwest. Gijón, on the coast, fell to the Muslims in 715 and had an Arab governor for years afterwards, as did Pamplona. Galicia too was in Arab hands for some time.

While all this was happening, other neglected fringes of the Iberian world were beginning their careers, including the little state of Navarra. Pamplona freed itself from Muslim rule in the Berber revolt of 740, and the Basques were independent once again. Once again, though, they had to fight to stay that way. After beating the Moors at Poitiers, the self-confident Franks soon came over the Pyrenees looking for new lands to conquer. One of their raids gave birth to the famous legend of Roland and Oliver, the famous knights of Charlemagne who perished at the hands of the Basques in an ambush at the pass of Roncesvalles in 778.

800–1000
The northern mountain boys tweak the moustaches of a powerful Emirate and then found some kingdoms

The endless conquests and confusions of the 8th century set the pattern for centuries of Spain's history to come. The new Emirate of al-Andalus developed a

24

02 History | 800–1000

policy of insulating itself from the wild north by a band of marches – no-man's-lands with military governors. At the beginning, these included what is now León, Castile and much of Aragón. The emirs might raid them every few years, but they could not keep Christian settlers from gradually filling in the empty spaces, laying the groundwork for the Reconquista.

While the Emirate (Caliphate after 929) was developing a brilliant Spanish-Muslim civilization in the middle of the Dark Ages, the northern kingdom was prospering and growing too, while economically and culturally drawing closer to Christian Europe. Not only was Asturias slowly and gradually expanding, but new centres of power appeared as well. In 800, the year Charlemagne was proclaimed emperor, the first written mention is made of the County of Castile, the 'Land of Castles'. The north may not have been so backward at all, comparatively speaking. The sophisticated and urbanized society of al-Andalus had a constant need for raw materials and food, and it spread prosperity and learning beyond its borders. One of the surprises of the Christian north was its pre-Romanesque architecture, as expressed in the famous 9th- and 10th-century churches around Asturias and Cantabria, built at a time when the rest of Europe was hardly building anything in stone. Design and clothing, however, were still heavily influenced by the latest fashions in Moorish Córdoba, Granada and Sevilla, and such educated princes as there were would more likely know Arabic than Latin.

In the 9th century, Muslim al-Andalus entered the golden age of its prosperity and power. Campaigns against the Christians in the north were frequent though inconclusive: Pamplona was taken again in 842, and León in 848, but neither could be held for long. Under ineffectual caliphs such as Abd Allah, the late 9th century was a time of civil strife and confusion in the south, and it permitted the new kingdom of Asturias to take its first steps on the way to the Reconquista – the retaking of all Iberia for Christianity that had already been predicted, against all odds, in a Christian work called *The Prophetic Chronicle*.

Christians began to resettle and hold lands south of the Cantabrian mountains; they also managed to found or refound a number of towns in the no-man's-land of the Duero Valley, notably Burgos (884). The reign of Alfonso III (866–910) was a watershed for the northerners, in which they pushed their boundaries into Portugal and resettled much of northern Castile (for convenience' sake, historians call Asturias the 'Kingdom of León', after that city was taken in 913, though interestingly for centuries the kingdom had no name at all, and such kings as could write would sign documents simply *Yo, el Rey*).

As for the Basques, by 824 Pamplona had chased the Franks out once and for all, forming the county of Navarra under a leader named Jimeno Aritza and his descendants. The Basques seem to have got on well enough with the Moors, and were often in alliance with them against the famous clan of the Banu Qasi – renegade Visigoths who had turned Muslim, and who held Zaragoza and much of Aragón not for the Emirate, but for themselves. Later, Basques would provide many of the favourite women in the palace harem at Córdoba, and consequently more than a few of the emirs were at least half Basque.

The reign of Abd ar-Rahman III (912–961), who declared himself caliph, marked the high point of the power of al-Andalus, and a setback for the northerners, though the caliph could do little to stop the resettlement of the new northern lands. Abd ar Rahman's notable contemporary in the north was Fernán González, *El Buen Conde*, the 'Good Count' of Castile (923–970) who despite continuous war with the Moors made his land into a kingdom independent of Asturias. More troubles for the north came with the rule in al-Andalus of al-Mansur, 'the Victorious', an ambitious vizier who had locked the weak young caliph Hisham II away in the palace at Córdoba and pulled all the strings himself. Al-Mansur defeated the Asturians and sacked León in 988, and Burgos in 1000. He forced most of the northerners to pay tribute, and on one raid his armies even occupied Santiago de Compostela, carrying off the church bells as a prize for the Great Mosque of Córdoba.

1000–1218
The northerners persist, and find that constant bellicosity brings big rewards

The Muslims definitely still held the real power in the peninsula, but the same al-Mansur who had won so many battles for them was unwittingly to be the downfall of the caliphate. By assuming personal power, he removed the main prop of the legitimacy of the state. When he died, his sons attempted to carry on in his place, leading to a revolution in 1009 that put an end to the political unity of al-Andalus forever, leaving a collection of small states quarrelling amongst themselves. That was all the opportunity the warriors of the north needed. Especially under Alfonso VI (1065–1109) they extended their boundaries ever farther; Alfonso crowned a long string of victories with the capture of Toledo in 1085, securing permanent control of the central *meseta*. Alfonso was the first Castilian king to mint coins (instead of using Moorish currency); he collected tribute money from the little kings of al-Andalus, and he began calling himself 'Emperor of All Spain', but he never would have done it without the help of the Castilian adventurer El Cid, Rodrigo Díaz de Vivar.

The new millennium had definitely got off to an auspicious start for Christian Spain. But for a while it looked as if the big victor among the Christian states would be little Navarra. Still Basque but becoming increasingly hispanicized and feudalized, Navarra had reached its zenith under Sancho el Mayor (1000–35), capturing all of La Rioja and even much of Castile. But like so many of the transient empires formed in the free-for-all of the Reconquista, Sancho's proved to be only a house of cards, and Alfonso VI cut Navarra down to size in the 1070s. In fact, every Christian state was taking advantage of al-Andalus's disarray to expand its boundaries: León/Castile (united by marriage), Navarra, Portugal and Aragón. Aragón and León/Castile eventually emerged as the main rivals for dominance in the new Spain that was growing. Under Alfonso I, *El Batallador*, Aragón emerged as a major power; in the 1110s Alfonso briefly controlled parts of Castile, including Burgos.

The new states could afford such rivalry; the new frontier life created by conditions on the *meseta* gave the Christians one particular military advantage:

a class of hard men doing well enough to afford heavy armour and a horse. The Spanish cavalry was small in number, but they could cover ground quickly, raid everywhere and often carry the day in pitched battles against Moorish forces that were numerically superior. Another advantage was the spirit of the Crusader, both in reinforcing morale and attracting fresh blood; early on, the popes had declared Spain a legitimate sphere of Crusading activity, as much as was the Holy Land.

Al-Andalus, however, was not finished yet. Before the Christians could completely swallow it up, the various little states were swept away by the new Almoravid (Murabit) empire. Originally an Islamic fundamentalist movement among the Berbers, dominated by a few powerful tribes, this grew into an emirate that controlled all of Morocco. After the fall of Toledo the Almoravids were invited into Spain, where they stopped the Christian tide – and added al-Andalus to their dominions. They lasted until 1147, falling into decay and being replaced by a nearly identical African sectarian empire, that of the Almohads (Muwahhid).

Although Muslim art and culture continued to shine, the Almohads suffered the same decay of reforming zeal as had the Almoravids, once introduced to the pleasures of Córdoba and Sevilla. The great disaster for al-Andalus came in 1212: the Battle of Las Navas de Tolosa, where a Christian alliance led by Alfonso VIII of Castile destroyed the Almohad power forever. The great cities of the south were gobbled up soon after, leaving the Muslims only the little kingdom of Granada, which held out by careful diplomacy and heavy tributes until 1492. Six years after Las Navas de Tolosa, in 1218, León and Castile merged once and for all under Ferdinand III el Santo.

1218–1516

In which medieval Spain creates a fat and happy civilization, and pride goes before a fall

It's the great historical paradox of the Reconquista, one of the examples of Cervantean irony that Spain is always bountiful in providing: the northwest, previously little more relevant to Spain's history than Novgorod or Baluchistan, suddenly takes centre stage in creating a new Spain, and then with success finds itself left behind on the periphery again with nothing to do. After Las Navas de Tolosa, all the money was to be made in the centre and south, in New Castile around Madrid, and in al-Andalus – now Spanish Andalucía.

Castile had tripled in size, and its kings, now by far the most dangerous ones on the chessboard, began spending much more of their time in central towns such as Toledo and Valladolid, and less in León or Burgos. For simple geographical reasons, the northwest would never be the real heartland of a nation. But for the time being it managed to share fully in Western Europe's blossoming during the 12th and 13th centuries.

Particularly striking was the growth of towns. Trade came back in the Atlantic in a big way, for the first time since the Romans, and little ports from A Coruña to San Sebastián reawakened from 600 years' slumber. Increasingly, they sent wool to England, France and Flanders. That was the big-money commodity of the age, and the northern plains were perfectly suited for raising sheep. Run under a sophisticated sort of royal cooperative called the *mesta*, this trade fuelled most of medieval Castile's remarkable prosperity, and the annual fair at Medina del Campo became one of the biggest in Europe. Many of the northern cities at least doubled in size in the 12th century, the biggest boom in all history for places such as León and Burgos. Though doomed never to make a role for themselves as capitals or great trade centres, both these cities took advantage of the good times to create notable monuments, including the finest Gothic cathedrals in Spain. León began its one in 1205, and Burgos followed in 1221.

With money came increasing power for the growing towns, and nearly all of them in this period were able to gain a high degree of independence from the kings, bishops or nobles who had formerly bossed them around. All over Spain, the towns were organizing themselves into *comunes*, as in the rest of Europe. A good example of the new type of medieval *comune* is Vitoria-Gasteiz, founded by King Alfonso VI of Navarra in 1181, soon after he had conquered the territory from Castile. Alfonso wanted a loyal town to consolidate his hold, and to keep the new settlers' loyalty, he granted it a charter of *fueros* (literally 'outsides', or exceptions to royal law) that gave the town rights of self-government and exemptions from some taxes and feudal responsibilities. This story was repeated literally hundreds of times across Christian Spain.

The *fueros* gave Spain a less oppressive government than most countries. They were made possible by the good example of the Basques. It was a good time for this incurably industrious people too, as they began to turn their talents to the sea. In 1296 a kind of Hanseatic league of Basque ports was founded, the Hermandad de las Marismas; shipping Vizcaya's iron and Castile's wool northwards, the Hermandad grew to control a disproportionate share of the Atlantic trade. But as in Navarra, the Basque language and culture were being pushed further into the background, in a world increasingly dominated by Spanish-speaking nobles and merchants. Navarra, condemned by geography to lose out in the Reconquista land grab, was now in full decline. French involvement in the kingdom dated from 1284, when an heiress of the kingdom, Juana I, married King Philip the Fair of France. Members of the Capetian dynasty ruled Navarra as a quaint Pyrenean Ruritania from then on.

Throughout the 14th and 15th centuries, the peninsula occupied itself with consolidating the gains of the Reconquista and trying to make some sense out of all the commotion that had occurred. Burgos and León got their tremendous cathedrals finished, but economically and culturally the northwest was increasingly left on the periphery of a Spain that was growing very large and complex. And already, some of the forces that would make this Spain go to pieces were in their larval forms – the big winners of the Reconquista, a bloated nobility and a dangerous but morally decayed Church, both exempt from taxes and loaded with privileges. On the whole, the experience of the Reconquista coarsened the life of Castile, creating a pirate ethos where honest labour was scorned, and wealth and honour were things to be snatched from one's neighbours.

The climax of unification came in 1469 with the marriage of *los Reyes Católicos*, Ferdinand of Aragón and Isabel of Castile. Under their reign Spain's borders were rounded out. Not only did they finally conquer the kingdom of Granada, the last remnant of al-Andalus, but Ferdinand's campaigns put an end to that medieval relic up north, the kingdom of Navarra. Spain was also embarking on its career as a grand imperialist, invading Italy and colonizing the Americas. All this cost a good deal of money, which Ferdinand and Isabel's ministers extorted out of the towns and cities of Castile. They whittled away at the communal lands and the *fueros*, and towns that had run their own affairs for centuries now found their assets carved up little by little among the crown and the local nobles. The religious bigotry of the 'Catholic Kings', Isabel in particular, put a perverse twist on Spanish life that was to last a long time. Under their reign the Inquisition was reintroduced, and the Jews expelled.

1516–1931
The north's history is dissolved into that of united Spain, and it isn't a pretty story

Worse was still to come. Whatever cash and valuables were left in Old Castile were soon relentlessly sucked out by Ferdinand and Isabel's grandson, the Habsburg Carlos I. Better known to history as Charles V, his title as Holy Roman Emperor, this rapacious megalomaniac gained the throne by declaring the rightful queen, his mother Juana, insane, and locking her up in a windowless cell for the next forty years. Charles and his Flemish minions then started squeezing Spain dry, to raise the gargantuan bribes that were necessary for an Imperial election in those days (even though there were only seven voters!). To accomplish the looting of his new country, Charles rescinded or ignored most of the remaining municipal *fueros*, wrecked the trade fairs and invented new taxes everywhere. The church and nobles jumped in for a share of the spoils, and Spain embarked on a rather remarkable and ultimately successful attempt to destroy its own economy.

A national financial collapse came in 1519, and an outraged Castile finally rose up in rebellion. The Comunero Revolt, a brave last attempt of the *comunes* to defend their purses and their liberties, began in 1520 and quickly spread through the towns of Old Castile. Charles' foreign troops put it down the following year, and though the king took a conciliatory line towards the rebels, there was no doubt now about who was boss. Castile was finished, its trade ruined and its once-thriving towns condemned to be the backwater relics they remain today.

Ripping out the heart of his country meant relatively little to Charles, who now had gold and silver flowing in from America to finance his endless aggressions across Europe. For a final note on one of history's bigger rotters, we see Charles after his abdication in 1556, living in a monastery at Yuste, in Extremadura, praying for his soul and gorging himself continually on eel pies. His favourite recreation in the later days was rehearsing his funeral, and at one practice session he caught a chill and died.

For Spain, still worse was yet to come. Under Charles's neurotic son Philip II, Spain reached the height of its book- and heretic-burning frenzy, while the economy stayed wrecked and military defeats piled up on every side. A particular blow against the northwest, motivated by corrupt ministers, was Philip's decision in 1573 to allow Seville to monopolize trade with the New World. The northern ports dwindled, and all the poor souls whose prospects had been ruined even had to find their way to the south to catch a boat just to emigrate.

This state of affairs lasted until 1788, by which time the northern towns had already undergone a steep decline along with the rest of Spain. Nevertheless, the northwest found ways to wring a penny from the Americas. The enterprising Basques, for example, created the Compañia Guipúzcana de Caracas, which wangled a monopoly over the chocolate trade and brought a lot of money home to the Basque country. For generations, Basques and Spaniards alike contributed their share to Spain's colonial adventures. Sons who went overseas to make their fortunes were called *indianos* – and *indianos*, or *casas de indianos*, is also the name for the houses built by the lucky ones who came home well off; you'll see them everywhere in the northwest, as early as 1650 and as late as 1920.

If little good happened in these centuries, at least the north was usually spared the curse of armies and wars. That is, until Napoleon crossed the Pyrenees in 1808. French occupation led to a spontaneous national revolt – the Spaniards call it their 'War of Independence'. The British pitched in to fight their mutual nemesis, at first catastrophically as their army under Sir John Moore, pursued by Maréchal Soult, beat a desperate retreat across the northwest to flee from A Coruña. When the British returned under Wellington, it was their turn to chase the French from Cádiz to Paris, the result as much a disaster for Napoleon as his winter in Moscow. Wellington is well remembered by the Spanish for kicking the French out (they made him a duke too), but his boys dealt with conquered land far worse than Napoleon or any contemporary army would have dreamed, distinguishing them-selves notably at the sack of San Sebastián. The French had been content with simply looting all the gold crucifixes and a lot of bad paintings.

But as the great chef Escoffier later expressed it, the only worthwhile thing France got out of the Peninsular War was the recipe for pheasant *à la Alcántara*. That did not stop the French from sending their army down again in 1823, with the blessing of the English and Austrians, to stamp out a democratic revolt against the despotic Bourbons. Nineteenth-century Spain became quite a wild place, often the very image of the banana republics that had just gained their independence from it in Latin America. The Basques, especially those of Navarra, did their best to keep the pot boiling. Supporting the claims of the pretender Don Carlos, they sided with the Church and reactionaries in the Carlist Wars of 1833–39 and 1872–6. Many Carlists only took up the cause in defence of what was left of their *fueros*, which liberal reformers in Madrid were trying to abolish. The generals of Isabel II put down both revolts, though there were some close moments, as in the Second Carlist War when the insurgents briefly besieged Bilbao.

Isabel II presided over the confusing height of the banana monarchy where rival generals and politicians could compete for her favours while issuing *pronuncia-mientos* and plotting backstage coups. But while the country as a whole was becoming an increasingly inconsequential backwater in Europe, some signs of life were stirring in unlikely places – not in the moribund Castilian centre, but on the periphery. Along with the Catalans, the Basques were doing their best to give the country a boost into the Industrial Revolution. Bilbao became a noisy boom town around its ironworks and shipyards, while a small echo was heard from tiny Asturias, which grew into Spain's most important mining region.

1931–the Present
The northerners choose sides, fight it out, and most finally conclude that pluralism isn't so bad after all

Along with industrialization came political change. The Basque Nationalist Party, or PNV, appeared to speak up for Basque concerns at the Cortes in Madrid, while Asturias with its strong unions became increasingly radicalized. The boom years of the First World War, provided by Spain's neutrality, were followed by a steep depression that brought social problems to a head, especially after the Second Republic was proclaimed in 1931. One famous event of the time, a prelude to the Civil War, was the bloody revolt of the Asturian miners in 1934, crushed by army troops under a general named Franco.

When the Civil War broke out in July 1936, the Basques and Asturians sided enthusiastically with the Republic, while Old Castile supported Franco. Until the end of the war the Nationalists kept their capital at Burgos. Most Galicians took the Nationalist side too – Franco was after all a native son, from Ferrol – and so did the Navarrese, whose politics still revolved around Carlism. Franco's armies soon reduced Republican territory in the northwest to a chain of small pockets along the coast. The Basques held out until 1937, when they succumbed to a campaign distinguished by the terror bombing of Guernica, performed by Franco's Nazi allies.

After the war the Basques suffered more than anyone for their loyalty to the Republic. As in Catalunya, the government suppressed even the casual use of the native language, forbade most festivals and cultural manifestations, and sent thousands of intellectuals to prison or into exile. State industrial schemes were consciously planned in a way to bring in large numbers of Spanish job-seekers to dilute the Basque population. The Basque response was the growth of the terrorist organization ETA, beginning in the 1950s. As the only active resistance to the dictatorship, ETA attracted widespread sympathy within Spain and elsewhere, especially in 1973 when they blew the car of Franco's hand-picked successor, Admiral Carrero Blanco, over the roof of a Madrid church.

In striking contrast, plenty of Navarrese, mostly Carlists, found posts in Franco's army and government until the end of the regime in 1975 (the Spanish fascists even borrowed the Carlists' yoke-and-arrows symbol for their own party). There are Carlists to be found even today, although the current pretender, Prince Hugo de Borbón, has tacitly acknowledged King Juan Carlos by paying him a social visit. Navarra remains the most politically reactionary part of Spain, maybe of all Europe; Pamplona, its bright and prosperous capital, is the mecca of Opus Dei, the shadowy Catholic organization that in Franco's later years attempted to gain control of the Spanish government by insinuating its members into high positions.

In Galicia, Cantabria and Castile, politics remain quietly Neanderthal; these are the only parts of Spain where you're still likely to see statues and streets named after Nationalist heroes. Since the restoration of democracy in 1977, the most dramatic change in Spain has been the reversal of centuries of centralization, with the creation of autonomous regional governments throughout the country, including Galicia, Asturias, Cantabria, the Basque country (Euskadi), Navarra and Old Castile – the latter the only part of Spain where a majority didn't want autonomy, and had it forced upon them by Madrid. The Basques got a special autonomy statute, and they have made the most of it, with their own schools, television and police force.

This wasn't enough for the die-hards of ETA, who still demand total independence, and who have continued their murders and bombing campaigns, almost always in other parts of Spain. The surprise truce declared in September 1998 brought 15 months of peace to Spain and the Basque lands, during which it was hoped that a peaceful solution could be found. Unfortunately, ETA found its marginalization in peace worse than the disgust it inspired when it was active, and in December 1999 the organization resumed the terror. The most spectacular loser in the May 2001 regional elections was Euskal Herritarok (ETA's political wing), which lost half of its 14 seats. Indeed, the record turnout of nearly 80 per cent of eligible voters gave a clear message to the rest of Spain: terrorism no, nationalism yes.

The message seemed to fall on deaf ears when, two days after the election, Basque journalist and anti-violence campaigner Gorka Landaburu lost part of his hand when a packet bomb sent to his home exploded. Then, in August of the same year, a municipal councillor in Leiza died when a bomb exploded beneath his van. Ten hours later an officer with the Basque police force was shot dead with a submachine gun as he parked his car in Tolosa. A further deadly attack took place in Madrid with the car bomb assassination of a national police office. A subsequent poll showed that terrorism had moved even further ahead of unemployment as the main concern of Spaniards.

Until the summer of 2002, most ETA attacks had taken place either in the capital or the Basque country. Tourism seemed to be the target that year when, during the height of the season, two car bombs exploded in Fuengirola on the Costa del Sol and a few weeks later in a resort near Alicante, resulting in the death of a child.

The Spanish government responded definitively on 26 July by applying the newly devised 'Ley de Partidos' to Batasuna, the political wing of ETA, effectively making the party illegal, on the grounds of its 'carrying out politics in connivance with terror' and for 'encouraging generalized intimidation' among other points. The group's offices were closed by the Basque police and its accounts frozen. Meanwhile the party moved to Bayonne, France where it is registered as an association. In a further development approximately three months later, the president of the (recognized) Basque government, Juan José Ibarretxe, put an end to the political ambiguity in the region and placed his cards clearly on the table, proposing that the European Union grant the Basque Country the status of free state, associated to Spain with shared sovereignty, a plan that no one except the Basques takes seriously. This was still a key issue in the Basque elections of April 2005, which Ibarretxe's party won – but only just. They lost their overall majority, and much of their bargaining power with it.

Meanwhile, Aznar's hardline Partido Popular (PP or People's Party) were ousted from government in the dramatic Spanish general election of 2004, when the Spanish people expressed their anger at the PP's deliberate attempts to implicate ETA in the terrible bombings at Madrid train stations on 11th March 2004, in which almost 200 people were killed. The attacks were claimed by Islamic fundamentalists in retaliation for Spanish involvement in the Iraq war (opposed by more than 90 per cent of Spaniards)

In early 2005, the new Socialist (PSOE) goverment under José Luís Rodríguez Zapatero promised to open peace talks with ETA if the group laid down its arms, but the announcement was followed by a series of car bombings in Madrid. These were widely perceived to be a gesture of defiance from ETA, and the government responded by arresting Arnaldo Otegi, the leader of the (still outlawed) Batasuna party, and by threatening to limit some areas of the Basque Country's current autonomy. Fragile hopes for peace were raised when ETA declared a 'permanent' ceasefire on March 2006 and a few months later, Zapatero's government showed signs that it was prepared to sit and talk with the armed separatists. But the sceptics were proved right when on December 30th ETA detonated a van bomb in a car park building at the Madrid Barajas international airport, killing two men. Although Zapatero discontinued talks immediately, it wasn't until June 2007 that ETA formally announced the end of the 'permanent' ceasefire. PSOE won the 2008 general elections, but the Basque terrorism question will remain high on the political agenda.

Meanwhile, the real story in Euskadi is not this relic of a troubled past, but the surprising rebirth of Bilbao as a symbol of the Basques' future. Long known only for industrial obsolescence and rust, the city has pulled itself up with such projects as Frank Gehry's Guggenheim Museum, a state-of-the-art metro and a huge riverfront redevelopment plan; in only a few years Bilbao has emerged from nowhere to become one of the most exciting cities in Spain, and the showcase for a small, ancient nation that in the past has always been able to absorb new ideas, innovate and prosper. The Basques, in spite of their troubles, seem poised to do it again.

Topics

03

The Pilgrimage to Santiago

The Official History

No saint on the calendar has as many names as Spain's patron – Iago, Diego, Jaime, Jacques, Jacobus, Santiago or, in English, James the Greater. James the fisherman was one of the first disciples chosen by Jesus, who nicknamed him Boanerges, 'the son of thunder', after his booming voice. After the Crucifixion, he seems to have been a rather ineffectual proselytizer for the faith; in the year AD 44 Herod Agrippa in Caesarea beheaded him and threw his body to the dogs. But Spain had another task in store for James: nothing less than posthumously leading a 700-year-old crusade against the peninsula's infidels.

In fact, the evidence suggests that it was really the French who put him up to it: the first mention of the Apostle's relics in Spain appears in an 830 annexe to the *Martirologio de Florus*, written in 806 in Lyon; after the fright of 732, when the Moors invaded as far as Poitiers and settled a good portion of France's Mediterranean coast, the French were ready to pull out all the stops to encourage their old Christian neighbours to rally and defeat the heathen. A new history of James emerged, one with links to Spain. First, before his martyrdom, he went to Zaragoza to convert the Spaniards and failed. Second, after his martyrdom, two of his disciples piously gathered his remains and sailed off with them in a stone boat (faith works wonders). The destination was Iria Flavia in remote Galicia, and the disciples buried Boanerges in the nearby cemetery of Compostela. In 814, a shower of shooting stars guided a hermit shepherd named Pelayo to the site of James's tomb; the bones were 'authenticated' by Bishop Theodomir. Another legend identifies Charlemagne (who died in 814) with the discovery of James's relics: in the Emperor's tomb at Aachen you can see the 'Vision of Charlemagne', with a scene of the Milky Way, the Via Lactea, a common name for the pilgrims' road.

In 844, not long after the discovery of the relics, James was called into active duty in the battle of Clavijo, appearing on a white horse to help Ramiro I of Asturias defeat the Moors. This new role as Santiago Matamoros, the 'Moor-Slayer', was a great morale booster for the forces of the Reconquista, who made 'Santiago!' their battle cry. In the churches along the *camino*, James is portrayed either as a humble pilgrim himself or as a mighty warrior trampling the Moors underfoot. Ramiro was so pleased by his divine assistance that he made a pledge, the *voto de Santiago*, that ordained an annual property tax for St James's church at Compostela.

Never mind that the bones, the battle and the *voto* were as bogus as each other; the story struck deep spiritual, poetic and political chords that fitted perfectly with the great cultural awakening of the 10th and 11th centuries. The medieval belief that a few holy bones or teeth could serve as a hotline to heaven made the discovery essential. After all, the Moors had some powerful juju of their own: an arm of the Prophet Muhammad in the Great Mosque of Córdoba (possession of it was Abd ar-Rahman's justification for declaring himself caliph in 929). Another factor in the early 9th century was the Church's need for a focal point to assert its doctrinal control over the newborn kingdoms of Spain, especially over the Celts in Galicia, stubborn followers of the Gnostic Priscilian heresy (*see* p.313). A third factor must have been the desire to reintegrate Spain into Europe – and what better way to do it than to increase human, commercial and cultural traffic over the Pyrenees? Pilgrimages to Jerusalem and Rome were already in vogue; after the long centuries of the Dark Ages, the Church was keen on re-establishing contacts across the old Roman Empire that it had inherited for Christianity.

The French were the great promoters of the Camino de Santiago (the Way to Santiago), so great in fact that the most commonly tramped route became known as the *camino francés*. The first official pilgrim was Gotescalco, bishop of Le Puy, in 950; others followed, including Mozarab Christians (those living under Moorish rule) from Andalucía, who emigrated north and put themselves under the protection of Santiago, founding some of the first churches and monasteries along the road in the province of León.

In the next century, especially once the frontier with the Moors was firmly pushed back to the south bank of the Duero, the French monks of the reforming abbey of Cluny did more than anyone to popularize the pilgrimage, setting up sister houses and hospitals along the way. Nor were the early Spanish kings slow to pick up on the commercial potential of the road; Sancho the Great of Navarra and Alfonso VI of Castile founded a number of religious houses and institutions along the way |and invited down French settlers to help run them. It was at this time too that the French stuck another oar in with their *Chanson de Roland*, which made Charlemagne something of a proto-pilgrim, although his adventure into Pamplona happened decades before the discovery of James's relics.

The 12th century witnessed a veritable boom along the *camino francés*: the arrival of new monastic and military orders, including the Templars, Hospitallers and Knights of Santiago, who all vowed to defend the pilgrim from dangers en route. In 1130, the Abbey of Cluny commissioned Aymery Picaud, a priest from Poitou, to write the *Codex Calixtinus*, the world's first travel guide, chock-full of prejudices and practical advice for pilgrims: he describes the four main roads through France and gives tips on where not to drink the water, where to find the best lodging, where to be on guard against 'false pilgrims' who came not to atone for crimes but to commit them. The final bonus for Santiago de Compostela came in 1189, when Pope Alexander III declared it a Holy City on equal footing with Jerusalem and Rome, offering a plenary indulgence – a full remission from Purgatory – to pilgrims on Holy Years (if you're planning a trip, the next will be 2010; other years you'll only get half time off). The favourite song they would sing along the way was the *Ultreya*:

Dum Pater familias, rex universorum
donaret provincias ius apostolorum
Jacobus Hispanias lux ilustrat morum
Primus ex apostolis, martyr Jerosolimis
Jacobus egregio, sacre et martyrio.
Herru Sanctiagu, grot Santiagu
e ultreia e suseia, Deus adiuva nos

(Our father, King of the Universe/Concede the land to apostolic right/Santiago of Spain is the light illuminating tradition/First among the Apostles, martyr of Jerusalem/Distinguished Santiago, holy and martyred/Lord Santiago, Great Santiago!/And Forward! and Onward! God help us!)

The Tour de Saint-Jacques in Paris was a traditional rallying point for groups of pilgrims (there was more safety in numbers); from there the return journey was 1,280km (800 miles) and took a minimum of four months on foot. It was not something to go into lightly, but for many it was more than an act of faith, a chance to get out and see the world. By the time of Aymery Picaud, the French had been joined by pilgrims from across Europe. Many were ill (hence the large number of hospitals), hoping to complete the pilgrimage before they died. Not a few were thieves, murderers and delinquents condemned by the judge to make the journey for penance. Sometimes dangerous cons had to do it in chains. To keep them from cheating or stealing someone else's indulgence (the Compostellana certificate), pilgrims had to have their documents stamped by the clergy at various points along the route, just as they do today (as a nice touch, the old stamps and seals have recently been revived).

An estimated half a million people a year made the trek in the Middle Ages (out of a European population of about 60 million) and, even in the 18th century, the so-called century of Enlightenment, the pass at Roncesvalles still counted 30,000 pilgrims a year. But in the 19th century numbers fell dramatically; most of the monasteries and churches were closed for ever with the confiscation of church lands in 1837; many were converted into stables or simply pillaged for their building stone. In the 1970s, just when it seemed as defunct as a dodo, the pilgrimage made a remarkable revival, due to a number of factors – the modern world's disillusion-ment with conventional religion; the search for something beyond what over-organized day-to-day life and church attendance can offer and, more prosaically, the growth of ecological and alternative tourism. In 1982 John Paul II became the first pope ever to visit Santiago; in 1985, UNESCO declared it the 'Foremost Cultural Route in Europe', helping to fund the restoration of some of the Romanesque churches that punctuate the trail. Although modern roads have changed the face of the pilgrimage for ever, efforts have been made to create alternative paths for pedestrians, marked every 500m with a stylized scallop shell; new inexpensive *hostales* have sprouted along the way for walkers or cyclists. The pilgrims' quest is back in business.

The Field of the Star

In the Middle Ages it took real courage to leave home and make such an arduous, perilous journey west to Finisterre; back then, as today, there was more to it than just picking up an indulgence to deposit as credit in the Bank of Grace. The pilgrimage was one of the few opportunities for the average Middle Ager to attain a consciousness and understanding beyond the strict limits of Church dogma. All the humbuggery over the 'discovery' of the Apostle's relics in the far northwest corner of Spain would never have caught the popular imagination so powerfully had it not been for the deep mythopoeic resonances already present; especially for the Celts, the far west was the abode of souls that pass on. It was an ancient Indo-European belief that a star appears in the Milky Way whenever a mortal is born, and shoots towards the west when they die, towards the realm of the dead in, as for example the Celts conceived it, the Castle of the Goddess Arianhrod (the constellation Corona Borealis). Similarly, according to Plato, the dead go to the celestial west, to the spot where the Milky Way meets the circle of the Zodiac – towards the real 'Compostela' (*campus stellae in finis terrae*), the 'field of the star at the world's end'. To make the journey to the end of the world *while still alive* was to come to terms with our ultimate destiny, to vanquish and harrow hell, to understand the mystery in a unique way with both the body and mind. There were certainly plenty of miracles and mysteries for the pilgrims to ponder as they followed the setting sun, both in legends and in the subject matter chosen by the sculptors who decorated the portals and capitals of the churches along the way. Much of their symbolism is enigmatic in the extreme. With the destruction, deterioration and ham-handed restoration of so many pilgrim churches and hospitals, many important clues left by the itinerant guilds of builders were lost, but the remains include Celtic and other pagan symbols, man-eating lions, eagles and snakes, two-headed monsters, jovial eroticism, labyrinths, figures from the zodiac or from the 'labours of the months', and much more, along with a wide range of orthodox and unorthodox depictions of scenes from scripture.

Aymery Picaud's *Codex Calixtinus* divided the *camino francés* into 13 days or stages. Some are rather long hauls, possible only with a fresh horse, others are short and walkable; some of the stages are to famous towns like León and Burgos, others to dusty one-horse nowheres, apparently chosen arbitrarily, which existed on their reputation only as long as the *Codex Calixtinus* was consulted. The number 13 has its own deep resonance, going back to the proto-pilgrimages of ancient Egypt, when a journey down the Nile was a living re-enactment of the journey made by an Egyptian after death. Egypt itself was a metaphor for the heavens, while the Nile was divided into 12 parts representing the Zodiac, as a lunar year is 12 or 13 months. As if to prove that such ideas reached Spain, a curious 9th-century BC Egyptian alabaster burial urn, found at Almuñécar and displayed in the Casa Castril in Granada, has hieroglyphs that suggest such a pilgrimage:

I have arrived from my foreign land. I have passed through countries and have heard about your being, you of the primordial state of the two lands, you who have engendered what exists. In you your two eyes shine. Your Word is the way of life that gives breath to all throats. Now I am in the horizon, flooded by the happiness of the harija oases, and I speak to it like a friend. In me there is a source of health, of life, beyond your shores.

The Wild Goose Chase
One theory has it that the Goose Game, a favourite children's pastime in Spain and most continental countries, is a playful memory of the pilgrimage, the medieval path of initiation. The Goose Game first became popular at the time of Philip II, the age when anything faintly outside church dogma was likely to lead to an auto-da-fé. In the Goose Game, the board has a path of 63 squares set in a spiral, leading inwards to the goal, with a picture of a goose in the centre, a total of 64. Twelve of the 63 squares also have pictures of geese, which are invariably good to land on; another nine have obstacles (the bridge, the inn, the dice, the well, the labyrinth, the prison, death, and the gateway to the goal). Players roll dice to move their markers around the board.

A number of writers on Compostela, beginning with Louis Charpentier who wrote *The Mystery of Compostela* (1973), have remarked on the persistency of the word 'goose' in the place names along the Camino de Santiago. *Oca* is Spanish for goose, *Ganso* is the Visigothic German, *Anser* the Latin, and a look at the map reveals that northwest Spain has far more than its share of goosey names: El Ganso, the Montes de Oca, Rio Oja, Puerto de la Oca, the river Anso.

Goosiness permeates the other side of the Pyrenees too. In France, *dévider les jars*, 'to spin the ganders', meant to speak in argot, the secret language of the builders' confraternities. The mysterious, now vanished Agotes (or Cagots in French), an outcast race who lived on either side of the Navarrese Pyrenees, were often forced to wear a goose foot around their necks. Basques had a race of lovely but goose-footed fairies, the *laminak*, and Toulouse was the home of the famous Visigothic queen Ranachilde, wife of Theodoric II. Better known as *la reine pédauque*, the 'goose foot', her story inspired the legend of goose-footed Berthe, Charlemagne's mum, a rather domestic queen who told children stories by her spinning wheel (French fairytales customarily begin with 'In the time when good Queen Berthe spun...'). Andrew Lang found the first reference to Mother Goose, *La Mere d'Oye*, in 1650.

So why choose, of all God's creatures, a goose as the key? One guess is that the goose is only a European adaptation of the Egyptian ibis, the bird sacred to Isis that destroyed the eggs of the Nile crocodile and annually battled winged serpents from Arabia (geese are pretty handy with serpents too, as every farmer knows). The figure of Isis distantly haunts the whole *camino*, which is littered with miraculous, usually dark-faced statues of the Virgin, her Christian equivalent. The Universal Way to Compostela, the Milky Way, the Starry Stairway to Heaven, was a path of initiation into the mysteries of life and death and unity of all things. A wild goose chase, for those who understood the cosmic joke. Why else would the figures Master Mateo carved on the cathedral of Santiago laugh so merrily?

Pilgrim Facts

To be considered a pilgrim you have three choices of transport: foot, horse or bicycle.

On foot, if you're reasonably fit and can clock up 30km (19 miles) a day, expect a journey of six weeks from Roncesvalles to Santiago; to enjoy the experience and take in all the monuments along or just off the way, give yourself two months. To get the Compostela certificate in Santiago (and the time off Purgatory that goes with it), genuine pilgrims are expected to bring a letter of accreditation from their parish priest, from one of the world-wide confraternities, including the **Confraternity of Saint James UK** (for members only), c/o Marion Marples, 27 Blackfriars Rd, London, SE1 8 NY, *www.csj.org.uk*. The 'credential letter' (*credencial* in Spanish) must be stamped along the way in order for pilgrims to qualify for the Compostela certificate (you must complete 100km on foot, or 200km by bicycle). The credential letter also entitles you to stay free or very cheaply in the *refugios* run by towns, churches or monasteries along the way, although the accommodation is often little more than a place to lay a sleeping bag; note that they can have fairly early curfews. The footpath is well marked, though bear in mind that in most parts of the trip, especially in Castilla y León, you won't have a footpath at all, but a dusty verge along a busy highway. July and August may have the best weather for the trip, but also bring the most traffic.

Spanish organizations devoted to helping pilgrims and answering questions include the **Federación Española de Asociaciones de Amigos del Camino de Santiago**, C/Ruavieja 3, Logroño-La Rioja, t 941 24 56 74, *www.caminosantiago.org*. There are numerous useful websites, including *www.jacobeo.net* (Spanish only), *www.csj.org.uk* (in English), and *www.americanpilgrims.com* (in English). Spanish tourist offices can also provide basic information.

To the insufficiently pious, the real revelation of the pilgrimage is that when you get to the end, there's simply nothing there – just a corpse that could be a mythical character's or anybody's. In the Goose Game, the square just before the goal is the Tomb, and if you land here you're dead and have to start again from the beginning. To those who see the pilgrimage as containing a secret teaching for a few, that's just the point. Once you have made it to Santiago de Compostela, it would hardly make sense not to go all the way to land's end. It isn't far, and the trail meets the sea at Noia, a place that was a holy site long before Compostela, with Neolithic dolmens, and a churchyard full of mysterious tombstones from the Middle Ages, carved with signs and motifs that no one has ever explained.

Roland the Rotter

All over the Pyrenees, you'll find memories of Roland – from the *Brèche de Roland* in the High Pyrenees, hewn with a mighty stroke of his sword Durandal, to a menhir on Mt Aralar that he tossed like Obélix. From here, his fame spread across Europe, remembered in everything from Ariosto's Renaissance epic *Orlando Furioso* to the ancient, mysterious statue of 'Roland the Giant' in front of Bremen city hall.

But who is this Roland really? Outside of the *Chanson de Roland*, information is scarce. The chronicler Eginhardt, writing *c.* 830, mentions a certain Roland, Duke of the Marches of Brittany – who perished in Charles the Great's famous ambush in the Pyrenees in 778 – without according him any particular importance. Two hundred years later this obscure incident had blossomed into one of the great epics of medieval Europe. Here is the mighty hero, with his wise friend and companion-in-arms Oliver. Here is the most puissant knight in the army of his uncle Charlemagne, come down from the north to crusade against the heathen Muslims of Spain. Charlemagne sweeps all before him, occupying many lands south of the Pyrenees and burning Pamplona to the ground before coming to grief at an unsuccessful siege of Zaragoza. On their return, Roland and Oliver and the peers of the rearguard are trapped at the pass of Roncesvalles, thanks to a tip from Roland's jealous stepfather Ganelon. Numberless hordes of paynims overwhelm the French; though outnumbered, they cut down Saracens by the thousands, like General Custer or John Wayne against the savage Injuns. Finally Roland, cut with a thousand wounds, smites his sword Durandal against the rock, meaning to keep it from the hands of the infidels (although in the *Chanson* he ends up heaving it in the air, whereupon it finally ends up stuck in the cliff at Rocamadour, a major site on the pilgrims' road in southwest France). He then sounds his horn Oliphant to warn Charlemagne, who alas is too far away to rescue them, puffing so hard that he blows his brains out as Michael and Gabriel appear to escort his soul to heaven, the archetypal warrior victorious in defeat. History says it wasn't a Muslim horde at all, but rather the Navarrese Basques who did Roland in. And why shouldn't they get their revenge on these uncouth Franks who were devastating their land, trying to force this democratic nation to kneel before some crowned foreign thug who called himself their king?

How this affair metamorphosed into an epic at the turn of the millennium or how the caterpillar Roland of history re-emerged as the mythological butterfly in the *Chanson* is murky, but as with most epics it involved a modicum of propaganda. The immediate source of the *Chanson* is said to have been a famous vision of Roland given to an 11th-century archbishop of Pamplona, which transformed Basque farmers into infidel knights (just in time for the Crusades). For the French there was another bonus: glorification of Carolingian imperialism provided poetic justification for the expansionist dreams of the Capetian kings.

Of Racial Purity and Pork

Spanish history is shot through with tragicomic implosions. One of the most destructive was the mania for *limpieza de sangre* (purity of blood), a doctrine that so undermined the national economy in the 15th–17th centuries that all the loot from the Americas couldn't patch the gaping wound. Purity of blood meant pure Christian ancestry, something probably only a few Asturian and Basque hillbillies could claim with a clear conscience. But as the Reconquista swept south, Castile, more than any of the other kingdoms of the northwest, began to define itself as a nation by religious segregation. Many Jews and Moors tried to conform by converting and, although at first they were accepted without stigma, bigotry raised its ugly head in the 1400s, just as the Christians achieved total control.

The Jews were the first to go. In Spain since the Diaspora, they were an educated and useful minority, many of them doctors and moneylenders (two of the few professions they were allowed to exercise). They were the subject of the first 'purity of blood' law, the 1449 Toledo decree, issued in spite of opposition from the king of Castile and the pope: 'We declare that the so-called *conversos*, offspring of perverse Jewish ancestors, must be held by law to be infamous and ignominious, unfit and unworthy to hold any public office or benefice within the city of Toledo.' Many cities followed suit. In 1480, Isabel and Ferdinand refounded the Inquisition to institutionalize discrimination against *conversos*: any of them suspected of backsliding in the faith – or often anyone merely accused of it – would have their property confiscated by the state, and would probably be burned at the stake. In 1492, Isabel celebrated the conquest of Granada by booting the Jews out of Spain. The kings of Navarra took them under their wing, at least until 1514, when Navarra itself was gobbled up by Ferdinand. Not satisfied with this, the Inquisition after 1530 began posting in the cathedrals the names of everyone who had any dealings at all with the Holy Office, so that people suspected of 'tainted blood' could always be readily identified – and not hired for any important post. In response, books of family trees were published, to prove one's own purity or to disparage someone else's. *Limpieza de sangre* contributed more than anything to the prevailing atmosphere in 16th-century Spain, which could be described as raging, surreal paranoia. The economic result was more concrete: by bankrupting and expelling the Jews and *conversos*, the perennially broke kings of Spain had to borrow money from Genoese bankers at calamitous rates. The annual silver fleet from the Americas would sail into Seville only to be sucked up whole by the Italians.

Muslims who refused to convert were given their walking papers in 1502. Those who did convert, the *moriscos*, were robbed and booted out a century later. The *moriscos* were excellent farmers, experts in irrigation, and willing to perform jobs no pure-blooded Spaniard would touch. Although the usual mafia of aristocrats, especially the Count of Lerma, picked up a tidy bundle from the sale of their confiscated lands, the *moriscos'* departure left many parts of Spain not far from Skid Row. Philip III, imbecile spawn of many generations of Habsburg family incest, was the king who allowed the *moriscos* to be put out. Philip, incidentally, died from sitting too close to the fire – so weighty was his concept of his own nobility that he couldn't imagine getting up and moving away from the flames on his own.

The blood obsession was becoming increasingly kinky. In Spain, a true aristocrat would bleed 'blue', while his younger brothers, poor *hidalgos* (and Christ himself, profusely, in a thousand horror-show Spanish statues) bled red, and everyone else bled 'plain blood' unless they were Moors, Jews or Lutheran heretics, whose blood was said to be 'black'. The *hidalgos* (from *hijo de algo*, 'son of somebody'), once the backbone of medieval Castile, were by now a mentally deranged caste of haughty layabouts. Located at the bottom of the noble ladder, with neither land nor vassals, they came to be the class most obsessed with blood and honour. It was their sole capital, all that they had from the ancestors who achieved the Reconquista. Some of them went to America as *conquistadores*, but most stayed, impoverished and futile like Don Quixote, guarding the iron-bound coffers where they kept their letters patent, attesting to their arms, rank, and privileges that exempted them from direct taxation and debtors' prison, all the time depriving Spain of productive men and poisoning society with their attitude.

> *My father was afflicted by a disgrace which he passed on to all his sons like original sin. He was a hidalgo. This is not unlike being a poet, for there are few hidalgos who escape perpetual poverty and continuous hunger. He possessed letters patent of his nobility so ancient that even he was unable to read them, and no one cared to touch them for fear of getting their fingers greasy from the bedraggled knots and ribbons of the tattered parchments. Even the mice took care not to gnaw them lest they were stricken with sterility.*
>
> Estebanillo González (1646)

Short of resorting to being bled by a barber to see what colour of *sangre* leaked out, there were two sure-fire ways to tell a true Christian Spaniard: he hardly ever washed (monks in particular never bathed, and called the inevitable result 'the odour of sanctity'), and he ate lots of pork. Bathing was Jewish, Moorish and effeminate: one of the first acts of Isabel and Ferdinand after the conquest of Granada was to close the baths. If a suspect hadn't bathed, the second test was to offer him a bit of pig meat. Now this was perhaps a more honest vetting; Spain has been known for pork since ancient times; and even a historian like Diodorus Siculus could rave about Iberian 'hams transcendently superlative' in the 1st century AD.

We can suppose that making the pig into a badge of the True Faith could not happen without some distortion of the national psyche. Pigs and Spanish strangeness went hand in hand, sometimes in uncanny ways. Extremadura was long Spain's hog heaven, and the best, most exquisite porkers there were fed on vipers. Like so many *conquistadores*, the great, unspeakable Pizarro came from there; he was suckled by a sow, and started his career as a swineherd. The Spanish national psychosis of the old days, a witches' brew of *limpieza de sangre*, lust for

03 | Topics | Of Racial Purity and Pork

gold, vicious imperialism, hatred and bigotry, found its reflection in the kitchen, in an obsession with pork that can be disconcerting, even today.

The Spanish Distemper

Home on the Range

If you want to see the best-preserved early medieval frescoes in Spain, you'll have to go to Gaceo, a dusty nowhere off the road from Vitoria to Pamplona. It's an unpromising spot, but, if you can find the man with the key, there is a wonderful cartoon vision of heaven and hell – a rare relic from a lost world. So often in Spain, the real treasures are hidden in out-of-the-way places. Gaceo is a somewhat special case – a Roman road, later the Camino Real (now the N1), once ran through it. Still, it would be only natural to ask why such a huge expenditure, by medieval standards, of money and talent should have been lavished on tiny Gaceo. That question itself is a key to understanding Spain.

All over Castile, in scores of cities and even villages, you will sense there were great expectations long ago, and greater disappointments afterwards. A dusty hamlet will sport an arcaded Plaza Mayor that never quite grew into a stone one like Vitoria's or Madrid's. Similarities with provincial American towns are obvious: a half-built feeling, streets ludicrously too wide for the traffic, laid out anticipating a boom that never came, and a couple of Plateresque palaces, sticking out from the humble tile roofs like the grand Victorian business blocks amidst the car parks of wasted American city centres. Like America, and unlike any European country save Russia, Spain has a heritage as a frontier society. Nearly every valley and plain south of the Cordillera Cantábrica knows a history of reconquest from the Moors and Christian resettlement. Romans, Vandals, Alans, Suevi, Byzantines, Franks, Visigoths and Arabs had all done their part to make Spain's central plateau into an empty waste. From the 800s, when the Asturians and others began to cross the mountains, to the final victory over the heathen Moor in 1492, the wave of the Reconquista spread gradually southwards; at one time every part of it was the scene of pioneers reclaiming land and founding villages and towns. And, as in the American West, the money that fuelled the expansion came largely from livestock – sheep, not cows. The biggest ranchers were the *hidalgos*, and they dominated frontier political life by influence and force; the towns found themselves constantly on the defensive against the *hidalgos'* attempted land grabs and extortions.

Few frontier expansions in history ever came off quite like this one, though. The people that started America's push west arrived logically from behind the frontier; many of Spain's, bizarrely enough, came from beyond it. The northwest was hardly overflowing with population at the beginning of the Reconquista, and the numbers were largely supplied by Mozarab Christians from Muslim-ruled Spain, from al-Andalus, looking for free land and a Christian atmosphere. Few facts were ever recorded about this trickling exodus, but it is reasonable to assume that Mozarabs with the gumption to pack up and move into the lonesome *meseta* were also likely to be the most fanatical supporters of Christianity and the new Christian states. And instead of half-naked Indians without towns or technology, the heathen enemy of the new Spanish frontiersmen happened to be probably the most delightful and sophisticated civilization in the Western world, led by caliphs whose greatest joys were writing lyrical poetry and planting pleasure gardens with tinkling fountains. Such irony can weigh on a nation's soul.

The pioneer warriors of the north had a secret weapon in their fight against the Moors – utter ruthlessness. Organized in highly mobile raiding parties, they could extort tributes from the Muslim lands simply by threatening to girdle their irreplaceable olive trees. Destroying crops and villages was another key tactic. The Christians expanded their boundaries by making the lands beyond uninhabitable. It all worked brilliantly, and behind the lines the new Spain gradually took shape. What happened in the end to all hopes of the frontiersmen can be read in Spain's sad history. The boom did come, fitfully and unequally, but nearly every village and town of Castile enjoyed at least a few decades of dizzying prosperity, enough to at least begin some grandiose projects. The woebegone church at Villalcázar de Sirga comes to mind. Santa María looks to have been planned to match the size of Burgos cathedral, and thrown up in a hurry. Sadly it never got more than a third finished, and the dust blows around it today. As always, after the boom came the bust, and what a bust it was. Castile has been busted ever since.

El Cid Campeador

In the Spanish pantheon El Cid Campeador comes in a close second to Santiago himself, but unlike Arthur, Siegfried, Roland and other heroes of national medieval epics, the Cid, Rodrigo Díaz de Vivar (1043–99), was entirely flesh and blood. Born in Vivar near Burgos, his unique title is derived from the Arabic *sayyidi* ('my lord'), and *Campeador*, which means 'Battler'. His fame spread widely among both Moors and Christians (in his career he served both Alfonso VI of Castile and the Emir of Zaragoza); even before his death, ballads celebrated his prowess. The greatest achievement of his life, the capture of Valencia from the Moors in 1095, took place when he was already 52 years old.

Through modern eyes, Rodrigo was little better than a gangster, but for the warrior class of the Reconquista he served as a model of virtue – fearless, with an exaggerated sense of honour, devoutly Catholic yet wholly pragmatic, a generous conqueror, devoted to his family, who paid his debts and always kept his word. The Cid was the perfect man for his time, living in the frontier society among Christians, Moors and Jews, where a king's powers were limited, and the main issues of the day were the simple pleasures of turf and booty.

For all that, 'O Born in a Happy Hour' – Rodrigo's other nickname – would not have had such a long shelf life, inspiring such diverse spirits as Corneille and Hollywood (where he was played, inevitably, by Charlton Heston), if there weren't something more to his character. This comes through in the epic *Poem of the Cid*, composed around 1140, less than half a century after his death. For 500 years the actual poem was lost, until 1779 when the royal librarian, through some literary detective work, located a copy from 1307, appropriately enough in Vivar, the Cid's home town. Not a single ounce of the magic or marvellous touches the text; the Rodrigo Díaz who emerges lies and cheats, but has a rustic sense of humour and a certain generous charm, always ready to praise another, happy to have his wife and daughters present to watch him 'earn his bread' fighting the Moors. You can't help liking the guy. His saga, though somewhat repetitive to read, is also the first known example of the Spanish gift for realism that would reach its climax in Cervantes' *Don Quixote*. Actually, even more realism would have been in order, for life on the frontier was not always the stuff of poetry.

Reconquista Man

Here he comes. Slouching in a rough woollen tunic, García Gómez is riding out of the sorrowful wilderness of the Cantabrian mountains and into history. García Gómez may look the Arkansawyer redneck of the American frontier, the sort that proverbially 'never had nothin', never learned nothin', and don't want nothin'', but he is a man on the make. He's got himself an iron sword, while his daddy had to get by with a big stick that he cut himself, like Little John – he carried it around, and anyone that gave him any lip was likely to get a taste of it with iron; such encounters are fewer but a little more dangerous. Of course being a Castilian, he is a *hidalgo*, really *hijo de algo*, a 'son of somebody'; we're all *muy noble y muy leal*, ain't we boys? At least as much as the big shot who owns the castle – he just came and nicked it from the former proprietor. Nicked his wife too.

The first thing to do is clear some land. And as you can see from the Castilian landscape today, there was something in García Gómez that didn't love trees. They used to say that a squirrel could go from Portugal to the Pyrenees, if he wanted, without touching ground. Juan José and his sons will do their best to blot out the offending forests, and the *coup de grâce* will be administered by the Habsburgs, who as we remember were always building armadas, and also creaming the profits off the timber trade for themselves and sending them home to Germany. Next thing to do is wrestle all the stones out of the fields, and build a dry-stone house. Piece of cake. In a generation or two, with a lot of luck and an eye constantly on the main chance, the family will be able to afford a little showplace – one of the hundreds of rude hilltop castles that gave Castile its name.

Unlike the settlers of the American West, García Gómez did not come over the mountains with his Bible in his hand. He couldn't really read it, and anyhow the Church doesn't exactly hand them out – a little later, when Ferdinand and Isabel bring in the Inquisition, a man could get himself incinerated just for reading one in Spanish. It might give him ideas. But García Gómez is content to let the learned clerics tell him what to believe. The mysteries of faith, all conducted in Latin of course, are too subtle for him, and the Church supplies the insistent propaganda that shapes his life: the triumph of the only faith over the godless Moors and Jews. Every now and then, fire-eating preachers like St Peter Martyr do the circuit, rousing the fools in the towns against the heathens, and our man will ride into town for the show; afterwards the good townspeople usually let off some steam, and any resident heathens are happy to escape with their lives. The towns are mostly of the one-horse variety (León, the biggest, counted a thousand souls at most in the early 11th century, maybe ten times that while they were building their cathedral) and they are not there to show a Gómez a good time. They're full of suspicious monks, merchants and officials, and, though they'd usually let him through the gate when he and the town weren't feuding, García Gómez hardly ever has reason to go.

Status in this neck of the woods is a horse. Being able to afford one of these most prized commodities ensures Garcia Gómez's position as one of the mounted warriors in the local count's retinue, ready to form an army for the king or a springtime expedition south to fight the Moors and grab some booty. A horse was the most significant investment the average man could have, but the men of the Reconquista knew how to make it pay. Then as now, Arabian blood was prized most of all – it was mainly through Spain that Arabian horses first came into Europe. The profits to buy the beast came from sheep. Gómez has a nice little spread, and a village of malodorous tenant farmers to kick in a little rent. They pay taxes and tithes, as do the townspeople. Gómez, being a *hidalgo*, does not.

Keep your eye on this boy, for he is blessed by the gods. Tucked away on a peninsula at the extremity of Europe, the *hidalgo* has nobody to bang away against except the hapless Moors, and eventually he will have all their land and goods. By 1500, flushed with ill-gotten wealth, he will be troubling the peace of Europe, and soon after he and his sword will be tramping around the Andes, up into Kansas and down the Amazon. And finally, before he rides off into the sunset he will burn himself out completely, tilting at windmills on the plains of La Mancha.

The Saving Grace

For all the sound and fury of the Reconquista, all the waste and futility, was anything left that would last? There are people capable of conjuring up beauty and delight in any age, and at the beginning of the Middle Ages Europe had the cash to do it in stone for the first time since the late Roman Empire. 'So it was,' wrote an 11th-century chronicler, 'as though the world had shaken herself and cast off her old age, and were clothing herself everywhere in a white garment of churches.' Spain shared fully in this flowering of Romanesque architecture and art; indeed the little Christian kingdoms of the north were the unlikely vanguard of the movement.

Where did the Romanesque come from? Unlike most parts of western Europe, northern Spain had very few Roman buildings left to serve as models. But from scattered examples around Europe and the Middle East it is easy to see a continuous progression everywhere, from late Roman architecture through the Dark Ages. The real homeland of Romanesque seems to be Syria, where Greek Christians built elegant basilican churches with plenty of rounded arches, windows and blind arcading up until the 7th-century Muslim conquest. Syrian monks, including most likely the architects and painters, spread across Christendom after that as refugees, taking the style with them. In this age buildings of any kind are few, and records almost nonexistent, and while early Romanesque works in Armenia, northern Italy and Asturias may show some striking similarities, it is impossible to say too much about how they got that way. Europe's first Romanesque churches appeared in the hills of Asturias in the 9th century, practically the only important architecture anywhere in Europe from that dark time. These showed classical elements, pediments, columns and arches, as well as considerable borrowings from the Muslim south: notably delicate double windows called *ajimeces*, divided by a column, and horseshoe arches, a native Spanish style that the Moors had adapted from the Visigoths.

In the sudden, explosive burst of energy and economic expansion after the magic year 1000, the impulse to build and create spread across Europe; in Spain, as elsewhere, the Romanesque churches were the symbol of the new civilization that had emerged from the chrysalis of the Dark Ages. One of the oldest Asturian buildings, San Miguel de Lillo at Oviedo, has carvings of what seems to be a circus scene, setting the tone for the wild imaginative freedom that characterizes all Romanesque art. The greatest charms of most churches are the carved portals, capitals and cloisters, on which you will see not only scriptural scenes, but legions of fantastical monsters, legendary heroes from Hercules to Roland, mermaids, farting monks, droll-looking insects, intricate floral designs and arabesques, demons, house cats, camels and leopards, spirals, labyrinths, hunting scenes, whales – everything in God's good creation, along with many things God never thought of, boiling up from the depths of the medieval unconscious. Unlike every age of religious art that followed, the Romanesque was never constrained by any narrow Church dogma; perhaps the most striking example is the number of frankly erotic scenes, as on the portal of the country church at Cervatos in Cantabria. Anything at all that could be experienced, or imagined, was a fit subject to decorate the House of God.

Expressive freedom in the Romanesque was hardly limited to stone-carving. The buildings themselves show a wide variety of ideas. Every province of Europe had its own distinct style and, within each, builders were often free to follow their fancy; eccentricities in northern Spain range from the octagonal churches at Eunate and Torres del Río in Navarra, modelled after the Holy Sepulchre in Jerusalem (these were either built or inspired by the Templars), to the outlandish Santa María del Sar at Santiago, built with the columns and walls of the nave tilted precariously outwards, or the Basque church of San Miguel de Arratxinaga in Markina, built over a huge dolmen – many early churches, most perhaps, replaced pre-Christian holy sites. What ties all the disparate Romanesque works together is a simple theory of proportion. Instead of the classical 'orders', medieval builders employed a new system of sacred architecture based on constructive geometry. Anyone with a mathematical bent will enjoy looking over the buildings, seeing how every point in them can be proved with a compass and straightedge, just as their builders designed them. Later ages of religious building may be more showy, more technically sophisticated, but none has the same hold over the imagination. The Romanesque is the art of springtime, of a new world where rules were few and fancy could wander where it liked.

The pilgrimage trail to Santiago is also a pilgrimage through some of medieval Europe's finest creations, from rustic one-aisled village churches to the great basilica of Santiago de Compostela, the biggest and most ambitious Romanesque work in Spain. Some of the other major attractions include Santo Domingo de Silos, south of Burgos, with the most beautiful Romanesque cloister in Spain; Estella, with a wealth of Romanesque buildings; San Martín at Frómista, west of Burgos; and the remote area called the 'Románico Palatino', north of Frómista, with the biggest concentration of Romanesque country churches in Europe.

Food and Drink

04

Fish Soup and Pig's Ear

The massive influx of tourists has had its effect on Spanish kitchens, but so has the Spaniards' own increased prosperity and, perhaps most significantly, the new federalism. Each region, each town even, has come to feel a new interest and pride in the things that set it apart, and food is definitely one of them. Northern Spain, with its markedly different personalities, is a special treat in this regard.

Seafood is undoubtedly the star of the show in the areas along the northern coast. The Atlantic has much more and better seafood than has the Mediterranean, and the ardent fishermen of this region are perfectly positioned to nab the best of it. They have plenty of practice cooking the stuff – archaeologists have found remains of sea urchins in settlements 10,000 years old. The bounty of the sea finds expression in famous **fish soups**, from the western *caldereta Asturiana* to the Basque *ttoro*, and there are any number of prized delicacies in every region: surprising things, such as *kokotxas*, 'cheeks' of the hake, or the Galician *vieiras de Santiago*, scallops cooked with almonds. On the whole, though, Spaniards try to keep their seafood simple. Galicians like to cook fish with potatoes and garlic; Basques do it with simple garlic and parsley sauces.

By popular acclaim, the champion cooks of northern Spain – really of all Spain – are the **Basques**, who coincidentally are also the most legendary eaters. Like the Greeks, the well-travelled Basques take their culinary skill with them everywhere. Basque restaurants turn up in unlikely places all over France, and it isn't unusual to drive through a dusty, one-horse town out in the American West where the only restaurant serves up good Basque home cooking.

Marseille may have its *bouillabaisse*, among a score of other exotic and treasured fish stews of southern Europe, but the Basques stoutly maintain their version, called *ttoro* (pronounced *tioro*), is the king of them all; naturally there is a solemn confraternity of the finest *ttoro* chefs. A proper one requires a pound of mussels and a mess of crayfish and congers, as well as the head of a codfish and three different kinds of other fish. Basque cuisine relishes imaginative yet simple sauces, including the legendary *pil pil* (originally named for the sound it made while frying), where somehow olive oil, garlic, and chillies magically meld with the cooking juices of salt cod. Another delight is fresh tuna cooked with tomatoes, garlic, aubergine and spices and *chipirones* (squid) – reputedly the only kind in the world that are all black, and better than they sound.

Each Basque chef knows how to work wonders with elvers (*angulas* or *txitxardin*) in garlic sauce, salmon and the famous *txangurro* – spider crab, flaked, seasoned, stuffed and served in its own shell. Gourmets especially recommend *kokotxas a la Donostiarra*, hake cheeks with a garlic and parsley green sauce, clams and slightly piquant red *guindilla* peppers. These peppers are another icon of the Basque kitchen; housewives still hang strings of them on the walls of their houses for drying (and for decoration). Peppers turn up everywhere: in omelettes, in sauces for seafood, or in the common stewed chicken. Basques like to wash it down with *txakoli*, a tangy green wine produced on the coast with just a modicum of sunlight.

The **Galicians** too have their talents in the kitchen, with the best of the best seafood, including some delicacies found nowhere else in the world. Throughout

Spain, Gallego restaurants command as much respect as Basque. The estuaries are rich in an extraordinary array of seafood, from the famous scallops of Santiago and lobster to some creatures unique to Galicia such as *zamburiñas* scallops, lobster-like *santiaguiños*, and ugly *percebes*, that have no names in English. Quantity is matched by quality: Galician seafood is considered the best in the world and preparation is kept as simple as possible. Another favourite served in every town are *empanadas*, large flat flaky pies filled with eels or lamprey (the most sought-after; try it before you knock it), sardines, pork, or veal. Turnip greens (*grelos*) are a staple, especially in *caldo gallego*, a broth that also features turnips and white beans; in winter, the heartier *lacón con grelos*, pork shoulder with greens, sausages and potatoes, holds pride of place. Galicia produces Spain's best veal and good cheeses, such as Roquefort-like *cabrales* and *gamonedo*, both mainly from cow's milk mixed with smaller quantities of ewe's or goat's milk; birch-smoked pear-shaped San Simón; or mild, soft *ulloa* or *pasiego*. A tapas meal to make a Gallego weep includes grilled sardines, *pulpo gallego* (tender octopus with peppers and paprika), roasted small green peppers (*pimientas de Padrón*), with chewy hunks of bread and lightly salted breast-shaped *tetilla* cheese, washed down with white Ribeira wine. For dessert try *tarta de Santiago* (almond tart), and to top it all off, a glass of Galician fire water, *aguardiente* – served at night after a meal to ward off evil spirits – properly burned (*queimada*), with lemon peel and sugar.

Inland, though you'll still find plenty of seafood, the cuisine is an entirely different world. Cooking can be heavy, almost medieval, with plenty of roasts and chops, stews and game dishes – partridge and pheasant are special favourites. Local dishes include *chuletas de cordero a la navarra* (lamb chops), *truchas con jamón* (trout stuffed with ham) or, for something out of the ordinary, *liebres con chocolate* (hare with chocolate), washed down by the good strong wines from Tudela and Estella. **Asturias** and **Cantabria** are the dairylands of Spain, and produce a number of cheeses, notably the Cabrales of Asturias, made from cow's, sheep's and goat's milk all mixed together. Asturias has its famous dishes too, including hake in *sidra* (the ubiquitous local cider) or *fabada*, a mess of beans usually served with pork.

You would do well to sharpen your taste for **pork** before venturing into **Castile**. Here not much of the pig gets thrown away. Besides the famous ham, the bacon, chops and such, Castilians take what's left to make endless sausages, smoked sausages, blood sausages, tripes and puddings. Castilians make the somewhat extravagant claim that pork 'spiritualizes the stomach' (back in the days of the Reconquista and Inquisition, eating it also confirmed one's status as a Christian), and the less expensive pig parts are the staple of cooking; big chunks of pig meat get thrown into all the heavy stews and casseroles that Castilians love. The apotheosis of the porker in Spain is *cochinillo asado*, roast suckling pig, and its capital is Segovia, where top *asadores* wear medals and cover their restaurant walls with parchment certificates that look like papal bulls, proclaiming their culinary achievements. *Cochinillo* can be a genuine treat, though from here the attractive-ness of the cuisine drops off rather sharply. Another favourite is the famous *botillo* of El Bierzo (*botillo del Bierzo*), which can include minced pork, sausages, fat, lips and ears. Wrap all this up in a pig's intestine, hang it in the chimney for two or three months, and there you are.

One of the symptoms of pork abuse is a permanent craving for **pulses** on the side. Red beans, white beans, chickpeas and lentils, the Spaniards' real staples are all those spirit-laden dried delights that Pythagoras and other philosophers warned us against (of course any Pythagoreans in Spain would have been tidied away by the Inquisition long ago). The 'musical fruit' adds much to the, let us say, expansive nature of much traditional cooking, as in the countryman's *olla podrida*, praised by Cervantes, or the 'Maragato stew' with chickpeas, pig's ears and trotters, and a few inches of blood sausage. Pork and beans is wagon cooking, the simple food of pioneers – pig-farming pioneers – and the presence of such a humble cuisine is another of the curious phenomena bobbing in the wake of Spain's curious history. It is the cuisine of the frontier experience.

Rioja, *Sidra* and Other Tipples

There are 55 areas in Spain under the control of the Instituto Nacional de Denominaciones de Origen (INDO), which acts as a guide to the consumer and keeps a strict eye on the quality of Spanish wine (DO, or *denominación de origen*, is the same as French AOC).

La Rioja is the best known and richest area for wine in Spain, producing a great range from young whites to heavy, fruity reds; it is divided into several sub-districts; east of Logroño, there is an extension of the La Rioja wine belt in Navarra. Rioja tastes like no other wine: soft, warm, mellow, full-bodied, with a distinct vanilla bouquet; its *vino de gran reserva* spends three years ageing in American oak barrels, and then another year in bottles, before release to the public. The Phoenicians introduced the first vines which, after the various invasions, were replanted under the auspices of the Church; the first law concerning wine was decreed by Bishop Abilio in the 9th century. The arrival of masses of thirsty pilgrims proved a big boost to business, much as mass tourism would do in the 1960s and 1970s.

Despite a long pedigree, the Rioja we drink today dates from the 1860s, when growers from Bordeaux, their own vineyards wiped out by phylloxera, brought their techniques south of the border and wrought immense improvements on the native varieties. By the time the plague reached La Rioja in 1899, the owners were prepared for it with disease-resistant stock. During the First World War, when the vineyards of Champagne were badly damaged, the French returned to buy up *bodegas*, sticking French labels on the bottles and trucking them over the Pyrenees. Rioja finally received the respect it deserved after Franco passed on to the great fascist parade ground in the sky. In the last 20 years, *bodegas* have attracted buyers from around the world and prices have skyrocketed. La Rioja's growing area covers 48,000 hectares, comprising three zones: Rioja Alta, home of the best red and white wines, followed by Rioja Alavesa (on the left bank of the Ebro in the Basque province of Álava) known for its lighter, perfumed wines, and the decidedly more arid Rioja Baja, where the wines are coarse and mostly used for blending – a common practice in La Rioja. The varieties used for the reds are mostly spicy, fruity tempranillo (covering some 24,000 hectares alone), followed by garnacha tinta (a third of the red production, a good alcohol booster) with smaller portions of graciano (for the bouquet) and high-tannin mazuelo (for acidity and tone). Traditional Rioja whites are relatively unknown but are excellent, golden and vanilla-scented like the reds: viura grapes are the dominant grape, with smaller doses of malvasía and garnacha blanca.

Unlike French wines, Riojas are never sold until they're ready to drink (although of course you can keep the better wines even longer). DOC rules specify that La Rioja's Gran Reserva, which accounts for only three per cent of the production, spends a minimum of two years maturing in American oak barrels (six months for whites and rosés) then four more in the *bodega* before it's sold. *Reservas* (6 per cent of the production) spend at least one year in oak and three in the *bodega*. *Crianzas* (30 per cent of the production) spend at least a year in the barrel and another in the bottle. The other 61 per cent of La Rioja is *sin crianza* and labelled CVC (*conjunto de varias cosechas*, 'combination of various vintages'): this includes the new young white wines and light reds (*claretes*) fermented at cool temperatures in stainless steel vats, skipping the oak barrels altogether and losing most of the vanilla tones.

Of course you'll find plenty of other Spanish wines in the region. **Euskadi** is known for its very palatable young 'green' wine called ***txacoli*** (in 1994 made a *denominación de origen*), which is poured into the glass with bravura from a height, like cider. *Txakoli* is made along the coast, around Getaria and Zarautz, as well as in small regions in Vizcaya and Álava provinces. In addition, there is a small, recently declared DO region around León, **El Bierzo**, with light and fruity reds (Casar de Valdaiga is a good one). Galicia's excellent **Ribeíro** (west of Ourense), made from aromatic albarino grapes, resembles the delicate *vinho verde* of neighbouring Portugal; other good wines from the region are **Rías Baixas** (areas on the coast near Pontevedra, and south of Vigo on the Portuguese border) and **Valdeorros** (east of Ourense) – pleasant, light vintages that complement the regional dishes, seafood in particular.

Much of the inexpensive wine sold throughout the country comes from **La Mancha** or the neighbouring **Valdepeñas** DO regions. And then there is **Jerez**, or what we in English call **sherry**. When a Spaniard invites you to *tomar una copa* (glass) it will nearly always be filled with this Andalucían sunshine. It comes in a wide range of varieties: *manzanillas* are very dry, *fino* is dry, light and young (the most famous is Tío Pepe); *amontillados* are a bit sweeter and rich; *olorosos* are very sweet dessert sherries, and can be either brown, cream or *amoroso*.

North of the Cordillera Cantábrica in Asturias, where apples grow better than vines, they produce hard **cider**, or ***sidra***, which can come as a shock to the taste buds for the first five minutes, then it goes down just fine. Cider means as much to Asturians as milk to babies; Basques are fond of good hard cider too. They claim to have taught the more famous cider-makers of Normandy and Asturias their secrets, and, back in the 1500s, Basque fishermen used to trade the stuff with the American Indians for furs.

Spanish **brandy** (mostly from Jerez too) is excellent; the two most popular brands, 103 (very light in colour) and Soberano, are both drunk extensively by Spanish labourers and postmen at about 7am (they throw a shot into their breakfast coffee and call it a *carajillo*). ***Anís*** (sweet or dry) is also quite popular. ***Sangría*** is the famous summertime punch of red wine, brandy, mineral water, orange and lemon with ice, but beware – it's rarely made very well, even when you can find it. Each region has its wine and liqueur specialities and nearly every monastery in Spain seems to make some kind of herbal potion or digestive liqueur that tastes more or less like cough syrup. In the Basque country, look for **Izarra**, a potent mix of Pyrenean herbs with exotic spices, which comes in either green or the less potent yellow; for something more unusual you can top off your meal with a tipple of deadly Basque hooch, *pacharán* (sloe brandy).

Practicalities

Learning to Eat the Spanish Way

Going to Spain, you may have to learn to eat all over again; dining is a much more complex affair here than in many countries. The essential fact to learn is that Spaniards like to eat all day long – this scheme spreads the gratification evenly through the day, and it facilitates digestion, which in Spain can be problematic. Give it some consideration. Start out with a big coffee, a *doble*, and a pastry (mostly poor French clones, with extra sugar) or find a progressive-looking bar where you might find a more fitting breakfast – a glass of wine or brandy, and a salami sandwich or *pincho*, or a glazed American doughnut. These bars will be around all day, their piles of treats under the glass cases on the bar growing by the hour, an eternal alternative to a heavy sit-down dinner. Ask around for the one that does seafood tapas. As if the bars weren't enough, there are *pastelerías* in the towns with all sorts of savoury pastries, *merenderos* (snack stands) in the countryside, and ice cream everywhere. You will never be more than a hundred feet from ice cream in a Spanish town. For a mid-morning or mid-afternoon energizer, there are sweet 'n' greasy *churros* (those inscrutable fried things that look like garden slugs) sold in bars and *churrerías*, dipped in thick cups of rich chocolate, for most non-Spaniards a once in a lifetime gut-gurgling experience.

The best **restaurants** are almost always those specializing in regional cuisine, though at the upmarket end of the scale you'll find plenty of new restaurants with innovative dishes heavily influenced by what the Basques call their *cocina nueva* – as with French *nouvelle cuisine*, expect a lot of surprising combinations, peculiar sauces and an obsession with appearances. There are still thousands of old-fashioned restaurants around – and many of the sort that travellers have been complaining about for centuries; Spanish cooking still usually comes a bit on the heavy side. The worst offenders are often those with the little flags and ten-language menus in the most touristy areas, and in general you'd do better to buy some bread, Cabrales cheese and a bottle of Rioja red and have a picnic. But the regions along the northern coast have a repertoire of traditional dishes as gratifying as any in the country, and seafood is undoubtedly the star of the show.

In any coastal town or village, the best seafood restaurants will be around the harbour. The fancier ones will post set menus, while at the rest you'll find only a chalkboard with prices listed for a plate of grilled fish, or prawns or whatever else came in that day. It's a convivial arrangement; just choose a plate, or negotiate a full dinner with the waiter. Don't expect seafood to be a bargain, though; a plate of prawns in garlic all by itself usually costs about €8–10.

If you dine where the locals do you'll be assured of a good deal if not necessarily a good meal. Almost every restaurant offers a *menú del día*, or a *menú turístico*, featuring an appetizer, a main course, dessert, bread and drink at a set price, always a certain percentage lower than if you had ordered the items *à la carte*. These are always posted outside the restaurant, in the window or on the plywood chef by the door; decide what you want before going in if it's a set-price menu, because these bargains are hardly ever listed on the menu the waiter gives you at the table. Unless it's explicitly written on the bill (*la cuenta*), service is not included in the total, so tip accordingly. Spaniards will just round up the bill by a few euros – 10 per cent is considered ludicrous, and 3–5 per cent is generous – but in tourist areas there are different expectations of visitors.

If you are travelling on a budget you may want to eat one of your meals a day at a tapas bar or *tasca*. **Tapas** (*caxuelitas* in Basque, though this is very unusual) means 'lids', and they started out as little saucers of goodies served on top of a drink. They have evolved over the years to form a main part of the world's greatest snack culture. Bars that specialize in them have platter after platter of delectable titbits, from shellfish to slices of omelette or mushrooms baked in garlic or vegetables in vinaigrette or stews. All you have to do is pick out what looks best and order a *porción* (an hors-d'œuvre) or a *ración* (a big helping) if it looks really good. It's hard to generalize about prices, but on average €15–20 of tapas and wine or beer will really fill you up. You can always save money in bars by standing up; sit at that charming table on the terrace and you'll find prices can jump considerably.

Another advantage of tapas is that they're available at what most Americans or Britons would consider normal **dining hours**. Spaniards are notoriously late diners; in the morning it's a coffee and roll grabbed at the bar, a huge meal at around 2 or 3pm, then after work at 8pm a few tapas at the bar to hold them over until supper at 10 or 11pm. After living in Spain for a few months this makes perfect sense, but it's exasperating to the average visitor. On the coasts, restaurants tend to open earlier to accommodate foreigners (some as early as 5pm) but you may as well do as the Spaniards do. Galicians are the early diners of Spain (8 or 9pm); Basques do it from 9 to 11 – if you can find a restaurant at all. In quieter non-touristy areas they will be inconspicuous and few. Just ask someone, and you will find a nice **comedor** with home cooking tucked in a back room behind a bar – if you hadn't asked you never would have found it. Such *comedores* (literally, dining rooms), where the food and décor are usually equally drab but cheap, are common everywhere, along with *cafeterías*, those places that feature photographs of their *platos combinados* (combination plates) to eliminate any language problem. Dinner will go for between €12 and €15, and you'll find as many good ones as real stinkers. *Asadores* are restaurants that specialize in roast meat or fish; *marisquerías* serve only fish and shellfish. Visit one in the countryside on a Sunday lunchtime when all the Spanish families go out to eat and make merry.

There are also many Chinese restaurants in Spain which are fairly good and inexpensive (though all pretty much the same), and American fast-food outlets in the big cities and resort areas; while Italian restaurants are 98 per cent dismal in

Spain, you can usually get a reasonable pizza. Don't neglect the rapidly disappearing shacks on the beach – they often serve up barbecued sardines that are out of this world. **Vegetarians** are catered for in the cities, which always manage to come up with one or two veggie restaurants, usually rather good ones too. In the countryside and away from the main resorts, proper vegetarians and vegans will find it hard going, though tapas make it easier to get your nutrition than in some other southern European countries. Navarra, perhaps the best producer of fruit and vegetables in Spain, is particularly good for veggies. Fish-eaters will manage just about everywhere.

What to Drink Where

No matter how much other costs have risen in Spain, **wine** has remained refreshingly inexpensive by northern European or American standards. What's more, the north produces much of Spain's best – the famous reds of La Rioja and a number of good whites from Galicia. A restaurant's *vino del lugar* or *vino de la casa* is always your least expensive option while dining out; it usually comes out of a barrel or glass jug and may be a surprise either way. Anyone with more than a passing interest in wine will want to visit a *bodega* or two. A good place to start would be Haro, the growing and marketing centre for the wines of Rioja Alta, with a clutch of *bodegas* near the train station (*see* p.124).

Northern Spain is not all wine, though. One bottle of Asturian **cider**, or *sidra*, is usually enough if you mean to do any walking afterwards; if not, the ritual of drinking it can make your evening. In any proper restaurant the waiter will hold the bottle over his head and pour it into a pint glass held behind his hip. The ones with the most *duende* do it without looking, splashing the stuff all over you, the floor, themselves, and people at three or four adjacent tables. This is done to air the stuff out; for the same reason they never put more than an inch in the glass, but it's a point of honour among them never to let your glass stay empty longer than fifteen seconds. In most bars they'll just leave the bottle (green, without a label and returnable) on the table and let you try it yourself. *Sidrerías* are the social centres of every Asturian town and village (there are also quite a few in Euskadi); to find one just follow your nose. In summer they migrate out onto the streets, and whole families gab around them until one in the morning, with small children bicycling between the tables.

Many Spaniards prefer **beer**, which is generally nondescript. The most popular brand is San Miguel, but try Mahou Five Star if you see it. Imported whisky and other **spirits** are pretty inexpensive, though even cheaper are the versions Spain bottles itself, which may come close to your home favourites.

Coffee, **tea**, all the international **soft drink** brands and the locally made Kas round off the average café fare. Spanish coffee is good and strong and if you want a lot of it order a *doble*; one of those will keep you awake even through the guided tour of a Bourbon palace. In summer look for the bars that make *blanco y negros* – coffee and ice cream treats that quickly become addictive in the hot sun. Ground almonds whipped to create ***horchata de chufa*** are also refreshing in summer.

Spanish Menu Reader

Entremeses (Hors d'œuvres)

aceitunas olives
ancas de rana frogs' legs
caldo broth
gambas pil pil shrimp in hot garlic sauce
gazpacho cold soup
huevos al plato fried eggs
huevos de flamenco baked eggs in tomato sauce
huevos revueltos scrambled eggs
sopa de ajo garlic soup
sopa de arroz rice soup
sopa de espárragos asparagus soup
sopa de fideos noodle soup
sopa de garbanzos chickpea soup
sopa de lentejas lentil soup
sopa de verduras vegetable soup
tortilla Spanish omelette, with potatoes
tortilla a la francesa French omelette

Pescados (Fish)

acedías small plaice
adobo fish marinated in white wine
almejas clams
anchoas anchovies
anguilas eels
angulas baby eels (elvers)
ástaco crayfish
atún tuna fish
bacalao codfish (usually dried)
besugo sea bream
bogavante lobster
bonito tunny
boquerones anchovies
caballa mackerel
calamares squid
cangrejo crab
centolo spider crab
chanquetes whitebait
chipirones baby squid
  ...en su tinta ...in its own ink
chirlas baby clams
cocochas hake cheeks
dorado sea bass
escabeche pickled or marinated fish
gambas prawns (shrimps)
langosta lobster
langostinos giant prawns
lenguado sole
lubina sea bass
mariscos shellfish
mejillones mussels
merluza hake
mero grouper
navajas razor-shell clams
ostras oysters
pejesapo monkfish
percebes barnacles

pescadilla whiting
pez espada swordfish
platija plaice
pulpo octopus
rape monkfish
raya skate
rodaballo turbot
salmón salmon
salmonete red mullet
sardinas sardines
trucha trout
ttoro Basque fish stew
veneras scallops
zarzuela fish stew

Carnes y Aves (Meat and Fowl)

Note: *cazuelas, cocidos, estofados, guisados, fabadas and potajes are all kinds of stew.*

albóndigas meatballs
asado roast
bistec beefsteak
buey ox
callos tripe
cerdo pork
chorizo spiced sausage
chuletas chops
cochinillo sucking pig
cola de toro see under 'rabo'
conejo rabbit
corazón heart
cordero lamb
faisán pheasant
fiambres cold meats
filete fillet
hígado liver
jabalí wild boar
jamón de Bayonne cured ham
jamón de York baked ham
jamón iberico cured ham
jamón serrano raw cured ham
lengua tongue
liebre hare
lomo pork loin
morcilla blood sausage
paloma pigeon
pato duck
pavo turkey
perdiz partridge
pinchitos spicy mini-kebabs
pollo chicken
rabo/cola de toro bull's tail with onions and tomatoes
riñones kidneys
salchicha sausage
salchichón salami
sesos brains
solomillo sirloin steak
ternera veal

Verduras y Legumbres (Vegetables)
ajo garlic
alcachofa artichoke
apio celery
arroz rice
   ...*a la marinera* with saffron and seafood
berenjena aubergine (eggplant)
cebolla onion
champiñones mushrooms
col, repollo cabbage
coliflor cauliflower
endibia endive (chicory)
ensalada salad
espárragos asparagus
espinacas spinach
garbanzos chickpeas (garbanzo beans)
judías (verdes) French beans
lechuga lettuce
lentejas lentils
patatas potatoes
   ...*fritas/salteadas* ...fried/sautéed
   ...*al horno* ...baked
pepino cucumber
pimiento pepper
puerro leek
remolacha beetroot (beet)
setas Spanish mushrooms
zanahoria carrot

Frutas y Nueces (Fruit and Nuts)
albaricoque apricot
almendras almonds
avelanas hazelnuts
cacahuetes peanuts
castañas chestnuts
cerezas cherries
ciruelas plums
ciruelas pasas prunes
dátiles dates
durazno nectarine
frambuesas raspberries
fresas strawberries
fruta de la pasión passion fruit
granada pomegranate
grosellas redcurrants
grosellas o casis blackcurrants
higos figs
lima lime
limón lemon
mandarina mandarin
mango mango
manzana apple
melocotón peach
melón melon
membrillo quince
moras blackberries
naranja orange
nueces walnuts
pera pear

picotas black cherries
piña pineapple
plátano banana
pomelo grapefruit
sandía watermelon
uvas grapes

Postres (Desserts)
arroz con leche rice pudding
bizcocho/pastel/torta cake
blanco y negro ice cream and coffee float
canutillos rolls of flaky pastry filled with custard
flan crème caramel
galletas biscuits (cookies)
helado ice cream
pantxineta almondy *gâteau basque* filled with cream or cherry jam
pasteles pastries
queso cheese
requesón cottage cheese
tarta de frutas fruit pie
turrón nougat

Miscellaneous
aceite oil
arroz rice
azúcar sugar
ensalada salad
huevos eggs
mantequilla butter
pan bread
pimienta pepper
sal salt
vinagre vinegar

Bebidas (Drinks)
agua con hielo water with ice
agua mineral mineral water
   ...*sin/con gas* ...still/sparkling
batido de leche milkshake
botella (media) bottle (half)
brandy brandy
café (con leche) coffee (with milk)
caña draught (beer)
cava Spanish champagne
cerveza beer
chocolate caliente/hecho hot chocolate
dulce sweet (wine)
granizado slush, iced squash
hielo ice
leche milk
seco dry
semi-seco semi-dry
spumoso sparkling (wine)
té (con limón) tea (with lemon)
vaso glass
vino (tinto, rosado, blanco) wine (red, rosé, white)
zumo de manzana/naranja apple/orange juice

Planning
Your Trip

05

When to Go

Climate

You have just one guess to figure out what makes the north coast of Spain so luxuriantly green. The Cordillera Cantábrica stops all the weather fronts coming over the Atlantic and squeezes out all the precipitation; the coast gets between three and four inches of rain in August – and the real rainy season doesn't start until September. Galicia seems to get a bit less rain than the coastal regions to the east, and the high Castilian plains are climatically another world – hot and dry most of the year, chilly and strange in winter. La Rioja enjoys a more reasonable climate between the two extremes, which is very good for the vines. For the coast as a whole, rain is spread around the calendar; plenty of it falls from September to January, with July the most reliable month (only an inch or two, if you're lucky). The rain champion is the Basque coast, which can get seven or eight feet a year, as much as Wales or the west of Ireland.

Spring and summer are the best times to visit; the winter can be pleasant, though damp and chilly. Most Spanish homes – and hotel rooms – are not made for the winter. High season is between June and September, when the ocean is warm enough for water sports, and the fiesta calendar is in full swing.

Festivals

One of the most spiritually deadening aspects of Francoism was the banning of many local and regional fiestas in Spain. These are now celebrated with gusto, and if you can arrange your trip to include one or two you'll be guaranteed an unforgettable holiday. The big holidays celebrated throughout Spain are *Corpus Christi* in late May or early June; Holy Week (*Semana Santa*), the week preceding Easter; 15 August (the Assumption of the Virgin); and 25 July (the feast day of Spain's patron, Santiago). No matter where you are, there are bound to be fireworks or processions on these dates, especially for *Semana Santa* and *Corpus Christi*.

Many village patronal fiestas feature *romerías* (pilgrimages) up to a venerated shrine. Getting there is half the fun, with everyone in local costume, riding on horseback or driving covered wagons full of picnic supplies. Music, dancing, food, wine and fireworks are all necessary ingredients of a proper fiesta, while the bigger ones often include bullfights, funfairs, circuses and competitions. In the Basque lands and Navarra, summer fiestas often feature a loose bull or two stampeding through the streets – an *encierro*. 'Giants' (10ft-tall dummies of Ferdinand and Isabel and a Moor) and 'fatheads' (comical or grotesque caricatures) pirouette through the throngs.

The Calendar of Events opposite is hardly complete: during the summer every village has its own special fiesta.

Tourist Information

After receiving millions of tourists each year for the last four decades, no country has more information offices, or more helpful ones, or more intelligent brochures and detailed maps. Every city will have an office, and you will almost always find someone who speaks English except in rural areas. Sometimes they'll be less helpful in the big cities in the summer. More often, though, you'll be surprised at how well they know the details of accommodation and transportation. Many large cities also maintain municipal tourist offices, though they're not as well equipped as those run by the Ministry of Tourism, better known as *Turismo*. Opening hours for most offices are Monday to Friday, 9.30–1.30 and 4–7.

Nearly all the provinces in Northern Spain have websites for everything you might want to see and do whilst there; some are more informative than others. Try: *www.bilbao.net*, *www.infoasturias.com*, *www.cfnavarra.es/ turismo*, *www.spain.info*, *www.euskadi.net/ turismo*, *www.liebanaypicosdeeuropa.com*, *www.turgalicia.es*, *www.turismo.cantabria.org*.

Average Maximum Temperatures °C/°F

	Jan	April	July	Oct
San Sebastián	15/58	27/81	34/93	24/75
A Coruña	16/61	25/77	27/81	26/79

Average Monthly Rainfall mm/in

	Jan	April	July	Oct
San Sebastián	142/5.5	84/3.3	92/3.6	142/5.5
A Coruña	125/4.9	78/3	35/1.4	135/5.3

Calendar of Events

Note that many of these dates are subject to change (to fit weekends, etc.); a call ahead to the tourist office is always a good idea.

January

6 *Los Reyes* (the Three Magi) procession, Baiona (Pontevedra).

15 *San Mauro*, big fiesta with fireworks, Villanova de Arousa (Pontevedra).

19–20 St Sebastian's Day, *Tamborrada*, when scores of drum corps bang their way through the streets, followed by feasting, San Sebastián (Guipúzcoa).

22 Fiesta, San Vicente de la Barquera (Cantabria).

Third Sun *San Vicente*, bachelors' party, Los Arcos (Navarra).

Last Mon and Tues *Zanpantzar*, pre-Christian dances of the *joaldunaks*, with pointed hats, sheepskins and big bells, Ituren and Zubieta (Navarra).

28 *San Tirso*, with dances and the burning of a papier-mâché *falla*, Villafranca del Bierzo (León).

30 *San Lesmes*, patron of Burgos.

February

Carnival A big affair everywhere in Spain. Some of the biggest celebrations are in Bilbao, San Sebastián, Vitoria, Tolosa (with a *pelota* championship). The entire week before Lent, Asturias puts on the biggest show in the northwest: at Avilés on Saturday and Tuesday; at Gijón on Monday; and in Oviedo on Tuesday, or Mardi Gras, the day before Ash Wednesday.

Every Sun Horse-racing in San Sebastián.

March

Two Sundays after 4th *Javierada*, two important pilgrimages for St Francis Xavier, Javier (Navarra).

March–April

Palm Sunday Procession at Monte San Tecla, A Garda (Pontevedra).

Semana Santa (Easter/Holy Week) In the north, it's the Castilians who really get into the processions, especially at León and Covarrubias (Burgos). Good Friday brings *Los Picaos*, medieval-style self-flagellants, San Vicente de la Sonsierra (La Rioja); Descent from the Cross, Vivero (Lugo); mystery plays, Balsameda (Vizcaya), processions in Hondarrabia and Segura (Guipúzcoa). In Avilés (Asturias), Easter and Easter Monday are celebrated with the

Fiesta del Bollo, with folklore groups, cake-eating and regattas.

First Sun after Easter *Fiesta de San Telmo*, including bull-running on the beach, Zumaia (Guipúzcoa); San Vicente de Barquera's *La Folia*, where the sailors transport an image of the Virgin at night in an illuminated maritime procession (Cantabria).

April

2nd Sun after Easter *Fiesta de San Isidoro*, León.

2nd Mon after Easter *Fiesta de San Telmo*, Tui (Pontevedra).

19 *Fiesta de Santísimo Cristo*, Finisterre.

End April Wine Festival, Ribadavia (Ourense).

May

First weekend *Día de las Almadías*: rafts are built and floated downriver to commemorate the ancient method of log transport, followed by picnics in the Irati and Salazar Valleys (Navarra).

10–15 Saint's day and parades, Santo Domingo de la Calzada (La Rioja).

22 *Santa Rita*, Vilagarcía de Arousa (Pontevedra).

23 Anniversary of the Battle of Clavijo (La Rioja).

Corpus Christi Usually falls at the end of May or early June (Thursday after Trinity Sunday), initiating four days of festivities. Also, *Procesión del Olé*, with dances, Frómista (Palencia); flower carpets in the streets, Ponteareas (Pontevedra). On the first day after Corpus Christi, *Los Corpillos* dances and celebrations at Las Huelgas, Burgos; Maragato festivals, Astorga (León) and surrounding areas.

June

11 *San Bernabé*, with the distribution of grilled fish, Logroño (La Rioja).

12 *San Juan*, with *encierros*, giants and Maragato bagpipers, Sahagún (León).

21–24 *La Magdalena*, with Basque sports, Bermeo (Vizcaya), followed by a nautical *romería* to the isle of Izaro; *San Juan*, bonfires and fishwives' festivities in Laredo (Cantabria); for midsummer's day, 'bonfires of San Juan' in many Basque villages; León celebrates St John's Day with parties and bullfights, bonfire in Plaza Alfonso II, Oviedo (Asturias).

24 *Fiesta de San Juan*, Laguardia (Álava); *Vueltas de San Juan*, Nájera (La Rioja).

26 *Fiesta de San Pelayo*, Zarautz (Guipúzcoa).

End of June *San Felices de Bilibio*, pilgrimage and drunken 'wine battles', Haro (La Rioja); *La Semana Gastronómica*, San Sebastián;

La Amuravela, satirical poems on the year's events in the local dialect and lots of drink Cudillero (Asturias).

29 *Fiesta de San Pedro*, Orio and Zumaia (Guipúzcoa); wine battle, Haro (La Rioja); beginning of two weeks of International Folklore *Feria*, Burgos, San Pedro.

30 *Fiesta de San Marcial*, Irún (Guipúzcoa); *El Coso Blanco*, processions and fireworks, Castro Urdiales (Cantabria).

July

All month International Jazz Festival, the biggest in Spain, San Sebastián.

All month Santander holds its International Music Festival.

First Sun *Rapa das Bestas* (Gallego wild horse round-ups, races and shearings), Viveiro and San Lorenzo de Sabucedo (Lugo). At La Estrada (Pontevedra), another *Rapa das Bestas*, with big festivities from Sat till Mon.

5–9 Getxo Jazz Festival, both international and national bands, Getxo (Vizcaya).

7–14 Famous running of the bulls and mad party for *San Fermín*, Pamplona (Navarra).

11 *San Benitiño de Lérez*, with river races and pagentry, Pontevedra (Galicia).

13 *Tributo de las Tres Vacas*, Piedra de San Martín, French mayors from the Baretous valley give Spanish mayors from the Roncal valley a tribute of three cows, renew their peace vows and name the keepers who will watch the common grazing land.

15 'Catch the goose' and other country fair-type festivities and humour, Comillas (Cantabria); Avilés (Asturias) has dances, entertainment and bullfights.

16 *Virgen del Carmen* with boat processions, Muros and Concubión (A Coruña).

Third week Jazz festival, Vitoria (Álava).

Second fortnight International horse-racing competition, San Sebastián.

Last half Historical sound and light pageant, Nájera (La Rioja).

22 Boat races, Basque sports and dancing, Bermeo (Vizcaya); *Fiesta de Santa María Magdalena*, Rentería (Guipúzcoa); fiesta with the dance of the *Zancos*, down the streets and steps on stilts, Anguiano (La Rioja).

24–30 *Santa Ana*, music and dancing for a week, Tudela (Navarra).

25 *Santiago de Compostela*, great celebrations for Santiago – national offering to the saint, the swinging of the *botafumeiro*, burning of a cardboard replica of Córdoba's Mezquita, fireworks and more; *Romería de Saniaguiño do*

Monte, with bagpipes and a sardine and pepper feast, Padrón (A Coruña); shepherds' festival, Cangas de Onís (Asturias). Also Vitoria and Bilbao's saint's day, Santiago.

Last Sun *Fiesta de la Playa*, Langosteira (Finisterre); *Fiesta de los Vaqueros*, La Braña de Aristébano, by Luarca (Asturias).

29 *Fiesta de San Pedro*, Mundaka (Vizcaya); *Vaqueiro* festival, mock wedding and dances, Luarca (Asturias); pilgrimage made in coffins by people who narrowly escaped death the year before, Santa María de Ribarteme (Pontevedra).

31 *Fiesta de San Ignacio*, Getxo (Vizcaya) and Azpeitia (Guipúzcoa).

August

3–9 Ancient fiesta, with giants, and the only *encierro* in Spain where women can run with the bulls, Estella (Navarra); Basque sport finals, Biarritz (Pays Basque).

First Sat Great kayak race on the Río Sella, Arriondas-Ribadesella (Asturias).

First Sun Asturias Day celebrations, with lots of folklore, Gijón. Festival of Albariño wine, Cambados (Pontevedra); Santa Cruz, Ribadeo (Lugo).

4–10 Giants, music, bonfires and more, for the *Virgen Blanca* – one of Spain's best parties (*see* p.176), Vitoria (Álava).

6 *Fiesta de San Salvador*, Getaria (Guipúzcoa).

9–11 *San Lorenzo* festivities, folklore and kayaking, Foz (Lugo).

10 *San Juan Dantzak*, procession and traditional dancing, Berástegui (Guipúzcoa); International Celtic Music Festival, Cudillero.

Second Sun Mountain Day folklore, song contests, Cabezón de la Sal (Cantabria); octopus-eating festival and bagpipe music, Carballino (Ourense); *romería* to the Ermita de Oca, Villafranca de Montes de Oca (La Rioja).

15 *Zikiro-Jatea* festival in Zugurramurdi (Navarra) with a popular picnic held in the caves on the 17th.

15–16 *Fiesta de San Rocco*, Gernika (Vizcaya); on the Saturday after the 15th, Bilbao starts its *Aste Nagustia* or *Semana Grande* ('Great Week'), with Basque sports and races; a week-long international fireworks festival starts in San Sebastián (Guipúzcoa); Assumption of the Virgin and San Roque festivities at Sada (A Coruña), with a big sardine roast; bagpipes and ancient dances, Llanes (Asturias); *El Rosario*, fisherman's fiesta, Luarca (Asturias).

15–19 Battle of flowers, Betanzos (A Coruña).

20 Running of the bulls, Tafalla.

26 *Festa da Istoria*, Ribadavia (Ourense); the whole village celebrates its origins with street pageantry and markets.

Last week Cider festival with free tasting and pouring competitions, Gijón (Asturias).

Last Sun Pilgrimage and music, Vivero (Lugo); *encierro*, Calahorra (La Rioja).

31 St Ignacio de Loyola Day, Loiola (Guipúzcoa); Battle of Flowers, Laredo (Cantabria).

September

First week Basque food festival, San Sebastián (Guipúzcoa).

1–8 Festival with Basque 'goose games', a contest between boatmen to pull the head off a goose with a greased neck, Lekeitio (Vizcaya).

6–10 *Fiestas del Portal*, Ribadavia (Ourense).

7–8 *Encierro*, Ampuero (Cantabria).

7–10 Pilgrimage of *Nostra Señora da Barca*, Muxía (A Coruña).

2nd week Basque games, Zarautz (Guipúzcoa).

8 *Fiesta de la Virgen de Guadalupe*, Fuenterrabía (Guipúzcoa); Virgin's birthday, celebrations in many places; *Fiesta de la Virgen de la Encina*, Ponferrada (León); pilgrimage at Cebreiro (Lugo); *San Andreu*, Cervo (Lugo).

8–10 *Fiesta de Santa Eufemia*, Bermeo (Vizcaya).

12 International Film Festival, San Sebastián.

14 Festival, Altsasu (Navarra).

16 Folk festival, Llanes (Asturias).

19 Vendimia wine festival of La Rioja, Logroño.

Second fortnight *Quincena Musicale*, classical music fortnight in San Sebastián.

Third weekend Americas Day, celebrating the many immigrants to the Americas from Asturias, Oviedo.

29 *Fiesta de San Miguel*, Oñati (Guipúzcoa); traditional Basque dancing, Markina (Vizcaya).

Last weekend San Cosme y San Damián, with antique dances, Covarrubias (Burgos).

October

First Sun *Las Cantaderas*, with medieval song and a sacred dance, León.

13 *Fiesta de San Fausto*, Durango (Vizcaya).

Second Sun Shellfish festival, O Grove (Pontevedra).

18–20 *As San Lucas*, big horse fair dating from the Middle Ages, Mondoñedo (Lugo).

November

19 *Fiesta de San Andrés*, Estella (Navarra).

Last Sun Oyster festival, Arcade (Pontevedra).

December

13 *Santa Lucía* fair, Zumárraga (Guipúzcoa).

Last week *O Feitoman*, handicrafts fair, Vigo (Pontevedra); *Olentzero* processions in many Basque villages.

31 The 'National Offering to the Apostle' – a major religious ceremony with the *bota-fumeiro*, Santiago de Compostela.

Spanish National Tourist Offices

UK: 22–23 Manchester Square, London W1V 3PX, t (020) 7486 8077, *www.tourspain.co.uk*.

USA: Water Tower Place, Suite 915 East, 845 North Michigan Avenue, Chicago, Illinois 60611, t (312) 642 1992, *www.okspain.org*; 8383 Wilshire Blvd, Suite 960, Beverly Hills, California 90211, t (323) 658 7188; 666 Fifth Avenue, New York, NY 10103, t (212) 265 8822; 1221 Brickell Avenue, Suite 1850, Miami, Florida 33131, t (305) 358 1992.

Canada: 2 Bloor St West, Suite 3402, Toronto, Ontario, M4W 3E2, t (416) 961 3131, *www. tourspain.toronto.on.ca*.

Japan: Daini Toranomon Denki Building, 6F, 3-1-10 Toranomon, Minato Ku, Tokyo 105-0001, t + 81 (3) 3432 6141, *www.spaintour.com*. Provides information for Australian and New Zealand nationals.

Embassies and Consulates

Foreign Embassies, etc. in Spain

UK: Alameda Urquijo 2, Bilbao, t 94 415 76 00, *www.ukinspain.com*.

Ireland: C/ Elcano 5, Bilbao, t 94 423 04 14.

USA: C/ Serrano 75, Madrid, t 91 587 22 00. Consulate: Paseo de la Castellana 52, *www. embusa.es*.

Canada: C/ Núñez de Balboa 35, Madrid, t 91 423 32 50, *www.canada-es.org*.

Spanish Embassies, etc. Abroad

UK: 20 Draycott Place, London SW3 2RZ, t (020) 7589 8989; 1a Brook House, 70 Spring Gardens, Manchester M2 2BQ, t (0161) 236 1262; 63 North Castle Street, Edinburgh EH2 3LJ, t (0131) 220 1843.

05

Planning Your Trip | Embassies and Consulates

Ireland: 17a Merlyn Park, Ballsbridge, Dublin 4, t (01) 269 1640.

USA: 545 Boylston Street, Boston, MA 02116, t (617) 536 2506; 180 North Michigan Avenue, Chicago, IL 60601, t (312) 782 4588; 2655 Le Jeune Road, 203 Coral Gables, Florida, t (305) 446 5511; 5055 Wilshire Blvd, Suite 960 Los Angeles, CA 90036, t (323) 938 0158; 150 East 58th Street, New York, NY 10155, t (212) 355 4080; 2375 Pennyslvania Avenue NW, Washington, DC 20009, t (202) 728 2330.

Canada: 1 West Mount Square, Montreal H3Z 2P9, t (514) 935 5235; 200 Front Street, Toronto, Ontario, t (416) 977 1661.

Entry Formalities

Passports and Visas

Holders of EU, US, Canadian, Australian and New Zealand passports do not need a visa to enter Spain for stays of up to three months; most other nationals do.

If you intend staying longer in Spain, you should report to the Foreign Nationals Office (*oficina de extranjeros*) at the local police station and apply for a community resident's card (*tarjeta de residente comunitario*). EU citizens are no longer required to obtain a resident's card, although it can be useful. Non-EU citizens had best apply for an extended visa at home, a complicated procedure requiring proof of income, etc. You can't get a *tarjeta* without this visa.

Customs

Duty-free allowances have been abolished within the EU. EU nationals over the age of 17 can now import a limitless amount of goods for their personal use. For travellers coming from outside the EU, the duty-free limits are one litre of spirits or two litres of liquors (port, sherry or champagne), plus two litres of wine and 200 cigarettes. Much larger quantities – up to 10 litres of spirits, 90 litres of wine, 110 litres of beer and 3,200 cigarettes – bought locally and provided you are travelling between EU countries, can be taken through customs if you can prove that they are for private consumption only.

Residents of the USA may each take home US$400-worth of foreign goods without attracting duty, including the tobacco and alcohol allowance. Canadians can bring home $300 worth of goods in a year, plus their tobacco and alcohol allowances.

Disabled Travellers

Eurotunnel is a good way to travel to northern Spain by car from the UK, since passengers are allowed to stay in their

---

Disability Organizations

Spain

ECOM, Gran Vía de les Corts Catalanes Principal 562, Barcelona, t 93 451 55 50, *www.ecom.es*. A federation of private Spanish organizations which offer services for disabled people.

ONCE (Organización Nacional de Ciegos de España), C/ José Ortega y Gasset 18, t 91 577 37 56, *www.once.es*. Association for the blind.

UK

Access Travel, 6 The Hillock, Astley, Lancashire M29 7GW, t (01942) 88 88 44, *www.access-travel.co.uk*. Travel agent for disabled people.

Tourism for All, Hawkins Suite, Enham Place, Enham Alamein, Andover, Hants SP11 6JS, t 0845 124 9971, *www.holidaycare.org.uk*.

RADAR (Royal Association for Disability and Rehabilitation), Unit 12, City Forum, 250 City Road, London EC1V 8AF, t (020) 7250 3222, *www.radar.org.uk*. Open Mon–Fri 10–4.

RNIB (Royal National Institute of the Blind), 105 Judd Street, London WC1H 9NE, t 0845 766 9999, *www.rnib.org.uk*.

USA

Alternative Leisure Co., 165 Middlesex Turnpike, Suite 206, Bedford, MA 01730, USA t (718) 275 0023, *www.alctrips.com*. Organizes vacations abroad for disabled people.

American Foundation for the Blind, 11 Penn Plaza, Suite 300, New York, NY 10001, t (212) 502 7600, or t 800 232 5463, *www.afb.org*.

Mobility International USA, 132 Broadway, Suite 343, Eugene, OR 97440, t (541) 343 1284, *www.miusa.org*. International educational exchange programmes and volunteer service overseas for the disabled.

SATH (Society for Accessible Travel and Hospitality), 347 5th Ave, Suite 610, New York, NY 10016, t (212) 447 7284, *www.sath.org*. Travel and access information; also details other access resources on the web.

vehicles. By train, **Eurostar** gives wheelchair passengers first-class travel for second-class fares. Most ferry companies will offer special facilities if contacted beforehand. Vehicles fitted to accommodate disabled people pay reduced tolls on *autoroutes* through France.

Once you arrive, the facilities for disabled travellers are limited. Spanish public transport is not particularly wheelchair-friendly, though the rail operator RENFE usually provides wheelchairs at main city stations, and many trains are slowly being upgraded to provide services for the disabled (lift access to platforms, etc.). The Spanish Tourist Office has compiled a fact sheet and can give general information on accessible accommodation; more useful is the official Spanish hotel guide (*Guía Oficial de Hoteles*), published annually, which covers hotels throughout the country (available in most bookshops, €10). For wheelchair-accessible beaches, see *www.esplaya.com*.

Insurance and EHIC Cards

No inoculations are required to enter Spain, though it never hurts to check that your tetanus jab is up to date.

Citizens of the EU are entitled to a certain amount of free medical care in EU countries if they have a free **European Health Insurance Card** or **EHIC** (available online at *www.dh.gov.uk/travellers*, or *www.ehic.org.uk*, or by calling t 0845 606 2030, or by post using the forms available from post offices). You will need a card for every family member.

On arrival in Spain you should take your EHIC to the local office of the Instituto Nacional de Seguridad Social, where you'll be issued with a Spanish medical card and some vouchers enabling you to claim free treatment from an INSS doctor. Canadians, US citizens and those of other nations should check their individual health policies. As an alternative, consider a **travel insurance** policy covering theft and losses and offering 100 per cent medical refund; check to see if it covers extra expenses if you get bogged down in airport or train strikes. Beware that accidents resulting from sports are rarely covered by ordinary insurance. Make sure you save all doctor's and pharmacy receipts., plus police reports for thefts.

Maps

Cartography has been an art in Spain since the 12th-century Catalans charted their Mediterranean Empire in Europe's first great school of map-making. The tourist offices give out detailed maps of every town. Unfortunately, for rural areas you will not find the detail you need for serious exploration of the countryside, and Spanish signposting isn't all it could be.

The maps available in Britain and America aren't very good, and you won't find much better general maps in Spain. On most, the road system in particular will be out of date, thanks to Spain's ambitious road improvement programmes. Topographical maps for hikers and mountaineers can be obtained from **CNIG** (Centro Nacional de Información Geográfica), part of the Instituto Geográfico Nacional (IGN). There are shops in all provincial capitals, and their maps are usually available in larger bookshops. You can buy maps and travel books online from the Spanish travel bookshop **Altaïr**, *www.altair.es*.

If in the UK, visit **Stanfords** at 12 Long Acre, WC2, for the biggest selection, or you can buy online at *www.stanfords.co.uk*.

Money and Banks

The currency of Spain is the **euro**. Coins are issued in denominations of 1, 2, 5, 10, 20 and 50 cents, and 1 and 2 euros. Notes are issued in denominations of 5, 10, 20, 50, 100, 200 and 500 euros. For the latest exchange rates, check out *www.xe.com/ucc*.

Traveller's cheques are the safest way to carry money. Major international **credit cards** are widely used in Spain, although American Express is often not accepted and Diners' Club cards are almost never accepted. For purchases, you will have to show some ID (a passport or identity card) when using a card. Smaller hotels, *pensiones*, restaurants, bars and cafés, particularly in rural areas, won't accept credit cards. Museums and sights still almost never have credit card facilities.

Cash withdrawals in euros can be made from bank and post office automatic cash machines (**ATMs**) using your PIN; the specific cards accepted are marked on each machine, and all give instructions in English. Credit card companies charge a fee for cash, but exchange rates are often better than banks.

Most banks will change **traveller's cheques** and cash, and are open Mon–Fri 9–2; a few open on Sat 9–1. You can sometimes change money at travel agencies, fancy hotels, restaurants, stations and big department stores like El Corte Inglés. Exchange rates vary, and nearly all take a commission of varying proportions. Beware of private exchange offices in tourist areas, which can be a rip-off despite the 'no commission' sign.

Getting There

By Air

There is an astounding variety of flight options to Spain these days, especially from the UK. A high-season **scheduled** return costs from around £80 on a no-frills carrier, up to around £200 on a national airline. However, even British Airways and Iberia offer special deals. No matter how you go, you can always save by booking in advance.

There are international **airports** in Bilbao, Santander, Santiago de Compostela and Asturias/Oviedo, and smaller airports that receive internal flights in San Sebastián, A Coruña, Pamplona, Vitoria, Vigo and Hondarribia.

Charter flights, which are often much cheaper than scheduled flights (roughly £100 for a high-season return to Bilbao), can be booked through travel agents (*see* below).

British Airways has a daily flight to Bilbao from London Heathrow (code-sharing with Iberia).

easyJet operates twice-daily flights to Bilbao from London Stansted, and daily to Asturias.

Iberia flies direct to Bilbao from London Heathrow daily, and to Bilbao via Barcelona or Madrid from Manchester. There are connections with major UK cities via London Heathrow. Also direct flights to Santiago de Compostela and to Santander, Vitoria, Pamplona, Vigo, San Sebastián and A Coruña (via Madrid or Barcelona).

Airline Carriers

UK
British Airways, t 0870 850 9850, www.ba.co.uk.
easyJet, t 0905 821 0905, www.easyjet.com.
Iberia, t 08706 090 500, www.iberia.com.
Ryanair, t 0871 246 0000, www.ryanair.com.

USA and Canada
Air Canada, t 1-888 247 2262, www.aircanada.ca.
American Airlines, t 1-800 433 7300, www.aa.com.
British Airways, t 1-800 247 9297, www.ba.com.
Continental Airlines, t 1-800 231 0856, www.continental.com.
Delta, t 1-800 221 1212, www.delta.com.
Iberia, t 1-800 772 4642, www.iberia.com.
United Airlines, t 1-800 864 8331, www.ual.com.

Discounts and Special Deals

UK and Ireland
CIE Tours International, Ireland t (01) 703 1888, www.cietours.ie.
Flightbookers, UK t 0821 223 5000, www.ebookers.com.
Trailfinders, UK t 08450 58 58 58, www.trailfinders.com.

Joe Walsh Tours, Ireland t (01) 241 0800, www.joewalshtours.ie.
www.cheapflights.co.uk; *www.expedia.com*; *www.flydeals.co.uk*; *www.lastminute.com*; *www.opodo.com*.

USA and Canada
Air Brokers International, USA t 800 883 3273, www.airbrokers.com.
Last Minute Travel Club, USA t 1-877 970 3500, Canada t 877 970 3500, www.lastminuteclub.com. Payment of an annual membership fee gets you cheap standby deals; there are also special rates for the major car rental companies in Europe, and train tickets.
Spanish Heritage Tours, 200 Broadacres Drive, Bloomfield, NJ 07003, t 1-800 456 5050, www.shtours.com.
www.traveldiscounts.com. Members get special discount rates on flights, hotels and tours.
www.orbitz.com. Cheap flights, hotels and car rental companies.

Student Discounts

Students and under-26s are eligible for considerable reductions on flights, train fares, admission fees to museums, concerts and more. Agencies specializing in youth travel can help you apply for the correct ID cards.

Europe Student Travel, 6 Campden Street, London W8, t (020) 7727 7647.
STA Travel, www.sta-travel.com/www.statravel.co.uk. Has over 450 branches in countries all over the world, including more than 50 in the UK. Check the website, or call intersales: UK t 0871 230 0040; USA t 1-800 781 4040.
Travel Cuts, 187 College St, Toronto, Ontario M5T 1P7, t 1-866 246 9762, www.travelcuts.com. Canada's largest student travel specialist.

USIT, Aston Quay, Dublin 2, t (01) 602 1906, www.usit.ie. Also: Belfast, t (028) 903 27111; Cork, t (021) 427 0900; Galway, t (091) 565 177; Limerick, t (061) 415 069; Waterford, t (051) 351 762.
Youth Travel, t 0870 887 0135, www.gapyear.youthtravel.com. Online travel agency specializing in youth/student fares, ideas for gap years, international student cards and working abroad programmes, etc.

Ryanair has flights to Santander, Vitoria and Santiago de Compostela from London Stansted.

There are no direct flights to northern Spain from the **USA and Canada**, but numerous carriers fly direct to Madrid, Barcelona and Paris. A high-season return will cost around US$1,100–2,000. Alternatively, it may be cheaper to fly to London and pick up an onward flight to Spain from there, especially off-season (October–April).

By Train

Travelling by high-speed train makes an attractive alternative to flying from the UK. **Eurostar** departs from London St Pancras with direct connections to Paris (Gare du Nord; 2hrs 15mins) and Lille (1hr 40mins). Fares are cheaper if booked in advance and/or include a Saturday night away. You must check in at least 30mins before departure or you will not be allowed on the train. Prices range from around £55 (more than 21 days in advance) to £300 for a standard return.

Once you reach Paris or Lille, France's high-speed **TGVs** (*trains à grande vitesse*) shoot along at an average of 180mph, when they're not breaking world records. From London to Bilbao or San Sebastián it's a full day's trip, changing trains in Paris and usually at Bordeaux or Hendaye in the small hours of the morning. For Bilbao you will have to change at San Sebastián for the slow but scenic **EuskoTren** service, which takes 2½ hours. The TGV service from Paris to Bordeaux can cut some hours off the trip if the schedule works for you. Another option is to take a direct train from Paris to Vitoria, and take a bus or local train from there.

If you plan to take some long train journeys, it may be worth investing in a **rail pass**.

The good-value **Inter-Rail** pass, www.interrail.net (for European residents of at least six months) offers 16 days', 22 days' or one month's unlimited travel in Europe, plus discounts on trains to cross-Channel ferry terminals, and returns on Eurostar from £59. Inter-Rail cards are not valid on UK trains. You can also get an Inter-Rail One Country Pass for three days (£109, under-26s £71) or eight days (£229, under 26s £149).

Visitors from North America have a wide choice of passes, including **Eurailpass, Europass** and **France 'n' Spain Pass**, which can all be purchased in the USA. A one-month Eurailpass costs around $925/1,089 for those aged under/over 26 years. There are also **Senior Passes** for the over-60s.

Note that rail passes are not valid on Spain's numerous narrow-gauge (FEVE) lines; you will also have to pay supplements for any kind of express train. For information on Spanish trains, see p.67.

For long-distance train travel, **bicycles** need to be transported separately and must be registered and insured. They can be delivered to your destination, though this may take several days. On Eurostar you need to check in your bike at least 24 hours before you travel, or wait 24 hours at the other end. For more details, call t 08705 186 186.

Rail Europe handles bookings for all services, including Eurostar and French Motorail (trains that carry your car), and sells passes.

Rail Europe, UK 178 Piccadilly, London W1V 0BA, t 08708 371 371 (calls cost at least 8p per minute), www.raileurope.co.uk.
Rail Europe, USA t 1-888 382 724; Canada t 1-800 361 RAIL, www.raileurope.com.
Eurostar, t 08705 186 186, www.eurostar.com.

By Coach

Eurolines offers departures several times a week in the summer (once a week out of season) from London to Spain (although most require a change, usually in Paris or Tours), along the east coast as far as Alicante, or to Algeciras via San Sebastián and Burgos. From either San Sebastián or Burgos, it will be easy to find further connections to any other town in the northwest. Journey time from London to San Sebastián is 21 hours. The fare goes from £107–119 return, or to Vitoria and Burgos from £85–101. There are discounts for anyone under 26, senior citizens and children under 12. The national coach companies operate services that connect with the local bus system.

Eurolines, t 08705 143 219, *www.nationalexpress.com/eurolines*.

By Sea

Good price-comparison websites are *www.ferrysmart.co.uk* and *www.ferrybooker.com*.

P&O Ferries, UK **t** 08705 980 333, Spain **t** 90 202 04 61, *www.poferries.com*. Sailing from Portsmouth to Bilbao, P&O's *Pride of Bilbao* is the UK's largest ferry, with accommodation for 2,500 passengers and 600 cars. It also offers several restaurants, a cinema, sauna and swimming pool, and has cabins for all passengers. The service is year-round and usually departs every three days. Although fares vary throughout the year, at the time of research a high season return for two adults, one child and a car in an economy 4-berth cabin was around £926 if booked well in advance. The Spanish terminal is at the port of Santurzi, 13km from the centre of Bilbao. In Bilbao, contact **Ferries Golfo de Vizcaya**, C/ Cosme Echevarrieta 1, **t** 94 423 44 77.

Brittany Ferries, t 0870 907 6103, *www.brittany-ferries.co.uk*. Ferries from Plymouth to Santander; prices and services are comparable to the P&O ferry.

If you prefer to cross the Channel to France, **Brittany Ferries** sail from Portsmouth to Caen and St-Malo, Poole to Cherbourg and St-Malo, and Plymouth to Roscoff; and **P&O** can transport you from Dover to Calais.

Norfolkline, UK **t** 08708 70 10 20, *www.norfolkline-ferries.co.uk*. Dover to Dunkirk.

Prices range from £38 return for a foot passenger to £134 return for a vehicle with two passengers (high season). Cheaper fares are available in advance, e.g. £99 return for a car and five passengers.

SpeedFerries, UK **t** 08702 200 570, *www.speedferries.com*. Offers a high-speed service between Dover and Boulogne, which starts at £20 one-way for a car and five passengers.

By Car

From the UK via France you have a choice of routes. If you get a ferry (*see* above) or the Eurotunnel train (*see* below) to Calais, you may face going through or around Paris on the abominable *périphérique*, a task best tackled either side of rush hour. To avoid this, you can get a ferry from Portsmouth to Cherbourg, Caen, Roscoff or St-Malo (*see* above). From any of these ports, the most direct route takes you to Bordeaux down the western coast of France, past Biarritz to the border at Irún and on to San Sebastián and Bilbao. For something different, opt for one of the routes the pilgrims to Santiago followed over the Pyrenees, through Somport-Canfranc (down the N134/E7/N330 south of Pau) or the classic route through Roncesvalles (on the D933 from St-Jean-Pied-de-Port) – you can get warmed up for Spain by inspecting the French Basque country along the way.

You may find it less tiring to take the ferry from Plymouth to Santander, which cuts out driving through France and saves expensive *autoroute* tolls.

Eurotunnel trains carry cars and their passengers through the Channel Tunnel from Folkestone to Calais on a simple drive-on, drive-off system (journey time 35mins). Payment is made at toll booths (which accept cash, cheques or credit cards). Prepaid tickets and booked spaces are available, but at off-peak times you can just turn up and take the next available service. Eurotunnel runs 24 hours a day, all year round, with a service at least once an hour through the night. Return fares range from around £98 (the cheapest standard return) to £199 (flexible return fare). Drivers must carry **registration** and **insurance** papers. If you're coming from the UK or Ireland, the dip of the **headlights** must be adjusted to the right (you can buy patches to

Drivers' Clubs

For more information on driving abroad, contact the AA, RAC or, in the USA, the AAA:

AA, t 0870 600 0371, *www.theaa.com*.

RAC, t 0870 572 2722, *www.rac.co.uk*.

AAA (USA), **t** 800 222 4357, *www.aaa.com*.

stick on the headlights). Carrying a **warning triangle** is mandatory, and it should be placed 50m (55 yards) behind the car if you have a breakdown. **Seat belts** are mandatory; in addition, all cars in France are required to have rear seat belts and these must be worn by rear seat passengers. Drivers with a valid licence from an EU country, Canada, the USA or Australia don't need an international **licence** for Spain or France.

Eurotunnel, info and bookings **t** 08705 35 35 35, *www.eurotunnel.com*.

Getting Around

If you're using public transport, there is usually an even choice between the bus and train. Buses are usually cheaper, and often faster, and are often the only way to reach smaller towns and villages. However, for long distances, trains are usually faster.

By Train

Democracy in Spain has made the trains run on time, but western Europe's most eccentric railway, RENFE, still has a way to go. The problem isn't the trains themselves – they're almost always clean and comfortable, and do their best to keep to the schedules – but that the new RENFE network remains phenomenally complex.

To start with, there are no fewer than 13 varieties of train, from the luxury **TEE** (Trans-Europe Express) to the excruciating *semidirecto* and *ferrobús*. Watch out for these; they stop at every conceivable hamlet to deliver mail. The best are the **Talgo** trains: speedy, stylish beasts in gleaming stainless steel, designed and built entirely in Spain. The Spaniards are very proud of them. **TER** trains are almost as good.

Then there are basically three kinds of train service: the high-speed inter-city trains; the slower and less expensive *regionales*, which link major towns and cities; *cercanías*, which

are local services connected to a major hub like Bilbao.

To add to the confusion, northern Spain has two private narrow-gauge railway lines: in Euskadi, the **EuskoTren** (Basque Railways) connects Bilbao and San Sebastián by way of Zarautz and Zumaia; and **FEVE** has tracks along the north coast of Spain connecting Bilbao to Oviedo via Santander. Both these lines show off rural Spanish life and scenery at their best. See 'Rail Excursions', below.

Every variety of train has different services and a different price – yet the system is efficient, albeit confusing for the visitor. There are **discounts** for children, large families, senior citizens and regular travellers, and up to 50 per cent discounts on *Días Azules* for round-trip tickets ('blue days' are posted in the RENFE calendars in every station – though really, almost every day is 'blue'). If you buy a single ticket, hang on to it, because if you decide to return you are still elegible for a discount. There is a **discount pass** for under-26s, the *tarjeta joven*; and BIGE or BIJ youth fares are available from **TIVE offices** in the large cities. Interpretations of the rules for these might differ from one ticket window to the next, so you may care to undertake protracted negotiations just as the Spaniards do.

Every city has a RENFE travel office in the centre, and you can make good use of these for information and tickets. Always buy tickets in advance if you can; one of RENFE's little tricks is to close station ticket-windows 10 minutes before your train arrives, and if you show up at the last minute, you could be out of luck. You can also book tickets online, or by telephone – although you must collect those booked over the phone within 48hrs.

RENFE, t 90 224 02 02, *www.renfe.es* (website has timetables, types of ticket available and fares, also in English). For international trains, visit *www.elipsos.com*.

Rail Excursions

FEVE has inaugurated a series of special trains designed to attract tourists. One of these, the **Transcantábrica**, takes in some of the loveliest parts of northern Spain, including the Picos de Europa.

The **EuskoTren** narrow-gauge line maintains an electric train from the 1920s with wooden carriages, and runs it in summer for excursions around San Sebastián; ask at the EuskoTren station there for details.

By Bus

Like the trains, buses in Spain are cheap by northern European standards. Usually, whether you go by train or bus will depend on simple convenience: in some places the train station is a long way from the centre; in others the bus station is out of town. Small towns and villages can normally be reached by bus only through their provincial capitals.

With literally hundreds of companies providing services all over Spain, expect confusion. Most bus stations have an information point (although it is unlikely you will find an English-speaker) which will provide you with schedules and fare information. Buy tickets from the window dedicated to the company providing the service. Tourist offices are the best sources of information.

By City Bus and Taxi

Every Spanish city has a perfectly adequate system of public transport. You won't need to make much use of it, though, for even in the bigger cities nearly all attractions are within walking distance.

City buses usually cost around €1, and if you intend using them often there are books of tickets called *abonamientos* or *bono-Bus*, or *tarjeta* cards to punch on entry, available at reduced rates from tobacconists (*estancos*). Bus drivers will give change if you don't have the correct amount (although most will only accept notes up to the value of €20). In many cities, the entire route will be displayed on the signs at each bus stop (*parada*).

Taxis are cheap enough for the Spaniards to use them regularly on their shopping trips. The average fare for a ride within a city will be €5–12. Taxis are metered and the drivers are usually quite honest; they are entitled to certain surcharges (for luggage, night or holiday trips, to the train or airport, etc.), and if you cross the city limits they can usually charge double the fare shown. It's rarely hard to hail a cab from the street, and there will always be a few around the stations. If you get stuck where there is none, or in a small village, call information (t 11882 is just one of the numbers in Spain for directory enquiries) for the number of a radio taxi. If you call a radio taxi, be aware that the fare will start as the taxi-driver makes his way to you.

By Car

This is probably the most pleasurable way of getting about, though the convenience is balanced by a considerable cost. **Petrol** is as expensive in Spain as anywhere else in Europe (apart from the UK). In cities, **parking** is often difficult; another problem is that only a few hotels – the more expensive ones – have garages or any sort of parking.

Spain's **highway network** is adequate and in good repair, and many major cities are now linked by motorways (*autopistas*) or dual carriageways. The government has invested a considerable sum on a full-scale motorway system, including one following the entire length of the northern coast. Oviedo sits at a motorway hub, which links it with Bilbao to the east, and León and Madrid to the south, with another motorway linking A Coruña and Vigo with Oporto and Lisbon. In some rural areas in western Asturias or Galicia, the road will suddenly disappear, leaving you stranded on a hellish road little better than a mule track, crammed with heavy trucks. The other motorist's nightmare is the Bilbao area; even if you're passing through, you'll probably get good and lost among the endless roadworks and bizarre topography. Be warned that tolls on the motorways (*autopistas*) are sheer highway robbery.

See pp.66–7 for **driving regulations** in Spain. The **speed limit** in Spain is 120kph (75mph) on the *autopistas*, and 100kph (62mph) on all other national highways unless otherwise marked.

Car Hire

This is slightly cheaper in **Spain** than elsewhere in Europe. Most of the big international companies are expensive, but budget firms like Auto Europe, Holiday Autos and **ATESA**, the government-owned Spanish firm (*www.atesa.es*), offer cheaper rates. Prices for the smallest cars begin at about €180 (£125) per week with unlimited mileage, but insurance can add considerably to the costs. Small local firms can sometimes offer

Car Hire Companies

Auto Europe, UK t 0800 223 5555, USA t 1-800 223 5555, www.autoeurope.com.
Avis, UK t 0844 581 0147, Spain t 94 427 57 60, www.avis.com.
Budget, UK t 08701 56 56 56, USA t 800 527 0700, www.budget.com.
Europcar, UK t 08706 075 000, USA t 877 940 6900, Spain t 91 343 45 12, www.europcar.com.
Hertz, in UK t 08708 44 88 44, Spain t 91 749 90 69, www.hertz.com.
Holiday Autos, UK t 0870 400 4461, Spain t 90 244 84 49, www.holidayautos.com.

a better deal, but should be treated with some caution.

Ask your travel agent about the 'Tour Spain' package that offers an inclusive price for ATESA car hire and accommodation in any of Spain's *paradores* for seven nights or more.

Car hire can also be booked through most of the airlines, including British Airways, Iberia and easyJet.

By Bicycle

Cycling is taken extremely seriously in Spain and you don't often see people using a bike as a form of transport. Instead, Lycra-clad enthusiasts pedal furiously up the steepest of hills on weekends, causing dire traffic hazards while they strive to reach the standards set by Miguel Indurain, the Navarrese winner of the Tour de France for three years running. In summer the moderate climate of the Basque lands, Cantabria, Asturias and Galicia, plus their greenery and network of coastal secondary roads, make them perfect spots for cycling. It's probably the current transport of choice among pilgrims to Santiago; pedalling across the frying pan of northern Castile in August is, appropriately, a lot like purgatory.

The main towns and holiday centres always seem to have at least one shop that hires out mountain bikes (BTT in Spanish) or touring/racing bikes; local tourist offices have lists. Be prepared to pay a fairly hefty deposit on a good bike, and you may want to enquire about theft insurance. Do take into account how fit you are. Wear a helmet.

Maps and information are available from the following federations and clubs:

Real Federación Española de Ciclismo, C/ Ferraz 16, 28008 Madrid, t 91 540 08 41, www.rfec.com.
Cyclists' Touring Club, Parklands, Railton Rd, Guildford, Surrey, t 0870 873 0060, www.ctc.org.uk.

On Foot

Spain has a network of long-distance paths, the *Gran Recorridos*, but they are poorly marked on the ground, the guides which cover them are usually out-of-date, and the paths are not marked on most maps.

Hitchhiking involves a long wait; few Spaniards ever do it.

If you are planning on following some or all of the pilgrimage route of the Camino de Santiago, *see* pp.34–9.

Where to Stay

Hotels in Spain are no longer the bargains they once were. However, overall rates are still pretty reasonable, and there are still some great bargains. For those travelling on a tight budget, there are plenty of *hostales* (generally one- or two-star places), rooms over bars, and rooms in private homes.

One thing you can still count on is a consistent level of quality and service; the Spanish government regulates hotels more intelligently, and more closely, than any other Mediterranean country. Room prices must be posted in hotel lobbies and in rooms, and if there's a problem you can ask for the complaints book, or *Libro de Reclamaciones*.

The prices given in this guide do not include **VAT** (IVA), charged at 15 per cent on five-star *hoteles*, and 7 per cent on other *hoteles*. No VAT is charged on other categories of accommodation. **Prices** for single rooms will average about 60 per cent of a double, while triples or an extra bed are around 35 per cent more. Within the price

Accommodation Price Ranges

Note that prices listed here and elsewhere in this book are for a double room in high season.

luxury	€€€€€	€180 and over
very expensive	€€€€	€130–180
expensive	€€€	€80–130
moderate	€€	€50–80
inexpensive	€	under €50

ranges shown, the most expensive are likely to be in the big cities, while the cheapest places are always in provincial towns. Look for the little blue plaques next to the doors of all *hoteles*, *hostales*, etc., which identify the classification and number of stars.

If you're travelling around a lot, a good investment would be the government publication *Guía de Hoteles*, a great fat book with every classified hotel and *hostal* in Spain, available in many bookshops (€10). The government also publishes similar guides to holiday flats (*apartamentos turísticos*) and campsites. Local tourist offices have complete accommodation lists.

Paradores

The government, in its plan to develop tourism in the 1950s, started this nationwide chain of classy hotels to draw attention to little-visited areas. They restored old palaces, castles and monasteries for the purpose, furnished them with antiques and installed fine restaurants featuring local specialities.

Paradores for many people are one of the best reasons for visiting Spain. Not all are historic landmarks; in resort areas, they are as likely to be cleanly designed modern buildings, usually in a good location with a pool and some sports facilities. As their popularity has increased, so have their prices; in most cases both the rooms and the restaurant will be the most expensive in town, though most offer substantial off-season discounts. There are also discounts for the over-60s and the under-30s (but these must be booked in advance, see under 'Offers and Promotions' at *www.parador.es*). There is also a good-value pass called the Five-night Card, offering five nights in any *parador* for a discounted price.

Parador Booking

Spain: Head office, C/Requena 3, 28013 Madrid **t** 91 516 66 66.

UK: Keytel International, 402 Edgware Road, London W2 1ED, **t** (020) 7616 0300, *www.keytel.co.uk*.

USA: Marketing Ahead Inc., 433 Fifth Avenue, New York, NY 10016, **t** 800 223 1356, *www.marketingahead.com*.

More information is available online at *www.parador.es*. Look out for special offers.

Hoteles

Hoteles (H) are rated from one to five stars, according to the services they offer. These are the most expensive places, and even a one-star hotel will be a comfortable, middle-range establishment. *Hotel residencias* (HR) are the same, only without a restaurant. Many of the more expensive hotels have some rooms available at prices lower than those listed; you'll have to ask. You can often get discounts in the off season but will be charged higher rates during big festivals. If you want to attend any of these big events, be sure to book as far in advance as possible.

Hostales and Pensiones

Hostales (Hs) and *pensiones* (P) are rated with from one to three stars. These are usually more modest places, often a floor in an apartment block; a two-star *hostal* is roughly equivalent to a one-star hotel, but not always. *Pensiones* may require full- or half-board; there aren't many of these establishments, only a few in resort areas. *Hostal residencias* (HsR), like *hotel residencias*, do not offer meals except breakfast, and not always that. Of course, *hostales* and *pensiones* with one or two stars will often have cheaper rooms without private baths.

Fondas, Casas de Huéspedes and Camas

The bottom of the scale is occupied by the *fonda* (F) and *casa de huéspedes* (CH), little different from a one-star *hostal*, though generally cheaper. Off the scale completely are hundreds of unclassified cheap places, usually rooms in an apartment or over a bar and identified only by a little sign reading *camas* (beds) or *habitaciones* (rooms).

You can also ask in bars or at the tourist office for unidentified *casas particulares*, private houses with a room or two. In fact, in most towns and resorts you will not have to look at all. Someone will probably find you in the bus or train station, and ask if you need a room. Almost all of these will be pleasant enough. Prices are usually negotiable (before you are taken to the place). Always make sure the location suits you – 'five minutes away' can mean five minutes on foot or in a car. In many villages these rooms will be the only accommodation on offer, but they're usually clean. In cities, the best places to look are right in the centre, not around the stations. Many will ask you to pay a day in advance.

Alternative Accommodation

Youth hostels exist in Spain, but they're rarely worth the trouble. Most are open only in summer, there are the usual inconveniences and silly rules, often they're in out-of-the-way locations – and they can be block-booked by schools. You're better off with the inexpensive *hostales* and *fondas*.

Ask at the local tourist office for rooms that might be available in **university halls**.

If you fancy some peace and tranquillity, the national tourist office has a list of 64 **monasteries and convents** that welcome guests. Accommodation and meals are simple and guests can usually take part in the religious ceremonies.

Camping

Campsites are rated from one to three stars, depending on their facilities and, in addition to the ones listed in the official government handbook, there are always others, rather primitive, that are unlisted. Facilities in most first-class sites include shops, restaurants, bars, laundries, hot showers, first aid, swimming pools, phones and, occasionally, a tennis court. Caravans (trailers) converge on all the more developed sites, but if you just want to pitch your little tent or sleep out in some quiet field, ask around in the bars or at likely farms. Camping is forbidden in many forested areas because of the danger of fire, as well as on the beaches. If you're doing some hiking, bring a sleeping bag and stay in the free *refugios* along the major trails. The government handbook *Guía Oficial de Campings* can be found in most bookstores and at tourist offices. See *www.spain.info*.

FEECPV (Federación Española de Empresarios de Campings y Parques de Vacaciones), C/ Valderribas 48, 1°C, 28007 Madrid, t 91 448 12 34, *www.fedcamping.com*.

Private Accommodation, Self-catering and *Casas Rurales*

With the rise in hotel prices, staying in private homes has become an increasingly popular way of holidaying in Spain. *Casas rurales*, rural accommodation in farms or country houses, has become extremely popular and is a wonderful way to enjoy the spectacular countryside of northern Spain. Some are rented whole, while others offer B&B accommodation. Provincial tourist offices have full lists of *casas rurales* and other self-catering properties. This type of accommodation is also called *Agriturismo*, or *Turismo Rural*, or in Basque (wait for it) *Nekazalturismoa*. Kitchen facilities may or may not be available, and prices generally fall in the range of €30–80 per day for a double room. A very useful website is *www.toprural. com*, which lists all kinds of rural accommodation throughout Spain and is also in English. You can also contact the following:

Asociacion Nekazalturismoa, Edificio Kursaal, Av. de Zurriola 1, San Sebastián-Donostia, t 90 213 00 31, *www.nekatur.net*.

Agroturismo de Navarra, C/ José Manuel Martínez de Irujo San Pedro 4, 31173 Izane (Cendea de Olzo), t 94 817 67 74, *www.agroturismosnavarra.com*.

There are numerous private firms offering all sorts of different types of self-catering accommodation. *See* the box below for some of the many travel operators who arrange self-catering holidays in the north of Spain.

Tour Operators

In the UK

Alternative Travel Group, 274 Banbury Road, Oxford OX2 7GH, t (01865) 315 678, *www.atg-oxford.co.uk*. Pilgrimages to Compostela on foot, and also other walking tours.

Arblaster & Clarke Wine Tours, Cedar Court, 5 College Street, Petersfield, Hants GU31 4AE, t (01730) 263 111, *www.winetours.co.uk*. Tours to the Rioja region, escorted by a wine expert, with lunches and visits to *bodegas*.

Exsus Travel, 23 Heddon Street, London W1B 4BQ, t (020) 7292 5050, *www.exsus.com*. Tailor-made tours of the Basque region.

Explore Worldwide Ltd, Nelson House, 55 Victoria Rd, Farnborough, Hants GU14 7PA, t 0870 333 4001, *www.explore.co.uk*. Exploratory holidays and treks in the Picos de Europa.

Martin Randall, Voysey House, Barley Mow Passage, London W4 4GF, **t** (020) 8742 3355, *www.martinrandall.com.* Lecturer-accompanied cultural tours.

Page & Moy, Compass House, Rockingham Rd, Market Harborough, Leicestershire LE16 7QD, **t** 0800 043 0234/**t** (0116) 217 8005, *www.pagemoy.com.* Cultural guided tours.

Pico Verde, 792 Wilmslow Road, Didsbury, Manchester M20 6UG, **t** (0161) 773 5335, *www.picoverde.com.* Walking holidays in northern Spain, including the Atlantic Pyrenees.

Plantagenet Tours, 85 The Grove, Moordown, Bournemouth BH9 2TY, **t** (01202) 521 895. Historical tour every spring of Castile, Galicia and Asturias.

Prospect Cultural Tours, 79 William St, Herne Bay, Kent CT6 5NR, **t** (01227) 743 307, *www.prospecttours.com.* Music and art tours.

Pyrenean Experience, UK **t** (0121) 711 3428, *www.pyreneanexperience.com.* Beginners' Spanish and walking holidays, painting and tailor-made holidays in the Spanish Pyrenees.

Ramblers Holidays, Lemsford Hill, Lemsford, Welwyn Garden City AL8 7TR, **t** (01707) 331 133, *www.ramblersholidays.co.uk.* Walking tours.

Sherpa Expeditions, 131a Heston Road, Hounslow, Middlesex TW5 0RD, **t** (020) 8577 2717, *www.sherpaexpeditions.com.* Guided walks in the Picos de Europa.

Waymark Holidays, First Choice House, London Rd, Crawley, West Sussex RH10 9GX, **t** 0870 950 9800, *www.waymarkholidays.com.* Guided walks on the Camino de Santiago.

The following companies organize group/individual walking tours/pilgrimages to Santiago de Compostela: *www.saranjan.com*; *www.experienceplus.com*; *www.petersway.com*; *www.easyridertours.com/walking.html*; *www.mccabe-travel.co.uk/pilgrimsantiago.*

In the USA

Cobblestone Tours, 757 St Charles Avenue, Suite 203, New Orleans, LA 70130, **t** 800 227 7889, or **t** (504) 522 7888, *www.cobblestonetours.com.* Small group culture tours in the Basque country, including Bilbao; also a wine and gastronomy tour.

NRCSA (National Registration Center for Study Abroad), PO Box 1393, Milwaukee, WI 53201, **t** (414) 278 0631, *www.nrcsa.com.* Language and cultural courses, San Sebastián.

Wilderness Travel, 1102 9th Street, Berkeley, CA 94710, **t** 800 368 2794, *www.wildernesstravel.com.* Hiking in the Basque country.

In Spain

Euro Adventures, C/Velázquez Moreno 9, Vigo, Pontevedra, Galicia, **t** 98 622 13 99, *www.euroadventures.net.* Gastronomic tours, walking tours, and tailor-made holidays.

Tenedor, PO Box 5070, San Sebastián, **t** 94 331 39 29, *www.tenedortours.com.* A superb range of cultural (art, food, wine and architecture) tours of the Basque country and Northern Spain, lasting from one to 13 days in length.

Totally Spain, Barrio Zoña, 39193 Castillo, Cantabria; Spain **t** 94 263 73 58, UK **t** 0871 666 0214, USA **t** (561) 828 0238, *www.totallyspain.com.* Tailor-made and themed holidays in Bilbao and the Spanish Basque lands, as well as tours and city breaks.

Self-catering Accommodation

In the UK

Casas Cantábricas, 31 Arbury Road, Cambridge, CB4 2JB, **t** (01223) 328 721, *www.casas.co.uk.* Holiday houses and small hotels.

Individual Travellers, Manor Court, Bignor, Pulborough, West Sussex, RH20 1QD, **t** 08700 780 194, *www.individualtravellers.com.* Village and rural accommodation.

Keytel International, 402 Edgware Road, London, W2 1ED, **t** (020) 7616 0300, *www.keytel.co.uk.*

Secret Destinations, Ulanor Hill, The Square, Grassington, N. Yorks BD23 5AQ, **t** 0845 612 9000, *www.secretdestinations.com.* Self-catering and hotels along the coast, in mountain villages and in the cities.

In the USA

EC Tours, 12500 Riverside Drive, Suite 206, Toluca Lake, CA 91602, **t** 800 388 0877, *www.ectours.com.* Flights and accommodation in villas and apartments as well as hotels.

Spain4Rent, *www.spain4rent.com.* Online villa rental company, with properties for rent in northern Spain.

Practical A–Z

06

Imperial–Metric Conversions

Length (multiply by)
Inches to centimetres: 2.54
Centimetres to inches: 0.39
Feet to metres: 0.3
Metres to feet: 3.28
Yards to metres: 0.91
Metres to yards: 1.1
Miles to kilometres: 1.61
Kilometres to miles: 0.62

Area (multiply by)
Inches square to centimetres square: 6.45
Centimetres square to inches square: 0.15
Feet square to metres square: 0.09
Metres square to feet square: 10.76
Miles square to kilometres square: 2.59
Kilometres square to miles square: 0.39
Acres to hectares: 0.40
Hectares to acres: 2.47

Weight (multiply by)
Ounces to grams: 28.35
Grams to ounces: 0.035
Pounds to kilograms: 0.45
Kilograms to pounds: 2.2
Stones to kilograms: 6.35
Kilograms to stones: 0.16
Tons (UK) to kilograms: 1,016
Kilograms to tons (UK): 0.0009
1 UK ton (2,240lbs) = 1.12 US tonnes (2,000lbs)

Volume (multiply by)
Pints (UK) to litres: 0.57
Litres to pints (UK): 1.76
Quarts (UK) to litres: 1.13
Litres to quarts (UK): 0.88
Gallons (UK) to litres: 4.55
Litres to gallons (UK): 0.22
1 UK pint/quart/gallon =
1.2 US pints/quarts/
gallons

Temperature
Celsius to Fahrenheit:
multiply by 1.8 then
add 32

Fahrenheit to Celsius:
subtract 32 then multiply
by 0.55

°C	°F
40	104
35	95
30	86
25	77
20	68
15	59
10	50
5	41
-0	32
-5	23
-10	14
-15	5

Spain Information

Time Differences
Spain: + 1hr GMT; + 6hrs EST
Daylight saving from last weekend in March
to end of October

Dialling Codes
*Note: to dial within Spain and within a province,
include the area code (9X).*
Spain country code 34
To Spain from: UK, Ireland, New Zealand 00 /
USA, Canada 011 / Australia 0011; then dial 34
and the full number
From Spain to: UK 00 44; Ireland 00 353; USA,
Canada 001; Australia 00 61; New Zealand 00
64; then the number without the initial zero
Directory enquiries: 11811
International directory enquiries: 176

Emergency Numbers
General EU emergency number: 112
Police: 112 or 091 (national)/092 (local)
Ambulance: 112 or 061
Fire: 112 or 080

Embassy Numbers in Spain
UK: 94 415 76 00 (Bilbao); **Ireland** 94 423 04 14
(Bilbao); **USA:** 91 587 22 00 (Madrid); **Canada** 91
423 32 50 (Madrid); **Australia** 91 353 66 00
(Madrid); **New Zealand** 91 523 02 26 (Madrid)

Shoe Sizes

Europe	UK	USA
35	2½ / 3	4
36	3 / 3½	4½ / 5
37	4	5½ / 6
38	5	6½
39	5½ / 6	7 / 7½
40	6 / 6½	8 / 8½
41	7	9 / 9½
42	8	9½ / 10
43	9	10½
44	9½ / 10	11
45	10½	12

Women's Clothing

Europe	UK	USA
34	6	2
36	8	4
38	10	6
40	12	8
42	14	10
44	16	12

Crime and the Police

General emergency number t 112

Crime is not really a big problem in Spain, and Spaniards talk about it perhaps more than is warranted. Pickpocketing and robbing parked cars are the specialities; except for some quarters of the largest cities, walking around at night is no problem.

Note that in Spain less than 8 grams of marijuana is legal; anything else may easily earn you the traditional 'six years and a day'. In Galicia, the traditional smuggling business has created a growing drug problem at home, along with some fierce vigilante efforts by locals to stop it.

There are several species of police, and their authority varies with the area. Franco's old goon squad, the *Policía Armada*, was reformed and relatively demilitarized into the *Policía Nacional*, known as 'chocolate drops' for their brown uniforms. Nowadays they wear blue and white, and their duties seem to consist largely of driving around and drinking coffee. The *Policía Municipal* (*Udaltzainzoa* in Basque) in some towns do control crime, while in others they are limited to directing traffic. Mostly in rural areas, you will see the *Guardia Civil*, with green uniforms. The *Guardia* is now most conspicuous as a highway patrol, assisting motorists and handing out tickets. Most traffic violations are payable on the spot; the traffic cops have a reputation for upright honesty. The Basques don't want anything to do with any of these and have set up their own police force, the *Ertzantza*. You'll see them looking dapper in their red berets, waiting by the roadsides for motorists in a barely legal hurry.

Report thefts (called making a *denuncia*) to the nearest police station: the reward is the bit of paper you need for an insurance claim. You can also call t 902 102 112. If your passport is stolen, contact the police and your nearest consulate for emergency travel documents.

Eating Out

Spaniards are notoriously late diners. In the morning it's a coffee and a roll grabbed at the bar, followed by a huge meal at around 2 or 3pm, then after work at 8pm a few tapas at the bar to hold them over until supper at

Restaurant Price Categories

Price categories in the 'Eating Out' sections throughout this book indicate the cost of the set menus, per person, without wine. It's safe to double the price for an *à la carte* meal.

expensive	€€€	over €40
moderate	€€	€20–40
inexpensive	€	under €20

10pm. On the coasts, restaurants tend to open earlier to accommodate foreigners (some as early as 5pm), while Galicians are the early diners of Spain (8 or 9pm); Basques do it from 9 to 11.

In non-touristy Spanish areas, restaurants are inconspicuous and few. Just ask someone, and you will find a nice *comedor* with home cooking tucked in a back room behind a bar. If you dine where the locals do, you'll be assured of a good deal if not necessarily a good meal. Almost every restaurant offers a *menú del día* (usually only available on week-days) or a *menú turístico*, featuring an appetizer, a main course, dessert, bread and drink at a set price. Unless it's explicitly written on the bill (*la cuenta*), service is not included in the total, so **tip** accordingly.

Since a 2006 extension to the ban on smoking in public spaces, many restaurants are also now largely **non-smoking**.

A wide array of snacking establishments will help fill in the gaps in your day, wherever you are. **Bars** and **cafés** collect much of the Spaniards' leisure time. They are wonderful institutions, where you can eat breakfast or linger over a glass of beer until four in the morning. Some have music – jazz, rock or flamenco; some have great snacks, or *tapas*, some have games or pinball machines. Some bars put on Parisian airs; others, including the *chigres* (another word for *sidrerías* in Asturias) are resolutely proletarian. Many night-time bars and clubs are totally invisible in the day, exploding into blue-light noise palaces punctually at midnight until 6am. This is the twilight world of *la marcha*, the all-night pub crawl of Madrid and Barcelona that finds a reflection in any Spanish city, especially if it has a university. Cities that can nourish a proper *marcha* include Santander, San Sebastián, Oviedo, Santiago, A Coruña, Pontevedra, Pamplona and León, while Burgos and Vigo are a little too staid to try.

06 Practical A–Z | Eating Out

For further information about eating and drinking in Spain, including local specialities and wines and a menu decoder, *see* the **Food and Drink** chapter, pp.47–56.

Electricity

The current is 225 AC/220V, the same as most of Europe. North Americans will need converters, and the British will need the usual two-pin adapters for the different plugs. Adapters and converters are sold in department stores and electrical shops.

Health and Emergencies

General emergency number t 112

The tap water in Spain is safe to drink, but at the slightest twinge of queasiness, switch to the bottled stuff.

Citizens of the EU are entitled to a certain amount of free medical care in EU countries if they have a European Health Insurance Card (EHIC). *See* **Planning Your Trip**, p.63.

In an emergency ask to be taken to the nearest *hospital de la seguridad social*.

Tourist offices can supply lists of local English-speaking doctors, but, if it's not an emergency, before resorting to a *médico* and his fat fee (ask at the tourist office for a list of English-speaking doctors), go to a pharmacy and tell them your woes; Spanish *farmacéuticos* are highly skilled.

Internet

Getting online is easy and cheap in **Spain**. Every city of any size has a couple of places, while heavily visited towns are likely to be infested with *cibers*, as the Spanish call their Internet cafés. Even the most unlikely and out-of-the-way, one-horse towns sometimes have Internet facilities. The average cost in cities is around €2.50 per hour, rising to an inflated €4 in places like Zarautz. Most hotels have their own websites with online booking.

Opening Hours, Museums and National Holidays

Shops usually open at 10am, boutiques an hour or so later. Spaniards take their main meal at 2pm and, except in larger cities, most

National Holidays

Everything closes on:
1 January New Year's Day
6 January Epiphany
Holy Thursday (March/April)
Good Friday (March/April)
Easter Sunday (March/April)
1 May Labour Day
Corpus Christi (May/June)
25 July *Santiago Apóstol*: St James' Day
15 August *Asunción*: Assumption
12 October *Día de la Hispanidad*: Columbus Day
1 November *Todos los Santos*: All Saints' Day
6 December *Día de la Constitución*: Constitution Day
8 December *Inmaculada Concepción*: Immaculate Conception
25 December *Navidad*: Christmas Day

shops close for 2–3 hours in the afternoon, from 1pm or 2pm. In the evening, most establishments stay open until 7 or 8pm.

Most **banks** are open Mon–Fri 9–2. A few open on Sat (mainly in winter), 9–1.

Officially, **post office** opening hours are Mon–Fri 8.30–8.30, Sat 9.30–1. This isn't necessarily the case outside the big cities. Many post offices close early in summer.

Museums and historical sites tend to follow shop hours, though they are shorter in winter. Nearly all close on Mondays. Seldom-visited sites have a raffish disregard for their official hours. Don't be discouraged: bang on doors and ask around. We've done our best to include opening hours in the text, but they are liable to change. Most close on national holidays and give discounts if you have a student ID card, or are an EU citizen under 18 or over 65 years old; most charge admission.

Most of the less important **churches** are always closed. If you're determined to see one, it will never be hard to find the *sacristán*, or caretaker. Usually they live close by and will be glad to show you around for a tip. Don't be surprised when cathedrals and famous churches charge for admission – just consider the cost of upkeep.

Post Offices

Every city in Spain, regardless of size, seems to have one **post office** (*correos*) and no more.

They will often be crowded, but unless you have packages to send you may never need visit one: most tobacconists sell **stamps** (*sellos*) and they'll usually know the correct postage for whatever you're sending. Send everything by air mail (*por avión*) and don't send postcards unless you don't care when they arrive. **Post boxes** are bright yellow.

Don't confuse post offices with the *Caja Postal*, the postal savings banks.

Sports and Activities

Football has pride of place in the Spanish heart, though you will not often find Athletic Club de Bilbao or any of the other northern teams except A Coruña challenging the dominance of Real Madrid and Barcelona.

Bullfighting and **cycling** vie for second place; all are regularly shown on television.

Bullfighting

The *corrida* is big in Spain. In Spanish newspapers, you will not find accounts of the bullfights (*corridas*) on the sports pages: you should look in the 'arts and culture' section, for that is how Spain has always thought of this singular spectacle.

There are only about 500 bullfights each year in Spain, mostly coinciding with holidays or a town's fiesta. Tickets can be astronomically expensive and hard to come by; sometimes touts buy the lot. Buy in advance, if you can, and directly from the *plaza de toros* to avoid the hefty commission charges. Prices vary according to the sun – the most expensive seats are entirely in the shade.

Bull-running

The biggest and most famous bull-running festival is **Los Sanfermines** in Pamplona (*see* pp.93–4), but bull-running is also a highlight of plenty of local festivals in the smaller villages of central Navarra. The custom dates back to the times when herds of cattle were chased down from their summer pastures in the mountains, a hair-raising journey which now takes place in the village streets. The most popular *encierros* outside Pamplona take place in Tudela (last week of July), Pilón (last week of August), Tafalla (20 August) and Sangüesa (mid-September).

Cycling

See 'Getting Around', p.69.

Fishing and Hunting

Fishing and hunting are long-standing Spanish obsessions, and you'll need to get a licence for both. **Freshwater fishing permits** (*permisos de pesca*) are issued from the Consejería de Agricultura y Pesca (Agriculture and Fishing Council), which has an office in each of the the provincial capital cities. A maritime recreational fishing licence (1st and 3rd Class) is required for fishing from the shore or from a boat near the coast; get it from the Delegación Provincial de la Consejería de Agricultura y Pesca, which also has an office in each provincial capital city (tourist offices can provide addresses).

Deep-sea fishermen need to obtain a **five-year licence** from the provincial Comandancias de Marina.

Spanish Fishing Federation (Federación Española de Pesca y Casting), Navas de Tolosa 3, 28013 Madrid, t 91 532 83 52, *www.fepyc.es.*

Directorate General of Sea Fishing (Subsecretaria de la Marina Mercante), Ministerio de Comercio, Calle Ruíz de Alarcón 1, Madrid. Information on the best fishing waters and boat rentals.

You may bring sporting guns to Spain, but you must declare them on arrival and present a valid firearms certificate with a Spanish translation bearing a consulate stamp. Hunters (boar and deer are the big game, with quail, hare, partridges and pigeons, and ducks and geese along the coasts in the winter) are obliged to get a **licence** (*permiso de caza*) from the local autonomous community, presenting passports and insurance.

Spanish Hunting Federation (Federación Española de Caza), C/ Francos Rodríguez 70, 28039 Madrid, t 91 311 14 11, *www.fedecaza.com.*

Golf

English settlers built Spain's first golf course at the Rio Tinto mines in Andalucía in the 19th century, and since the advent of Severiano Ballesteros Spaniards too have gone nuts for the game. The sunny, warm winters, combined with greens of international tournament standard, attract golfing enthusiasts from all over the world throughout the year. Most places hire out clubs. Green fees have taken a leap in recent years, however, and even the humblest clubs will charge at least €20. Many hotels cater specifically for the golfer and there are numerous golf-package tour operators.

Royal Spanish Golf Federation, Capitán Haya 9–5, 28020 Madrid, **t** 91 555 26 82, *www. golfspainfederation.com.*

Hiking and Mountaineering

Spain's sierras attract thousands of hikers and mountaineers. Los Picos de Europa and the Pyrenees are by far the most popular, though there are also some lovely hikes in El Bierzo of western León and Os Ancares of eastern Galicia. *See* pp.71–2 for tour operators who organize walking holidays.

The tourist office or the Spanish Mountaineering Federation provide a list of *refugios*, which offer mountain shelter in many places. Some are well equipped and can supply food. Most, however, do not, so take your own sleeping bags, cooking equipment and food with you. Hiking boots are essential, as is a detailed map of the area, issued by the Instituto Geográfico Nacional, or the Servicio Geográfico Ejército.

Spanish Hiking and Mountaineering Federation (Federación Española de Deportes de Montaña y Escalada), C/Floridablanca 84, Barcelona, **t** 93 426 42 67, *www.fedme.es.*

Tennis

There is equal fervour in Spain for tennis as for golf, inspired by recently retired international champions Arantxa Sánchez Vicario and Conchita Martínez, and current favourites led by Rafael Noda. Every resort hotel has its own courts; municipal ones tend to be rare or hard to get to.

Royal Spanish Tennis Federation, Avenida Diagonal 618, 08021 Barcelona, **t** 93 201 08 44, *www.rfet.es.*

Telephones

Calls within **Spain** are expensive (25–80 cents for a short local call), and overseas calls from Spain are among the most expensive in Europe: calls to the UK cost about €2 a minute, to the USA substantially more. Most tobacconists sell PIN-**phonecards** that make international phone calls much cheaper.

Public **phone booths** have instructions in English and accept phonecards, available from news stands, tobacconists and post offices. In some Spanish phone booths, there will also be a little slide on top that holds coins. In every big city in Spain, there are also **calling centres** (*locutorios*) where you telephone from a metered booth. These offer cheap international calls, but national calls are expensive. They can usually be found around bus and train stations. Expect to pay a big surcharge if you make any calls from your hotel. For directory enquiries, dial **t** 11811.

Telephone codes have now been incorporated into the telephone numbers. All numbers in this guide are listed as they must be dialled. If you're ringing from abroad, the code for Spain is 34 followed by the number.

For international calls from Spain, dial **t** 00, wait for the higher tone and then dial the country code and the rest of the number (omitting the zero in any area code).

Time

Spain is one hour ahead of UK time and six hours ahead of North American EST. Summer time runs from the last Sunday in March to the last Sunday in October.

Toilets

Apart from bus and train stations, public facilities are rare in Spain. On the other hand, every bar on every corner has a toilet; just ask for *los servicios* and take your own toilet paper.

Women Travellers

On the whole, the horror stories of sexual harassment in Spain are a thing of the past – unless you dress provocatively and hang out by the bus station after dark. All Spaniards seem to melt when they see blondes, so if you're fair you're in for a tougher time. Apart from in resorts on the coast, it often tends to be older men who comment on your appearance as a matter of course. Even Spanish women sunbathe topless these days at international resorts, but be discreet elsewhere.

Navarra and La Rioja

Europe's traditional front door to Spain, Navarra combines a sizeable, often nationalistic Basque minority up in the misty western Pyrenees with a conservative, non-Basque Navarrese majority tending the sunny vineyards and gardens of the Ebro valley flatlands to the south. The combination hasn't always been comfortable, and only now that much of the population has abandoned the countryside have tensions between the two groups loosened up.

As everyone must know by now, much of this 'loosening up' is concentrated in Pamplona, the capital both groups share, into an ecstatic week-long bacchanalia of inebriated recklessness, bull running and partying known as Los Sanfermines.

Roads from Navarra – most importantly, the Camino de Santiago – flow naturally southwest into the autonomous comunidad of La Rioja, celebrated far out of proportion to its size for its red wine with the distinctive vanilla flavour.

07

Don't miss

⭐ **Running the bulls**
Pamplona **p.90**

⭐ **The atmospheric 'town of the star'**
Estella **p.107**

⭐ **Striking Wild West scenery**
Bárdenas Reales **p.103**

⭐ **Chickens in church**
Santo Domingo de la Calzada **p.122**

⭐ **Wine *bodegas***
Rioja Alta **p.124**

See map overleaf

Navarra: A Potted History

To understand the standoffish, weird James Dean role Navarra traditionally plays, you need a bit of Spanish history, which is full of the phrase 'except Navarra'. Even in 'the nation of nations' the region has stood apart ever since 605, when the Franks tried to harness it as part of the Duchy of Vasconia, a huge untenable territory that extended from the Garonne to the Ebro. Charlemagne himself came down in 778, either to discipline the unruly duchy or to force it to join his fight against the Moors, and after razing the walls of Pamplona he went stumping back to

France – except for his rear guard, which the furious Basques of Pamplona ambushed in 778 at the pass of Roncesvalles.

Charlemagne taught the Navarrese that owing nothing to nobody was the way to go, and within a few years of his passing they created the independent kingdom of Navarra. Its most talented king, Sancho III 'the Great' (1004–34), firmly established the *camino francés* through Navarra and controlled much of French Basque country and Galicia, and pocketed Castile and León after the death of its last count, setting up his son Ferdinand I as the first to take the title of 'King of the Spains'. The centre was too precocious to hold, and by the time of Sancho IV (1054–76) Navarra was once again a fierce rival of Castile, but avoided entanglements – marital or martial – by playing the French card. 'The Flea between Two Monkeys', as it became known, was ruled by three different French dynasties between 1234 and 1512, when Ferdinand the Catholic slyly demanded that Navarra let his armies march through to France. His demand, as he anticipated, was refused and he used the refusal as an excuse to grab Navarra south of the Pyrenees. France was left with only Basse Navarre, a thimble-sized realm but one that gave her a long line of kings, with the accession of Henri IV (1589–1610). Ferdinand kept the Navarrese happy by maintaining their *fueros* (or privileges), which in practice gave the region an independence enjoyed by no other in Spain; it was ruled by a viceroy, minted its own coins and had its own government. Napoleonic and Liberal attempts to do away with the *fueros* in the cause of central unity turned the Navarrese into fierce reactionaries and the most ardent of Carlists (supporters of the pretender, Charles III). In the 1930s Navarra rejected the Republic's offer of autonomy; instead, the Navarrese Carlist *requetés* in their distinctive red berets became some of Franco's best troops, fighting for their old privileges and Catholicism – just as the Basques were, only on the Republican side. Franco rewarded Navarra by leaving the *fueros* intact, making it the only autonomous region in Spain until his death.

Approaches from France: Down the Valleys of the Pyrenees

The Navarrese Pyrenees don't win altitude records, but they're green, wooded and shot through with legends, many lingering in the mists around Roncesvalles, for centuries the pass most favoured by French pilgrims to Santiago. Much of Navarra's Basque population is concentrated in the three valleys of Roncal, Salazar and Baztán, where seemingly every house in every hamlet is emblazoned with a coat of arms – for the Basques have traditionally considered themselves all equal and all noble.

The Eastern Valleys: Valles del Roncal and de Salazar

Like many Pyrenean valleys, the Roncal was so remote for centuries that the central authorities were content to let it run its own show. Time has changed a few things: timber logged on its thickly forested slopes now travels by truck instead of careering down the Esca river, and the valley's renowned sheep's cheese, *queso de Roncal*, is now made in a factory (but according to farm traditions). Mist often envelops **Isaba**, the Valle del Roncal's biggest town, gathered under its fortress-church of San Cipriano (1540). Every 13 July since 1375, at stone frontier-marker no.262, the mayor of Isaba and his colleagues don traditional costume, march up to meet their counterparts from the Vallée de Barétous in France, and ask them three times for the 'Tribute of the Three Cows' in exchange for the right to graze their herds in the Valle del Roncal in August – something both sides used to kill for before the annual tribute was agreed on. Isaba provides an excellent base for exploring the magnificent mountain scenery: hike up the region's highest peaks, **Pic d'Anie** (8,200ft/2,500m) and **Mesa de los Tres Reyes** (7,900ft/2,408m), or take the most beautiful walk of all, into the Parque Natural Pirenáico to the **Refugio de Belagua**, set in a stunning glacial amphitheatre.

Refugio de Belagua
t 94 839 40 02

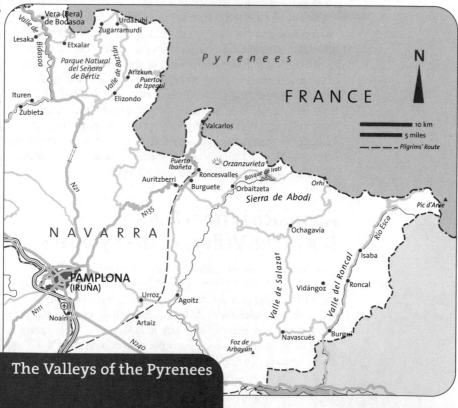

The Valleys of the Pyrenees

Getting to and around the Eastern Valleys

There are no **trains** here, and in most cases the **buses** from Pamplona go only once a day.

La Tafallesa (t 94 822 28 86/t 94 870 01 99) and **La Roncalesa** (t 94 821 20 79) both serve the Valle del Roncal; they stop at Yesa, near the lake, and 4km from the monastery of Leyre (*see* p.100). There are twice-daily services (one on Sat, none on Sun) to Roncesvalles with **Artieda** (t 94 830 02 87).

For the Valles de Salazar and Aezkoa, **Río Irati** (t 94 830 35 70) has one bus daily to Ochagavía and one to Orbaitzeta. **La Baztanesa** (t 94 858 01 29) serves the Valle de Baztán.

Casa-Museo Julián Gayarre
open April–Sept Tues–Sun 11.30–1.30 and 5–7; Oct–Mar Sat–Sun 11.30–1.30 and 4–6; adm

Roncal, once the capital of the valley, is a pretty village surrounded by pine forests. The great, amiable Basque tenor Julián Gayarre (1844–90) was born here and lies buried in a suitably high-operatic tomb just outside town; the **Casa-Museo Julián Gayarre** contains costumes and photos from his glory days. **Burgui**, south, has a Roman bridge and two roads that cut over to the Valle de Salazar: an easy one westward to Navascués and a narrow one northward by way of the remote village of Vidángoz.

The sparsely populated **Valle de Salazar** is much less visited but just as lovely, abubble with trout streams, beech forests and old white stone Basque *caserones*, or mansions, with their pompous coats of arms. The best of them line the riverfront and cobbled lanes in **Ochagavía**, the local metropolis and another good base for walks. An easy one is up to the 13th-century chapel of **Santa María de Muskilda**, topped by an unusual square tower with a round roof: its *romería* (pilgrimage) on 8 September is celebrated with some of Navarra's most ancient dances.

To the north, a road twists through the Sierra de Abodi to the snow-white hermitage of **Nuestra Señora de las Nieves** (1954): from here, trails of varying length and difficulty lead into the vast beech and ancient yew **Forest of Irati** (Bosque de Irati), the largest primeval forest in Spain, with majestic Mount Orhi (6,618ft/2,017m) as a backdrop. This is one of the richest wildlife habitats in the Pyrenees, full of red squirrels, deer and wild boar, with lesser populations of wildcat and beech marten. The area also contains a couple of real rarities: the white-backed woodpecker, found only where there are plenty of insect-ridden beech trees, and the endemic Pyrenean desman, an aquatic shrew with a nose like a dragon's snout. Besides the usual Basque fairy folk, the forest is haunted by a rather unexpected ghost: that of Jeanne d'Albret, queen of French Navarre and mother of Henri IV, a nasty, die-hard Protestant fanatic. Poisoned in 1572, Jeanne tours her old domain on windy nights with an escort of lovely Basque *lamiaks*, the mischievous nymphs with whom she never would have been caught dead while still alive. On the other side of the forest, the picturesque village of **Orbaitzeta** makes a good base; nearby, a dolmen called **Azpegi I** is surrounded by a circle of 123 stones.

In the south of the valley, the spectacular 1,000ft sheer-sided limestone gorge, the **Foz de Arbayún**, extends for 10km below the

Where to Stay and Eat in the Eastern Valleys

ⓘ **Ochagavía >>**
Centro Interpretación de la Naturaleza, on the main road, opposite the river, **t** *94 889 06 41,* oit.ochagavia@navarra.es

ⓘ **Roncal >**
Centro Interpretación de la Naturaleza, **t** *94 847 52 56,* oit.roncal@navarra.es

Navarra as a whole has made efforts to improve the provision of reasonably priced accommodation in rural areas. Traditional houses have been restored as *casas rurales*, or bed and breakfasts: write to the Pamplona tourist office for their *Guía de Alojamientos de Turismo Rural*, or see www.navarra.es.

Valle del Roncal ✉ 31680

There are several *casas rurales* in and around Roncal: visit the website (Spanish only) www.roncal-salazar. com or contact the tourist office. The website www. toprural.com is available in several languages.

***Isaba**, C/ Bormapea 51, Isaba, **t** 94 889 30 00, www.husalamontana.com (€€€–€€). Modern and luxurious, with every facility including sauna/gym.

*Hs Lola**, C/ Mendigatxa, Isaba, **t** 94 889 30 12, www.hostallola.com (€€). Welcoming little place with comfy rooms and a decent restaurant.

Pensión Txiki, C/ Mendigatxa 17, Isaba, **t** 94 889 31 18 (€€). Reasonable half-board rates above restaurant and bar.

*Hotel Ezkaurre**, C/ Garagardoia 14, Isaba, **t** 94 889 33 03 (€€–€). Tucked away down a back street, this classic mountain *hostal* has comfortable rooms and a top-floor sitting room, with fireplace and mountain views.

Pensión Txabalkua, C/ Izargentea 16, Isaba, **t** 94 889 30 83 (€). One of the cheapest options for half-board rates.

Tapia, C/ Bormapea 23, Isaba, **t** 94 889 30 13 (€). Regional dishes and *platos combinados*, reliably good.

*Hs Zaltua**, C/ Castillo 23, Roncal, **t** 94 847 50 08 (€). A pleasant, if basic, *hostal* in the centre of town.

Ochagavía ✉ 31680

Most accommodation in the Salazar valley is in *casas rurales*.

Auñamendi, Plaza Gurpide 1, **t** 94 889 01 89, auniamendi@jet.es (€€€–€€). As well as offering rooms, this place serves trout with ham and a good asparagus and prawn pie. *Closed mid-Sept–mid-Oct.*

Hs Salazar, C/ Mayor s/n, Oronz, **t** 94 889 00 53, hotelsalazar@jet.es (€€). Traditional chalet-style hotel just south of Ochagavía, with a pool and pretty views.

*Hs Orialde**, C/ Urrutia 6, **t** 94 889 00 27 (€€–€). A 12-room place featuring Basque cooking in the kitchen. *Closed mid-Dec–mid-Mar.*

Casa Ballent, **t** 94 889 03 73 (€). One of the best, with just three cosy bedrooms, a welcoming owner and views from the terrace over the Pyrenees and the vegetable patch.

Casa Sarbide I and **II**, **t** 94 889 03 42 (€). A tiny place with two rooms and lots of character, and a *casa rural* for four.

Orbaitzeta ✉ 31670

There are no hotels here, and only a handful of *casas rurales*.

Casa Mujurdín, C/ Mendikoa 5, **t** 94 876 60 46 (€). Has just two rooms with shared bath in a classic Basque stone house.

Casa Sastrarena, C/ San Juan, **t** 94 876 60 93 (€). Offers rooms with private bath and a pretty garden at a slightly higher price.

road, home to Spain's largest colonies of rare griffon vultures (*buitres leonados*), with their 8ft wing span, and an assortment of smaller eagles; you can nearly always spot them floating around the roadside belvedere between Navascués and Lumbier. Man-made wonders Leyre and Sangüesa are just south (*see* pp.98–101).

Roncesvalles (Orreaga)

Of all the passes over the Pyrenees, introverted Roncesvalles ('Bramble Valley') is the most renowned, thanks to the *camino francés* to Compostela (*see* pp.34–8). French pilgrims would mumble verses from the *Chanson de Roland* as they paid their respects to the sites associated with Charlemagne and his nephew Roland (*see* **Topics**, pp.39–40), then say their first prayer to another gallant knight, Santiago. From Roncesvalles' Colegiata it's 781km to Santiago, a distance the fittest pilgrims could cover in 20 days.

Not so long ago the Colegiata had a sad, has-been look. Although in the 18th century, Roncesvalles still counted 30,000 passing pilgrims a year, numbers fell dramatically in the 19th century. Most of the monasteries and churches along the route were closed forever with the national confiscation of church lands in 1837; many were converted into stables or pillaged for their building stone. By the 1970s, the medieval floods of pilgrims had dried to a trickle of eccentrics. But just when it seemed that the pilgrimage was ready to be pushed into Europe's closet of forgotten traditions, it came roaring back. A number of factors seem to be involved – modern disillusionment with conventional religion, the restless search for something beyond the routine of over-organized day-to-day lives and, more prosaically, the growth of ecological and alternative tourism. In 1982, John Paul II became the first pope ever to visit Santiago; in 1985, UNESCO declared this the 'Foremost Cultural Route in Europe', helping to fund the restoration of the churches that punctuate the trail. Although modern roads have changed the face of the *camino francés* for ever, efforts have been made to create alternative paths for pedestrians, marked with scallop shells, and new inexpensive *hostales* have sprouted along the way for walkers or cyclists. No one predicted that in the 1990s the number of pilgrims who stopped to have their documents stamped in Roncesvalles would grow by thousands each year. There is a large refuge here and camping facilities for up to 1,000 pilgrims. The pilgrims' quest is back in business; even Shirley MacLaine has done it and written a book about her experience.

The three main pilgrims' routes through France converged at Saint-Jean-Pied-de-Port and then continued up to the busy frontier town of **Valcarlos**, the 'carlos' in its name referring to Charlemagne, who was camped here when he heard the dying Roland's horn blast. From here, the road winds up through lush greenery to Roncesvalles, where the 12th-century **church of Sancti Spiritus** (the 'Silo de Charlemagne') is said to have been first built as Roland's tomb. According to legend, by the time the emperor arrived, not only were Roland and the peers dead, but so were all the Saracens; since he couldn't tell who was who (poor Charlemagne – his legends always make him seem as thick as a pudding), he asked heaven for a sign to make sure he gave all the Franks a Christian burial, and all at once the Christian corpses looked up to heaven, with red roses sprouting from their lips. Equally unlucky pilgrims were laid in the 7th-century **ossuary** underneath the church;

Santiago
open summer daily 10–2 and 3.30–7; winter except Jan daily 10–2 and 3.30–5; Jan Thurs–Tues 10.30–2.30, closed Wed; adm

according to Aymery Picaud (*see* p.37), many were done in by 'false pilgrims', mostly locals. Adjacent, the tiny church of **Santiago** is a plain Gothic chapel from the 13th century.

Set back from the road, at the foot of the pass, the **Colegiata de Roncesvalles** is a French-style Gothic church consecrated in 1219, which replaced the first Colegiata, built up at Puerto Ibañeta in 1112 and abandoned by the frostbitten monks after five ghastly winters. What was originally the front of the Colegiata caved in under the snow in 1600 (hence the incongruous corrugated zinc roof on the rest) and was replaced by a **cloister**, from where you can pop into the 14th-century chapterhouse to see the stained glass (1960) showing a scene from the 1212 Battle of Las Navas de Tolosa, where Sancho VII 'the Strong' led the Navarrese to their great victory over the Moors. The chains in the chapel are among those that bound 10,000 slaves at the ankle and wrist, forming a human shield around the emir's tent, a scurvy tactic that failed to prevent the Christians from leaping over and carrying off the tent as booty. The chapterhouse holds the **tomb of Sancho the Strong**. Apparently, in life the king was exactly as tall as his 7ft 4in effigy: pilgrims used to think that his battle maces, now in the museum, belonged to Roland. Sancho financed the Colegiata, which over time has been stripped of its costly gifts, with the exception of a much-revered 13th-century image of the Virgin under her baldachin. Its jumbled, anachronistic, pious legend goes that after the battle at the pass, Charlemagne founded a monastery up at Ibañeta. When the Moors poured through to attack France in 732, the monks hid the statue, and it remained hidden until 1130, when the hiding place was revealed to a Basque shepherd by a red stag with a star shimmering between its antlers.

Museum
open daily 10–2 and 3.30–7; adm

The fascinating **museum** contains such medieval treasures as the emerald which fell from the emir's turban when giant King Sancho burst into his tent at Las Navas de Tolosa; an 11th-century *pyx*, or golden box used to hold the Host; and a reliquary of gold and enamel (*c.* 1350) called 'Charlemagne's chessboard' for its 32 little cases, each designed to hold a saintly fingertip or tooth. Among the paintings there's an excellent 15th-century Flemish triptych and a *Holy Family* by Morales, and two books on Confucianism, purchased in India in the time of St Francis Xavier.

An easy and beautiful path from the monastery leads up in half-an-hour to the **Puerto Ibañeta** (3,150ft/960m), from where the Basques, hidden on Mounts Astobizkar and Orzanzurieta, dropped boulders on the heads of the Franks. A modern chapel replaces the monastery of San Salvador, where the monks would toll a bell to guide pilgrims through the mists and snowstorms. Heading south, the pretty villages of **Auritz** (**Burguete**) and **Auritzberri** (**Espinal**) were the pilgrims' next stops and are still good places to stay.

Where to Stay and Eat in Roncesvalles

ⓘ Roncesvalles >
Antiguo Molino,
t 94 876 03 01,
oit.roncesvalles@
navarra.es.

Roncesvalles ✉ 31650

If you have no luck at any of the places listed below, then try one of several *casas rurales* in the vicinity.

Hs Loizu, Avda Roncesvalles 7, in Auritz (3km from Roncesvalles), **t 94 876 00 08, *www.hotelloizu.com* (€€€–€€). Pretty little hotel-restaurant with plenty of atmosphere.

Hostal Burguete, C/ Única s/n, Auritz, **t 94 876 00 05, *hburguete@ auritz-burguete.org* (€€–€). Whenever

Hemingway decamped to the Pyrenees, he stayed here. Though its elegance is mostly faded, this antiques-bedecked old place is still a great choice for slumming it in style.

*Hs Casa Sabina, t 94 876 00 12, *www.casasabina-roncesvalles.com* (€€–€). Next to the monastery gate, with six pleasant rooms and good Navarrese cooking.

Hs La Posada, t 94 876 02 25, *www.laposadaderoncesvalles.com* (€). Charming, with spacious rooms in the Colegiata, and a fine **restaurant (€€) in the medieval inn which formerly served the pilgrims.

Western Valleys: Valle de Baztán and Valle de Bidasoa

Frequent rains off the Atlantic make these valleys so lush that they're called the 'Switzerland of Navarra'. Both are dotted with well-preserved, unspoiled white Basque villages, trout streams and quietly beautiful scenery. One of the best-known smugglers' routes ran from the caves of Sare, just over the border in France, to the caves of Zugarramurdi; it still makes a pretty and easy walk today.

But what **Zugarramurdi** is most famous for is its role as the Salem of the Basque lands. The **Valle de Baztán** once had Spain's largest Agote population (*see* p.99) and perhaps not entirely coincidentally a supposed colony of witches in the early 17th century, based in Zugarramurdi, 'the Hill of Elms', a pretty place just in from the French frontier. As in Salem, the witchcraft scare began with the dubious confessions of a young woman in 1608, and spread like wildfire from denunciation to denunciation in a kind of mass hysteria. It wasn't long before 10 witches had confessed to a whole slew of heinous crimes, taking responsibility for nearly every death and trouble in Zugarramurdi that had occurred over the past 50 years. According to Basque law, they were tried and pardoned. Then the Inquisition, based in Logroño, got wind of it. Thirty-one hapless souls, mostly women and children, were arrested and 'put to the question' in 1609; of those condemned, 13 died under torture, and six, who refused to confess, survived to be burned alive at an *auto-da-fé*. Another 11 were burned the following year. That year, the Inquisition claimed to have discovered 1,590 witches in Navarra alone. No one really knows how many died.

Cuevas de Zugarramurdi
t 94 859 91 70;
open summer daily 9–dusk; adm

Just outside the village, carved out of the mountain by the *Infernuko Erreka* ('Hell's Stream'), the vast **Cuevas de Zugarramurdi** were the scene of black sabbaths, or *akelarres*, in which the participants smeared themselves with an unguent made of human brains and bones – mixed with belladonna, toads, salamanders and snakes – and flew through the night to join in outrageous orgies with a Satanic black billy goat, *akerbeltz* – at least according to the confessions extracted by the Inquisitors.

Basque witchcraft enjoyed a revival in the post-Franco 1970s, when the cult was seen either as a feminist revolt against an oppressive male-dominated society and religion, or as an instance of pocket survivals of the old pagan beliefs, demonized by the Church, perhaps even practised as underground rituals of Basque solidarity. Whatever the case, the inhabitants of Zugarramurdi have decided that it was all a splendid excuse for a hugely popular *Sorginak Besta* (Fiesta of Witches), to dress up and party on the Saturday closest to the summer solstice, and thousands still gather in the caves for an old-fashioned re-enactment of an *akelarre*, complete with all kinds of philtres and magic potions. Even older magic was built into the **cromlechs of Mairuillarrieta**, dedicated to the Basque goddess Mari, reached by a path from the village. There

Cuevas de Urdax
guided tours run roughly every 20mins in summer

are other caves, including the lovely stalactite **Cuevas de Urdax** just south at Urdazubi/Urdax, where fish-tailed *lamiaks* once frolicked in the stream, or perhaps still do when no one's looking.

Elizondo, one of the prettiest villages in the Baztán valley, has an informal tourist office where you can pick up a map that pinpoints the historic houses: those along the river are especially impressive. **Arizkun**, 7km northeast, has the fortified stone house of one of Spain's busiest *conquistadores*, Pedro de Ursúa, leader of the search for El Dorado up the Amazon in 1560 when he was killed by rebel leader Lope de Aguirre. The parish church has a striking Baroque façade. Further north a road turns east to France by way of the

Izpegui pass
accessible in summer only

spectacular **Izpegui pass**.

Navarra's westernmost Pyrenean valley, the **Valle de Bidasoa**, embraces streams filled with salmon and trout and, more prosaically, the main San Sebastián–Pamplona road. Bus services in the area offer a chance to visit charming old Basque villages such as **Bera (Vera) de Bidasoa**, only a couple of miles from the French frontier, with the former summer home of Basque novelist and doctor Pío Baroja (1872–1956). A member of the Generation of '98, Pío Baroja was a firm supporter of the Republic from the beginning (*Memorias de un hombre de acción*), but he was also fascinated by Basque witchcraft, and made it a feature of one of his novels, *La Dama de Urtubi*. **Lesaka**, equally pretty, claims one of the best-preserved fortified feudal houses in Navarra. Tiny **Etxalar (Echalar)**, a hamlet that time forgot, is on a stream on the pretty, seldom-used road to Zugarramurdi – seldom used except in October, during the annual wild pigeon and wood-cock holocaust. The church at Etxalar is surrounded by 100 Basque funerary steles with their distinctive solar symbol discs.

Parque Natural del Señorío de Bértiz
t 94 859 24 21, www. parquedebertiz.es; open summer daily 10–8; winter daily 10–6

Farther south, the **Parque Natural del Señorío de Bértiz**, a former private estate, has foot, bicycle and riding paths through thousands of acres of oak, beech and chestnut forests; the gardens near the manor boast over 120 species of exotic trees. Note the coat of arms of the lord of Bértiz, showing a mermaid holding a mirror and comb; Charles III ordered her to be placed there in 1421 in honour of his ambassador, Micheto de Bértiz.

Two villages just west of here, **Zubieta** and **Ituren**, are famous for a late-January ritual ushering in spring that could have been invented by Dr Seuss: young unmarried men and boys (starting as young as five) called *joaldunaks* dress up in dunce's caps and lacey smocks or sheepskins and fasten a pair of copper *polunpaks* (giant bells) to their backs with an intricate network of laces. Thus arrayed, for two days the *joaldunaks* make a *zanpantzar*, a group of 20 or so, who dance and march from village to village across the frosty land, their *polunpaks* clanging with deep resonance.

Sports and Activities in the Western Valleys

The old **smugglers' path** to Sare is easy to follow and waymarked with silhouettes of the little Basque horse, the *pottok*.

Orbela, at the Albergue Beintza, Beintza-Labaien ✉ 31753, t 94 845 00 14, *orbela@alberguesnavarra.com*. Organizes full- or half-day guided excursions into the mountains of Baztán-Bidasoa; they also offer mountain-bike tours down the old Bidasoa railway line, and potholing excursions into one of the local caves.

BKZ, at the Albergue Bertiz Aterpea in Narbarte, t 94 859 23 22, *bkz@navarraaventura.com*. White-water rafting and canoeing trips at all levels.

Where to Stay and Eat in the Western Valleys

Zugarramurdi ✉ 31710
Alzatenea, C/ Basaburua 3, t 948 59 91 87 (€). Charming restaurant: roast meats cooked over a wood fire.

Urdazubi ✉ 31711
Hostal Irigoienea, C/ Salvador, t 94 859 92 67, *www.irigoienea.com* (€€). This old, whitewashed Navarrese farmhouse furnished with a handful of antiques is a charming place to stay. *Closed 4th week June, and Mon–Wed in Oct–May.*

Restaurante La Koska, C/ San Salvador, 4, t 94 859 90 42, *http://lakoska. restaurantesok.com* (€€). Traditional Navarra fare is served in this well-established, family-run restaurant. The owners pride themselves on their use of an authentic wood stove. *Closed Mon, Tues–Thurs eves, Sun eve, and last 2 weeks Nov.*

Elizondo ✉ 31700
Señorío de Ursúa, Caserio Ikazatea, Arizkun, t 94 845 35 00, *www.hotelursua.com* (€€€€–€€€). Sumptuous rooms and a fine restaurant in this beautifully renovated 17th-century Basque farmhouse.

★★★Baztán, on the main road, t 94 858 00 50, *www.hotelbaztan.com* (€€€). Modern, with panoramic views, a pool and a garden. *Closed Nov–Mar.*

★★Hs Saskaitz, C/ M. Azpilijueta 10, t 94 858 04 88, *hotelelizondo@biazpe.net* (€€€–€€). Cosy and calm, despite being in the centre of town.

Casa Rural Urruska, 10km away in Barrio de Bearzún, t 94 845 21 06, *www.urruska.com* (€€). People come from all over Spain to stay here. Simple but solid home cooking served upstairs while livestock baa and moo on the ground floor.

Casa Galarza, C/ Santiago 1, t 94 858 01 01 (€). A rival to Roncal's offerings, this haven of traditional Baztánian cuisine and cheese serves *txuri-tabeltz*, a stew of lamb's tripe for which Elizondo is famous. *Closed Thurs.*

ⓘ **Elizondo ❯❯**
Palacio de Arizkunenea,
t 94 858 12 79

Pamplona (Iruña)

11 Pamplona

Whether you call it Pamplona, the town founded by Pompey in 75 BC, or by its older name of Iruña, which means simply 'the city' in Basque, the capital of Navarra sits on a strategic 1,400ft pimple on the beautiful fertile plain, its existence as inevitable as its nickname, the 'Gateway of Spain'. For a few years in the 730s, the Arabs used it in reverse, as the gateway to France, until their dreams of Europe were hammered at Poitiers.

Over the next decades, the Basques regained control of Pamplona, clobbered Charlemagne after he burnt their walls, and set up their own king. In 918 the Moors came back and razed Pamplona to the ground again. To encourage rebuilding, Sancho the Great invited his subjects over the Pyrenees, in what is now Basse-Navarre, to come and start trades in what became the two new districts of Pamplona, San Cernín and San Nicolás. The fact that the three districts of the city were practically independent and had their own privileges led to violent rivalry between them, so much so that in 1521 the French, coming to the rescue of the French Navarrese, unsuccessfully besieged Pamplona in an effort to regain San Cernín and San Nicolás. Wounded while fighting for Castile was a certain Captain Iñigo López de Recalde (or Loyola), who got religion in a militant way and founded the Jesuits (*see* p.149).

Pamplona seems to have been naturally conducive to that sort of thing, with a reputation for being crazily austere, brooding and puritanical. To anyone who knows the city only for throwing the wildest party in Europe, this comes as a shock of *desfase*, or maladjustment, a word that means (and gleefully celebrates) the unresolved contradictions that coexist in post-Franco Spain. Stern Catholicism is part of the city's fabric. 'From the top to the bottom of Pamplonese society, I have found the whole place poisoned by clerical alkaloid,' grumped Miguel de Unamuno. 'One drop in the eye is enough to infect you forever.' In the 1950s, the shadowy Opus Dei, Christianity's conservative fifth column, chose Pamplona to build their Universidad de Navarra, their most important educational institution in Spain, especially since the late Pope John Paul II's beatification of the founder, Josemaría Escrivá. Today, the head prelate of the order is a Basque, Bishop Javier Echevarría. In the 1960s, Pamplona's new tennis club still built separate swimming pools for men and women. Forty years on, the city prides itself on having set up Spain's first shelter for battered women, the first city workshops for training disadvantaged youths and the first urban recycling programme. It is also the seat of the Udako Euskal Unibertsitaea (Basque Summer University), which has led the way in higher education in Euskera and has promoted the printing of over 180 university textbooks in Basque. 'Pamplona

Getting to and around Pamplona

By Air

Pamplona's **airport** (t 94 816 87 00/50 (information) is 6km south of the city, with daily connections to Madrid and Barcelona. The cheapest way to get to the airport is to take no.21 bus from the bus station (every half-hour) to Noaín, which drops you 800m from the airport.

By Train

The **train station** is 2km out of town on Avda San Jorge. Bus no.9 makes the connections from it to the centre every 10mins (t 90 224 02 02 for train information). Tickets and information can also be had at the railway office in town, at C/ Estella 8, t 902 240 202.

By Bus

The **bus station** (t 94 822 38 54) is in town, near the citadel, at C/ Conde Oliveto 8. Besides provincial connections, there are ten buses daily to Vitoria, six to Bilbao, ten to San Sebastián (plus five slower services) and six to Zaragoza. There are fewer services at weekends, particularly on Sundays.

---

is a city that gives much more than it promises,' said Victor Hugo. It certainly will if you come in the second week of July for *Los Sanfermines*, but expect it also to take your money, your sleep and a lifetime's supply of adrenaline.

A Walk through the Casco Viejo

Pamplona was squeezed into a tight girdle of walls until the early 1900s, when the city spread in all directions and accumulated around 185,000 inhabitants in the process. But for all its 20th-century flab the vital organs in the historic Casco Viejo remain intact, curled tightly around the city's heart, the spacious **Plaza del Castillo**. Off the southwest corner extends the **Paseo de Sarasate**, populated by stone kings and queens and the overwrought **Monumento a los Fueros**, erected by popular subscription after Madrid tried to mess with Navarra's privileges back in 1893. The bronze allegory of Navarra holds a copy of the *Ley Foral*, or *Fueros'* Law, surrounded by the broken chains from the Battle of Las Navas de Tolosa, symbolizing freedom; these also feature on Navarra's coat of arms. Historical frescoes decorate the neoclassical **Palacio de Navarra** at one end of the Paseo; its archives contain one of the best caches of medieval documents in Spain and the garden boasts a massive sequoia.

Off the eastern end of Plaza del Castillo, the narrow streets jammed with shops and bars were once the **Judería**, where Pamplona's Jews, 'a gentle and reasonable race' according to the king of Navarra, lived unmolested until Navarra was gobbled up by the intolerant, Inquisitor-infested Spain of Ferdinand and Isabel. Behind these, tucked up near the ramparts, the gracious 14th–15th-century Gothic **cathedral** hides behind a dull neoclassical façade, slapped on in the 18th century by a misguided do-gooder; a shame, because the original front, according to travellers' descriptions, was as lusty as the one at Cervatos (*see* pp.195–6).

Cathedral
entrance on C/ Dormitaleria; open mid-July–mid-Sept daily 10–7; May–mid-July and mid-Sept–Oct daily 10–1 and 4–7; Nov–April daily 10.30–1.30 and 4–6; adm, includes cloister and Museo Diocesan

Pamplona

When completed, this was the second-largest cathedral in Spain after León's, and suitable shelter for the beautiful alabaster tombs of the cathedral's sponsors, big-nosed Charles III 'the Noble' and his big-nosed queen Leonora de Trastámara, sculpted in the 15th century by Jean de Lomme of Tournai. The kings of Navarra were crowned before the Romanesque statue of Santa María La Real, carved and gilded in silver in the 12th century, who peers out from beneath a spidery neo-Gothic canopy in the presbytery. The delicacy of the Gothic **cloister** (1280–1472) approaches gossamer in stone and reaches a climax of decorative bravura in the justly named **Puerta Preciosa** (1350–60), carved with a superb *Dormition of the Virgin*. The **Museo Diocesano** occupies the kitchen and refectory where pilgrims once dined; the refectory is filled with sweet-faced 12th–15th-century carvings of the Madonna and Child, while the kitchen is remarkable for its enormous chimneys. The Cillería (behind the ticket desk) contains two remarkable reliquaries – the 1258 *Relicario del Santo Sepulcro* and the 1401 *Relicario del Lignum Crucis*, adorned with precious stones.

The narrow old lanes around the cathedral belong to the **Navarrería**, the original Basque quarter, populated in the Middle Ages by cathedral-builders and farmers who tilled the bishop's lands. Here, on the promontory of the Rincón del Caballo Blanco, you'll find the most impressive segment of the surviving **walls** built by Philip II, with a reputation for impregnability so powerful that no one challenged it until the French tried to hole up here against Wellington; the views stretch for miles over the plain. Just west, the 13th-century **Palacio del Virrey** started out as the royal palace and is now being completely refurbished and expanded.

Past the attractive **Portal de Zumalacárregui** (16th century, but renamed after the heroic Carlist general who died at the siege of Bilbao), the **Museo de Navarra** occupies a huge 16th-century hospital and contains everything from Navarrese prehistory to contemporary art, with Roman mosaics, Gothic wall paintings, carved capitals from Pamplona's original Romanesque cathedral (minus the naughty bits), an ivory coffret from Leyre made in Córdoba in the 11th century and a fine portrait of the *Marqués de San Adrián* by Goya. A pretty courtyard with Roman mosaics offers views of a stretch of the old city walls. Just below the museum, wooden barricades remind you that this is the beginning of the *encierro*; the bulls leave their corral near Plaza Santo Domingo and head up C/ Mercaderes and C/ Estafeta. Follow their route and you'll come to Plaza Consistorial and the colourful Baroque **Casa Consistorial**, topped with jaunty allegorical figures. Pamplona's nobles built their finest escutcheoned palaces just off this square, along C/ Zapatería and C/ Mayor. Plazas de Consejo and San Francisco, set diagonally opposite each other, are also worth a look, the latter with a Modernista (Art Nouveau) hotel converted into a bank. Nearby in C/ Ansoleaga, the well-preserved Gothic **Cámara de los Comptos Reales**, the king's mint in the 12th century, has a magnificent porch opening onto a vault and patio.

Museo de Navarra
t 848 42 64 99, www.cfnavarra.es; open Tues–Sat 9.30–2 and 5–7, Sun and hols 11–2; adm

Cámara de los Comptos Reales
open Mon–Fri 8–3

07 Navarra and La Rioja | Pamplona (Iruña)

Pamplona's Annual Meltdown: *Los Sanfermines*

Before Hemingway there was Fermín, son of a Roman senator and first bishop of Pamplona. His family had been converted by San Saturnino (or Sernin, or Cernín) of Toulouse, who was martyred by being dragged by a bull. Fermín, for his part, travelled as a missionary to the Gauls and was beheaded in Amiens. Some time between then and 1324, when Pamplona held its first fiesta, Fermín decided to take bullfighters under his saintly cape; by 1591 his festival had found its current dates and form. Although it's the insanely dangerous running of the bulls that has made *Los Sanfermines* world-famous, this is only a tiny portion of the nine days of non-stop revelling when 'Pamplona becomes the world capital of happiness', a state of hyper-bliss fuelled by three million litres of alcohol.

There is some order to the madness. The *Sanfermines* officially start at noon on 6 July, when thousands of Navarrese in their festival attire (white shirts and white trousers or skirts, red sashes and red bandanas) gather in front of the town hall to hold their bandanas aloft as a rocket called *El Chupinazo* is fired off the balcony and a city councillor cries in Spanish and Basque: 'People of Pamplona! Long live San Fermín!' The city explodes with a mighty roar, while popping tens of thousands of champagne corks (and smashing the bottles on the pavement).

In the afternoon, the giants and big heads (*gigantes y cabezudos*) – as essential to the fiesta as the bulls – leave their 'home' in the bus station. The eight 13ft plaster giants supported by dancers date from 1860 and represent kings and queens, whirling and swirling to the minuet, their sweeping skirts flowing in the air. They are accompanied by the *cabezudos* and *kilikis*, big-headed figures in tricorn hats, with names like Napoleon and Patata, who wallop children on the head with foam rubber balls tied to bats. This is also the prerogative of the *zaldikos*, the colourfully dressed men wearing cardboard horses around their waists; all are accompanied by dancers, *txistularis* and *gaiteros*.

At four o'clock a massive scrum, the *Riau Riau*, begins when members of the Corporación de San Fermín dressed in all their finery try to proceed 400m down the Calle Mayor to the chapel of San Fermín at San Lorenzo for vespers, but everyone else tries to prevent them in a gung ho defiance of authority, to the extent that it's often late at night before the Corporación achieves its goal. The mayor of Pamplona has tried for several years to ban the chaotic *Riau Riau*, but it seems to be unbannable. After a first night of carousing and dancing in the streets, the dawn of 7 July and every following day is welcomed with the *dianas*, a city-wide wake-up call performed on screeching pipes.

The *encierro*, or *zezenketa*, the running of the bulls, begins daily at 8am, but, if you want a good place to watch, wedge yourself into a spot along the route – Cuesta de San Domingo, Mercaderes and Estafeta – at least an hour earlier. Before running, the locals sing a hymn to Fermín and arm themselves with a rolled-up newspaper to distract the bull's attention, since the animals – 1,200lbs of muscle and fury – charge at the nearest moving object, ideally at a flung newspaper instead of a falling runner. A rocket goes up as the first bull leaves the corral; a second rocket means that all are released, and a third signals that all have made it to the bullring – on a good run the whole *encierro* only lasts three minutes. The most dangerous moments are when the runners and bulls have to squeeze into the runway of the bullring, or when a bull gets loose from his fellows and panics. People (and not all of them tourists) get trampled and gored every year; if you run you can hedge your bets by running on weekdays, when it's less crowded, and by avoiding the *toros* of the Salvador Guardiola ranch, which have the most bloodstained record.

The spirit of abandon is so infectious that, even if you come determined not to run, you may find yourself joining in on a self-destructive spur of the moment. Women do defy the authorities and run, although the police try to pull them out. During the *encierro* the lower seats of the bullring are free (again, arrive early), except on Sunday; from here you can watch the bulls and runners pile in and, afterwards, more fun and games as heifers with padded horns are released on the crowd in the ring. The traditional breakfast is huge (bull stews, lamb's sweetbreads, ham and eggs in tomato sauce, washed down with gallons of chilled rosé and *patxaran*).

The bullfights themselves take place daily at 6.30 in the evening – tickets sell out with the speed of lightning and are usually only available from scalpers. The *sombra* seats are for serious aficionados, while members of the *peñas* (clubs devoted to making noise and in general being as obnoxious as possible) fill up the *sol* seats and create a parallel fiesta if the action in the ring isn't up to snuff, or create pandemonium if it is. Afternoons also see other bull sports that are bloodless (for the bull, at any rate): the dodging, swerving *concurso de recortadores* and leaping *corrida vasca-landesa*.

Between the bullfights there are concerts, Navarrese dance (*jotas*) and Basque dances, processions of the relics of San Fermín and other religious services, parades and activities for young children and senior citizens. At night, fireworks burst over the citadel and the *toro de fuego*, or 'fire bull', carried by a runner and spitting fireworks, chases children down the route of the *encierro*. Then there's the midnight *El Estruendo de Irún*, led by an enormous drum called the *bomba*, in which hundreds of people – just about anyone who can lay their hands on anything that makes a sound – gather and let loose in an ear-bashing sonic disorder.

At midnight on 14 July, Pamplona winds down to an exhausted, nostalgic finale, a ceremony known as the *Pobre de mí*; everyone gathers in front of the town hall (or in the Plaza del Castillo for the livelier, unofficial ceremony), with a candle and sings: 'Poor me, poor me, another San Fermín has come to an end.' As the clock strikes 12 everyone removes their red scarves and agrees, like Hemingway, that it was 'a damned fine show' and promises to do better and worse next year. Die-hards party on until 8am the next day, and perform one last feat, the *encierro de la villavesa*: the bulls are all dead so they run in front of a bus.

**San Saturnino/
San Nicolás/
San Lorenzo**

*all churches open
roughly 8.30–12 and
6.30–7.30*

The not always tremendously popular *francos* invited to
Pamplona by Sancho the Great lived just to the east in their two
rival quarters named after, and defended by, 13th-century churches
that doubled as fortresses when their fellow citizens went on the
warpath. These are **San Saturnino** (or San Cernín) in C/ San
Saturnino and **San Nicolás** in lively, bar-lined C/ San Nicolás; a
plaque by the former marks the site where the first Pamplonans
were converted by San Saturnino. To the west, **San Lorenzo** is best
known for its chapel dedicated to San Fermín, built by the city in
1717, where his bust reliquary quietly resides 51 weeks of the year,
presiding over weddings; so many Pamplonese want to be married
under his protective eye that there's a two-year waiting list.

Pamplona is well endowed with parks. The oldest, the French-
style **Parque de la Taconera**, closes the west end of the Casco Viejo
and has one of the city's nicest cafés, the **Vienés**. Just south, the
star-shaped **Ciudadela**, built on the orders of Philip II, now has a
green park inside and outside the steep walls. The immaculate
new **Parque Yamaguchi** is named after Pamplona's Japanese 'twin'
and has a neat Japanese garden complete with lakeside wooden
house for the tea ceremony. Also here is one of Pamplona's newer
attractions, a tall, fat red-and-blue tower containing the **Planetario**.

The city's prettiest garden, **Parque Media Luna**, lines the river east
of the city and has a path ending at the medieval bridge, the
Puente de Magdalena, used by the pilgrims. The park in front of the
Plaza de Toros was renamed Paseo Hemingway and has a grizzled
bust of the writer whose novel *The Sun Also Rises* (1926) made
Pamplona a household name.

The influential sculptor Jorge Oteiza (1908–2003) is remembered
in the new **Museo Oteiza**, close to the village of Navarra de Alzuza.
The collection includes more than 1,600 pieces.

Planetario
*t 94 826 26 28, www.
pamplonetario.org;
open Aug–Sept 11–1.30
and 6–9; Oct–June Mon
9.30–1.30, Tues–Fri
9.30–1.30 and 4–7.30,
Sat 11–1.30 and 5–8.30;
closed Sun and
July; adm*

Museo Oteiza
*t 94 833 20 74,
www.museooteiza.com;
open Oct–May Tues–Fri
10–3, Sat–Sun and hols
11–7; June–Sept
Tues–Sun 11–7;
adm, free on Fri*

Tourist Information in Pamplona

ⓘ **Pamplona** >
*C/ Eslava 1, Plaza
San Francisco,
t 84 842 04 20, oit.
pamplona@navarra.es*

The staff at the **tourist office**
operate a booking service for *casas
rurales* throughout Navarra, **t** 90 219
64 62 (*daily 11–4*).

For up-to-date info on *Los
Sanfermines, see www. sanfermin.com*.

Cultural/historical walking tours:
Erreka, C/ Curia 18, **t** 94 822 15 06,
info@incomingnavarra.net; **Estafeta
Tours**, C/ Estafeta 45, **t** 94 822 57 68.

Post office: Paseo de Sarasate 9,
t 94 820 72 17.

Internet access: Naveganet, Travesía
de Acella 3, **t** 94 819 92 97. *Open
Mon–Sat 10–1 and 4–10.*

Markets in Pamplona

Mercado de Santo Domingo, next to
the town hall in Plaza de los Burgos.
The oldest and most popular market
in the city (*Mon–Sat*).

Mercadillo de Landaben, Polígono
Landaben. This Sunday-morning
open-air market (*not July and Aug*)
has everything from clothes to fruit.

Where to Stay in Pamplona

Pamplona ✉ **31300**
During *Los Sanfermines*, hotel
prices double and often triple, supplemented by scores of overpriced rooms

in *casas particulares*, advertised weeks ahead in the local newspapers, *Navarra Hoy* and *Diario de Navarra*. If you end up sleeping outside, any of the gardens along the walls or river are preferable to the noisy, filthy, vomit-filled citadel. Keep a close eye on your belongings (petty criminals, unfortunately, go into overdrive along with everyone else during the fiesta) and check in what you don't need at the *consigna* in Plaza San Francisco, next to the tourist office; everyone else does too, so get there early. Two free campsites are set up along the road to France, but again, don't leave anything there you might really miss. If you stay outside Pamplona and drive into town, beware that theft from cars is widespread.

****Iruña Palace Los Tres Reyes, C/ de la Taconera, **t** 94 822 66 00, *www.hotel3reyes.com* (€€€€€). Conveniently located a short walk from the old town, this big modern hotel pampers its well-heeled guests with every possible convenience, including an indoor heated pool and tennis.

*La Perla, Plaza del Castillo, **t** 94 822 30 00, *www.granhotellaperla.com* (€€€€€). Hemingway always stayed at this, Pamplona's oldest hotel, with its high ceilings and plaster mouldings.

***Yoldi, Avda San Ignacio 11, **t** 94 822 48 00, *www.hotelyoldi.com* (€€€€–€€€). A modern business hotel that has long been the favourite of *toreros* and aficionados in general.

***NH El Toro, Berrioplano (5km from Pamplona on the Guipúzcoa road), **t** 94 830 22 11, *nhtoro@nh-hotels.es* (€€€). Quiet rooms in a traditional-style mansion, overlooking a statue group of the *encierro*.

Casa Otano, San Nicolás 5, **t** 94 822 50 95, *www.casaotano.com* (€€€). Popular for years, for its nice rooms with baths, and a good, inexpensive bar-restaurant.

Hostal Navarra, C/ Tudela 9, **t 94 822 51 64, *www.hostelnavarra.com* (€€). Next to the bus station, this offers immaculate cream-painted rooms with sage-green furnishings and all the conveniences. Five minutes' walk from the Casco Viejo. Recommended.

Meson del Barro, C/Acella 2, **t** 92 825 63 66 (€€). Good-value rooms, with or without bath, above a restaurant close to the Parque Yamaguchi. They also offer self-catering apartments.

Castillo de Javier, San Nicolás, 50-52, **t** 94 820 30 40, *www.hotelcastillodejavier.com* (€€). A new, delightful and well-priced hotel in central location. Rooms are stylish, comfortable and clean. The street-side rooms can get noisy so, if you are a light sleeper, insist on a back room.

Hs Príncipe de Viana I and **II, Avenida Zaragoza 4, **t** 94 824 91 47 (€€–€). Clean but faded rooms with baths; run by a pair of sisters in the same building.

Arriazu, Comedias 14, **t** 94 821 02 02, *www.hostalarriazu.com* (€€–€). The fresh and clean rooms in this charming *hostal* suggest a more upmarket place to stay than its price category. Next to the Plaza del Castillo and a popular eating area, this is a good bargain.

Cheaper *hostales* and *fondas* are mostly on C/ San Gregorio and C/ San Nicolás.

*Pensión Casa García, C/ San Gregorio 12, **t** 94 822 38 93 (€). Offers very plain double rooms without bath, and a decent *menú del día* in its restaurant.

*Hs Bearán, San Nicolás 25, **t** 94 822 34 28 (€). One of the few decent *hostales*, where newly renovated doubles come with baths, TV, and air-conditioning.

Pension Santa Cecilia, C/ Navarrería 17, **t** 94 822 22 30 (€). Located in an 18th-century palace, and providing one of the nicest economy sleeps, under lofty ceilings in huge rooms.

Pensión Sarasate, Paseo Sarasate 30, **t** 94 822 30 84 (€). Small and personal; the decent but unspectacular rooms all have a private bath.

Ezcaba, **t** 94 833 03 15, *www.ezcaba.com*. The nearest campsite, 7km north.

Eating Out in Pamplona

Josetxo, Plaza Príncipe de Viana 1, **t** 94 822 20 97 (€€€). A local gourmet institution in Pamplona for 50 years. Try to book one of the small Belle Epoque dining rooms upstairs, and choose between delicacies such as *ajoarriero con bogavante* (lobster

(★) Hostal Navarra >

(★) Josetxo >>

Baserri >>

cooked with dried cod, tomatoes, garlic and peppers) or the chef's prize *solomillo a la broche con salsa de trufa* (steak fillet on a spit with truffle sauce). *Closed Sun and Aug.*

Hartza, C/ Juan de Labrit 19, **t** 94 822 45 68 (€€€). Very close to the bullring, this is a traditional, welcoming establishment serving up fresh Basque-Navarre dishes made with ingredients selected daily by the now rather elderly Hartza sisters. It's famous for its *bonito encebollado* (tuna with onions). *Closed Mon, 1–25 Aug and Xmas/New Year.*

Alhambra, C/ Francisco Bergamín 7, **t** 94 824 50 07 (€€€). Look out for the more imaginative dishes at this fashionable place, a favourite with local gourmets: potatoes stuffed with truffles and scampi. *Closed Sun and mid-July–early Aug.*

Rodero, C/ Arrieta 3, **t** 94 822 80 35 (€€€). Currently the best restaurant in the city, serving modern variations on Navarrese, Basque and French recipes prepared with the finest seasonal ingredients. Try the *corona de alcachofas fritas* (lightly fried artichokes) to start, followed by the *canelón de bacaloa con ajo* (cod baked with garlic). The wine list is excellent. *Closed Sun, plus 2nd week July.*

Enekorri, C/ Tudela 14, **t** 94 823 25 47, *www.enokorri.com* (€€€). An attractive mixture of old and new furnishings, echoed in the food, a creative mix of traditional recipes with new twists.

Casa Manolo, C/ García Castañón 12, **t** 94 822 51 02, *www.restaurantecasa manolo.com* (€€€–€€). Traditional, welcoming and good value, with a range of set menus offering fine local cuisine.

Bodegón Sarria, C/ Estafeta 50, **t** 94 822 77 13 (€€). Fronted by a wonderful old bar (with some of the best tapas in town) with black and white pictures of Hemingway and bulls on the walls, the restaurant here dishes up solid traditional fare.

Erburu, C/ San Lorenzo 15, **t** 94 822 51 69 (€€). This is a quiet, wooden-beamed retreat at the height of the *marcha*; it serves Navarrese-style seafood and excellent beef, and there's also a popular tapas bar. *Closed Mon and last two weeks of July.*

Baserri, C/ San Nicolás 32, **t** 94 822 20 21, *www.restaurantebaserri.com* (€€). Hard to beat for *cocina en miniatura*; this restaurant's fine creations have repeatedly walked away with the top honours at Pamplona's annual *Concurso de Pinchos*. You can try a selection of them, and delicacies such as fresh rocket and smoked cod salad, plus a choice of more than 80 wines.

San Fermín, C/ San Nicolás 44, **t** 94 822 21 91 (€€). This is one of the best places to try Navarra's famous vegetables, all freshly prepared. They also offer tasty meat and fish, and there's a lunch menu for €12. *Closed Mon.*

Sarasate, C/ San Nicolás 19, **t** 94 822 57 27 (€€). Come here for the best vegetarian meals in Pamplona. *Closed Sun and evenings, except Fri and Sat.*

Tapas/*Pintxos* in Pamplona

As well as elegant cafés, Pamplona had some 700 bars at the last count, or one for every 280 inhabitants – many of whom seem to be always in them, day and night.

Café Iruña, Plaza del Castillo 44, *www.cafeiruna.com*. You can tuck into inexpensive light meals until 2.30am at this famous 1888 Modernista place, with etched glass and chandeliers. It also boasts the best terrace in the city.

Mesón del Caballo Blanco, Rincón del Caballo Blanco (behind the cathedral), in Redín, east of Pamplona. An atmospheric old stone house with a terrace. In winter, sandwiches are served around the fireplace. Dine in the restaurant upstairs, or enjoy a drink downstairs.

Café Roch, C/ Comedias 6. One of the oldest cafés in the city, this is small, lively and usually packed at the start of the *marcha*, thanks in part to their superb *fritos de pimiento pintxos*.

Letyana, Travesía de Bayona 2. Excellent, award-winning *pintxos*, a great atmosphere.

El Molino, Avda Bayona 13. A much-loved classic, with fabulous *pintxos* and a regular crowd of locals.

Fiterro, C/ Estafeta 58. This is the best tapas bar on legendary Estafeta, with an array of mouthwatering *pintxos*.

East of Pamplona:
Sangüesa, Javier and Leyre

Pilgrims to Santiago from Mediterranean lands would cross the
Pyrenees at Somport in Aragón and enter Navarra at Sangüesa,
home of one of the very best Romanesque churches and one of the
craziest palaces in all Spain, but these days, if the wind's wrong, the
pong of the nearby paper mill hurries visitors along; note that if
you go by bus from Pamplona (*see* p.91) there are only three a day.

Aoiz (Agoitz)

The area due east of Pamplona, crossed by the Río Irati, gets few
tourists, but, if you're driving, the undulating landscapes and
nearly deserted villages make an interesting alternative to the
more direct N240 to Sangüesa. Aoiz itself has fine old houses, a
medieval bridge and the 15th-century **San Miguel Arcángel**, worth
a look for its excellent *retablo mayor* (1580) by Basque master Juan
de Achieta and for its unusual 12th-century painted stone font.
Romanesque connoisseurs should go out of their way to **Artaiz**, a
tiny blip to the southwest (due south of Urroz), where the church
of **San Martín** has the finest sculpture in rural Navarra.

Sangüesa

Sangüesa was a direct product of the pilgrimage, purposely
moved from its original hilltop location in the 11th century to the
spot where the road crosses the Río Aragón. In 1122, Alfonso el
Batallador, king of neighbouring Aragón, sent down a colony of
francos to augment Sangüesa's population, and 10 years after that
ordered the Knights of St John to build a church well worth
stopping for: **Santa María la Real**. This possesses one of the most
intriguing and extraordinary portals anywhere, so strange that
some writers believe that its symbols (knotted labyrinths,
mermaids, two-headed beasts symbolizing duality, etc.) were
sculpted by Agotes (*see* box, opposite), or by a brotherhood of
artists, into something deeper than orthodox Catholicism. Even the
damned are laughing in the *Last Judgement* on the tympanum,
presided over by a Christ in Majesty with a secret smile. Below, the
elongated figures on the jambs show stylistic similarities to
Chartres cathedral, although again the subjects are unusual: on
the left the three Marys (the Virgin, Mary Magdalene and Mary
Salome, mother of St James), on the right Peter, Paul and Judas,
hanged, with the inscription *Judas Mercator*. The upper half of the
portal is by another hand altogether, crossed by two tiers of
Apostles of near-Egyptian rigidity and another Christ in Majesty.
If the church is open, ask the sacristan to show you the capitals in
the apse, hidden behind the Flemish Renaissance *retablo*, and note

Getting East from Pamplona

Around three **buses** a day are run by **La Veloz Sangüesina**, t 94 887 02 09, from Pamplona to Sangüesa.

---

the well in the corner. Walk around to see the beautiful carved corbels on the apse and the octagonal tower.

When Aragón and Navarra went their separate ways, the kings of Navarra made Sangüesa one of their several residences. Its arcaded Rúa Mayor is lined with palaces, including the **Casa Consistorial**, built over the old royal patio of arms, today a leafy square; behind this is the austere 12th-century, twin-towered **Palacio del Príncipe de Viana**. The 12th-century **church of Santiago** has a huge battlemented tower and carved capitals, and conserves a large stone statue of St James, discovered buried under the floor in 1965. The slightly later, Gothic **San Salvador** has a pentagonal tower and a huge porch, sheltering a carved portal; its Plateresque choir stalls come from Leyre. Just around the corner, in C/ Alfonso el Batallador, the brick **Palacio Vallesantoro** catches the eye with its corkscrew Baroque portal and the most extraordinary wooden eaves in Spain, carved with a phantasmagorical menagerie.

Javier and Leyre

Sangüesa is the base for visiting two of Navarra's holy sites. **Javier**, 13km away, is topped by a picturesque if over-restored

07

Navarra and La Rioja | East of Pamplona: Sangüesa, Javier and Leyre

---

Europe's Untouchables: the Agotes

Some of Europe's best-known outcasts, the Agotes (Cagotes in French) lived in the valleys of Navarra and especially across the Pyrenees in Basse Navarre and Gascony. Apartheid-style laws forced them to live separately and only marry other Agotes; to enter church only by a certain door and hear Mass in a special corner; to dress differently, with a goose foot sewn on to the backs of their coats; to play castanets at all crossroads and other public places to warn passers-by of their presence. Trades were forbidden them – except as builders and carpenters, a craft they excelled at to the extent that they were often called 'the Master Carpenters' instead of Agotes.

Guesses as to who the Agotes actually were and how they came to be pariahs vary in the extreme: some say they were dwarves, or albinos covered with a blond down, or Visigoths who failed to give up their Arian heresies and took refuge in the mountains when the Moors invaded. A strong tradition linking the Agotes to leprosy suggests that they were descended from a colony sent to live up in the remote valleys; but leprosy is not hereditary, and the Agotes who lived in Sangüesa and other towns were not lepers, although the stigma may have remained. In the Middle Ages, their ranks may have been swollen by all the loose ends of Europe who landed up along the road to Santiago. Or it may have been that the Agotes were only symbolic lepers, kept at a distance for the stigma of their heresies (curiously, they were also Crestias, or Christians, as if emphasizing that they were still, really, in the fold). This heresy may have been a highly contagious kind of universal mysticism practised by the Templars or the Order of the Knights of St Lazarus, an order founded in the East before the Templars, and devoted to the care of lepers, using Lazarus as their symbol of death within life. Whatever the real reason for their pariah status, it was forgotten by the 16th century, when the fed-up Agotes petitioned the pope to give them the same rights as other citizens. The pope agreed, but it was only in the 20th century, after a long civil rights struggle, that the Agotes were fully integrated into society, intermarrying with non-Agotes and vanishing without trace.

Castle
open 9–1 and 4–7; adm

battlemented **castle**, the birthplace in 1506 of Francisco de Javier (Xavier), Jesuit apostle of Japan and the Indies. Although the castle is now a Jesuit college, you can take the tour and learn a lot, about both St Francis and castles. Perhaps most fascinating is the fresco of the *Dance of Death*, a grim reminder that the Pyrenees were especially hard hit by the plague.

Just north of Javier, at **Yesa**, the Río Aragón has been dammed to form the vast **Yesa Reservoir**. A road from Yesa leads up into the Sierra de Leyre and to the **Monasterio de San Salvador de Leyre**. Its foundation predates the Moors, and in the 8th century its most famous abbot, San Virila, so constantly prayed to heaven for a peek into infinity that he was granted his wish, by the lovely warbling of a bird. To the abbot, the vision was a sublime moment, but when he went down to tell his monks about it he found that his eternal second had lasted 300 years. Leyre essentially dates from the 11th century, when Sancho the Great reformed the rule according to that of Cluny and declared it 'the centre and heart of my realm'. The first kings of Navarra were buried there, and the abbot of Leyre served as the bishop of Pamplona. Abandoned in the 19th century, the monastery was reoccupied in 1950 by the Benedictines, who began a restoration programme that unfortunately obscures much of the older building. Visits begin in the startling, 11th-century crypt, where the first impression is that the church is sinking into the ground. The columns are runty little stubs of columns of unequal height weighed down by heavy block capitals, carved with simple geometric designs that stand at about chest level. The chancel above was consecrated in 1057 and supplemented two centuries later with a single-aisled nave; the effect is harmonious, light and austere, providing the perfect setting for the Benedictines' beautiful 7th-century **Gregorian chant**, still sung at matins and vespers. The bones of the first 10 kings of Navarra lie in a simple wooden casket behind a fine grille; the 13th-century statue of the Virgin of Leyre sits on the altar. The west portal, the **Porta Speciosa**, is finely carved with a mix of saints and monsters.

It's a 10-minute walk up to the **Fountain of San Virila** for the magnificent view of the artificial lake and the Navarrese countryside that the abbot contemplated during his prayers, although the warbling birds have been replaced by hang-gliding Spaniards. Nature is a big attraction in eastern Navarra. The Sierra de Leyre divides the Roncal and Salazar valleys (*see* p.83), but there are two splendid gorges quite close at hand. The **Foz de Lumbier**, formed by the Irati river, has a pleasant riverside trail, and is a breeding site for griffon vultures. The even more spectacular, sheer-sided, 6km **Foz de Arbayún** (*see* p.83) lies further to the north along the Río Salazar, with more griffon and a few Egyptian vultures; both gorges are accessible from Lumbier.

Monasterio de San Salvador de Leyre
www.monasteriode leyre.com; open Mon–Fri 10.15–2 and 3.30–7; Sat and Sun 10.15–2 and 4–7; adm

Gergorian chant
t 94 888 41 50; Mon–Wed and Fri–Sat at 7pm and 9.10pm, Thurs at 7.30pm and 9.10pm, Sun at 12 noon, 7pm and 9.10pm

Where to Stay and Eat East of Pamplona

(i) **Aoiz** >
C/ Arriba 5,
t 94 833 66 90,
oitaoiz@hotmail.com

(i) **Sangüesa** >
C/ Mayor 2, t 94 887
14 11, oit.sanguesa@
navarra.es; guided
visits – a good way
of ensuring the
monuments are open –
are organized by the
tourist office

Aoiz ✉ 31430

*Hs Beti Jai, C/ Santa Agueda 2, t 94 833 60 52, *www.beti-jai.com* (€). 14 rooms and an excellent restaurant (€€), a soul-satisfying, good-value mix of the best regional traditions with the most modern techniques. Riverside views. *Closed Mon.*

Sangüesa ✉ 31400

**Yamaguchi, on the road to Javier, t 94 887 01 27, *www.hotelyamaguchi.com* (€€). A modern hotel with a pool, *frontón*, and a pleasant restaurant.

**Hs Las Navas, C/ Alfonso El Batallador 7, t 94 887 00 77 (€). A handful of basic but spotless rooms for a very low price.

Mediavilla, C/ Alfonso El Batallador 15, t 94 887 02 12 (€). A Basque *asador* serving delicious charcoal-grilled fish and meat with local wine. *Closed Mon.*

Javier/Leyre ✉ 31411

****Hotel Señorío de Monjardín, Ctra de Leyre 4, t 94 888 41 88, *www.hotelsenoriodemonjardin.com* (€€€). Large, modern hotel, 3km from Leyre on the N240, with some luxurious suites and a restaurant featuring Navarrese cuisine and game dishes.

***Xabier, Plaza de Javier, t 94 888 40 06, *www.hotelxabier.com* (€€€–€€). You can stay and eat next to the castle at this charming, historic hotel-restaurant.

**El Mesón, t 94 888 40 35, *www.hotelmeson.com* (€€). Also next to the castle, but rather more basic. *Closed mid-Dec–mid-Feb.*

**Hospedería de Leyre, t 94 888 40 11, *www.hotelhospederiadeleyre.com* (€€). This charming former pilgrims' *hostal* at Leyre is the perfect antidote to stress; its restaurant specializes in traditional Navarrese cuisine. *Open Mar–mid-Dec.*

South of Pamplona to Tudela

The green Basque hills are a distant memory south of Pamplona; here the skies are bright and clear, the land arid and toasted golden brown after the winter rains, except for the green swaths of vineyards in La Ribera, cradle of Navarra's finest, freshest rosés.

Tafalla and Olite

In the 17th century, a Dutchman named E. Cock described Tafalla and Olite as the 'flowers of Navarra'. Old **Tafalla** has wilted a bit over the centuries and grass grows between the cobbles, but it still has an impressive Plaza Mayor and claims one of the finest and biggest *retablos* in the north: a masterpiece by Basque artist Juan de Ancheta tucked away in the austere church of **Santa María**.

Northwest of Tafalla, **Artajona** has the air of an abandoned stage set: majestic medieval walls with startlingly intact crenellated towers defend little more than the 13th-century fortress church of **San Saturnino**. The Hispano-Flemish *retablo mayor* dates from 1515. This is the second church on the site. Artajona's walls, redone in the 14th century, were first built between 1085 and 1103 by the Templars and canons of St-Sernin (San Saturnino) of Toulouse.

Near Artajona, the **Ermita de la Virgen** shelters a bronze and enamel 13th-century Virgin holding a bouquet of roses. There are two megalithic gallery tombs nearby.

Getting around South of Pamplona

Trains linking Pamplona and Zaragoza call at Tafalla, Olite and Tudela. **Conda buses** (t 94 822 10 26, *www.conda.es*) stop at Tafalla, Olite and Tudela on the way to Zaragoza. Hire a **bicycle** or mountain bike from **Chiqui-bike** in Tudela and Arguedas, t 94 882 52 01, or t 68 969 56 60.

**Palacio Real
de Olite**
*open July and Aug
10–8; spring and
autumn 10–7;
winter 10–6; adm*

Olite, south of Tafalla, is a fabulous medieval town dwarfed by its bewitching, lofty-towered **Palacio Real de Olite** built for the king of Navarra in 1407. Each of its 15 towers and turrets has its own character, and restorers have made the whole thing seem startlingly new. Inside, the décor is *mudéjar*; hanging gardens were suspended from the great arches of the terraces, and there was a *leonera*, or lion pit, and a very busy set of dungeons; the Navarrese royal families led messy, frustrated lives. At night the whole complex is illuminated with a golden light, creating a striking backdrop to performances in the summer Festival of Navarra.

**Santa María
la Real**
open 9.30–12 and 5–8

San Pedro
open 9.30–12 and 5–8

The castle's Gothic chapel, **Santa María la Real**, has a gorgeous 13th-century façade, and the Romanesque church of **San Pedro** has an octagonal tower and portal adorned with two large stone eagles, one devouring the hare it has captured (symbolizing force) and the other, more friendly, representing gentleness.

Eastwards, the village of **San Martín de Unx** has a superb crypt under its 12th-century church. From here a byroad branches south for the spectacular medieval village of **Ujué**, set on a hill corrugated with terraces, where a shepherd, directed by a dove (*ujué*), found the statue of the black Virgin now housed in the powerful 13th-century Romanesque-Gothic church of **Santa María**. The doorway has finely carved scenes of the Last Supper and the Journey of the Magi, and the altar preserves the heart of King Charles II of Navarra. Every year since 1043, on the first Sunday after St Mark's day (25 April), the Virgin has been the object of a solemn pilgrimage that departs from Tafalla at 2am.

Tudela

Founded by the Moors, Tudela, the second city of Navarra and capital of La Ribera region, was the last town in Navarra to submit to Ferdinand the Catholic, and it did so most unwillingly. Before the big bigot, Tudela had always made a point of welcoming Jews, Moors and heretics expelled from Castile or persecuted by the Inquisition, and it was no accident that its tolerant environment nurtured three of Spain's top medieval writers: Benjamin of Tudela, the great traveller and chronicler (1127–73); the poet Judah Ha-Levi of the same period; and doctor Miguel Servet (1511–53), one of the first to write on the circulation of the blood. Head straight for the picturesque, labyrinthine Moorish-Jewish kernel, around the elegant 17th-century **Plaza de los Fueros**; the decorations on the façades recall its use as a bullring in the 18th and 19th centuries.

Cathedral
*open Tues–Sat 9–1
and 4–7, Sun and
Mon 9–1; adm*

The Gothic **cathedral** was built over the town's Great Mosque in the 12th century and topped with a pretty 17th-century tower. It has three decorated doorways, and the delightful choir, behind its Renaissance grille, is considered the finest Flamboyant Gothic work in Navarra, carved with geometric flora, fauna and fantasy motifs; note, under the main chair, the figures of two crows picking out the eyes of a man – the dean who commissioned the work but refused to pay the sculptors the agreed price. The main altar has a beautiful Hispano-Flemish *retablo* painted by Pedro Díaz de Oviedo, and yet more chains from Las Navas de Tolosa. There's an ornate Gothic *retablo* of Santa Caterina and a chapel of Santa Ana, patroness of Tudela, with a cupola that approaches Baroque orgasm. The cool, plant-filled 13th-century cloister, with twin and triple columns, has capitals on the Life of Jesus and other New Testament stories, while the Escuela de Cristo, off the east end of the cloister, has *mudéjar* paintings and decorations. The square is pedestrianized and filled with a sea of café tables.

Among the best palaces are the 16th-century **Casa del Almirante**, near the cathedral, and, in the C/ de Magallón, the lovely Renaissance **Palace of the Marqués de San Adrián**. An irregular, 17-arched, 13th-century bridge spanning the Ebro still takes much of Tudela's traffic, with help from an ultramodern suspension bridge.

Around Tudela: a Desert, Water and Wine

 **Bárdenas
Reales**
*www.bardenas
reales.es; open
8am–1hr before dusk*

Just east of Tudela is a striking desert straight out of the American Far West known as the **Bárdenas Reales**, where erosion has sculpted steep tabletops, weird wrinkled hills and rocks balanced on pyramids. You might recognize it, since it's a popular location for everything from Bond films to pop videos. The best way to see it (and not get lost) is by the GR13 walking path, which crosses its northern extent from the Ermita de Nuestro Señoro del Yugo. An easier way, however, is to go on an organized excursion, by horse, mountain bike or 4x4 (*see* box, overleaf).

South of Tudela, **Cascante** is known for its wines and the lofty church of the **Virgen del Romero** (Our Lady of the Rosemary Bush), built in the 17th century and reached by way of an arcaded walk-way from the village below. The small spa town of **Fitero** (the waters are used in treating tuberculosis) grew up around the 11th-century Cistercian monastery of **Santa María la Real**, whose abbot, San Raimundo, founded the famous Order of the Knights of Calatrava in 1158. Don't miss the Romanesque Sala Capitular, a monumental *retablo* from the 16th century, the 18th-century chapel of the Virgen de la Barda and, among the treasures, a 10th-century ivory coffer from the workshop of the Caliph of Córdoba. **Cintruénigo** and **Corella**, just north, are important producers of DO Navarra wine, with a good dozen *bodegas* in the environs.

Market Days
South of Pamplona

Tafalla: Fri, Plaza Navarra.
Olite: Wed, Paseo del Portal.
Fitero: Tues and Fri, Plaza San Raimundo.

Sports and Activities
South of Pamplona

A number of firms offer excursions into the Bárdenas Reales, in a 4x4 or on horseback. For more info, see *www.bideak-navarraactiva.com*.

Novotur, t 94 826 76 15. Offers mountaineering as well as excursions.

Nattura, t 94 813 10 44, *www.nattura. com*. Also offers mountaineering.

Erreka, t 94 822 15 06, *www.erreka.net*. Half-day programmes to 3- or 5-day study trips of Las Bárdenas.

Hípica Arbayún, t 94 888 02 71, and **Hípica La Laguna**, t 94 856 28 76. Excursions on horses to visit the surrounding beauty spots, including the Bárdenas Reales.

Where to Stay and Eat
South of Pamplona

Tafalla ✉ 31300

**Hs Tafalla, on the Zaragoza road, t 94 870 03 00, *www.hostaltafalla. com* (€€€–€€). Modern roadside hotel. The food is delicious, especially when the dishes involve asparagus, lamb and hake. *Closed Fri.*

Túbal, Plaza de Navarra 6, t 94 870 08 52 (€€€–€€). Chef Atxen Jiménez draws in diners from Pamplona and beyond with her variations on classic Navarrese themes. Book well in advance. *Closed Mon and late Aug.*

Olite ✉ 31390

***Parador de Olite, Plaza de los Teobaldos 2, t 94 874 00 00, *olite@ parador.es* (€€€). Next to the castle of Carlos III in the converted 13th-century Castillo de los Teobaldos. A garden, air-conditioning and beautiful furnishings make castle-dwelling a delight, as do Navarrese gourmet treats in the dining room.

La Joyosa Guarda, C/ de los Medios 23, t 94 874 13 03, *www.eljoyosaguardo. com* (€€€). Chic new hotel in a renovated mansion, with a stylish mix of antiques and contemporary furnishings and a very elegant restaurant.

**Hotel Merindad de Olite, Rúa de la Judería 11, t 94 874 07 35 (€€). In a restored old building, incorporating part of the 12th-century walls.

**Casa Zanito, Rúa Revillas 16, t 94 874 00 02, *zanito@cmn.navarra.net* (€€). A modern hotel with simple, cheerful rooms and excellent meals, based on market availability, with home-made desserts. *Closed mid-Dec–mid-Jan.*

Ujué ✉ 31390

Casa El Chofer I and II, t 94 873 90 11 (€). Simple rooms with private bath.

Mesón las Torres, t 94 873 90 52 (€€). Has long been the place to eat, with Navarrese treats and Ujué's special candied almonds. *Lunch only.*

Tudela ✉ 31500

*Hs Nueva Parrilla, C/ Carlos III el Noble 6, t 94 882 24 00 (€€–€). Friendly, basic; functional rooms.

**Hs Remigio, C/ Gaztambide 4, t 94 882 08 50 (€). Simple *hostal*, not far from the Plaza de Fueros, decorated with an old-fashioned rusticity.

Restaurante 33, C/ Capuchinos 7, t 948 82 76 06 (€€€). Widely regarded as the best in Navarra when it comes to local produce – they even offer a *menú* entirely of vegetable dishes. Carnivores will be more than satisfied with lamb dishes and country stews. *Closed Sun and first 3 weeks Aug.*

Casa Ignacio, C/ Cortaderos 11, t 94 882 10 21 (€€). Long-established favourite: try the famous *menestra de verduras*: asparagus, artichokes, peas, celery and lettuces. *Closed Mon eve.*

La Estrella, C/ Carnicerías 14, t 94 882 18 58 (€). Serves up good home cooking based on garden vegetables. *Closed Sun eve and 16–30 Sept.*

Cintruénigo ✉ 31592

Hotel Restaurante Maher, C/ La Ribera 19, t 94 881 11 50 (€€€). One of Navarra's best restaurants. Delicious Navarrese dishes with an imaginative *nouvelle cuisine* touch.

ⓘ **Tudela »**
C/ Juicio 4, t 94 884 80 58, www.tudela.es; exhibitions on local interests

ⓘ **Olite »**
Plaza de los Teobaldos 10, t 94 874 17 03, oit.olite@cfnavarra.es

The Knight, the Dragon and the Archangel

In the 9th century, Count Teodosio de Goñi went off to fight the Saracens with his Visigothic overlord King Witiza. He was returning home when he met a hermit (the devil in disguise) who warned him that his wife was unfaithful. Seething with rage, the knight stormed into his castle, saw two forms lying in his bed and without hesitation slew them both (this was endemic in the Middle Ages; the same thing happened to St Julian the Hospitaller). When Teodosio ran out he met his wife returning from Mass, who told him, to his horror, that she had given his own aged parents the bed. Horrified, Teodosio went to Rome to ask the pope what penance he could possibly do to redeem his soul, and after three nights the pope had a dream that he should wear heavy chains in solitude until God showed his forgiveness by breaking them.

Binding himself in chains, Teodosio went up to the top of Mount Aralar and lived as a hermit for years. One day, when he was sitting next to a cave, a scaly green dragon emerged, smoke billowing from its nostrils. Teodosio implored the aid of St Michael, who suddenly appeared with his sword in hand and spoke to the dragon in perfect Basque: '*Nor Jaunggoitkoa bezaka?*' ('Who is stronger than God?'). The dragon slunk back into its cave and the archangel struck off the knight's chains and left a statue of himself – an angelic figure with a large cross on its head and an empty glass case where the face ought to be. Every year between March and August the figure goes on a fertility-blessing tour through a hundred Navarra villages; and on Corpus Christi pilgrims walk or cycle up to the chapel.

Northwest of Pamplona: Aralar and San Miguel in Excelsis

Navarra's magic mountain, **Aralar**, now a natural park, is a favourite spot for a picnic or Sunday hike from Pamplona, gracefully wooded with beech, rowan and hawthorn groves. It has been sacred to the Basques since Neolithic times, when they erected 30 dolmens and menhirs in the yew groves around Putxerri. On top is Navarra's holy of holies, the **Sanctuario de San Miguel in Excelsis**, on a panoramic south–north road (NA751) that climbs over Aralar between Huarte Arakil and Lekunberri. The gloomy stone chapel built by the count of Goñi was consecrated in 1098. Traditionally guarded by mastiffs, the chapel has had an empty air ever since French Basques plundered it in 1797, when they knocked off St Michael's head (or so say apologists who find the crystal head too weird); the hands of the desecrators were chopped off before they were put to death, and nailed over the

Sanctuario de San Miguel in Excelsis
open 9.30–8

Where to Stay and Eat Northwest of Pamplona

(i) **Lekunberri >**
Plazaola 21,
t 94 850 72 04,
oit.lekunberri@
navarra.es.

Lekunberri ✉ 31870

**Hs Ayestarán II, C/ Aralar 22, t 94 850 41 27, *www. hotelayestaran.com* (€€). A pleasant, old-fashioned atmosphere, with tennis, children's leisure facilities, a pool and garden, and tasty local food. *Closed Oct–Mar.*

*Hs Basa Kabi, C/ Alto de Leitza, t 94 851 01 25, *basakabi@jet.es* (€€).

Reasonable, rural, good hotel-restaurant in the hills. *Closed Sept–May.*

Asador Epeleta, Aralar s/n, t 94 850 43 57 (€€–€). Possibly the finest roast meats in Spain, along with seafood. Book well in advance. *Closed Mon, second fortnight of June.*

Venta Muguiro, Autopista A15 (exit 123), t 94 850 41 02 (€). Old-fashioned 19th-century inn, with country cooking and plenty of atmosphere.

Getting around Northwest of Pamplona

Most Pamplona–Altsasu **trains** stop at Huarte Arakil. Daily **buses** go to Lekunberri and Aldatz from Pamplona (La Muguiroarra, **t** 94 850 40 66)

chapel door. You can see the chains worn by Teodosio de Goñi (*see* above) and the hole through which the dragon appeared. A high-tech alarm system protects the recently stolen and recovered enamelled Byzantine *retablo*, showing the Virgin on a rainbow in a mandorla with the Christ Child; the only comparable work in Europe is the great altarpiece in St Mark's in Venice. Tentatively dated 1028, it was probably originally stolen from Constantinople by a Crusader and sold to Sancho the Great.

In art, heaven's *generalísimo* is often shown with a spear, not slaying so much as *transfixing* dragons to the earth. A recurrent theme in the endless mysticism surrounding St Michael has it that his cult took over ancient religious centres concerned with water sources and underground streams (and, if you like, 'telluric forces' within the earth); the act of fixing the 'dragon' symbolizes the capture and manipulation of these forces. Sure enough, the Sierra de Aralar is so karstic as to be practically hollow: under the sanctuary there's an immense subterranean river that makes moaning dragonish sounds, feeding an icy lake in a domed cavern.

Around Aralar

Of the villages under the mountain **Lekunberri** is the most orientated to tourism, but **Leitza**, just north, is a prettier choice, besides being the home of Basque legend Iñaki Perurena, the *arrejazotzale* or champion heavy-stone weightlifter. **Zudaire**, south of Aralar, is the head town in a broken terrain called **Las Améscoas**, the refuge of the Carlists and delight of speleologists: most of the caves are located above Zudaire around **Baquedano**.

Southwest of Pamplona: The Camino de Santiago

Few places in Europe can boast such a concentration of medieval curiosities as this stretch of the famous road (*see* pp.34–8), where the mystic syncretism of Jews, Knights Templars, pagans and pilgrims was expressed in monuments with secret messages.

Santa María de Eunate

July–Sept 10.30–1.30 and 5–8; Mar–June and Oct 10.30–1.30 and 4–7; Jan–Feb and Nov 10.30–2.30; closed Mon and Dec

From Pamplona to Estella

A short turn off the N111 (about 15km from Pamplona) leads to the old village of **Obanos**, and 1.6km beyond that village to a lonely field and **Santa María de Eunate**, a striking 12th-century church built by the Templars. The Templars often built their chapels as

Getting along the Camino de Santiago

La Estellesa buses (t 94 832 65 09, *www.laestellesa.com*) from Pamplona stop at Puente la Reina and Estella (with a fancy neo-Moorish station), en route to Logroño, five times a day.

Bideak, t 94 822 17 73, *www.bideak-navarraactiva.com*. Organizes guided tours of Estella and the surrounding area, as well as bicycling and 4x4 trips throughout the region.

octagons, but this one was purposely made irregular and is surrounded by a unique 33-arched octagonal cloister – hence its name 'Eunate' ('the hundred doors'). Many knights were buried here, and it's likely that its peculiar structure had deep significance in the Templars' initiatory rites. There are only a few carved capitals – some little monsters, and pomegranates on the portal, which, oddly, faces north. During the church's restoration, scallop shells were discovered along with the tombs – the church also served as a mortuary chapel for pilgrims. The lack of a central keystone supporting the eight ribs inside hints that Arab architects were involved in the building.

The *camino francés* from Roncesvalles (*see* p.84) and the *camino aragonés* converged at the 11th-century bridge in pretty **Puente la Reina**, which hasn't changed much since the day when pilgrims marched down the sombre Rúa Mayor, where many houses preserve their coats of arms. The pilgrims traditionally entered Puente la Reina through the arch of another Templar foundation, **El Crucifijo**, a church with scallops and Celtic interlaced designs on the portal and two naves. The smaller one was added to house a powerful 14th-century German crucifix left by a pilgrim. Towards the bridge, the church of **Santiago** has a Moorish-style lobed portal and, inside, two excellent polychrome 14th-century statues.

From Puente la Reina, the path (although not the road) continues up to atmospheric old **Cirauqui** propped on its hill. The ancient road to the west of Cirauqui, paved with Roman stones, predates even the pilgrims.

Estella (Lizarra): the Town of the Star

 Estella

A stop at Estella, known as Estella la Bella for its beauty, was much looked forward to by the pilgrims. It owes its foundation in 1090 to a convenient miracle: nightly showers of shooting stars, that always fell on the same place on a hill, intrigued some shepherds, who investigated and found a cave hidden by thorns, sheltering a statue of the Virgin. Returning from the siege of Toledo the same year, King Sancho Ramírez founded Estella on the opposite bank of the Río Ega from the old settlement of Lizarra (coincidentally the Basque word for 'star') and populated it with *francos*, or freemen: artisans, merchants and others who owed allegiance to no feudal lord (although, confusingly, most of these *francos* were also Franks from Gascony, who fought in the

Reconquista for pay or piety's sake). Thanks to them, Estella has numerous fine medieval buildings; if many have been cropped, thank the Grand Inquisitor of Castile, Cardinal Cisneros, whose troops literally cut Navarra down to size in 1512 for Ferdinand the Catholic. The most exciting time to visit Estella is the Friday before the first Sunday in August, when it holds the only *encierro* where women are welcome to join in the run, even if the bulls are really heifers with padded horns.

The arcaded **Plaza Fueros** is the town's bustling main square, full of terrace cafés and overlooked by the Gothic church of **San Juan**, with a dour early 20th-century façade and bells which ring ear-splittingly on the hour. To the west is the **Basílica de Nuestra Señora de Puy**, a must on the pious pilgrim route, being built on the point where the stars fell on Navarra. The 14th-century Virgin is still there, but the old basilica was replaced in 1951 with a concrete and glass star-shaped church, and a *mirador* offering lovely views across the old town. South of Plaza Fueros, the highlight for art pilgrims is 12th-century **San Miguel**, the parish church of the *francos*, set on a craggy rock atop its original set of steps (which lead up from C/ Chapitel). March right up them for the magnificent portal, where Christ in Majesty holds pride of place among angels, Evangelists and the Elders of the Apocalypse. On the left, St Michael pins the dragon and weighs souls; on the right, an angel shows the empty tomb to the three Marys. The top, sadly, fell to the Cardinal's tower-bashing squad, but the brackets are good, especially the man-eating wolf. Near San Miguel you'll find a faithful 19th-century copy of Estella's **medieval bridge**, which pilgrims crossed to the Lizarra side to visit the 12th-century **San Sepolcro**, with a fascinating façade added in 1328 but again truncated by Cisneros. The tympanum has an animated Last Supper, Crucifixion, Resurrection and what looks to be the Harrowing of Hell; statues of the 12 Apostles flank the door; one of them appears to be holding a stack of pancakes. To the right of the bridge is the piquant centre of old Lizarra, with churches and palaces bearing proud coats of arms, most now occupied by antiques shops, along Calle de la Rúa ('street of the street'). The finest palace is the Plateresque **Casa Fray Diego**, now used as the Casa de Cultura.

Off to the left was the **Judería**, or ghetto, its 12th-century synagogue converted into **Santa María de Jus del Castillo**, where the apse is decorated with a rich assortment of Romanesque modillions. The church is dwarfed by the adjacent 13th-century, austere **monastery of Santo Domingo**, now a retirement home. Further up, near the new bridge, a 16th-century fountain under a canopy of linden trees in **Plaza de San Martín** is a delightful place.

A curving flight of stairs leads up to the 12th-century **San Pedro de la Rúa**, defended by a skyscraper bell tower. The Moorish-

Casa Fray Diego
open Tues–Fri 6.30pm–8.30pm, Sat 12–2 and 6.30–8.30, Sun 12–2

San Pedro de la Rúa
open for Mass or guided visits only; see tourist office

inspired foiled arch of the portal is crowned by a relief of St James in a boat with stars. Inside, the church has its share of curiosities: a unique column made of three interlaced 'serpents', and the black *Virgen de la O*, a cult figure of the masons, who left their marks all over the church. The Baroque chapel to the left houses St Andrew's shoulderblade; the story goes that the bishop of Patras took it with him for good luck while making the pilgrimage in 1270. Luck failed him in Estella, where he died and was buried in San Pedro's cloister, along with his relic. The holy shoulderblade wasn't going to have any of this and made itself known by a curious light that appeared over the tomb; in 1626, the day when Andrew was proclaimed patron of Estella, a burning vision of his X-shaped cross hovered over the church. Of the cloister, only two galleries survive, reconstructed after the castle above was blown up in 1572 and crashed down on top of it. The twisted column is a copy of a famous one in Santo Domingo de Silos in Burgos.

Over the years, Estella became a favourite residence of the kings, whose 12th-century **Palacio de los Reyes de Navarra**, opposite San Pedro, is one of the best-preserved civic buildings from the period. Prominent at street level, a capital bears the oldest known depiction of Roland (*see* pp.38–9), clad in scaly armour, fighting the equally scaly giant Ferragut; further up, another capital shows a scene of devils and animal musicians, including a donkey playing a harp. The palace now houses the **Museo Gustavo de Maeztú**, devoted to works by Estella's best-known painter (1887–1947).

Museo Gustavo de Maeztú
t 94 854 60 37; open Tues–Sat 11–1 and 5–7, Sun 11–1.30; closed Mon

Around Estella

Estella is an important producer of DO Navarra wine, and the most interesting *bodega* to visit just happens to be the Benedictine **Monasterio de Irache**, 2km south at Ayegui. First recorded in 958, it later received a generous endowment from Sancho the Great, who helped finance one of the very first pilgrims' hospitals here. In 1569, Philip II moved the university of theology here from Sahagún (near León), where it remained, enjoying the same privileges as Salamanca until it closed down with the expropriation of monasteries in 1824. The complex is a handsome mix behind an eclectic façade. The entrance is through an elegant Plateresque door, leading into an austerely beautiful Romanesque church with three apses under a Renaissance dome; the church is stripped of centuries' encrustation of altarpieces. The small wine museum preserves Irache's 1,000-year-old custom of offering free drinks to pilgrims.

Twelve kilometres up the San Sebastián road in Abarzuza, the **Monasterio de Santa María de Iranzu** was founded in the 11th century by Cistercians, who chose to live in a dramatic ravine true to their preference for wild, remote settings. It was recently

Monasterio de Irache
monastery open summer Tues 10–1.30, Wed–Fri 10–1.30 and 5–7, Sat–Sun 9–1.30 and 4–7; winter Tues 10–1.30, Wed–Sun 10–1.30 and 4.30–6; wine museum open Sat–Sun 10–2 and 4–8

Monasterio de Santa María de Iranzu
open summer daily 10–2 and 4–8; winter daily 10–2 and 4–6; adm; to arrange guided visits call t 94 852 00 47;

restored by the government of Navarra and given to the Theatine order. The monks will show you the Romanesque-Gothic cloister with a hexagonal fountain, the medieval kitchen, and church.

South of Estella on the Ebro, **Lodosa** is famous for its red peppers, *pimientos del piquillo*, which are dried in long garlands over the white façades of the houses.

Los Arcos, Sorlada and Torres del Río

After Estella, the pilgrims walked to **Los Arcos**, where, tucked off the N111, there is an arcaded *plaza* and a 16th-century church, **Santa María**, with a pretty cathedral-size Gothic cloister, carved choir stalls and frantic Baroque *retablos*. Seven kilometres north of Los Arcos at **Sorlada**, a grand 18th-century Baroque basilica belongs to **San Gregorio Ostiense**, a once immensely popular saint who lost much of his influence to modern fertilizers. His story is told in the basilica's naïve paintings: back in 1039 locusts plagued the region so badly that a group of farmers walked to Rome and asked the pope for help. The pope had a dream that Cardinal Gregory of Ostia was the man for the job, and off he was sent to Navarra, where he preached and dispersed the locusts, an exertion that killed him after five years. He was buried at Sorlada and forgotten, until a light redirected farmers to his tomb. Remembering his good juju against the locusts (and their ancestral Celtic head cult), they would cart his skull reliquary around their fields, pouring water through the hole which made it into 'holy Gregory water'. Philip II had gallons of it sent down to water the orchards of the Escorial.

Agricultural tour
t 94 864 00 21,
Los Arcos tourist office

Farming is so big here that you can take an **agricultural tour** of the local *bodegas*, ostrich farm, preserve-makers and distilleries.

West of Los Arcos, **Torres del Río** has a striking, tall octagonal church, **Santo Sepolcro**, built in the late 12th or early 13th centuries by the Knights of the Holy Sepulchre, or some say the Templars; like **Santa María de Eunate** (*see* p.106) it may have been a mortuary chapel for pilgrims.

Viana: where Cesare Borgia Bit the Dust

Viana, the pilgrims' last stop in Navarra, fits a lot of monumentality into a small space. Founded by King Sancho VII 'the Strong' in 1219 to defend his frontier with Castile, it became the hereditary principality of the heir to the throne of Navarra in 1423. Although its once-proud castle fell to Cardinal Cisneros' demolition programme, nobles and courtly hangers-on stayed on and built themselves splendid mansions with big coats of arms, the elegant 17th-century **Casa Consistorial**, crowned with an escutcheon the size of an asteroid, and the 13th–14th-century church of **Santa María**, hidden by a magnificent concave Renaissance façade based on a triumphal arch, with a coffered ceiling designed and carved by

The Last Days of Cesare Borgia

How did Pope Alexander VI's son and Machiavelli's hero end up in Viana? With the papacy and central Italy in his pocket by 1502, married to Charlotte, sister of the king of Navarre, and supported by France, Cesare had embarked on a brilliant career as a ruthless Renaissance prince-assassin. When his father pulled the rug out from under him by dying suddenly in 1503, Cesare himself was too ill to get to the Vatican and influence the conclave to elect a Borgia candidate; according to Machiavelli's *The Prince*, it was the only political mistake he ever made. It proved to be fatal. Once Julius II, arch-enemy of the Borgias, was elected in late 1503, Cesare's conquests in Italy were frittered away in anarchy, the French turned against him, and he went from being on top of the world to a man whose life was in danger. He fled to Aragón, cradle of the Borgias, only to be imprisoned by Ferdinand. The still-independent kingdom of Navarra proved to be his refuge, and he died in a skirmish in Viana, fighting Castilian rebels.

Juan de Goyaz (1549). Inside, the Gothic interior is quite airy and lovely, culminating in an intricate gilded Baroque *retablo*. The façade could be considered the tombstone of Cesare Borgia (1475–1507, *see* box), whose memorial, all that is left of his desecrated remains, lies buried under the marker in front of the church.

Where to Stay and Eat on the Camino de Santiago

(i) **Puente la Reina >**
C/ Mayor 105,
t 94 834 08 45;
closed Jan–Mar

(i) **Los Arcos >>**
in the Ayuntamiento,
Plaza de los Fueros 1,
t 94 864 00 21

(i) **Estella >**
C/ San Nicolás 1,
t 94 855 63 01,
oit.estella@navarra.es

(i) **Viana >>**
Bajos Ayuntamiento,
t 94 844 63 02

Puente la Reina ✉ 31100

**Mesón del Peregrino, on the Pamplona road, t 94 834 00 75, www.hotelelperegrino.com (€€€). This stone and timber place isn't as old as it looks, but it has air-conditioned rooms and a pool. *Closed Sun eve and Mon.*

Hotel Rural Bidean, C/ Mayor 20, t 94 834 11 56 (€€). A pretty stone building that has been recently refurbished to create a cosy, country atmosphere.

Estella ✉ 31200

***Irache, Ayegui (3km away on the Logroño road), t 94 855 11 50, www.hotelirache.com (€€€). The largest and most comfortable hotel, set in a 1970s urbanización, with air-con and pool.

*Hôtel Yerri, Avenida Yerri 35, t 94 854 60 34 (€€–€). Another modern and well-equipped if rather bland establishment, next to the bullring.

*Pensión San Andrés, Plaza Santiago 58, t 94 855 41 85 (€). Excellent value, clean and central, with family-size rooms overlooking the square.

*Hs Cristina, C/ Baja Navarra 1, t 94 855 07 72 (€). A simple but clean place run by a kindly woman. May be noisy on a Saturday night.

Fonda Izarra, C/ Caldería, t 94 855 06 78 (€). The cheapest doubles in town.

La Navarra, C/ Gustavo de Maeztú 16, t 94 855 00 40 (€€). A good bet, perhaps more for its medieval atmosphere than food, which is good if a bit pricy. *Closed Sun eve and Mon.*

Restaurante Richard, Avda Yerri, 10, t 94 855 13 16 (€€). Traditional cooking using fresh local produce. *Closed Mon and first week Sept.*

Los Arcos ✉ 31210

**Hotel Monaco, Pza del Coso 1, t 94 864 00 00, www.monacohotel.net (€). Recently refurbished modest hotel in the centre, with crisp modern rooms.

**Hs Ezequiel, Avda General Uda s/n, t 94 864 02 96 (€). A friendly, family-run hotel, with large restaurant/bar.

Viana ✉ 31230

Hôtel Casa Armendariz, C/ Navarro Villoslada 19, t 94 864 50 78 (€). A cosy little spot in the centre of town; the rooms are small, but the management is charming. Traditional and modern cuisine in their *sidreria* (€€–€).

Borgia, C/ Serapio Urra 1, t 94 864 57 81 (€€–€). Avant-garde décor is the setting for Aurora Cariñanos' temple of personal, imaginative cuisine, where you can dine on delectable dishes such as *pochas con caracoles al tomillo* (fresh haricot beans with snails and thyme). The cellar is excellent. *Closed Sun eve and Aug.*

La Rioja

La Rioja may be named after the river Oja, one of the seven tributaries of the Ebro, but to most people it means wine, wine and more wine. The banks of the Ebro are frilly with vineyards and pinstriped with rows of garden vegetables on the flat, fertile plains of Rioja Baja around Calahorra. In the Sierra de la Demanda in the southwest, mountains are high enough to ski down; in the gullies of Rioja Baja, dinosaurs once made the earth tremble. Wedged up against the Ebro between Navarra and Castile, who once so hotly contested its fields and vineyards, the *comunidad* of La Rioja is now the smallest autonomous region in Spain (5,000 sq km) – not that there is any distinctive Riojan language or race, although in the 11th century a king, one of the four sons of Sancho the Great of Navarra, sat in Nájera. This was a brief period of independence, when Riojans began the history of Castilian Spanish as a written and poetic language and contributed to the invention of Santiago.

Logroño

More than half of all the 250,000 Riojans live in Logroño, their shiny, up-to-date capital famous not only for wine but also coffee caramels. It began under the Visigoths as Gronio, 'The Ford', but really bloomed only with the advent of the pilgrimage, when a stone bridge was built over the Ebro by San Juan de Ortega, one of La Rioja's two building saints. A prosperous modern agricultural centre, it nonetheless contains a pleasant little historic centre huddled around the graceful cathedral.

Logroño is a big long sausage of a town, but the interesting bits are concentrated in a small area near the Ebro. Barely an arch survives of San Juan's first bridge, which was replaced in the 1800s by the **Puente de Hierro**, or iron bridge. Just off this the pilgrims would pass in front of the 16th-century fountain and lofty Gothic **Santiago**, the oldest church in town. This was rebuilt in 1500, with a single nave a startling 53ft wide and still standing, in spite of the fact that its architect had no confidence in his handiwork and left town as soon as it was completed. It has a Renaissance *retablo*, and at the front a mighty 18th-century statue of Santiago Matamoros ('St James Moor-killer') who rides a steed with *cojones* as big as beach balls. The sculptor of the equestrian statue of General Espartero (in Logroño's central park, the **Espolón**) took them into consideration and equipped the mortal general's mortal horse a few degrees less generously.

The skyline of Logroño is stabbed by church towers, including two slender 18th-century Churrigueresque towers by Martín de Beratúa that frame the magnificent Baroque façade of the

**Santa María de
la Redonda**
*open Mon–Sat 8–1
and 6.30–8.45, Sun 9–2
and 6.30–8.45*

cathedral, **Santa María de la Redonda** in Plaza del Mercado, a front
that belies the Gothic-inspired gloom inside; the rotundity of its
name (the first Romanesque church was octagonal) is recalled in
an exuberant round rococo altar. Near here, in a high-security
strongbox, is the *Tabla de Calvario*, supposedly painted by
Michelangelo for his friend and muse Vittoria Colonna. Logroño's
most distinctive landmark is its nubby pyramidal 'Needle', the 149ft
13th-century spire atop the lantern of **Santa María de Palacio**, in
C/ Marqués de San Nicolás, a church said to have been founded by
no one less than Emperor Constantine. If it's open, pop in to see the
Renaissance choir stalls, the 13th-century *Nuestra Señora de la
Antigua*, and what remains of the Gothic cloister. Another tower,
brick 11th-century *mudéjar* this time, looks over **San Bartolomé**
with a ruggedly carved, time-blackened 14th-century Gothic
façade; the smooth white interior has lovely shallow choir vaults.

**Museo Provincial
de La Rioja**
*closed until at least
2009; call* **t** *94 129 12 59,
museo@larioja.org*

The 17th-century **Palacio del General Espartero** in Plaza San
Agustín now holds the **Museo Provincial de La Rioja**, full of art
from disappeared churches (14th-century painting from San Millán
and *San Francisco with Brother Lion* by El Greco), Flemish coffers
and orphaned academic 19th-century paintings from the Prado's
storerooms. There are a number of wine cellars in the area,

**Bodegas Marqués
de Murrieta**
*www.marquesde
murrieta.com, Ctra de
Zaragoza, Km.5,*
t *94 127 13 70*

including **Bodegas Marqués de Murrieta**, at Ygay, founded in 1852
and famous for its 35–40-year-old Gran Reservas, and the striking
Bodegas Juan Alcorta, designed by Ignacio Quemada.

Getting around Logroño

Several **trains** a day link Haro, Logroño and Calahorra on the Bilbao–Zaragoza route. The RENFE station (with a left luggage office) is at Plaza de Europa: **t** 902 24 02 02, or *www.renfe.es*.

Logroño's **bus** links are faster and more frequent than train services. Several buses a day run to Burgos (via the towns on the pilgrims' route), Zaragoza, Vitoria, Pamplona and Rioja's villages. In Logroño the bus station is at Avda de España 1, **t** 94 123 59 83.

Hire car: Atesa, Avda Lope de Vega, 31, **t** 94 124 29 29, *www.atesa.es*; Ebrorent, Siete Infantes de Lara, 16 bajo, **t** 94 128 60 73.

Taxis: Radio Taxi: **t** 94 122 21 22; Tele Taxi: **t** 94 150 50 50 .

Markets in Logroño

Logroño: country produce, Mercado del Campo, Marqués de la Enseñada 52, Tues and Fri 8–2.

Where to Stay in Logroño

ⓘ Logroño >
*Paseo del Espolón,
t 94 129 12 60,
www.logroño.org (for
city information) or
www.lariojaturismo.
com (covers all tourist
offices in La Rioja)*

Logroño ✉ 26000

Logroño has a surprising number of luxury modern hotels, but few of them possess much charm.

****Carlton Rioja**, Gran Vía del Rey Juan Carlos I 5, **t** 94 124 21 00, *www.pretur.es* (€€€€–€€€). Glassy modern block located on the edge of the Casco Antiguo.

***Hotel Portales**, C /Portales 85, **t** 94 150 27 94, *www.hotelportales.es* (€€€€– €€€). Bright maroon rooms add warmth to this new, sleek hotel. Centrally located, close to the tapas bars. Check offers even in summer.

*****Gran Hotel AC La Rioja**, C/ Madre de Dios 21, **t** 94 127 23 50, *www.ac-hotels.com* (€€€). The only 5-star hotel in Logroño, this is modern and geared towards business travellers – but it offers guests every necessary convenience.

***Hotel Marqués de Vallejo**, Marqués de Vallejo 8, **t** 94 124 83 33, *www.hotelmarquesdevallejo.com* (€€€). A handsome place near the cathedral, with a sleek contemporary interior hiding behind a historic façade.

***Hotel Murrieta**, Marqués de Murrieta 1, **t** 94 122 41 50, *hotels@pretur.es* (€€€–€€). A bland, modern hotel, but central and offering guests free Internet access.

***Ciudad de Logroño**, C/ Menéndez Pelayo 7, **t** 94 125 02 44, *www.pretur.es* (€€). Central, modern and comfortable, with views over a park.

Residencia Daniel, C/ Juan 21, **t** 94 125 29 48 (€€). Has spotless rooms amid the bustle of the *casco viejo*.

****Hs la Numantina**, C/ Sagasta 4, **t** 94 125 14 11 (€). Modest, but attractively priced *hostal* in the centre. *Closed Christmas and Jan.*

Eating Out in Logroño

For tapas, try C/ Laurel and C/ San Juan.

El Cachetero, C/ Laurel 3, **t** 94 122 84 63, *www.cachetero.com* (€€€–€€). A popular choice for four generations, Logroño's best restaurant serves mouthwatering *menestras* and local delicacies such as pigs' trotters stuffed with mushrooms, capers and paté; book ahead. *Closed Sun and Wed eve and last week of Aug.*

El Rincón del Vino, Marqués de San Nicolás 136, **t** 94 120 53 92 (€€). As well as a vast selection of the promised *vino*, they have a fine *asador* serving delicacies like sirloin steak with wild mushroom stuffing. *Closed Sun eve, Mon and Aug.*

Los Gabrieles, C/ Bretón de los Herreros 8, **t** 94 122 00 43 (€€). Grand traditional restaurant off the main square with dishes like *cazuela de pimientos* (pepper stew) and *pisto riojana* (Rioja-style ratatouille)

Las Cubanas, C/ San Agustín 17, **t** 94 122 00 50 (€). Come here with the locals for a delicious *menestra*; the place owes its popularity to excellent regional cuisine, its friendly atmosphere and good value. *Closed eves.*

Calahorra and La Rioja Baja

Down the Ebro, east of Logroño, La Rioja Baja is flat, fertile, well watered and endowed with a sunny Mediterranean climate. Olive oil and wine are the two mainstays of the economy, with the kind of peppers the Spanish devour by the kilo coming in a close third.

Calahorra

Despite its down-at-heel appearance, Calahorra has an interesting history. In fact, it has been inhabited for so long (since Palaeolithic times) that St Jerome speculated that it was founded by Tubal, grandson of Noah. It first makes history as Kalauria, an important Celtiberian fortress town under Carthaginian sway that, thanks to the Ebro, traded with the Greek colonies on the Mediterranean coast. In 187 BC the town was grabbed by Rome and renamed Calagurris; then, in a dispute between Pompey and Sertorius in AD 72, it held out against Pompey until all its defenders were dead through starvation. The Romans rebuilt it, and Calahorra returned the favour by giving Rome Marcus Fabius Quintilian (42–118), the first salaried professor of rhetoric in Rome and author of *Institutio Oratoria*, the empire's textbook on the fine art of talking. In the Middle Ages Calahorra was a prize craved by both Aragón and Castile; in a famous incident in the romance of *Las Mocedades del Cid* (and in the film *El Cid*, 1961, starring Charlton Heston), the Cid fought one-to-one for the city against Aragón's champion, vowing to lose not only the town but his head if he were defeated, but gaining both Calahorra and the hand of his beloved Ximena if he won. Which of course he did.

Calahorra has been an episcopal see since the 5th century, but the **cathedral** has been fussed with frequently. Behind a fruity, floral neoclassical façade pasted on in 1700, the nave with graceful star vaulting is a product of 1485. The furnishings are equally eclectic: the Gothic *Cristo de la Pelota*, 'Christ of the ball', is part of a Deposition from the Cross, the alabaster statues of the saints are 17th century, and there are paintings attributed to Titian and Zurbarán. The Plateresque cloister houses the **Museo Diocesano** with a 12th-century bible and 15th-century Custodia called *El Ciprés*, made of gold and silver, donated by Henri IV.

Museo Diocesano *open Sun and hols only, call t 94 113 00 98*

Just over the Río Cidacos, note the 13-spout fountain. Near the cathedral, the church of Santiago and its *retablo* of St James is considered the finest neoclassical work in La Rioja. Nearby, the **Museo Municipal**'s archaeological collection stars the serene Roman bust of the Dama Calagurritana, symbol of the city. Just north of this, the church of **San Andrés** has a Gothic portal illustrating the triumph over paganism, and the **Arco del Planillo** is the only gateway surviving from the Roman walls of Calagurris.

Museo Municipal *open Tues–Sat 12–2 and 6–9, Sun 10–2*

East of Calahorra: the Alhama Valley

**Colegiata de
San Miguel**
*closed for restoration
until at least 2009; call
t 94 118 01 33 for
an update*

Down the Ebro holding down the east end of La Rioja, **Alfaro** was known as Ilurcis in the 5th century BC but kept its Arab name even after the Reconquista. Its chief monument is the enormous twin-towered **Colegiata de San Miguel**, built in the 16th and 17th centuries and reminiscent of colonial churches in South America. The Colegiata's chief claim to fame is, it has more stork nests on its generous roof than any other in Spain, a colony of some 250 birds.

Further south, **Cervera del Río Alhama** long had an Arab majority and still has a Moorish feel to it: villagers speak *cerverano* (the town website, *www.riojainternet.com/cervera*, has a great little dictionary), with hundreds of words that are a last relic of the lost language of the Mozarabs, or Christians living in Moorish Spain. Between **Aguilar del Río Alhama** and **Inestrillas**, the Celtiberians, fleeing after the conquest by Mantis Acidinus (181 BC), holed up from the Romans for a hundred years at **Contrebia Leucada**, built on terraces, defended on one side by the river and the others by a vast ditch. It is a rare surviving example of Celtiberian town-planning and water systems, and is currently being excavated.

La Rioja's Dinosaurs

Museo de Calzado
*closed for restoration
and a planned move to
Paseo de Constitución
60; call the tourist
office on t 94 138 39 88*

South of Calahorra, **Arnedo** is a shoe-making town with a **Museo de Calzado** (shoe museum) to prove it. Every 27 September the town's patron saints Cosme and Damián are honoured in the usual Spanish effigy procession, only here the parade is combined with a scrum: villagers from Navarra come in to attack the procession and make three bold attempts to make off with the saints' statues, claiming that the Riojans stole them centuries ago.

South of Arnedo, **Arnedillo** has been La Rioja's most important spa since 1847. This is all recent history compared to the main attraction in these parts. 'When there is no trace of Spielberg left,' reads the tourist brochure, 'the dinosaur tracks will still be here.' Take that, Hollywood! La Rioja Baja has 5,000 footprints – Europe's largest concentration of dinosaur tracks, or ichnites as they're called – dating back 120 million years to when La Rioja was lush, warm and wet and the denizens of the Cretaceous (post-Jurassic) period stomped through the marshes. Somehow conditions for preserving their prints in these broken hills were better than most places. In the Middle Ages, the ichnites were said to be the hoof marks of Santiago's horse or prints left by giant chickens that lived in the time of the Moors. The best places to find them are in **Préjano** just east of Arnedillo and the Los Cayos gully at **Cornago**. **Enciso** has the largest number, especially at the Valdecevillo bed, and also houses the **Museo Paleontogólico**, a significant collection of prehistoric relics. Other sites are just north in **Munilla** in a gully called Peñaportillo; **Igea** has more tracks and petrified plants.

**Museo
Paleontogólico**
*www.dinosaurios-
lariga.org; open winter
Mon–Sat 11–2 and 3–6,
Sun 11–2; summer daily
11–2 and 5–8; adm*

ⓘ **Arnedo** >>
Palacio de la
Baronesa, C/ Carrera 9,
t 94 138 39 88,
www.arnedo.com

ⓘ **Calahorra** >
C/ Ángel Olivan 8,
t 94 114 63 98,
www.ayto-calahorra.es

Markets in La Rioja Baja

Calahorra: Pza del Raso, Thurs.
Alfaro: Fri.
Cervera de Río Alhama: Fri.
Arnedo: Mon and Tues.

Where to Stay and Eat in La Rioja Baja

Calahorra ✉ 26500

****Parador de Calahorra**, t 94 113 03 58, calahorra@parador.es (€€€). A modern, red-brick *parador* near the scanty Roman ruins of Calagurris, with good views, newly renovated rooms and air-conditioning. It has a good restaurant serving regional cuisine.
****Chef Nino**, C/Padre Lúcas 2, t 94 113 20 29 (€€). A modest hotel, which boasts the best restaurant (€€) here.
Casa Mateo, Pza del Raso 15, t 94 113 00 09 (€€). Delicious fresh produce, including the local vegetables for which the region is famed.
La Taberna de la Cuarta Esquina, Ctra Esquinas 16, t 94 113 43 55 (€€). Calahorra's best-known restaurant is justly renowned for its well-prepared fish, game and vegetable dishes and reasonably priced wines. *Closed Tues eve, Wed and July.*

Arnedo ✉ 26580

*****Victoria**, Pso de la Constitución 97, t 94 138 01 00, www.hvictoria.com (€€€). Recent and comfortable, offering good value with a pool.
*****Molino de Cidacos**, Ctra de Arnedo Km.14, Arnedillo (14km from Arnedo), t 94 139 40 63, www.pegarrido.com (€€€). A lovingly restored 17th-century flour mill; one of the prettiest hotels.
****Virrey**, Pso de la Constitución 27, t 94 138 01 50, www.hvirrey.com (€€€). Ultra-modern façade; one of the few hotels in the *comunidad* with facilities for the disabled. Also has a restaurant.
****Hospedería Las Pedrolas**, Plaza Félix Merino 16, Arnedillo, t 94 139 44 01 (€€). An enchanting and stylish little inn in a whitewashed 18th-century building next to the church.

Enciso ✉ 26580

Posada de Santa Rita, Ctra de Soria 7, t 94 139 60 71, www.posadadesanta rita.com (€). This little red 19th-century house is cosy, with a small library devoted to dinosaurs.
La Fábrica de Harinas, Ctra de Soria 10, t 94 139 60 51 (€). Offers delicious meals based on game dishes, served in an atmospheric old flour mill. *Open daily in summer, otherwise weekends and holidays only.*

South of Logroño: Into the Sierra

Dry history and misty legend are often one and the same in three-digit years in northwest Spain. Although the western bit of La Rioja was reconquered by Alfonso I of Asturias back in the 8th century, the Christians' hold on the land was tenuous and often lost for long periods to the Moors, whose caliph made the Christians pay a tribute of a hundred maidens into their harem in return for the right to worship. This humiliating loss of young womanhood was the source of the legendary Battle of Clavijo, where Santiago Matamoros made his famous début on his white horse to lead Ramiro and the Christians to victory. In gratitude, Ramiro decided to donate to Santiago a measure of wine and wheat for every *yugada* of land he reconquered, in a document known as the *Voto de Santiago* dated May 844 – a 13th-century forgery by the monks of guess where. The hamlet of **Clavijo** is on a dead-end road south of Logroño under a rocky outcrop and a ruined castle, with crenellations that look like a witch's teeth. The end of the tribute is celebrated on the third Sunday in May in the village of **Sorzano**, just west of the N111, when a hundred girls dressed in white make a pilgrimage to the Hermitage del Roble. The N111 ascends through the forested **Valley of Iregua**, which narrows between the sheer cliffs and buttes of the Sierra de Cameros, dotted with old, now partly abandoned villages of shepherds, who still follow the old transhumance paths to Extremadura in the winter. There are especially lovely views of the square-cut natural gorge, the Peñas de Isallana, and the Vega del Iregua below it from the heights of **Viguera**.

The Pilgrim Route West of Logroño

Beyond Logroño, the segment of the Camino de Santiago that crosses La Rioja is short but choice and full of interest.

Navarrete

Eleven kilometres west of Logroño, Navarrete is known for its ceramics and rosé wine. In the Middle Ages it made pilgrims comfortable in its hospital of San Juan de Arce. Of this, only the gate survives, doing duty as the entrance to the cemetery. The older houses in Navarrete look narrow and poky but are actually quite spacious (owing to a tax on façade sizes). The 16th-century church of the **Asunción**, sometimes attributed to Philip II's architect Juan de Herrera, contains an elaborate Churrigueresque *retablo* and a triptych (in the sacristy) by Rembrandt's student Adriaen Ysenbrandt.

Nájera: the Residence of Kings

Arabic Náxara, or 'between two hills', Nájera is a bustling furniture-making town with an illustrious pedigree. It straddles both banks of the trout-filled Najerilla, where the Moorish giant Ferragut was defending the bridge like the troll in *Three Billy Goats Gruff* when Charlemagne's knights tried to cross it. Ferragut picked them up by the armour and gathered them under his arm – at least until Roland arrived on the scene and gave him what for.

After the Moors flattened Pamplona in 918, the kings of Navarra chose to live in Nájera, mainly to keep an eye on the ambitious upstart kingdom of Castile. The first *Rex Hispaniorum*, Sancho III the Great (1004–35) held his court in both Nájera and Pamplona; in 1020 he diverted the Camino de Santiago to pass through Nájera's centre, assuring it of a good income. When he divided his kingdom between his sons, one took Pamplona and another, García III, made Nájera his capital and reconquered Rioja Baja. His grandsons were squeezed by these two medieval powerhouses, and in 1076 Nájera was snatched by Alfonso VI of Castile and the Cid. The Cid's daughter, Doña Elvira, made a happy second marriage with the son of the last king of Nájera and their son, García V, became king of Navarra in 1134.

In 1052 García III was hunting on the banks of the Najerilla when he saw a dove fly past over the thick woods on a hill. He sent his falcon after it and followed the birds through the trees into a cave, from which a bright light emanated; inside he found the dove and falcon cooing side by side and a statue of the Virgin and Child, a jar of fresh lilies, a lamp and a bell. To celebrate the miracle, García founded an order of knights, the Caballeros de la Terraza ('Knights of the Jar' – a mystic receptacle like the Holy Grail) and the church,

Santa María la Real
open Tues–Sat 10–2 and 5–8; adm

which was rebuilt in the 15th century as the monastery of **Santa María la Real** and restored after 1895 by the Franciscans. The entrance is through a beautiful Flamboyant Gothic door, the **Portal of Charles V**, crowned with the emperor's coat of arms. Through here waits the serene and lovely Gothic-Plateresque **Claustro de los Caballeros**, with 24 arches half-veiled by intricate sculpted screens carved to imitate lace: no two are alike. Cloister chapels hold the elegant effigy tomb of a 13th-century Queen of Portugal. From here a Plateresque walnut door leads into the solemn 15th-century **church**. The original Flemish *retablo mayor* was sold for a piece of bread when the monastery was dissolved in 1835, but the 17th-century wowser in its place still holds the miraculous 11th-century statue of Santa María la Real. Originally she wore a large ruby. This was pinched by Pedro the Cruel in 1367 to pay the Black Prince and the English for whipping the French-supported army of his brother Enrique de Trastámara in a battle near Nájera. The ruby now glows on the State Crown of England, but it cost the Black Prince his life – from a Spanish fever.

Near the high altar are the **tombs** of the Dukes of Nájera, King Ferdinand of Aragón's right-hand men, who gave Ignatius of Loyola his first job as a soldier. At the entrance of the holy cave are 16th-century tombs of the 10th–12th-century dynasties of Pamplona and Nájera, among them the original sarcophagus of Sancho III's 21-year-old wife Blanca. This is the finest Romanesque Spanish tomb to come down to us. Behind the kings is the **holy cave**; up the spiral stair is the remarkable Isabelline Gothic choir (1493–95), believed to have been carved by Jewish *conversos* (note the Hebrew letters on chair 23), a masterpiece of grace, detail and fantasy. The armour-clad King García figures on the main chair and Gothic paintings of kings and queens around the top create a charming *trompe l'œil* effect. History buffs may want to check out the town's **archaeological museum** on Plaza de Nájero in the centre.

Archaeological museum
open Mon–Sat 11–2 and 5–8, Sun 11–2; adm

Basilica Santa María de Arcos
open Tues–Sat 10.30–1.30 and 4.30–7.30, Sun 10.30–1.30

Just outside Nájera, hill-top **Tricio** was an important Roman town known as Tritium Megalon. Its small mortuary temple was converted wholesale in 1181 into the **Basilica Santa María de Arcos** to house a miraculous dark-skinned statue of the Virgin; mellow Roman columns support Visigothic arches covered with Baroque stuccoes that at first glance seem to be made of white icing. Traces of Romanesque paintings (the only ones found so far in La Rioja) remain·on the walls.

San Millán de la Cogolla: Yuso and Suso

From Nájera it's 17km south into the Sierra de la Demanda and San Millán de la Cogolla, a village that grew up around two ancient monasteries, Yuso ('The Lower' in old Castilian) and Suso ('The Upper'); *Cogolla* was a nickname for the monks' habit. San Millán (473–574) spent much of his 101 years living in the caves on the hill, his sanctity attracting numerous male and female anchorites.

Suso monastery
open summer
Tues–Sun 10–1.30 and
4–6.30; winter
Tues–Sun 9.30–1.30 and
3.30–6.30; adm

In the 7th century the anchorites built the first monastery at **Suso**, signposted up a 2km narrow road, and soon became known for their literary efforts when the 7th-century monk San Baudelio wrote the *Life of San Millán*. Carved out of a wooded hill, the shadowy little church has a cloister at the entrance, containing the tombs of three queens of Navarra and those of the Seven Infantes de Lara and their tutor Nuño Salido, who met a tragic end after a game played at their uncle's wedding went wrong and a member of the bride's family was accidentally killed. Poet Gonzalo de Berceo loved to sit and write in the Visigothic portico. The church was heavily damaged by al-Mansur in the Reconquista and rebuilt in the 10th and 11th centuries, with Romanesque arches on one end and Mozarabic and Visigothic down the second aisle. Because of the lack of security, Suso's treasures – notably its golden Flemish diptych – have been removed.

Even the 11th-century tomb with its recumbent alabaster effigy of San Millán is empty, not due to any 20th-century security precautions, but rather because in 1053 King García III decided that San Millán's relics belonged in Nájera. The bones were loaded onto a cart, but the oxen, once they reached the bottom of the hill, refused to budge another inch. Realizing that 'the saint didn't want to leave his lands', García built a new, more splendid, monastery on

Yuso monastery
www.monasteriode
yuso.org; open summer
daily 10.30–1.30 and
4–6.30; winter
Tues–Sun 10–1
and 4–6; adm

the spot where the oxen stopped. This is **Yuso**, known as the 'Escorial of La Rioja' after it was rebuilt on a grand scale in the 16th century, its main entrance crowned by an equestrian relief of San Millán in the guise of Santiago Matamoros.

In the Middle Ages Yuso continued Suso's reputation as a literary centre: the monastery is proudest of its one anonymous monk who, in the 10th century, was writing a commentary in the margins of his Latin text or, to be precise, on folio 72 of the *Emilian 60 Codex*, when for 43 words he lapsed into the vernacular – the first known use of Castilian. It's engraved on stone along with other exhibits (mostly portraits of kings) in the **Salón de Reyes**.

The Cradle of Spanish

When the Arabs invaded Iberia, the Christians who fled into the mountainous regions of the north were isolated for several centuries. Latin-speakers and Visigoths found themselves among pagan speakers of Iberia's pre-Roman languages, cut off from the Moors and from each other. Several languages developed in addition to the Stone Age tongue of the Basques: Catalan, Gallego, Babel and Aragonese. From Babel, the first language of the Reconquista, evolved the tongue that would dominate: Castilian, or *castellano*, or what most people know simply as Spanish.

The predominance of Castilian owes as much to Castile's conquering role in history as to the fact that the language is one of the most efficient means of communication ever devised. The Visigoths endowed it with aspirates and a stricter framework than any other Romance language, 'a dry, harsh, stone-cracking tongue', according to V.S. Pritchett, 'a sort of desert Latin chipped off at the edges by its lipped consonants and dry-throated gutturals...and each word is as distinct and hard as a pebble.' It was the first modern language to have a grammar written for it. When a copy was presented to Queen Isabel in 1492, she understandably asked what it was for. 'Your Majesty,' replied a perceptive bishop, 'language is the perfect instrument of empire.'

In the centuries to come, this concise, flexible and expressive language would prove just that: an instrument that would contribute more to Spanish unity than any laws or institutions, while spreading itself effortlessly over much of the New World. In 1870, the aforementioned Emilian gloss long held in Yuso was carted off to the Royal Academy of History in Madrid, and La Rioja still wants it back. But Yuso has another feather in its cap: Gonzalo de Berceo, the shepherd-priest born in the nearby village of Berceo in 1198 and educated as a choirboy at San Millán, who took Castilian out of the margins and made it into poetry. Gonzalo's verses on the lives of local saints have a simple, sweet quality and, as befits a good Riojan, were inspired by a draught of wine.

Interestingly, Yuso also has the first known example of written Basque; both languages were current in medieval La Rioja.

The Renaissance church has weighty ogival vaulting and a 16th-century *retablo* on the life of San Millán; you can learn more about him in the paintings along the upper cloister, built in 1572. The library has hundreds of old codices and manuscripts, if not the precious Emilian gloss, while the small **museum** contains Yuso's prizes: the ornate wooden reliquary chests of San Millán and San Felices de Bilibio, commissioned in 1063, originally covered with ivory plates, gold and precious jewels. They were stripped of their gold and jewels by Napoleon's plundering troops, who fortunately had no eye for medieval ivories.

There are two other important religious houses in the vicinity. Just north of San Millán and Berceo, **Santa María de Cañas** was founded in 1169 and has a fine tall Gothic church with two floors of windows filling the nave with light. Off the cloister, the chapter-house has the superb 14th-century tomb of the abbess-daughter of the founder, Doña Urraca López de Haro. The nuns have long been famous for engraved ceramic work.

South of San Millán, 15km from Anguiano in the verdant foothills of the Sierra de la Demanda, the 12th-century Benedictine **Monasterio de Valvanera** was built to shelter its much-venerated Virgin, the patroness of La Rioja, discovered in a hollow tree by a thief named Nuño who became a saint. On her knee baby Jesus in regal robes is turned to the left, to avert his gaze, they say, ever

Monasterio de Valvanera
open daily 9–7; double rooms available (€€–€) as well as a good menú del día (€13)

since a couple fornicated in the church, a sin that led the monks to erect a circle of white crosses, which no woman was allowed to cross, around the church. Other works of art were pillaged by the French or lost when the monks abandoned the monastery in 1839. They returned in 1885 and have been distilling their herbal Valvanera liqueur ever since, plucking the herbs according to the phases of the moon.

Santo Domingo de la Calzada and its Chickens

⭐ **Santo Domingo de la Calzada**

As they made their way across La Rioja, pilgrims especially looked forward to Santo Domingo de la Calzada, a delightful walled village, now famous for its *muebles* (furniture) but that owes its name and existence to the first road saint. Born a shepherd, Domingo (1019–1109) applied for a monkish career at Valvanera and San Millán. Rejected, he devoted his life to building bridges and making the pilgrims' way easier, clearing paths with a magic sickle just like a druid, making him the patron saint of engineers and public works, hence *de la Calzada* ('of the causeway'). His village grew up by a complex of his works: a long stone bridge over the Río Oja, a hospital (now a *refugio*), a guesthouse (now a *parador*) and a church. The local people call him their *abuelito*, or little grandfather. His church, now the **Catedral de Santo Domingo**, was founded on land donated in 1098 by King Alfonso VI. Recon-

Catedral de Santo Domingo
open Mon–Sat 9.30–1.30 and 4–6.30; adm, includes adm to cloister and museum

struction began in 1158 and took centuries to finish: the first tower was destroyed by lightning in 1450; the second one, completed in 1750, sagged menacingly, and was torn down in 1760; the third, 243ft high, freestanding and neoclassical to match the façade, was built by Basque tower-master Martín de Beratúa in 1762 on boggy ground, shored up with sand, limestone and a ton of cow horns.

The Gothic interior is simple but lavishly decorated, but what everyone remembers best are the rooster and hen, cackling in their own late-Gothic henhouse. Their presence recalls the miracle that took place in Santo Domingo's *hostal*: a handsome 18-year-old German pilgrim named Hugonell, travelling with his parents, refused the advances of the maid, who avenged herself by planting a silver goblet in his pack and accusing him of theft. Hugonell was summarily hanged by the judge while his parents sadly continued to Compostela. On the way back, they passed the gallows and were amazed to find their son still alive, telling them it was a miracle of Santo Domingo. They hurried to the judge and told him; the judge, about to dig into a pair of roast fowl, laughed and said their son was as alive as the birds on his table, upon which both came to life and flew away. Since then, a white hen and cock have been kept in the church, and are replaced every month; pilgrims would take one of their feathers and stick it in their hats for good luck. Under the window you can even see a piece of the gallows.

Opposite the henhouse is the magnificent tomb of Santo Domingo, designed by Felipe de Vigarni (1517–29); the saint's recumbent statue suggests he could be a starter in heaven's basketball league. On the high altar, the huge Plateresque *retablo* (1540) is the last and best work of Damián Forment, one of Spain's finest Renaissance painters. The carved choir is another excellent, detailed Plateresque work (1530s), decorated with painted scenes on the life of St Domingo, while the chapels are equally beautiful and ornate, especially the screen of the Capilla de la Magdalena. The Gothic-*mudéjar* cloister is now used as a **museum** (same hours as cathedral).

Outside the cathedral, take a look at its ornate Romanesque **apse**, at the nearby walls, erected by Pedro the Cruel, and at the arcaded *plaza*, with a stately 16th-century **Casa Consistorial**. At the west end of town, the Renaissance **Convento de San Francisco** was built by Philip II's favourite architect, Juan de Herrera, to house the elaborate tomb of the king's confessor, Fray Bernardo de Fresneda.

South of Santo Domingo, the most dramatic of La Rioja's seven valleys, the Oja, slices through the lofty Sierra de la Demanda up to the handsome stone village of **Ezcaray**. Ezcaray made its fortune on merino wool but now serves as a centre for mountain excursions, with the ski resort of **Valdezcaray** on Mount San Lorenzo (7,451ft), and picnic tables in the beech and pine forests. Don't miss a trip up to the **Ermita de la Virgen de Allende**, site of recent archaeological digs and where some delightful paintings by a well-meaning artist show St Michael dressed up like an 18th-century *generalísimo*, his avenging sword replaced by a harquebus. The Virgin is celebrated on the 24 and 25 September, with traditional dances and parades and a pilgrimage to the hermitage.

Valdezcaray
ski info
www.valdezcaray.es

07 Navarra and La Rioja | La Rioja: The Pilgrim Route West of Logroño

Where to Stay and Eat West of Logroño

(i) **Nájera** ›
C/ Constantino Garrán 8, t 94 136 00 41, www.aytonajera.es

(i) **Santo Domingo** ››
C/ Mayor 70, t 94 134 00 33, www.santodomingodelacalzada.org

(i) **San Millán**
Monasterio de Yuso, t 94 137 32 59

Nájera ✉ 26300
****Hostería Monasterio de San Millán**, t 94 137 32 77, *hostería@sanmillan.com* (€€€).In the monastery itself, with a good restaurant.
****San Fernando**, Pso San Julián 1, t 94 136 37 00 (€€). A modern hotel on the Najerilla river with recently renovated rooms. *Closed Dec.*
****Hs Hispano**, La Cepa 2, t 94 136 36 15, *hispano@najera.net* (€). A good choice, plus restaurant.
La Parra (*casa rural*), La Canal 4, Campróvin (8km from Nájera), t 94 136 16 11 (€). Simple B&B in a pleasant family house.

El Mono, C/ Mayor 43, t 94 136 30 28 (€€). Nájera's favourite for local dishes like roast lamb, or leek and prawn tart. Buzzy bar at the entrance.
Los Parrales, C/ Mayor 52, t 94 136 37 30 (€). A few doors down, this family-run restaurant has an excellent, good-value menu, plus a summer terrace.

Santo Domingo ✉ 26250
****Parador de Santo Domingo de la Calzada**, Pza del Santo 3, t 94 134 03 00, *santodomingo@parador.es* (€€€€). This elegant *parador* occupies the pilgrim's *hostal* built by Santo Domingo; the restaurant serves a delicious, if pricey menu.
****Hospedería Cistercense**, C/ Pinar 2, t 94 134 07 00, *www.cister-lacalzada.com* (€€–€). A pleasant guesthouse run by Cistercian nuns.

*Hs Río, Echegoyen 2, t 94 134 00 85 (€). Try this for something cheaper.

El Peregrino, C/ Zumalacárregui 18, t 94 134 02 02 (€€). Local dishes are served in a garden. *Closed Mon, plus Nov–mid-Mar except for holidays.*

El Rincón de Emilio, Pza de Bonifacio Gil 7, t 94 134 09 90 (€€). A well-known restaurant specializing in the regional cuisine. It does a wonderful set menu featuring organic produce (€35). *Closed Tues eve and 3 wks Feb.*

(i) Ezcaray >
C/ Sagastia 1, t 94 135 46 79, www.ezcaray.org

Ezcaray ✉ 26280

***Echaurren, C /Héroes del Alcázar 2, t 94 135 40 47, info@echaurren.com (€€€). Since the beginning of the 20th

century, this has been the place to sleep and eat; recently it has been renovated. It's usually essential to book a table at the hotel's restaurant (€€€), known for its spectacular, contemporary cuisine. *Closed 2 wks Dec; restaurant closed Nov also.*

***Hostería Valle del Oja, Ctra Posadas-Ezcaray, t 94 142 74 16, www. hosteriavalledeloja.com (€€€). In a beautiful riverside setting 6km from Ezcaray, this converted mill has comfortable rooms, a pool and tennis.

**Iguareña, C/ Lamberto Felipe Muñoz 14, t 94 135 41 44 (€€). A good choice; quiet, with a moderately priced Basque restaurant.

Wine Towns in La Rioja Alta

(✪) Rioja Alta *bodegas*

To the north along the Ebro lies the Rioja Alta, a lush region of abrupt natural features rising above rolling hills, carpeted with vineyards and roads lined with brash spanking new wine *bodegas* that speak of La Rioja's rising reputation.

Haro

Bodegas Bilbaínas
Barrio de la Estación 3, t 94 131 01 47, www. bodegasbilbainas.com

Bodegas Roda
t 94 130 30 01; www.roda.es

CVNE
t 94 130 48 00

López de Heredia
t 94 131 02 44, www. lopezdeheredia.com

Rioja Alta
Avda Vizcaya, t 94 131 03 46, www.riojalta.com

Federico Paternina
Avda de Santo Domingo 1, t 94 131 05 50

Martínez Lacuesta Hnos
C/ Ventilla 71, t 94 131 00 50, www. martinezlacuesta.com

At the confluence of the Ebro and Tirón, Haro is a working wine town built around a large arcaded square. Its chief monuments are a handful of noble houses, the attractive **Casa Consistorial** (1775) and the 16th-century church of **Santo Tomás** up in Plaza Iglesia, bearing a handsome, recently restored Plateresque façade with sculpture and reliefs in several registers, paid for by the Condestables de Castilla.

Haro is the growing and marketing centre for the wines of Rioja Alta, with a clutch of *bodegas* near the train station. While most *bodegas* welcome visitors, they usually require advance notice (the tourist office has a useful booklet listing them all). An exception is **Bodegas Bilbaínas**, with a pretty façade in *azulejos*, usually open mornings and late afternoons. Nearby, you'll find one of the newest – and already among the most praised – wine-producers: **Bodegas Roda**. Along Costa del Vino, you'll find the celebrated cellars of the CUNE, or **CVNE**, home of a fine bubbly; Chilean-owned **López de Heredia**, makers of one of the best Riojas, Viña Tondonia and with a tasting room designed by award-winning architect Zaha Hadid; and the vast, French-founded **Rioja Alta**, with 25,000 barrels. The even larger **Federico Paternina**, founded in 1896 by the Plaza de Toros, houses four million bottles, and welcomes visitors daily except for Monday. Another, **Martínez Lacuesta Hnos**, is in the old gas company that became obsolete back in 1891, when

Haro became the first city in Spain to have public electric street

Selección Vinos de Rioja
Pza Paz 5,
t 94 130 30 17

Wine Museum
C/ Bretón de los Herreros 4, t 94 130 57 19; open Tues–Fri 10–2 and 4–7, Sat and Sun 10–7; adm

lighting. Among the shops, **Selección Vinos de Rioja**, offers tastings and a wide variety of different Riojas.

Since 1892, Haro's **Estación Enológica** (just behind the bus station) has tested new wine-making techniques and varieties; its excellent **Wine Museum** offers detailed explanations of the latest high-tech processes used in La Rioja. For a far less serious initiation, or rather baptism, in Rioja, come on 29 July when San Felices is celebrated with a Batalla del Vino. Everyone dresses in white and, after the Mass, fortified with *zurracapote* (Rioja sangría, made with red wine, citrus fruit and cinnamon) and armed with every conceivable squirter, splasher and sprayer, opposing groups douse one another with 100,000 litres of wine. This Dionysian free-for-all takes place 3km from Haro at the **Peña de Bilibio**, below the striking rock formation and pass of the **Conchas de Haro**, 'the Shells of Haro', where Felices, a hermit-follower of San Millán, lived in a cave. Archaeologists have recently discovered a 10th-century church and the ruins of a Roman town, Castrum Bilibium, or Haro la Vieja, just under the rocks.

Around Haro: the Sonsierra

There aren't many landmarks around Haro, but a handful of villages are worth a look if you're trawling about looking for that perfect bottle. A good place to start is the Sonsierra, a pocket of La Rioja on the left bank of the Ebro. **Briñas**, just north of Haro, has a number of noble escutcheoned manors left over from the days when it was the playground of the Haro nobility. These days wine is the be-all and end-all; there's even a *bodega* under the church.

Don't confuse Briñas with **Briones** further south, where there is a nubbly church tower and a bridge to **San Vicente de la Sonsierra**, a village best known in La Rioja since 1499 for its Guild of Flagellants, Los Picaos, headquartered at **Ermita de Vera Cruz**. During Holy Week, clad in anonymous hoods, the Picaos whip themselves across the shoulders, then pique the bruises with wax balls full of crystal splinters until the blood runs. Just outside San Vicente, the curious 12th-century Romanesque church **Santa María de la Piscina** was founded by Ramiro Sanchez, son-in-law of the Cid, who allegedly brought back a piece of the True Cross from the Crusades. Over the door there's a shield carved with mysterious numbers and symbols. Paintings inside represent the *piscina probática* (waters of

Bodegón de la Real Divisa
t 94 125 81 33

Marqués de Riscal
t 94 160 60 00, www. marquesderiscal.com

the flock) of Jerusalem and the Holy Grail. Just east, **Abalos** has one of the oldest cellars in Spain, the **Bodegón de la Real Divisa**, owned by descendants of the Cid, and a 16th-century church, **San Esteban Protomártir**, decorated with dragons. In **Elciego**, 9km southeast of Abalos, you'll find the *bodega* of the **Marqués de Riscal**, a famous producer who helped establish the reputation of Riojas in the 19th century. The vineyard has a reputation for knowing just how to age wines, and some 30,000 barrels sit in the cellars here, some for as long as 50 years. An added attraction is a new complex designed by none other than Frank Gehry, architect of the Guggenheim Museum in Bilbao. Gehry has once again used titanium for the undulating roof of the building, which now houses a shop, museum and Basque restaurant and a luxury hotel (*see* below).

Back on the south bank of the Ebro, **Cenicero** is another important wine town which has proudly borne the sobriquet the 'Humanitarian' since the 1920s, when the inhabitants went out of their way to care for victims of a train wreck. It has some of Rioja's grandest *bodegas*: ultra-modern **Berberana**, and **Amezola de la Mora**, on the San Asensio road, a fine example of old *bodega* architecture, ideal for its *crianzas* and *reservas*. West of Haro, **Sajazarra** boasts a 13th-century castle, and **Cellórigo**, 'the Pulpit of La Rioja', has views as far as Logroño and an 11th-century castle under the pointed crags of Peña Lengua. **Casalarreina** is a little Renaissance hamlet around the Renaissance convent of La Piedad (1508); 2km west in **Cihuri** the Río Tirón is crossed by a pretty Roman bridge.

Berberana
t 94 145 31 00

Amezola de la Mora
t 94 145 45 32

Markets in Rioja Alta

Haro: Tues and Sat, Arco de S. Bárbara.

Where to Stay and Eat in Rioja Alta

(i) **Haro >**
Plaza Hermanos F. Rodríguez, t 94 130 33 66, www.haro.org/turismo

Haro ✉ 26200
****Ciudad de Haro**, Ctra N124, Km 41, t 94 131 12 13, *www.hotelciudaddeharo. com* (€€€€). Along the highway, overlooking Haro, this modern hotel has been newly restored.
****Los Agustinos**, Plaza de San Agustín 2, t 94 131 13 08 (€€€). Superbly restored, occupying a former Augustinian monastery that later served as a prison.
***Hs Aragón**, La Vega 9, t 94 131 00 04 (€). Basic, but the better of the couple of *hostales* on this street.
Beethoven I and II, C/ Santo Tomás 3–5 and Pza de la Iglesia 8, t 94 131 11 81 (€€). Traditional mushroom, fish and vegetable dishes at these two good dining establishments across the street from each other.
****Hospederia Señorio de Casalarreina**, Plaza Santo Domingo de Gúzman 6, Casalarreina (5km from Haro), t 94 132 47 30 (€€€€). A charming rural hotel in part of the 16th-century monastery, with luxurious rooms and a pool.

Briñas ✉ 26200
****Hospedería Señorio de Briñas**, Travesía de la Calle Real 3, t 94 030 42 24 (€€€). Has some unique split-level rooms in a carefully restored mini palace, decorated with antiques.
***El Portal de La Rioja**, Ctra de la Vitoria, km 42, t 94 130 34 86 (€€–€). As well as rooms with baths, there is an excellent restaurant, a craft shop and a wine museum.

Elciego ✉ 01340
Hotel Marqués de Riscal, Calle Torrea 1, Elciego, t 94 518 08 80, *www. starwoodhotels.com* (€€€€€). The owners asked Frank Gehry to design a 'chateau for the 21st century' but even they couldn't have envisaged this futuristic construction with its glittering silver, yellow and red titanium exterior. Each of the 43 rooms is uniquely shaped and the two sections of the hotel are connected by a suspended footbridge. Even if you can't stay (and there are special deals if you plan way in advance), you can savour some of the surreal ambience at the fine gourmet restaurant.

The Basque Lands (Euskadi)

When it isn't raining, Euskadi is one of the most charming corners of Spain – rural for the most part, lush and green, crisscrossed by a network of mountain streams that meander every which way through steep, narrow valleys in their search for the sea. Great stone country houses resembling Swiss chalets dot the hillsides and riverbanks – though the next valley over may have a grotty little town gathered about a mill. Spain's industrial revolution began in Euskadi, and even today the three Basque provinces are among the most industrialized and wealthy in Spain.

08

Don't miss

⭐ The *Fiesta de la Virgen Blanca*
Vitoria p.176

⭐ Glorious Gothic frescoes
Gaceo p.181

⭐ A titanium wonder
Guggenheim Museum, Bilbao p.167

⭐ Colourful fishing villages
Getaria and Mundaka pp.151 and 157

⭐ *Belle époque* elegance and New Basque cuisine
San Sebastián p.138

See map overleaf

pp.184–5

pp.244–5

Pilgrims' Route

20 km
10 miles

N

Bay of Biscay

Plentzia
Bakio
Isla de Izaro
Bermeo
Elantxobe
Santurtzi
Getxo
Mundaka
Ispaster
Lekeitio
Costa Vasca
Cabo Higuer
Portugalete
Mungia
Gernika
Ondarroa
Mutriku
Zumaia
SAN SEBASTIÁN
(DONOSTIA)
Hondarribia
BILBAO
(BILBO)
Basauri
Vizcaya
Getaria
Zarautz
Orio
Irún
Errenteria
Balmaseda
Bolívar
Markina
Oikia
Hernani
Llodio
Durango
Bérriz
Ermua
Elgoibar
Eibar
Azkoitia
Azpeitia
Régil
Oyarzun
EUSKADI
Elorrio
Loiola
Tolosa
Amurrio
Urkiola
Arrasate
(Mondragón)
Bergara
Zumárraga
Guipúzcoa
Amboto
Otxandio
Oñati
Ordizia
Beasain
Leitza
Bóveda
Embalse de Urrunaga
Uribarri
Segura
Azpirotz
Arcángazu
Embalse de Ullivarri
Aizkorri
Zegama
Sierra de Aralar
Espejo
Mendoza
Iruña
Trespuentes
Á l a v a
Argómaniz
Eguilaz
Altsasu
VITORIA
(GASTEIZ)
Gaceo
Salvatierra
Alaiza
Arrizala
Armiñón
Treviño
County of Treviño
Antoñana
Urturi
Santa Cruz de Campezo
Estella
Miranda de Ebro
Toloño
Peñacerrada
Bernedo
Briñas
Laguardia
Sierra de Cantabria
Balcón de la Rioja
Samaniego
Haro
Ábalos
Leza
Elvillar
Lanciego
San Vicente de la Sonsierra
Villabuena
Laguardia
Briones
Elciego
Oyón
Viana
N A V A R R A
Logroño

FRANCE

PORTUGAL

SPAIN

p.80

Don't miss

⭐ Vitoria **p.176**

② Gaceo **p.181**

③ Guggenheim Museum, Bilbao **p.167**

④ Getaria and Mundaka **pp.151 and 157**

⑤ San Sebastián **p.138**

Euskadi

The Basque lands, known in the Basque language as 'Euskadi' ('Collection of Basques'), contain, according to the autonomy agreement of 1981, the three provinces of Vizcaya, Guipúzcoa and Álava. To the Basques themselves, however, 'Euskadi' means all lands inhabited by Basques – the 'Seven Provinces' that include Labourd, Haute-Navarre and the Soule in France and northern Navarra.

Note that both the Spanish and Basque names for towns and provinces are official, and both are used on road signs: San Sebastián/Donostia, Bilbao/Bilbo, Vitoria/Gasteiz, etc.

In most places in Euskadi, industry and finance seem remote. Basque nationalism, on the other hand, is ever present; every bridge, underpass, and *pelota* court has been painted with the Basque flag and slogans of the Euskadi Ta Askatsuna ('Freedom for Basques'), the notorious ETA, the small but violent minority that has given this ancient people a bad press.

An Introduction to the Basques

Nomansland, the territory of the Basques, in a region called Cornucopia, where the vines are tied up with sausages. And in those parts there was a mountain made entirely of grated Parmesan cheese on whose slopes there were people who spent their whole time making macaroni and ravioli.

Boccaccio,
The Decameron, VIII

When did the inhabitants of Basqueland become Basques? Wild stories like Boccaccio's have often been told about the Basques and their inscrutable ways, but the conclusions reached by many scholars are almost as hard to believe. It seems likely that the Basques are no less than the aborigines of Europe, the descendants of Cro-Magnon hunter-gatherers and painters, having survived in their secluded valleys during the great Indo-European migrations of peoples from the east thousands of years ago. This theory has had a big boost from the discovery that the Basques have the highest proportion of type O blood in the world, as do other people pushed long ago into Europe's corners – the Irish, the Scots, and Cretans. Yet even more peculiarly, the Basques also have the world's highest incidence of Rh negative blood, a factor characteristic of the indigenous prehistoric European race. Other clues are the slight but telling physical differences between the Basques and their neighbours: they have long noses and long earlobes, are bigger and stronger, and the distinct shape of their skulls is matched only by those of their ancestors, buried under dolmens in 2000 BC.

One doesn't visit the Basque country to see the sights, which are few and far between. The real attraction is the Basques themselves, a taciturn though likeable lot, and their distinctive culture and way of life. The setting also helps to make the trip worthwhile; emerald landscapes well tended by the same people for millennia.

History

'The Basques are like good women; they have no history.' So runs the old saying. Another of their jokes is that, when God created the first man, he got the bones from a Basque graveyard. No one knows for sure just how far back they go – only that someone, incredibly, must have been around even before them. For the areas around the Pyrenees are one of the oldest inhabited places on earth, and one of the cradles of human culture. The first European yet discovered, 'Tautavel Man', parked his carcass in a cave at the western end of the chain some 450,000 years ago. Traces of habitation in the Basque lands go back at least 100,000 years, and somebody was painting pictures on cave walls as early as 35,000 BC. While the most famous examples yet discovered are in southwestern France and Cantabria, the Cro-Magnons in the Basque provinces were no slouches, as the painted caves at Santimamiña and elsewhere show. Genetic research, perhaps less subjective than phrenology, has confirmed a unique persistence of the European Palaeolithic DNA markers in the ethnic Basque population. Even the Basque language, with no known relatives, offers its hints of extreme antiquity; practically every word for common tools, for instance, comes from the ancient root *haiz*, meaning stone, even *haiztur*, scissors.

Sheep, not native to Basqueland, arrived around 5000 BC, followed by horses and cattle, part of the Neolithic agricultural and cultural revolution that spread across western Europe. Today scholars believe that those with farming know-how migrated slowly out of Turkey, and hunter-gatherer traditions slowly disappeared through intermarriage. This is when the ancestors of the Basques remained aloof. But if they didn't mingle, they did learn agriculture, the domestication of animals, and building – their lasting monuments include dolmens, tumuli and menhirs.

About 800 BC, Celtic peoples started moving through the region, probably intermarrying with the original people as well as conquering them. Again the ancestors of the Basques for some reason remained unassimilated while picking up tips from the newcomers, on metalworking and cultivating wheat. When the Romans came, they found a nation they called the Aquitanians or Vascones, speaking a non-Indo-European language and occupying much of the land between the Ebro and the Garonne.

The Romans never really exercised much control over the Basques' mountain fastnesses, and the Visigoths and Franks who followed found the Basques a permanent headache. Charlemagne pacified the inhabitants of the plains by 781, but the mountain Basques held out, and taught the aggressive emperor a costly lesson in the legendary battle of Roncesvalles (*see* pp.39–40). As the medieval states that claimed Basque property – Navarra, Asturias/Castilla, England, Béarn and France – grew in wealth and power, there was increasingly little chance that an event like Roncesvalles could be repeated. This was a world dominated by a feudal aristocracy, one made up of foreigners, the descendants of Germanic invaders and Roman landowners, and with such bossy

Folklore

The Basques are not alone. In fact, their long intimacy with their land has forced them to share it with an unreasonably large number of gods, demons, spirits and fairies, creatures of one of the richest mythologies of Europe.

Many tales are connected to the dolmens and other Neolithic monuments that grow so thickly on the mountains here; often their names connect them to **Mari**, the ancient Basque great goddess. The dolmens were built by the *jentillak*, the race of giants that once lived side by side with the Basques. The *jentillak*, often a great help to their neighbours, invented metallurgy and the saw, and introduced the growing of wheat. One day a strange storm cloud appeared from the east, and the wisest of the *jentillak* recognized it as an omen and interpreted it as the end of their age. The giants marched off into the earth, under a dolmen still visible in the Arratzaran valley in Navarra. One was left behind, named Olentzero, and he explained to the Basques: 'Kixmi [Jesus] is born and this means the end of our race.' Olentzero lives on today, as the jolly fat doll or straw figure seen prominently in the Basques' celebrations of Christmas and New Year's Day, the leader of all the processions. You will find Olentzero in Basque homes and even in the churches, often bearing an unusual resemblance to the Michelin man; he'll probably be surrounded by food because, of course, being one of the *jentillak*, Olentzero likes to eat all day. Other familiar creatures include the *laminak*, originally small female fairies with a capacity to help or harm, now a sort of leprechaun, which get blamed for everything that goes wrong. And where mythology fades off into nursery-lore, we have the '**man with the sack**' who comes to carry off naughty children, and a large bestiary with jokes like the elusive *dahu*, a kind of lizard with legs that are shorter on one side – the better to walk the mountain slopes.

Along with the myths goes a remarkable body of pre-Christian religious survivals, including rituals that lasted well into the 20th century; many old Basques in isolated villages can remember festivals with midsummer bonfires in their childhood, and in some villages the custom is coming back, just as it is in the Catalan Pyrenees. (Any excuse for a party!)

Basques are passionately fond of **music**, whether it's choral music at Mass (which they do extremely well), Basque rock (rare, fortunately), or traditional tunes played by village bands. Dozens of traditional dances are still current, and small groups in many villages keep them up; you'll have a chance to see them at any village fête – especially in Guipúzcoa, where you can tour the villages on a Sunday morning and usually find a couple with traditional dances going on in the square. Traditional Basque instruments include the *txistu*, a three-holed flute played with one hand, the other hand beating the rhythm on the tambour; another is the *dultzaina*, a primitive bagpipe. When they're in the mood, the Basques dance some of the most furiously athletic dances in the world, especially the *Bolant Dantza* ('Flying Dance') or *La Espata Dantza* ('Sword Dance').

The real monument of Euskadi is the *etxe*, a word that means much more to a Basque than just 'house'. Set on its own on the velvet hillsides, the traditional Basque farmhouse is one of the most distinctive characteristics of the whole region: pretty, simple, functional and nearly always painted white, they are usually two storeys high, with a distinctive long, low gable along the façade. The upper section often has half-timbering and shutters – trimmed, of course, with green and *rouge basque*. Most *etxes* face east, towards the rising sun. In the old days, it was the heads of households who met to make laws at the assemblies, and it is common to find families whose home has been on the same site for over a thousand years. The cemeteries have been around even longer. Basques have distinctive 'discoidal' or round-headed tombstones. Archaeologists have dug up models 4,500 years old, and they've been using the same style ever since. The earliest ones often had human figures, sun symbols or other symbols carved on them; since the coming of Christianity the stones usually show crosses. You will see them in any churchyard, usually turned south so that the sun shines on the carved face all day.

neighbours that it is not surprising the Basques never coalesced into a nation. The Basques at this time are practically invisible, their language merely the patois of countrymen, and nobody paid much attention to them. All through the Middle Ages, the Basque boundaries shrank gradually but inexorably as the natives were either pushed out or assimilated by Spaniards, Gascons and Catalans. Many place names, especially in the eastern Pyrenees, give clues of a Basque origin, but by the 1300s the Basque lands had contracted roughly within the boundaries they retain today.

Despite the decline, the Basques survived as a nation throughout. When they finally did agree to recognize the suzerainty of Castilla it was on their own terms, retaining *fueros* (privileges) and ancient laws, one of which was that every king, once crowned, should come to Gernika and swear under the sacred oak tree to uphold their laws. Since then, Basques have always played an important role in Spanish affairs, far out of proportion to their numbers. They were great sailors and explorers, shipbuilders and whalers, *conquistadores* and pirates, and nowadays they run most of Spain's banks. The Basques organized the first whale fishery, in the Middle Ages. At first they only took whales that came too close to the shore, but as the whales got wise the Basques began chasing them farther out to sea. The Basques claim they landed in the Americas long before Columbus (who took a Basque pilot along); Basque sailors helped the English conquer Wales, built the Spanish Armada, and founded a number of Spanish colonies, including the Philippines, as well as cities like Buenos Aires. The *conquistadores* Lope de Aguirre and Pedro de Ursúa were Basques; the Basque captain Sebastián Elcano became the first man to sail around the world. Two of Spain's most important saints, St Ignatius of Loyola and St Francis Xavier, were also Basque.

In the 19th century, the Basque lands suffered as much as any other part of France or Spain from rural poverty and depopulation. Young Basques from the mountain uplands went in great numbers to the Americas, especially to Argentina and the United States, where the Basque connection goes back to the 1,500 sailors who came to join Lafayette and fight for American independence. Simón Bolívar, liberator of Venezuela and Colombia, was of Basque descent. In the bayous of Louisiana and east Texas, and on the Argentine pampas, Basques became some of the first cowboys in the 1840s, setting the model and contributing much to the image (*lariat*, among other cowboy terms, is a Basque word, and exotic cinema locales such as Durango, Colorado and Laredo, Texas were named after Basque villages). Later in the century they moved further west, taking lonely jobs as shepherds in the Rockies. There are still large Basque communities in Idaho, Utah, California and other states.

Throughout history, the Basques have wanted only to be left alone, and they always support any politics that promise to uphold their ancient rights and liberties. In modern times, this has meant adventures with both the far right and the far left. In the 19th century, when progress meant doing away with quaint relics like Basque culture and *fueros*, the Basques remembered their pious nature and took the side of Fernando VII's reactionary brother Don Carlos in the second Carlist war (1876), and lost the *fueros* as a result. At the same time Euskadi, with its iron deposits and port towns, began to industrialize, and, while many prospered, the majority of workers, seeing their traditional society threatened on all sides, flocked to the banner of Basque Nationalism.

Nationalism is hardly a recent phenomenon. It started in the 18th century, with a community of liberal bourgeois in Bilbao and the other outward-looking port cities; these supported Enlightenment thinkers such as Manuel de Larramendi, who developed a concept of Basque nationhood based on language and tradition. Throughout the 19th century, nationalist thought and the development of Basque culture proceeded apace in Spain, while, at least on the political side, it ran into a stone wall in the much more repressive

Basque Diversions

Basques definitely know how to eat. Go into a village restaurant at 9am on a market day, and watch the boys tuck into their three-course breakfasts – soup, tons of meat, fish and potatoes, with a gallon or so of wine for each. Fortunately for them, the Basques also know how to cook. Their distinctive and world-renowned cuisine will be one of the delights of your visit to the Basque country (*see* p.48).

The real national sport, of course, is smuggling sheep over the border. But the Basques love to play, and over the millennia they have evolved a number of outlandish games that are unique in the world. Many of these are based on pure brute strength, a major element of the national mystique. Even today, especially strong, tall people are said to be descendants of the *jentillak*. One can imagine them, back in the mists of time, impressing each other by carrying around boulders – because that's what they do today, in a number of events generally called the *harri altxatzea*, literally 'stone-lifting'. In one, contestants see how many times they can lift a 500lb stone in five minutes; in others, they roll boulders around their shoulders. Related to this is the *untziketariak*, in which we see how fast a Basque can run with 100lb weights in each hand. They're fond of the tug-of-war too; they probably invented it. You will also see them at the village festivals pulling loaded wagons, racing with 200lb sacks on their shoulders, or chopping huge tree trunks against the clock. Don't fool with these people.

The miracle is that at the same time they could develop a sport like *pelota*, the world's fastest ball game. Few sports in the world can offer an image as beautiful and memorable as the *pelotari* in his traditional loose, pure white costume, chasing down the ball with a long, curving *chistera*. Pelota takes a wide variety of forms, but the basic element is always the ball: a hard core, wrapped tightly with string and covered with hide – like a baseball, only smaller and with much more bounce; in a serious match it can reach speeds of 150mph. The oldest form of the game is *rebot*, played without a wall. This is done bare-handed; other versions, played in an outdoor *frontón*, may be bare-handed, with a leather glove (*pasaka* or *joko garbi*), or with the *chistera*, made of leather and osier, which enables a player to scoop up the ball and fling it back in the same motion.

Whatever the game, it usually requires teams of two players each. The ground in front of the wall is marked off in *cuadros* every 4m from it; to be in, a ball bounced off the wall must hit between the 4th and 7th *cuadros*, if it is not returned on the fly. Games are usually to 35 points. Every Basque village has a *frontón*, usually right in the centre. On some village churches from as far back as the 1600s, you can see how the architects left one smooth, blank wall to accommodate the game. It may also be played in a covered court, or on one with another wall on the left side, a *jaï-alaï*, when the game is called *cesta punta*, the fastest and most furious form of *pelota*. Thanks to Basque immigrants this is now a popular sport around the Caribbean and some areas of the USA.

climate of France. French Euskadi thus became a sideshow to main events, while in Spain the PNV, the first Basque nationalist party, controlled a majority of the region's parliamentary seats from 1917 on. In 1931, when supporters of a republic offered the Basques autonomy in exchange for support, they jumped at the chance, despite reservations about the new Second Republic's secularism. When the Civil War broke out, they remained loyal to the Republic and even the priests fought side by side with the 'Reds'. To break their spirit, the German Condor Legion practised the world's first saturation bombing of a civilian target at Gernika (see p.155).

Franco later took special pains to single out the Basques for reprisals of all kinds, outlawing their language and running the region as a police state, so that even the thousands of Castilians who immigrated to Euskadi to work in the factories felt oppressed enough to sympathize with Basque Nationalist goals. Franco's rule was a catastrophe for the Basques: there were over 100,000 prisoners and 200,000 exiles after the Civil War, including the entire intelligentsia and political leadership. Resistance groups did not start forming until 1952, and Francoist repression determined the equally poisonous nature of the antidote. ETA (Euskadi Ta Askatsuna) was founded in 1959. Its bombing campaign near the end of Franco's reign was singularly effective – notably when they blew the car carrying Franco's anointed successor, Admiral Carrero Blanco, over the roof of a Madrid church.

The repression of the Basques during the Franco years caused the Spanish state to lose any claims to legitimacy in the eyes of many, and, when called upon to ratify the new constitution in 1978, most Basques abstained from the ballot box; those who voted, voted no. Although they regarded the autonomy imposed on them as second rate, they have made the best of it, and today Euskadi has the greatest autonomy of any region in Spain. Taxes are collected by local governments, and local rule covers education, culture, industry, health services, police, agriculture and fishing, etc. Most parents, even Spanish, choose to have their children educated in Basque and Spanish. The Basque government at Gasteiz (Vitoria) is held up in Spain as a model of efficiency and progressiveness.

Today 70 per cent of Basques vote for nationalist parties, mostly for the moderate PNV and the more nationalist but still peaceful Eusko Alkartasuna (Basque Solidarity); on the whole they are progressive-left on most issues, strongly anti-nuclear and anti-NATO. The left wing opposition, Herri Batasuna (now Euskal Herritarok), the only party to openly support ETA, regularly gets some 15 per cent of the vote; their garish posters are on every wall. Terrorist ETA has gone steadily downhill since its failure to make an impression during Spain's year of celebrations in 1992. Widespread disgust with terror tactics has made ETA fall out of favour, though support for a totally independent Euskadi remains considerable. Most people, however, are in no hurry for it, and would rather see independence brought about as part of a peaceful and evolutionary process.

Language

Speaking the local language is an art! The Basques point out with great pride that their language is not only Europe's oldest, but also the most difficult; the only language ever found to have any similarity to it is Berber. There are four distinct dialects, and in each the grammar is Kafkaesque, to put it mildly. Verbs, for example, can vary according to the gender of the person you are addressing. The vast number of grammatical tenses includes not only a subjunctive, but two different potentials, an eventual, and a hypothetical. But grammatical complexity permits beauty and economy; you can express anything in Basque in fewer words than in most other languages.

Basque is maddeningly, spectacularly indirect. For example, 'I am spinning', comes out as *Iruten ari nuzu*', or literally, 'In the act of spinning doing you have me!' Or try out this proverb: '*Izan gabe eman dezakegun gauza bakarra da zoriona*'... 'Having without, give (*Izan gabe eman*) we can (*dezakegun*), one thing only is (*gauza bakarra da*), happiness (*zoriona*)' – 'Happiness is the only thing we can give without having.' Pronunciation, thank heavens, is not such a problem; it's phonetic, and there are only a few letters you need to know: *e* as long *a*; *u* as *oo*; *j* as *ee*; *s* as something halfway between *s* and *sh*; *tz* or *z* as *s*; and *x* as *sh*. Pronounce all the vowels, and don't make any soft consonant sounds.

Peculiarities of the language include the habit of doubling words for effect, unknown to any European tongue but common among the Polynesians, and some entertaining onomatopoeia. In Basque, something very hot is *bero-bero*, and when a Basque walks on all fours it is called *hitipiti-hatapata*. Looking at a menu in a Basque restaurant (they have the best cuisine in Spain, so you'll want to do this often), you may well be *keko-meko* (undecided); if you choose *birristi-barrasta* (carelessly), you might get *ttattu* (little cat), a supposed speciality in Bilbao in the 19th century. Basques can put it away; other Spaniards accuse them of *mauka-mauka* (gluttony). Like eskimos, who know no generic word for 'ice', the Basques have no word for 'tree' or 'animal'. And being democratic folk, there's no word for 'king' either – they had to borrow one from the French and Spanish potentates they were forced to pay taxes to.

Owing to the severe cultural oppression under Franco, the percentage of Basque speakers is higher on the French side, according to a recent survey: 64 per cent in Basse-Navarre, 54 per cent in the Soule, and 26 per cent in Labourd, as opposed to 45 per

08 The Basque Lands (Euskadi) | An Introduction to the Basques

A Basque Outline

Very few Basque words have made it into English, although one, 'silhouette', is derived in a most roundabout way from a Basque word, *zuleta*, which means 'many holes'. The surname Zulueta or Zuloeta was probably given to a family who lived among the holes, or caves. One branch of the Zulueta family in France adopted the spelling Silhouette. Their most famous member, Etienne de Silhouette (1709–67), was a writer and politician who held the powerful post of controller-general. He wasn't very good at it and didn't keep his office long, and his meagre policies cast but a shadow (according to one explanation), although others say Silhouette himself liked to draw portraits in outlines and hang them on the walls of his château.

cent in Guipúzcoa, 18 per cent in Vizcaya, 10 per cent in Navarra, and only 9 per cent in Álava. However, for the first time, the numbers are rising in a revival that has touched all aspects of Basque culture. In Euskadi, the language is now mandatory in school, and in the past decade 100,000 adults have learned to speak it. Basque TV and radio are broadcast on both sides of the border; there are Basque newspapers, including *Gara* and *Berria*, and over 1,000 books of all kinds published annually, a remarkable statistic for a population of only a million potential readers: one novel, *Obabakoak* (1989), by Basqueland's best-known living writer, Bernardo Atxaga, is the first ever to be translated into English. Equally encouraging is the continuing popularity of the *bertsulari*, poets (often scarcely literate shepherds) who have memorized a vast repertoire of traditional pieces and are especially skilled at complex improvisions at festivals and competitions.

Along the Coast: France to San Sebastián

If you are driving in from France, there is a choice of routes: the A8 (also signposted, confusingly, as the E5/E70 and E80) motorway which is expensive though occasionally dramatic, or the old routes through Hendaye and Hondarribia.

Hondarribia (**Fuenterrabía** in Spanish) gets overlooked with all the border confusion, but this is one of the most agreeable destinations on the coast; the village glows with colour – in its brightly painted houses, especially along Calle San Nicolás, or Calle Pampinot, in its flower-loaded balconies and in its fishing fleet that has taken on France in the EU's battles over fishing rights. The town has had its share of sieges – you can still see the ancient walls and a **castle** of Charles V, now a *parador* – and every summer sees an invasion of French tourists. In the evening, head out towards the lighthouse on **Cabo Higuer** – the northeasternmost corner of Spain – for views of the sunset over the bay.

Irún, on the French border, is inland on the Bidasoa. It was bombed to bits by Franco and his German friends in the Civil War

Getting along the Coast to San Sebastián

It's only 20mins by **bus** to San Sebastián from Irún or Hondarribia on the frontier; connections are frequent by bus and **train**, and not a few people watching their euros stay in Irún (or in France) rather than in the more pricy resort. If you're not in a hurry, take the narrow-gauge EuskoTren for a leisurely ride.

and has little to recommend it. Further inland you can climb **Monte San Marcial** for a memorable view over the Bay of Biscay (there is a road to the top), or else flee the bustling coast for the serene **Valley of Oyarzun**, one of Euskadi's rural beauty spots, with the pretty villages of **Oyarzun**, **Lesaka** and **Vera de Bidasoa**. There are neolithic monuments all through this region, on both sides of the border; the spot where the Pyrenees meet the sea was a holy spot. A site called **Oianleku**, off the main road near Oyarzun, includes some small stone circles among the dolmens.

If you're driving, you can take the coastal road from Hondarribia along **Monte Jáizkibel**, offering superb views over the Bay of Biscay, the French coast and the Pyrenees. Just east of San Sebastián, the ribbon town of **Pasajes de San Juan** (**Pasai Donibane**) lines the east bank of an estuary, where there are more picturesque old houses. Victor Hugo lived in one for a while, and the Marquis de Lafayette lodged in another before sailing off to aid Britain's American colonists in their revolution. Philip built part of the Armada here, although now all such business affairs are handled by San Juan's ugly stepsister across the estuary, **Pasajes de San Pedro**.

(side margin) 08 The Basque Lands (Euskadi) | Along the Coast: France to San Sebastián

Where to Stay and Eat along the Coast from San Sebastián

(i) **Hondarribia >**
Javier Ugarte 6,
t 94 364 54 58,
www. bidasoaturismo.
com (website has
information for
Hondarribia, Irún and
Hendaia/Hendaye)

Hondarribia ✉ 20280

***Parador Imperador Carlos V, Plaza de Armas 14, t 94 364 55 00, *www.parador.es* (€€€€€). Prettily situated at the very top of town, in the castle of Charles V. The decoration is medieval, including fine tapestries.

***Hotel Obispo, Pza del Obispo, t 94 364 54 00, *www.hotelobispo.com* (€€€€–€€€). A 14th-century mansion, in the old residence of the Bishop of Hondarribia, built on the Bastion San Felipe, with sumptuously refitted rooms and splendid views.

***Pampinot, Kale Nagusia 5, t 94 364 06 00, *www.hotelpampinot.com* (€€€€–€€€). A smaller, but just as noble, historical monument, with eight rooms in a restored 15th-century mansion in the old quarter.

**San Nikolas, Pza de Armas 6, t 94 364 42 78 (€€). A little blue-and-pink hotel with attractive rooms right on the *plaza*, with sea views.

Txoko Goxoa, C/ Margolari Etxenagusia, t 94 364 46 58 (€€–€). Lovely *hostal* in the Casco Histórico.

**Hostal Álvarez Quintero, C/ Bernat Etxepare 2, t 94 364 22 99 (€). In the old fishing quarter, one of a small number of *hostales*; dependable and good value, it even has a small pool.

Alameda, C/ Alameda 1, t 94 364 27 89, *www.restalameda.com* (€€€). Rustically furnished, this is the best restaurant in the region, serving imaginative and award-winning New Basque cuisine with a strong local flavour, such as *manitas de cerdo braseadas* (braised pigs' trotters) or a scrumptious lasagne with squid and pumpkin. *Menú degustación* €65. *Closed Sun eve, Mon, and Tues eve.*

Beko Errota, C/ Barrio de Jaizubia, t 94 364 31 94 (€€€–€€). Traditional Basque dishes are on offer here, with a good selection of fish dishes. An elegant restaurant surrounded by beautiful gardens. *Closed Sun eve and Mon.*

Arraunlari, Butroi Pasealekug 3, t 94 364 15 81 (€€). Next to the sea. Offers fine, traditional fish dishes. *Closed Sun eve and Mon, plus mid-Dec–mid-Jan.*

Restaurant Danontzat, C/ Las Tiendas 6, t 94 364 56 63 (€). Budget snack/tapas bar downstairs, with tasty *platos combinados* for under €6. More formal dining upstairs.

ⓘ **Irún >**
Puente de Santiago (Barrio de Behobia s/n), t 94 362 26 27, and in the train station, t 94 361 67 08

Irún ✉ 20300

Cheaper rooms in Irún are no longer the bargain they once were, and very little is available for under €36.

***Alcazar, Avda Iparralde 11, t 94 362 09 00, *hotelalcazar@euskalnet.net* (€€€). Top of the range.

**Lizaso, C/ Aduana 5, t 94 361 16 00 (€). Possibly the best deal in Irún, with decent rooms.

Mertxe, C/ Francisco Gainza 9, t 94 362 46 82 (€€€). A pretty chalet-style building with a winter garden, one of the finest restaurants here. *Closed Sun eve, Wed, and first 2 wks July.*

Ramon Roteta, Villa Ainara, Irún 1, t 94 364 16 93 (€€€). Gracious dining in a lovely villa with a garden; grand cuisine and superb desserts. *Closed Sun eve and Tues, plus Feb.*

Larretxipi, Larretxipi 5, t 94 363 26 59 (€€). Excellent fish, though a number of places nearby are cheaper. Gourmet menu €17. *Closed Sun eve, Tues, last 2 weeks Mar, last 2 weeks Nov.*

Bar Oiarso, C/ Mayor 17, t 94 362 61 81 (€). The best place to fill up on tapas.

San Sebastián (Donostia)

⭐ **San Sebastián**

At the beginning of the 21st century, it is difficult to imagine that a place like San Sebastián (Donostia in Basque) could ever exist. The *belle époque* may be a hundred years away, but in San Sebastián the buildings still seem to be made of ice-cream, with trim in Impressionist colours and florid brass streetlights; people still dress up instinctively for the evening *paseo*. This confection embraces one of the peninsula's most enchanting bays, the oyster-shaped Bahía de La Concha, protected from the bad moods of the Atlantic by a wooded islet, the Isla de Santa Clara, and by Monte Urgull, the humpbacked sentinel on the easternmost tip of the bay. It looks a bit like Rio de Janeiro, and it's a movie set when the sun's shining, which is most of the time.

San Sebastián has probably been around as long as the Basques, but the earliest mention of it is as a Roman port called Easo. The town resurfaced in the Middle Ages; in the 12th century, when the Navarrese controlled this part of the coast, they built the first fortress on Monte Urgull, one that has been rebuilt and reinforced many times since. The first recorded tourist came against his will – François Ier, king of France, was locked up in the fortress for a time by Charles V after being captured at the Battle of Pavia in 1527. In the 19th century, the city found a new role as the cynosure of fashion: a century before there were any such thing as '*costas*', wealthy Spaniards were coming here to spend their summers. In the 1850s it was blessed by the presence of Queen Isabel II, who brought the government and the court with her in summer. It was during her reign that San Sebastián was made capital of the

Getting to and around San Sebastián

By Air

San Sebastián's airport (t 94 366 85 00, *www.aena.es*), 20km to the east near Hondarribia, has connections to Madrid and Barcelona. The bus to the airport, Hondarribia and Irún (t 94 364 13 02) departs from Plaza Gipúzkoa every 12mins – note that it sets you down across the road from the airport.

By Train

RENFE trains depart from the **Estación del Norte** (t 90 224 02 02), on Paseo de Francia. There are frequent connections with Irún and Hendaye, Burgos and Madrid; and less frequent trains to Paris, Barcelona, Pamplona, Salamanca, Vitoria, Zaragoza and León. *Talgos* whizz all the way to Madrid, Málaga, Córdoba, Algeciras, Valencia, Alicante, Oviedo and Gijón.

EuskoTren (t 90 254 32 10) runs services to Hendaye and Bilbao from **Amara** station on Plaza Easo: trains stop everywhere on the way.

By Bus

A bewildering number of buses leave from the station on Plaza de Pio XII at the southern end of town. The ticket office for **Pesa**, which runs the services to Bilbao, Biarritz and Bayonne, is nearby at C/ Sancho el Sabio 33, though some lines (including La Roncelesa, t 94 346 10 64, for buses to Pamplona and Vitoria) have their offices on Paseo de Vizcaya. There are five buses daily to Oviedo, seven to Burgos and five to Galicia. Within Euskadi, buses depart every half-hour to Bilbao and Vitoria, and up to 10 times a day to Pamplona. For information on buses in San Sebastián itself, call t 94 328 71 00. No.16 goes to Igueldo and the funicular (*daily in summer 10–10, every 15mins*).

By Taxi

Radiotaxi Donosti, t 94 346 46 46.
Radio Sutal, t 94 339 68 40.
Vallina Teletaxi, t 94 340 40 40.

By Bike

Cycling is a great way to explore San Sebastián, especially along the 12km seafront promenade: it's possible to get from one end of the city to the other without having to cross a road. Bikes can be hired from Avenida de la Zurriola 22, t 94 327 92 60.

Motor Boats

Boats make 30-minute excursions out to the Isla de Santa Clara every hour (*summer only*) from the pier (*muelle*), where you can also rent a rowing boat to do the same yourself.

Sebastian bat ba da zeruan

Donosti bat bakarra munduan

(There's only one St Sebastián up in heaven And there's only one Donostia here on earth)

from The March of St Sebastian, 1861

province and the Paris–Madrid railway was completed, making the city convenient to holidaymakers from both capitals.

Queen Regent María Cristina again made San Sebastián the rage in 1886 – following the example of Empress Eugénie of France, who had popularized nearby Biarritz. The sister city of Reno, Nevada, it's still a classy place to go: a lovely, relaxed seaside resort in a spectacular setting.

Playa de la Concha, the Comb of the Winds and the Centro Romántico

Sheltered within the bay is the magnificent golden crescent of the **Playa de la Concha**, San Sebastián's centrepiece and its largest beach, beautifully hemmed by the Paseo de la Concha, an elegant promenade with flouncy balustrades, dotted with creamy *belle époque* cafés and the matronly **bath house**. On its western end

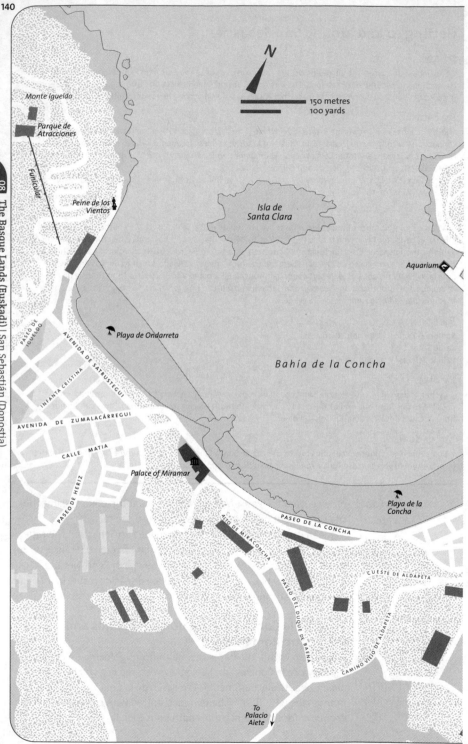

Monte Igueldo

Parque de Atracciones

Funicular

Peine de los Vientos

Playa de Ondarreta

PASEO DE IGUELDO

AVENIDA DE SATRUSTEGUI

INFANTA CRISTINA

AVENIDA DE ZUMALACÁRREGUI

CALLE MATIA

PASEO DE HERIZ

Palace of Miramar

ALTO DE MIRACONCHA

PASEO DE LA CONCHA

PASEO DEL DUQUE DE BAENA

CAMINO VIEJO DE ALDAPETA

CUESTE DE ALDAPETA

Isla de Santa Clara

Aquarium

Bahía de la Concha

Playa de la Concha

N

150 metres
100 yards

To Palacio Aiete

Mar Cantábrico

British Cemetery

Monte Urgull

Castillo de Santa Cruz

Museum of
San Telmo

Santa María
del Coro

Museo Naval

PLAZA DE
TRINIDAD

CALLE 31 DE AGOSTO

San Vicente

PASEO NUEVO

PASEO DE SALAMANCA

LA PARTE VIEJA

PUERTO

PLAZA
DE LA
CONSTITUCIÓN

IÑIGO

ALDAMAR

CALBETÓN FERMÍN

El Muelle

CALLE MAYOR

SAN JERÓNIMO

MARI

Playa de Gros

Playa de
Zurriola

Palacio de Congresos
Kursaal y Auditorio

PUENTE
DE
ZURRIOLA

AVENIDA DE LA ZURRIOLA

ALAMEDA DEL BOULEVARD

PASEO REPÚBLICA ARGENTINA

Ayuntamiento

Parque de
Alderdi Eder

PEÑA FLORIDA

PLAZA DE
GIPÚZKOA

CALLE ANDÍA

CALLE OQUENDO

PASEO DE COLÓN

CALLE DE ZABALETA

BERMINGHAM

GEN. ARTECHE

C NUEVA

CALLE DE SAN FRANCISCO

GROS

SECUNDINO ESNAOLA

CENTRO ROMÁNTICO

CALLE MIRAMAR

PUENTE
DE SANTA
CATALINA

PLAZA DE
LUSKADI

CALLE   MIRACRUZ

PLAZA DE
CERVANTES

PASEO DE LA CONCHA

AVENIDA   DE   LA   LIBERTAD

CALLE LOIOLA

CALLE DE SAN MARCIAL

FUENTERRABIA

ETXAIDE

PASEO DE LOS FUEROS

Mercado de la
Brecha

PLAZA DE
ZUBIETA ZARAGOZA

CALLE DE SAN MARTÍN

PASEO DE FRANCIA

CALLE DE SAN BARTOLOMÉ

CALLE DE EASO

CALLE DE URBANETA

CALLE DE URBANETA

Catedral del
Buen Pastor

CALLE REYES
CATÓLICOS

PUENTE
DE MARÍA
CRISTINA

Estación
del
Norte

PASEO DEL DUQUE DE MANDAS

PLAZA
EASO

CALLE MORAZA

CALLE DE PRIM

PASEO DEL ÁRBOL DE GUERNICA

Río Urumea

Estación de
Amara

Parque de
Cristina Enea

To
Bus Station

Río Urumea

stands a promontory topped by the mock-Tudor **Palace of Miramar of María Cristina**, built as a summerhouse for the royal family, now owned by the city and used for receptions and special exhibitions. A tunnel under the Miramar leads to the **Playa de Ondarreta**, a traditional society retreat. Ondarreta beach itself comes to a dead end at seaside **Monte Igueldo**, crowned by a **Parque de Atracciones**. You can get to the top by road or by the rickety old **funicular** from the end of the beach, and the reward is a spectacular view over San Sebastián, the Bay of Biscay and the Cantabrian mountains.

Back on the shore, beyond the beach and the funicular, stands one of the most talked-about monuments of modern Spanish sculpture, Eduardo Chillida's *Peine de los Vientos* (*Comb of the Winds*). The work is a series of terraces, built into the rocks that guard the entrance to the bay, decorated with cast-iron constructions, the 'teeth' of the comb that smooths the winds coming from the sea towards the city. Chillida was a native of San Sebastián (he was once goalie for the local football side), and lived in a house on the cliffs above the monument.

Nearly all the city behind the beaches of La Concha and Ondarreta dates from the 19th century. San Sebastián is an ancient place, but it has been burned to the ground twelve times in its history, lastly by Wellington's drunken soldiers, who celebrated their conquest with their accustomed murder and mayhem. The city was rebuilt and even expanded soon after, in a neat neoclassical grid now called the **Centro Romántico**, with the **Catedral del Buen Pastor**, completed in the 1880s, at its centre. The **Mercado de San Martín** squats nearby. At the heart of this district is the arcaded Plaza de Gipuzkoa, sternly overlooked by the neoclassical **Palacio Foral**.

A promenade-lined river, the Urumea, divides 19th-century Sanse (as the city is affectionately known) from the newer quarter of **Gros**, once the working men-student-bohemian enclave, a lively place full of bars and restaurants and endowed with its own beach, the **Playa de Gros**, which is always less crowded but lies outside the sheltered bay, subject to the wind, waves and filthy debris. Still, it's great for surfers, who come in droves. Of the three charming bridges that span the Urumea, the **María Cristina** (near the station) most resembles a cream pastry.

With its imposing main façade facing the Cristina-Enea Park and its back to the north railway station is Donostia's old tobacco factory, **Tabacalera**, which at the time of writing was getting ready to become one of the region's most important contemporary art centres. The idea is to make use of the vast area occupied by the former tobacco factory to serve several purposes: as a research centre for all types of artists including cooks, a media library and space for temporary art exhibitions.

Tabacalera
for updates, info and current exhibitions, consult www. tabacalera-donostia.eu and the tourist office

La Parte Vieja and Monte Urgull

Most of the action in town takes place under Monte Urgull in the narrow streets of the Parte Vieja, or old town (also known as the Casco Viejo). From **La Concha** beach, its entrance is guarded by a beautiful, well-manicured square, the **Parque de Alderdi Eder**, and the enormous 19th-century **Ayuntamiento**, or town hall, formerly the casino that María Cristina built (the new one is on Calle Mayor). What remains of the city's fishing fleet may be seen in the harbour behind the Ayuntamiento, a picturesque tumble of whitewashed cottages rimmed by souvenir shops, pricy tourist restaurants – although it's worth trying the freshly grilled sardines – and a pair of salty museums. The **Museo Naval** is set in the 18th-century consulate and is devoted to the Basques' proud naval history, with models, photographs and biographies of famous Basque seafarers. At the far end of the port, the **Aquarium** is stuffed with model ships, the skeleton of a Basque whale that went belly-up in San Sebastián's port and, downstairs, tanks of fish and other sea creatures from around the world.

Museo Naval
open Tues–Sat 10–1.30 and 4–7.30, Sun 11–2; adm

Aquarium
open July–Sept 10–10; Oct–April Mon–Fri 10–8, Sat and Sun 10–9; May–June Mon–Fri 10–7, Sat and Sun 10–8; adm

From here you can stroll along the outer edge of **Monte Urgull** on the Paseo Nuevo, a splendid little walk between turf and surf. In the late afternoon, when the light is best, stroll up one of the numerous paths to the summit of the rock; Monte Urgull is really the city's park, closed to traffic and including surprises along the way, such as a British cemetery from Wellington's campaign and some of the old bastions and ancient cannons of the city's defences. Up at the top is the half-ruined **Castillo de Santa Cruz de la Mota** (16th-century), topped with an ungainly kitsch statue of Christ (from the Franco era) called the **Sagrado Corazón**, which keeps an eye on the holidaymakers on La Concha beach below.

The centre of the Parte Vieja is the arcaded **Plaza de la Constitución**, which once did double duty as the local bullring. Within a few blocks of this local centre of Basque nationalism stand San Sebastián's three best monuments. From Calle Mayor, the distant neo-Gothic spires of the **Catedral del Buen Pastor** outstare the hyper-ornate façade of **Santa María del Coro** (18th century) on Vía Coro. At the other end of the Calle 31 de Agosto, the only street left standing after the great fire of 1813, is the solid Gothic church of **San Vicente** (16th century), the oldest building in the city. Nearby, the old Dominican monastery of San Telmo is now the fascinating **Museum of San Telmo**, currently being expanded and modernized. The monastery's church is adorned with golden murals by the Catalan artist Josep Sert (1930) on the history of the Basque people. Old Basque discoidal tombstones are lined up in the cloister; upstairs, the museum contains three El Grecos, two bear skeletons, Basque lucky charms and amulets, Basque sports paraphernalia, the interior of a Basque cottage and more.

Museum of San Telmo
t 94 348 15 80 to check if reopened

08
The Basque Lands (Euskadi) | San Sebastián (Donostia)

Isla de Santa Clara
ferry from El Muelle, the dock behind the Ayuntamiento; summer 10–8.30

The main attraction of the Parte Vieja is its countless bars, where the evening crowds hasten to devour seafood tapas and Basque goodies. A fun excursion is to gather up some of that good food and row it out to **Isla de Santa Clara** for a picnic.

Around San Sebastián

Museo Chillida Leku
take the N1 from San Sebastián and turn off onto the GI 2132 to Hernani, or get the half-hourly G2 bus from C/ Okendo; t 94 333 60 06, www.museo chillidaleku.com; open July–Aug Mon–Sat 10.30–8, Sun 10.30–3; Sept–June Wed–Mon 10.30–3; adm

About 8km from town, the open-air **Museo Chillida Leku** (Chillida Museum) is devoted to the works of San Sebastián's favourite son. Creator of a slew of monumental sculptures adorning boulevards and museums across the world, Eduardo Chillida (1924–2002) was the international standard-bearer of the Escuela Vasca (Basque School) founded by Jorge de Oteiza, who exhorted Basque artists to define an aesthetic rooted in the Basque character. Chillida's use of iron, granite and wood follows the same tradition as the Basque ironworkers and shipwrights, and their predecessors who worked in stone, leaving dolmens and cromlechs in the mountains and finely worked tools in the caves. Chillida restored this 16th-century farmhouse with its old oak beams, lit by a sheet of natural light which pours in from a glass wall and illuminates works spanning half a century. The lawns, shaded by huge old trees, are dotted with more than 40 massive pieces, sculpted mostly from iron and granite, yet light and graceful.

Tourist Information in San Sebastián

(i) **San Sebastián >**
C/ Reina Regente 3, t 94 348 11 66, www.donostia.org

The tourist office sells the **San Sebastián Card**, which offers free public transport plus discounts on museums and attractions, and is valid for 3 days (€10).
Post office: C/ Urdaneta, behind the cathedral.

Shopping in San Sebastián

Along with the tourist shops in the Parte Vieja, there are a number of more original places that sell a range of items, from surf-punk paraphernalia to exquisite home-made chocolates. The Centro Romántico has a wide range of fashionable boutiques, from chains like Zara and Mango to chic individual establishments selling Spanish designers.
Trip, C/ 31 de Agosto 33, t 94 342 94 43. Small, intriguing shop selling everything from snazzy bags to scented candles.

Casa Ponsol, C/ Narrica 4. An institution in the world of Basque berets, established in 1832.
Barrebnetxe, Plaza de Gipúzkoa 9, t 94 342 44 82. Fabulous Basque pastries, cakes and chocolates, and wonderful bread. Café area.
Hontza, C/ Okendo 4. If you're inspired by all the seafood you've been eating, this place sells books on Basque cooking in English.
Saski-naski, Calbetón C/ Fermín 45, t 94 342 28 91. Delightful boutique run by kindly staff specializing in hand-made Basque gifts, including ceramics, sculpture, linens and jewellery.

Where to Stay in San Sebastián

San Sebastián ✉ 20000
San Sebastián is not the place to look for bargains – many of the cheaper *hostales* and *fondas* are packed full of university students most of the year. In general, the farther back you are from the sea,

the less expensive the accommodation is likely to be.

Luxury–Very Expensive (€€€€€–€€€€)

*****María Cristina, C/ Okendo 1, t 94 343 76 00, www.westin.com (€€€€€). For a touch of *belle époque* elegance, this old *grande dame* is one of Spain's best hotels; it looks onto the Río Urumea's promenade.

****Hotel Londres y Inglaterra, C/ Zubieta 2 (on La Concha beach), t 94 344 07 70, www.abbalondreshotel.com (€€€€€–€€€€). The city's other most luxurious address, with splendid views, first-class service, as well as one of the city's best restaurants.

****Gudamendi Park, Plaza de Gudamendi, Barrio de Igueldo, t 94 321 40 00, www.hotelgudamendi.com. Quiet, comfortable and attractive, located halfway up Monte Igueldo: the best rooms have sea views.

Expensive (€€€)

**Pensión Gran Bahía, C/ Embeltrán 16, 1°, t 94 342 02 16, www.paisvasco.com/granbahia. Run by delightful, chatty Teresa, this elegant *hostal* is cosy and comfortable.

**La Galería, C/ Infanta Cristina 1–3, t 94 321 60 77, www.hotellagaleria.com. A couple of minutes from Playa Ondarreta on a lovely quiet street, this French-inspired *palacete* has rooms full of antiques, art and individuality.

Moderate (€€)

The best you'll find will be at the higher end of the moderate range, and there are a fair number both in the Parte Vieja and in the centre.

**Pensión Bikain, C/ Triunfo 8, t 94 345 43 33, www.pensionbikain.com. Top-notch facilities at a very good price, close to the beach and Parte Vieja, as well as spotless rooms, parking facilities and a helpful owner.

**Pensión Alameda, Alameda del Boulevard 16, t 94 342 64 49, www.pensionalameda.com. The charming new owners of this central *pensión* have kitted out the newly decorated rooms with all kinds of thoughtful extras including hairdryers, free wifi Internet access and mineral water.

**Pension Lorea, Alameda del Boulevard, 16, www.pensionlorea.com.

An intimate choice (only six doubles and one single) in a centrally located part of town. Rooms are decorated in white and pink traditional style.

*Pensión Amalur, C/ 31 de Agosto 44, t 94 342 96 54. Covered in flowers, this is a charming little spot in the Casco Viejo, with simple rooms, some with pretty balconies. A little noisy, but a good choice all the same.

*Pensión Urgull, C/ Esterlines 10, t 94 343 00 47. Delightful choice; just five immaculate rooms with two shared bathrooms. The charming owners are kind, friendly and more than happy to help with local information.

Pension Bellas Artes, C/ Urbieta, 64, 1°, t 94 347 49 05, www.pension-bellasartes.com. Leire and her mother Carmen could well win the competition for most friendly hosts, more than compensating for the smallish rooms. If you are sensitive to street noise, ask for an interior-facing room.

Pensión Anne, Esterlines 15, 2nd floor, t 94 342 14 38, www.pensionanne.com. Also centrally located, with clean rooms. There is a bathroom for every two rooms.

Inexpensive (€)

**Pensión San Lorenzo, C/ San Lorenzo 2, t 94 342 55 16/ t 62 734 32 08. A very popular choice, with brightly decorated rooms (which come with fridge and kettle) and friendly owners.

Eating Out in San Sebastián

As eating is the local obsession, it's not surprising the city claims several of Spain's most renowned, award-winning restaurants – cathedrals of Basque cuisine. Be sure to book weeks if not months in advance. For cheaper dining, follow the crowds through the tapas bars of the Parte Vieja.

Expensive (€€€)

Arzak, Alcade Elosgui 273, t 94 327 84 65, www.arzak.com. Often described as the finest restaurant in Spain; offers a constantly changing menu of delights. Chef Juan Mari Arzak is often at hand to make suggestions, as dishes change with the seasons and availability. Book weeks in advance.

Closed Sun eve, Mon; Jan–June also closed Tues; closed 2 weeks in June and 3 weeks in Nov.

Akelarre, Paseo Padre Orkolaga 56 (in the Barrio de Igueldo), t 94 331 12 09, *www.akelarre.net.* This restaurant is celebrated for its mixture of some of the most remarkably innovative New Basque cuisine with a delicious array of traditional local dishes – look out for the wonderfully prepared langoustines. Beautiful mountainside setting with views over the sea to boot. *Closed Sun eve and Mon, Tues Jan–June, Feb and first fortnight in Oct.*

Casa Nicolasa, C/ Aldamar 4, t 94 342 17 62. Another culinary shrine, founded in 1912. Specializes in classic Basque cookery and offers a large choice of dishes. *Menú del día €46. Closed Sun, Mon, 3 weeks Feb.*

Urepel, Paseo de Salamanca 3, t 94 342 40 40. This is another of San Sebastián's most eminent restaurants, serving classic Basque cuisine with original touches. The house speciality is the *sopa de pescados* (fish soup). *Closed Sun, Tues, Christmas, Easter and 3 wks in July.*

Rekondo, Paseo de Igueldo 57, t 94 321 29 07, *www.rekondo.com.* A superb choice, this classic *mesón*-style restaurant specializes in grilled fish and meat and has a huge wine cellar. Come here for elegant dining at around €50. *Closed Tues eve and Wed.*

Martín Berasategui, C/ Loidi Kalea 4, Lasarte (8km from San Sebastián), t 94 336 64 71. Although some may murmur that Berasategui has spread himself a little too thin with his countless enterprises in the Basque lands, his own restaurant remains a temple to New Basque cuisine at its finest. The *menú de degustación* is a hefty €142, but this is a dining experience you won't forget. *Closed Sun eve, Mon and Tues, plus mid-Dec–mid-Jan.*

Moderate (€€)

Casa Urola, C/ Fermín Calbetón 20, t 94 342 34 24, *www.restauranteurola. com.* This is a wonderful old favourite, a good, refined restaurant with a decently priced *menú del día*, and a less expensive bar area. The wine list is particularly good. *Closed Wed, and Sun eve.*

Bodegón Alejandro, C/ Fermín Calbetón 4, t 94 342 71 58, *www. bodegonalejandro.com.* This is where famed chef Martín Berasategui started out, and offers excellent traditional cuisine with innovative touches. The speciality is a succulent *marmita de bonita* (tuna stew), and there's a lunchtime deal at €13.

Inexpensive (€)

Portaletas, C/ Puerto 8, t 94 342 42 72. Fronted by a hugely popular tapas bar, the restaurant has an excellent menu. The *pastel de verduras* is delicious (and vegetarian).

Tapas/*Pintxos*

The Parte Vieja is proud of its reputation for having more bars per square metre than anywhere else in the world. Perhaps the gastronomic heart of the Parte Vieja is Calle Mayor and C/ 31 de Agosta.

Clery, Plaza de la Trinidad 1, t 94 342 34 01. One of San Sebastián's most-loved restaurants, with an attractive bar and terrace where you can sample tasty *pintxos* like little fried balls of cod with a green pepper sauce.

La Cepa, C/ 31 de Agosto 7–9, t 94 342 63 94. With a ceiling dripping with cured hams and a liberal splashing of taurine memorabilia, this is one of the most down-to-earth of the local bars.

Ormazábel, C/ 31 de Agosto 22, t 94 342 99 07. A family-run *bodega* with an excellent selection of local wines to accompany the unusual spinach *croquetas*, or *chipirones* (baby squid), which have been everyone's favourite for over 40 years. *Closed Wed.*

Gaztelu, C/ 31 de Agosto, t 94 342 14 11. Next to the Ormazábel, this friendly, neighbourhood bar where everyone seems to know everyone else has got a big reputation for its *cazuela de caracoles* (snail stew). *Closed Wed.*

Bideluze, Plaza de Guipúzcoa, 14, t 94 342 28 80. Given its key location and reputation, you'll be hard pushed to find a table. But the long wait will all be worth it when you try '*El Tigre*' ('The Tiger'), a *pintxo* based on mussels, green pepper and onion.

La Cuchara de San Telmo, Calle 31 Agosto 28, t 94 342 08 40. You'll have to squeeze your way inside to sample

 La Cuchara de San Telmo >>

some of the immaculately presented *pintxos* but there is a fantastic terrace used in the summer.

Casa Gandarias, Calle 31 de Agosto, 25, **t** 94 342 81 06. Another classic *pintxos* bar where you have to try a '*Solo Mio*', a tiny piece of immaculate beef.

Txapetxa, C/ Pescadería 5, **t** 94 342 22 27. This bar has become a 'temple of anchovies', and you can get them prepared in every imaginable way.

Casa Alcade, Calle Mayor 19, **t** 94 342 62 16. Lined with bullfighting memorabilia and hanging hams, this bar has remained virtually unchanged for 80 years. Wafer-thin slices of cured ham make a fine accompaniment to the excellent Riojas on offer.

Nightlife in San Sebastián

For listings, check out the back pages of *El Diario Vasco*.

Be Bop, Paseo de Salamanca 5, **t** 94 342 98 69. One of several bars in the area with live music.

La Kabutzia, Paseo de la Concha, *www.lakabutzia.com*. The sleek Real Club Náutico is the setting for this crowd-pleasing disco, which offers everything from salsa to pop.

Altxerri Bar & Jazz, Reina Regente 2, **t** 94 342 16 93. Located between the Kursaal and the old town, this is one of the emblematic haunts for jazz-lovers in the whole Basque country.

Inland from San Sebastián

Tolosa and Oñati

Guipúzcoa, San Sebastián's province, is the most densely populated rural part of the Basque country, where plenty of fat villages bear unpronounceable, unimaginable names. To see them, you'll have to invest a lot of time on some lovely, lazy back roads, and stay off the motorways from San Sebastián to Tolosa and to Pamplona. Despair will probably set in at a corner with signs pointing you to Aizarnazabal, Azpeitia, Azkoitia, Azkarate, or Araiz-Matximenta; you'll think the Basques are doing this just for you.

One of the first Basque towns to join the Industrial Revolution, **Tolosa** (named after Toulouse) is still fairly industrial and the largest town on the Oria river, thriving on paper mills (which explain the aroma). Tolosa also makes wicker *chisteras* for *pelota*, and sweets, especially *tejas* (almond biscuits) and *delicias*. You can learn all about them in the **Museo de Confitería** at C/ Lechuga 3, next to the Plaza del Ayuntamiento, run by Tolosa's *pastelería* of renown, Gorrottxategui, in the Plaza Zarra. Dining out is the main reason to stop, though, as the town itself is fairly drab.

Southwest of Tolosa on the N1, there's the pretty mountain village of **Segura**, its main street lined with the palaces of a locally powerful family, the Guevaras, and other nobles. Segura lay on the original pilgrim route. Up in the mountains beyond Zegama, bits of the original Roman road to Vitoria are still visible, but today there's no road at all, and this valley has become something of a dead end.

Before Segura, at Beasain, the main road branches westwards for **Oñati (Onate)**, beautifully set in a rich, rolling valley, dominated in the distance by the bluish pointed peaks of Mount Amboto and Udalaitz. It served as the capital of the pretender Don Carlos in the

Carlist Wars and was one of the few towns in Euskadi to be ruled by a noble; it retained a degree of independence until 1845. For many years the town had the only Basque **university**, founded in 1540; Oñati's landmark, it has a beautiful Plateresque façade and a *mudéjar*-style arcaded courtyard. The parish church of **San Miguel** (15th-century) contains the alabaster tomb of the university's founder, Bishop Zuázola de Ávila, attributed to Diego de Siloé, and an attractive Plateresque cloister. Other noteworthy buildings include the Baroque rococo-style **Ayuntamiento** and the Franciscan **Convento de Bidaurreta**. Oñati is known also for its well-preserved Renaissance palaces, one of which saw the birth in 1511 of the *conquistador* Lope de Aguirre, perhaps best known these days as the deranged 'Wrath of God' in the film by Werner Herzog.

University
Universidad Sancti Spiritus, open Mon–Thurs 9–5, Fri 9–2; adm, includes guided visit; to book, call t 94 378 34 53

Sanctuary of Aránzazu
open daily 8.30–8

A scenic road up from Oñati climbs 9km to the **Sanctuary of Aránzazu**, usually filled with tour buses and pilgrims. Here, in 1469, a shepherd found an icon of the Virgin by a thorn bush and a cow bell, and the Virgin of Aránzazu became the patron saint of Guipúzcoa. The church that houses the icon has been rebuilt innumerable times since, lastly in 1950. This curious temple of Basque modernism is striking in its lonely and rugged setting, its two towers covered with a distinctive skin of pyramidal concrete nubs, creating a waffle-iron effect – a reference to an eccentric Renaissance conceit popular in Spain, seen in many buildings from Salamanca to Naples. Some of the best-known Basque artists contributed to the church: there are sculptures on the façade by Jorge Oteiza, the main doors are by Eduardo Chillida and the crypt holds paintings by Nestor Basterretxea.

Arrasate (Mondragón) and Bergara

The only town of any size in the region has two names: Basques call it **Arrasate**, Spaniards **Mondragón**. Though a nondescript industrial town these days, Arrasate used to be a spa – a Spanish prime minister, Antonio Cánovas del Castillo, was murdered here by an anarchist in 1897 while taking a cure. Arrasate still has some of its medieval walls and gates, along with the 14th-century Gothic church of San Juan. It's under the name of Mondragón that the town has made its mark, synonymous with one of the most successful, innovative cooperative ventures in the world, founded in the early 1960s, now the eighth largest firm in Spain, and employing a fifth of all workers in Euskadi.

Farther north, as a contrast, the pretty village of **Bergara** has palaces, churches and other monuments from the 16th and 17th centuries; note the Palacio Arrese, with its cut-out corner window in the best Spanish Renaissance style. Were it not for the University of Bergara, in fact, you would be reading this by candlelight: here, in 1783, at the University of Bergara, the first secular university in

Spain, the Elhuyar brothers from the French Basque country isolated tungsten, the element used in the filaments of light bulbs. East of Bergara, near the village of **Zumárraga** is the unusual 15th-century fortress church of Santa María, popularly known as La Antigua. The hewn-oak interior is rustic and spartan, with carved geometric patterns running along the balustrades and beams.

Loyola: St Ignatius' Home Town

From Zumárraga the GI631 heads north, passing through Azkoitia before reaching the ancient village of **Azpeitia** and the nearby hamlet of **Loyola** (**Loiola**), birthplace in 1491 of Ignatiusa, and now home of the **Santuario de Loyola** (Sanctuary of St Ignatius). Ignatius, or Íñigo López de Loyola, was born here in 1491, the last of 13 children of a noble family, who became the founder of those intellectual stormtroopers of Christ, the Jesuits. The actual birth house, built by the saint's grandfather after a four-year exile among the Moors, is a fortress-like *mudéjar* structure, redesigned inside as a museum with solemn chapels and over-the-top gilded ceilings. Next to it stands the **basilica**, one of the outstanding Baroque works in all Spain. Carlo Fontana, a student of Bernini who had worked on many of the great Baroque building projects in Rome, was the main architect, and the costs were borne by a Habsburg queen of Austria; her family's coat of arms in stone hangs over the main door. Begun in 1689, this circular temple with its 211ft-high dome took almost 50 years to complete. To give an Italian building the proper Spanish touch, the ornate rotunda is flanked by two plain, broad wings of monastery buildings, making a façade almost 500ft wide – creating the sharp contrast of vast, austere surfaces and patches of exuberant decoration that marks so many of the best Spanish buildings. At the entrance, a monumental stairway guarded by stylized lions leads up to a porch under three arches; in it are five niches with statues of early Jesuit heroes, including St Francis Xavier, another Basque who met martyrdom, proselytizing the Japanese. Nothing on the exterior, however, prepares you for the overwrought stone carving that covers every part of the dome inside, designed by a group of masters that included Joaquín de Churriguera, one of the three brothers whose taste for ornament gave Spanish architecture the word *churrigueresque*. As in most Jesuit monuments, no expense was spared, from the fine Carrara marble frieze around the rotunda to the elaborate pavement in coloured stone. Over the main altar, a life-size statue of St Ignatius is covered with silver sent by the Basques of Caracas, Venezuela.

On the way back east to Tolosa, the twisting GI2634 passes through **Régil**, a pretty mountain town with beautiful views from the Col de Régil, the 'Balcón de Guipúzcoa'.

Santuario de Loyola
t 94 302 50 00; open daily 10–1 and 3–7; adm free, audioguide €3

08 The Basque Lands (Euskadi) | Inland from San Sebastián

(i) Oñati >>
Foru Enparatza 11,
t 94 378 34 53,
www.oinati.org

(i) Tolosa >
Santa Maria Plaza 1,
t 94 369 74 13,
www.tolosaldea.net

Where to Stay and Eat Inland from San Sebastián

Tolosa ✉ 20400

*Oria and Oria 2, C/ Oria 2, t 94 365 46 88, www.hoteloria.com (€€). Central, comfortable hotel with modern main building and annexe in a pretty 19th–20th-century villa.

Hs Oyarbide, Plaza Gorriti 1, t 94 367 00 17 (€). Functional rooms.

Casa Julián, Santa Klara Kalea 6, t 94 367 14 17 (€€€). Tolosa's oldest restaurant, still one of the best, specializing in grilled steaks, with a good list of Rioja wines. *Closed Mon–Thurs eves.*

Frontón, Paseo San Franciso 4, t 94 365 29 41 (€€). Longstanding classic from the 1930s with an Art Deco interior and New Basque cuisine. Fantastic lunch menu. *Closed Sun eve, Mon.*

Nicolás, Zumalacárregui 6, t 94 365 47 59 (€€). Does delicious things with fresh and dried cod, as well as charcoal-grilled steaks. The house speciality is succulent grilled meat (*chuletón*). *Closed Sun and Aug.*

Sausta, Paseo Belate Ibiltokia 7, t 94 365 54 53 (€€). The chef here has trained with some of the region's most formidable chefs, and for some of the most innovative New Basque cuisine at very decent prices, this is a must. Try the *mero a la plancha sobre salsa de marisco* (sea bass with shellfish sauce). *Closed Sun eve and Mon, plus last 2 weeks Feb and first 2 weeks Aug.*

Oñati ✉ 20400

**Etxe Aundi, Torre Auzo 10, t 94 378 19 56, www.exteaundi.com (€€€). Traditional, stone-built hotel with a fine local restaurant.

Hospedería de Aránzazu, t 94 378 13 13, ostatua@arantzazu.org (€). A large place for pilgrims at the Sanctuary of Aránzazu; simple, clean doubles with bath.

Mertxe Esnaola Zubeldia, Garagaltza Auzoa 19, t 94 378 08 24 (€). Located 2km from Oñati and 9km from the sanctuary of Aránzazu (*see p.148*), this newly built house looks older than it is, as it has been built in the traditional stone and wood combination of the area. The set-up is cosy with six double rooms and two living areas with chimney and TV, as well as parking space and a garden.

Iturritxo, Atzeko Kalea 32, t 94 371 60 78 (€). A well-loved local establishment; the secret is superb regional cooking and reasonable prices.

Azpeitia ✉ 20730

**Loiola, C/ Loiolaka Inazio 47, t 94 315 16 16, www.hotelloiala.com (€€). Crisp, modern hotel with a garden.

Larrañaga, Elosiaga 392, t 94 381 11 80, www.hotel-larranaga.com (€). For heaped plates of great home cooking, follow the locals to this haunt.

Juantxo, C/ Loiola Inazio Hiribidea 3, t 94 381 43 15 (€€€–€€). Welcoming, old-fashioned restored 18th-century country house with a reputation for fine traditional cuisine. Set meals for €15. Also offers rooms (€€). *Closed Sun, eves from Mon–Thurs, plus Aug.*

Along the Coast: San Sebastián to Bilbao

San Sebastián to Zumaia

West of San Sebastián, the coastal cliffs keep all roads inland as far as **Orio**, a venerable fishing village that looks like an industrial town, at the mouth of the Río Orio, one of the most polluted rivers in Spain. Although the beach by Orio's very popular camp ground is clean enough, rough seas can bring out the no-swimming flags. If

20 km
10 miles

Bay of Biscay

San Juan de
Gaztelugatxa
Isla de Izaro
Río de Gernika
Playa de Laga
Lemoiz
Bakio
Playa de Laida
Plentzia
Bermeo
Costa
Vasca
Santurtzi
Algorta
Getxo
Butrón
Mundaka
Elantxobe
Ispaster
Lekeitio
Playa de Cerraspio
Mungia
Forua
Cueva de
Santimamiñe
Portugalete
Saturrarán
SAN SEBASTIÁN
Cabo
Higuer
BILBAO
(BILBO)
Gernika
Ondárroa
Mutriku
(DONOSTIA)
Pasajes
Jaizkibel
Hondarribia
Basauri
V i z c a y a
Zumaia
Getaria
Monte Igueldo
A8
Zarautz
Irún
Errenteria
Markina
Deba
Orio
San Marcial
Bolívar
Río Oka
Oikia
Oyarzun
Cueva de
Ekain
Hernani
Elgoibar
N634
A8
Bérriz
Ermua
Azpeitia
Río Urola
Río Oria
Río Urumea
Durango
Eibar
Azkoitia
GI634
Loyola
Régil
Elorrio
EUSKADI
Bergara
N621
Tolosa

you're planning a picnic, drive up to the lush hilltop Parque de
Pagoeta, signposted along the N634.

These same waves and a mile and a half of sand draw surfers to
nearby **Zarautz**. Whaling and shipbuilding in the Middle Ages put
Zarautz on the map, while more summering royalty – this time
Belgium's King Baudouin and Queen Fabiola – inaugurated its
international reputation as a resort. Now the second biggest resort
in Euskadi after San Sebastían, Zarautz is especially popular among
well-to-do Basque nationalists – hence summer courses in Basque
language and folklore events, to go with the golf course, riding
stables, and good food (with some harder-to-swallow prices).
In the historic centre of Zarautz, look for its trio of tower houses,
especially the **Torre Luzea** in Calle Mayor and the one incorporated
into the 16th-century **Palacio de Narros**. The most important
church, **Santa María la Real**, has a half-Plateresque, half-
Renaissance *retablo*; the campanile was added atop yet another
medieval tower house in the 18th century.

Getaria (Guetaria)

⭐ Getaria

Zarautz's shipbuilders built the *Vitoria*, the first ship to circum-
navigate the globe, while the next fishing town to the east,
Getaria, produced the man who captained it, Juan Sebastián
Elcano: approaching from the east, a massive stone monument in
his honour will be your introduction to this petite and utterly
charming resort.

From the coastal road, you wouldn't think there was much to
Getaria at all. Only pass through the old gate next to the monument, and you will find one of the loveliest villages of Euskadi,
hugging the steep slope down to the harbour. Whenever the
Getarianos go to Mass in the church of **San Salvador**, in the centre
of the old town, they step on Elcano's grave, located just inside the
door. He was lost in the Pacific in 1526, so there probably isn't much

The First Man to Sail Around the World

In the Age of Discovery, no Spanish or Portuguese captain worth his salt would set out without a Basque pilot, the heirs of centuries of experience in whaling boats off Europe's westernmost shores – they may actually have found the American coast in the Middle Ages, but kept the knowledge a closely guarded secret. Basques were deeply involved in all four of Columbus' voyages, from building the ships to outfitting them and providing the crews.

Juan Sebastián Elcano, like many seamen in Getaria, started off as a deep-sea fisherman and smuggler to French ports, but he sought even greater adventures. He was in Seville in 1519, and got a job on an expedition backed by Charles V to send Portuguese navigator Ferdinand Magellan on what they hoped would be a quick western shortcut to the Indies by sailing southwest around America to the spice-laden Molucca Islands. Charles supplied five ships and 239 men, and in August they set out. As they wintered on the coast of Brazil there was a mutiny against continuing any further. By then Magellan and Elcano avidly hated one another, and most of the blame fell on Elcano, who was chained up and forced to do hard labour. One ship turned back before attempting the turbulent straits that took Magellan's name (October 1520). If already dismayed by the distances involved just crossing the Atlantic, Magellan must have been appalled at the extent of the Pacific. Even worse, by the time hs little fleet made it to the Philippines in 1521, a civil war had just broken out, which soon numbered Magellan among its dead. After several other Portuguese leaders fell victim to the intrigues of the war, Elcano took over the helm and sailed halfway around the world from the Moluccas to Seville in the only surviving ship, the *Vitoria*. He arrived in October 1522, the holds stuffed to the brim with spices, some 1,124 days after setting out (Elcano was surprised to realize he had lost a day somewhere according to the ship's log, the first inkling of an international date line).

In spite of his singular feat, Elcano was destined to remain forever in Magellan's shadow – except of course in the eyes of his fellow Basques. Besides the aforementioned monument, they erected a statue of Elcano just outside the gate of the old town, and stage a historical re-enactment of his homecoming every four years on 7th August. Below the monument lies Getaria's port, sheltered by a peninsula and an islet known for its shape as El Ratón, the mouse.

of him in there anyway. Once beyond Elcano's tomb, this church has other surprises. Founded in the 13th century, it was rebuilt in 1429 in a curious off-kilter fashion: the wooden floor lilts as if on rough seas, and the choir vaulting is just as tilted. No one knows why. Along the right wall, near the suspended ex voto of a ship, is something you rarely see in a church: a menorah. A double flight of stairs rises in the back, and the crypt and another chapel lie along the alley descending to the port. The crypt contains the remains of the ancestors of the same Queen Fabiola who made nearby Zarautz a resort. Getaria doesn't mind; although it has two small beaches of its own, it picked up all of Zarautz's fishing business. From the port, with its brightly painted boats and seafood restaurants, a path leads up to the top of Mouse Island, a pretty wooded natural area with flitting birds and fine views.

Museo Zuloaga
t 94 386 23 41, open mid-April–mid-Sept Wed–Sat 4–8; for visits rest of year call to arrange an appointment; adm

Zumaia

West of Getaria the N634 rises dramatically over the sea before descending to **Zumaia**, a pleasant town set at the mouth of the River Urola. A kilometre before Zumaia itself, keep an eye out for the town's chief attraction, the **Museo Zuloaga**, a cosy villa set in a small park of ancient trees, surrounded by a wall. This was the

Getting around from San Sebastián to Zumaia

The coast is served by frequent **buses** from San Sebastián. The narrow-gauge **Eusko Tren** stops 4 or 5 times a day at Zarautz, then Zumaia, Deba and Durango on the way to Bilbao.

---

home of the Basque painter Ignacio Zuloaga (1870–1945), and it holds not only a selection of his own works, but also the masterpieces he collected over the years: several El Grecos, Goyas, Moraleses, two saints by Zurbarán and an excellent collection of medieval statues and *retablos*. Adjacent, the little 12th-century church and cloister of **Santiago Etxea** was a stop for pilgrims taking the coastal route to Compostela. Below stretches the pine-rimmed beach named after the painter, **Playa Zuloaga**. There's more art in the middle of Zumaia, in the 15th-century church of **San Pedro**: two triptychs on either side of the altar, the one on the right Flemish, and a dark, Gothic St Christopher on the back wall. There's another beach to the west at **San Telmo**, a dramatic swath of sand under sheer red cliffs, known for the strength of its pounding surf.

The coastal scenery between Zumaia and **Deba** is considered the best in Euskadi, with cliffs arcing gracefully from a choppy ocean in great vertical bands of pink and golden sandstone. A good way to explore it is by walking the cliff-top path that links Zumaia with Mutriku and Deba, passing through green fields and tiny hamlets and affording magnificent views. **Mutriku** is a quiet village set back on a narrow inlet 3km from the quiet beach at **Saturrarán**. Deba, a favoured resort at the turn of last century, nowadays lies happily in the shadows of the other coastal centres. The local church, **Santa María la Real**, is of late Gothic construction and has a spectacular painted portal; less elaborate, but somewhat older, are the Palaeolithic scratchings in the nearby **Cueva de Ekain**.

Cueva de Ekain
t 94 312 29 45; accessible only to groups of max 6 people, by prior appointment, tours in Spanish

Where to Stay and Eat from San Sebastián to Zumaia

ⓘ **Zarautz >**
Nafarroa Kalea, t 94 383 09 90, www.turismo. zarautz.com

ⓘ **Getaria >>**
Parque Aldamar 2, t 94 314 09 57, www. paisvasco.com/getaria; open summer only

Zarautz ✉ 20800

★★★★**Karlos Arguiñano**, C/ Mendilauta 13, t 94 313 00 00, www.hotelka.com (€€€€). A lavish mock castle on the beach owned by the eponymous celebrity chef. Its restaurant (€€€) is one of the best along this stretch of coast, with sophisticated seafood dishes. *Closed Sun eve in Nov–Feb; Sun eve and Wed in Mar–Oct.*

Pensión Txiki-Polit, Musika Plaza s/n, t 94 383 53 57, www.txikipolit.com

(€€–€). A central option, in a modern building in the old town. Spacious rooms and a good restaurant (€).

Aiten-Etxe, C/ Elkano 3, t 94 383 18 25 (€€€). Fine, uncomplicated seafood dishes and magnificent views along Zarautz's main beach. *Closed Sun eve.*

Argoin-Txiki, Argoin Auzoa s/n, t 94 389 01 84 (€€–€). Friendly cider house that offers different variations of traditional home cooking.

Getaria ✉ 20808

★★**Pensión Guetariano**, C/ Herrerleta 3, t 94 314 05 67 (€€). In the cheerful green and yellow house at Getaria's main crossroads; a friendly place with magazines in the lounge.

08 The Basque Lands (Euskadi) | Along the Coast: San Sebastián to Bilbao

(i) **Zumaia >>**
Plaza Zuloaga,
t 94 314 33 96, www.
zumaiaturismo.com;
open summer only

**Pensión Iribar, C/ Aldamar 23, t 94 314 04 51 (€€–€). Four simple rooms in a great location on the quiet street leading down to the port. Has a good restaurant (€€).

Agote Aundia, Askizu, t 94 314 04 55, *www.agoteaundi.com* (€). Just 3km from Getaria, in the Askizu district, which is dotted with country houses, cattle farms and *txakoli* vineyards. Overlooking the sea, this country house offers a well-priced, intimate (six rooms, three bathrooms and a living room) stay. Home cooking.

Elkano, C/ Herrerieta 2, t 94 314 00 24 (€€€). This traditional *asador* serves superb fish and meat grilled over charcoal and is justly considered one of the finest restaurants in the the Basque Lands. *Closed Sun and Mon eves in Nov–May, plus first 2 weeks Feb and first 2 weeks Nov.*

Kaia, Gral. Arnao 10 (upstairs), t 94 314 05 00, *www.kaia-kaipe.com* (€€€). Spectacular Basque seafood, elegant surroundings, charming staff and

beautiful harbour views. The ground floor has a cheaper grill house (**Kai-Pe**), where you can dine outside on fresh seafood. *Closed first 2 weeks Mar, second 2 weeks Oct.*

Zumaia ✉ 20808
Some of the bars in the main square have inexpensive rooms, and cheaper food can be found on C/ Erribera.

***Zelai, C/ Itzurun, t 94 386 51 00, *www.talasozelai.com* (€€€). A modern thalassotherapy centre with comfortable rooms in an unbeatable location high up on the cliffs.

Agroturismo Jesuskoa, Barrio de Oikia, t 94 314 32 09, *rjesuskoa@terra.es* (€€–€). Six rooms in a restored farmhouse outside town; also has an apartment to rent.

Marina Berri, Puerto Deportivo, t 94 386 56 17, *www.marinaberri.com* (€€€–€€). Elegant restaurant, café-bar and *sidrería* in one, with splendid views. Excellent *menú del día* (€10). *Closed Mon–Thurs eves, and Jan.*

Ondarroa to Bilbao

Crossing into Vizcaya province at **Ondarroa** used to mean paying duty at the provincial customs house near the medieval stone Puente Vieja. The village is another pretty fishing port, one of Vizcaya's busiest and a popular spot on sunny weekends, but most people press on west to **Lekeitio** (**Lequeitio**), with its promenade flanked by restaurants and lovely beaches, **Isuntza** and **Carraspio**, further out. The well-preserved palaces in Lekeitio's old quarter stand as testimony to its Belle Epoque popularity, but the elegant old port still catches more fish than tourists. Don't miss the early 16th-century Gothic church of **Santa María** and its impressive Flemish *retablo mayor*.

Lekeitio is famous for its *antzareguna*, which takes place during the San Antolines festival in early September. This goose rodeo, however, is not an event for the faint-hearted – although now, thankfully, they use a dead goose. A rope is stretched over the port, held on either side by strong tug-of-war veterans. In the middle a goose, liberally smeared in grease, is suspended by its feet over the port. Competitors, not allowed to weigh more than 70kg, are rowed up under the goose. One by one they attempt to grab the slippery bird by the neck, and tuck its head under their armpit.

From Lekeitio a detour off the main road leads northwards to **Elantxobe**, huddled beneath sheer cliffs, an immaculate little fishing village that funnels down to a bijou harbour. Geographical challenges have helped Elantxobe retain its remote atmosphere – there's only one way in, down the serpentine main street – and traditional fishermen's houses adorn the narrow lanes that wind down to the little port. Above loom the tall cliffs of **Cabo Ogoña**.

Gernika (Guernica)

Guernica is without doubt the most powerful and driving symbol in the entire Basque political culture. For an American, it would be Pearl Harbor, the Alamo and Bunker Hill combined in a single, searing metaphor.
Robert Clark

Beautifully set in the Mundaka valley, the ancient, sacred city of the Basques is mostly rebuilt now, and the majority of the inhabitants are too young to remember the horror that occurred one market day in 1937, when some 1,645 people were killed in a concentrated three-hour aerial bombardment by state-of-the-art German aircraft (*see* box, below).

The **Tree of Gernika**, the seedling of an ancient oak by the 19th-century Basque parliament building (*Las Casas Juntas*), is the symbol of Basque democracy; under it the representatives of the Basque provinces met in assembly from the early Middle Ages on, and proclaimed the laws that governed them. After 1300, the kings of Castile would come to Gernika's oak to swear to uphold Basque *fueros* and ancient laws. When the tree died in 1860, it was immediately replanted with a sapling from one of its acorns; the stub of the original's 300-year-old trunk can be seen under a

---

Experiments in Saturation Bombing

Gernika in 1937 became the kind of symbol for its times that Sarajevo was for the 1990s, a civilized little place that a band of thugs had chosen to flatten. Almost as soon as it happened, the Nationalist propaganda machine began sending out stories that the Communists had really destroyed the town by placing bombs in the sewers. It may have been the only time in his life that Francisco Franco was actually embarrassed. Just how much responsibility the Generalísimo had for Gernika will probably never be known, but there is nothing in his long, shabby career that suggests he was capable of such a stunt – Franco could massacre prisoners and stuff prisons with priests and professors, but Gernika, and Durango, which preceded it, were evil on a Nazi scale.

Hitler had sent his 'Condor Legion' to Spain not only to give Franco a hand, but to test the new *Luftwaffe*'s theories of terror bombing, and his commanders coldly determined Gernika to be the site of lesson number two (on a market day too). Though the town had no military significance whatsoever, as a symbol of Basque nationhood it was the perfect spot for a bombing designed especially to destroy the enemy's morale – by breaking their hearts, perhaps. While Gernika had little effect on the Civil War – the isolated Basque pocket was bound to fall anyhow – the Nazis were pleased enough with the results and the notoriety they gained from them to make such bombing the centre of their strategy; after Gernika came Warsaw, Rotterdam and Coventry, among many others.

Picasso's famous great painting, resting safely in New York during the Franco years, did as much as the bombing itself to catch the world's attention when it was displayed the following year in the Republic's pavilion at the Paris World Fair. Since 1981 it has been proudly displayed in Madrid, perhaps the ultimate exorcism of the War and the General. The *Guernica* that seemed so mysterious and revolutionary in its time now seems quite familiar and eloquent to us, so much have our ways of seeing changed since that distant age. The black and white gives it the immediacy of a newspaper photo. Picasso's preliminary sketches show that the central figures in the painting, the fallen horse and rider, were in his mind from the beginning. We can see in them the image of Gernika's destroyers: the eternal bully on horseback, the *caudillo*, the conqueror. In a way, *Guernica* may have been Picasso's prophecy – with such an atrocity as this, the man on horseback may finally have gone too far.

Getting from Ondarroa to Bilbao

The coast is served by frequent Bizkaibus **buses** to Bilbao's Paseo del Arena. The narrow-gauge **Eusko Trenbideak** line runs to Bilbao from Bermeo, via Mundaka and Gernika (don't get off at Gernika-Lumo).

nearby pavilion. The young tree somehow survived the bombing, and serves as a potent symbol of freedom and hope, not only for the Basques but for everyone.

Gernika was rebuilt in the Franco era, though neither the planning nor the architecture win any prizes. However, the hilltop area near the Tree of Gernika survived the onslaught comparatively unscathed and the regal 18th-century Palacio Alegría, built on the remnants of a much older fortified mansion, now contains the **Museo Euskal Herria**, dedicated to the history of the Basque Country from prehistoric times. It's an engaging little museum, describing Basque language, customs and traditions. Behind it spreads the **Parque de los Pueblos de Europa**, a shady green expanse with lofty trees and a pretty wooden bridge. Cross it to find a pair of modern memorials: *Gure Aitaren Etxea* (*Our Father's House*), an eloquent contribution by Eduardo Chillida, dedicated to peace, and a piece by Henry Moore, *Large Figure in a Shelter*. Behind, another palace contains the information centre for the Urdaibai Biosphere Reserve (*see* below). Near the park entrance, there's a ceramic copy of Picasso's masterpiece; the Basques, who feel that they are the rightful owners, have been lobbying Madrid to send them the original to hang in the Guggenheim.

Down the hill, on the edge of the tiny pedestrianized old quarter, full of boutiques and cafés, you'll find Gernika's new **Museo de La Paz**, focusing on the 1937 bombing. The centrepiece is a moving audiovisual exhibit (in Spanish and English) recounted by a local woman musing on her life just before her home is reduced to rubble. A gallery contains documents, uniforms and photos, and there are several exhibits related to peace around the world.

Surrounding Gernika is the 220 sq km **Urdaibai Biosphere Reserve**, created in 1984 to prevent the destruction of habitats in the Ría de Mundaka. The reserve is hardly a pristine wilderness – besides Gernika it counts 18 towns within its boundaries – but the sympathetic interaction between inhabitants and their environment is an embodiment of that most elusive of eco-ideals: sustainable development. Farms and factories share Urdaibai with wetlands and lush oak forests; greenshank and bar-tailed godwit stalk the mud flats, while observers may get a glimpse of the nocturnal genet, an odd mixture of raccoon and tabby cat.

About 5km northeast of Gernika, the **Cueva de Santimamiñe** has Euskadi's best Upper Palaeolithic art: two rooms with engravings of bison, horses, arrows, a bear and a deer, and geometric designs; they are rather faint, as only some of the black paint of the outlines

Museo Euskal Herria
t 94 625 54 51; open Tues–Sat 10–2 and 4–7, Sun 10–3; adm

Parque de los Pueblos de Europa
open daily 10–7, until 9 in summer

Museo de La Paz
Foru Plaza 1, t 94 627 02 13; open Tues–Sat 10–2 and 4–7, Sun 10–2; call in advance for guided visits in English; adm

Urdaibai Biosphere Reserve
Parque de los Pueblos de Europa, t 94 625 71 25, www.urdaibai.org; open Mon–Thurs 9–1.30 and 3–5, Fri 9–2

Cueva de Santimamiñe
t 94 406 77 37; guided tours Mon–Fri 10 and 11.15am, 12.30, 4.30 and 6pm; note that due to the fragility of the art, only 15 people are allowed in at a time

has survived. It is said that these caves are also the home of the Beigorri, a huge, hairy red bull with a militant stare, the protector of the goddess Mari. A path leads from the cave entrance into the **Forest of Oma**, where local artist Agustín Ibarrola has fused art with nature by painting luminous multicoloured bands and symbols on the trees, to achieve an array of perspective tricks.

Along the Coast to Bilbao: the Castle of Butrón

 Mundaka

Just north of Gernika the Río Oka becomes a broad flat estuary (Ría de Gernika), snaking towards the Cantabrian Sea. Near the mouth lie the pretty beaches of **Laida** and **Laga**; there are others on the western shore at **Pedernales** and **Mundaka**, the latter famous among surfers for having the longest left-hand break in Europe. In Mundaka, enjoy wandering through labyrinthine alleys and soaking up the views from its charming waterfront promenade. In the mouth of the estuary the tiny island of **Izaro** used to be home to a band of hardy monks.

Museo del Pescador

open Tues–Sat 10–2 and 4–7, Sun 10–2.15

Continuing round the coast, **Bermeo** is Euskadi's largest fishing port, a colourful, working town that makes few concessions to tourism. The long history of Basque seafaring is celebrated in the **Museo del Pescador**, which relates stories of whaling expeditions from the Bay of Biscay to Newfoundland.

Further towards Bilbao lies **Bakio**, another *txakoli*-producing new town tucked into a little bay. Nearby, the hermitage-topped islet of **San Juan de Gaztelugatxa** is linked to the mainland by a bridge and offers magnificent views along the dark coastal cliffs.

Where to Stay and Eat from Ondarroa to Bilbao

(i) Lekeitio >
Independentzia Enparantza, t 94 684 40 17, www.learjai.com; open summer only

(i) Gernika >>
C/ Arte Kalea 8, t 94 625 58 92, www.gernika-lumo.net

Lekeitio ✉ 48280
★★★Zubieta, Portal de Atea, t 94 684 30 30, www.hotelzubieta.com (€€€). Charming hotel on the grounds of a castle, in the former gatehouse, with lovely rooms and lovely owners. Café-bar, too. *Closed mid-Nov–early Feb.*

★★★Emperatriz Zita, C/ Santa Elena Etorbidea s/n, t 94 684 26 55, www.aisiahoteles.com (€€€). A plush modern palace of a place, complete with a thalassotherapy centre, built over the ruins of the home of the last Austro-Hungarian empress.

Piñupe, Avda Abaroa 10, t 94 684 29 84 (€€–€). Simple rooms, but a really handy location, just five minutes from the beach.

Méson Arropain, Ctra Marquina, Ispaster, t 94 684 03 13 (€€€). 5km from Lekeitio, this friendly restaurant serves fish dishes smothered with salsas. *Closed Sun eve and Wed.*

Gernika ✉ 48300
Boliña, C/ Barrenkale 3, t 94 625 03 00, www.hotelbolina.net (€). In the heart of the pedestrian area, this offers simple rooms with or without bath and a good restaurant with a *menú de degustación* for €32.

Baserri Maitea, Ctra. BI 635 (near Forua, on the way to Mundaka), t 94 635 34 08 (€€€). A wonderful restaurant in a 300-year-old farmhouse with wooden beams; the fish is particularly good. Book in advance. *Closed Sun eve in May-Oct; Sun–Thurs eves Nov–April.*

Zallo Berri, C/ Juan Calzada 79, t 94 625 18 00, www.zallobarri.com (€€). A delightful restaurant serving excellent regional cuisine with

08 The Basque Lands (Euskadi) | Along the Coast: San Sebastián to Bilbao

ⓘ Mundaka >
Plaza Lehendari Aguirre, t 94 617 72 01, www.mundaka.org; open Tues–Sun

ⓘ Bermeo
C/ Lamera, t 94 617 91 54, www.bermeo.org

innovative touches (excellent value *menú del día* €20; *menú degustación* €40). *Closed eves Sun–Wed.*

Mundaka ✉ 48360

**Atalaya, Itxaropen Kalea 1, t 94 617 70 00, *www.hotel-atalalya-mundaka.com* (€€€). One of the loveliest hotels in the region, on the river in one of those glorious Basque buildings of a century ago, with glass galleries all around.

*Mundaka, Florentino Larrínaga 9, t 94 687 67 00, *www.hotelmundaka.com* (€€). More down-to-earth, but with bar and Internet facilities.

*El Puerto, Portu Kalea 1, t 94 687 67 25, *www.hotelelpuerto.com* (€€).

Pretty, whitewashed hotel with bright rooms overlooking the port.

Asador Zaldua, Sabino Arana 10, t 94 587 08 71 (€€). Serves a wonderful array of fresh fish and succulent steaks grilled to perfection. *Menú de degustación* €58. *Lunch only Sun–Thurs during Nov–June; closed all day Sun in July–Sept.*

Bakio ✉ 48130

Hotel Joshe Mari, C/ Bentalde 31, t 94 619 40 05, *www.bakio.com* (€€). This unusual little hotel has only a handful of rooms, each individually decorated with locally gathered antiques; the restaurant offers good food in a relaxing atmosphere.

Inland: San Sebastián to Bilbao

If you drive from San Sebastián to Bilbao along the coast, the narrow, twisting roads will take you nearly a day. The more common routes west are the A8 (also signposted, confusingly, as the E5/E70 and E80) motorway, with its exorbitant tolls, and the slower, parallel N634, both of which cut inland near Deba and follow some of the more somnolent landscapes of Euskadi.

If you avoid the tolls and follow the latter you'll get an object lesson in the life of the average Basque, passing through tidy, grey little industrial splotches like **Elgoibar** and **Eibar**, a typically peculiar Basque factory town stuffed in a narrow valley, with plenty of tall apartment blocks around Spain's biggest sewing machine plant.

Further south, on the BI2632, **Elorrio** is an attractive village of grand palaces and impressive little squares, adorned with a set of unique crucifixes from the 15–16th centuries. The façade of the **Ayuntamiento** bears a curious verse from Matthew 12: 36: 'I tell you, on the day of judgment men will render account for every careless word they utter.' From the centre it's a lovely walk out to the hermitage of **San Adrián de Argiñeta**, where you can see the 9th- and 10th-century tombs of Argiñeta, carved out of rock, some adorned with pinwheel-like stars or Latin inscriptions.

It's another 6km to the biggest town in the area, **Durango**, a name that conjures up cowboys and Westerns in the New World (besides the Durango in Colorado, there is another in Mexico, which in colonial times was capital of the province of 'Nueva Vizcaya': there must have been a lot of Basques about). The original has nothing to detain you long, though there is an attractive Baroque centre behind its **Portal de Santa Ana**, an ornate survival from the old walls. In the centre, note the brightly painted

Getting around Inland from San Sebastián to Bilbao

Durango and Elorrio are both served by **BizkaiBus** from Paseo del Arenal in Bilbao, and slow but scenic **EuskoTren** services between San Sebastián and Bilbao call at Durango.

Ayuntamiento, and the stone mosaic maze under the portico of **Santa María de Uribarri**. The most unusual single monument is the 19th-century **Kurutziaga Cross**, just outside the centre.

South of Durango, the Duranguesado massif juts abruptly out of rolling green hills, creating Vizcaya's most dramatic mountain scenery. Protected as the **Parque Natural Urkiola**, the range offers plenty of opportunities for sweaty assaults on the high peaks, or leisurely ambles through birch forest.

North of Durango, in the heartland of old Basque traditions, is the minute village and valley of **Bolívar**, where the family of the great Liberator of South America, Simón de Bolívar, originated (he was born in Venezuela in 1783). His Art Deco monument dwarfs the village square, and down the village's one lane, the site of his ancestral house has been fixed up as a **Museo Bolívar**. Near the old parish church of **Santo Tomás** you can see the 'cattle trial yards' and the huge stone weights hauled by oxen at festivals.

Markina (Marquina), further north, is nicknamed the 'University of Pelota'; its historic *frontón* has produced champions who have made their mark around the world. On the right bank of the Río Artibay, stands the uncanny, hexagonal church of **San Miguel de Arretxinaga**, built around an enormous altar constructed by the giant *jentillak* (or, according to some, fallen from heaven) that consists of three massive rocks propped against one another.

Museo Bolívar
t 94 616 41 14; open Tues–Fri 10–1, Sat and Sun 12–2; July and Aug also 5–7

08

The Basque Lands (Euskadi) | Inland: San Sebastián to Bilbao

Where to Stay and Eat Inland from San Sebastián to Bilbao

 Durango >
Askatasun Etorbidea 2, t 94 603 39 38, www. durango-udala.net

 Alto de Urkiola
Caserio Toki-Alai, t 94 681 41 55

Durango ✉ **48200**

★★★★ Gran Hotel Gran Durango, Gasteiz Bidea 2, t 94 621 75 80, *www. granhoteldurango.com* (€€€). 19th-century mansion converted into a hotel with gardens, pool, restaurant.

★★★ Hotel Kurutziaga, C/ Kurutziaga 52, t 94 620 08 64, *www.kurutziaga.com* (€€€). Central 18th-century mansion, transformed into a modern hotel with a decent restaurant.

Hotel O Camiño, C/ Olleria 8, t 94 621 60 36 (€€). Modern, basic, with a restaurant serving Galician food.

Txacoli Larrinagatxu, Larrinagatxu Auzoa 4, t 94 681 49 66 (€€€). There isn't much in workaday Durango, but this family-run restaurant offers delicious local dishes, including a fine €8 lunch menu.

Pedro Juan, C/ San Antonio 1, in Bérriz, t 94 682 62 46 (€€). In a lovely stone house, fine regional dishes and fabulous home-made desserts.

Markina ✉ **48200**

★★ Vega, Abesúa 2, t 94 686 06 15 (€). Central place, with large, airy rooms overlooking the main *plaza*.

Niko, Abesúa 2, t 94 616 75 28, *www. niko-jatexte.restaurantesok.com* (€). Good cooking with a bargain *menú* (downstairs from the Vega).

Bilbao (Bilbo)

Tucked in the lush clefts and folds of Euskadi's coastal mountains, and stretched along the Nervión, once a notorious industrial by-product resembling chocolate milk and now clean enough to support a few fish as it discharges its last effluents into the flushing tide, you'll find Bilbao. The name is Bilbo in Basque, but its inhabitants lovingly call it the *botxo*, the Basque for hole, or orifice.

The orifice was originally a scattering of fishing hamlets, huddled on the left bank of a deep *ría* where the hills offered some protection from the Normans and other pirates. In 1300, when the coast was clear of such dangers, the lord of Vizcaya, Diego López de Haro, founded a new town on the right bank of the Ría de Bilbao. It quickly developed into the Basques' leading port, its main link to northern Europe, exporting Castile's wool to Flanders and the swords Shakespeare called 'bilbos'. In 1511 the merchants formed the Consulado de Bilbao to govern their affairs, an institution that survived and thrived until 1829.

The 19th century had other treats in store: the indignity of a French sacking in 1808 and sieges by the Carlists in both of their wars; Bilbao was the 'martyr city' of the Liberal cause. But this century also made Bilbao into a city. Blessed with its tremendous iron mines, forests, cheap hydraulic power and excellent port, Bilbao got a double dose of the Industrial Revolution. Steel mills, shipbuilding and other industries sprang up, quickly followed by banks and insurance companies and all the other accoutrements of capitalism to finance them. Workers from across the country poured into the tenements, and smoke clogged the air. It was Spain's Pittsburgh, and just as full of worker misery and exploitation. Franco punished it for its support of the Republicans, then in the 1960s whipped it forward as the industrial centre of Spain.

Of late, the rusting machinery has been removed and the once-seedy dock area gentrified. Meanwhile Greater Bilbao/Bilbo/*botxo*, with its population of over a million, the fourth city of Spain and its greatest port, not to mention the sister city of Boise, Idaho, is not twiddling its thumbs awaiting obsolescence. Thanks to banking, insurance and such less obviously dirty business the economy is doing pretty well, and the city has ambitiously redeveloped and reclaimed vast areas of the centre formerly devoted to industry. The hugely popular Guggenheim Museum, which opened in October 1997, has by itself significantly boosted the city's economy, attracting almost a million and a half visitors in its first year. Other new projects include cleaning up the Nervíon, a concert hall and convention centre (completed in 1998), and a library, park, hotel, offices and residential buildings all to be built on the site of the old shipyards. The metro, with sleek modern stations designed by Sir

Getting to and from Bilbao

By Air

Bilbao's **Loui airport** lies 10km north of the city centre and is the busiest in northern Spain, with daily flights from London, Brussels, Frankfurt and Milan, and most airports in Spain (for information, t 94 486 96 63/64, *www.aena.es*). A **taxi** into Bilbao costs around €20–25. There is also an **airport bus** service (no. A-3247, t 90 222 22 65), which runs roughly every 30mins from 6am to midnight to the Plaza Moyúa (with a metro connection) before terminating at Termibus (for tram connections).

By Ferry

The P&O Portsmouth–Bilbao ferry operates twice weekly and arrives in the suburb of Santurtzi, 13km from the centre of town. There is an information and booking office (t 94 423 44 77) on C/ Cosme Echevarrieta 1, in the centre of town.

By Train

Bilbao has several train lines and about a dozen stations, although as a non-suburban commuter you have to be aware of only three of them.

The main **RENFE** station, **Estación de Abando** (t 90 224 02 02, *www.renfe.es* for information), on Plaza Circular, has connections to France, Madrid, Barcelona and Galicia. Next to Abando, at C/ Bailén 2, facing the river with a colourful tiled front, is the **Estación de Santander** (t 94 423 22 66, *www.feve.es*), also known as **La Concordia**, where scenic, narrow-gauge FEVE trains set off for Santander and Oviedo.

The pretty little **Estación de Atxuri**, at C/ Atxuri 6 in the Casco Viejo, is used by the Basque regional line, **EuskoTren**, t 90 254 32 10, *www.euskotren.es*, running slow but scenic services to San Sebastián by way of Durango, Zarautz and Zumaia. A separate line serves Gernika, Mundaka and Bermeo.

By Bus

All inter-city bus lines arrive and depart from **Termibus** (t 94 439 42 00, *www.termibus.es*) near San Mamés stadium. There are hourly services to San Sebastián, Vitoria and Santander, and several buses a day to Pamplona, Madrid, Barcelona, Galicia and Castilla-León. **BizkaiBus** (t 90 222 22 65, *www.bizkaia.net*) serves destinations within Vizcaya, including Durango, Gernika and the coastal villages, from a separate terminal on Paseo del Arenal, near the Casco Viejo.

Norman Foster, was completed in 1995. The airport got an elegant new terminal designed by Santiago Calatrava in 2000, and the port has been given a boost as part of a vast harbour expansion project which includes an excellent Maritime Museum (opened 2004). Bilbao is shaping up to be one of the cities of Europe's future.

The Casco Viejo

The Casco Viejo, the centre of the city from the 15th to the 19th century, is a small, snug region on the east bank of the Nervión; tucked out of the way across the Puente del Arenal from the bustling centre, it remains the city's heart. The bridge leaves you in **Plaza de Arriaga**, known familiarly as **El Arenal** from the sand flats that stood here long ago. Fittingly for a Basque city, its monuments are both musical: the opera house, or **Teatro Arriaga**, and a glorious Art Nouveau **pavilion** in steel and glass. Adjacent to the Arenal is arcaded, enclosed **Plaza Nueva**, now a bit down-at-heel, but in its day the symbol of Bilbao's growth and prosperity.

Philosopher Miguel de Unamuno was born on nearby Calle La Ronda, not far from the **Museo Vasco**. Located in an old Jesuit cloister, this offers for your perusal a scale-model of Vizcaya, a

Pavilion
concerts every Sunday afternoon

Museo Vasco
Plaza Miguel de Unamuno 4; open Tues–Sat 11–5, Sun 11–2; adm

AVENIDA DE MAURICE RAVEL

VÍA VIEJA DE LEZAMA

VÍA VIEJA DE LEZAMA

URIBARRI

PLAZA
DE LA SALVE

CASTAÑOS

AVENIDA DE MAURICE RAVEL

TRAVESÍA DE URIBARRI

MONTE ZARO

Funicular de
Artxanda

HUERTAS DE LA VILLA

CASTAÑOS

PUENTE DE LA SALVE

PLAZA DE
MORAZA

PASEO CAMPO DE VOLANTÍN

TÍBOLI

URIBARRI

ANSELMA DE SALCES

MATIKO

MUELLE DE MARZANA

MUELLE DE URIBITARTE

LOS HEROS

UNDI

C ECHEBARRIETA

ALAMEDA DE MAZARREDO

URIBITARTE

PUENTE DE ZUBIZURI

TÍBOLI

AVENIDA DE ZUMALAKARREGI

Parque
de Etxebarria

AVENIDA DE ZUMALAKARREGI

LOS HEROS

ERCILLA

HENAO

URIBITARTE

PÍO BAROJA

PLAZA
PÍO BAROJA

Ayuntamiento

PLAZA
ERNESTO
ERKOREKA

QUITANA

PLAZA
ENSANCHE

COLÓN DE LARREÁTEGUI

DIPUTACIÓN

ASTARLOA

PLAZA
SAN
VICENTE

San Vicente
Mártir

PUENTE DEL
AYUNTAMIENTO

SENDEJA

VÍA DE DON DIEGO LÓPEZ DE HARO

LEDESMA

ALAMEDA DE MAZARREDO

BERASTEGUI

Jardines
de Albia

PUENTE ERREINA ZABALETA

VILLARÍAS

RIPA

ESPERANZA

VIUDA DE EPALZA

ROZA

ALAMEDA DE URQUIJO

EUSKALDUNA

PLAZA
CIRCULAR

HURTADO DE AMEZAGA

NAVARRA

PUENTE DEL ARENAL

Paseo
del
Arenal

San Nicolás

LOS FUEROS

CAMINO IRALA-MARKINA

VIRGEN DE BEGOÑA

BEGOÑA

DE AMEZAGA

Estación de
Abando

Estación de
Santander

LA RIBERA

BIDEBARRIETA

PLAZA DE
ARRIAGA

Teatro
Arriaga

CORREO

PLAZA
NUEVA

To Basílica Nuestra
Señora de Begoña

AMADEO DEPRIT

DE GARCÍA SALAZAR

BAILÉN

SANTA MARÍA

JARDINES

VÍCTOR

SOMBRERERÍA

PLAZA DE
MIGUEL DE
UNAMUNO

PRIM

ITURRIBIDE

PRIM

ITURRIBIDE

SAN FRANCISCO

LAS CORTES

DOS DE MAYO

HERNANI

PUENTE DE
LA MERCED

PERRO

PELOTA

LOTERÍA BANCO DE ESPAÑA

CASCO VIEJO

Museo Vasco

SOLOKOETXE

SOLOKOETXE

SOLOKOETXE

LA CONCEPCIÓN

SAN FRANCISCO

PLAZA
CORAZÓN
DE MARÍA

Museo de
Reproducciones
Artísticas

LA RIBERA

PUENTE DE
LA RIBERA

PLAZA
SANTIAGO

JULIÁN ECHEVARRÍA

Catedral

ARTEKALE

CAMARÓN

SOMERA

LA RONDA

ZUMÁRRAGA

PLAZA
ZUMÁRRAGA

ZUMÁRRAGA

FIKA

ZABALBIDE

ZABALBIDE

SANTUTXU

LA CONCEPCIÓN

SAN FRANCISCO

Río de Nervión

MUELLE DE MARZANA

Mercado

PLAZA
SANTOS
JUANES

PUENTE DE
SAN ANTÓN

ATXURI

FIKA

FIKA

Estación de
Atxuri

PLAZA DE LA
ENCARNACIÓN

Diocesan
Museum of
Sacred Art

ATXURI

PLAZA DEL
CARMEN

N

Monte de Miribilla

250 metres
250 yards

Getting around Bilbao

Nearly all of Bilbao's attractions are within walking distance of each other in the centre; the efficient city bus line (**Bilbobus**), the metro and the shiny new tram will take you there if you're elsewhere. There is a card available, the **Creditrans**, which offers reduced fares (51 cents per ride, 85 cents for the airport bus) on the bus, tram and metro services. It can be bought at machines in metro stations, bus and tram stops, or at some tobacconists. Cards cost €5, €10 or €15, and can be topped up with any amount once purchased.

A new card is now also available, the **BilbaoCard**, which provides low fares on city transport as well as discounts to museums, shops, restaurants, leisure facilities and shows. Cards cost €6 (1 day), €10 (2 days) and €12 (3 days). Buy online at www2.bilbao.net/bilbaoturismo/ingles, at Bilbao tourist offices or Bilbao International Airport.

By Metro

The metro consists of two lines: a main line (L1) from Etxebarri to Plentzia, and a branch line (L2), which splits off at Sarriko to head up the left bank of the river to Setsao. The metro offers the easiest way to the beaches at Getxo and Plentzia; there are stations at the Casco Viejo, Abando (for long-distance trains), Plaza Moyúa (closest to the Guggenheim), Indautxu and San Mamés (for Termibus). A single ride costs €1.20–1.45 depending on the distance travelled. There is also a €3 ticket which offers unlimited metro travel for one day, or you can buy a Creditrans card (see above). Metro services run about every 2 minutes within the centre, and every 30 minutes to Plentzia.

For information call **t** 94 425 40 25, or visit the website www.metrobilbao.net.

By Tram

A new tram system, the **EuskoTran**, **t** 90 254 32 10, fills the last gap in inner Bilbao's public transport network. The line runs alongside the Nervión, connecting Estación Atxuri with San Mamés via Abando, the Guggenheim and Abandoibarra. Trams run every 10 minutes and you can buy tickets from machines at tram stops, or use the Creditrans card (see above). Date-stamp your ticket before boarding.

By Bus and Taxi

It is unlikely you will need the local **bus** service in this pocket-sized city with such an efficient metro. The local buses have red and white stripes and each stop has a route map.

To continue around the coast from Plentzia without your own transport, take a taxi to Mungia (€15–20) from where buses go to Bermeo. **Taxis** in Bilbao are white with a red stripe. A green light on the roof indicates they are free. For a **radio taxi**, call **t** 94 426 90 26, **t** 94 444 88 88, **t** 94 410 21 21, or **t** 94 480 09 09.

Tours

The tourist office offers two **walking tours**, one around the Casco Viejo (departures from the tourist information office at the Teatro Arriaga) and the other around the Ensanche (departures from the tourist office in front of the Guggenheim). Both last around 1½ hours and cost €3. For times and more information, call **t** 94 479 57 60, or email bit@ayto.bilbao.net.

Bilbao Paso a Paso, **t** 94 415 38 92, www.bilbaopasoapaso.com, organizes walking tours around the city, including the Casco Viejo, as well as guided visits of the Guggenheim, gastronomic tastings and special trips into the surrounding hills. Phone in advance for prices and timetable information.

---

reconstruction of the rooms of the consulate, the old merchants' organization, as well as tools, model ships and Basque gravestones. In the middle of the cloister, the ancient Idolo de Mikeldi is the museum's treasure – it looks like a primitive depiction of the cow that jumped over the moon.

Around the back of the museum, the **Catedral de Santiago** sends its graceful spire up over the centre of the Casco Viejo. Begun in the 1200s, most of this understated but elegant grey stone church is 14th–15th-century Gothic (though the façade was added in the 1880s). It matches its setting perfectly; everything to the south is the calm grey world of the 'Seven Streets' (*Siete Calles*), the core of

Bilbao when it was still a village. All the colour and animation is concentrated in the 1929 **Mercado de la Ribera** on the river front, the largest covered market in Spain.

Diocesan Museum of Sacred Art
9 Plaza de la Encarnación; open Tues–Sat 10.30–1.30 and 4–7, Sun 10.30–1.30; adm

Nearby, the **Diocesan Museum of Sacred Art**, occupying the former Convento de la Encarnación, displays over eight centuries' worth of religious art and finery; vestments of gold brocade and embroidery; hundreds of pieces of glittering silverware and a large collection of sculptures and paintings by Basque artists.

The Seven Streets being closely hemmed in by cliffs, Bilbao's centre spread over the bridge as the city grew, while garden suburbs were on the cliffs. Behind the large church of **San Nicolás**, off El Arenal, an elevator ascends to the upper town, from where it's a short walk to the Viscayans' holy shrine, the 16th-century **Basílica de Begoña** with its unusual (later) spire. Inside, there is a venerated statue of the Virgin and huge paintings by Luca Giordano, who was very popular in his day. There are fine views.

The Ensanche

Nobody in the 19th century had a sharper sense of urban design than the Spaniards, and wherever a town had money to do something big, the results were impressive. Like Barcelona, Bilbao in its industrial boom years had to face exponential population growth, and its mayors chose to plan for it instead of just letting things happen. The area across the river from Bilbao, the '**Anteiglesia de Abando**', was mostly farmland in the 1870s when the city annexed it. A trio of planners, Severino de Achúcarro, Pablo de Alzola and Ernest Hoffmeyer, got the job of laying out the streets for what came to be known as the **Ensanche**, or 'Extension', and they came up with a simple-looking but ingenious plan, with diagonal boulevards dividing up the broad loop of the river like orange segments.

The Ensanche begins across from El Arenal; just over the bridge from the old town, a statue of Bilbao's founder, Diego López de Haro, looks benignly over the massive banks and circling traffic in the **Plaza Circular**. This has become the business centre of the city, with the big grey skyscraper of the Banco Bilbao Vizcaya, built in the 1960s, to remind us who is the leading force in the city's destiny today. The RENFE station occupies one corner of the square; you'll have to walk around behind it on the river front to see one of the city's industrial age landmarks: the tiny **Bilbao–Santander rail station**, a charming Art Nouveau work with a wrought iron and tile façade, designed by Severino de Achúcarro.

Museo Taurino de Bilbao
open Mon–Fri 10.30–1 and 4–6; adm

South of the stations, Plaza Zabálburu marks the beginning of Bilbao's less salubrious quarters. On the cusp lie the **Vista Alegre** bull ring and the **Museo Taurino**, which holds mementos from 250 years of bullfighting history; the highlight is a magnificent embroidered cape by Goya, created for the Enlightenment-era matador Joaquín Rodríguez.

08 The Basque Lands (Euskadi) | Bilbao (Bilbo)

From Plaza Circular, the main boulevard of the Ensanche extends westwards: the **Gran Vía de Don Diego López de Haro**. A block to the north, the façade of the **Corte Inglés** department store is one vast high relief mural evoking the industry and history of Bilbao. The centre of the Ensanche scheme is **Plaza de Federico Moyúa**, better known as La Elíptica. The **Hotel Carlton** here, still one of the city's posh establishments, served as the seat of the Basque government under the Republic and during the Civil War. From La Elíptica, C/ Elcano takes you to the **Museo de Bellas Artes**.

Museo de Bellas Artes
Plaza del Museo 2; open Tues–Sat 10–8, Sun 10–2; adm; for guided tours (also in English) call t 94 439 61 37

It contains a worthy collection ranging from Flemish paintings (Metsys' *The Money Changers* is one of the best) to Spanish masters like Velázquez, El Greco, Zurbarán and Goya, to modern art by Picasso, Gauguin, Léger and the American Impressionist Mary Cassatt, and efforts by 19th- and 20th-century Basques. Overflow from the Guggenheim has brought more visitors, and the museum has been elegantly enlarged to accommodate them. The large and beautiful **Parque de Doña Casilda Iturrizar** next to the museum is an agreeable place to spend an hour or two, with exotic trees labelled, a lagoon, and a light-and-colour 'Cybernetic Fountain'.

Along the Nervión

When Bilbao's urban planners embarked on post-industrial regeneration in the late 1980s it was inevitable that the riverbank would be the project's linchpin. The significance of the Nervión (which becomes the Ría de Bilbao) to Bilbao is as much symbolic as practical; for years it has been synonymous in Spain with massive industrial pollution, but clean-up efforts since 1981 have succeeded in making the river habitable to fish for the first time in nearly a century. Major developments have taken place above water too, as several kilometres of old rusting jetties and dock installations have been torn out to make room for a riverside park, stretching downstream from Arenal bridge to the Guggenheim museum. Bilbaínos have taken to the development with gusto – thousands of them pour on to the riverbanks every evening to walk their dogs and eat ice cream – and when the trees grow, and the estuarine pong disappears, it's likely to be a very pleasant space.

Halfway along, the new glass-floored **Puente Zubi Zuri** ('White Bridge' in Basque) was one of the first additions to the riverfront landscape; its nautical theme – the bridge billows out like a great sail – has become a widespread motif in the architecture of New Bilbao. Across the river a **funicular** glides up to the hilltop park on **Monte Artxanda**, where there are several restaurants and extensive views of the Casco Viejo, the Guggenheim and, on really clear days, the sea, 16km to the north. For an authentic cultural experience go up on a weekend, when half of Bilbao squeezes into the rattling cars and hangs out on the mountain.

Funicula de Artxanda
every 15 minutes from Plaza Funicular, off C/ Castaños; runs Mon–Sat 7.15am–10pm, Sun 8.15am–10pm, until 11pm in summer on Sat, Sun and hols, www. funicularartxanda.com

The Guggenheim Museum

**🛈 Guggenheim
Museum**
*Avenida Abandoibarra
2, t 94 435 90 80, www.
guggenheim-bilbao.es;
open Tues–Sun 10–8,
daily in July and
Aug; adm*

*The greatest
building of
our time.*

Philip Johnson

Downstream from Zubi Zuri a 6oft tower of steel and golden limestone heralds the presence of Bilbao's new art Mecca, and the centrepiece of its biggest riverfront redevelopment, Frank O Gehry's Museo Guggenheim. Gehry's titanium clipper ship occupies the Abandoibarra flats, until 1987 home to Bilbao's biggest shipyard and now a worldwide symbol of successful urban renewal; the museum fits in to the landscape perfectly, looking utterly futuristic and yet in keeping with the city's industrial past. Its massive popularity and high public visibility have helped to spawn an economic boom, the so-called 'Guggenheim Effect', which has been felt throughout the Basque Lands.

A major part of the museum's success is due to its innovative design, which continues to attract universal curiosity – most visitors spend as much time wandering around the **exterior**, comparing opinions and examining angles, as they do looking at the art works inside. Like the three blind men and the elephant, your interpretation will depend on which part of the building you are looking at: ships' hulls, truncated fish bodies, and palm trees all protrude from the bulging mass, the juxtaposition of natural forms and 21st-century technology suggesting a new genre of 'bio-architecture'. Some of the best views are to be had from the **Puente de la Salve**, a classic lump of 1960s concrete that Gehry's design embraces, by way of the aforementioned limestone tower. One of his skylights looms up towards the bridge, looking for all the world like a giant open-mawed basking shark.

The **interior** spaces are no less remarkable. Access is by a broad flight of steps sweeping down from Avenida Abandoibarra through the entrance bottleneck and into the building's heart, a 150-foot-high atrium of white light and swooping curves. This is in every sense the museum's centre – galleries radiate from it on all

08 The Basque Lands (Euskadi) | Bilbao (Bilbo)

Puppy, or Life Imitates Art, Again

Before you even get a chance to step through the doors of the museum, you'll be mugged by the Guggenheim's first (and biggest) exhibit, a 40ft mountain of flowers and love created by kitsch guru Jeff Koons and answering to the name of '*Puppy*' (pronounced 'poopy'). *Puppy*, presumably a West Highland terrier, is a familiar sight at galleries worldwide – he's made appearances in New York and Sydney, amongst other cities – a kind of vegetarian version of the Littlest Hobo, who wanders from city to city lending his support wherever art exhibitions need him, before turning tail and trotting off into the sunset. But, like the Littlest Hobo, eventually the time came to settle down, and *Puppy* has put down his roots firmly in Bilbao, to the delight of almost everyone. He's been adopted as the city's de facto mascot, his image decorating everything from T-shirts to Vizcaya government literature.

Puppy's meteoric rise to mass adulation no doubt amuses his creator. When Koons came across the dog, it was no more than a tacky porcelain souvenir, a mass-produced piece of commercial crassness. Having based a career on taking just this kind of tat and elevating it to the status of High Art, Koons saw potential in *Puppy*; a couple of months, one CAD program and a few thousand begonias later and, *voilà*! a star was born. Yet just as junk can be made into art, art can be made into junk and before long the poor pooch was back where he came from; cuddly *Puppys* are the hot souvenir in Bilbao.

> *He is an architect of immense gifts who dances on the line separating architecture from art but who manages never to let himself fall.*
>
> Paul Goldberger,
> *New York Times*
> architecture critic

sides, and you'll inevitably pass through time and again at different levels – but it is also a sculptural work of art in itself, Frank Gehry's contribution to the Guggenheim legend. Light floods in through glass curtain walls, and cascades down from skylights in the roof. Whatever the interpretation, Gehry's atrium is a worthy successor to Frank Lloyd Wright's legendary spiral design; watch out for his cheeky nod of the head to Frank senior. Outside the atrium, the Nervión is incorporated into the museum's design by way of an ingenious raised walkway, rising and curving and creating a union between river and water garden. The architect has also created some unique gallery spaces, especially the cavernous 'Fish Gallery', 420ft long by 100ft wide with whalebone-like ribs supporting the ceiling, designed to hold the biggest and heaviest works of modern art. *Snake*, a heavy iron sculpture designed especially for the gallery by Richard Serra, throws down the gauntlet to future artists; too heavy to move and too big to fit anywhere else, it's one of the few exhibits that's guaranteed to be on show. *Snake* has recently been augmented with Serra's seven-part sculpture *A Matter of Time* (2005), seven huge (they even dwarf the *Snake* itself) swirls of steel that were also created specifically for this space. A meditation on time, both physical and experiential, a journey to the centre of these swaying steel ellipses and spheres is curiously dislocating – walls appear and fall away when you least expect them to.

The Collection

After Gehry's architectural fireworks, and Koons' giant dog, the collection itself has a hard act to follow; whether or not it succeeds will depend on when you go. Thanks to its links with major galleries in New York, Venice and Berlin, the Guggenheim has access to more masterworks of 20th-century art than a museum of its tender age has any right to. Yet the shifting nature of its exhibits means there's no guarantee that the piece you're desperate to see will be on show. In any event, the site-specific works by Koons and Serra will be there, as will Jenny Holzer's *Installation For Bilbao* (1997), a characteristically spiky LED monologue carrying implications of abuse, obsession and violation, scrolling upwards into a reflective ceiling via nine vertical columns.

Guggenheim Practicalities

Don't underestimate the Guggenheim's popularity. Attendance rates have vastly exceeded those projected, and long **queues** to get in – up to an hour – have become frequent, especially at weekends.

Once you're through the door it's easy enough to wander round the galleries independently; alternatively, **audioguides**, included in the admission price, have recorded information on the key works. There's a **visitor information desk** in the main entrance hall. Free **guided tours** in English, Spanish and Basque take place four times per day, but there's a definite skill to getting on one – spaces are limited to 20 people and you cannot register until 30 minutes before the tour.

If the **permanent collection** is up, look out for a good selection of European avant-garde art: there's a pivotal work by Miró, *The Tilled Field* (1923–4), a bold and relatively accessible prelude to his later, more figurative style; a selection of Kandinskys; some elongated heads by Modigliani and scattered works by Picasso and Klee, mostly on permanent loan from the Guggenheim in New York. Underpinning these is Bilbao's own distinguished collection of abstract expressionists, including pieces by some of the movement's leading figures, among them Robert Motherwell's stark assessment of the Civil War, *Elegy to the Spanish Republic IV* (1955–60), a swirling late-period Pollock (*Ocean Greyness*, 1953) and De Kooning's forceful *Composition* (1955), a gestural riot of primary colours. The polychromatic chaos is balanced by a tranquil Rothko (*Untitled*, 1956) and Yves Klein's *Large Blue Anthropometry* (1960), which the artist created by smearing naked women in paint (the famously patented *International Klein Blue*) and dragging them across the canvas while a 20-piece orchestra played his own *Symphonie Monotone*, a single note sustained for 10 minutes alternating with 10 minutes' silence.

There's a fairly patchy collection of pop art, perhaps best represented by Lichtenstein's unusually subdued *Interior With Mirrored Wall* (1991); some fine pieces by Schnabel, Dubuffet and Basquiat; and a moving monographic exhibition devoted to Anselm Kiefer. This juxtaposes the historically laden works of his early period – the notorious faces of Nazi Germany glare down from a chaotic monochrome swirl in *The Paths to Worldly Wisdom: Hermann's Battle* (1982–3) – with the unburdened, redemptive inner landscapes that characterize Kiefer's work in the 1990s. In *Sun Ship* (1994–5), a dried sunflower glides over devastated landscapes of ash and fallen trees, heading off to a brighter future, a future perhaps realized in the cracked desert colours of *Alone With Wind, Time and Sound* (1997).

Elsewhere, there's a small collection of works by Basque and Spanish artists: sculptures by Eduardo Chillida and Cristina Iglesias, a few textural paintings by Tapiés; and some startling mixed-media still lifes and landscapes from Miguel Barceló – which the museum's directors have pledged to augment with future purchases. They tried hard to get the one work that the Basques feel really belongs here – Picasso's *Guernica* – but Madrid refused to send it even on loan for the opening in 1997, out of fears, they say, that the Basques wouldn't give it back.

Nothing draws the crowds to Bilbao like a big new **temporary exhibition** – until the collection matures, they're the best guarantee of seeing a really strong body of work – and the Guggenheim has achieved a few stunning successes. Features in the past have included a major exhibition of photographs by

German cult cinematographer Wim Wenders, wide-ranging retrospectives of Chillida and Iglesias, and an assemblage of sculpture and photography by Picasso, Degas and Rodin. But nothing so far has been able to compete with the runaway success of 2000's 'The Art of the Motorcycle' exhibit, featuring highly polished machines from an 1894 Hildebrand and Wulfmüller to turn of the millennium superbikes, with a floor plan designed by Frank Gehry in the shape of a Scalextric track. All of a sudden, half the Basque country was in gallery 104, dribbling over the lusty iron horse, and for a time leather and long hair shared the halls of high culture.

The Guggenheim Effect

The Guggenheim's success has spawned an ambitious series of restoration projects throughout Bilbao, none of which are bigger than the transformation taking place on the **Abandoibarra flats**. Acres of railway sidings and container trucks have disappeared, making way for a new development under the direction of Argentinian architect Cesár Pelli; office blocks, a hotel, shopping malls and a 30-storey tower block are sprouting up alongside the Guggenheim. An extensive park area is unfolding, completing the 'green corridor' between Parque de Doña Casilda Iturrizar and Paseo del Arenal. The thick-set **Palacio de Congresos y de la Musica** completes the project, its massive hulk evoking the days when rusty freighters churned up the waters of the Nervión.

More tangible reminders of the old trade are housed in a spectacular new museum devoted to Bilbao's maritime history, the **Museo Marítimo Ría de Bilbao**, downriver towards Olabeaga in the old Euskalduna dry docks. Here a permanent collection, displayed both in immense indoor galleries and out in the docks, traces the city's maritime history, with restored fishing boats, sailing ships, historic nautical instruments and maps on show, accompanied by film clips and all kinds of high-tech exhibits. The old lock system which once operated on the river is still kept in working order. Temporary exhibitions are always huge crowd-pullers, and the museum is in general a family pleaser.

It's difficult to miss Bilbao's **San Mames stadium**, also known as 'the Cathedral' which is now open for guided tours (includes box seats, press room and changing rooms).

Museo Marítimo Ría de Bilbao
Muelle Ramón de la Sota 1, **t** *90 213 10 00,* *www.museomaritimo bilbao.org; open Tues–Sun 10–8; adm*

San Mames stadium
guided tours at 10.30, 11.30, 12.30, 4.30, 5.30 and 6.30

Around Bilbao: Getxo and the Hanging Bridge

Only a third of Bilbao's million-odd souls live within the city itself. Bilbao is the heart of a sprawling conurbation that lines the Nervión for 32km, with factories and tower blocks squeezing in wherever the terrain permits. The fancier suburbs are found near the coast, where there are dramatic cliffs and a number of beaches. The most distinguished of these is **Getxo** (Neguri, Algorta and

Bidezabal Metro stations), a combination suburb, marina and beach resort whose waterfront is lined with lovely villas; Getxo claims one of the youngest populations in Vizcaya, and the closest beaches to downtown Bilbao, yet retains a distinctly refined atmosphere. Traces of the town's more earthbound past continue to linger, especially in the graceful old fishing port of **Algorta**, cascading down the cliffs from a defiantly modern *urbanisación*. Look out for 19th-century, late neoclassical **San Nicolás de Bari**, where stoups made of giant clam shells prop up the walls.

Almost everything else in Getxo was built in the 20th century, including the grandiose villas that line the waterfront between Ereaga and Las Arenas beaches. New money from iron and the shipyards paid for these mansions; it couldn't guarantee good taste, but at least in the 1920s it bought a nice view. Nowadays, however, the crumbling old castles look across to the proletarian suburbs of Bilbao's superport, sprawling along the estuary.

Puente Colgante
Areeta metro station; open daily 10–9, t 94 463 88 54, adm; for group discounts call t 94 480 10 12

The *ría*, and a social chasm, are bridged at the Nervión's mouth by one of Vizcaya's great industrial age landmarks, the **Puente Colgante**, or 'Hanging Bridge'; the name refers to a system (unique in its day) of transporting people and goods across the river by way of a suspended gondola. This is Bilbao's proudest monument from the 19th century, and was as much a symbol of a vigorous economy in its day as the Guggenheim is now. Modern-day visitors can take a lift to the uppermost span, for a commanding view of the estuary.

The **beaches** continue eastwards along the coast. Though they're jam-packed with Bilbaínos on weekends, they can be fun; both the beaches and the water are surprisingly clean. Two of the most popular are at **Sopelanas** and **Plentzia**; the latter is an agreeably sleepy town on weekdays, with a handsome medieval quarter. Plentzia lacks any real sights, but it's a good place to wander when the beach scene gets too frantic. If you are spending much time in Bilbao, might we recommend (though not for the faint-hearted) a ride around the mountains that hem in the city. On **Monte Artxandamendia**, or in the hills above Erandio or Portugalete, you will see incredible landscapes of steel mills perched on mountain tops, grazing sheep, Victorian castles, shantytowns and roads on stilts – scenes from some surrealist comic book.

Tourist Information in Bilbao

Bilbao >
Plaza Ensanche 1, t 94 479 57 60, www.bilbao.net

Airport, t 94 471 03 01

The **main tourist offices** are in Plaza Ensanche, in front of the Guggenheim at Abandoibarra 2, and in the Teatro Arriaga, Plaza Arriaga, on the edge of the Casco Viejo. There is also an **airport** office, near the luggage carousel. As well as the official city site, *www.guggenheim-bilbao.es* (the official Guggenheim site) and *www.spain.info* (the official Spanish tourist office site) are useful. Best of all is *www.euskadi.net*, a Basque government website with excellent links to other sites and a wide range of useful information.

Post offices: The main post office is at Alameda de Urquijo 19.

Shopping in Bilbao

The Siete Calles of the Casco Viejo are a good place to start, particularly C/ Bidebarrieta and C/ Correo, with plenty of upmarket clothing and shoe shops, and tacky souvenir places knocking out ceramic *Puppys* (*à la* Guggenheim). For something slightly funkier, try C/ Somera, where youthful fashions dominate. The trendiest boutiques are concentrated in the Ensanche, mostly south of the Gran Vía around Plaza Indautxu; C/ Ercilla is a good place to start. Best buys are leather goods, food and wine.

El Corte Inglés, Gran Vía Pastelería 7–9. Everything you would expect from Spain's department store chain.

Calzados Ayestaran, Gran Vía 27. High quality shoes and leather garments designed by established, local chain.

Mica, C/ Lotería 2. A showcase of Spanish designers.

La Casa del Libro, Colón de Larreategui 41. A wide range of maps and books.

Almacen Coloniales y Bacalao Gregorio Martín, C/ Artekale 22. A wonderful old shop in the Casco Viejo, still with its old fittings, almost overtaken by the sheets of *bacalao* (salted cod) hanging from the ceiling.

Arrese, Gran Vía 24. An old and very famous confectioners.

Chocolates de Mendaro, C/ Licenciado Poza 16. Luxury chocolates since 1850.

Basandere, C/ Iparraguirre 4. Near the Guggenheim, this attractive Basque boutique has ceramics, glassware, hand-crafted jewellery, and linens.

Where to Stay in Bilbao

Bilbao ✉ 48000

The 'Guggenheim Effect' has filled Bilbao's hotels with the kind of educated, culture-seeking tourist other cities dream of, so book in advance.

Luxury–Very Expensive (€€€€€–€€€€)

Bilbao has quite a few luxury hotels catering for the businesspeople who pass through; some offer up to 50 per cent discount at weekends.

*****Gran Hotel Domine Bilbao, Alameda de Mazarredo 61, t 94 425 33 00, *www.granhoteldominebilbao. com*. Currently the hottest place to stay in town, with a fabulous location right opposite the Guggenheim. The excellent restaurant and hip bar are open to non-residents.

*****Lopez de Haro, C/ Obispo Orueta 2, t 94 423 55 00, *www.hotellopezde haro.com*. This classically elegant hotel has one of the city's finest restaurants, **Club Náutico**.

****Hotel Miro, Alameda Mazarredo, 77, t 94 661 18 80, *www.mirohotel bilbao.com*. Opposite the Guggenheim museum, this boutique hotel is the work of fashion designer Antonio Miró. Weekend rates include tickets to the Guggenheim and a massage.

Expensive (€€€)

****Hesperia Bilbao, Campo Volantín 28, t 94 405 11 00; *www. hesperia-bilbao.es*. It's difficult to miss the multicoloured window panes of Bilbao's trendy newcomer, which is located next to Santiago Calatrava's footbridge over the Nervión River. Like Miro, the hotel is located near the Guggenheim but has lower rates.

****Hotel Indautxu, Plaza del Bombero Etxaniz, t 94 444 00 04, *www.hotelindautxu.com*. This giant glass cube has all the comforts in a good, quiet location. The house restaurant, **Etxaniz**, is very good.

*****Carlton, Plaza de Federico Moyúa 2, t 94 416 22 00, *www. aranzazu-hoteles.com*. This plush 19th-century hotel has lodged famous bullfighters, along with Hemingway, Ava Gardner and Lauren Bacall.

Moderate (€€)

**Bilbao Jardines, Jardines 94, t 94 479 42 10, *www.hotelbilbaojardines. com*. A clean, light and modern hotel in the Casco Viejo, conveniently located close to the *pintxos* circuit. One of the historic centre's best deals.

**Sirimiri, Pza de la Encarnación 3, t 94 433 07 59, *www.hotelsirmiri.com*. A peachy little hotel that offers a comfortable, reasonably priced option, situated on a pretty square near the old church of San Anton and Atxuri train station. Small gym and sauna.

**Hotel Artetxe, Carretera Enékuri-Artxanda Km.7, t 94 474 77 80, *www.hotelartetxe.com*. A delightful option, this is a traditional Basque house on a hill above the city with charming rooms and fabulous views. Best if you have your own transport. Good restaurant and they also rent apartments in an annexe.

Hostal Iturrienea Ostatua >

Hostal Iturrienea Ostatua, C/ Santa María 14, **t 94 416 15 00. Definitely the best choice in the Casco Viejo; great care has gone into equipping the rooms with a mix of antique and new furniture, while flowering plants trail from the balconies. You can't miss its bright blue-and-yellow façade.

Pension Central, Alameda Recalde, 35a, 1°, **t 94 410 63 39, *www.hostal central.com*. The price is fair for the modern, clean rooms with internet access. Just off Moyúa square.

Hostal Begoña >

Hostal Begoña, C/ Amistad, 2, **t 94 423 0134, *www.hostalbegona.com*. An intimate choice (only 15 rooms) in a boarding house that was founded in the 1920s but recently renovated in bright colours that come straight out of an Almodóvar film.

*Hotel Ripa, C/ Ripa 3, **t** 94 423 96 77, *www.hotel-ripa.com*. On the riverfront opposite the Casco Viejo; nice, renovated rooms with balconies overlooking the old opera house.

*Hotel Arriaga, C/ La Ribera 3, **l** 94 479 00 01, *www.hotelarriaga.com*. On the edge of the Casco Viejo, very close to the Teatro, this offers plush, comfortable rooms and parking. It is run by a slightly eccentric family.

Inexpensive (€)

*Hostal Estrella, C/ María Muñoz 6, **t** 94 416 40 66. Refurbished, clean and bright *hostal* near the cathedral. Can be a bit noisy.

Pension Mendez I and II, Santa Maria 13, fourth floor (Pension I) and first floor (Pension II), **t** 94 416 03 64, *www.pensionmendez.com*. The rooms are rather small but clean and painted an elegant turquoise blue. You pay more for the Pension II because it's on the first floor and rooms have baths and TV. The higher options (fourth floor) come with shared baths.

Getxo ✉ 48990

***Gran Hotel, C/ María Díaz de Haro 2, Portugalete, **t** 94 401 48 00, *www.*

granhotelpuentecolgante.com (€€€). Across from the great Getxo neighbourhood, this is one of the city's latest hotels, situated in a sumptuous historical building at the foot of the Vizcaya Bridge. Excellent value.

Artaza, Avda Los Chopos 12, Neguri, **t 94 491 28 52, *www.hotelartaza.com* (€€€). Elegant comfort in a refined mansion surrounded by tranquil parkland, a short walk from Neguri metro station.

Eating Out in Bilbao

This city may not get as wild about cuisine as San Sebastián, but eating is still a pleasure in Bilbao. For the purest Basque cuisine, look for the strangest names.

Expensive (€€€)

Zortziko, Alameda de Mazarredo 17, **t** 94 423 97 43, *www.zortiko.es*. Splurge at this, the city's finest (Michelin-starred) restaurant, in an historic building. The lunch menu is a relative bargain. *Closed all day Sun, Mon eve, last week in Aug and first 2 weeks Sept.*

Bermeo, C/ Ercilla 37 (Hotel Ercilla), **t** 94 470 57 00. This offers a delicate blend of new and old Basque cuisine in sumptuous surroundings. If it's on the menu, this is the place to try one of the ultimate Basque treats, *kokotxas* – the 'cheek and throat' of a hake in a garlic and parsley sauce. *Closed Sat lunch, Sun eve and first 2 weeks Aug; open Semana Grande.*

Guría, Gran Vía 66, **t** 94 441 57 80, *www.restauranteguria.com*. Old favourite serving traditional Basque fare on offer (lunch menu €30). They also run the cheaper but excellent **El Bistrot** (same address). *Closed Sun eve.*

Goizeko-Kabi, C/ Particular de Estraunza 4–6, **t** 94 441 11 29, *www. goizekokabi.com*. The name sounds right; innovative cooking to match. *Closed Sun and first 2 weeks Aug.*

Gorrotxa, Alameda de Urquijo 30, **t** 94 422 05 35. In spite of its shopping mall setting, offers spectacular New Basque cooking in a sophisticated ambience. *Must book. Closed Sun, first 2 weeks Sept, and Holy Week.*

Víctor, Plaza Nueva 2, **t** 94 415 16 78, *www.restaurantevictor.com*. An enviable reputation as one of the Casco Viejo's best restaurants. *Closed Sun (exc May), Easter, last 2 weeks Jan and first 2 weeks Sept.*

Guggenheim, Guggenheim Museum, t 94 423 93 33, *www.restaurante guggenheim.com*. Full of light, designed by Frank Gehry; the food, created by chef Martín Berasategui, is an excellent snapshot of some of the best of Basque cooking. Two *menús degustaciones* on offer (€56–65), and a good-value lunchtime *menú del día* (€18). *Closed Sun, Mon and Tues eves, and 2 weeks Jan.*

El Perro Chico (Perrotxico), C/ Arechaga 2, t 94 415 05 19. Close to Ribera market and overlooking the river, this is one of Bilbao's most talked-about restaurants. Deep blue walls, tiles and lots of paintings give it a boho-chic atmosphere in which to dine on traditional Basque favourites. *Book in advance. Closed Sun–Mon.*

Moderate (€€)
Metro-Moyúa, C/ Gran Vía 40, t 94 424 92 73. Family-run restaurant serves good Basque cooking with flair.

Yandiola, Paseo del Campo Volantín 15, t 94 413 4013, *www.yandiola.com*. Along the Bilbao estuary; the minimalist décor across two floors is upstaged by the colourful creations of young chef Ricard Perez. *Menú del día* €20. *Closed Sun and Mon eve.*

Harrobia, C/ del Perro 2, t 94 679 00 90, *www.harrobia.com*. Busy, buzzy restaurant serving *nueva cocina vasca* in elegant surroundings.

Inexpensive (€)
Saibigain, Barrencalle Barrena, 16, t 94 415 01 23. Well established since the 1950s; from €8 for a standard *menú del día* to €32 for the most elaborate. If you have less time, the bar serves a tasty range of *pintxos*. *Closed Sun.*

Café Boulevard, C/ Arenal 3, t 94 415 31 28. Elegant Art Deco interior for an afternoon coffee or early evening *copa*.

Tapas/*Pintxos*

One of the city's greatest pleasures is the *txikiteo*, the ritual bar crawl, selecting titbits from the groaning bar tops. There are three main areas to enjoy this: in the Casco Viejo, in the streets around C/ Ledesma in the Ensanche, and the central area around C/ Licenciado Poza and the Plaza Indautxu. Many of the city's finest restaurants also serve *pintxos* at the bar, a great way to taste some of the best cuisine in the city.

Víctor Montes, Plaza Nueva 8, t 94 415 70 67. One of the city's most celebrated eating places, a *belle époque* classic *Closed Sun eve.*

Berton, C/ Jardines 11, t 94 416 70 35. Filled with locals at weekends; brimming with a zillion varieties of pieces of heaven. *Closed Sun pm and Mon.*

Gatz, C/ Santa María 10. Tiny little bar in the heart of the Casco Viejo with fabulous and unusual tapas, including cherries stuffed with blue cheese.

Iruña, C/ Berastegui 5, t 94 423 70 21. A stunning tribute to the Alhambra, this legendary, beautiful *mudéjar*-style café comes alive in the evening.

El Huevo Frito, Calle García Rivero Maestro, t 94 441 22 49. This bar's name, 'Fried Egg', belies the sophistication of its elaborate *pinxtos*.

Entertainment and Nightlife in Bilbao

Bilbao is a serious working city and nightlife is generally limited to weekends, mainly in the streets of the Casco Viejo. For listings, check the back pages of the local newspaper, *El Correo*, or pick up the bi-monthly *Bilbao Guide*, available at tourist information offices. The city is fond of opera.

C/ Barrenkale is a busy place with a number of music bars and clubs, while C/ Somera has friendly and funky bars that are very popular with the Basque nationalist community. In the Ensanche there are more on C/ Pérez Galdós and C/ Licenciado Poza.

The Cotton Club, C/ Gregorio de la Revilla 25. Offers live music (everything from funk to jazz).

Palladium, C/ Iparraguire 11, t 94 424 61 65. Live jazz and blues.

Kafé Antzokia, C/ San Vicente (by the Jardínes de Albia), *www.kafeantzokia. com*. In a former cinema and is a Basque-speaking café by day, this is a bar and club by night, with DJs and live music and theatre performances.

Vitoria (Gasteiz)

Vitoria has style. It also has the air of a little Ruritanian capital – because it is one. The seat of the inland province of Álava and, since 1980, the capital of Euskadi, Vitoria has grown to be one of Spain's modern industrial centres, a phenomenon that has so far done little harm to one of the most surprisingly urbane cities in the nation. Although Wellington soundly defeated the forces of Joseph Bonaparte here in 1813, Vitoria's name has nothing to do with

Getting to and around Vitoria

By Air

Foronda airport (*www.via-vitoria-airport.com*), 9km northwest of Vitoria, has connections with Madrid and Barcelona (**t** 905 505 505, *www.aena.es*).

By Train and Bus

Vitoria's stylish **train station** (**t** 90 224 02 02 for information) is at the head of C/ Eduardo Dato, six blocks from the old town. Trains between San Sebastián and Madrid pass through Vitoria, with at least eight daily services heading for the capital (approx. 5hrs 30mins), and Salvatierra is a stop along RENFE's Vitoria–Pamplona run. Otherwise you'll have to take the bus. The **bus station** (**t** 94 525 84 00) is at C/ Los Herran 50, a short walk east of the old town via the pedestrian street Cantón de San Francisco Javier. There are regular services to San Sebastián, Bilbao and Logroño, as well as to the provincial villages, and, because of the city's position on the main route north from Madrid, you can get a bus to nearly anywhere.

victory, but recalls the height (*Beturia* in Basque) on which the city was built. In the Middle Ages this was a hot border region between the kingdoms of Navarra and Castile. Navarrese King Alfonso VI founded a fortress and town here in 1181, but the Castilians managed to snatch it away from them soon after. Like everything else in medieval Castile, Vitoria boomed, and extended itself logically in concentric rings of streets. Hard hit by the wars and plagues of the 1300s, Vitoria stagnated for centuries, and began its recovery only with the industrial boom of the 1890s. It has preserved itself beautifully throughout, probably an important factor in getting Vitoria named the Basque capital in the autonomy agreement of 1981.

⓫ *Fiesta de la Virgen Blanca*

The important thing to know about Vitoria is the *Fiesta de la Virgen Blanca*, from 4 August. It's a berserk six-day Basque blowout, with high-powered fireworks and parties until dawn, but the image of it that sticks in the mind is Celedón, a dummy in a beret and workman's clothes. Celedón holds an umbrella aloft, which is attached to a wire from the top of the cathedral tower; from this he descends like Mary Poppins, gliding across the *plaza* to start the festival. On the morning of 10 August, he glides up the wire and pops back into the bell tower, and it's all over for another year.

The Casco Viejo

The old city, with its core of neat, concentric streets, begins with **Plaza de la Virgen Blanca**, a delightful example of asymmetrical medieval town design. Adjacent to it, the enclosed symmetrical **Plaza de España** provides a perfect contrast; this grand neoclassical confection was built at the height of Spain's flirtation with the Enlightenment, in the 1780s, and now houses mostly city offices. Plaza de la Virgen Blanca is the centre of Vitoria's big party from 4 August; it takes its name from the statue in the niche over the door of **San Miguel**, the 14th-century church that turns a lovely portico towards the top of the square. An 18th-century arcade called **Los Arcillos**, reached by a stair, runs under some graceful old glass-fronted buildings to connect Plaza de la Virgen Blanca to yet a third connected square on the slope of the hill, **Plaza del Machete**, named after the axe over which city officials would swear their oaths of office. Behind San Miguel, Calle Fray Zacarías leads north into the medieval streets. This was the high-status street for palaces, as evidenced by two 16th-century Plateresque beauties, the **Palacio Episcopal** and the **Palacio Escoriaza-Esquivel**, built by a local boy who became physician to Charles V.

Catedral Santa María
t 94 525 51 35; www. catedralvitoria.com; for tours book online or through the tourist office; adm

At the top of the street is the 14th-century **Catedral Santa María**, currently undergoing an extensive restoration programme which is not expected to be completed until 2010: the cathedral is not holding services during this period, but you can visit it by guided tour. There is a beautifully carved western doorway and impressive central nave, and the aisles are lined with the tombs of Vitoria's notables from medieval times. Archaeological excavations in the cathedral have unearthed remains of an ancient fortified church.

A couple of streets west of the cathedral, on C/ del Herrería, the **Torre de Doña Otxanta** is a defensive tower of the 15th–16th centuries. Italian early-Renaissance cities, with their skylines of skyscraper-fortresses, set a fashion that found its way to other countries. Fortresses like these were private castles in town, and city officials had to fight hard to keep their owners from acting like rustic barons on their manors. Now fully restored, the tower is home to the province's **Natural Science Museum**. Another tower nearby, the **Torre Hurtados de Anda**, lurks just to the north of the cathedral on C/ Correría: this is a blank-walled fort with a half-timbered house planted on top. Also on C/ Correría, a rambling brick and timber structure called **El Portalón**, built in the early 16th century, is one of the oldest buildings in town. Just across the street at No. 116, the **Archaeology Museum** occupies a lovely half-timbered house containing Roman finds and Basque discoidal tombstones, as well as some fascinating medieval finds, such as the exceedingly strange *Relief of Marquinez*. There are over a hundred artificial caves in the province of Álava, and exhibits recount the story of the religious hermits who occupied them.

Natural Science Museum
open Tues–Fri 11–2 and 4–6.30, Sat 10–2, Sun 11–2

Archaeology Museum
open Tues–Fri 10–2 and 4–6.30, Sat 10–2, Sun 11–2

Palaces are fewer in the eastern quarter of old Vitoria, across C/ Las Escuelas; the houses here are generally plainer, though older, especially those in the former **Judería**, the medieval Jewish ghetto that covered much of this area. On C/ de la Cuchillería, in the Plateresque Palacio Bendaña, Spain's biggest manufacturer of playing cards (a Vitoria speciality) has opened the **Museo Fournier de Naipes**, which has the oldest surviving card (14th-century), as well as card-making machinery and paintings. The collection includes Tarot decks too; originally there was no difference between the cards for fortune-telling and those for playing games.

Museo Fournier de Naipes
open Tues–Fri 10–2 and 4–6.30, Sat 10–2, Sun 11–2

08

The Basque Lands (Euskadi) | Vitoria (Gasteiz)

Artium
www.artium.org;
open Tues–Fri 11–8, Sat
and Sun 10.30–8; adm,
'you decide' on Wed

Just east of here, at C/ Francia 24, is Vitoria's exciting new **Artium** (Basque Museum of Contemporary Art), with a permanent collection of more than 1,600 contemporary paintings, sculptures, drawings and photos by Basque and Spanish artists.

The New Cathedral and the Museum of Fine Arts

The tourist information office shares the pretty **Parque de la Florida**, Vitoria's monumental centre, with the stern, no-nonsense **Basque Parliament** building and the remarkable 'new cathedral', the **Catedral de la María Inmaculada**. Here, the Basques show their devotion to the Middle Ages by building a completely 'medieval' building, by medieval methods, beginning in 1907. Most of it is already finished, although there is enough decorative work to do inside to last them another century or two. The style seems to be part English Gothic, part Viollet-le-Duc, and the most endearing feature is the rows of comical modillions around the cornices. It

Museo Diocesano
de Arte Sacro
open Tues–Fri 10–2
and 4–6.30, Sat 10–2,
Sun 11–2

contains the **Museo Diocesano de Arte Sacro**, with an appealing collection of medieval Madonnas, over-the-top Baroque religious paintings, and lavish church plate and ornaments.

Vitoria is a city of unexpected delights; one example, completing the park's monumental ensemble, is one of the most resplendent **Art Deco petrol stations** in Europe, just behind the cathedral. Another, a few blocks southeast on Calle Eduardo Dato, is the fantastical **RENFE station**, done in a kind of Hollywood-Moorish style with bright tiles. The city has finally finished constructing the **Plaza de los Fueros**, a square just southeast of Plaza de la Virgen Blanca, designed and decorated by Eduardo Chillida. It's a strange space – part Roman amphitheatre, part basketball court; it seems to get most use after the bars have closed. At one end, an untitled Eduardo Chillida sculpture is enclosed within angular walls.

The wonderful **Parque de la Florida**, laid out in 1855, retains much of the Romantic spirit of its times, with grand promenades, hidden bowers and viewpoints. It was the centre of the city's fashionable district, and a shady walkway from the southern end of the park, the Paseo de la Senda, takes you to the elegant **Paseo de Fray Francisco de Vitoria**, lined with the Hispano-Victorian mansions of

Museo de
Bellas Artes
open Tues–Fri 10–2
and 4–6.30, Sat 10–2
and 5–8, Sun 11–2

the old industrialists. One of these houses, now the **Museo de Bellas Artes**, features a well-displayed collection ranging from early paintings to Picasso and Miró, with a handful of great Spanish masters in between; all in a beautifully restored space, with original features such as a Tiffany-style stained-glass skylight. Some of the finest works are of the type that museums here call *Escuela Hispanoflamenca*, paintings from the early 16th century, at a time when the influence from the Low Countries was strong; most are anonymous. One of the finest works, a triptych of the *Passion* by the 'Master of the Legend of Santa Godelina', shows the same sort of conscious stylization as an Uccello; the longer you look at it, the stranger it seems. Medieval painted carved-wood figures are well represented, and you'll also find some surprises, such as a great early 20th-century Basque landscapist named Fernando de Anarica, or his contemporary Ramon Zubiaurre, whose *Autoridades de mi Aldea* shares the not-quite-naïve sensibility of Rousseau or Grant Wood. The façade of a 13th-century hermitage has been reconstructed in the museum's garden. Back along the Paseo at No.3, the **Museum of Arms** houses suits of armour, medieval weapons and dioramas.

Seeing the last of Vitoria's little secrets means a pleasant 20-minute walk southwest (from the Paseo de Fray Francisco, take Paseo de Cervantes and Avenida de San Prudencio), to the **Basílica of San Prudencio**, in Armentia, a village swallowed up by the city's suburbs. The church was built at the end of the 12th century, with a fine doorway and curious reliefs and carved capitals inside.

West of Vitoria you can visit Roman ruins, including a long, 13-arched bridge at **Trespuentes**, near the remains of a pre-Roman town, the *oppidum* of Iruña. Two kilometres away at Mendoza, near the airport on the A3302, a 13th-century defensive tower with great views over the countryside has been restored to house the **Museo de Heráldica**, Spain's only museum dedicated to the origins and graphic styles of heraldic escutcheons.

Museum of Arms
open Tues–Fri 10–2 and 4–6.30, Sat 10–2, Sun 11–2

Oppidum **of Iruña**
open Tues–Sat 11–3; Sun 11–2; adm

Museo de Heráldica
open Tues–Sat 11–3; Sun 10–12; adm

08 The Basque Lands (Euskadi) | Vitoria (Gasteiz)

Where to Stay in Vitoria

(i) **Vitoria** >
Plaza General Loma 1, t 94 516 15 98, www.vitoria-gasteiz. org/turismo

(★) **La Casa de Los Arquillos** >>

Vitoria ✉ 01000

****Hotel Ciudad de Vitoria**, Portal de Castilla 8, t 94 514 11 00, *www.hotel ciudaddevitoria.com* (€€€€). More character than most, with friendly staff and an indoor garden. Good discounts.

****NH Canciller Ayala**, C/ Ramón y Cajal 5, t 94 513 00 00, *www.nh-hotels.com* (€€€). Modern tower hotel next to the Florida Park, with standard chain décor but little in the way of charm. Still, it's central.

***General Álava**, Avda de Gasteiz 79, t 94 521 50 00, *www.hga.info* (€€€). Another of the large hotels in the new part of town, with modern rooms geared towards business travellers.

***Almoneda**, C/ de la Florida 7, t 94 515 40 84, *www.hotelalmoneda.com* (€€€). Welcoming hotel with simple, tasteful rooms and a pleasant lounge with an eclectic collection of antiques.

***Hotel Palacio de Elorriaga**, C/ Elorriaga 15, t 94 526 36 16, *info@palacioelorriaga.com* (€€€). Charming hotel on the outskirts of the city, in an elegant 17th-century mansion surrounded by gardens. Rooms are stylishly decorated in a mix of the traditional and the contemporary.

La Casa de Los Arquillos, C/ Los Arquillos 1–2°, t 94 515 1259, *info@lacasadelosarquillos.com* (€€€). A delightful new, intimate hotel housed on the second floor of a medieval building which used to be a tailor's workshop. The décor blends exposed stone walls and solid wooden floors with pristine white linen and comfortable bathrooms. Book early, as there are only eight rooms. Only avoid if you dislike the ringing of church bells.

****Hotel Desiderio**, C/ San Prudencio 2, t 94 525 17 00 (€€). Functional rooms, but close to the old town and friendly.

****Dato 28**, C/ Eduardo Dato 28 (near the train station), t 94 514 72 30, *www.hoteldato.com* (€€). Conveniently located, with imaginative Art Deco furnishings. Reserve, or you will be sent to the less attractive **Residencia Dato 2**.

**Guesthouse Casa 400, Florida 46, 3ºD, t 94 523 38 87, *www.telefonica. net/web2/casa400* (€). A great find if you are on a budget. Close to the cathedral and medieval town.

**Pension Araba II, C/ de la Florida 25, 1st floor, t 94 523 25 88 (€). Bright and breezy *hostal* in the centre of town; with or without bathrooms.

Eating Out in Vitoria

Most of the most atmospheric bars and restaurants in Vitoria are in the old town. Look out for the *'Semana Del Pincho'* ('Pintxo Week'), an annual gastronomic competition launched in 2003 where tapas bars have a chance to show off elaborately prepared miniature tapas. Ask the tourist office.

Ikea, C/ Portal de Castilla 27, t 94 514 47 47, *www.restauranteikea.com* (€€€). One of the most renowned restaurants in Euskadi; original cuisine prepared with the finest seasonal ingredients. Push the boat out with the *menú de degustación* (€70). *Closed Sun eve and Mon, plus last 3 wks Aug.*

Zaldiarán, Avda de Gasteiz 21, t 94 513 48 22, *www.restaurantezalidiaran.com* (€€€). Smart restaurant serving award-winning traditional cuisine. Widely considered one of the best in town. *Closed Tues eve and Sun.*

El Portalón, C/ Correría 151, t 94 514 27 55, *www.restauranteelportalon.com* (€€€). Especially good, with tables on three floors of a 15th-century building and traditional Basque food. *Closed Sun and 2nd week Aug.*

Dos Hermanas, C/ Madre Vedruna 10, t 94 513 29 34 (€€). A local institution for over a century. *Closed Sun eve.*

Mesa, C/ de Chile 1, t 94 522 84 94 (€€). Flavoursome, down-to-earth local dishes including game and mushrooms in season. *Closed Wed, and mid-Aug to 1st week Sept.*

Olarizu, C/ Tomás de Zumárraga 54, t 94 521 75 00, *www.olarizu.com* (€€). Creative, elegant cuisine based on old Alavesa recipes. *Closed Sun eve, Mon and Tues.*

Zabala, C/ Mateo Moraza 9, t 94 523 00 09 (€€). An old-fashioned, family-run spot with simple but delicious regional dishes. *Closed Sun and Aug.*

Oleaga, C/ Adriano VI 15, t 94 524 68 53 (€). Counters heaving with *pintxos* and a dining room with home cooking at bargain prices. *Closed Sun eve and Mon, and 2nd half Aug.*

Nightlife in Vitoria

Vitoria has its share of nightlife, mostly in the Casco Viejo, though C/ Dato, near the station, can also be noisy after hours. Outside the centre, Lakua is a popular area for nightlife.

Álava Province

Just because the Basque capital is located here, you might think that Álava (*Araba* in Basque) is the Euskadi heartland. In fact, speakers of Basque make up precisely 4 per cent of the population, by far the lowest in the seven Basque provinces. One senses that, having lost ground to the Spaniards for centuries during their long economic decline, the Basques purposely planted their parliament here as part of a careful plan to reclaim the soil. Álava is home to the historical oddity of the County (*Condado*) of Treviño, an enclave of Castilian Spaniards smack in the middle of the province, making Álava the only province in Spain that is shaped like a doughnut.

Gaceo and Alaiza

There aren't a lot of sights here, but for anyone interested in things medieval the province offers something truly outstanding –

**⚁ San Martín
de Tours**
*guided tours available
through Tour Agurain;
for details call t 94 531
25 35 or t 608 90 16 70*

and almost totally unknown outside the area. The minuscule village of **Gaceo**, on the N1 east of Vitoria, offers nothing less than one of the finest ensembles of Gothic fresco painting anywhere in Europe. The frescoes are in the simple church of **San Martín de Tours**; covered in plaster, they were not rediscovered until 1966.

Research places these works some time between about 1325 and 1450. The style, a bit archaic with its Romanesque attention to flowing draperies, is distinctive enough for scholars to speculate about an obscure 'Basque-Navarrese' school of artists, perhaps centred in Vitoria. Byzantine influence is also strongly present, though details like the gnarled, rugged cross are uniquely Spanish (such a cross was the symbol of the 19th-century Carlist rebels). Thanks to the plaster, most of the paintings are well preserved, though oddly enough many of the faces have vanished. True fresco work requires that the plaster underneath the paintings, applied fresh each morning for an artist's day's work, be absolutely right. The secrets were just being rediscovered in the 14th century in Italy; artists elsewhere hadn't got it quite right.

Gaceo is not such an illogical spot for art as it seems. The modern N1 that connects Vitoria to Burgos and Pamplona roughly follows the course of the main Roman road into the north. Enough of this survived in medieval times to keep it an important route, heavily used by pilgrims on their way to Santiago de Compostela. It may well have been that the village was a popular pilgrim stop, and some pious gentleman or lady paid for the paintings.

The figures around the *Trinity* on the apse seem to be arranged to represent the commemoration of All Saints' Day. On the right, note the conspicuous figures of St Michael and Abraham, gathering the fortunate to his bosom. The choir vault too is entirely covered in frescoes, stock images from the Life of Christ divided by charming borders of *trompe l'œil* designs and fantasy architecture. At the bottom right is something no medieval mural picture book could be without: the souls of the damned getting variously swallowed up in the mouth of hell or cooked in a big pot.

While you're out in Gaceo, you might as well carry on a little further and see some quite different paintings at another tiny hamlet, **Alaiza** (from the N1, take the A3100 south from Salvatierra). The **Iglesia de la Asunción** here is a barn-like 13th-century building; it too has a painted apse and choir, but the contrast with Gaceo's is like day with night. Instead of flowing Gothic draperies, Alaiza has one-colour cartoons so weird and primitive they might have been done by a Palaeolithic cave artist on a bad day. The central work, on the apse, shows soldiers besieging a castle, while on the choir vault and walls bizarre hooded figures joust, murder or indulge in bodily functions. There is a contrastingly precise inscription underneath in Gothic letters, but no one has ever managed to decipher it.

The closest village in this region, **Salvatierra**, is a pleasant place of warm stone near two of Euskadi's best dolmens – **Aizkomendi** at Eguilaz, in a little roadside park off the N1, and **Sorginetxe** in Arrizala. North of Vitoria, the biggest features on the landscape are the dams and lakes of **Urrunaga** and **Ullívarri**. Farther north, on the road to Durango, **Otxandio** was the original Basque iron town, commemorated by a statue of the god Vulcan in the main square.

South of Vitoria: The Ebro Valley

Some of the best Rioja vines actually come from the province of Álava, a region known as **La Rioja Alavesa**, along the Ebro river facing the real La Rioja. Perched high over the river, the key wine town here is walled, medieval **Laguardia (Biasteri)** where you can learn all about local wines and their production at **La Casa del Vino**, and visit more *bodegas*, including the wave-shaped cedar and glass **Ysios Bodega** designed by Santiago Calatrava Don't miss the 14th-century apostles carved in the portal of Laguardia's Gothic **Santa María de los Reyes**. Near Laguardia, an Iron Age village is still being excavated: the **Poblado de la Hoya**. Although the site is not open to the public, you can visit the adjacent small **museum**.

Poblado de la Hoya Museum
t 94 518 19 18/t 94 562 11 22; open May–Oct Tues–Fri 11–2 and 4–8, Sat 11–3, Sun 10–2; Nov–April Tues–Sat 11–3, Sun 10–2

As for the **County of Treviño**, though this forgotten fief looks strangely compelling on the map, in reality there's plenty of oak woods and good farmland, but unhappily no greater attractions.

Where to Stay and Eat in Álava Province

ⓘ **Laguardia >**
Palacio Samaniego, Plaza de San Juan, t 94 560 08 45, www.laguardia-alava.com

★ **Hotel Castillo El Collado >**

Argómaniz ✉ 01192

***Parador de Argómaniz**, Ctra N1 Km 363, t 94 529 32 00, argomaniz@parador.es (€€€€). Small and simple, with some rooms in the original building, a 17th-century mansion with iron balconies. Tiny Argómaniz is 10km east of Vitoria, near the paintings of Gaceo. Great restaurant.

Laguardia ✉ 01300

Hotel Castillo El Collado, Paseo El Collado, t 94 562 12 00, www.euskalnet.net/hotelcollado.com (€€€€). The pick of the hotels: a 1920s palace full of antiques and luscious fabrics, with an incredibly welcoming owner The restaurant (€€€) serves Basque and Navarrese dishes.

Posada Mayor de Migueloa, C/ Mayor de Migueloa 20, t 94 562 11 75, www.mayordemigueloa.com (€€€). In a 17th-century mansion with antique furnishings; also has an excellent restaurant (€€€) and wine cellar.

Antigua Bodega de D. Cosme Palacio, Ctra Elciego, t 94 562 11 95 (€€). Delightful little hotel with a fine restaurant in the original *bodega*. Rooms are rustically decorated.

*Pachico Martinez, C/ Sancho Abarca 20, t 94 160 00 09, www.pachico.com (€€). In the same family since 1806.

*Marixa, C/ Sancho Abarca 8, t 94 560 01 65, www.hotelmarixa.com (€€). The best dining in town, with air-conditioning and expensive meals.

Elciego

Hotel Marqués de Riscal, Calle Torrea 1, t 94 518 08 80, www.starwoodhotels.com (€€€€€). The owners asked Frank Gehry to design a 'château for the 21st century' but even they couldn't have envisaged this futuristic construction with its glittering silver, yellow and red titanium exterior. Each of the 43 rooms is uniquely shaped and the two sections of the hotel are connected by a suspended footbridge. There is a rooftop lounge with spectacular views of the church of the sleepy Elciego and of the surrounding vineyards.

Cantabria
and the Picos de Europa

Spain's steep emerald-green dairy-land, Cantabria is wedged between the extraordinary Picos de Europa, the Cordillera Cantábrica and a coastline of scenic beaches. Santander, the capital and only large city, is a major summer resort but, while there are a handful of other tourist spots, much of Cantabria is serenely rural, claiming to have the highest density of cows in Europe. The majority of the bovine population lives indoors, and in the evening a common sight is the farmer or his wife, often wearing wooden clogs, driving home an ox-cart laden with grass that they have cut from their several Lilliputian plots of land scattered over the hills. On rainy winter evenings in the more remote areas they gather to hear the strains of the rabel, a three-stringed instrument from the Moors, made only of wood cut by the light of a full moon.

09

Don't miss

1 Palaeolithic masterpieces
Altamira p.201

2 Catalan Modernista architechure
Comillas p.202

3 An aristocratic village
Santillana del Mar p.199

4 Dramatic gorges and monasteries
Picos de Europa p.206

5 Erotic medieval church carvings
Colegiata, Cervatos p.197

See map overleaf

Costa Verde

Costa

San Vicente
de la Barquera

Colombres
Unquera

Comillas

Cuevas de
Altamira

Santillana
del Mar

Torrelavega

Arenas de
Cabrales

Cabezón
de la Sal

Lago de la
Ércina

Poncebos

Tresviso

Bulnes

Sotres

Naranjo de Bulnes

Desfiladero de la
Hermida

La Hermida

Puentenansa

Ruente

Lebeña

Reserva Nacional de Saja

Mirador del Cable

Turieno

Posada
de Valdeón

Fuente Dé

Espinama

Santo Toribio
de Liébana

Potes

Bárcena Mayor

Alto Campóo

Fuente del Ebro

Fontibre

Reinosa

Bolmir

Suano

Retortillo

Salcedillo

Cervatos

Valberzoso

Reserva
Nacional
de Fuentes
Carrionas

Aguilar de
Campoo

Cervera
de Pisuerga

pp.218-19

N611

N621

A67

S614

FRANCE

PORTUGAL

SPAIN

pp.244-5

Don't miss

1 Altamira p.201

2 Comillas p.202

3 Santillana del Mar p.199

4 Picos de Europa p.206

5 Colegiata, Cervatos p.197

Humanity has found Cantabria to its liking literally since its first cows, or prehistoric aurochs, came home some 38,000 years ago. It has Spain's greatest concentration of Upper Palaeolithic cave art, from indecipherable scratches to the masterpieces in Altamira. Back in the Iron Age, just before the arrival of the Romans, the Cantabrians carved star reliefs on large stone discs that still mystify everybody: were they part of a Celtic astral cult, remembered from the primordial night in the pilgrimage to Compostela, the Field of the Star?

Like La Rioja, Cantabria historically considered itself part of greater Castile. When the government was dividing up Spain into autonomous regions, the devolutionists feared that, if La Rioja and Cantabria were added to the new region of Castilla y León, they would feel insignificant and peripheral and liable to be lured by the wily Basques into joining Euskadi. A provision in the constitution allows Cantabria and La Rioja to change their minds and join Castilla y León if they care to, but so far autonomy suits them just fine.

Note that although areas of the **Picos de Europa** *are in Asturias and León, for convenience the whole mountain range is grouped together in this chapter.*

Eastern Cantabria
Bilbao to Santander: The Costa Esmeralda

If this eastern stretch of coast is all you see of Cantabria, you may think what you have just read about rural serenity is pure fiction. This seems to be the busiest coast in all northern Spain in the summer and especially at the weekend, when half of Bilbao is out here looking for a bit of beach; they all seem to end up on the endless sweep of sand at Laredo.

Castro Urdiales

Just half an hour west of Bilbao, Castro Urdiales is one of Cantabria's most scenic fishing ports, endowed with a beach and seafood restaurants that draw hordes of *bilbaínos* every summer weekend. Magdalenian-era graffiti, discovered in the 1960s in a cave near the Plaza de Toros, dates Castro Urdiales' first inhabitants back to 12,000 BC. In ancient times, the Romans muscled in on the native Cantabrians to found Flavióbriga, located where the castle stands today.

A stronghold of the Templars in the Middle Ages, the town declined in the 14th century as Pedro I and Enrique II de Trastámara fought for this stretch of coast. It suffered even more grievously in 1813 when the French punished Castro's resistance in the War of Independence by burning most of it to the ground. Only a few streets near the harbour escaped the flames, beyond the 18th-century **Ayuntamiento**, at the top of the Paseo Marítimo.

From here, walk up to the fortress-like church of **Santa María de la Asunción**, a magnificent Gothic temple with massive buttresses and pinnacles. Constructed almost entirely in the 13th century, its Templar touches are most obvious in the unusual symbolism of

Santa María de la Asunción
open June–Sept daily 10–1.30 and 4–7.30; Oct–May daily 4–6 only

Getting around the Costa Esmeralda

The two daily FEVE **trains** between Santander and Bilbao stop at Treto (5km from Laredo), departing from Santander's Plaza de las Estaciones s/n, **t** 90 224 02 02.

Several Turytrans **buses** a day run along the coast between Santander and Bilbao; from Santander they also depart from Plaza de las Estaciones s/n, **t** 90 242 22 42.

the figures carved in the lovely frieze wrapped around the top of the church – rabbits kissing oxen, dragons devouring serpents devouring birds and more, although to see them properly you'll need binoculars. Inside there's a 13th-century sculpture, the *Virgen Blanca*, and a series of Gothic woodcarvings. You can also see the Santa Cruz, or 'Holy Cross', the Christian standard at the battle of Las Navas de Tolosa (1212). A Roman milestone remains in place in front of the church, while over the striking Roman/medieval bridge most of the walls of Castro's pentagonal **Templar castle** have survived and now shelter a lighthouse.

Castro Urdiales' beach, **Playa Brazomar**, is at the other end of town, and fills up so quickly that a new artificial beach, the **Playa de Ostende**, has been created at the western end of town. If you want a top-to-toe tan, there's also a naturist beach just outside town at **El Pocillo** (but you have to scramble down the cliffs). The best beach, however, is 8km west up at **Islares**, a small village with a magnificent strand of sand under the cliffs, interspersed with shallow lagoons ideal for young children. Just west of Islares, at **Oriñón**, there's another beach worth stopping for, and a campsite.

Laredo

Cantabria's biggest resort has little in common with its name-sake on the Río Grande. The scenery in fact isn't too different, but on its streets there is hardly a cowboy alive or dead to be seen. This Laredo does have an old town, hidden somewhere among the *urbanizaciones*, but you'll remember it mostly as a haphazard Legoland of modern apartments with a frightening dearth of shops, restaurants and bars.

Laredo was the Roman Portus Luliobrigensium, the place where the Romans finally subdued the last die-hard Celtiberians in a great sea battle. The medieval **Puebla Vieja** over the harbour was walled in by Alfonso VIII of Castile to safeguard the region from pirates; its 13th-century church of **Santa María de la Asunción** has five naves (rare for the period) and curiously carved capitals. In the sacristy note the two eagle-shaped lecterns, donated by Charles V, who landed here on his way to his retirement at Yuste. The late-Renaissance **Ayuntamiento** in Plaza Cachupín is said to mark the location of the harbour quay that the megalomaniac Emperor actually stepped on; behind it is the attractive tiled market building erected in 1902. Not really glossy or chic, Laredo especially attracts families, who cover its splendid beach and fill the scores of cafés, bars and discos in the Puebla Vieja. *Urbanizaciones* have almost reached the tip of Laredo's wide, sheltered pride and joy: **Playa de Salvé**, a gentle 5km-long crescent of sand.

From Laredo to Santander

West of Laredo the beaches continue: **Santoña** is another fishing-port resort and home town of Juan de la Cosa (b. 1460), the cartographer who accompanied Columbus on his second voyage to America (1493) and is remembered with a suitably large monument. Santoña also claims that its shipbuilders made the *Santa María* for Columbus.

Another lovely area, **Noja**, has another stretch of fine, sandy beaches and a considerable villa and apartment *urbanización* along the shore – which seems to grow daily. Local legend says that the village takes its name from Noah, whose ark, they say, washed up on one of the mountains nearby.

The rest of the way to Santander there are plenty of unexploited beaches, reachable on back roads off the main coastal route: the **Playas de Arnuero**, near the lighthouse at Cape Ajo, and the **Playas de Barayo**, west of Ajo.

Markets on the Costa Esmeralda

Castro Urdiales: Thurs.
Laredo: Mercado Municipal, daily except Sun.

Where to Stay and Eat on the Costa Esmeralda

(i) **Castro Urdiales >**
Avda de la Constitución 1, t 94 287 15 12, www.castro-urdiales.net

Castro Urdiales ✉ 39700
Castro is a more pleasing place to stay than Laredo, though inexpensive places are hard to find (ask at a bar). Bars are concentrated along C/ de la Rúa and the Paseo Marítimo.

****Las Rocas, Paseo de la Playa s/n, t 94 286 04 00, *www.lasrocashotel.com* (€€€€). This luxurious, tranquil place overlooks the beach. Prices outside August are cheaper (€€€).

***Miramar, Avda de la Playa 1, t 94 286 02 04, *www.miramardecastro.com* (€€€). A smart, modern hotel on the beach with attentive service.

***Hostal Vista Alegre, Brazomar, t 94 286 01 50 (€€). A cheaper option than Miramar but still comfortable and not far from the sea. There is also a restaurant.

**La Sota, C/ La Correría 1, t 94 287 11 88 (€€). Light and attractive *pensión* two blocks from the harbour, with sea views from most rooms.

*Pension Alberto, Avda de la República Argentina 2 (near the park), t 94 286 27 57 (€). The bathless doubles are fine. *Open Mar–Sept only.*

Camping Playa Arenillas, Ctra Bilbao–Santander, 8km from Castro Urdiales, t 94 286 31 52, *www.camping playaarenillas.com* (€). A large and comfortable campsite, by the beach. *Closed Oct–Mar.*

Mesón El Marinero, Correría 23 (in the Casa de los Chelines, by the port), t 94 286 00 05 (€€). The place to go for heaped plates of fresh seafood at reasonable prices. For less than the typical €30 meal, feast on a wide selection of tapas at the bar.

El Segoviano, La Correría 19, t 94 286 18 59 (€€). Castro's second culinary shrine, close by. Come here for roast suckling pig or a seafood grill.

El Faro de Castro, La Plazuela 1, t 94 286 72 32 (€). A good tapas place with tables overlooking the harbour. Locals flock here for the fried *calamares* at weekends.

Islares ✉ 39798
**Hs Arenillas, t 94 287 09 00 (€). A quiet and pleasant *hostal* near the beach.

(i) **Laredo** >
Alameda de Miramar s/n, **t** 94 261 10 96, www.laredo.es

(i) **Santoña**
Palacio Manzanedo, **t** 94 266 00 66, www.aytosantona.org

(i) **Noja**
Avda del Ris 79–81, **t** 94 263 15 16

Laredo ✉ 39770
Hotels here are small and quite expensive, and reservations are essential in the summer.

****Parador de Limpias, Fuente del Amor s/n, Limpias, **t** 94 262 89 00, limpias@parador.es (€€€€). A new (2004) *parador*, 10km from Laredo (on the FEVE line), in a 19th-century palace surrounded by extensive parkland. Gym, tennis and pool.

***Risco, C/ La Arenosa 2, **t** 94 260 50 30, www.hotelrisco.com (€€€). Good rooms with views over the protected bay and beach; the restaurant (€€) is Laredo's top seafood palace, offering

elaborate dishes such as a *capricho* of lobster, chicken and figs.

***Miramar, Alto de Laredo s/n, **t** 94 261 03 67, www.hmiramarlaredo.com (€€€–€€). Modern, mid-size, with huge windows to take in the huge sea views.

Montecristo, C/ Calvo Sotelo 2, **t 94 260 57 00 (€€€–€€). One of the better mid-priced beach hotels in town. *Open mid-May–mid-Sept.*

Hotel Cortijo, C/ Gonzalez Gallego 3, **t** 94 260 56 00 (€€€–€€). Plush marble décor at this modern hotel, not too far from the beach. Ask for a room with a terrace to enjoy the view.

*Pensión Salomón, C/ Menéndez Pelayo 11, **t** 94 260 50 81 (€€). With immaculate rooms and wooden floors, this is the best deal in the centre.

Casa Felipe, Travesía José Antonio 5, **t** 94 260 32 12 (€€). Deliciously fresh seafood and shellfish and a wonderful range of local cheeses are on offer at this welcoming spot.

Eastern Cantabria: Inland

This corner of the *comunidad* can offer absolutely nothing but scenery, but it is some of the sweetest and greenest cow country you'll ever see. The villages are tiny and the roads little more than paved mule tracks, meandering exasperatingly up and down the mountains, in and out of the eternal fog and mists. Almost all the houses are the lovely traditional Cantabrian type, with carved and painted wooden balconies on the front.

El Hombre Pez

In Liérganes (*see* overleaf), you might note the unusual name of the main street, the Paseo del Hombre Pez, which commemorates a wonderfully strange story from the 1700s. The 'Fish Man' was a native of this village, Francisco de la Vega Casar, who went off to Bilbao to work as a carpenter. One day he went out for a bathe in the river and never returned; his friends and family assumed he'd drowned. Nine years later some fishermen trawling in the Bay of Cádiz, way down in Andalucía, pulled up their nets and found an odd sort of fish inside, a damp and chilly man with scales covering most of his body. When they brought him back to Cádiz, a Cantabrian who had known him recognized him by a birthmark. The fish-man had lost the power of speech, but he understood enough to agree that he was in fact Francisco de la Vega Casar of Liérganes. He lived on land for nine more years, and it seems that he was exploited as a curiosity. De la Vega stayed chilly and damp until the end, and never accepted any food but raw fish. Needless to say, the people who were looking after him never let him get anywhere near the water. One day he simply slipped away and was never seen again.

Now, all this happened in the middle of the Age of Enlightenment, and Spain was full of learned sceptics, including the famous writer Fray Benito Feijóo, who couldn't let a chance like this slip by without looking into the common belief in the miraculous. The Hombre Pez's career was thoroughly investigated and plenty of witnesses confirmed all the details of the case. So did it really happen, or was it simply one of the most successful carnival tricks of all time?

(i) **Liérganes >>**
Pso del Hombre Pez,
t 94 252 80 21, www.
aytolierganes.com

Markets in Inland Eastern Cantabria

Solares: Wed.

Where to Stay and Eat in Inland Eastern Cantabria

Ramales de la Victoria
✉ 39800

This is the unlikely setting for one of Cantabria's best restaurants.

**Río Asón, Barón de Adzaneta 17, t 94 264 61 57, *www.hostalrioason.com* (€€€–€€). The restaurant's daily three-course menu is an excellent bargain, with game dishes, grilled meats with *cèpes* and a rarity – fresh salmon from the nearby Asón; it also has nine rooms and one suite. *Restaurant closed Sun eve and Mon (open Mon lunch in summer).*

Liérganes ✉ 39800

Liérganes is a thermal spa, and consequently the most dependable place to look for a hotel in these little-touristed parts.

***Gran Hotel Balneario, C/ José Antonio s/n, t 94 252 80 11, *www. grupocastelar.com* (€€€). The most luxurious of the spa hotels, with every modern facility.

***Posada del Sauce, C/ José Antonio s/n, t 94 252 80 23, *www.grupocastelar. com* (€€€). A century-old stone inn with attractively decorated rooms, a pool and a good restaurant.

***Casona El Arral, C/ Convento 1, t 94 252 84 75, *www.casona-elarral. com* (€€€). A charmingly converted 19th-century mansion surrounded by gardens on the river.

**El Cantábrico, Pso del Hombre Pez 8, t 94 252 80 48 (€€€–€€). A modern and relatively luxurious place.

Small Nowheres and Secret Caves

Cueva de Covalanas
open summer roughly 10–8; winter Wed–Sun 10–2; times vary according to season, arrange a visit through the tourist office on t 94 264 65 04; adm

South of Laredo the N629 for Burgos heads into the rugged and empty valley of the Soba. Near Ampuero you can visit one of the major sanctuaries of Cantabria, **Nuestra Señora de la Bien Aparecida**, a 17th-century chapel commemorating a miraculous appearance of the Virgin. Near **Ramales de la Victoria**, on the borders of Euskadi, there are a number of Palaeolithic painted caves, although only the **Cueva de Covalanas** is open to the public.

The area directly south of Santander is an odd region. Once it was one of the biggest mining areas in the north, but it is finally being allowed to recuperate; there are mineral springs everywhere, and a small, modern spa resort, **Liérganes**, the biggest village in the area.

Santander

The capital of Cantabria, Santander has a lot in common with San Sebastián – a large city beautifully situated on a protected bay, popularized by royalty as a summer resort. The story has it that Queen Isabel II first came down in the 1860s in the hope that the sea air would help with a bad dose of the clap (which she probably got from General O'Donnell, the prime minister, or another up-and-coming politician). Again, after the First World War, it was *the* fashionable place to go for Madrileños, especially with the founding of an international summer university (named after

Getting to and around Santander

By Air

Santander's **airport** is 7km away at Maliaño (no buses), with daily connections to Barcelona and Madrid with Iberia (**t** 94 220 2156) and to London Stansted with Ryanair (**t** 94 220 24 12). Airport information *www.aena.es*, **t** 94 220 21 00.

By Ferry

From Santander, **Brittany Ferries** sail to Plymouth twice-weekly from mid-March to mid-November. For information in Santander, call **t** 94 236 06 11, *www.brittanyferries.es*, or visit the ticket office at the Estación Marítima.

By Train

The train stations are both on Plaza de las Estaciones s/n. **RENFE**, **t** 902 240 202 for information, has connections with Madrid, Palencia, Reinosa, Segovia and Valladolid. The narrow-gauge **FEVE**, **t** 94 209 51 11, *www.feve.es*, has trains to Bilbao, Oviedo, Torrelavega and Unquera; unfortunately they miss out the coastline towns east of Santander, which are served instead by buses.

By Bus

The central bus station is conveniently opposite the train stations on Navas de Tolosa, **t** 94 221 19 95, *www.santandereabus.com*. Connections from here include: **Continental Auto** to Burgos, Madrid and Ontaneda-Vejores; **Turytrans** to nearly all the coastal towns and resorts, and also to Bilbao, Zarauz, San Sebastián, Llanes, Oviedo, Gijón, Vitoria and Pamplona; **Intercar** to Galicia, Asturias and Euskadi; **Fernández** to León and **Autocares de Cantabria** to Logroño.

The main line up into the Picos de Europa is **Palomera**, with runs to Potes and Fuente Dé. Within Santander itself there are frequent buses and trolleys (nos.1, 2 and 7) that run from the centre to El Sardinero, just 20 minutes away.

By Boat

Lanchas Reginas, **t** 94 221 67 53, runs a service to the beaches across the bay, with boats leaving every 15 minutes from 10.30am to 8.30pm from the Muelle de Ferrys, two blocks from the cathedral. They also offer tours of the bay and excursions around the Río Cubas. Call for details.

By Taxi

For a radio taxi, call **t** 94 233 33 33, and **t** 94 236 91 91.

Menéndez Pelayo, Santander's favourite son and Spain's greatest antiquarian), offering holidaymakers highbrow culture to complement its wide beaches. Still, despite this and its widely acclaimed International Music Festival in August, Santander lacks the excitement and *joie de vivre* of San Sebastián.

On the other hand, Santander has been a great town for disasters. Two of the most recent were the explosion of a ship full of dynamite in 1893, killing 500 and clearing most of the harbour area, and the fire of 1941, which started in the Archbishop's Palace and destroyed most of the old centre. No city in northern Spain shows a more striking split personality. At the centre it's a gritty, workaday town rather like Bilbao without the smokestacks, but stray a few streets to the other side of the peninsula and you'll be in what seems to be a Belle Epoque dream resort, casino and all. The Santander of the festivals shows a bright and modern face to the world, but the real atmosphere of the place is still best represented by the pigeon-spattered statue of Franco in the centre

09

Cantabria and the Picos de Europa | Santander

Cathedral
C/ Casmiro Sainz 4;
open Mon–Fri 10–1 and
4–7.30, Sat 10–1 and
4.30–8, Sun 8–2

Santísimo Cristo
open June–Sept, daily
8–1 and 4–8; Oct–May
daily 8–1 and 5–8

Museo de
Prehistoria y
Arqueología
www.cultura-cantabria.
org; open Tues–Sat 9–1
and 4–7, Sun 11–2

Museo de
Bellas Artes
C/ Rubio 6; open
summer Mon–Fri 11.15–1
and 5.30–9, Sat 10.30–1;
winter Mon–Fri 10.15–1
and 5.30–9, Sat 10–1

(currently one of only three in the whole of Spain, although the local government have promised to dismantle it), and the grey streets still named after Nationalist hoodlums of the Civil War.

The Cathedral and Museums

In the centre, next to the Diputación Regional, Santander's much-altered and rebuilt **cathedral** is interesting mostly for its early Gothic crypt; this now forms the separate church of **Santísimo Cristo**, where a glass floor has been installed over the remains of a Roman building.

The **Museo de Prehistoria y Arqueología** has exhibits devoted to Cantabria's prehistoric cave-dwellers, including tools, reproductions of their art, and two disc-shaped star tombstones the size of tractor tyres made just before the Roman conquest, discovered in the valley of the Buelna.

The best parts of old Santander lie to the north of the fishing port and the railway station, across the main Avda Calvo Sotelo. Near the Ayuntamiento, the **Museo de Bellas Artes** has, besides a contemporary art collection of dubious merit, a good Zurbarán and

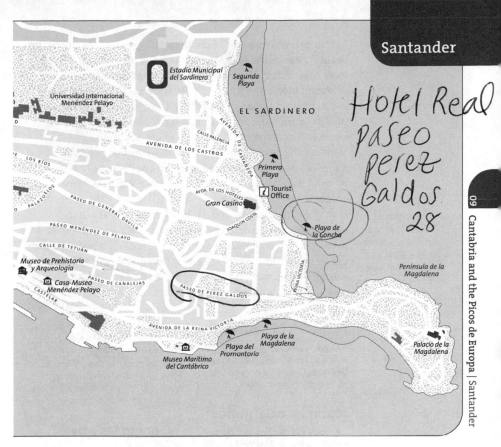

Santander

09

Cantabria and the Picos de Europa | Santander

several Goyas, including a portrait of Ferdinand VII, commissioned by the city to flatter the king.

Casa Museo de Menéndez Pelayo
open Mon–Fri 9.30–11.30, guided tours available

Nearby, the **Casa Museo de Menéndez Pelayo** has an extensive collection of books, many of them by great Catalan writers, which were donated to the city by the scholar himself. Behind the Ayuntamiento, the iron and glass **market** is the most colourful sight in Santander, especially the pride of the town: the glorious fish market.

Museo Marítimo del Cantábrico
open May–mid-Sept daily 10–9; mid-Sept–April daily 10–7; adm

On the way out to the beaches, Avenida Reina Victoria passes Santander's new **Museo Marítimo del Cantábrico**, which has an array of model ships, exhibits on the local maritime tradition and an aquarium.

El Sardinero

The 1941 fire destroyed most of Santander's character but it spared the suburb of **El Sardinero**, with its fine twin beaches, imaginatively named **Primera** (First) and **Segunda** (Second), backed by the enormous Belle Epoque **casino**, recently refurbished in an effort to revive some of the city's lost panache.

El Sardinero is separated from the working end of the city by the beautiful **Peninsula de la Magdalena**, a city park fringed by two more splendid beaches, the **Playa de la Magdalena** and the **Playa del Promontorio**. The Tudor-style **Palacio de la Magdalena** at the end of the peninsula was a gift from the city to Alfonso XIII; when the king accepted it, Santander's return to fashion as a summer resort was guaranteed. Today it is part of the university.

Besides the beaches in the city, there are several miles of golden dunes across the bay at **Somo**, **El Puntal** and **Pedrena**, linked every 15 minutes by boat from the centre of town; **Playa las Atenas** nearby is a naturist beach. Just west of Santander at Liencres, there is another fine and very popular beach, **Valdearenas**, a huge expanse of sand bordered by pine woods. And if you have children in tow you will probably be visiting the **Parque de la Naturaleza de Cabárceno**, 10km south of the city at **Obregón**, where a bit of land wasted by strip mining has been recycled into an attractive and enormous zoo, with more than 400 species from ape to zebra.

Parque de la Naturaleza de Cabárceno
www.parquedecabarceno.com; open daily summer 9.30–7; winter 9.30–6; adm

Facilities in Santander

The **post office** is on the corner of Avda Alfonso XIII and C/ Calvo Sotelo. **Ciberlope**, C/ Lope de Vega 14, **t** 94 203 79 10, offers Internet access.

Markets in Santander

Plaza de la Esperanza behind the Ayuntamiento on Tues, Wed, Fri and Sat for food; Mon and Thurs for clothes; in Plaza de México on Mon, Wed, Fri and Sat for food; Tues and Fri for clothes (by the bullring at the end of Calle de San Fernando).

Shopping in Santander

Santander is a good city for shopping and it is very easy to while away an afternoon strolling along streets such as C/ San Francisco in the city centre and others in the vicinity.

A former covered market on C/ General Mola is also now an upbeat shopping centre with bars and boutiques.

Lucio Herrezuelo, C/ Calvo Sotelo 23. A good place for quality shoes and leather goods.

El Oso Goloso, C/ Calderón de La Barca 19. Gourmet deli selling goodies like chestnuts and goat's cheese.

La Ruta del Vino, C/ Peña Herbosa 23. A wide selection of wines and liqueurs.

Librería Estudio, C/ Calvo Sotelo 21. Has a good selection of maps and books, including a number of walking guides to the Picos de Europa.

ⓘ Santander >>
Regional: *Plaza de Velarde 5,* **t** *94 231 07 08*

Municipal: *Jardines de Pereda (in the city centre, facing the port),* **t** *94 220 30 00, www.ayto-santander.es; at the beach in El Sardinero,* **t** *94 274 04 14; and in the bus station opposite the train stations on Navas de Tolosa; they offer free guided walking tours*

Where to Stay in Santander

Santander ✉ 39000

July to September are the busy (and expensive) months here, especially the first two, when the music festival and International University are in full swing. Prices are as high as in San Sebastián, though there are plenty of *casas particulares* to preserve your budget. Hang around the bus and train stations and someone will probably lead you to one.

Luxury (€€€€€)

Santander's most elegant hotels are all found on the back side of town by the beaches. There are countless expensive chain hotels, with lots of amenities but little charm.

*****Hotel Real**, Pso de Pérez Galdós 28, **t** 94 227 25 50, *www.hotelreal.es*. A lovely Belle Epoque-style hotel located near the Playa de la Magdalena offering marvellous bay views, fine rooms and a well-kept garden.

****Hotel Bahía, Avda de Alfonso XIII 6, t 94 220 50 00, www.grupo sardinero.com. Stately modern hotel towering like a lighthouse between the old town and the port.

Very Expensive (€€€€)
****Hotel Hoyuela, Avda de los Hoteles 7, t 94 228 2628, www.gruposardinero.com. Perhaps the prettiest hotel overlooking El Sardinero's beach, in a turn-of-the 20th-century mansion.

***Hotel Sardinero, Plaza de Italia 1, t 94 227 11 00, www.gruposardinero.com. Popular and near the beaches of Sardinero and the casino.

Expensive (€€€)
Hotel Vincci Puerto Chico, Castelar 25, t 94 222 52 00, www.hotelvincci puertochico.com. The new owners of the former Castelar have updated the hotel which enjoys sea views and excellent location in the old town.

Silken Rio Hotel, Avenida Reina Victoria 153, t 94 227 43 00, www.hoteles-silken.com/santander_rio. The former Rhin hotel has been renovated to make the most of its smart location on Avda Reina Victoria, the main street facing the Sardinero beachfront.

***Hotel Central, General Mola 5, t 94 222 24 00, www.elcentral.com. Good summer choice with spacious terraces and sea views.

**HR Paris, Avda de los Hoteles 6, t 94 227 23 50, inforeservas@hparis.net. Elegantly-furnished rooms in a rambling old queen of a building near the casino.

Piñamar, C/ Ruiz de Alda 15, t 94 236 18 66. Modern, functional and located near the train station.

Moderate (€€)
The cheaper hotels have gained a notoriety for being either dreary or rip-offs. If the price you are quoted seems ridiculously high, find out what it includes: a common sting, especially among the pensiónes around El Sardinero, is to include a 'secret' breakfast for which you will be charged even if you don't know about it. An official room-only price list should be posted somewhere near the front door.

**Hs La Mexicana, C/ Juan de Herrera 3, t 94 222 23 50. Good value choice in the centre, with friendly management and comfortable rooms. Big enough to have space when others in this price range are full. Budget out of season.

**HR San Glorio, C/ Ruiz Zorilla 18, t 94 231 29 62, www.sanglorio.com. Centrally located, with simple rooms and a restaurant.

**Hs Rocamar, Avda de los Castros 41, t 94 227 72 68, www.hostalrocamar.com. Classic 1960s-style hostal located on a street in El Sardinero where there are several other inexpensive places to choose from.

Inexpensive (€)
*Pensión La Porticada, C/ Méndez Núñez 6, t 94 222 78 17, www.hlaporticada.com. Sparkling rooms with balconies set in a building that speaks of vanished glory. Cheaper rates are available with shared bathrooms.

Pension La Corza, Hernán Cortés 25, t 94 221 29 50. Only eight rooms, so book early if you want a good deal in a central location.

Camping Cabo Mayor, t 94 239 15 42, www.cabomayor.com. Located by the Cabo Mayor lighthouse. Closed mid-Oct–Mar.

Eating Out in Santander

Unlike San Sebastián, Santander is hardly known for its cuisine. The seafood, however, is always good, and the traditional place to get it is at the rather piquant Barrio Pesquero, an area rebuilt after the fire, just behind the stations. Around the beaches, the restaurants are more elaborate.

El Serbal, C/ Andrés del Río 7, t 942 22 25 15, www.elserbal.com (€€€; menu degustación €55). The swankiest restaurant in town, with elaborate contemporary cuisine in elegant surroundings. Winner of numerous awards, so it is always worth booking in advance.

Restaurante Cañadio, C/ Gómez Oreña 15, t 94 231 41 49, www.restaurante canadio.com (€€€–€€). For that special

09 Cantabria and the Picos de Europa | Santander

seafood moment – one of the best in town. Try the *croquetas de bacalao* (croquettes filled with cod) as a taster at the bar.

Bar del Puerto, Hernán Cortés 63 (in the Puerto Chico), t 94 221 30 01 (€€). The seafood here is worth stopping off for.

Bodega del Riojano, Río de la Pila 5 (north of the Jardines de Pereda), t 94 221 67 50 (€€). One of Santander's typical *bodegas* in the old quarter, offering healthy servings of tapas. Specialities are *rabo de buey* (oxtail), *morcillo estofado* (a blood sausage stew), and stuffed peppers. *Closed Sun eve and Mon.*

La Sardina de Plata, Glorieta del Dr Fleming 3 (in El Sardinero), t 94 227 10 35 (€€; *menu degustación* €33). A fashionable place in a very pretty setting, offering imaginative renderings of traditional dishes such as *bacalao* with red peppers. *Closed Feb, Sun eve and Mon, except in summer.*

Bodega Cigaleña, C/ Daoíz y Velarde 19, t 94 221 30 62 (€€–€). A typical dark *bodega* which harbours a wine museum; come here to get a feel for traditional fare. *Closed Sun.*

Zacarías, C/ General Mola 1, t 94 221 23 23 (€€–€). Offers a total '*mar y montaña*' Cantabrian culinary experience, including the region's excellent cheeses.

El Diluvio, General Mola 14, t 94 221 85 63 (€). One of the best bars in town for mouthwatering canapés and tapas; always packed with locals.

⭐ **La Gaviota** >

La Gaviota, C/ Marqués de la Ensenada 32, t 94 222 11 32 (€). A favourite in the *barrio*, where you can try the seafood *menú del día* for under €10 or, for a little more, you can order a plate of whatever delicacy has come home with the fishermen.

Restaurante Modena, C/ Eduardo Benot 5, t 94 231 33 71 (€). A rare Italian restaurant with the usual pizza/pasta plus a few surprises, like crêpes.

Entertainment and Nightlife in Santander

Nightlife in Santander is concentrated in two places: first the proper *marcha* grounds in the old town, with a vast number of bars and clubs around C/ de la Pila and Pza de Cañadío. This is the place where you're most likely to find live music and a raucous good time. Somewhat more staid entertainment can be had around El Sardinero; the Plaza de Italia attracts the older set, while the overdressed young in search of fun head for the numerous bars and discos in Calle Panamá.

Festival Internacional de Santander. Since 1951, this August festival has showcased an extraordinary variety of music, dance and spectacle from around the world. Along with all the big-league culture, popular Spanish and Latin American song, dance, magic shows and fireworks take place every night throughout August at the Auditorium and the Finca Altamira. For information contact the Oficina del Festival, Palacio de Festivales de Cantabria, C/ Gamazo s/n, 39004, t 94 221 05 08, *www.festivalsantander.com*. Tickets are on sale in advance from the ticket booth at the Palacio de Festivales, from any branch of the Caja Cantabria bank, or from the special Festival booth in the Jardines de Pereda, near the library, t 94 222 34 34 (*open 11–2 and 5–8*).

Bodega La Montaña, San Fernando 28 (the park boulevard northwest of the RENFE and FEVE train stations), t 94 223 10 39. A typical wine *bodega*, with restaurant, full of big old barrels.

Canela, Plaza de Cañadío. One of many bars on this buzzy, late-night square, where there's always plenty going on.

La Conveniente, C/ Gómez Oreña 9. An 18th-century *bodega* resurrected into an evocative, cavernous bar, lined by 8,000-plus bottles, with live piano nightly. *Closed Sun.*

Gran Casino, Plaza de Italia s/n, t 94 203 05 00. You can risk your euros from 7pm to 4am at this lavish nighttime haunt (dress up and bring your passport).

La Luna, C/ General Mola 35. A classic place for those wanting to avoid the strictly young scene.

El Rocambole, C/ Hernán Cortés 10. An especially popular venue, which offers plenty of space to party until the rosy-fingered Aurora appears in the sky.

South of Santander: The Heart of Cantabria

South of the capital the land gradually rises to the Montañas de Santander, a pretty, hilly region that supports only a handful of villages. There are plenty of wide open spaces along these high roads of the old County of Castile, but there are a few attractions besides the solitude: caves of prehistoric art, untouched forests, the source of the Ebro and one of the sexiest churches in Europe.

The Caves of Puente Viesgo

If you haven't made an appointment in advance to see the caves of Altamira (see p.201), you can at least get into Cantabria's second most spectacular set of prehistoric grottoes at **Puente Viesgo**. There are five caves altogether, but the only one open to the public is the **Cueva del Castillo**. Decorated with graceful line drawings of stags, horses and other animals, this ensemble is believed to predate the even more eloquent art at Altamira.

Cueva del Castillo
open May–Sept Wed–Sun 10–2 and 4–6.30; Oct–April Wed–Sun 9.30–5; adm

Reinosa, on the rail line and just off the A67 motorway, is the main hub in this part of the Cantabrian mountains, with most of the area's hotels and restaurants. The source of northern Spain's longest river, the **Nacimiento del Ebro**, is signposted to the northwest in **Fontibre**; you can clamber down in the trees to stick your toes in the stream gurgling out of the ground. The river has barely begun when, just on the other side of Reinosa, it is dammed to form the massive **Embalse del Ebro**, the grass on its jagged shore cropped by horses and dairy cows, following the outline of a prehistoric lake. **Corconte**, on the eastern end of the lake, bottles mineral water next to an old spa.

The most beautiful part of the region lies west of Fontibre, in the virgin valleys of the **Saja National Reserve**, where beech, oak and birch forests follow the courses of clear streams. Real explorers can make for **Suano** and the **Población de Suso**, villages that figure on few maps but can claim a large number of dolmens, a huge cromlech and the ruins of a Templar castle. The region's most important ski installation, **Alto Campóo**, lies to the west.

Alto Campóo
www.altocampoo. com for ski resort information; also phone t 94 277 92 39 or t 699 90 62 20

A Trinity of Romanesque Churches

South of Reinosa you'll find good Romanesque churches – in **Bolmir** and more significantly in **Retortillo**. Retortillo is near the scanty remains of the Roman city of **Julióbriga**, once the most important city of Cantabria. Set amidst the low walls is the church, with a unique sloping stair leading up to its campanile. Over the door, note the carving of two animals shaking hands.

Julióbriga
open Wed–Sun 10.30–12.30 and 4–7; adm

But the most extraordinary Romanesque church of all is south in **Cervatos**: the singular 12th-century **Colegiata**, at the top of a newly

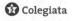 **Colegiata**

Getting around South of Santander

Reinosa's **bus station**, at the south end of town, is served from Santander by García, t 94 221 09 60, and Alsa, t 902 42 22 42. Donato, t 94 275 14 32, links Reinosa to Espinilla and La Lomba in the Alto Campóo.

cobbled lane. It has a tympanum with an oriental design, a frieze of lions and, carved on to the corbels and capitals in the apse, unabashedly erotic figures that a respectable guidebook hesitates to describe. This unique medieval tantric temple probably survived clerical prudishness over the centuries because of its remote location and the explanation that such exhibitionism was meant to frighten rather than tempt parishioners with the horrors of sin.

South of Cervatos, the narrow CA272 soon meets up again with the Ebro. It's a lovely road, with lots of trees and local swimming holes by tiny villages. One of the largest is **Polientes**, with a road-side statue of a spotted dog and one of Cantabria's 'rupestrian churches' in a cave, although here little old ladies have set up a table by the altar to play cards. Follow the road and Ebro east to an even more remote region and the 12th-century church at **San Martín de Elines**, with a lofty cylindrical tower, keyhole windows, more modillions and carvings by the same school as Cervatos but without any bawdy flashers and sexual contortionists. The kindly caretaker lives in the house nearest the church and will take you around the cloister, with a 9th-century wall and tombs excavated from the garden in the centre; the most impressive is the fancy sepulchre of a pilgrim who died along the route.

Markets South of Santander

Reinosa: *Mon.*

Where to Stay and Eat South of Santander

Puente Arce ✉ 39478

One of the best restaurants in Cantabria can be found at this village, 12km inland from Santander on the road to Torrelavega:

⭐ **El Nuevo Molino** >

El Nuevo Molino, Barrio Monsignor 18, t 94 257 50 55, *www.elnuevomolino.es* (€€€–€€). In an old mill on the river, this long-established restaurant has been overhauled by the energetic management of El Serbal in Santander (*see* p.195). It's the perfect place to treat yourself, with exceptional cuisine, a superb wine list, and great service. *Closed Sun eve and Tues.*

Puente Viesgo ✉ 39478

***Gran Hotel Balneario, C/ Manuel Pérez Mazo s/n, t 94 259 80 61, *www.balneariodepuenteviesgo.com* (€€€€€). If you have come to see the caves, you can stop at this sumptuous modern establishment connected to a spa that's good for your rheumatism and neurological troubles; swimming pool, sauna and all the amenities. Great online deals available.

***Casona Azul de Toranzo**, C/ General Díaz de Villegas 5, Corvera de Toranzo, t 94 259 64 00, *www.casonaazul.com* (€€€). A pair of elegant *indiano* villas 3km from Puente Viesgo have been converted into a stylish small hotel set in gardens with a croquet lawn.

Pensión Carrion, at neighbouring Alceda, t 94 259 40 16 (€€). A more realistic alternative in town.

Mesón El Cazador, Ctra General s/n, t 94 259 42 50 (€€€–€). A good country restaurant in San Vicente de Toranzo, south of Puente Viesgo; offers boar, pheasant and other game dishes.

(i) Reinosa ›
*Avenida Puente
Carlos III 23, t 94 275 52
15, www.ayto-reinosa.es*

Reinosa ✉ 39200

****Casona de Naveda de Campóo**, Plaza del Medio Lugar 37, t 94 277 95 15, *www.casonadenaveda.com* (€€€). An immaculate country hotel in an old stone house, with elegant rooms and friendly staff who can organize all kinds of activities.

***Vejo**, Avda Cantabria 83 (in the newer part of town), t 94 275 17 00, *www.hotelestrebol.com/reinosa* (€€€). The most comfortable place in town, with a garden, bar and good restaurant.

*La Casona**, C/ Campóo 3, in Nestares, t 94 275 17 88 (€€). This old inn on the Reinosa–Cabezón de la Sal road is a scenic place to stay if you're driving.

The Coast West of Santander

This lush and lovely seaside stretch has been spared any Laredo toadstools, and what tourist development there is remains fairly discreet. When the summer hordes have vanished and the little winding roads belong to you alone, it is haunting and strange in a fairylike way. Even in the rain.

Santillana del Mar

Jean-Paul Sartre, who had always wanted to be a guidebook writer but couldn't get a break, practised on Santillana del Mar, pronouncing it 'the most beautiful village in Spain'. Sooner or later someone in town will remind you of this, and it's best not to argue. The tour buses disgorge their hundreds daily upon this tiny village (which despite the 'del Mar' is not on the sea), and in summer it can be a ghastly tourist inferno, with no place to put your car for a mile around. If you come at all, do it out of season, or spend the night after the day-trippers have all gone.

Santillana is both an evocative medieval town of grand palaces and a country village of dairy farmers, whose pastures lie on the hills just beyond the mellowed stone and half-timbered houses that line Santillana's patchwork of ancient streets and squares. Its past distinctions come from great wealth in medieval times, which was earned from wool and linen. By 1600 nearly every man in town was a noble, or *hidalgo* (from *hijo de algo*, 'son of somebody'), courtesy of easily purchased titles of nobility in the time of Charles V (1516–56) and his son, Philip II (1556–98). So they stopped doing any work, and Santillana has changed little since. In the 1920s Juan Antonio Güell López, grandson of the famous Marquis of Comillas (*see* box, p.203), became minister for tourism under the dictatorship of Primo de Rivera. He took a special interest in Santillana, and began the restoration of its old buildings.

The village is famous as the birthplace of Spain's favourite fictional rogue, Gil Blas, and home of the real Marqués de Santillana, Íñigo López de Mendoza, the Spanish Sir Philip Sidney,

Getting along the Coast West of Santander

FEVE **trains** from Santander go to Torrelavega, with frequent bus connections to Santillana. Another FEVE station is 3km from San Vicente – a lovely walk if you're not carrying a lot.

Suances, Santillana, Comillas and San Vicente are linked around six times daily to Santander by La Cantábrica de Comillas or SA Continental **buses**, from Santander's main bus station.

Colegiata
open April–Oct daily 10–1.30 and 4–7.30; Nov–Mar Tues–Sat 10–1.30 and 4–6.30; adm

Museo Diocesano
across town near the car park, t 94 284 03 17; open Mar–Jan Tues–Sun 10–1.30 and 4–7.30; closed Feb

a warrior and poet and courtly lover whose house still stands on the Calle del Cantón. Other houses have equally noble pedigrees; an archduchess of Austria owned the one across from the **Colegiata**. The latter is a 12th-century masterpiece, dedicated to St Juliana (or Iliana), an Anatolian martyr under Diocletian whose remains have lain here since the 6th century, and who gave her name to the town; the monks who built the cloister for themselves owned most of the town and ran its affairs until the 1400s.

The church has a fine weatherbeaten façade, rebuilt in the 1700s with bits and pieces of the Romanesque original tacked on; inside, the impressive altar is made of silver from Mexico – plenty of the *hidalgos'* younger sons went off to America to make their fortune, and many of the family mansions in the village are *casas de indianos*. There is a beautiful, ivy-draped **cloister**, with capitals carved with biblical and hunting scenes. The ticket to the cloister will also get you into the **Museo Diocesano**, which is installed in the 17th-century Convento de Regina Coeli. It is Gothic in style and displays an exceptional collection of ecclesiastical artefacts from all over Cantabria, some Templar in origin, and all perfectly restored by the nuns.

In the eloquent Plaza Ramón Pelayo, the tower house of Don Borja holds the **Fundación Santillana**, which organizes temporary exhibitions on local themes – particularly on the region's seafaring past and its relationship with the Americas. This makes up in a way for the town's anomalous name 'del Mar' when it's 3km from the sea. On the same *plaza* stands the **Ayuntamiento**, rebuilt in 1770, and, from the same century, the **Palacio de Barreda-Bracho**, now the Parador Gil Blas (*see* p.204).

Twenty or so years ago, residents of Santillana still kept cattle on the ground floors of their homes and sold delicious rich milk by the glass and tasty *bizcocho* (cake) by the piece to tourists. You'll see less of that today, but there are still plenty of souvenirs to buy. If you're in a hurry to get to the promised Mar, the closest beaches are at **Suances**, just 5km away; it's a fishing village and a small resort. Although the sea here isn't the cleanest, people come here for water sports, including surfing. Suances began life as Portus Blendium, the chief Roman port on this part of the coast, though there's nothing Roman to be seen.

The Caves of Altamira

🌟 Altamira

¡Mira, papa!
¡Bueyes!
(Look, papa!
Oxen!)
María de Sautuola,
discoverer of the
paintings at Altamira

From Santillana you can walk up to Altamira in 20 minut
though don't expect to get in unless you've written three)
advance (*Centro de Investigación de Altamira, Santillana del Mar,*
✉ *39330 Santander*) and are one of the 20 chosen ones allowed the
15-minute glimpse at one of the sublime masterpieces of Upper
Palaeolithic art. Still, an extraordinary number of people show up
at the caves anyway, pilgrim-like, to pay homage to the genius of
the artists of *c.* 12,000 BC who covered the undulating ceiling with
stunningly exuberant, vividly coloured paintings of bison, horses,
boars and stags. Only at Lascaux, up at the northern end of the
Franco-Cantabrian arc of Magdalenian cave painting, will you find
such powerful, masterful technique; the movement and strength
in the coiled, startled and galloping bisons, the attentive deer, the
frisking horses are awesome. As they say, 'This is the infancy of art,
not an art of infancy.'

The story of the discovery of Altamira, however, is a parable of
perceptions. As at Lascaux, an ancient landslide sealed the
entrance of the caves and tunnels (and more or less vacuum-
packed the paintings) until it was rediscovered by a hunter and
his dog in 1868. In 1875, Don Marcelino de Sautuola, an amateur
prehistorian, was intrigued by the black drawings on the walls in
the outer rooms and, over the years, explored them, in 1879 taking
his nine-year-old daughter María along. The child wandered a little
deeper into the caves, and lifted her eyes to find the superb
polychrome paintings. Although no one had ever seen the like, the
marquis at once recognized the ceiling for what it was: a ravishing
work of genius from the Stone Age. Excited, he published a
description of Altamira but, rather than receiving the expected
response of awe and wonder from the 'experts' in the field,
Sautuola was mocked, ridiculed, viciously attacked, and even
accused of forging the paintings; the scholars simply refused to
believe that people who used stone axes were capable of painting,
one of the 'civilized arts'.

Undaunted, the marquis held his ground, insisting Altamira was
for real, and died heartbroken in 1888, vilified and as forgotten as
the caves themselves. Fifteen years later, the discovery of a dozen
painted caves in the Vézère Valley in the Dordogne led to a
change of mind, beginning in 1902 with one expert, E. Cartailhac,
making a public apology to Sautuola's memory in his *Mea Culpa
d'un sceptique*.

Although the 'white disease' caused by the moisture in the
breath of visitors has restricted admission to the caves, you can do
the next best thing at Altamira: visit an exact replica, including
videos and a holographic tableau detailing the history of the caves
and offering explanations of the stunning reproductions of the

paintings. Picasso, for one, would not have approved – he visited the caves back in the 1920s, declaring that 'not one of us is capable of painting like this' – but his posthumous hand-wringing is unlikely to deter the extra 400,000 tourists who show up annually to visit the fascinating **museum**. You can also explore a small stalactite **cave** which is prettily lit to emphasize nature's wonders as compensation for the inaccessibility of the more fragile works of man.

Altamira museum
www.museodealtamira.
mcu.es; open June–Sept
Tues–Sat 9.30–7.30;
Oct–May Tues–Sat
9.30–5, Sun
9.30–3; adm

Comillas, with a Little Modernista Madness

⓲ Comillas Definitely *the* place to be on this stretch of the coast, the seaside resort of Comillas offers a bit of Catalan quirkiness in a gorgeous setting, framed by two endearing beaches – the Playa Comillas and the longer Playa de Oyambre. Comillas's old town, with its rough cobbled streets and arcaded mansions, has been a quiet watering hole for the Madrid and Barcelona aristocracy for a long time; the latter brought along their favourite architects in the 19th century to add a Modernista flair.

The peculiar legacies of the robber barons are up on the hills to the west of the village centre. There you will see Gaudí's **El Capricho**, built for a relation of the Marquis de Comillas, and subsequently restored and pressed into service as a restaurant (*see* p.205). If not one of the architect's more ambitious works, it is a delightful house, exciting the envy of the crowd of Spanish tourists usually milling about it. The main feature is an eccentric, perfectly non-functional tower, half-lighthouse and half-minaret. The decorative theme, held together by lovely ceramic tiles in green and gold and by extravagant wrought-iron balconies and cornices, has a repeated sunflower motif.

Next to El Capricho you can have a peek into the vanished lifestyle of Comillas' rich and shameless at the summer palace of the Marqués de Comillas, the **Palacio de Sobrellano**. A work of another Catalan, Gaudí's friend Joan Martorell, this ponderous palace in a quirky Modernista neo-Gothic style is protected by an imitation castle wall with oubliettes. It's worth taking the guided tour to see Gaudí's grinning Modernista dragons, which adorn the walnut fireplace in the marquis' old billiard room; more wicked specimens lurk on the arms of his fireside chairs. Next door, the marquis' **chapel** adds the perfect touch of discreet surrealism to the ensemble. It's bigger than Comillas' parish church, and inside there are furnishings by Gaudí himself and marble sepulchres of the marquis and his family.

Palacio de
Sobrellano
open July–early Sept
daily 10.30–1.30 and
4–7.30; mid-Sept–June
Wed–Sun 10.30–1.30
and 4–7.30; adm

The third member of this singular trio stands on the opposite hill, across the main road through Comillas, but it commands the views for miles around. Construction of the **Universidad Pontificia** began in 1883, with a plan by Martorell and some financial help from

Universidad
Pontificia
opening times vary –
check at tourist office

The Instant Marquis

The Spain of the Industrial Revolution is a land not very well known, but if the nation's capitalists never could match the mills of the Midlands or Massachusetts in the 19th century they certainly produced some marvels, and some incredible robber-baron careers. Antonio López was a local boy who went off to Cuba and made a fortune in shipping and slaves (slavery wasn't abolished in Spanish-run Cuba until 1886), and then moved out and made another pile running a monopoly, the Philippine National Tobacco Company. He came back home, and purchased the title of Marquis of Comillas.

The new marquis' son married the daughter of Joan Güell, the richest man in Barcelona, who had also started in Cuba and ended up as Spain's biggest textile magnate. If the name is familiar, you're thinking of Antoni Gaudí's famous surreal Güell Park in Barcelona. Like Cosimo de' Medici in old Florence, this robber baron had a talented aesthete to succeed him, whose sponsorship of Gaudí sparked the golden age of Modernista architecture in Catalunya. It was the Güell connection that brought Gaudí to Cantabria, where he helped with the López family palace in 1878 and came back to build El Capricho in 1883. The centre of the López interests was Barcelona, where they ran factories, banks and the Transatlántica shipping line (which later fell into the grasp of the greatest of all Spanish robber barons, Juan March, and still runs most of the Spanish island ferries). The Lópezes lived on the Ramblas in Barcelona, but they spent their summers here, bringing along their Catalan friends and making Comillas a genteel upper-class resort; locals called them the 'Transatlánticos'.

López's castle-like summer mansion, on the hill overlooking the town, was one of the most spectacular private homes in its day, and the centre of the glittering social season Comillas knew at the turn of the 20th century. But modern capitalist glories never seem to last more than a generation or two, and today López's palace stands as empty and weird and forlorn as *Citizen Kane*'s Xanadu.

Antonio López. The pope's university moved to Madrid in 1964, leaving a huge complex of buildings with no specific use; still the people of Comillas maintain the site and give tours of the sumptuous main building containing decorations by a third major figure of Catalan Modernism, Lluis Domenech i Montaner. There are frescoed rooms and a chapel, but the best features are the figures carved in wood over the main stairway in the form of gargoyles: fearsome monsters share space with, among others, a house cat, a chicken and a fly.

If you like Domenech i Montaner there's a wonderfully florid **Monument to Antonio López** by him near the beach, within sight of Comillas' peculiar **cemetery**, built in a Gothic ruin and topped with a huge marble angel. Domenech i Montaner is responsible for some of the funerary statues inside too, and it isn't difficult to guess which ones are his.

San Vicente de la Barquera

The next resort to the west, San Vicente de la Barquera is still as much a fishing port as a holiday retreat, though it's hugely popular with Madrileños in summer – you won't find a place to park your car. Marvellously sited on a hill in the last elbow-bend of the wide and marshy Río Escudo (arriving on the coastal road from the west provides the best view), it is linked by a long causeway to the eastern coast, near the town beach. The older, upper town is dominated by the rose-coloured parish church **Nuestra Señora de**

los Ángeles, a 13th-century transitional work containing the finely sculpted Renaissance tomb of the Inquisitor Antonio Corro. Below, interwoven branches of plane trees add a French touch to the main *plaza*. Every quarter of an hour the bell tower of the San Vicente church booms out a recording of the first phrase of Schubert's *Ave María*, guaranteed to drive you nuts. The locals claim an enemy of their town had it installed – with any luck it will be a bad memory by the time you get there.

If you want to take a dip inland in this western end of Cantabria, the first town south of San Vicente is **Cabezón de la Sal**, a town where the *pozos de sal* – 'salt wells' – have been mined since before the Romans came. Cabezón is little more than an industrial centre, but nearby both the landscapes and the area's modest attraction remind you of Cantabria's more rural side: at **Carrejo**, the **Museo Regional de la Naturaleza** has exhibits of local flora and fauna in an 18th-century *palacio*.

Museo Regional de la Naturaleza open April–Oct Tues–Sat 11–2 and 4–7, Sun 11–2; Nov–Mar Tues–Sat 11–2 and 4–6

Beyond that come two rather refined villages, each with a number of fine mansions and other works: **Ruente** and **Bárcena Mayor**. Bárcena especially, on a back road in the mountains, retains a medieval ambience, with arcaded streets, wooden balconies and woodworkers' shops. Legend claims it as one of the first towns of Cantabria and a stronghold of the *foramontanos*, as they call the mountaineers who resisted the Moors in the Dark Ages; the village has a fountain that goes back to Visigothic times.

Markets on the Coast West of Santander

Suances: Tues.
Torrelavega: Wed.
Comillas: Thurs.
San Vicente and **Cabezón**: Sat.

⭐ La Casa del Organista >>

ⓘ Santillana del Mar >
C/ Jesús Otero 20, t 94 281 82 51, santillana@cantabria.org

⭐ La Casa de Güela >>

Where to Stay and Eat on the Coast West of Santander

Santillana ✉ 39330

Ask at the tourist office for a list of *casas particulares*, though many of them are in the newer suburbs en route to Altamira; or head for C/ Los Hornos or Avda Le Dorat, which have plenty of rooms.

*****Casa de Marqués**, C/ Canton 24, t 94 281 88 88 (€€€€). Magnificent new hotel in a 15th-century building with a stone and beam interior. *Closed mid-Dec–Mar.*

***Parador de Santillana Gil Blas**, Plaza Ramón Pelayo 11, t 94 281 80 00, *santillana@parador.es* (€€€€). Wonderfully atmospheric with medieval rooms and an elegant dining room; reserve well in advance in season; request a room on the first or second floor.

La Casa del Organista, C/ Los Hornos 4, t 94 284 03 52, *www.casadel organista.com* (€€€). Gorgeous wood-panelled rooms with sloping ceilings, in a medieval mansion overlooking fields on the edge of town.

***Hotel Altamira**, C/ Cantón 1, t 94 281 80 25, *www.hotelaltamira.com* (€€€–€€). A good choice, in a palace with a patio and garden; an elegant dining room serves big plates of roast meats and is possibly the best restaurant in town.

***La Casa de Güela**, C/ Los Hornos 9, t 94 281 82 50 (€€€–€€). A beautiful boutique-style hotel with just 10 rooms in a handsome old stone palace. With pool, tennis and gardens.

Pensión El Cantón, C/ De La Carrera 3, t 94 284 02 74 (€€). A lovely and welcoming *posada*, boasting the cheapest rooms with bath in Santillana's old quarter.

Posada La Cerrá de San Roque, t 94 284 00 65 (€). A charming inn set in lovely countryside halfway between Suances and Santillana del Mar. A good family option, with pool and gardens.

Camping Santillana, t 94 281 82 50 (€€). Just north of the village, this is a more pricey campsite, but it has all amenities, including a pool and tennis courts.

La Joraca, C/ Los Hornos 20, t 94 284 0137 (€€). An atmospheric restaurant serving fine traditional cuisine prepared with flair: go for the *menú degustación* (€32).

Los Blasones, Pza de la Gándara 8, t 94 281 80 70 (€€). Feast on local and mountain specialities here – from *fabada* to grilled *langostinos* (crayfish). *Closed mid-Dec–mid-Mar.*

La Robleda, C/ Revolgo, t 94 281 83 36 (€). You pay even less for *fabada* and *langostinos* here. Otherwise the bar nearest the Colegiata offers good tapas and reasonable meals.

(i) Suances >
C/ Ceballos 12,
t 94 281 09 24

(i) Torrelavega
C/ Juan José Ruano 9,
t 94 289 29 82, www.
aytotorrelavega.es

(i) San Vicente de
la Barquera >>
Avda Generalísimo 20,
t 94 271 07 97, www.
sanvicentedelbarquera.org

(i) Comillas >
Bayos del Joaquin del
Ayuntamiento Piélago 1,
C/ Aldea 6,
t 94 272 07 68

Suances ✉ 39340

Most rooms here go for about €40.

*Castillo de Suances, C/ Acacio Gutiérrez, t 94 281 03 83, www.turismosuances.com (€€€). This 19th-century crenellated folly by the beaches offers interesting, individually decorated rooms, some with TV.

Casa Sito, Pso de la Marina Española, t 94 281 04 16 (€). This good seafood restaurant is as popular with the locals as the tourists; it offers a good-value menu and dishes like paella with lobster (*paella bogavante*) for a splurge. *Closed Mon, Feb.*

Comillas ✉ 39520

Ask at the tourist office for a list of *casas particulares.*

***Marina de Campíos, C/ General Piélagos 14, t 94 272 27 54, www.marinadecampios.com (€€€). A handsomely renovated villa with elegant, individually styled rooms and suites and a piano-bar.

***Casal del Castro, San Jerónimo, t 94 272 00 36, hccastro@infonegocio.com (€€€). Right in the centre of town in a fine old building, with a pretty garden and comfortable rooms. *Closed Jan.*

**Hs Esmeralda, C/ Antonio López 7, t 94 272 00 97 (€€). A good cheaper choice, which is close to the beach and has a pleasant bar/restaurant. *Closed Nov–Mar.*

*Fuente Real, Barrio de Sobrellano 19, t 94 272 01 55 (€). A basic alternative behind El Capricho.

Adolfo, Avda Las Infantas, t 94 272 20 14 (€€). A good choice, with traditional cooking for a few more euros. *Closed Tues and Nov.*

El Capricho de Gaudí, Barrio de Sobrellano, t 94 272 03 65 (€€). Comillas is the only place where you can dine in a building designed by Gaudi. The interior, if not entirely as he meant it to be, has been beautifully restored. The food is mostly seafood with a *nouvelle cuisine* touch; the set menu is a bargain. Ring ahead in season as it's usually booked solid. *Closed Sun eve and Mon in winter, plus mid-Jan–mid-Feb.*

Gurea, C/ Ignacio Fernández de Castro 11, t 94 272 24 46, www.restaurantegurea.com (€€). A good alternative to El Capricho, serving excellent and unusual Basque dishes like *merluza* (hake) in crayfish sauce and fig ice cream. *Closed Sun eve and Mon.*

Fuente Real, Plazuela Fuente Real 4, t 94 272 21 59 (€). Just outside the grounds of El Capricho, this cheerful seafood haunt with its décor of *azulejo* tiles has been a favourite for over a century.

San Vicente de la Barquera ✉ 39540

***Miramar, Pso de la Barquera 20, t 94 271 00 75, miramarhoteles@arrakis.es (€€). Modern, with great views of the bay and the Picos de Europa; the restaurant allows you to enjoy the vista. *Closed Nov–mid-Mar.*

**Luzón, Avda Miramar 1, t 94 271 00 50 (€€) A solid, square stone inn smack in the centre of town facing the tidal basin.

ⓘ Cabezón de la Sal
Pza de Ricardo Botin s/n, t *94 270 03 32, turismosanvicente@ cantabria.org*

*La Paz, C/ del Mercado 2, t 94 271 01 80 (€€). Has been remodelled and offers stylish, if bathless, rooms.

Camping El Rosal, Playas de San Vicente, t 94 271 01 65, *www. campingelrosal.com* (€). Conveniently located near the beaches, on the main road just outside San Vicente.

Boga-Boga, Pza José Antonio, t 94 271 01 35 (€€). Expect more seafood at this place, where the chef turns out delicious Cantabrian favourites along with a very good *solomillo con verduras.* The upstairs hotel (€€€) is good. *Closed Tues in Oct–May.*

Maruja, Avda Generalísimo s/n, t 94 271 00 77 (€€). For a less serious seafood attack, you can do well here for under €30, and there's a bargain menu for €16. The restaurant also has 15 **rooms** (€€).

Bárcena Mayor ✉ 39500
Posada La Franca, C/ La Franca, t 94 270 60 67, *www.lafrancaposadarural. com* (€€€). Come here for the village's famed mountain cuisine – stuffed haunch of venison and other game dishes in season. The comfortable **rooms** are in the inexpensive range.

The Picos de Europa

✪ Picos de Europa

They are not the highest mountains in Spain, or even in the Cantabrian-Pyrenean *cordillera,* but the Picos de Europa have a certain cachet. So many peaks, closely packed in a small area of Cantabria, Asturias and León, make a memorable landmark for Spain's north coast. No one knows the origin of the name, though it may have been that they were the first sight of the continent for Atlantic sailors. To the Asturians they are known as the Urrieles.

Thank Asturian ecologists for their efforts in keeping Spain's most beautiful mountains enchanting and unspoiled: what development there is (ski resorts, hotels) is mostly in western Cantabria. The Picos are divided by rivers into three tremendous massifs – **Andara,** mostly in Cantabria, **Urrieles,** in the middle, and **Cornión,** to the west. The highest peak, **Torre de Cerredo,** stands 8,606ft. But for sheer beauty and rugged grandeur, for the contrast of tiny rural villages in fertile green valleys against a backdrop of sheer, twisted stone peaks snow-crested year round, the Picos de Europa are hard to beat.

The range seems to have been dropped from heaven, especially for hikers; there are trails for Sunday walkers and sheer cliffs for serious alpinists. Hiking boots, however, are universally recommended because of frequent patches of loose shale on the trails and slopes. If you're going for an extended holiday in the Picos, get the detailed maps published by the Federación Española de Montañismo, generally available at Potes, the main base for visiting the mountains. The guide *Picos de Europa* by Robin Collomb (West Col, Reading) is a great help, and up-to-date detailed information on guides, itineraries and mountain *refugios* (free overnight shelters) is available from the **Federación Asturiana de Montañismo,** the **Federación Cántabra de Montaña,** and the **Delegación Leonesa de Montaña.**

Federación Asturiana de Montañismo
C/ Melquiades Álvarez 16, Oviedo, t *98 525 23 62, www.fempa.net*

Federación Cántabra de Montaña
C/ Sánchez Díaz 1, Reinosa, t *94 275 52 94, www.fcdme.com*

Delegación Leonesa de Montaña
Paseo de la Facultad 3, León, t *98 725 00 52*

Hiking in the high Picos is practical only from the end of May to October, but even then you may get a soaking – the Picos are only 32km from the rainy Atlantic seaboard. Low-level walks can be done at any time of year. Bring warm clothes and a lightweight plastic poncho, a sleeping bag and a food supply for any nights you may spend in the *refugios*, and a pair of binoculars to take in the wonderful array of wildlife and birds.

The Eastern Picos de Europa

Potes and the Valley of Liébana

The eastern mountains of the Picos are the most visited and the most accessible. The main entrance from the coast begins at **Unquera** (a FEVE stop on the coast to the west of San Vicente de la Barquera); the N621 from here climbs up through the **Desfiladero de La Hermida**, a dramatic, high, narrow gorge walling in the River Deva, and the hamlet of **La Hermida**, famous in sunny Spain for not seeing *el sol* at all from 26 October to 8 March.

The road climbs up from here into the idyllic little **valley of the Liébana**, more happily fated by geography to have an unusual 'Mediterranean' microclimate. Vines and even olives grow here, though you'll see mostly apple orchards with the vineyards around the first village, **Lebeña**, with its parish church – the 10th-century Mozarabic **Santa María** – signposted south of the village on the

Getting to and around the Eastern Picos de Europa

By Bus

Palomera buses, t 94 288 06 11, *www.autobusespalomera.com*, serve Potes up to four times daily from Santander, via Unquera, San Vicente and Torrelavega. There are two buses (one in the winter) daily between Santander and León that stop at Potes and Lebeña. From Potes there are three buses in high season from the central square to Fuente Dé and the *teleférico* (times change according to the season, so check in advance).

By Jeep, Horse and Bike

Jeeps make the link between the upper station of the *teleférico* to the *refugio de Áliva*. Arenas de Cabrales (in Asturias) is the main hub in the northern Picos, with Land Rover services to Poncebos and Sotres and daily buses to Cangas de Onis and Panes. **4WD jeeps** can be hired in Potes for journeys deeper into the mountains with **Europicos**, *www.europicos.com*, t 94 273 07 24, or with **Picostur**, *www.picostur.com*, t 94 273 8091, two of several companies offering adventure activities in the region.

Also, a stable in Turieno next to Potes offers several guided riding excursions in the Picos. If you want to do it yourself, Viajes Wences and other firms in Potes rent **mountain bikes**.

N621. This is one of the finest pre-Romanesque churches, a little jewel in the middle of nowhere that is the perfect expression of the strange little mountainous state of Asturias and, perhaps, its dreams of future greatness. Built in 925 for a Count Alfonso, Santa María is as impressive a work as any of the more famous churches around Oviedo. Most of the exterior was restored a century ago, but the original roof corbels and decorated parts of the exterior are carved with originality, and inside the simple Greek-cross plan – with horseshoe Visigothic arches and not too much regard for precision – is a delight. A few years ago, the stone step up to the altar was raised and found to be carved with geometric symbols, along with a human figure apparently painted on the stone in blood. The information card the caretaker hands out claims that the stone is 2,000 years old, and carved with Celtic sun symbols; the symbols may be that old, but the stone probably came as the original altar when the church was built. You'll see a photo of a lovely carved wood Virgin, the work of the great Renaissance sculptor Gil de Siloé. Unfortunately the picture is all Lebeña has left; someone nicked the icon in 1993. Two venerable companions, an olive and yew tree, stand next to the church; they were both planted at the time the church was built – over 1,000 years ago.

Potes, the capital of the Valley of Liébana, is the metropolis of the Picos, where you can garner information, catch buses, change travellers' cheques and stock up on supplies. For all the tourist traffic Potes is still a gracious town, with stone arcades to shelter the cafés on the main street and a warren of medieval lanes behind. There are also a number of jeep excursions on offer. The main monument in Potes itself is the 15th-century **Torre del Infantado**, a massive, square defensive-residential work in the centre of town.

The most popular excursions from Potes include the 4½ up to the **Monasterio de Santo Toribio de Liébana**. Don't m. because this is the only place in Cantabria where a visit will e. you an indulgence – time off from purgatory. It is a long established pilgrimage site, allegedly the home of the world's largest chunk of the True Cross. In the early days of the Kingdom of Asturias the Liébana was a kind of monastic preserve, and this monastery was its centre, founded early in the 8th century. What you see today, though, is mainly Romanesque and Gothic. The 'world's largest sliver of the True Cross' is kept in an ornate Baroque chapel where Masses are said daily. In its earliest days the monastery was ruled by the Abbot Beato de Liébana, whose *Commentaries on the Apocalypse* were popular in Spain throughout the Middle Ages. Girona and El Burgo de Osma have beautiful 10th-century illuminated editions of the manuscript, but in the cloister here you can see a full set of copies of one of them – mad and brilliant pictorial prophecies from an age when people were convinced the world would soon be meeting its end.

The nearby **Mirador de Santo Toribio** takes in splendid views over the Andara massif. Another, longer walk south will take you through **Cabezón de Liébana**, where some of the houses have coats of arms, and two medieval bridges cross over to the lovely church of **Santa María de Piasca**, built in 1172 with fine Romanesque carvings on the capitals within. The monastery was shared by monks and nuns, which was typical for the mountains but unusual elsewhere.

Beato de Liébana Defends the Faith

Back in the grim 8th century, when the heathen Normans were attacking from the north, the godless Magyars from the east and the infidel Moors from the south, and the Faith was in gravest peril, just what were the Christians up to? Well, they were arguing amongst themselves as usual. Christian Spain in that age may not seem to have been really big enough to generate a proper theological controversy, but somehow it managed. At issue was something called Adoptionism, the doctrine that Jesus the man was only the 'adopted son' of God. In the far corner, wearing the black trunks, we see Bishop Helipandus of Toledo, then under Muslim rule, who argued for Adoptionism. In the near corner, in the white trunks, stands Beato of Liébana, who isn't about to let anybody say his Saviour does not participate fully in Godhood.

Like all such controversies, this brouhaha masked some more mundane conflicts – between the mountaineer Asturians and the more sophisticated Mozarabic Christians of the south, over who was boss in matters of faith and politics. This particular conflict caught the attention of all Western Christianity, though, and it found a solution, surprisingly, not with the pope in Rome but at the court of Charlemagne. In those days, if you were lucky enough to find someone with the necessary wisdom and erudition to decide on such a case, he would probably have been (another surprise) an Englishman. The king of the Franks was fortunate enough to have in his services the greatest doctor of Christendom, Alcuin of York, who was busy trying to reform the Carolingian educational system and, with less success, to teach Charlemagne how to write his name. In 799 Alcuin pronounced that Adoptionism was just a rehash of the old Nestorian heresy, and awarded a clean decision to Beato, who thereupon retired from the ring of Church politics and went home to write about the End of the World.

From Fuente Dé to Arenas de Cabrales

The classic excursion from Potes is to take the bus west up to the stunning old village of **Espinama** and, 1.6km beyond, to **Fuente Dé**. Here you can catch the *teleférico* for an awesome, vertigo-inducing ride 2,568ft up the sheer cliff to the **Mirador del Cable**.

Mirador del Cable
teleférico runs daily, July–Sept 9–8; Oct–June 10–6; in peak season arrive very early or you'll get stuck waiting, maybe for hours

Once at the top, walk 4km (2½ miles) up to the **Hotel-Refugio Áliva**, a modern version of the old mountain refuge; a path from here leads down to Espinama – a pleasant day's circuit, and very popular with gnarly mountain bikers, who consider this one of the best rides in Europe.

From Espinama or the hotel, you can make a longer, more serious hike through the eastern and central massifs north to Sotres, a pleasant mountain village in spectacular scenery (jeep excursions also available from Espinama). **Sotres** has a couple of basic *pensiones* and places to eat, and makes an excellent base for walks deeper into the mountains; a good one is the 11km (7-mile) haul up to **Tresviso** on the eastern edge of Andara massif, where there's a magnificent view 3,000ft down into the Desfiladero de la Hermida. Most people head west, though, across the Pass of Pandébano and into the majestic central cirque of Los Urriellos; the big landmark in this area is **Naranjo de Bulnes** (Pico Urriellu on some maps), a distinct sheer-sided, tower-like pinnacle, loved and hated by daredevil alpinists. Below the Naranjo, **Bulnes** is a classic mountain village, set in a steep green valley surrounded by towering cliffs; until recently, the only way to get there was to walk, but in 2001 a **funicular** was finally built – to the delight of locals and the despair of environmentalists – which links the village with **Poncebos**.

Funicular
runs daily 10–12.30 and 2–6, until 8pm Easter Week and July–Sept; trains leave every 30 mins; adm

The most important village in the area is **Arenas de Cabrales**, connected by Land Rover with Poncebos and Sotres and the centre of an area renowned for its stinking mountain cheese – 'never matured in manure, never contains worms', the tourist literature boasts. *Raciones* of the stuff are served everywhere, and almost everyone finds themselves trying it before they can get out of town. Hikers will be more interested in the classic traverse of the Divine Gorge from Poncebos, more commonly approached from the south by way of Posada de Valdeón in León province (*see* p.215).

Markets in the Eastern Picos de Europa

Unquera: Wed.
Potes: Mon.

Where to Stay and Eat in the Eastern Picos de Europa

It may be paradise for hikers, but there's no need to rough it. Nearly every village in the Picos has at least one *casa particular* or *fonda* or a place to camp, and you can purchase supplies or dine out in a traditional restaurant. Every village has its specialities, and the shops under the arches on the main street of Potes are treasure-houses of the mountains' finest; you can buy local cheeses and *charcuterie*, honey in various original flavours and *orujo*, the Cantabrian firewater sold in dangerous-looking bottles all over town. It's made from the stems and pulp of grapes after the wine harvest, like French *marc* or Italian *grappa*.

(i) Unquera

(Val de San Vicente)
Ctra N-639 Km 279,
t 94 271 96 80,
turismounquera@
cantabria.org

(i) Potes >

C/ Independencia 12,
t 94 273 07 87,
turismopotes@
cantabria.org; also try
Bustamente, C/ Capitán
Palacios 10, a photo-
and bookshop
specializing in the Picos
de Europa with a wide
range of maps and
guides; also check out
www.liebanaypicosde
europa.com

(i) Turieno

National Park Office,
Urb. La Molina, t 94 273
05 55; the National Park
runs free daily guided
walks in summer in the
Liébana valley and
Cabrales, covering
various routes

(i) Arenas de Cabrales >>

Ctra General, t 98 584
64 84, turismo@
cabrales.org
(summer only)

Potes ✉ 39570

Potes has by far the most accommodation in the region.

**Infantado, Ojedo (1km from Potes), t 94 273 09 39 (€€). Modern, stone-built and one of the best here.

**Picos Valdecoro, C/ Roscabao, t 94 273 00 25 (€€). Also excellent.

**Picos de Europa, C/ Arco Iris 3, t 94 237 10 15, *www.grupopicosdeeuropa.com* (€€). A small place run by a friendly, knowledgeable fellow with an adjoining agency for advice on hiking and a range of outdoor activities.

La Casa del Frama, Frama (8km from Potes), t 94 273 04 65 (€€). A lovely stone mountain house with just six pretty rooms and friendly owners.

*Casa Cayo, C/ Cántabra 6, t 94 273 01 50, *www.casacayo.com* (€€–€). A modernized mountain hotel, with simple but comfortable rooms overlooking the river and a very popular *comedor* downstairs that serves huge portions.

*Hotel Rubio, C/ San Roque 31, t 94 273 00 15, *hotel_rubia@yahoo.es* (€€–€). Slightly more expensive, but has rooms in an attractively restored village house. Pets allowed.

**Hs La Serna, C/ La Serna 9, t 94 273 09 24 (€). A budget choice, with good restaurant downstairs.

Posada de Bistruey, La Vega (9km south of Potes), t 94 273 60 95 (€). If Potes is too hectic, head for this peaceful roadside *posada*, run by a friendly family who provide a hearty breakfast, free sweets, and spotless rooms with bath at bargain prices.

Camping El Molino, La Vega, t 94 273 60 09 (€. Offers pitches and bunga-lows in a leafy setting.

El Fogon de Cus, Plaza Capitán Palacios 2, t 94 273 00 60 (€€). Has the best name in town for local dishes and Basque cooking. It also has rooms (€).

Paco Wences, C/ Roscabao 5, t 94 273 00 25 (€€). A good place to try the local speciality, *cocido liebaniego*, a hearty stew of garbanzo beans, chorizo, black pudding and anything else that happens to be on hand.

Los Camachos, C/ El Llano, t 94 273 0064 (€). For dinner, this place has an honest menu with *fabada*, trout and other local treats.

Fuente Dé ✉ 39588

***Parador Río Deva, t 94 273 66 51 (€€€). Since 1965, this magnificently sited hotel has been a part of the Picos experience. A modern building at the end of the *teleférico*, many of its rooms have grand views; the hotel organizes Jeep excursions into the peaks, and its restaurant specializes in mountain and Castilian dishes. *Closed mid-Nov–Mar.*

***Hotel del Oso, Cosgaya (12km from Fuente Dé), t 94 273 30 18, *www.hoteldeloso.com* (€€). Amid stunning mountain scenery, this modern but traditionally stone-built place is owned by the famously welcoming Rivas family and the restaurant is perhaps the best in the area.

Espinama ✉ 39500

Refugio de Áliva, about 7.5km up from Espinama, t 94 273 09 99 (€). Has a restaurant (€) and 24 rooms available on a first-come, first-served basis. Ring in advance; a Land Rover from Espinama will take you up (or take the *teleférico*). *Open June–mid-Oct. (For other refugios in the Picos, ask at the Potes tourist office.)*

Arenas de Cabrales and around ✉ 33554

***Picos de Europa, Ctra General s/n, t 98 584 64 91, *www.hotelpicosde europa.com* (€€€–€€). The poshest choice here, with smart rooms, a pool and a good restaurant.

**Hotel Villa de Cabrales, Carretera General s/n t 98 584 67 19, *villacabrales@hotmail.com* (€). Large bright rooms with views of the Picos.

La **Casa del Chiflón**, Bulnes, t 98 584 59 43, *www.casadelchiflon.com* (€€). The only places to stay in Bulnes are in *casas rurales* or *hostales* – this traditional stone-built house has attractive, if simple, rooms and can arrange guided tours and excursions. **Pensión La Perdíz**, Sotres, t 98 594 50 11 (€€). Has doubles with bath; two rooms have private balconies and fantastic mountain views.

Casa Cipriano, at Sotres, t 98 594 50 24, *www.casacipriano.com* (€€). Run by Cipriano López, the mountaineering mogul of Sotres, so you can come to this simple *pensión* and *hostal* for information on outdoor activities; the staff can arrange Land Rover taxis and climbing guides. Good hearty stews and *raciones* are served in the bar.

The Asturian Picos de Europa: Cangas and Covadonga

The salmon-filled Río Sella defines the west edge of the western Massif de Cornión. Most easily reached from Ribadesella on the Asturian coast, or through the stunning narrow **Desfiladero de los Beyos** gorge (N625) from León and Riaño, the region lacks the high drama of the mountains further east, but is nonetheless green and tranquil, and for Spaniards constitutes a pilgrimage.

Desperately Seeking Pelayo

Cangas de Onís claims to be the first capital of Christian Spain, where the Asturian kings set up shop right after their victory at nearby Covadonga. The most beautiful things in Cangas are the high **medieval bridge** (erroneously called Roman) with its great arch spanning the Río Sella, and the **Capilla de Santa Cruz**, where the kings worshipped. It was built over a dolmen, and according to legend its founder was Favila, the successor of Pelayo. The original building may really be as early as the 5th century, though it was completely rebuilt in the 15th (get the key at the Ayuntamiento, and they might also let you have the key for the cave of Buxu). On a pillar near the entrance, an old relief shows a cross over a crescent moon, symbolizing the Christians' victories over Islam. As for the dolmen, it is still clearly visible in the chapel's crypt, carved with religious symbols.

Capilla de Santa Cruz
open Easter Week and June –Sept Tues–Sun 11–2 and 4–7.30; closed rest of year, but contact the tourist office for guided visits t 98 584 80 05

From Cangas it's 3km north to **Villanueva**, where Alfonso I founded the **Monasterio de San Pedro** in 746. Recently restored and converted into a *parador* (*see* p.214) it has a 12th-century doorway, with capitals carved with bear-hunting scenes. East of Cangas, the AS114 follows the narrow valley of the Río Güeña, providing the northern part of the circuit around the Picos. In Cardes, the **cave of Buxu** contains rare, very abstract paintings from the Solutrian era (20–15,000 BC).

Cave of Buxu
open all year, Wed–Sun, 10.30, 11.30, 12.30, 3.15, 4.15; maximum of 25 visitors per day; adm, free Wed

From here it's 10km to **Covadonga**, dominated by an enormous, kitschy 19th-century basilica. Here Pelayo, supposedly the son-in-

Getting to and around the Asturian Picos de Europa

ALSA buses, t 902 42 22 42, *www.alsa.es*, serve Cangas de Onís several times daily from Oviedo and Gijón with a less frequent service from Llanes and one daily from León. There's a direct bus from Oviedo to Covadonga, or change at Cangas de Onis for services to Covadonga and Arenas de Cabrales. The ALSA website lists seasonal timetables. ALSA also run buses from Arenas de Cabrales to the Bulnes **funicular** at Poncebos. There are no bus services to Ponga, where you will need your own transport to explore properly. **Taxis** can be hired in San Juan de Beleño on **t** 98 584 30 17.

law of Roderick, the last Visigothic king, and 300 followers managed to ambush a small Moorish expedition and defeat them, according to legend. The Moors, who didn't much care for the climate to begin with, made the mistake of letting the Christians stay and consolidate their power, preferring to seek richer spoils in France. Next to the basilica is the **cave** where Pelayo fought with his back to the wall and now rests in peace in a sarcophagus next to his wife.

From Covadonga it's a beautiful 12km drive through the national park to the mountain lakes of **La Ercina** and **Enol**, with the huge Peña Santa mountains as a backdrop. In response to the huge summer traffic jams, a **shuttle bus** service now ferries the endless surge of families up to the lakes. The bus runs from 10am–6.30pm from end July to early Sept; outside these times you can drive up. On sunny weekends the lakes pack out with day-trippers, but a stroll around the shore of La Ercina should see you well away from the picnicking throng, and surrounded instead by wild flowers. There are plenty of longer walks from the lakes; try the four-hour descent into the gorgeous **forest of Pome**, home to eagle owls and capercaillie.

Shuttle bus
€6/€3 for children

A more serious proposition is to hike right across the Cornión massif to 6,340ft Jultayu, beyond which the mountains collapse precipitously into the Garganta Divina. In summer there is a frequent bus service from Cangas and Covadonga; the rest of the year there's just one a day. Back on the AS114, the next village east is **Corao**; nearby, at a place called Abamia, the church of Santa Eulalia has parts going back to the 8th century, along with fragments of medieval frescoes.

Ponga and the Desfiladero de Los Beyos

South of Cangas de Onís the N625 follows the crystalline Rio Sella towards León, passing some hidden swimming holes that most people drive straight past; the best one is near **Ceneya**, a deep ice-blue pool reached by way of a tiny bridge across the gorge.

A couple of miles before Ceneya, in the hamlet of **Santillán**, the AS261 turns off to the west and makes its narrow and sinuous way through the *concejo* of **Ponga**, a little-known and rarely visited land of sparkling brooks, enchanting green valleys and tiny villages plastered to steep hillsides. A good overview of the area can be had from the *mirador* of **Les Bedules**, a short walk off the main road 3km beyond Beleño; to the east, the central ranges of the Picos heave their crests skyward in a crescendo of limestone extravagance; to the west the tranquil Valle de Ponga is dominated by massive, craggy **Tiatordos**. An easy trail continues from Les Bedules into the beautiful **forest of Peloño**; die-hards can tackle the ascent of Tiatordos itself, a tough uphill grunt from the village of Taranes for which a guide must be hired. Beyond Les Bedules the road passes through raggle-taggle **Viego** before narrowing to a single lane and dropping steeply to rejoin the main road at Puente La Huera. This is the start of the **Desfiladero de los Beyos**, a narrow cleft through the mountains which Spain's engineers are pleased to announce is the narrowest motorable gorge in Europe. It's an exhilarating piece of highway, threading between cliffs that rise vertiginously to 3,000ft above the canyon floor, with plenty of pullouts and tantalizing views; snow finch and wallcreepers can be spotted flitting around the walls. After six twisting kilometres the road emerges into the wide open **Valle de Sajambre**, and León province.

Markets in the Asturian Picos de Europa

Cangas de Onís: Sun.

Where to Stay and Eat in the Asturian Picos de Europa

(i) **Cangas de Onís >**
Jardines del Ayuntamiento,
t 98 584 80 05, www.
cangasdeonis.com; free
guided walks daily from
the car park at Lago de
La Ercina to areas of
the Peña Santa range

National Park
information: Casa
Dago, t 98 584 86 14,
in summer

Cangas de Onís ✉ 33550

*****Parador de Cangas de Onís**, in Villanueva (2km from Cangas), t 98 584 94 02, *cangas@parador.es* (€€€€). The 12th-century Monasterio de San Pedro de Villaneuva is now one of Spain's most luxurious *paradores*, with palatial guest quarters. The views over the river and Picos are superb, as is the traditional Asturian cuisine.

****Los Lagos**, Jardines del Ayuntamiento 3, t 98 584 92 77, *www.loslagos.as* (€€). A good choice in the centre of Cangas, in a traditional building with friendly staff and an excellent restaurant 'Los Arcos' (*see* right).

***Plaza**, La Plaza 7, t 98 584 83 08 (€€). Small, friendly, and well located in the middle of town.

Piloña, San Pelayo 19, t 98 594 71 56 (€€). Cangas has pricey hotels and a score of *hostales* where the going rate is about €75 in high season, considerably less the rest of the year; this is one of the more central ones.

Casa Juan, Avda de Covadonga 20, t 98 584 80 12 (€€). *Fabada* and other Asturian dishes are to be had at this restaurant, open since 1943. *Closed Tues and Wed eves and June.*

Los Arcos, Hotel Los Lagos, Avda Covadonga 17, t 98 584 92 77, *www. loslagos.as* (€€). This place is one of the very best in the region, and has established an enviable reputation for its imaginative interpretations of traditional Asturian cuisine. *Closed Sun eve, plus Mon in Nov–Mar.*

Sidrería El Polesu, C/ Angel Tárano s/n, t 98 584 9248 (€). A traditional old *chigre*, full of locals and easily identified by the stench of cider wafting from the doors, with good *raciones* of local meats and cheeses.

Covadonga ✉ 33589

Accommodation here is scarce. Bars and restaurants hang out *camas* (beds) signs along the main road.

***Hotel Pelayo, t 98 584 60 61 (€€€). Basic and perhaps a bit overpriced.

Casa Priena, Santuario de Covadonga, t 98 584 60 70 (€€). A delightful B&B close to the sanctuary, with four small, stylish rooms, hearty breakfasts and a decent traditional restaurant, open to the public.

⭐ La Casona de Con >>

El Colladín, in Llerices, t 98 584 90 97 (€€). A traditional, antique-filled country house in a tiny village close to the Santuario de Covadonga. Simple rooms and lavish home-cooked breakfasts.

El Huerto del Ermitaño, Cruce a los Lagos, t 98 584 60 97, *www.elhuerto delermitano.com* (€€). Surrounded by trees and mountains with a real alpine feel. Excellent *fabada* and home-made desserts.

Hospedería del Peregrino, 200m below the sanctuary in Covadonga, t 98 584 60 47, *peregrino@ picosdeuropa.net* (€€). Has a well-deserved name for its *fabada*, seafood and mountain dishes. Rooms are without bath.

Ponga ✉ 33557

La Casona de Con, Mestas de Con, t 98 594 40 74, *www.lacasonadecon. com* (€€). A wonderful rural retreat in a tiny village 10km easy of Cangas de Onís, in a typical 18th-century farmhouse with stylishly furnished bedrooms and delicious breakfasts. *Closed Nov–Feb.*

Pensión Fonda de Ponga, San Juan de Beleño, t 98 584 30 04 (€). A basic but funky *pensión* above a restaurant.

The Leonese Picos de Europa

At the southern end of the *desfiladero*, pyramidal Pica Ten dominates the Sajambre valley and its main village, **Oseja de Sajambre**, a pretty place that sees few visitors. Most people pass through on their way to the isolated mountain hamlet of **Soto de Sajambre**, high above Oseja and bang in the middle of the Picos' most pristine forest. Soto attracts plenty of hikers, who come to tackle the **Senda del Arcediano**, an epic high-altitude traverse of the Sierra de Beza. The trail can also be walked from its Asturian end in **Amieva**; this used to be the main route between Cangas de Onís and the *meseta*, and traces of the original paving remain. It takes less effort to wander out through densely wooded territory to **Vegabaño**, where a lonely *refugio* looks out over spectacular views of the central Picos.

Posada de Valdeón

From Oseja it's a short drive across the Puerto de Pontón to Posada de Valdeón, chief village of the high valley of Valdeón and a serenely magnificent place to rest up in before or after the Cares Gorge; here tiny farming villages and their rustic granaries, or *hórreos*, built on stilts to protect their contents from moisture and mice, look like mere toys under the loftiest mountains in the Picos. One of the most stupendous views of these is from the **Mirador del Tombo**, 1.6km from Posada de Valdeón towards Caín, framed by a statue dedicated to the chamois goat, an animal occasionally seen

Getting to and around the Leonese Picos de Europa

Buses (about five weekly, more in high season) from Cangas de Onís to Madrid pass through Oseja de Sajambre, as does the summer-only service from Cangas to Posada de Valdeón; Posada is also served by daily buses from Riaño, where there is a twice-daily service to León.

Beyond the main villages the only transport is by **taxi**; in Oseja **t** 98 774 03 59, or in Posada (for Land Rovers to Caín), **t** 98 774 26 09 or **t** 609 569 647/661.

in the flesh frisking over the steep slopes. The **Chorco de los Lobos** nearby was used to trap the mountains' most fearsome predator, the now-rare wolf. Across the river is the tiny hermitage of **Corona**, according to Leonese legend the true site of Pelayo's coronation after the battle of Covadonga.

The Divine Gorge

Between Caín and Poncebos, the **Cares Gorge** (better known as simply the 'Garganta Divina') extends north-to-south across the Picos. It is a spectacular 12km (7-mile) walk over sheer drops down to the Río Cares, made relatively easy by a footpath sculpted into the mountainside (although 80 per cent of all accidents in the Picos de Europa happen here, so make sure you are well prepared for the trek). The classic approach is from **Caín** in the south, itself linked to Posada de Valdeón by a regular four-wheel-drive service. Walking south from **Poncebos** isn't much more strenuous – but you risk either spending the night in Caín, which has limited lodgings, or walking the 9km (5½ miles) further south to sleep in Posada de Valdeón.

ⓘ **Posada de Valdeón >>** *National Park information office: Travesía Los Llanos, t 98 774 05 49; free guided walks into the hills around Posada daily in summer, courtesy of the National Park (call in advance for information)*

Where to Stay and Eat in the Leonese Picos de Europa

Oseja de Sajambre ✉ 24916

*Hs Pontón, Ctra Nacional 625, **t** 98 774 03 16 (€). Has great views and a good value *menú del día*.

Soto de Sajambre ✉ 24916

*Hs Peñasanta, C/ Principal s/n, **t** 774 03 95 (€). A lovely traditional *hostal*, with flowers on the balconies. The restaurant (for guests only) serves up slabs of *cabrito asado* (roast goat) for a minimum of 6 people, and Asturian stews; information about hiking trails is available next door in the *albergue*.

Posada de Valdeón ✉ 24915

Hs Casa Abascal, El Salvador, **t 98 774 05 07 (€). This offers the most comforts. Posada has several *casas particulares* and some fine *fondas*.

Hs Campo, Amador Campo Pérez, **t 98 774 05 02 (€). Has good-value modern rooms with bath, and wonderful views from the terrace. The cafeteria serves decent stews and *fabadas*.

Pensión Begoña, Amador Campo Pérez, **t** 98 774 05 16 (€). Offers an authentic mountain experience – small and spartan rooms with goatskins on the floor, terrific meals and a warm welcome.

Camping El Cares, Santa Marina de Valdeón, **t** 98 774 26 76 (€). Has 400 pitches and plenty of facilities, including horse-trekking. *Open June–Oct.*

Asturias

The principality of Asturias is the Spanish Wales, a rugged country of stupendous mountains, mines and a romantically beautiful coastline. The inhabitants have traditionally been a hardy lot, beginning with the Iberian tribe of Astures, after whom the province is named, who defied both the Romans and Visigoths. One of the last areas to be touched by tourism, it is fighting to maintain its integrity and environment against big developers who would exploit the magnificent Picos de Europa and the coast; instead, Asturias would have you stay in a rural village, to learn something of its culture and architecture.

10

Don't miss

⭐ The capital of cider country
Villaviciosa **p.222**

⭐ Unique 9th-century churches
Near Oviedo **p.231**

⭐ Lammergeyers, eagles and bears
Somiedo National Park **p.235**

⭐ The perfect seaside hideaway
Cudillero **p.240**

⭐ In the footsteps of dinosaurs
Lastres **p.222**

See map overleaf

Costa Verde

Cabo Peñas

Playa del Castro Tapia de Casariego Ortiguera Playa de Bozo Capo Vidio Playa de Salinas
Ribadeo Figueras Navia Luarca Cudillero San Juan de Nieva
Castropol Coaña Avilés

N640

Boal Navelgas Salas Pravia Posada

Taramundi Bárcena del Monasterio Grado

Obona Tineo A S T U R I A S Trubia

Pola de Allande Belmonte de Miranda Tuñón

Grandas de Salime Berducedo Llamas del Mouro Proaza

C630 Caranga

Cangas del Narcea La Plaza

Pola de Somiedo Reserva Nacional de Somiedo

Puerto del Connio Puerto Ventana

Moal Cordillera Cantábrica Torrestio Peña Ubiña Tuiza

Bosque de Muniellos

Río Navia

Río Negro

Desfiladero del Teverga

FRANCE

PORTUGAL SPAIN

p.302

pp.244–5

Don't miss

- ①️ Villaviciosa **p.222**
- ②️ Near Oviedo **p.231**
- ③️ Somiedo National Park **p.235**
- ☆️ Cudillero **p.240**
- ④️ Lastres **p.222**

The proudest date in Asturian history is 718, when a band of Visigoths, led by the legendary Pelayo, defeated the Moors in the mountain glen of Covadonga, officially beginning the Reconquista and founding the first tiny Christian kingdom in Muslim Iberia. Their beautiful churches are Asturias's chief artistic heritage; the language they spoke, *el Bable*, or 'Babel', survives only as a dialect against the modern dominance of Castilian, its direct descendant.

Since the 14th century, the Spanish heir-apparent has borne the title of 'Prince of Asturias', a practice initiated by John of Gaunt when his daughter married the son of Juan I. Not long after that, pp.184-5

pp.244-5

Asturias fell into an obscurity that lasted centuries. The discovery of iron ore and coal in the 19th century rapidly transformed its traditional agricultural economy into a mining one with radical tendencies. These brought about the second great date in Asturian history: an epic miners' revolt in October 1934 that served as a prelude to the Civil War. Even after the war, resistance to Franco continued in the wild mountains of the province.

The modern autonomous region of Asturias is, in its quiet way, one of the most progressive in Spain. In 1985, the Asturian wildlife protection fund received the European Preservation of Nature (FAPAS) prize for its efforts to preserve the rare Cantabrian bear and the capercaillie from extinction. One of the gentlest ways to get acquainted with the Asturian countryside is on a **pony trek**, especially along the Roman road of Lamesa, between the districts of Somiedo and Teverga. **Cyclists** can get advice on the best routes by visiting the useful official website or calling their information line, which also has tips on the national parks and countless other activities. **Canoeing** to suit all standards can be found all over, from

Pony trekking
www.cuadrosobia.com, or call t 63 054 42 41 in Teverga for information

Cycling
www.infoasturias.com (also in English) or information line t 902 300 202

Fishing
*www.infoasturias.com
for general information
including where to
get permits*

**Surf and
Bodyboard
Federation**
*www.costasurf.com/
fsbpa*

**Real Club de Golf
Castiello**
*t 98 536 6313,
www.castiello.com*

La Barganiza, Siero
t 98 574 24 68

the tumbling rapids of the mountains to the gentle streams in the valleys – Asturias has a full national and international programme. Asturias is a **fishing** paradise; the waters teem with trout, salmon and eel. If you like your watersports with a flavour of salt, head for the gusty Bay of Biscay for sailing and windsurfing. Surfers should contact the **Surf and Bodyboard Federation** based in Gijón. There are several golf courses in the region, including those at Gijón (**Real Club de Golf Castiello**) and Siero (**La Barganiza**).

At least once, visit an old Asturian *chigre* or *sidrería* to taste the local poison, *sidra* (cider) – natural but dangerous stuff always poured at arm's length to give it the proper bounce. If you drink enough of it, it even begins to taste good. In recent years the principality has promoted rural tourism by way of a network of *'casas de aldea'* or country homes. These houses, some of historical interest, usually have between two and four rooms for rent, with meals also available. An official guide to these homes is put out each year and is available at any tourist office. The word **pola** in this chapter is the local Asturian word for *pueblo* (village).

Note that although the Picos de Europa are partly in Asturias, the whole range has been grouped together in **Cantabria and the Picos de Europa** *(see pp.212–15).*

The Asturian 'Costa Verde': East to West

Although the Picos de Europa attract mountaineers and hikers from all over the world, the very attractive coast of Asturias sees relatively few foreigners. There are over 50 sandy beaches, most of them on unmarked roads just off the main coastal highway; some have spectacular locations, and a few can offer relative peace and quiet even in the middle of August. It's a mountainous and rugged coast for the most part, and the lack of a good road along it (until recently) has kept development to a minimum.

Llanes to Villaviciosa

Llanes

This eastern section of the coast is well endowed with beaches and quiet coves, especially around Llanes, the first sizeable town. Llanes gets busy in summer – in fact when this agreeably funky old town becomes loaded with *madrileños* it becomes charmingly anarchic. Llanes is so popular because the coast around it contains some of the best beaches in Asturias: the town beach, El Sablón, is a pretty arc of golden sand, but it's small and quickly fills up in

Getting around from Llanes to Villaviciosa

22

By Train and Bus

FEVE **trains** along the coast take in much of the marvellous scenery. Two trains a day run between Santander and Oviedo, with stops at Unquera, Colombres, the beaches at Nueva and Villaharmes and Ribadesella; a further two a day go from Oviedo to Llanes.
To continue west up the coast from Ribadesella, you take a Gijón-bound **bus**. FEVE has frequent connections between Gijón and Avilés, and west to Cudillero, Luarca, Soto de Luiña and Ortigueiro. ALSA buses link all these towns with Oviedo as well, while RENFE links Gijón with Oviedo, Madrid, Barcelona and the rest of the peninsula.
FEVE timetables and information at *www.feve.es*, t 94 220 95 22 (Santander), t 98 534 24 15 (Gijón) and t 98 529 76 56 (Oviedo).

By Car

Turning the old N632 along the coast into the big A8 motorway has been the biggest road project in this region for some years. Most of it is already finished and driving is not a problem.

---

summer. Head east for bigger beaches near two pretty villages. At **Cué**, signs point to the less frenetic Playa de Toró, set among pinnacle-like rock formations; at **Andrín**, 3km further, you can find two good beaches not yet crowded and commercialized: Playa de Andrín and Playa de Ballota.

The area's two antiquities lie east of Llanes: near Vidiago and the Playa de France, there's a peculiar Bronze Age monument called **Peña-Tú** or the 'Cabeza del Gentil' (Gentile's Head). Even older are the cave drawings in the **Cueva del Pindal** near **Colombres**, featuring the only known painting of a mammoth in Spain.

West of Llanes, at **Celorio**, the unspoiled Playa de Borizu faces a small islet you can swim to, and you can find another string of beaches, some ideal for children, around the charming village of **Niembro**, along with the ruins of a 12th-century monastery, San Antolín de Bedo. For more isolation, try the **Playa de Torimbia**, situated in a perfect crescent of cliffs and accessible from a path down the rock face.

Cueva del Pindal
t 60 817 52 84; open Wed–Sun 9.30–1.30 and 3–4.45; a maximum of 200 people per day are allowed in; guided tours in Spanish

Ribadesella

The next town, Ribadesella, at the mouth of the meandering Río Sella, makes an excellent base for forays along the coast or into the western Picos. Split in two by the river and bridge, with a picture-postcard backdrop of mountains, Ribadesella has a handful of old streets, a long protected beach, and plenty of chances for hiking, pony trekking, canoeing and fishing. The beaches lie just across the Sella to the west of town. Just outside town are the stalactitic **Tito Bustillo Caves**, where some 15–20,000 years ago the residents painted the walls with stylish animals and humans in the Altamira fashion, worth a visit although their burnt sienna, purple and black tones have faded.

Tito Bustillo Caves
t 986 86 11 20, www.titobustillo.com; open April–mid-Sept Wed–Sun 10–4.30; adm, free Wed

Farther west, into what is officially known as the 'Costa Verde', you'll find quiet beaches in the tiny hamlets of **Caravia** (Baja and

10 Asturias | The Asturian 'Costa Verde': Llanes to Villaviciosa

Alta), and near **Colunga**: La Isla, La Griega and Lastres. You'll also find evidence of Asturias' Jurassic inhabitants – fossilized shells, tree trunks, and dinosaur tracks – all along the coast between Ribadesella and Villaviciosa. The best-preserved remains are around **Playa de la Griega** near **Lastres**, including footprints left in the coastal mud by giant sauropods. Overlooking the beach, you

⭐ Museo del Jurásico de Asturias
www.museojurasico. com; open Easter week and July–mid-Sept daily 10.30–2.30 and 4–8; mid-Sept–Nov Wed–Sun 10.30–2.30, and 4–7; rest of year Mon 10.30–2.30, Wed–Sun 10.30–2.30 and 4–7; adm

can find out more in the slick new **Museo del Jurásico de Asturias**, with huge bones and dinosaur skeletons, models and plenty of interactive exhibits. Equally renowned for its clams and *sidra*, Lastres' stack of red-tile-roofed houses and noble mansions overlooks one of Asturias' most picturesque fishing harbours.

There is a small beach at the village, but a better one just to the west at **Rodiles**, a half-mile of sand lined with eucalyptus trees, very popular in season. Some rare Asturian horses, descendants of the hardy creatures used by the Romans for mountain duty, survive in the **Reserva Nacional de Sueve**, 3km south of Colunga, where you'll also find the **Mirador del Fito** with splendid views of the Picos de Europa and the coast. There is a small pre-Romanesque church, built in 921, in the village of **Priesca**, off the N632 or the A8 12km west of Colunga.

Villaviciosa

⭐ Villaviciosa

Apple orchards line the coast around Villaviciosa, and as you enter the town you'll pass a sign welcoming you to the 'Apple Capital of Spain'. They grow every sort of apple around here, but most common are the ones that feed the town's dozen cider manufacturers. No town makes more of Asturias's favourite sauce, and none seems more devoted to drinking it – particularly during the Fiesta de la Manzana, held every year in mid-October. Every warm evening the tables go out from *chigres* (cider bars) onto the streets around the market, and the noise goes on half the night. Children run around; cider is splashed everywhere. You can visit

El Gaitero
www.gaitero.com, t 98 589 01 00 and t 98 589 29 38; call for times

El Gaitero, one of the most famous cider manufacturers; the tourist office has a list of others that also offer tours.

O villa más viciosa, as an old drinking song chides it, is really a quite pleasant place, with a lively centre built around the Parque Vallina, and a small collection of old streets and palaces, including the attractive 13th-century **Santa María de la Oliva**. Not much has changed since 1517, when Villaviciosa became the first town in Spain to see the handsome but all-too-intense face of their new king, Charles V, who was sailing to Santander from his home in Flanders and was blown off course. There is a plaque on the house where the king stayed to mark the biggest surprise in Villaviciosa's history. If you want to swim, there are two beaches near Villaviciosa: long **Rodiles**, facing the sea and the *ría*, and, across the *ría*, **Tazones**, a picturesque fishing village on a little cove.

Villaviciosa was a more important town a thousand years ago than it is today, and, although nothing from that time survives in the place, its surroundings have a number of early Asturian churches that can serve as an introduction to the better-known pre-Romanesque churches around Oviedo. One kilometre south, signposted off the O121, the Romanesque **San Juan de Amandi** is noted for its beautiful sculpture: graceful geometric patterns on the portal and the usual vigorous but mystifying scenes on the capitals. The lovely rounded portico was added in 1796. Other churches can be sought out in the nearby villages of Ambás and La Piñeda.

San Juan de Amandi
*open Tues–Sun
11.30–1.30 and 5.30–7.30*

Valdediós was probably an ancient site from the earliest times, and in the days of the Kingdom of Asturias it was the religious centre of the region. Nine kilometres southwest of Villaviciosa, in the pretty Puelles valley, it contains two separate churches. The oldest is the oratory of **San Salvador**, built in 893 by Alfonso III. It's an interesting building, one that shows some of the influences behind Asturian architecture. The top still shows a memory of Roman times with its neat classical pediment, though below this has been amplified into a basilican-style three-aisled church. The windows have stone latticework and *ajimeces* (mullioned windows) derived from al-Andalus. A Cistercian monastery was later built nearby, around the 11th-century basilica of **Santa María** (better known as El Conventín); the glorious Romanesque portal and the apse survive from the original building, though most of the interior is much later. The monastery is still in use, and the church interior, usually shut off behind an iron *reja*, glitters like a cave of mystery with its gilt Baroque *retablo* and other furnishings – an effect heightened when the organist monk is practising.

San Salvador
*open Tues–Sun 11–1
and 4.30–6; adm*

Markets from Llanes to Villaviciosa

Llanes: Tues.
Ribadesella and **Villaviciosa**: Wed.

Where to Stay and Eat from Llanes to Villaviciosa

ⓘ **Llanes** ›
Alfonso IX, La Torre
t 98 540 01 64,
www.venallanes.com
and www.llanes.as/guia

Llanes ✉ 33500
***Don Paco**, Parque Posada Herrera 1, t 98 540 01 50, *www.llaneshotel donpaco.com* (€€€). In a graceful 17th-century palace; it's quiet, with a garden, and the main hall is now an elegant restaurant, serving mostly seafood. *Closed Nov–Mar.*

***Hotel Sablón's**, El Sablón, t 98 540 07 87, *www.hotelsablon.com* (€€€). Perched on the rocks above the Playa El Sablón, with comfortable rooms and a restaurant with terrace.
***Arcea Hotel La Arquera**, s/n Llanes, t 98 540 24 24, *www.hotelarquera.com* (€€€). Part of the Asturian Large Houses Quality Club, this is an attractive, friendly and intimate place to stay, with stunning views over Llanes from its hilltop location. A special treat is the breakfast room located in the former 'hórreo' (a raised granary) and the cider press.
***Posada de Babel**, La Pereda (4km from Llanes), t 98 540 25 25, *www. laposadadebabel.com* (€€€). An elegant country house in its own tree-filled grounds, with stylish rooms

★ **Ribadesella Playa Hotel >>**

(including the glassy ultra-modern 'Cube') and a wonderful restaurant for hotel guests only.

***La Posada del Rey, C/ Mayor 11, t 98 540 13 32 (€€€). One of the nicest places to stay in the old quarter, its stylish modern rooms occupy a converted 16th-century town house. Charles V stayed next door on his way to Santander, hence the 'del Rey'.

**Hotel Quinta, in Cué, t 98 540 20 11, *www.laquintallanes.com* (€€). Both Llanes and the villages near the beaches have lots of inexpensive accommodation, such as this place in the pretty village of Cué.

**Pensión La Guia, Pza de Parres Sobrino, t 98 540 25 77 (€€). Decent rooms in a lovely old building on a square in the centre of town.

Casa Moran, at Puente Nuevo (on the road from Posada to Robadella), t 98 540 60 93 (€€). In season there are some wonderful instant restaurants, nothing more than a roof and a few tables, where you can get anything finned at bargain rates. Not far from Llanes, try this popular place with a traditional menu featuring items like *fabada asturiana* and roast lamb. *Closed Oct–Mar.*

El Jornu, C/ Cuetu Molín 43, Pancar (1km from Llanes) t 98 540 1615 (€€). A much-loved local classic, with traditional dishes like rice with clams and freshly grilled fish of the day served out on the terrace. It also rents apartments. *Closed Sun eve, Mon, Nov.*

El Pescador, C/ Manuel Cué 4, t 98 540 22 64 (€€). Serves wonderfully unusual seafood dishes (for example, try the sea urchin omelette), with décor and music to match.

Mesón El Galeón, C/ Mayor 24, t 98 540 16 50 (€€–€). It may look ordinary but the chef is superb and creative. Try the goat's cheese salad with pine nuts as a starter.

(i) **Ribadesella >**
El Muelle, t 98 586 00 38 (summer only), www.ribadesella.com

Ribadesella ✉ 33560

Ribadesella has more accommodation than most villages around the coast.

****Gran Hotel del Sella, La Playa, C/ Ricardo Cangas 17, t 98 586 01 50, *www.granhoteldelsella.com* (€€€). A posh, air-conditioned beachside hotel in a converted palace, once belonging

to the Marquesses of Argüelles. With a pool, tennis courts and garden – a bit of Costa del Sol luxury on the Atlantic. *Open April–Sept.*

***Ribadesella Playa Hotel, C/ Ricardo Congas 3, t 98 586 07 15, *www. ribadesella-playahotel.com* (€€€). A grand residence from the turn of last century, this hotel has a lovely waterfront location on the peninsula and rooms with all modern luxuries.

Hotel El Carmen, s/n Ribadesella, t 98 586 12 89, *www.hotelcarmen.com* (€€). Inside, the meticulously chosen antique furniture creates the feel of a traditional Asturian *casona* but the hotel is newly built so you also enjoy up-to-date bathrooms and modern comforts. Set in large gardens facing the Santianes mountain range, this is difficult to beat at the price.

*Boston, C/ El Pico 7, t 98 586 09 66, *www.ovio-boston.com* (€€–€). Good-value doubles with bath.

La Huertona, C/ de la Piconera 2, t 98 586 05 53 (€€€–€€). On the edge of town, this lovely restaurant sits on the banks of the river and serves superb local cuisine, including seafood and a fine *fabada*.

La Parrilla, Avda Palacio Valdés 33, t 98 586 11 84 (€€). Ribadesella's favourite restaurant: wonderfully fresh fish and shellfish is served simply grilled. Reservations essential.

Sidrería Carroceu, Marqueses de Arguelles 25, t 98 586 14 19, facing the harbour (€). The place to go for tapas and cider; noisy and convivial.

Lastres ✉ 33330

This growing resort can still be your best bet for a peaceful place to spend a few days. There are *casas particulares* and rooms over bars.

***Hotel Palacio de Vallados, C/ Pedro Villarta s/n, t 98 585 04 44, *www. palaciodevallados.com* (€€€–€€). A restored 16th-century palace with lovely lounge but somewhat spartan rooms overlooking the port. *Closed Oct–mid-April.*

Hotel Eutimio, C/ San Antonio s/n, t 98 585 00 12, *www.casaeutimio.com* (€€). This lovely old stone residence has individually decorated rooms with views over the sea. Its restaurant, **Casa Eutimio (€€), is something of a tradition round these parts, serving a marvellous *sopa de marisco*.

Tazones ✉ 33330

*****Hotel El Pescador**, San Miguel 6, t 98 589 70 77 (€€–€). Pleasant rooms in an old harbourside house with port views; the restaurant serves seafood, or you could try one of the myriad similar places along the main drag.

Villaviciosa ✉ 33300

It may be a couple of miles away from the beach, but this is an agreeable place to stay.

******La Corte de Lugás**, Lugás, t 98 589 02 03, *www.lacortedelugas.com* (€€€€). A beautiful stone country manor, with large, elegant rooms (some with four-poster beds) and a fine restaurant.

La Casona de Amandi, at Amandi, C/ San Juan 6, t 98 589 01 30 (€€€). A *casa de indiano* (a house built by a returned emigrant to the Americas); now a very charming nine-room hotel in a lovely formal garden. The owners

dealt in antiques and the rooms are full of their finds.

*****Casa España**, Plaza Carlos I, t 98 589 20 30, *www.hcasaespana.com* (€€). Occupies a converted *casa de indiano* in the monumental centre of town, with antique-furnished rooms and a pleasant café on the plaza.

****Carlos I**, Pza Carlos I, t 98 589 01 21 (€€). A handsome hotel in a 17th-century *palacio* in the centre. *Closed mid-Nov–mid-Mar.*

*****El Manquín**, Plaza Santa Carla 2, t 98 589 05 06, *www.hotelmanquin.com* (€€). Has quiet rooms and a restaurant on a pretty square with fountain; seafood and properly poured cider.

Sol, C/ Sol 27, t 98 589 11 30 (€). Pleasant rooms at bargain rates with spit'n'sawdust bar below.

Sidrería La Oliva, C/ Eloisa Fernández 6 (€). A friendly and atmospheric *sidrería* (one of many), full of local families, couples and friends knocking back cider and filling up on *raciones*.

ⓘ Villaviciosa ›
La Casina de La Oliva,
t 98 589 17 59,
www.villaviciosa.es

Gijón and Avilés

With some 270,000 people, Gijón (pronounced Hee-Hon) is the largest city in Asturias and a major industrial centre and port, a salty, slightly gritty town with few sights but plenty of personality. Built on a rock projecting from the sea called the Cimadevilla, Gijón goes back to the Romans and possibly the Phoenicians – Cimadevilla is often referred to as the '*atalaya*'. When coal began to boom it grew into one of Spain's biggest ports. It was the home of the Enlightenment reformer Jovellanos. Parts were almost totally rebuilt after the Nationalists devastated it in the Civil War. Lately, regionalists have painted over the road signs to remind us that the Asturian spelling is *Xixón*.

What sets Gijón apart are the excellent beaches stretching east from the Cimadevilla. Lined with the slick *urbanizaciones* of the newer town, they give the industrial city a carnival air in the warm months – hordes of locals, mostly red as lobsters, decorate the beaches in a way reminiscent of Reginald Marsh's famous caricatures of Coney Island.

Almost everything worth seeing in Gijón is within walking distance of Cimadevilla, starting with the birthplace and home of the city's most famous reformer, the 16th-century **Museo Casa Natal Jovellanos**. As well as a collection of Jovellanos' belongings, the museum has a good cross section of 19th- and 20th-century

Museo Casa Natal Jovellanos
www.jovenallos.net,
open July–Aug Tues–Sat
11–1.30 and 5–9, Sun
11–2 and 5–8; Sept–June
Tues–Sat 10–1 and 5–8,
Sun 11–2 and 5–7

Getting to and around Gijón and Avilés

By Air

There is an **airport** (the Aeropuerto de Asturias) 14km west of Avilés near Piedras Blancas, **t** 98 512 75 00; daily flights to Madrid, Barcelona and Malaga, and three weekly flights direct to London with Iberia, plus daily flights to London Stansted with easyJet. ALSA buses link the airport with Gijón, Avilés and Oviedo, €10.65 return; taxi from airport is €40.

By Train and Bus

There are frequent FEVE **trains** to Avilés and Cudillero, **t** 90 210 08 18 or *www.feve.es*, hourly RENFE services to Oviedo and less frequent long-distance RENFE trains to León and Madrid (**t** 902 24 02 02 for timetables and reservations). The FEVE and RENFE stations are close together on the Avda de los Telares on the edge of town. The main **bus station** is also here, with services (ALSA is the main bus operator) to Oviedo, into the mountains of Asturias, and along the coast as far as San Sebastián and Galicia.

By Car

Finding a place to **park** can be a problem in the centre of Gijón. If your hotel doesn't have parking, there is a convenient garage under Plaza 6 de Agosto.

For a **taxi**, try Radio Taxi Gijón, **t** 98 514 11 11, or Radio Taxi Jovellanos, **t** 98 516 44 44.

Termas Romanas
*open July–Aug Tues–Sat
11–1.30 and 5–9, Sun
11–2; Mar–June and Sept
Tues–Sat 10–1 and 5–8,
Sun 11–2 and 5–7;
Oct–Feb Tues–Sat 10–1
and 5–8, Sun 11–2
and 5–8; adm*

Pueblo de Asturias
*Paseo Dr Fleming 877,
bus no.10; open Tues–
Sat 10–1 and 5–8, until
9 in July and Aug, Sun
and hols 11–2 and 5–7
(until 8 in July); adm*

**Museo del
Ferrocarril**
*open July–Aug Tues–Sat
10–2 and 5–9, Sun 11–2
and 5–9; Sept–June
Tues–Sat 10–2 and 4–8,
Sun 11–2 and 4–8; adm,
free Sun; train trips
with lunch, €30, reserve
on t 98 517 89 29*

Asturian painting and a selection of sculptures by José María Navascués. However, what everyone comes for is the *Retablo del Mar* by local woodcarver Sebastian Miranda, a misty-eyed evocation of a fishing port that takes up a whole wall. Old photographs next to the *retablo* suggest that Miranda mellowed with age – his original, carved in the 1930s and destroyed in the Civil War, was full of leering faces and grotesque posture, a stark contrast to his 1970s version.

There's not much else to see in Cimadevilla, which suffered greatly in the Civil War. The *atalaya*, also called the hill of Santa Catalina, has a park overlooking the sea, with the obligatory sculpture by Eduardo Chillida; this one's called *Elogio al Horizonte*, 'Tribute to the Horizon'. The rest of the hill is taken up with an abandoned cigar factory where *farias*, the most noxious of smokes, used to be made. The centre occupies the isthmus leading to the newer quarters; there you will find the enclosed and arcaded **Plaza Mayor**, surrounded with restaurants and cafés. Behind it, and cleverly landscaped underground, are the **Termas Romanas**, part of a 2nd-century baths complex notable for its underfloor hypocaustal central heating. Computer animations explain how the baths worked. This is the start of the main beach, the **Playa de San Lorenzo**. At the other end, in the **Pueblo de Asturias** on the far side of the Río del Piles, there is a display of traditional Asturian architecture, from *sidrerías* and *hórreos* (raised granaries) to 18th-century farmhouses: one contains the **Museo de la Gaita**, which displays a host of bagpipes from Celtic northwestern Spain and around the world, as well as a workshop.

If you have children, you'll probably end up at the **Museo del Ferrocarril**, in the old Estación del Norte, home to over 50 pieces of rolling stock and other memorabilia from the Steam Age. On

Saturdays in July and August, it organizes special trips with the FEVE narrow-gauge railway across the road, when a historic train chugs out along the old Langreo rail line to San Vicente and the Museo de la Mineria. Lunch on board is included.

Up to Cabo Peñas and Down Again

Between the industrial centres of Gijón and Avilés the Asturian coast juts northwards for a bit; the coastal road from Gijón may take hours to find, but eventually it will take you out beyond the new port district to **Candás**, an old tuna-fishing village famous for its *corridas marineras* – bullfights on the beach that were unique in Spain, but are no longer practised. **Luanco**, just up the coast, had similar beginnings, but has now become much more of a resort; acres of holiday cottages surround the tidy, small centre. Luanco is famous for lace and embroideries, which you will see in shops and even in the tourist office. There is a small **Museo Marítimo** in Calle Gijón, with model ships and old maps. Luanco has two beaches close to the centre, but there are quieter ones around the tip of the peninsula, at **Cabo Peñas**: the prettiest, Playa de Ferrero and Playa de Llumere, are found on either side of the cape.

At the opposite side of the peninsula is **Avilés**, another large and friendly industrial town with disheartening sprawl that includes a dilapidated steel mill covered in red dust, right across the *ría*. But, unlike Gijón, Avilés has a beautiful and well-preserved historic centre: this medieval town still has a copy of its *fueros*, its charter of rights, kept proudly in the Ayuntamiento. Look especially for the arcaded **Plaza de España**, and the expressively sculpted 16th-century fountain, **Caños de San Francisco**, in little Plaza San Nicolás, next to the 13th-century church of **San Nicolás de Bari**. Inside, note the tomb to favourite son Pedro Menéndez de Avilés, who founded St Augustine, Florida, the oldest city in the USA. Avilés can be lively at night, especially in the *chigres* and clubs around Calle Galiana, on the western side of the lovely **Parque de Ferrera**. This was the garden of the Marqués de Ferrera, whose refined 17th-century palace still stands at the edge, across from the Ayuntamiento.

Just north of Avilés, an old lighthouse guards the entrance to the *ría*, at **San Juan de Nieva**, and a long, gorgeous beach at **Salinas** (an otherwise nondescript modern resort).

Museo Marítimo
open summer Tues–Sun 11–2 and 6–9; winter Tues–Sat 11–2 and 5–8, Sun 11–2

10 Asturias | The Asturian 'Costa Verde': Gijón and Avilés

ⓘ Gijón >
*General information on **Asturias**: C/ Marqués de San Esteban 1, t 98 534 60 46*

InfoGijón, in the port, t 98 534 17 71, www.gijon.info

Tourist Information in Gijón and Avilés

Gijón: general information on Asturias at C/ Marqués de San Esteban; municipal information from **InfoGijón**, in the port; they also have a series of booths along the beaches and waterfront. They organize free daily walking tours in summer, and also sell the **Gijón Card**, valid one day (€10), two days (€12) or three days (€15), which offers free entry to museums, plus unlimited local bus travel and discounts in shops and restaurants.

Gijón's **post office** is on Plaza 6 de Agosto. For Internet access, try

Clickea, Avda Pablo Iglesias 39, or Ciber del Muelle, C/ Claudio Alvargonzález 4, on the harbour.

Markets in Gijón and Avilés

Gijón: La Camocha, C/ La Camocha s/n, Mon, and a Sun am flea market in the car park of Estadio El Moliñón, in Gijón's eastern suburbs. Avilés: Mon.

Where to Stay and Eat in Gijón and Avilés

Gijón ✉ 33200

There are plenty of places to stay in Gijón and also some of the best restaurants in Asturias.

****Parador Molino Viejo, in the pretty Parque Isabel La Católica, t 98 537 05 11, gijon@parador.es (€€€€). An old mill with a modern annexe, it has the best rooms in town and all the usual facilities (except a pool, but the beach is a 10min walk). It serves Asturian food in its restaurant.

***Hotel Quinta Duro, Camino de las Quintas, Cabueñes, t 98 533 04 43, www.hotelquintaduro.com (€€€). Beautifully set in a park; Carlos Velázquez-Duro and his family have converted their old country house into an intimate, smart hotel with modern amenities (a lift and solar power-run hot water). Close to the botanical gardens and university.

***Asturias, Plaza Mayor 11, t 98 535 06 00, www.hotelasturiasgijon.com (€€€). A handsome old building with plain rooms but grand public spaces in the historic centre.

***La Casona de Jovellanos, Plazuela de Jovellanos 1, t 98 534 18 20, www.lacasonadejovellanos.com (€€€–€€). Offers history along with modern comforts: built to house the great reformer's Asturian Institute of Navigation and Mineralogy, renovation work turned up remains of Cimadevilla's original Roman walls, which can now be seen in the fancy restaurant. Next door is one of the city's most popular chigres, a good place to begin the festivities.

**Hotel Miramar, C/ Santa Lucía 9, t 98 535 10 08, www.hotelmiramar gijon.com (€€€–€€). Gracious town house bang in the centre with tasteful revamped décor.

**La Ermita de Deva, C/ San Antonio, Deva (3km from Gijón), t 98 533 34 22, www.hotel-laermita.gijon.com (€€€–€€). A lovely country hotel, with just a handful of pretty rooms, a café-bar and welcoming owners.

**Castilla, C/ Corrida 50, t 98 534 62 00 (€€€–€€). Smart modern rooms with bath on the classiest street in Gijón; good out-of-season rates.

**Hs Manjón, Plaza del Marqués 1, t 98 535 23 78 (€). Friendly but a bit run-down; some rooms overlook the harbour.

Casa Gerardo, Ctra Nacional in Prendes (8km from Gijón), t 98 588 77 97, www.casa-gerardo.com (€€€). Breathes new life into traditional Asturian cooking, with innovative dishes, like rodaballo en aceite de canela (turbot in cinnamon oil), accompanied by tomato marmalade happily sharing a menu with old favourites. Closed winter Mon and Sun–Thurs eves, plus 3 wks in Jan; in August, open Tues–Sat plus Sun lunch.

Las Delicias, Camino de las Dalias (in the suburb of Somió), t 98 536 73 78 (€€€–€€). you'll find this long-established upmarket eaterie, which mixes surf and turf – lubina al horno (sea bass from the oven), medallones de solomillo (sole), escalopines de ternera a la sidra (veal in cider) – and very good service. Closed Tues.

La Colegiata, C/ Melquíades Álvarez 3, t 98 535 44 35 (€€€). Fashionable restaurant and café, good for vegetarians, with an excellent ensalada primavera (spring salad). Closed Sun.

La Pondala, Avda Dionisio Cifuentes 58, Somió, t 98 536 11 60, www.lapondala.com (€€). La Pondala has existed for nearly a century. Specialities are the rice and seafood dishes – try the arroz con almejas (rice with clams) and the delis merluza rellena de mariscos (hake filled with shellfish). There are also plainer options and a good wine list. You have a choice of three smart dining rooms and, in summer, dining on the terrace. Closed Thurs, plus 2 wks June and 2 wks Nov.

(i) **Avilés >>**
C/ Ruiz Gómez 21,
t 98 554 43 25

Torremar, C/ Ezcurdia 120 (one block back from the beach), t 98 533 01 73 (€€). Come here for something kinder on the pocket but just as interesting to the taste buds; offerings include seafood and Asturian dishes such as *fabes con almejas.*

La Galana, Plaza Mayor 10, t 98 517 24 29 (€€–€). A fine old *sidrería* and restaurant with dark wooden beams and huge barrels.

Sidrería Plaza Mayor, Travesía Jovellanos 10, t 98 535 0938 (€€). One of several convivial places around Plaza Mayor; good for a basic dinner.

Avilés ☒ 33400
This unlikely destination has a few good restaurants.

***Hotel de la Villa-Arga, Plaza Domingo Álvarez Acebal 4, t 98 512 97 04 (€€). A good, central option in a much-modernized old building.

La Capilla, Plaza de España 9, t 98 551 06 84 (€€). Inventive cuisine from an up-and-coming young chef is on offer at this stylish restaurant.

La Fragata, C/ San Francisco 18, t 98 555 19 29 (€€–€). Pause at the bar with the locals, or head to the *comedor* for a wide range of tasty local dishes.

Oviedo

The modern capital of Asturias, Oviedo is an elegant and delightful town wrapped around a charming old centre of crooked, tavern-lined streets opening into unexpected squares. Not long ago, the historic core was grimy and neglected, but a determined city council have cleaned it up beautifully, restricting traffic and restoring many of its graceful palaces and churches. It has a fine cathedral, a university almost 400 years old, and two of Europe's most exquisite pre-Romanesque churches, built when the rest of the continent was still living in the Dark Ages. Founded by Fruela I in 757 as a fortress guarding the key road over the mountains to the coast, Oviedo became the capital of Christian Spain when Alfonso II 'el Casto' (the Chaste) built himself a palace in 810, and stayed capital until the Asturian kings conquered León in 1002.

The city suffered terribly in the insurrection of 1934 and during the Civil War. It used to earn a living from the surrounding coal and iron mines, but today Oviedo has its sights firmly set on the tourist euro. It continues to take up a variety of causes – walls are covered with graffiti encouraging the revival of *el Bable*; a helter-skelter mix of pro-choice, 'Viva la Virgen' and 'Europa Blanca' rally posters are pasted side by side on the walls of the numerous *chigres*.

The shining results of the clean-up and new focus have not gone ignored by the outside world. When world-renowned film director Woody Allen visited Oviedo in 2002 to pick up an arts prize at the annual Prince of Asturias Awards (Spain's most prestigious awards), he described the city as 'delicious, exotic, beautiful and pedestrianized: it's as if it didn't belong to this world... Oviedo is like a fairy tale.' The city paid back the compliment by erecting a life-size statue of him in C/ Milicias Nacionales. But the mutual love affair didn't end there. In the summer of 2007, Allen chose Oviedo to shoot several scenes of his new film starring Scarlett

Getting to and around Oviedo

All **trains** leave from the station at the head of C/ Uria in the centre of town. RENFE, t 90 224 02 02, has hourly connections to Gijón and fewer links to Barcelona, Zaragoza, Burgos, León, Pamplona, Madrid, Valladolid and Palencia. FEVE trains, t 98 529 76 56, run east to Santander and Bilbao, and west along the coast to Ferrol.

The new **Estación de Autobuses** is next to the train station, info t 98 596 9696, *www.estaciodeautobuses deoviedo.com*. ALSA, the biggest company, t 90 249 99 49, *www.alsa.es*, serves destinations throughout Asturias and Northern Spain, as well as Madrid, Seville, Barcelona, Valladolid and Valencia; international buses go as far as Paris, Geneva, Zürich and Brussels.

Parking and getting around can be a pain in Oviedo. Almost all of the old centre is closed to traffic; as a last resort there is a parking garage underneath the Campo de San Francisco.

For a **Radio Taxi**, call t 98 525 00 00.

Johansson. Filming took place in key locations including the pre-Romanesque church of San Julián de Los Prados, the central Corrada del Obispo square, the century-old café 'Camilo de Blas', the Fontán market and the luxury Reconquista hotel.

The Cathedral

The middle of Oviedo (take C/ Uría, the main shopping street, from the station) is occupied by the tranquil, shady **Campo de San Francisco** – a typically lavish Spanish city park with fervent memorials to past literati, grand promenades, carefully labelled exotic trees, ducks to feed, and children getting ice cream all over their best clothes. From here C/ San Francisco leads to the oldest part of the city, and the asymmetrical **cathedral**, an attractive Gothic temple from the 14th century; its lovely tower with its delicate stone latticework is Oviedo's landmark. King Fruela began the first church on this site when he founded the city, and Alfonso el Casto enlarged it, but the current incarnation, recently restored, is a high Gothic work begun in 1388. In the Capilla Mayor, look for an enormous florid 16th-century *retablo* of the *Life of Christ* sculpted by Giralte of Brussels.

Best of all, a door in the right transept leads to the original church of Alfonso el Casto, now known as the **Cámara Santa**, strange and semi-barbaric, with fine carvings of the Apostles attributed to Master Mateo on the capitals of the outer chamber and disembodied heads on the walls. The Capilla de San Miguel was built by el Casto in 802 to house the relics of Visigothic Toledo rescued after its capture by the Moors, and largely rebuilt in the 12th century. Today it contains the cathedral's treasures: the *Cruz de la Victoria*, supposedly borne by Pelayo at Covadonga, and today on Asturias's coat of arms; the *Cruz de los Angeles* (808), a golden cross embedded with huge rubies and carved gems, reputedly made by the angels themselves and donated by Alfonso II; a beautiful, silver-plated reliquary chest of 1073, as well as a phial of the Virgin Mary's milk and one of Judas's 30 pieces of silver.

Cámara Santa
*open July–Sept
Mon–Fri 10–8, Sat 10–6;
Oct–June Mon–Fri 10–1
and 4–6, Sat 10–6; adm
to the Cámara Santa
only, or combined adm
to Cámara Santa,
museum and cloister*

Oviedo cathedral was always famous for its collection of relics, although none has attracted as much attention of late as the Sudarium, a bloodstained cloth reputedly used to cover Jesus's head after he was crucified. In recent years, it has been put forward as supporting evidence for the authenticity of the Shroud in Turin – unlike the Shroud, the Sudarium is documented back to the 1st century AD, and laboratory studies have shown the two were used to wrap the same body and are stained with same rare AB blood group (see www.shroud.com/guscin.htm). The **museum** includes Romanesque sculptures and glittering liturgical plate, and the **cloister** is pale and lovely. Just off the cloister, the Crypt of Santa Leocadia contains the plain tomb of the 3rd-century martyr-saint from Toledo. The crypt is part of the ancient cathedral under the Cámara Santa, with a pair of carved Visigothic stone reliefs.

Behind the cathedral the old convent of San Vicente houses the **Museo Arqueológico**, featuring finds from the Palaeolithic era to the days of the Asturian kingdom. There are a few attractive old streets to the south of the cathedral around the **Plaza del Fontan**, an enclosed square that was starting to fall down before restoration works were started.

Museo Arqueológico
closed indefinitely for restoration, call **t** *98 521 54 05 for updates*

The Asturian Pre-Romanesque Churches

Pre-Romanesque churches

Oviedo has the finest of Asturias's post-Visigothic pre-Romanesque churches. Enjoying the patronage of its kings, this little capital can claim the beginnings of sophisticated medieval architecture, at a time when most of Christian Europe was still scratching its carrot rows with a short stick. The two most important churches were built on Mount Naranco as part of the palace that Alfonso el Casto built for himself and Ramiro I (842–50) expanded, and it's fascinating to think of these pocket potentates throwing up a summer pleasure-dome in the hills in imitation of the great sultans of al-Andalus.

Some scholars have found a Carolingian influence in their structures, although this is hard to see. The major influence clearly comes from North Africa or the Middle East, via Christian refugees from those newly Islamized countries. The classical pediment common atop Asturian churches was also common there; it goes back to the origins of Christian building, to the basilicas of Constantine and Theodosius in the Greek east. Hints of later Byzantine elements can be seen in many of the details, but this is all – Byzantium was 2,700km away. The only building that has anything in common with Santa María de Naranco and its unusual plan is a unique, mysterious little chapel in central Italy called the Tempio del Clitunno, built a century earlier. Even with these influences, much in these provocative prototypes that never made it to the assembly line is original and beautiful. In 1985 UNESCO

10

Asturias | Oviedo

declared them the best architecture produced in 9th-century Christian Europe, protected as part of the 'Heritage of Humanity'.

San Julián de Los Prados
open summer Mon–Fri 10–1, Sat 9.30–12.30 and 2.30–5.30; winter Tues–Sat 9.30–11.30, Mon 10–12.30; closed Sun; adm

Alfonso el Casto built the oldest of these, **San Julián de Los Prados** (also called Santullano), northeast of the centre; C/ de Martínez Vigil from the back of the cathedral takes you there. This is a simple, solid building with three square apses, a secret compartment in the wall, and interesting murals by an artist influenced by Roman monuments.

If you're pressed for time, head in the opposite direction up the **Cuesta de Naranco**, a hill overlooking the town (facing the RENFE station, turn left to the sign at the bridge over the tracks and continue 3km (2 miles); city bus no.10 makes cameo appearances on the hour. Pick it up from C/ Uría and get off by the car park at La Cruce). The two churches here, Santa María de Naranco and San Miguel de Lillo, can be found halfway up the mountain with a view over Oviedo. Both of these churches were built by Alfonso el Casto's successor, Ramiro I; incredibly, the perfectly proportioned

Santa María de Naranco
open Tues–Sat 9.30–1 and 3.30–7, Sun and Mon 9.30–1; adm, free Mon

Santa María de Naranco is believed to have been part of the king's summer palace. Built of a fair golden stone and set in a small clearing, it is an enchanting building, supported by unusual flat buttresses and flanked by two porches. The lower level is believed to have been a waiting chamber and bath; the upper, with a rough-hewn altar on the porch, was the main hall. Inside are blind arches of subtly decreasing height, topped by round medallions. An **Interpretation Centre** is nearby in an old schoolhouse, where you can organize guided visits and pick up information.

San Miguel de Lillo
open summer Tues–Sat 9.30–1 and 3.30–7, Sun and Mon 9.30–1; winter Tues–Sat 10–1.30 and 3–5, Sun 10–1; adm

Just up the road, **San Miguel de Lillo** is a more traditional cruciform church, although of stunted proportions after an ancient amputation removed two-thirds of the original length. Its round windows are adorned with beautiful stone traceries, and what the guides claim to be a circus scene is carved on the door jamb, along with some Visigothic arabesques.

Facilities in Oviedo

(i) Oviedo >>
'El Escorialin',
C/ Marqués de Santa Cruz s/n, t 98 522 75 86, www.ayto-oviedo.es

The **post office** is on C/ Alonso Quintanilla 1.

Cheap **Internet** access is available at Laser, C/ San Francisco 9; there are several other cybercafés, including the **Café Oriental**, C/ Jovellanos 8.

Markets in Oviedo

Oviedo: There is a covered market on Plaza del Fontán. A flea market is held outside on Sundays.

Where to Stay in Oviedo

Oviedo ✉ 33000

*****Hotel de la Reconquista**, C/ Gil de Jaz 16, t 98 524 11 00, *www. hoteldelareconquista.com* (€€€€€). A couple of blocks from the Parque de San Francisco, this lovely 17th-century palace has been converted into a super-luxury hotel.

****Gran Hotel España**, C/ Jovellanos 2, t 98 522 05 96, *www.granhotel espana.com* (€€€€). Plush and comfortable, this classic hotel is in the heart of the old centre.

****Gran Hotel Regente, C/ Jovellanos 31, t 98 522 23 43, *www.granhotel regente.com* (€€€€). This offers traditional elegance opposite the Monastery of San Pelayo. It is geared towards business travellers, hence good website deals.

****Libretto Hotel, C/ Marqués de Santa Cruz 12, t 98 520 20 04, *www. librettohotel.com* (€€€€). An elegant Modernista building, now a stylish hotel, with a chic mixture of the contemporary and antique.

****M Hotel, C/ Comandante Vallespín, t 98 527 40 60, *www.mhotel. es* (€€€€). An ultra-modern hotel by the Palacio de Congresos, with quirky contemporary rooms and a spa.

Hotel Fruela, C/ Fruela 3, t 98 520 81 20, *www.hotelfruela.com* (€€€). The late 19th century façade, painstakingly restored, couldn't be more different from the sleek, minimalist interior valued by trendy boutique hotels. The central location is also excellent.

***Hotel Vetusta, C/ Covadonga 2, t 98 522 22 29, *www.hotelvetusta.com* (€€€). An excellent central option, in a traditional building with slick, modern décor and Jacuzzis in some rooms.

Palacio de la Viñona, C/ Julián Clavería 14, Barrio Colloto, t 98 579 33 99 (€€€). A graceful 18th-century stone manor on the outskirts, with a garden and beautiful rooms (most with Jacuzzi).

**Santa Clara, C/ Santa Clara 1, t 98 522 27 27 (€€€). In the centre, this friendly, well-equipped place offers weekend discounts.

*Hotel Favila, C/ Uría 37, t 98 525 38 77, *www.hotelfavilaoviedo.com* (€€). A good family-run option close to the bus and train stations, with immaculate rooms and a decent restaurant (€) downstairs.

*El Ovetense, C/ San Juan 6, t 98 522 08 40, *www.hotelovetense.com* (€€–€). A welcoming little hotel close to the cathedral, with its own *sidrería* and restaurant.

**Hs Arcos, C/ Magdalena 3 (just off Plaza de la Constitución), t 98 521 47 73 (€€–€). One of the cheapest central options, with rooms with or without bath and very friendly staff.

*Hotel Alteza, C/ Uría 25, t 98 524 04 04 (€€–€). Another reliable, if rather worn, option by the train station. All rooms with bath and TV.

*Hs Belmonte, C/ Uría 31, t 98 524 10 20, *calogon@telecable.es* (€€–€). Family-run, one of the best of several *hostales* that cluster on and around C/ Uría, near the RENFE station. Recently renovated.

Pensión Riesgo, C/ 9 de Mayo 16, t 98 521 89 45 (€). Cheap and cheerful rooms with shower, on a pedestrianized street near the centre.

Eating Out in Oviedo

Casa Fermín, San Francisco 8 (near the park), t 98 521 64 52 (€€€). Although there are plenty of restaurants and tapas bars in Oviedo, this remains the oldest and the best, offering award-winning Asturian cuisine and seasonal Spanish regional dishes in a refined atmosphere. *Closed Sun.*

El Cabroncín, Ctra Paredes 1 (in Lugones, 2km from Oviedo), t 98 526 63 80 (€€€). Drive out to this charmingly rustic *comedor*, and try the inventive interpretations of traditional Asturian cooking; kidney beans with rabbit cutlets and slivers of calamari, followed by truly decadent chocolate ravioli smothered with orange cream. *Closed Sun eve and Mon.*

La Mar del Medio, C/ Mon 18, t 98 522 55 75 (€€). Has excellent fish and seafood in a suitably nautical ambience; arrive early as it fills up quickly during lunch times, or pop in and try the tasty *pinchos. Closed Sun night and Mon.*

El Raitán, Plaza de Trascorrales 6, t 98 521 42 18 (€€). A classic that specializes in grilled meats along with homemade desserts like the *carbayones* (made with almonds).

Cervantes, C/ Jovellanos 4, t 98 522 00 11. (€€–€). A good choice for traditional fare for 40 years. *Closed Sun and Aug.*

Villaviciosa, C/ Gascona 7, t 98 520 44 12 (€). Hearty Asturian stews and good *fabadas* bubble away at all the *sidrerías* around C/ Gascona. This is one recommendation.

Entertainment and Nightlife in Oviedo

Oviedo is the centre of Asturian rock, and you can see what the local groups are getting up to in the desperate-looking clubs all along C/ Rosal, one street south of the Campo de San Francisco. Otherwise, the action is on the nearby streets in the old town, with more clubs and bars for the younger set. The best places for a simple drink are the informal bars around Fontan.

Cervecería Asturianu, C/ Carta Puebla 8. Serves every different kind of beer and whisky imaginable, with décor that includes pieces of the Berlin Wall.

Danny's Jazz, La Luna 11. Funky café/bar with live jazz.

El Pigüeña, C/ Gascona 2. On this street of *sidrerías*, one of the best.

La Real, C/ Cervantes 19. A mythical, massive disco, with excellent DJs.

Salsipuedes. A lively disco-bar, which is good for an early evening drink on the outdoor terrace on Ildefonso Martínez. Busy later on.

Southern Asturias

The principality, beyond the coast and the Picos, is *terra incognita* for most foreigners: a hilly, wooded land of small mining towns and agricultural villages, crisscrossed with walking paths. Much of it is protected, especially in the national hunting preserves that cover the northern slopes of the Cordillera Cantábrica. The coast is excellent – rugged cliffs, few tourists, and plenty of shellfish and beaches. Public transport is limited here, and you'd do well to rent a car – and pack a big lunch – before setting out. Be sure to pick up one of the large detailed maps at the tourist office in Oviedo.

Around Oviedo: Miners' Valleys and More Churches

Southeast of Oviedo, the AS17 passes **Langreo** and **Pola de Laviana**, both typical Asturian copper-mining towns. Langreo is home to the **Museo de Minería y Industria**, with exhibits on the history of mining; there are scale models of old machinery, a recreated explosives laboratory, and a replica of a copper mine.

Beyond Pola de Laviana the road continues to Reres National Reserve and the beautiful mountain pass, **Puerto de Tarna**. The next pass to the west, **Puerto San Isidro**, has a major ski installation. Both passes can be reached by bus from Pueblo de Lillo in León province. **Collanzo**, some 12km below the pass, is set near an idyllic little gorge, the **Hoces de Río Aller**.

Directly south of Oviedo, along the train route and recently built highway to León (an engineering feat Spain is not a little proud of), the views become increasingly magnificent as you ascend to the dramatic **Puerto de Pajares**, another ski spot on the border with Léon. But before you get there, look for the signs 6km south of the grim industrial town of **Pola de Lena** for another of Ramiro I's lovely churches, the hilltop **Santa Cristina de Lena**, a cruciform temple built around 845, with blind arches similar to Santa María de Naranco, Visigothic decorations and an intricate iconostasis of Mozarabic inspiration.

Museo de Minería y Industria
www.mumi.es; open July–Aug Tues–Sat 10–8, Sun 10–2; Sept–June Tues–Sat 10–2 and 4–7, Sun 10–2; adm, see Gijón, p.226 for days out by historic train

Puerto San Isidro
in the province of León, see www.san-isidro.net for information

Santa Cristina de Lena
open summer Tues–Sun 11–1 and 4.30–6.30; winter Tues–Sun 4.30–6

Getting around Southern Asturias

The RENFE **train** between Oviedo and León stops at Pajares and Pola de Lena; Pola de Lena is linked by frequent *cercanías* (local trains). Call t 902 24 02 02 for information and reservations.
All the main towns in southern Asturias can be reached by **bus**. ALSA buses from Oviedo's main bus station, t 902 42 22 42, *www.alsa.es*, go to Salas, Puerto de Somiedo, Cangas del Narcea, Tineo and Pola de Allande. Empresa Fernández, t 98 523 83 90, has buses to Mieres, Pola de Lena and Turón; there are also a half-dozen or so daily buses down the western coast to Cudillero and Luarca, and as many from Gijón. Alcotán, t 98 521 76 17 and t 98 560 02 68, runs buses to Pola de Laviana.
If you're **driving** when the snow is flying, it's essential to call ahead for road conditions, t 98 525 46 11.
To **rent a car**, the main companies in Oviedo are along C/ Ventura Rodríguez.

The landmark in this part of the Cantabrian mountains is the jagged 7,855ft **Peña Ubiña**, which sturdy walkers can tackle in around 4–5hrs from **Tuiza de Arriba** for incomparable views over the Picos de Europa and Somiedo (to reach Tuiza, take the side road from the highway at Campomanes). From Pajares, you can make the much shorter climb up the 5,580ft **Pico de los Celleros**.

Up to the Cordillera, and Somiedo National Park

Southwest of Oviedo, in the highest part of the Cantabrian mountains, is the **Parque Natural de Somiedo**. This vast wild area stretches from Puerto de Pajares in the east to Pola de Somiedo in the west, encompassing 7,000ft peaks, dense beech and oak forests, and several *brañas*, ancient villages of straw-roofed huts built by the *vaqueros* (*see* p.240). Although not a true National Park – much of Somiedo is protected as a hunting reserve – this is the Cordillera Cantábrica's great wildlife stronghold; it has the healthiest population of brown bears in Spain, and the Iberian wolf is so successful it is considered common. For birdwatchers too it is a paradise: middle-spotted and black woodpeckers make their home in the forests, ultra colourful bee eaters reach the northern limit of their range on the lower slopes, and wallcreepers flit around the vertical crags. The very fortunate may get a glimpse of the rare lammergeyer or bearded vulture, the largest bird of prey in Europe – a startling sight, with its black wings, fierce expression, and habit of dropping bones on rocks to get access to the marrow inside; the Spanish call it *quebrantahuesos*, the 'bone-breaker'. There's a **park information office** in Pola de Somiedo.

Parque Natural de Somiedo

Park Information Office
t 98 576 37 58; open Easter week and mid-June–mid-Sept 10–2 and 4–9; rest of year 10–2 and 4–7

One approach to Somiedo is by way of **Trubia**, a village known mostly for its enormous armament works (*see* box, overleaf). Ten kilometres south of Trubia on the road to the park you can stop at **Tuñón** for one of the last of the 'Asturian' churches, **Santo Adriano**, built by Alfonso III (866–910). Sombre in design and Mozarabic in style, it features clerestory windows and pretty latticework crosses. Inside are some of the oldest frescoes anywhere in Spain, traces of what seem to be sun symbols over the altar and zigzag motifs taken straight from the Grand Mosque of Córdoba. The tobacco

The Dress Rehearsal

The event of the 20th century in Asturias was the epic miners' revolt of 1934, a full-scale battle that eerily prefigured the Spanish Civil War. Because of the large numbers of workers in mining and industry, Asturias was politically the odd man out, an island of belligerent Marxists in the middle of the arch-conservative northwest. Mining and metalworking go way back in Asturias, but really took off at the beginning of the 20th century, when *indianos* forced home by Spain's loss of Cuba and the Philippines began to invest their money here. In the First World War, Spanish neutrality made for a boom in the mining areas, one which collapsed in the 1920s, leaving Asturias with the angriest proletariat in Spain.

Along with the Basques and Catalans, Asturians were strong supporters of the Republic when it appeared in 1931 but, for many of their leaders, the new regime was only a stepping-stone to Socialism. The depression increased popular discontent, but what really set the workers boiling was the radical right-wing national government elected in 1934. Under prime minister Gil Robles, it began dismantling all the reforms of its leftist predecessors and openly postured for the restoration of the monarchy. On 4 October 1934 the trade unions declared a general strike in Asturias in protest. Barcelona and Madrid also rose up but failed to follow through, leaving the Asturians on their own and in a fighting mood. The main centres of the revolt were Mieres, Sama and Oviedo, but it was the munitions works at Trubia, near Somiedo, that turned the strike into a war. The workers occupied it and seized some 30,000 rifles inside. Soon there was a 30,000-man 'Red Army', and a revolutionary committee was formed to govern the province.

The government sent in a dependable general named Mola, leading a force made up mainly of Moroccan troops – northern Morocco was still a Spanish protectorate. The Moors were mercenaries who had fought against their own people, but they were fiercely loyal to their commander, one Francisco Franco. Franco, a Galician married to an Asturian woman, felt right at home. He had already led troops, using the Spanish Foreign Legion, to crush a general strike in Asturias in 1917. The Legion was also present in 1934. An outfit not much like the romantic French version, this one was now led by a fascist psychopath named Millan Astray, famous for his missing arm and eye-patch. As for the Moors, some of them must have enjoyed the irony of a Spanish commander, an heir to Pelayo, bringing them to a place where they hadn't set foot for a thousand years. The government had to make its point, and the revolt was crushed quickly and with the utmost ferocity. Many of the mining towns were thoroughly wrecked, and the troops slaughtered nearly 1,300 Asturians in reprisals after the surrender on 19 October. A year and a half later, after new elections brought the leftist Popular Front to power, the coup that began the Civil War started with the same cast of characters: General Mola, who was to be the new dictator, but who died in an air crash at the start; the Foreign Legion; and the inevitable Francisco Franco, whose Moroccans won him the title of *caudillo* (leader). The best-equipped and -trained forces in Spain, they used their practice in Asturias to get the jump on the disorganized government and citizens' militias, and gained control of much of Spain within a month, an advantage that helped assure the Nationalists' final victory.

shop opposite has the key, but the only guide is the unusually friendly bat that lives in the choir.

Further south, **Proaza** has a number of medieval buildings; it is separated from the next village, **Caranga**, by a pretty gorge you can walk through, the **Desfiladero del Teverga**. The road continues south through La Plaza, site of the 12th-century **Colegiata de San Pedro**, where elements of Asturian pre-Romanesque combine with early French Romanesque; on the capitals are sculpted local animals, and there are two 18th-century mummies.

From La Plaza, the road south cuts through a magnificent forest to the **Puerto Ventana**, perhaps the least-used Asturian mountain pass. Just on the other side of the pass, from the Leonese village of **Torrestio**, you can hike in three hours into the lovely heart of Somiedo and its mysterious lakes, where *xanas*, or mermaids, guard the sunken treasures they use to please their lovers on the night of St John. The first lake, **Lago de la Cueva**, is the source of the Río Sil; the third and largest is the eerie, dark **Lago Negro**.

A second approach to Somiedo is via the N634, the main road west from Oviedo. This will take you through the village of **Grado**, where everybody comes on Wednesday and Sunday for the markets, and lovely **Salas**, with its medieval monuments and palaces, as well as the fine Renaissance **Colegiata de Santa María**, home to the beautiful alabaster tomb of the Inquisitor Valdés-Salas. The surrounding countryside is rich in picturesque *hórreos* (granaries), and to the west are the lovely pasturelands and hills around **Navelgas** and **Bárcena del Monasterio**, where the *vaqueros* (*see* p.240) winter their herds.

From Salas head south and follow the valley of the Pigüeña towards Somiedo. The big village in this iron-mining area is **Belmonte de Miranda** (C633); a curiosity in the region is the **Machuco de Alvariza** (near Belmonte village), an oak-built hydraulic hammer used in the 18th-century iron works. Many *vaqueros* still live here – some of their conical-roofed *pallozas* (huts), along with several Celtic *castros* (hill forts) lie towards **Pola de Somiedo**, the district's major town (where the Natural Park information office, *see* p.239, is located).

One of the best excursions in this area is to **Lago del Valle**, an easy four-hour ramble through a fantasy valley plucked from the pages of Tolkien; eagles soar above twisted peaks, a dusty road winds through wild flower meadows, and dogs as big as horses stand guard over the livestock. There are a few scattered *pallozas* along the way; a better collection can be found west of Pola de Somiedo in the ancient *braña* of **La Pornacal**, Somiedo's largest and best-preserved *vaquero* hamlet, reached by a farm track from Villar de Vildas. Two kilometres beyond La Pornacal lies the much older **Braña de los Cuartos**, its circular walls in a state of poetic semi-dereliction at the head of the valley.

West of Oviedo: Ancient Pottery and Primeval Forests

Back on the main route west from Oviedo, after Salas the next village is **Tineo**, a great trout-fishing area crossed by a branch of the Santiago pilgrimage route. Several medieval churches survive from that era – Tineo's 13th-century parish church and the ruined monastery and church of San Miguel in nearby **Obona**. Further south, a dirt road leads up to the tiny borough of **Llamas del Mouro**, where potters, isolated from the rest of the world, still create the shiny black ceramic jugs and bowls made by their

Celtiberian ancestors. The pieces are fired in the ancient style, in circular ovens buried in the earth. Only the family of Jesús Rodríguez Garrido continues to make and fire pottery; they sell it too, at very good prices, in a little shop adjacent to the workshop.

Cangas del Narcea, the largest town in southwest Asturias, is modern and has little to waylay you; head instead further south to **Pico de la Masa** (near Puerto del Connio) for the view over the magnificent 5,000-hectare **Bosque de Muniellos**, one of Europe's last and most extensive forests of primeval oak and beech. A strictly protected wildlife preserve, the forest is home to rare species like capercaillie, otter and pine marten, while larger mammals and predators inhabit the area's higher regions: chamois, wolves, and a few itinerant brown bears. There's only one trail through the forest, beginning at **Tablizas**, a short hike from Moal; from here it's a delightful scramble up a ferny green canyon to the edge of the woods, beyond which lie three glorious subalpine lakes. The whole hike takes about five-and-a-half hours and will leave you mourning for the ancient times, when (they say) a squirrel could cross the whole of Iberia without ever touching the ground. Like Altamira, Muniellos is accounted such a threatened treasure that only 20 people a day are allowed inside the forest; make sure you call well in advance or submit a *petición del permiso de acceso* through the website. East of Muniellos lies the **Reserva Nacional de Degaña**, another lovely, wooded area, with pretty meadows and small lakes formed by glaciers. In the Roman era Degaña was heavily mined for its gold.

Gold was also mined in the most westerly zone of the province, around **Pola de Allande** and **Grandas de Salime**, both enchanting, seldom-visited villages. Grandas has a partially Romanesque church, San Salvador, and a **Museo Etnográfico y Escuela de Artesanía**, with exhibits on country life in old Asturias and craft-workers there in person weaving, making baskets and carving wood. In **Celón**, 5km from Pola, there's a fine 12th-century church, **Santa María**, with impressive frescoes and carvings. One of Asturias' best-preserved Celtic *castros* is up on **Pico San Chuis** to the west near Berducedo, whose ancient inhabitants, like the modern, exploited the region for its supply of minerals.

Bosque de Muniellos
t 98 527 91 00, www.asturias.es (Spanish only)

Markets in Southern Asturias

Mieres: Sun.
Pola de Somiedo: Tues.
Tineo: Thurs.
Cangas del Narcea: every other Sat.

Skiing in Southern Asturias

Valgrande Pajares, 3km from the Busdongo train station. Offers 15 slopes from the very difficult to the very easy, 10 lifts and two chairlifts. Info at *www.valgrande-pajares.com*. **San Isidro**, near Puebla de Lillo (León province). With a total of 23 ski-runs,

(i) Tuñón
t 98 576 15 34

(i) Pola de Somiedo >>
Centro de Recepción e Interpretación del Parque, t 98 576 37 58

(i) Tineo >>
Calle Mayor, t 98 580 01 87 (summer only)

(i) Cangas del Narcea >>
C/ Mayor 48, t 98 581 14 98, www.narceaturismo.com

(i) Salas >
Pza de la Campa, t 98 583 09 88, www.ayto-salas.es

of which about half are difficult, three chairlifts and several ski lifts. There are a couple of hotels at Puebla de Lillo (you can book accommodation online), but no public transport. Info at *www.san-isidro.net*.

Leitariegos Pass, San Emiliano. A small ski installation on the slopes of Peña Ubiña. Info at *www.leitariegos.com*.

Where to Stay and Eat in Southern Asturias

Puerto de Pajares ✉ 33693
La Rectoral de Tuiza, in Tuiza de Arriba, t 98 545 14 20 (€€€; between €100–120 per night for the whole house; only let whole). Groups tackling the heights of Peña Ubiña can try something a bit different: set up base in a complete *casa rural* with space for up to six people, in a beautiful setting high up in the mountains.

**Puerto de Pajares, Puerto de Pajares, t 98 595 70 51 (€€€). A little further away from the slopes than La Rectoral de Tuiza, with comfortable basic rooms and central heating.

Albergue Toribión de Llanos, Brañillín, t 98 595 70 40, *www.toribiondellanos.com* (€€–€). Dormitories and some double, triple and quadruple rooms; you can step straight out of the hotel and into the ski lifts.

Mieres ✉ 33600
**Hotel Rural Cenera, Cenera, t 98 542 63 50, *www.valledecenera.com* (€€€–€€). Traditional country inn in a tiny village close to Mieres, with comfy rooms and sturdy home cooking in the *mesón* below.

**Hs Villa de Mieres, C/ Teodoro Cuesta 33 (off the Oviedo–León road), t 98 546 11 08 (€). Good home cooking in modern, smart surroundings.

Salas ✉ 33600
Salas is a convenient stopover on the N634, with a few inexpensive *hostales* over bars. There are basic campsites within the Somiedo Park at Valle de Lago and Saliencia.

**Castillo de Valdés, Plaza Campa, t 98 583 01 73/01 74, *www.castillovaldesalas.com* (€€, with lunch and dinner included). A restored 16th-

century palace (formerly a castle), with a popular restaurant. Servings include imaginative Asturian dishes.

Casa Soto, C/ Arzobispo Valdés 9, t 98 583 00 37 (€). Pleasant large rooms in a historic building in the centre.

Pola de Somiedo ✉ 33840
**Casa Miño, C/ Rafael Rey López, t 98 576 37 30, *www.hotelcasamino.com* (€€). A comfortable traditional hotel, with nicely furnished spacious rooms and a friendly local bar.

**Hotel Rural el Meirel, C/ Fernández Álvarez s/n, t 98 576 39 93 (€€). Small but perfectly formed, with individually decorated rooms and three apartments for longer stays. The restaurant serves hearty mountain meals and wicked *fabadas*.

Casa Cobrana, in Valle del Lago, t 98 576 37 48 (€). A rural *hostal* which also offers good meals, at the head of the beautiful trail to Lago del Valle.

Tineo ✉ 33870
*Hotel Don Miguel, Avda de Oviedo 6, El Viso, t 98 580 03 25 (€). Pleasant hotel with good rooms.

**Hs Casa Sole, Navelgas, on the main road, t 98 580 60 44 (€). Simple and old-fashioned, offering pleasant rooms above a café-bar.

*Casa Lula, El Crucero, t 98 580 16 00 (€). A cosy spot.

Cangas del Narcea ✉ 33800
**Hotel La Casilla, Limés, t 985 81 26 80, *www.hotellacasilla.com* (€€). A traditional, pretty hotel in a small village just outside Cangas del Narcea plus good local restaurant.

**Pensión Virgen del Carmen, C/ Mayor 46, t 98 581 15 02 (€). Small, with seven good rooms with heating and air-conditioning.

*Peña Grande, Ctra Leitariegos (1km from the centre), t 98 581 23 92 (€). A comfortable place, with lovely views, flouncy rooms and a large restaurant.

*Hotel Rural La Pista, Vega de Rengos (20km south), t 98 591 10 04 (€). Near the entrance to Bosque de Muniellos, this is a cosy place to stay, with bright rooms, a budget restaurant and an extremely welcoming owner.

*Hs Acebo, C/ Hermanos Flórez 1, t 98 581 05 46 (€). Has rooms without bath.

Asturias' Western Coast

The Asturian coast west of Avilés could be the best chance in this book for a peaceful and agreeable seaside holiday. The shoreline does not seem dramatic until you see it close up – wild cliffs of jumbled, glittering metamorphic rock, mixed with long stretches of beach where you can find uncrowded spots even on August weekends. Cudillero in particular happens to be one of the most delightful seaside villages on earth, and there are plenty of isolated beaches all along the rugged coast between them.

Cudillero and Luarca

⭐ Cudillero   The first resort west of Avilés, **Cudillero** was for many years well protected from the tourist hordes by its geography; the only way into this fishing village was along its narrow, cobbled main street, which snakes down almost vertically for around three kilometres. The hordes can now sweep down to Cudillero on a smooth new road, into the picturesque little harbour with its Portofino-style coloured houses at the bottom of the cliffs. Except for the summer days when it fills up with Madrileño day-trippers, Cudillero is a perfect place to hide away for a few days. If you have your own car you can find plenty of good beaches nearby, especially the broad **Playa de la Cueva** (visible from a high viaduct on the coast highway, though in fact it is many miles away).

Asturias has no shortage of souvenirs. The most common things you'll see are traditional wooden clogs, or *madreñas*, but recently the hot item seems to be whole cow hides; the roadside stand by the viaduct has a wide selection. Just to the west, a road branches off to Soto de Luiña and **Cabo Vidio**, from where there are views of the coastal mountains; on a clear day it's possible to see as far as the Estaca de Bares, the northernmost point in Spain, an incredible 112km away in Galicia.

The *Vaqueros*

The territory around Luarca is the land of the *vaqueros*, one of Iberia's marginal peoples, first mentioned in the Middle Ages. The *vaqueros* were cowherds who spent half of the year in the mountain pastures with their cattle, transporting all of their worldly goods in ox carts and building *pallozas* (huts with conical thatched roofs), which you can still see in rural regions further inland.

Although ostracized from society (in most parishes they weren't even allowed to hear Mass inside a church or be buried in holy ground), they themselves claimed to be far older than God, and returned disdain for disdain. Recent research based on their dialect places them as 1st-century AD immigrants from Italy. Those still living around Luarca have traded in their ox carts for pick-ups, though curiously enough Franco, abolisher of so many ancient Spanish festivals, inaugurated a new one, ostensibly to preserve their customs in the form of a 'vaquero wedding' in La Braña de Aristébano, 6km south of Luarca. On the last Sunday in July, prominent citizens are chosen to play the parts of the *vaqueros*, who are duly married and escorted home with a procession that includes the neatly made matrimonial bed pulled by oxen.

Luarca, with its sheltered harbour at the mouth of the Río Negro, is a little more tourist-orientated, but it is still a satisfactory place for a stay on Spain's northern coast. The village was an important place in medieval times, first as a whaling port and then from trade with the Americas. The best way to see it is to follow the first signposted road in from the east – a back road that will take you to the cemetery, high on a cliff with a stunning view over the village below. Luarca is still an important fishing port, mostly for tuna, and the harbourfront ensemble makes a pretty photograph. Old Luarca stretches inland from there, with some stately palaces from the 17th and 18th centuries, and some old quarters with narrow alleys climbing up the steep hills. There is a quite acceptable beach right in the centre of Luarca, but for something special head for **Playa del Barayo**, a beautiful natural area to the west of Luarca.

Continuing westwards, **Navia** is the next fishing village. Southwest of here at **Coaña** you can visit the extensive remains of another Celtic *castro* – foundations of stone walls, paved streets and the foundations of houses. The similarity between these and the *vaquero* huts led some to believe that the *vaqueros* were a lost Celtic tribe.

The Asturian coast ends with Figueras del Mar and then **Castropol**, another attractive fishing port sheltered on the broad Ría de Ribadeo. Inland, south beyond Vegadeo, tiny **Taramundi** up in the mountains has long been famous for the manufacture of knives which have become popular Asturian souvenirs.

10

Asturias | Asturias' Western Coast

Markets on Asturias' Western Coast

 La Casona de la Paca >>

Cudillero and **Navia**: Fri.

Tapia de Casariego: Mon.

Where to Stay and Eat on Asturias' Western Coast

(i) **Cudillero >**
Puerte del Oeste,
t 98 559 13 77,
www. cudillero.org

Cudillero ✉ 33150

**Azpiazu, Playa de Aguilar, t 98 558 32 10, *www.azpiazu.com* (€€€). Well-known hotel at Playa de Aguilar; the restaurant specializes in seafood and has a breezy terrace where you can tuck into shellfish soup, hake and cider-marinated dishes. *Closed 10 Dec–10 Mar.*

**Hotel Casona Selgas, Avda Selgas s/n, El Pito, t 98 559 01 13 (€€). A charming hotel with a pretty sky-blue façade, set 1.5km from the port. The friendly owners offer a wealth of activities.

**La Casona de la Paca, El Pito, t 98 559 1303, *www.lacasonadelapaca.com* (€€). A charming hotel in a converted *indiano* mansion, surrounded by flower-filled gardens. Choose from stylish rooms and suites or equally elegant self-catering apartments.

**La Casona de Pio, C/ Río Frío 3, t 98 559 15 12, *www.arrakis.es/ ~casonadepio* (€€). Sympathetically designed to fit into the old port, this traditional establishment provides style and comfort, right in the centre of Cudillero. Great restaurant.

*La Lupa, in San Juan de la Piñera (2km east of the village), t 98 559 09 63 (€€–€). A modest hotel with a good restaurant.

Pensión El Camarote, C/ Garcia de la Concha 4, t 98 559 12 02, *www. elcamarote.es* (€€–€). Has impressively

ⓘ **Navia**
Plaza del Ayuntamiento,
t 98 547 37 95,
www.ayto-navia.es

ⓘ **Luarca >**
Olavarrieta 27,
t 98 564 00 83, www.
luarcaturismo.com;
open summer only

★ **Villa**
La Argentina >

★ **Palacete**
Peñalba >>

ⓘ **Castropol**
C/ La Fuente 15, t 98
563 51 13, www.ayto-
castropol.com

ⓘ **Taramundi**
Avda de Galicia,
t 98 564 68 77,
www.taramundi.net

large rooms with baths, and is run by a friendly family.

Pensión Alver, C/ García de la Concha 8, t 98 559 00 05, *www.pensionalver. com* (€). Colourful paintings adorn the breezy rooms in this welcoming and recently renovated central *pensión*. Discounts for pilgrims.

Casa Mariño, t 98 559 11 88, *www. concha-artedo.com* (€€–€). In a lovely setting with a view of the sea and mountains, Concha de Artedo has one of the many pretty beaches in the area (off the coastal road west of Cudillero). The restaurant (€€) serves top-class seafood, and a memorable *zarzuela de mariscos y pescados* (shellfish and fish casserole).

Taberna del Puerto, Calle Ribera 4, t 98 559 04 77 (€€). Excellent seafood is served at this restaurant, one of many that line the tiny harbour.

Los Arcos, Plaza de la Marina, t 98 559 00 86 (€). Popular restaurant with scrubbed wooden tables overlooking the harbour, and offering an excellent seafood tapas (and menu) choice.

Luarca ✉ 33700

El Gurugú, C/ de la Peña 93, t 98 547 06 13 (€€€). Another *casona de indiano* lovingly restored in bright pastel colours to create an elegant and intimate (only 10 rooms) setting. All comforts are catered for, including a swimming pool and a small cinema viewing room.

Villa La Argentina, Villar de Luarca s/n, t 98 564 01 02, *www.villalargentina. com* (€€€). A charmingly if eccentrically refurbished *indiano* villa, with cosy rooms and suites (some with Jacuzzi) plus an outdoor swimming pool and gardens. *Closed 7 Jan–mid-Mar.*

***Gayoso**, Paseo Gómez, t 98 564 00 50 (€€€–€€). Actually, this is two hotels: the older one-star frontage is cheaper, while the modern annexe is bland, but more comfortable.

Casa Consuelo, at Otur (6km west of town on the N634), t 98 547 07 67, *www.casaconsuelo.com* (€€€–€€). One of the best hotel-restaurants in the area, where the food attracts people from miles around with classic Asturian *fabada* and cider. The wine list is exceptional. *Closed 7 Jan–mid-Mar.*

*****Hs Rico**, Pza Alfonso X, t 98 570 05 59 (€€). A pleasant, comfortable choice.

La Colmena, C/ Uría 2, t 98 564 02 78, *www.lacolmena.com* (€€). Newly refurbished with warm earth colours and plenty of wood and tile; offers Internet access.

Los Cantiles, at Villar, Ctra 634, Km502.7 (on the cliffs above Luarca), t 98 564 09 38 (€). The closest campsite. *Open year-round.*

La Mesón del Mar, Paseo del Muelle 32, t 98 564 09 94 (€€). As at Cudillero, for dinner in Luarca you need look no further than the row of seafood restaurants on the harbour; nearly all of them have outside tables, allowing you to enjoy the view. This restaurant on the far end offers a wonderful seafood *menú gastronómico* with a bit of everything that was landed in the day's catch.

La Dársena, Paseo del Muelle 11, t 98 564 11 60 (€). The least expensive restaurant on the harbour (with a tiny terrace) and a good one for fish and seafood. *Closed in winter.*

Figueras del Mar ✉ 33793

****Palacete Peñalba**, Granada s/n, t 98 563 61 25, *www.hotelpalacete penalba.com* (€€€). At the farthest western limit of Asturias, near Castropol, you'll find the region's loveliest hotel. Set in a pair of glorious Art Nouveau mansions designed by a follower of Gaudí, it is a listed monument, and retains its gardens and much of its original furnishings; all rooms have TV and minibar.

Old Castile and León

Old Castile and León encompasses two ancient kingdoms of Spain and the meseta *– a flat, semi-arid table-top 2,300–3,300 feet above sea level, where the climate, summed up in an old Castilian proverb, is 'nine months of winter and three months of hell'. It looks like no other place in Europe: endless rolling dun-coloured plains, spotted with scrub and patches of mountains, but few trees; during the mindless free-for-all of the Reconquista nearly all of the forests were axed. Depending on your mood you will find the* meseta *romantic and picturesque, or brooding and eerie, but you'll never forget it.*

11

Don't miss

❶ Lace-like Gothic spires
Burgos cathedral **p.256**

❷ The perfect Romanesque church
Frómista **p.271**

❸ Haunts of the mysterious Maragatos
Near Astorga **p.294**

❹ Spain's refined ancient capital
León **p.283**

❺ Benedictine Gregorian chant
Santo Domingo de Silos **p.265**

See map overleaf

Old Castile and León

Pola de
Somiedo · Collanzo · Oseja de
Sajambre
Reserva
Nacional de Somiedo · Puerto de
San Isidro · Puerto
de Tarna
Bosque de
Muniellos · Moal · C a n t á b r i c o · Peña Ubiña · Tuiza · Pajares · Riaño
Villablino · Puerto de
Pajares
Balouta · Peranzanes · Mora · Cistierna
Burbia · Ancares Leoneses · Marzán · L E Ó N
Doiras · Sierra de Ancares · Almanza
Pedrafita
do Cebreiro · Vega de
Espinareda · Abano
Balboa · Riofrío
Villafranca
del Bierzo · Carracedo · A6 · LEÓN
Corullón · Villasbariego · San Miguel
de Escalada
Ponferrada · Acebo · Mansilla de las Mulas
Carucedo · Montes de · Rabanal del
Camino
Las Médulas · Montes · Astorga · Hospital
de Órbigo
Peñalba de
Santiago · CASTILLA
El Teleno · La Bañeza · Sahagún
Valencia de Don Juan
Villada

N

PORTUGAL

20 km
10 miles
– – – Pilgrims' Route

FRANCE

PORTUGAL

SPAIN

Don't miss

1 **Burgos cathedral p.256**
2 **Frómista p.271**
3 **Near Astorga p.294**
4 **León p.283**
5 **Santo Domingo de Silos p.265**

From this unlikely land came the culture, language and people who would dominate in their day not only the nations of Iberia, but a good part of two continents. Even today Burgos, seat of the first counts of Castile, is the headquarters of all that is pure Castilian and *castizo*, down to the proper lisping pronunciation of the name of Castile's hero, the Cid, or 'El Theed'.

In early times Castile not only resembled America's Far West, but played the same kind of frontier role twice in European history. After the Romans whipped the native Iberians, retired legionaries were given land to raise wheat (any place named Quintanilla recalls one of their settlements, as in *quinta*, a rural villa or farm). The Visigoths followed in their tracks, but the Moors found little to like in Old Castile and conquered it without settling it. The Christian kingdoms to the north erected a string of border fortifications that gave the region its name Castile ('Land of Castles') some time around 800. In 882 the first part of Castile was reconquered by Alfonso III of Asturias; two years later, Diego Porcelos founded Burgos and became the first count of Castile. According to the medieval *Romance de Fernán González*, the

Good Count Fernán González obtained Castile's independence from Asturias-León in the 10th century by selling the king of Asturias a horse and goshawk. The king, lacking any handy cash, promised Fernán González he'd pay him double the price for every day that he didn't pay. The king forgot his promise, and by the time Fernán González reminded him the sum was so vast that all the king could do was give him Castile.

Fernán González formed his fledging state politically into seven counties, the Antiguas Merindades de Castilla. Unlike the feudal Christian kingdoms to the north, where the land was owned by great lords, or the Church, or the military orders, Castile was settled by free men or *hidalgos*, each of whom owned their farms and bore the responsibility for defending them. The difficulties in repopulating vast expanses of empty land was greatly eased by the development of the Camino de Santiago (the medieval road equivalent of the Union Pacific, America's first transcontinental railroad), especially after Castile was 'tamed' by the reconquest of Toledo by Alfonso VI and the Cid in 1085. It set off a medieval boom: settlers moved in and towns sprouted along the length of the road.

Northwest Spain includes only the oldest parts of Castilla y León, the provinces of Burgos, Palencia and León, a region that encompasses some of the most striking, weird and unknown landscapes in Spain. In between are picturesque little towns that have been collecting dust since Charles V sucked them dry in the 16th century; others have changed little since the medieval pilgrims wended their way to Compostela.

Approaches to Burgos

This section covers the approaches to Burgos from the east and north, whether you're coming in slowly along the pilgrims' road from La Rioja, quickly on the *autopista* from Bilbao, or through the mountain scenery of the Cantabrian range from Santander.

Along the *Camino*, from Redecilla to Burgos

The pilgrimage road follows the N120 from Santo Domingo de la Calzada (*see* p.124) and enters Castile at medieval **Redecilla del Campo**, built like an old strip frontier town along the road. Houses still bear their *hidalgos*' crests, but as usual the main focus is the church, Virgen de la Calle, not much in itself but notable for its sublime 12th-century baptismal font, intricately carved with the towers and windows of a city presumed to be Jerusalem. The

Getting around on the Approaches to Burgos

There are four or five **buses** a day from Burgos to Belorado, fewer to Miranda de Ebro, a major rail junction. At least one bus a day goes to Oña and Briviesca; services are less frequent to Frías, Espinosa de los Monteros and Poza de la Sal.

church in the next town, **Castildelgado**, has interesting Gothic *retablos*; while beyond, **Viloria de Rioja** preserves the font where Santo Domingo de la Calzada was baptised. Further west, the much larger, leather-making town of **Belorado** (the Belfuratus of the *Codex Calixtinus*) attracts a different kind of pilgrim these days with its factory outlets. The ruins of a monastery and a hospital recall its former vocation, along with two churches, San Pedro and Santa María, built in the 1500s in the wide, airy Catalan Gothic style. Hermits lived in the caves by **Tosantos**, around the church of the Virgen de la Peña, built into a cliff, while to the west in **Espinosa del Camino** you can see the 9th-century ruins of the Mozarab monastery of **San Félix de Oca**, where the first count of Castile, Diego Porcelos, was buried.

Just west of the Sierra de la Demanda, the deeply forested **Montes de Oca** (Mountains of the Goose) mark the traditional border of Castile. At their foot, **Villafranca Montes de Oca**, a town settled by Franks, was once a major pilgrims' halt; today both Franks and pilgrims have gone, leaving a church and the 14th-century Hospital de San Antón to recall its glory days. A path leads up to the **Hermitage of the Virgen de Oca**, a pretty, leafy place with plenty of picnic tables. At Villafranca the N120 and the walking path split; the latter, heading up the pine-forested slopes (enjoy it: it's the last shade before the mountains west of León) eventually emerges at **San Juan de Ortega**.

San Juan de Ortega is named after Santo Domingo's architecturally minded sidekick, who, after a pilgrimage to Jerusalem, came back to Spain determined to build chapels, bridges and hostels along the *camino*, especially in places like this, where wolves devoured more than a few pilgrims. A couple of miles from the N120, the hamlet he founded is all but abandoned, although, unlike the hostel (now *parador*) built by Santo Domingo de la Calzada, San Juan's still serves its original purpose, thanks to the local priest who feeds and lodges pilgrims. In 1142 the saint designed the church, of which most notably the apse survives, an original, elegant design of slender round columns and three receding arches around alabaster windows. Inside, San Juan is buried in a magnificent tomb, with an effigy and delightful cartoon-like scenes from his life carved in the base and crowned by an Isabelline Gothic baldachin, paid for by Isabel the Catholic herself, who got pregnant for the first time in 1477 after praying by the saint's Romanesque tomb (now down in the crypt). At 5pm on the day of the spring and autumn equinoxes (21 March and 22 September), pilgrims come to see the *Milagro de la Luz*, when a sunbeam illuminates the womb of the Virgin of the Annunciation, carved on a triple capital in the crossing. Isabel also paid for the chapel of San Nicolás, designed to hold the tomb now removed to the old church; in exchange the Renaissance grille from the old church has been installed in the chapel. Just to the west, the walking path continues to one of San Juan de Ortega's bridges in the tiny hamlet of **Agés**.

In **Atapuerca**, the next town (13km east of Burgos), excavations since 1990 in a complex of limestone caves and railway cuttings have thrown up incredibly important palaeontological finds, including, in 2008, the oldest human remains ever found in western Europe – a jawbone and teeth dated 1.1 to 1.2 million years, that resemble the even earlier human remains recently found in Dmanisi, Georgia – suggesting an immigration out of Africa far, far earlier than anyone previously thought, by a species generally known as *Homo antecessor* or Pioneer Man. Current studies are under way to see if *Homo antecessor* was the missing link between Neanderthals and *Homo sapiens sapiens* (Cro-Magnons), our direct ancestors. The area was recently designated a UNESCO World Heritage site which can be visited by **guided tour**. Finds will be displayed in the new **Museo de la Evolución Humana**, currently being built in Burgos and expected to be completed by 2009 at the earliest.

Beyond the Sierra of Atapuerca are the sprawling eastern suburbs of Burgos (*see* p.255).

Atapuerca area tours
www.atapuerca.com; tours Sat, Sun and hols 11, 1, 5.30, extra tours July–Sept; for more info, call t 90 202 42 46, consult the tourist office in Burgos; adm, a guided tour is included with the Burgos Card, see p.262

To Burgos from Bilbao: The Gate of Pancorbo

The Bilbao–Madrid motorway A1 runs into Castile near **Miranda de Ebro**, a major town surrounded by dreary industrial suburbs with little to see besides the glass balconies of its old houses hanging over the river. It grew up around a medieval bridge, which was replaced in 1777 by the Puente de Carlos III. The 16th-century church of **Santa María** is Miranda's most beautiful monument, while the Ebro itself sculpted the stunning gorge, the **Hoces del Sobrón**, through the nearby Montes Obarenes.

The road, the *autopista* and the train funnel dramatically through the pass at **Pancorbo**, for V.S. Pritchett 'a place of horror, for the rock crowds in, comes down in precipitous, yellow shafts, and at the top has been tortured into frightening animal shapes by the climate'. A ruined Moorish **castle** and an 18th-century **fort** that played a role when Wellington's army chased the French through the gorge in 1813 survive above the homely old town. Most of the Pancorbans work in the big truck stops, where drivers tuck into a bowl of *sopa castellano* to prepare themselves for their long ride in the night to beat the heat of the *meseta* beyond. Or, as Pritchett put it: 'Pancorbo is the moment of conversion. Now one meets Spain, the indifferent enemy.'

Between Pancorbo and Burgos, **Briviesca** on the River Oca was on the *camino francés* until the 11th century, before Sancho the Great prompted a change of route through Nájera. The regular rectangular plan of Briviesca, with its pleasant Plaza Mayor, was the model for several towns founded in South America; its octagonal church, **Santa Clara** (1565), has star vaulting and a florid carved *retablo mayor* (a rare, unpolychromed one, with a central figure dreaming of the tree of Jesse); another fine 16th-century *retablo* is in the Capilla de Santa Casilda in the **Colegiata de Santa María**. In 1388, the Cortes Generales of King Juan I were held in Briviesca, and here he bestowed on his eldest son, Enrique, the title of 'Prince of Asturias' for his wedding to Catherine of Lancaster, a title, like the Prince of Wales, that has been held ever since by the heir to the Spanish throne.

Farther west towards Burgos, the Benedictine Monasterio de Rodilla has vanished, leaving only its lovely Romanesque church, **Nuestra Señora del Valle**, set in a meadow with picnic tables.

Northeast Approaches

Oña

Briviesca is the chief town of the Bureba, where the foothills of the Cantabrian mountains begin. This bulge of the map in northeast Burgos province, the cradle of Old Castile, is full of curiosities and remarkable scenery; a good place to start is medieval Oña, 'La Villa Condal', north of Briviesca. Founded by the Romans on the River Oca, Oña had one of the first castles of Castile and was granted its *fueros* or privileges in 950 by Fernán González, Castile's first king. In the early days, the king's travelling court often stayed here; in 1033, Sancho the Great of Navarra, heir of Castile, ordered the old royal stronghold replaced by the Benedictine **Monasterio de San Salvador**. He meant this to serve as a royal pantheon, a status he encouraged by spending his dying days in Oña.

Oña's main *plaza* is picturesquely laid out on three different levels. Behind an old pilgrims' cross, the monastery, rebuilt in 1640 and decorated with four squat kings who would look perfectly at home on a deck of cards, is now a psychiatric hospital. However, the town offers guided tours of its **church**, atop a flight of steps. The entrance is through the 15th-century Pórtico de los Reyes, carved with figures of kings and counts, leading into an open atrium; beyond is the oldest Romanesque façade in Castile (1072), with Flemish-Gothic paintings just inside, and a *mudéjar* door. Although the walls of the long narrow church date from the 11th century, the interior was redone in the 15th by Fernando Díaz. The second Baroque *retablo* on the right marks the tomb of Santa Tigridia, San Salvador's first abbess; its expressive Romanesque *Cristo de Santa Tigridia* is attributed to sculptors from the Toulouse school.

Further up, charming 14th-century Gothic frescoes depict the legend of St Mary of Egypt (really Isis, they say, dressed in Christian

Monastery church
tours Tues–Sun 10.30, 11.30, 12.45, 4, 5, 6, Sat 10.30, 11.30, 12.30, 1.15, 4, 5, 6.15; adm

clothing). Fernando Díaz's starry dome measures 4,300sq ft and is the second largest in Spain after Tarragona; below are filigree choir stalls in walnut, and flanking the ultra-florid 18th-century Baroque *retablo* is the magnificent **Panteón Real**. Sancho the Great (d.1035) and his wife are here, among others, their tombs arranged by Fernando Díaz into charming little temples, richly carved and decorated with elaborate tracery and Hispano-Flemish paintings by Fray Alonso de Zamora. Behind the *retablo*, the **Capilla de San Íñigo** contains the 16th-century silver reliquary of Íñigo (Eneco), persuaded to be first abbot of Oña by Sancho the Great and whose death, they say, grieved Christian, Jew and Saracen alike. The **museum** in the sacristy contains the alabaster tomb of Bishop López de Mendoza, by Italian Mannerist master Leone Leoni, a fragment of 10th-century cloth once belonging to Sancho the Great, with Arabic writing, the figures of an alchemist and the horse and goshawk of Castile's independence.

The **cloister**, built by Simón de Colonia in 1508, is a rich piece of Isabelline Gothic. Presiding over the door is the Gothic statue of Santa María de Oña, whom the poet-king Alfonso the Wise praised in his *Cantiga 221*; when his son Fernando, the future saint, was given up for dead by his doctors, the statue, brought into his presence, restored him. She was also known as sovereign against worms in Infantes. One wing of the cloister holds the tombs of the counts of Bureba, cousins to the counts of Castile and the granddaughters of the Cid. One of their epitaphs translates:

> Gómez, who defended the Spanish coasts
> Like Hector you guarded them, while your faithful wife Urraca
> Remained here, and contemplated how the cold winters
> and pleasant springs passed
> And how nothing under heaven endures.

Down towards the river, you can see a little more of Oña's past: the last of its medieval gates, the **Arco de la Estrella**, and the Gothic church of **San Juan**, with a carved portal under the porch.

Up the Ebro: Frías and Medina de Pomar

East of Oña, built high over the banks of the Ebro, medieval **Frías** looks beautiful on postcards: a ruined 12th-century castle spirals up a rocky outcrop known as 'the Molar' high above the hanging whitewashed houses, arcaded lanes and intimate vegetable gardens. Because it's on the way to nowhere, few people ever vis̵ ̵ and if it's hot you can join the locals for a dip in the Ebro in ̵ shadow of Frías' magnificent **medieval bridge**, compl̵ mighty gate and central guard tower. Between ̵ north 16km to **Trespaderne** for 12th-century **Sa** site of a curious hermitage set over the village o̵ capsized boat. Odd carvings decorate the capitals (dragons' heads, masks and a speak-no-evil figure). Further up the valley, by the **Orduña pass,** is one of the highest waterfalls in Europe.

Another road north of Trespaderne leads to **Medina de Pomar,** site of a powerful, two-towered castle containing a museum, the **Museo de las Merindades,** built in the 14th century by the Velasco family, the hereditary Constables of Castile; a *mudéjar* stucco frieze in the main hall is decorated with inscriptions in Gothic and Arabic letters. The Constables founded the **Monasterio de Santa Clara** in 1313, and lie buried in tombs with alabaster effigies in its early Gothic church with an octagonal star-vault; Santa Clara's lovely 16th-century Capilla de la Concepción has a Renaissance grille and *retablo* by Diego de Siloé and Felipe de Vigarni. In the convent **museum,** you'll find paintings attributed to Rogier van der Weyden, an ivory Christ of Lepanto, a dead Christ by Gregorio Fernández, and goldwork. Medina de Pomar is also proud of Juan de Salazar, who went to the New World in 1547 and founded Asunción, the capital of Paraguay.

Museo de las Merindades
open Oct–May Tues–Sat 12.30–2 and 5.30–7.30, Sun 12–2; June–Sept Mon–Sat 12–2 and 6–8.30, Sun 12–2; adm

Monasterio de Santa Clara
open daily 11.30–1.30 and 5.30–7.30; adm

The Canyons of the Ebro

San Pedro de Tejada
visits by appointment only, t 94 730 32 00

Up the Ebro from Oña, just outside Puentearenas, **San Pedro de Tejada** is one of the province's finest Romanesque churches, its portal carved with a Last Supper and Ascension of Christ. Its other carvings are flagrantly erotic, in the same vein as the church at Cervatos, just over the mountains in Cantabria (*see* p.197). Further up, above Incinillas, **Villarcayo** (due west of Medina de Pomar) was the capital of the Merindad de Castilla la Vieja, one of Fernán González's original counties, but it was burned in the First Carlist War. Only bits of its medieval past survive, especially in the **Museo-Monasterio de Santa María la Real de Vileña,** founded to hold the treasures and fragments of the 13th-century Cistercian monastery that burned down in 1970.

Museo-Monasterio de Santa María la Real de Vileña
open daily 10.30–12.30 and 4–6.30

Villarcayo is in easy striking distance of a pair of sites associated with the archaic judges of Castile who, in this isolated pocket in the 8th and 9th centuries, played a role somewhere between chieftain, lawmaker and general sage. One of them, *juez* Laín Calvo, was buried in the Romanesque **Hermitage of the Virgen de la Torrentera** in **Villalaín;** when disinterred, the chronicles write, all were amazed at the giant stature of his body, which turned to dust on contact with the air. The church, with a square apse and inscription dated 1130, has a lovely portal and interesting murals inside. Sculptures of the five judges of Castile decorate the elegant doorway of the large Renaissance church in nearby **Bisjueces;** one judge, Nuño Rasura, wears a striking Chinese hat. North of Villarcayo in **Torme,** the 12th-century Romanesque church of Butrera is one of the best preserved in the province.

To the northwest, you can pick up the 6318 into the mountains (*see* below). For the Ebro Canyons, however, cut over to **Soncillo**, then drive southwest through the Puerta de Carrales towards **Rúerrero** (along the CA274), at the beginning of the **Canyons of the Ebro**. The cliffs grow increasingly majestic and fantastical as you drive towards **Orbaneja del Castillo**: vultures and eagles circle high over the ruddy canyon walls, sculpted by aeons of wind and rain to form a bizarre natural roof line of soaring bridges, castle walls, haunted towers or hollow snaggle-toothed caves. In Orbaneja an enchanting, lush waterfall cascades, even in August; from here the road does a semicircle through the canyon before climbing up to the N623, the main Santander–Burgos highway. The main highway is not an unattractive route, but for something even better pass it by and cross the Ebro at **Pesquera de Ebro**, make your way east to Pesadas de Burgos and turn right onto the CL629.

For the next 14km the road is surreal – perfectly straight, in the middle of absolutely nowhere, yet each kilometre is systematically marked off with an impressive 10ft monument in stone, all identical, all bearing no identification whatsoever. The sensation of wandering across the middle of a bizarre games table for giants is confirmed when, after the last monument, you turn east and it's as if the world has suddenly dropped out beneath your feet, leaving you to wind down the edge of the table, with tremendous views across to the **Castillo de las Rojas**, an impressive ruin piled high on a rocky outcrop. The castle, where Charles V imprisoned the ambassadors of Pope Clement in 1528, defends **Poza de la Sal**, a town founded by the Romans, who first extracted salt from its marshes along the Río Torca Salada. Fortified in the 10th century, the town and its salt were so important that in 1530 its lord was made Marqués de Poza. In its web of tiny lanes there's a Gothic church with a Baroque façade, the 18th-century salt administration offices, a pair of old gateways and a panoramic view from Plaza Nueva; along the river, the old salt works, abandoned in the mid-19th century, are near an interesting Roman aqueduct. From here the road continues south towards Briviesca.

The Far Northeast Corner: in the Cordillera Cantábrica

Near Soncillo the 6318 leads into the secret corner of Burgos province; if you're coming from the north, the N629 from Laredo will take you straight there. Some day, perhaps, the most extraordinary attraction, the massive karstic **cave complex of Ojo Guareña** by **Quintanilla-Sotoscueva**, with its prehistoric paintings and Upper Palaeolithic footprints, will be open to visitors. The caves extend some 40km underground and are still not fully explored. For now you can only get as far as the subterranean **Hermitages of SS. Bernabé and Tirso**, set on a panoramic esplanade

Hermitages of SS. Bernabé and Tirso
open Mar–June Thurs–Sun 11–1.30 and 5–7.30; July–mid-Sept Tues–Sun 11–1.30 and 5–7.30; Nov–Dec Thurs–Sun 11–2; closed Jan–Feb; adm

with their façades built into the cliffs; inside are 17th- and 18th-century paintings and wax *ex votos*.

The 6318 continues east to medieval **Espinosa de los Monteros**, the local market town, with its 14th-century **Castillo de Los Condestables** on the far bank of the river Trueba, and the Constables' Baroque palace in town; there are several tower houses, and a good 15th-century *retablo* by Fray Alonso de Zamora in the church of **San Nicolás**. The fifth of August is the best time to come, when the citizenry indulge in what the tourist office describes with trepidation as 'strange dances of pagan origin'.

Portillo de Lunada
ski info at
www.lunada.es.vg

Some 15km north there's a small ski station at **Portillo de Lunada**, where the old Roman road once passed between the *meseta* to Cantabria; the incredible views down the valley of the Miera are well worth the trouble of visiting at any time of year. On the other hand, if you venture east, interesting Romanesque churches are your reward: San Miguel at **Bercedo**, with a good portal and beams carved into animals; a 12th-century Templar church of Santa María at **Siones**, with an elegant double archway in the apse, strange and beautiful capitals and other carvings, a 12th-century statue of the Virgin and a Visigothic baptismal font; and the church of San Lorenzo at **Vallejo de Mena**, founded by the Knights of St John with a gallery of arcades along the top of the south façade and a handsome apse. The parish church of the big town in these parts, medieval **Villasana de Mena**, has a good relief of the Three Magi.

Markets on the Approaches to Burgos

Oña: Fri.
Medina de Pomar: Thurs.

Where to Stay and Eat on the Approaches to Burgos

Villafranca Montes de Oca ✉ 09240

La Alpargatería, C/ Mayor 2, t 94 758 20 29 (€). A sweet little *casa rural* in the centre; B&B or rent the whole place.

El Pájaro, Ctra Logroño–Burgos, t 94 758 20 29 (€). Your best bet for a simple room and meal.

Pancorbo/Briviesca ✉ 09240

**Hotel Isabel, C/ Santa María Encimera 2, Briviesca, t 94 759 29 59, *www.hotel-isabel.com* (€€). A modern, central hotel with comfy rooms.

ⓘ **Villarcayo**
C/ Laín Calvo 22,
t 94 713 04 57.
www.ayuvillarcayo.org

ⓘ **Medina de Pomar >>**
C/ Mayor 14, t 94 714 72 28, www.medinadepomar.org

Casa Rural El Ferial, C/ San Nicolás 59, Pancorbo, t 94 735 42 02, or t 94 735 42 76 (after 9pm) (€). This place, lying on the edge of the old town, is the best lodging choice. Fronted by a gallery, it's really a cheap bed and breakfast overlooking a garden, but the best thing about it is the charming owners, Vicente Cardiñanos and his wife, who must be the most hospitable people in the whole of Castile.

El Concejo, Pza Mayor 14, Briviesca, t 94 759 16 86, *www.restauranteel concejo.com* (€). Prettily set in a 15th-century mansion in town, this restaurant serves a tasty leek and prawn pasta in cheese sauce and imaginative desserts; good value *menú del día* (€12).

Medina de Pomar ✉ 09500

***Ciudad de Medina, Pza Somovilla, t 94 719 08 22, *www.ciudademedina. com* (€€). In a pretty, historic building with the village's best, moderately priced restaurant downstairs.

Burgos

First it must be said that Burgos is a genteel and pleasant town, its river, the Arlanzón, so filled with frogs in the spring and early summer that they drown out the traffic with their croaking; and that the favourite promenade, the Paseo del Espolón, is one of Spain's prettiest, adorned with amazing topiary hedges. Burgos contains one of the greatest collections of Gothic art and monuments in southern Europe, and it is the city in Spain where you are most likely to see a nun riding a bicycle.

Yet throughout much of its history Burgos' role has been that of a stern military camp, from the days of El Cid Campeador to Franco el Caudillo who, during the Civil War, made it his temporary capital, the city where, it was said, 'the very stones are Nationalist'. Here, in 1970, Franco held the infamous Burgos trials in which 16 Basque separatists (two of them priests) were tried in a kangaroo court; six were sentenced to death but their sentences later commuted.

The Kingdom of Castile was born in Burgos, and it is fitting that the city itself began as a castle erected on the Moorish frontier in 884. In 926 it took its first step away from Leonese rule, electing its own judges; in 950, one of the judges' successors, Fernán González, declared his independence as Count of Castile. His descendant, Ferdinand I, elevated the title to king and married the heiress of León. Burgos remained sole capital of Castile until 1087, when Alfonso VI moved to Toledo (perhaps to put some distance between himself and the overbearing Cid). The frontier was moving south and this city that had done so much to create the ethos of Spain now found itself a backwater. But Burgos has always remained true to the cause. It is still Spain's most aristocratic, pious, polite and reactionary city. Franco rewarded it with a programme of state-financed expansion, an attempt to drag it into the 20th century that may well succeed some day.

Arco de Santa María

Burgos' glistening white, fairytale front door, the **Arco de Santa María**, was originally part of the medieval walls, but after the Comunero revolt it was embellished to appease Charles V; triumphal arches like this were a Renaissance conceit (the first one was made at Naples for a Spanish king), and they were especially favoured by the vainglorious and ambitious Charles. The Emperor himself is portrayed in a Burgos pantheon that includes its first judges, King Fernán González, and El Cid. The arch was designed by Francisco de Colonia and Juan de Vallejo, two artists you are going to know well before you leave Burgos – along with Francisco's father Juan, responsible for the great openwork spires of the cathedral, looming just behind the arch.

Getting to Burgos

By Train

RENFE is on Avda Conde Guadalhorce, across the river from the cathedral, t 90 224 02 02; tickets are also sold at the office at C/ Moneda 21, t 94 720 91 31. Burgos is on the main rail line from Irún to Madrid (connections to Pamplona, Vitoria, Bilbao, Valladolid, etc.), with less frequent links with Zaragoza, Palencia, León, and La Coruña; also to Salamanca, Barcelona, Málaga, Madrid, Córdoba and Vigo on various Talgos.

By Bus

The bus terminal is on C/ Miranda, across the river from the Arco de Sta María, t 94 728 88 55. There are daily buses to León (1), Santander (at least 3), Madrid (12), San Sebastián, Soria, Bilbao and Vitoria (4 or more), and the provincial villages. Even if there may be only one bus a day to places not on a main route, such as Frías, they're often conveniently timed for a day trip but check in advance to avoid stranding.

The Cathedral

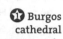 **Burgos cathedral**
main entrance for mass only on Plaza Santa María; visitor entrance and ticket office on Plaza Rey San Fernando; open Mon–Sat 9.30–1 and 4–7, Sun 9.30–11.45 and 4–7

Along with León and Toledo, Burgos has one of Spain's greatest Gothic cathedrals. Yet while León has an instant, sublime appeal, Burgos' power lies in its awesome number of master works and details from the tiniest carving in the choir stalls to its beautiful star-vaulted domes. In 1221, in honour of his marriage to Beatrice of Swabia, Ferdinand III and the English bishop Maurice laid the first cornerstone. On the north side, a stair leads up to the **Puerta del Sarmental**, its 13th-century tympanum showing Christ and the four Evangelists (sitting studiously at their desk, writing the Gospels). The first portal to be finished, the south-side **Puerta Alta de la Coronería** (1257) is the most interesting, with its Apostles, the Almighty, and a peculiar row of mere mortals, the Blessed and the Damned, in between. Around the corner of the transept, the **Puerta de la Pellejería** is part of the original 13th-century work.

These doors are rarely opened; Burgos is prey to a biting wind in the late afternoon, and the cross-current would blow the congregation away. From up here, though, you can get a good view of the forest of spires, especially on the lantern, adorned with scores of figures. Three generations of the Colonia family devoted themselves to moulding the soft grey stone of Burgos into the cathedral's intricate towers and pinnacles. Colonia is Cologne, in Germany; Hans of Cologne began the works in the late 1400s, and his son Simón and grandson Francisco carried on, followed by Juan de Vallejo, who built the Plateresque crossing tower. These, and the **Arco de Santa María**, are illuminated at night.

The **west façade** incorporates two Stars of David, an unintentional reminder that more than one of Burgos' bishops hailed from a Jewish family before 1492, as did the city's greatest sculptors, Diego and Gil de Siloé, the undisputed masters of Isabelline Gothic. Their work inside is one of the cathedral's main attractions. Tragically, the three portals of the west façade were 'improved' in the 'Age of Enlightenment' of the 18th century, and replaced with pallid substitutes. But around the back, another monument of late

500 metres
500 yds

Gothic excess survives, the huge Capilla del Condestable (*see* overleaf), attached to the apse.

Along with the cathedral of Santiago, this is one of the two great treasure houses of Spain. De Vigarni, who also designed the choir, carved the tomb of Don Gonzalo de Lerma in the 16th-century **Capilla de la Presentación**, the largest and most beautiful of the chapels on the southern aisle. Look out for the famous 15th-century mechanical clock across the nave (look up in the dim corner by the rose window), the **Papamoscas** ('Flycatcher'), a grinning devil who pops out of a hole in the wall to strike the hour. The extravagantly Baroque Capilla de Santa Tecla on the northern aisle can be glimpsed through glass doors – it, like the celebrated Capilla de Santo Cristo (*see* p.259) is reserved for services. Next, the lovely **Capilla Santa Ana** has a *retablo* of the Tree of Jesse by Gil de Siloé and a fine bishop's tomb by his son Diego. One of Diego de Siloé's masterpieces, the diamond-shaped, drippingly Plateresque

Golden Stair (1523), is the most strikingly original feature of the interior, the perfectly proportioned solution to the **Puerta Alta**, 30ft above the floor of the cathedral. The idea of stairways as architectural showpieces was just beginning in 1523; Michelangelo was working on his famous one at the Laurentian Library in Florence at the same time.

The enclosed **choir** is almost entirely shut off from the rest of the church, but nonetheless accessible on the visitor. Lift your gaze above the grille work to see the magnificent gold-trimmed star vault of Juan de Vallejo's **lantern**, under the central tower, which Felipe II declared couldn't have been built by men but only by angels. Four stately round piers support a profusion of intricate carved decoration – a Spanish twist on Renaissance styles, married harmoniously into a Gothic building. Underneath its majestic beauty a simple slab marks the **tomb of the Cid and his wife Ximena**, their bones relocated here with great pomp in 1921. The other tomb in the *coro* belongs to Bishop Maurice, topped by his enamelled copper effigy; try to get in to see the magnificent carving on the wood and inlaid stalls – unabashed pagan figures on the seats, New Testament scenes above. They were done by Felipe de Vigarni, who also sculpted the dramatic scene on the ambulatory behind the main altar.

The most spectacular chapel, the octagonal **Chapel of the High Constable of Castile (Capilla del Condestable)**, was built by Simón de Colonia for Pedro Hernández de Velasco in 1482–94. The tomb, accompanied by that of the Constable's wife, Doña Mencía de Mendoza, faces the elaborate altar by Vigarni and Diego de Siloé. The constable, the head of the Castilian army, clutches his sword even after death; his lady's little dog sleeps at her feet. Velasco was constable during the conquest of Granada, whose Moorish craftsmen inspired the great, geometric star-vaulting that crowns

A Building Trying to Disappear

If you have the time, take a good, long look at the exterior of this cathedral (preferably from up the stairs on the edge of the *plaza*). This is the Gothic idea stretched to its wildest extreme – in its day it must have looked as outrageous as Gaudí's Sagrada Familia when its first parabolic towers went up in the 1900s.

In the first blossoming of Gothic building in the Île-de-France, they concentrated on the interior – soaring arches and acres of stained glass to make the walls disappear and create a kind of spiritual union of inside and outside. Spain, the land of extremes, naturally had to take the principle a step further. The virtuoso stone lace spires, finished to Juan de Colonia's design in the 19th century, are only the crowning glory of the most diaphanous church ever built. Note how the windows in the bell towers were made so wide that from most points of view you can actually see through the towers. Hundreds of pinnacles, as electric as any of Gaudí's, pattern out the sky, while between the towers hangs an equally transparent, thoroughly over-the-top gallery of statues of Spanish kings, under the biggest, most delicate stone traceries ever perched over a façade. Imagine the master mason directing the works in the 1200s, dreaming of a building that would be built half of stone, half of light and air.

the chapel. Among the works of art within the chapel is a wonderfully voluptuous auburn-haired *Magdalen* by Giampetrino, a pupil of Leonardo da Vinci.

The nearby **Sacristía Mayor** – the cathedral's sacristy – is adorned with one of the cathedral's lighter scenes, a Baroque bubble bath of a heaven. Off the cloister, the **Museo Diocesano** is housed in a series of Gothic chapels: the Capilla de Corpus Christi contains the famous leather-bound coffer the Cid filled with sand and locked tight, then passed off as gold as security to Raquel and Vidas, two Jewish money-lenders, who made him a sizeable loan; another prized possession is the Cid's marriage agreement in the next-door chapel of Santa Catalina. The most prized possessions, including a series of vivid paintings from a medieval reliquary, are gathered in the adjoining chapels of San Juan and San Diego.

Museo Diocesano
adm included in ticket to cathedral

The cathedral's main draw, however, is just inside the west door, in the part of the cathedral kept separate for religious services only. To the right is the glass-doored **Capilla del Santo Cristo**, where ladies gathered to worship one of the strangest cult idols of any religion – the 13th-century Cristo de Burgos, a figure made of buffalo hide (long reputed to be human skin), real hair and fingernails (according to an old tale, both had to be trimmed regularly), in a green frock and warm to the touch. The head and arms can move, like a doll's; these were probably somehow manipulated to impress the faithful, back in the golden age of miracles. Still the focus of enormous veneration, the only way to get a glimpse is to re-enter the cathedral via the west door and peer through the chapel's glass doors, or else attend a service.

Around the Cathedral

Just to the northwest of the cathedral on Calle Fernán González, **San Nicolás de Bari** contains an incredible wall-sized alabaster *retablo* by Francisco de Colonia (1505), depicting 36 scenes from the Bible and more angels than could dance on a head of a pin. **Santa Águeda**, a plain 15th-century church on Calle Santa Águeda, is the successor of the church where the Cid forced Alfonso VI to swear on a silver lock that he had nothing to do with the assassination of his brother Sancho – an iron copy of the lock is hung over the door inside. The Cid's ancestral mansion, the **Solar del Cid**, was demolished in 1771, though two obelisks mark the site. Between his two banishments and innumerable campaigns, he probably had little leisure to enjoy it anyway.

San Nicolás de Bari
open July–Sept Mon–Fri 9–2 and 4–6; Oct–June Mon–Fri 11–2 and 6–7, Sat 9.30–2 and 5–7, Sun for a short time before or after mass

Santa Águeda
open only before and after mass

The **castle** was blown up by the French in 1813 – an explosion that shattered most of the cathedral's stained glass, and little remains to be seen up here besides the fine view of the city. In its day, however, the castle saw many important events – Edward I of England and Leonora of Castile were married here. It is reached through the horseshoe **Arco de San Esteban**; also near the arch are two 14th-century Gothic churches: **San Esteban** and **San Gil**, both with fine interiors. San Esteban also houses a museum of altarpieces, the **Museo del Retablo**.

Museo del Retablo
open summer 10.30–2 and 4.30–7, rest of the year Sat 10.30–2 and 4.30–7; adm

Near San Gil, in Plaza Alonso Martínez, you'll notice a grim little building called the **Capitanería**, guarded by military police and adorned with commemorative plaques dedicated to Franco and Mola. This was the Nationalist capital during the Civil War; here Franco assumed total power among the rebels and directed his campaigns in the north. Calle Santander is Burgos' main shopping street; at its head is the **Casa del Cordón**, named after the rope (really a Franciscan monk's belt) carved over the door in honour of St Francis. This palace was built by the Condestable de Velasco in 1485. Ferdinand and Isabel received Columbus here after his second voyage, and 18 years later, an ageing Ferdinand sent Ponce de León off to discover the Fountain of Youth.

Nearby, the attractive, arcaded **Plaza Mayor** has been refurbished and pedestrianized, although the shady **Paseo del Espolón** along the riverfront is the city's real centre; at the far end, a mighty equestrian **statue of the Cid** seems ready to fly off its base and attack any enemy crossing **San Pablo bridge** towards the Plaza Primo de Rivera. The bridge is embellished with stone figures of the Cid's wife, his companions and a Moorish king. Across the bridge (and past the site of the new Museum of Evolution, due to open in late 2008) the lovely **Casa Miranda** (1545) houses an archaeological collection. In the adjoining Casa de Iñigo Angulo is the **Museo de Bellas Artes**, with four floors of local art from the 12th to 20th centuries. The best is the medieval art in the first gallery, which includes some exquisite treasures from the Monasterio de Santo Domingo de Silos (*see* p.265).

Casa Miranda
open June–Sept Tues–Sat 10–2 and 5–8; Oct–May Tues–Sat 10–2 and 4–7, Sun 10–2; adm

Museo de Bellas Artes
same opening times, adm with same ticket

Monasterio de Las Huelgas

Monasterio de Las Huelgas
open Tues–Sat 10–1 and 3.45–5.30, Sun 10.30–2; adm, free Wed for EU citizens

On the outskirts of Burgos lie two of Spain's richest monasteries, both well worth a visit. A 20-minute walk to the west will take you to the Cistercian monastery of Las Huelgas, founded by Alfonso VIII in 1187 at the behest of his wife Leonor, daughter of England's Henry II (*huelga* in Spanish means a strike now, but, back then *Las Huelgas Reales*, the monastery's true name, meant 'The Royal Repose'). The abbess of Las Huelgas had more power and influence than any other woman in Spain except the queen herself, until her powers were revoked in the 19th century. In 1219 Ferdinand III 'the Saint' began the custom of Castilian kings going to Las Huelgas to be knighted into the Order of Santiago by Santiago himself; in the cloister you can see the statue of the saint with a moveable arm holding out a sword made for this purpose. Guided tours (in Spanish) will take you through the English-Gothic church: statues of Alfonso VIII and Leonor kneel before the altar, and there's a curious painted iron pulpit of 1560 that gyrated to allow the priest to address the nuns in the choir or congregation. The church also serves as a royal pantheon of Castilian kings and royal ladies. The French, as usual, desecrated the tombs, though the one they missed, that of Alfonso X's son Ferdinand de la Cerda, produced such a fine collection of goods as to form the nucleus of Las Huelgas' **Museo de Ricas Telas**, a fascinating collection of fabrics and medieval dress, showing considerable Eastern influences.

Museo de Ricas Telas
reopening in 2008 – same hours as monastery

These are not the only Moorish touches in Las Huelgas: note the geometric tomb of the Infanta Doña Blanca, the peacock and stars in the *mudéjar* **cloister**, and the **Capilla de Santiago**. The grandest chamber, the **Sala Capitular**, contains a trophy from Alfonso VIII's great Battle of Las Navas de Tolosa – the silk flap of the Moorish commander's tent – and Don Juan's banner from Lepanto, which he gave to his daughter Ana, abbess of Las Huelgas. If the guide's in a good mood, he'll play a scale on the well-tuned columns in the halls. Some 44 nuns still live at Las Huelgas, painting porcelain and baking cookies. Noble and wealthy pilgrims would receive a fair welcome at Las Huelgas, but for the needs of poor pilgrims Alfonso VIII also built the **Hospital del Rey**, a short walk from Las Huelgas, facing the road to León. Most impressive here are the 16th-century Plateresque gateway and the court.

La Cartuja de Miraflores

Cartuja de Miraflores
open daily 10.15–3 and 4–6, Sun 11–3 and 4–6

Burgos' second great monastery is a 3.5km walk to the east, through a lovely park of shady trees. Miraflores was founded by Juan II in 1441 and is still in use, so you can see only the church, built by the Colonia family; yet this alone contains more great art than many cathedrals. Here Isabel la Católica commissioned the great Gil de Siloé to sculpt the **tomb of Juan II and Isabel of Portugal** as a memorial to her parents and, after four years' work, he created the most elaborate, detailed tomb of all time, 'imprisoning Death inside an alabaster star' as a local guidebook poetically put it. Instead of a chisel, it looks as if Siloé used a needle to sew the robes of the effigies – Juan pensive, his wife reading a book. Isabella owed her succession to her brother's death and, as a posthumous thank you, had Siloé carve his memorial too. The tomb of the Infante Don Alfonso shows the young prince (1453–68) kneeling at prayer among a playful menagerie of animals, *putti* and birds entwined in vines. Master Siloé also did most of the gilt *retablo* of the high altar, said to be made with the gold Columbus had presented to the Catholic kings at the Casa de Cordón.

Other works of art include a lovely painting of the Annunciation by Pedro Berruguete; carvings on the stalls of the lay brothers' choir (the middle section of the Carthusian church's traditional

11 Old Castile and León | Burgos

three divisions – the monks' choir is in the front, the general public at the back), a painting of the Virgin sending the infernal spirits packing and a wooden polychrome **statue of St Bruno** in the side chapel by the Portuguese Manuel Pereira, so lifelike 'it would speak if it weren't a Carthusian monk', as the *burgaleses* like to say.

Below Miraflores, 10km further down the road is the abbey of **San Pedro de Cardeña**, founded in 899 and now a Trappist monastery. Here the Cid left his family when banished by Alfonso VI, and here he was buried beside his wife Ximena. The French stole the bones and when the Spanish government finally got them back it was to inter them in the more secure precincts of the cathedral. You can visit the tombs with their effigies in a chapel off the **Cloister of Martyrs**, where 200 Benedictines were beheaded in a 10th-century Moorish raid. The Cid's faithful charger Babieca is buried just outside the gate.

San Pedro de Cardeña
open April–Oct Mon–Sat 10–1 and 4–6, Sun 12–1.30 and 4–6; Nov–Mar Mon–Sat 10–1.30 and 3.30–5.30, Sun 12–1.30 and 3.30–5.30; adm

Tourist Information and Facilities in Burgos

The tourist office can sell you a **Burgos Card** (one day €13, two days €17), which will give you free entry to many local attractions.

The **post office** is on Plaza Conde de Castro, across the river from Paseo del Espolon; **Ciber Café Cabaret**, C/ La Puebla 21, has **Internet access**, at €4/hr (*open 12pm–1am, Sat 5pm–4am, Sun 5pm–1am*).

(i) **Burgos >**
municipal offices: both t 94 728 88 74: Teatro Principal, Paseo del Espolón s/n; also Plaza del Rey de San Fernando

provincial office: Plaza Alonso Martinez 7, t 924 720 31 25

www.aytoburgos.es www.jcyl.es/turismo

Where to Stay in Burgos

Burgos ✉ 09000
*****Landa Palace**, just outside on the Madrid road (N1), **t** 94 725 77 77, *www.landapalace.es* (€€€€€). A member of the prestigious Relais et Châteaux, offering a memorable stay in an over-the-top pseudo-medieval tower full of antiques, an indoor atrium and pool, and beautiful all-mod-con rooms. A meal in the equally palatial restaurant, the region's finest, will set you back some €50.
****Abba Burgos**, C/ Fernán González 72, **t** 94 700 11 00, *www.abbahoteles.com* (€€€€ – look out for special offers). Luxury hotel in a converted palace with all the extras, including a gym and swimming pool.

****Hotel Almirante Bonifaz**, C/ Vitoria 22/24, **t** 94 720 69 43, *www.almirantebonifaz.com* (€€€€). In the centre of town.
***Meson del Cid**, Pza Santa María 8, **t** 94 720 87 15, *www.mesondelcid.es* (€€€€). Magnificent location opposite the cathedral, with well-equipped modern doubles, garage space and a secret tunnel to their excellent restaurant next door. They have opened a new four-star hotel, **Meson del Cid II**, which is more luxurious, but has a little less character.
***Cordón**, La Puebla 6, **t** 94 726 50 00, *www.hotelcordon.com* (€€€). A classic Spanish hotel with glass balconies on a quiet street. It has triples and rooms with private sitting room. It's geared towards business people and offers good deals at weekends.
***La Puebla**, La Puebla 20, **t** 94 720 00 11, *www.hotellapuebla.com* (€€€). A truly delightful little boutique hotel in the centre with chic décor.
Norte y Londres, Pza Alonso Martínez 10, **t** 94 726 41 25, *www.hotelnorteylondres.com* (€€€). Charmingly old-fashioned hotel, offering a whiff of elegance right in the middle of town.
***Hotel Cabildo**, Avda Del Cid No 2, **t** 94 727 3521, *www.hotelcabildo.com* (€€). Centrally located, this new hotel was built to service business travellers

but the sleek yet snug décor is also attractive for leisure travellers and there are good weekend deals.

*Hotel España, Paseo de Espolón 32, t 94 /20 63 40, *www.hotelespana.net* (€€). Pleasant, good-value hotel on a tree-lined pedestrian street. It also has a restaurant.

**Hs Manjón, Gran Teatro 1, t 94 720 86 89 (€). Has good budget rooms close to the river; most have private bath. Run by two friendly sisters.

*Hs Hidalgo, Almirante Bonifaz 14, t 94 720 34 81 (€). A well-kept, old-fashioned *hostal* on a relatively quiet street off the Plaza Mayor. Shared baths only.

Pensión 196, Avda Vitoria 196, t 94 722 94 74 (€). This *pensión* has spotless rooms with en-suite baths at bargain rates, though it's a trek from the centre; take the bus marked 'Gamonal' from Avenida Arlanzon.

Residencia Juvenil Gil de Siloé, Avda Cantabría s/n, t 94 722 03 62 (€). The town's youth hostel. *Open July–Aug.*

Eating Out in Burgos

El Ángel, C/ La Paloma 24, t 94 720 86 08 (€€). Perhaps the best in town: highly creative cuisine in the elegant dining room upstairs, and a popular tapas bar downstairs. *Closed Sun eve, Mon (except summer), 1st fortnight June (menu degustacion € 42)*

Casa Ojeda, Vitoria 5, t 94 720 90 52, *www.restauranteojeda.com* (€€). The most popular place in town, with the best tapas in its bar and good local cuisine in its dining room, including several veggie options. *Closed Sun.*

Mesón del Cid, Pza Santa María 8, t 94 720 87 15 (€€). For a medieval atmosphere in a 15th-century building facing the cathedral, and delicious roast suckling-lamb, this is the place to go. *Closed Sun.*

Mesón de los Infantes, just inside the Arco de Santa María, t 94 720 59 82 (€€). Offers Castilian specialities like *olla podrida* and 'medieval lentils'; outdoor summer dining.

Gaona, C/ La Paloma 41 (near the cathedral), t 94 720 40 32 (€€–€). Has Basque cooking in a glassed-in terrace; try peppers stuffed with cod.

Mesón de Los Herreros, C/ San Lorenzo 20, t 94 720 24 48 (€). Fill up on delicious tapas and *raciones* at this popular local favourite.

Tapa, Avda del Cid 22 (€). A wide range of tasty tapas including some of the best *patatas bravas* in town.

Southeast of Burgos

The most popular corner for a day out from Burgos is the mountainous region to the southeast, on or off the N234 towards Soria, where it's hard to tell where one *sierra* begins and another ends. Covarrubias and Santo Domingo de Silos are firmly marked on the tourist map, but you'll need a car to take in the prizes just off the beaten track such as San Quirce or the Visigothic church of Quintanilla de las Viñas.

A Scatological Abbey and a Visigothic Beauty

Abadía de San Quirce
inside open only the first Tues of each month, 9.30–6

The **Abadía de San Quirce** is not easy to find; signposts guide you from **Hontoria de la Cantera**. Set in a quiet wooded valley, it was founded by Count Fernán González after his defeat of the Saracens on this spot in 929. Abandoned in 1835, the church conserves its original structure, with a stout fortified tower in the centre; the west door has 11 modillions showing the Creator, Adam and Eve, Cain and Abel and, in between, earthy reliefs of men squatting and defecating, with inscriptions reading *io cago* and *mal cago* ('I shit',

Getting around Southeast of Burgos

Transport here is sketchy. There are several **buses** daily from Burgos to Aranda de Duero, and usually one a day to Santo Domingo de Silos (except on Sundays) and Caleruega, and about three a day to Lerma and to Covarrubias. Services are reduced at weekends. Otherwise you'll need to hire a **car**, National Atesa, t 94 720 18 43, discounts with Burgos Card, see p.262, or a taxi, t 94 727 77 77, to get around.

and 'I shit badly'); one thinks of the anarchical shitting figure, the *caganer*, that accompanies every Catalan Christmas crib. Other reliefs decorate the north door and modillions supporting the charming bubble of an apse, unusually illuminated by two round bull's-eye windows and a regular Romanesque window, which was probably originally a bull's eye as well; inside, the capitals are carved with the legend of San Quirce and a naked woman who suckles serpents, with lions on either side.

Further south on the N234, there's an unusual corridor-dolmen at the ghost town of **Mazariegos**, where the big stones are engraved with what could be horses. Aim your next stop for **Quintanilla de las Viñas**, where 4km up, under the steel-toned Montes de Lara and the ruins of the Castilla de Lara, the gold-stoned Visigothic **Nuestra Señora de las Viñas** drinks up the sun. This is the last Visigothic basilica in Spain, dated 7th century or just before the invasion of the Moors. Made of large blocks incised with Christian graffiti, only the square apse and part of the transept have survived the past 1,300 years. The exterior of the former is girdled with three friezes, the lowest band of vines and grapes, the middle band decorated with plants and birds – ducks, peacocks, doves, and what are thought to be the monograms of the founders, in round medallions of curling tendrils. The upper band has a Persian air with griffons, leopards, lions, bulls and rams. Inside, on the triumphal arch, there's another bird frieze and a rare example of Visigothic syncretism: angels with rocket wings, Byzantine in style or perhaps even more like the winged figures on Roman tombs, holding up portraits identifying Christ with the moon (a bearded figure, with a crescent moon LVNA on his head like horns) and the Virgin (or Church) with the sun SOL, topped by a Latin inscription: 'I, modest Flammola, offer this modest gift.' Blocks in the apse show heavily coiffed, symmetrical but inexplicable 'astral' figures, sculpted by another artist who had trouble getting the arms and hands right.

Nuestra Señora de las Viñas
t 94 728 15 00;
open July Wed–Sun
10–2 and 4–8; Aug–Sept
Wed–Sun 10–2 and 4–7;
May–June and Oct–
April Wed–Sun 10–5;
closed Mon, Tues and
last weekend of month

Fernán González Country: San Pedro de Arlanza and Covarrubias

South of Quintanilla de las Viñas, the Arlanza river runs east–west through a valley known in the 10th century as the Valley of Towers, the frontier of old Castile, pushed this far south by 'the Good Count' Fernán González, the founder of the realm. His exploits are described in an epic poem, written in the 13th century

San Pedro de Arlanza

t 689 596 064; open July–Sept Wed–Sun 10–2 and 4–8; April–June Wed–Sun 10–2 and 4–7; Oct–Mar Wed–Sun 10–5; closed Mon, Tues and last weekend of month

by a monk in the large, now romantically ruined abbey of **San Pedro de Arlanza** founded in 912 by the count's father, Gonzalo Fernández, below a cave where the hermit Pelagio predicted the illustrious destiny of his line. The guardian will let you in to see what's left of the church, its tower, cloister and nave.

Medieval **Covarrubias** is Old Castile's half-timbered showcase of porticoed squares and lanes, guarded by the only surviving 10th-century Mozarab tower in the Valley of Towers, the sturdy **Torreón de Doña Urraca**, whose countess was walled up inside in 965 and left to die. The **Ayuntamiento** has a Romanesque doorway that once belonged to Fernán González's palace. Behind this, the ex-

San Cosme y San Damián

open Mon and Wed–Fri 10.30–2 and 4–7, Sun 10.30–12 and 4–7; closed Tues and Sat; adm

Colegiata, **San Cosme y San Damián**, was rebuilt in 1474 as the pantheon for the count's descendants, the Infantes de Covarrubias, whose tombs line the nave; in 1848, the remains of Fernán González and his wife Sancha were brought from San Pedro de Arlanza and placed next to the altar in a 4th-century Roman sarcophagus. The 17th-century organ, one of the most beautiful in Spain, still works, although you'll have to attend Mass to hear its sweet antique sound. The cloister contains the tomb of a 13th-century Norwegian princess, promised to Alfonso the Wise but married to his ex-bishop brother Ferdinand (*see* p.272). The prize in the museum is the Flemish-inspired *Triptych of the Magi*.

Santo Domingo de Silos and its Sublime Cloister

South of Covarrubias at **Santibáñez del Val**, the road to Barrious leads 2km to the River Ura and the 10th-century Mozarabic hermitage of **Santa Cecilia de Barriosuso**, with a square apse and window made of five rings and a horseshoe arch inside. The attraction in these parts, though – one that brings many pilgrims

⭐ **Santo Domingo de Silos**

www.abadiasilos.es; open for guided visits only Tues–Sat 10–1 and 4.30–6; adm; Gregorian chant sung six times a day: times on the website, or call t 94 739 00 49

down on a special detour – is **Santo Domingo de Silos**, a Benedictine monastery founded in 954 by Fernán González and ruled in the 10th century by the abbot who gave it its name. Rebuilt after al-Mansur razed it to the ground, the monastery was re-founded in the 19th century by French Benedictines from Solesmes, who have made it famous for Gregorian chant. They inherited the most beautiful Romanesque **cloister** in Spain, elegant, two-tiered and ivory-coloured, built around an ancient cypress tree. The lower section dates from the late 11th–early 12th centuries and has fascinating capitals on twin columns carved by a sculptor so well versed in animals and other motifs of the Córdoba caliphate and Middle East that he may have been a Moor. On the corners of the cloister, eight large reliefs on the life of Jesus are in a similar style; one shows the only known representation of Christ in pilgrim's garb. The cloister's *mudéjar* ceiling, painted with scenes of everyday life in the Middle Ages, has been restored. Off the cloister, the **museum** houses Mozarabic illuminations (Santo Domingo is a study centre of Mozarabic art, liturgies and manuscripts), the Romanesque tympanum from the first church, a 12th-century paten with Roman cameos, an 11th-century chalice and the 18th-century **pharmacy** (*botica*) with big jars. After all this, the church, rebuilt in the neoclassical style in the 18th century, seems dull.

A mere 2.5km from Santo Domingo towards Caleruega, a narrow gorge, the **Desfiladero de la Yecla**, has been fitted with some rather battered wooden walkways, making for an easy and spectacular walk; the stair descends just before the tunnel and the end of the walkway emerges just after it. The gorge is part of a nature park with colonies of vultures, hawks and buzzards, the largest *sabina* (shrubby juniper) forest in the world, and remains of a Celtic *castro*. Beyond hilltop **Hinojar de Cervera**, the Cueva de San García has even older traces of civilization, dating back to the Upper Palaeolithic era. **Caleruega**, further south, was the birthplace in 1170 of yet another canonized Domingo, the one who went into the heavenly big time, Santo Domingo de Guzmán. It was his theological battles against the heretical Cathars in Toulouse that led, in 1216, to Domingo's founding of his preaching order, the Dominicans or Black Friars, who took on the job of the Inquisition. The Guzmán tower house is still intact, and the exact spot of the saint's birth is marked in the crypt of the church of Dominican Madres.

The Bloody Cucumber of Vengeance

The seven sons of Gonzalo Gustios, the Lord of Salas, were known for their chivalry and prowess, in no small thanks to their tutor, the judge Nuño Rasura. In 986 their troubles began at the splendid wedding of their uncle Ruy Velázquez to Doña Lambra, when the youngest of the seven brothers quarrelled with a kinsman of the bride. Doña Lambra took the quarrel as a personal insult and, as the brothers rode away, she ordered her slave to heave a bloody cucumber at them. This was the ultimate deadly insult in 10th-century Castile (discretion forbade the romancers to explain exactly why); the outraged brothers slew the slave, even though he tried to 'hide even in the folds of her garment'.

Now it was Ruy Velázquez's turn to feel insulted by the brothers, and he schemed to avenge himself on the whole family. First he sent the father to Córdoba with a message in Arabic for the king, asking him to slay the bearer; but the Moorish king took pity on Gustios and merely put him in prison, where the king's sister fell in love with him and bore him a son named Mudarra. Meanwhile, Ruy Velázquez plotted an ambuscade with another Moorish king, so that when he sent the seven brothers and Nuño Rasura out to fight the Moors they were headed off at the pass by a far superior force and killed. The Moorish king sent Velázquez their eight heads, and he forwarded them to Gustios as a homecoming present. After 14 years, Mudarra came north to find his father and promised to avenge the deaths of his seven brothers. When Ruy Velázquez heard of Mudarra, he thumpingly declared, in Lockhart's translation of the Spanish Ballads:

> Oh, in vain have I slaughter'd the Infants of Lara,
> There's an heir in his halls – there's the bastard Mudara.
> There's the son of the renegade – spawn of Mahoun:
> If I meet with Mudara, my spear brings him down.

Of course it was Mudarra who brought down Velázquez instead. He then stoned and burned Doña Lambra at the stake for the bloody cucumber insult, and became lord of Salas. The parish church of Salas de los Infantes keeps the heads of the Seven Infantes and Nuño Rasura in a reliquary; their trunks are stored in the weird old tombs at San Millán de la Cogolla (*see* p.122).

East of Santo Domingo de Silos, **Salas de los Infantes** is named after the legend of the Siete Infantes de Lara, a favourite subject of Spanish ballad and romance (*see* box, left). There are some strange things around Salas, including a Visigothic hermitage covered with weird symbols on a hill just south of **Barbadillo del Mercado** (on the N234), under cliffs where you can see lammergeyers. East, in **Palacios de la Sierra**, the parish church has a collection of indecipherable Palaeochristian tombstones. **Jaramillo de la Fuente**, towards the Sierra de la Demanda, has a fine 12th-century Romanesque church.

Way Down South in Burgos Province

The N1 south of Burgos to Madrid passes through **Lerma**, another town on the Arlanza river, founded by the son of Fernán González in 978. It owes its impressive appearance to the unusually successful Dukes of Lerma, one of whom (Francisco Gómez de Sandoval y Rojas) ruled Spain between 1598 and 1618 for Felipe III. It was the duke's idea to expel the *moriscos*, and devote a part of the proceeds from their expropriated property into making Lerma (effectively, the capital of Spain during his lifetime) a unique monumental complex, with at least six monasteries and a four-towered **Palacio Ducal**, recently converted into a luxurious *parador*. This is linked by a flying walkway (so the duke could attend mass without mingling with the commoners) to the **Colegiata de San Pedro**, bearing the duke's crest over the door. Inside, the church contains its original organ of 1616 and a statue in bronze of the archbishop of Seville, the uncle of the duke. The tourist office (*see* p.268) offers daily guided tours of the town.

Much further south, **Gumiel de Izán** has a fine 15th-century parish church with monumental stairs and a beautiful Renaissance *retablo* by an unknown master; the adjacent museum, open when the priest is around, has Romanesque capitals salvaged from its long-gone monastery. Gumiel marks the northern limits of DO Ribera del Duero, the largest and finest wine region in Castile, producing a variety of reds, especially from a local grape known as *tinto del país*; mixed with garnacha, malbec, merlot and cabernet sauvignon, it becomes a fresh rosé, a purplish young wine or a mellow well-aged wine; '95, '96, '99 and 2001 are excellent; Vega Sicilia is the most illustrious name. **Aranda de Duero**, the third town of the province, has a number of old *bodegas* and a pair of good churches: Santa María has a beautiful portal attributed to Simón de Colonia and an excellent Renaissance *retablo*.

Downriver, the Augustinian **Monasterio de la Vid**, 'of the vine', boasts an 18th-century Baroque façade with spiralling leaves and roses on the sides of the elegant belfry and octagonal dome. East of Aranda, picturesque **Peñaranda de Duero** is built around the

Monasterio de la Vid
guided tours all year Tues–Sat 10.30, 11.30, 12.30, Sun 11.30, 12.30; plus winter 4.30, 5.30, 6.30, summer 5, 6 and 7; closed Mon

11

Old Castile and Léon | Southeast of Burgos

sprawling castle of its medieval lords, the Avellaneda, who in the safer 16th century decided to move down into the arcaded Plaza Mayor. A fine Plateresque portal marks their **Palacio de los Zúñiga y Avellaneda**, built around an elegant two-storey patio; rooms are adorned with superb *artesonado* ceilings and plasterwork. Around the corner, the 17th-century **Botica de Jimeno** is the second-oldest pharmacy in Spain, and has been in the same family for seven generations; of its original fittings, there are some 230 pharmaceutical jars, stills and books.

North of Peñaranda, the half-ruined silhouette of a castle tops **Coruña del Conde**, where in the 18th century a local inventor named Diego Marín made the first manned flight in Spain. The equally isolated 11th-century **Ermita del Santo Cristo** is made out of stones cannibalized from the Roman city of **Clunia**, just north, near **Peñalba de Castro**, where the guardian lives. Founded under the reign of Augustus, it counted 30,000 inhabitants at its peak. In AD 69 Galba, governor of Nearer Spain, rose up here against Nero and was proclaimed emperor by his legionaries; the Senate concurred, leaving Nero to run himself through. He was the first ruler to come from outside the Julian and Claudian families, although he adopted the names Caesar and Augustus. Managing to displease nearly everybody by the time he got to Rome, he was brutally murdered the next year by Otho, his successor – another, more ominous precedent. Clunia was abandoned with the fall of Rome, leaving the forum, a large if eroded rock-cut theatre, baths, temples, and houses with mosaics dusty and mute.

Palacio de los Zúñiga y Avellaneda
open Tues–Sun 10–1.30 and 4–7

Clunia
www.arqueoturismo clunia.com; open summer Tues–Sun 10–2 and 4–8; winter Tues–Sun 11–2 and 3–6; adm

Where to Stay and Eat Southeast of Burgos

ⓘ **Santo Domingo de Silos >>**
C/ Cuatro Cantones 10, t 94 739 00 70; open April–Oct

ⓘ **Covarrubias >**
Monseñor Vargas s/n, t 94 740 64 61, www.ecovarrubias.com; open Mar–Dec Tues–Sun, closed Mon

ⓘ **Lerma**
C/ Audiencia 6, t 94 717 70 02, www.citlerma.com

Covarrubias ✉ 09346

★★★Arlanza, Pza Mayor 11, t 94 740 64 41, www.hotelarlanza.com (€€). Occupies a handsome old mansion in the town centre; its restaurant serves medieval banquets on Saturday nights with music and ancient Castilian dances; book ahead.

★★Doña Sancha, Avda Victor Barbadillo 31, t 94 740 64 00, www.hoteldon sancha.com (€€). A welcoming rural hotel, built in traditional style. Every room has a balcony with lovely views.

Restaurante de Galo, C/ Monseñor Vargas 10, t 94 740 63 93 (€€). Atmospheric restaurant with medieval open chimney, serving typical Castilian fare. Closed mid-Nov–mid-Mar Tues–Thurs eves; mid-Mar–mid-Nov Mon eve and Wed.

Santo Domingo de Silos ✉ 09610

★★★Tres Coronas, Pza Mayor 6, t 94 739 00 47 (€€). In a charming 18th-century stone house, with 16 intimate rooms. There's a classic restaurant which serves a filling *menú del día*.

★★★Santo Domingo de Silos, C/ Santo Domingo 14, t 94 739 00 53 (€). Choose from the 3★ hotel or the *hostal*; all rooms are flouncy in classic Spanish style, but those in the hotel are better equipped. The restaurant serves hearty Castilian classics and a good-value lunch menu.

★★Arco de San Juan, Pradera de San Juan 1, t 94 739 00 74, www. arcosanjuan@wanadoo.es (€). Near the famous cloister, this is a quiet place with a delightful garden.

Hospedería de Monasterio, t 94 739 00 49 (€). Men 'in need of spiritual exercise' can eat and sleep for a song (well, almost) in the monastery; ring in advance.

① Aranda de
Duero >
Plaza Mayor s/n,
t 94 751 04 76

Aranda de Duero ✉ 09400

Aranda gets plenty of business travellers en route to Madrid and concentrates its functional hotels near the highway; most have cheap weekend rates.

****Torremilanos, Ctra N122 km 274, t 94 751 28 52, *www.torremilanos.com* (€€€€). A pretty, pastel-painted *bodega*-hotel in its own gardens just outside the centre. Elegant rooms and a fine restaurant featuring their own highly respected wines.

**Hotel Julia, San Gregorio 2, t 94 750 12 50 (€€). A modest, but conveniently central hotel, with comfy rooms and a decent old-fashioned restaurant.

Mesón de la Villa, C/ La Sal 3, t 94 750 10 25 (€€). Serves some of the best food around, including poultry and garden vegetables raised on owner Eugenio Herrero's own farm, accompanied by the finest bottles of Rioja. *Closed Mon and 2nd week Oct.*

Rafael Corrales, C/ Carrequemada 2, t 94 750 02 77 (€€). An *asador* that opened in 1902, serving lamb baked in a wood oven, washed down with Ribera del Duero. *Closed Thurs eve.*

West from Burgos along the Pilgrim Route

If the medieval pilgrim survived the storms, cut-throats and wolves at Roncesvalles, the Navarrese who exposed themselves when excited and the dupers and fleshpots of Burgos, then they faced the dustiest, flattest, hottest and most monotonous landscape in Europe. The idea is that, with nothing to look at, one becomes introspective and meditative, altogether in a proper state to receive enlightenment. On the other hand, nearly all the route between Burgos and León is off the highways, on paths and lonely back roads where 20th-century intrusions are rare; their straggling hamlets of humble adobe houses, church towers crowned with storks and huge dovecotes (pigeon was the only meat country folk could afford) evoke the Middle Ages as powerfully as any cathedral.

From Burgos to Frómista

After Burgos, the pilgrims' path goes straight to Castrojeriz, leaving the N120 in Tardajos; by car the first important stop is **Sasamón**, 33km west of the capital. This was the Celtiberian Segisamo, where Augustus camped with his Macedonian legions, en route to pummel the Cantabrians. The town's pride is its church of **Santa María la Real**, with an exact 12th-century copy of the Sarmental door on the cathedral of Burgos (*see* p.256); it has a good, if damaged, cloister and a statue of St Michael attributed to Diego de Siloé. The **Ermita de San Isidro Labrador** has a superb 16th-century cross, the Cruz del Humilladero. Of the third church, the 15th-century **San Miguel**, only the portal survives with its seven archivolts isolated in a field like a lost triumphal arch.

Getting along the Pilgrim Route West of Burgos

Daily **buses** run from Burgos to Aguilar de Campóo and Cervera de Pisuerga (twice a day on Thurs and Sat), to Palencia, Frómista, Sahagún, Saldaña and Carrión (on the Burgos–León route), to Sasamón and Grijalba. Frómista can also be reached by **train** on the Palencia–Santander line.

In nearby **Olmillos**, the stately 15th-century castle belonged to the Leví, a noble family of *conversos*; the current owner has converted it into a pilgrims' guesthouse (*see* p.272). A few kilometres northwest, at **Grijalba**, the 13th-century Gothic church of **Santa María de los Reyes** has plenty of gargoyles and carved capitals with New Testament themes; inside, the ribs of the vaults are painted with alligators with sharp teeth. The font is a pretty 12th-century work carved with interlacings, and supported by a lion and a serpent.

The main road, however, heads south of Tardajos, passing through the village of **Hornillos del Camino**, home to an old pilgims' hospital, the Espíritu Santo. After Hornillos the road passes through the haunting, ravaged remains of the 14th-century **Monasterio de San Antón**, its once-magnificent vaults hanging miraculously in the void. Its monks were famous for treating pilgrims afflicted with 'St Anthony's fire' or erysipelas, inflammations on the body, associated with leprosy. What really went on is a medieval mystery. The Order of St Anthony was founded in France in 1093, named after a 5th-century anchorite in the Egyptian desert, often depicted holding fire in his hands, symbolic of spiritual force and energy. His followers went about dressed in blue with the Greek **T** or *tau*, the cross of St Anthony, sewn on their habits, bearing a staff and bell; they would not only give passing pilgrims a meal but little *tau*-shaped amulets holding 'St Anthony's fire'. As St Anthony was also the patron of domestic animals (when not shown with fiery hands, he is accompanied by his pet pig), his monks kept pigs, or rather let them run wild, a practice that ended when one jaywalking porker in Paris tripped up the horse bearing the dauphin and caused him to break his neck.

West is the medieval castle and village of **Castrojeriz**, an old Iberian settlement that once had seven hospitals and a residence of Pedro the Cruel along its long Calle de los Peregrinos. In 974 Fernán González wrote down its privileges in a charter, giving equal rights to Christians and Jews. Its finest monument is at the village entrance: the Gothic church of **Santa María del Manzano**, named after the apple-tree trunk where its statue of the Virgin was found when Santiago on his white horse, leapt from the castle to the tree; note the horseshoes on the door. Inside there are 16th-century tapestries and a *retablo* by Mengs; other tapestries, 17th-century and Flemish, are displayed in the parish museum

note the 16th-century **Santa María del Castillo** with its elaborate painted Hispano-Flemish *retablo* with 29 panels.

Near Frómista, you can visit four sets of locks of the Castilian Canal, dug in the 18th and 19th century and the inspiration for Lesseps' rather bigger ditch in Panama.

West of Frómista

Beyond Frómista, the tawny little villages of Palencia merge into the tawny earth. **Villarmentero de Campos** has a delightful picnic ground, with a lawn for a siesta to prepare yourself for the next stop at **Villalcázar de Sirga**, once a thriving town and key Templar possession. The Knights, at the start of the 13th century, built the enormous church of **Santa María la Blanca** with what must be the tallest porch in Spain, to shelter a richly decorated double portal with a double frieze. Pilgrims made a beeline for the Capilla de Santiago and its miraculous Virgin (now a little the worse for wear), to whom Alfonso X the Wise dedicated his *Cantigas*, but modern visitors tend to head to the beautifully carved tombs sculpted by Antón Pérez de Carrión of the Infante Don Felipe (son of Ferdinand III the Saint) and his second wife, Leonor Ruiz de Castro, curiously gagged. Don Felipe, fifth of 14 children, was pursuing a meteoric ecclesiastical career and had just been made archbishop of Seville when he reversed course and married the Norwegian princess promised to his brother, the future Alfonso X. The princess died after four years and is buried in Covarrubias; Felipe soon remarried, but not long after, in 1271, was murdered by Alfonso, the next in line to the throne, who got away with it (no wonder he celebrated the Virgin's miracles). Here too is the tomb of a Knight Templar, with his hawk and sleeping lion: a rare burial, as most Templars were buried face down in the earth without a casket. The magnificent *retablo mayor* was painted by the school of Berruguete.

Santa María la Blanca
open May–mid-Oct daily 10.30–2 and 5–8; mid-Oct–April Sat–Sun 12–2 and 4–6

Where to Stay and Eat from Burgos to Frómista

(i) **Frómista >>**
Paseo Central 11,
t 97 981 01 80,
www.fromista.com

Olmillos ✉ 09123

Hotel Señorío de Olmillos, Camino Santa Lucía s/n, Olmillos de Sasamón, t 94 737 40 09, *www.castillodelaflor delys.com* (€€€€). A chance to stay in a 15th-century castle built by Don Pedro de Cartagena, a converted Jew of Burgos, that has been recently transformed into a comfortable 28-room hotel. If you can't stay the night, there is a banquet hall-like restaurant.

Castrojeriz ✉ 34440

**Mesón de Castrojeriz, C/ Cordón 1, t 94 737 86 10 (€). Offers a handful of rooms in a lovely old stone building, a peaceful setting. Simple traditional fare in the dining room (€€).

Frómista ✉ 34440

*Hotel San Martín, Plaza San Martín 7, t 97 981 00 00 (€). Modern, but built in traditional style, this is a friendly, central spot.

Fonda Marisa, Plaza de San Martín 3, t 97 981 00 23 (€). Costs even less and cooks up good menus.

Hostelería de Los Palmeros, Plaza San Telmo 4, t 97 981 00 67 (€€). Fine restaurant that began as a *hostal* for pilgrims, although the medieval décor has undergone several style changes since; furnished with antiques; the set lunch is €18. *Closed Tues.*

Villalcázar de Sirga ✉ 34440

There's limited accommodation here, besides a pilgrims' shelter behind the town hall and a couple of *casas rurales* nearby.

Hostal Infanta Doña Leonor, C/ Condes de Toreno 1, t 97 988 80 48 , *www.hostalinfantaleonor.com*(€€–€). A delightful little *hostal* with café-bar in the centre. They also run the cosy and simpler *hostal* **Los Cantigos** (€) geared towards pilgrims.

Mesón Los Templarios, Plaza Mayor, t 97 988 80 89 (€€–€). This popular, charming former grainhouse offers Castilian favourites, including baked suckling pig with almonds. *Closed eves in winter, exc Fri–Sun.*

North of Frómista:
The Románico Palentino

If you've the time or inclination, you could wander off the beaten track into the northern part of Palencia province, into the foothills of the Cantabrian mountains, known as the Románico Palentino for its rare collection of some 200, mostly untouched, never remodelled Romanesque churches (nothing less than the greatest concentration in Europe). It seems that the masons who built churches along the *camino* came up here to build churches in the new villages, founded to repopulate the region. Aguilar de Campóo, linked by bus from Burgos or Palencia, or train from Santander, makes the best base, although you really need a car and patience, and that most elusive object of desire: a good map of Spain.

North to Aguilar

Northwest of **Alar del Rey** (on the Santander–Palencia N611) you can easily see two of the finest Romanesque works in the region. **San Andrés de Arroyo** is a Bernardine convent founded in 1190 with an small, interesting museum; the chapterhouse entrance is beautiful and the cloister has extraordinary twin columns and capitals, decorated with fretwork, zigzags and exotic flora. The second church, the golden-stone **Iglesia de San Juan** at **Moarves de Ojeda** has a superb portal, with a Christ in a mandorla, four Evangelists and 12 Apostles; the capitals are crowded with people and inside there's a 13th-century baptismal font and a Gothic Virgin and Child. Other prime stops on the Romanesque trail are north of Moarves: **Cozuelos**, with a simple early 12th-century church; **Vallespinoso de Aguilar**, home to a fortified 12th-century hermitage on a rock with a cylindrical tower and pretty door; and **Barrio de Santa María**, a handsome village where the **Ermita de Santa Eulalia** is a pristine example of a 13th-century church with a lovely apse, the narrowest windows in Spain and murals. Its parish church underwent a Renaissance remodelling and has good

San Andrés de Arroyo
open Tues–Sun 10–12.30 and 3–6; adm

Iglesia de San Juan
get the key from the warden across from the entrance

15th-century paintings inside and a finely carved Renaissance *retablo mayor*. From Vallespinoso the road skirts the Aguilar reservoir to Aguilar de Campóo (*see* below).

Alternatively, if you stick to the N611, north of Alar del Rey, you'll find (just to the left) **Becerril del Carpio** with two Romanesque churches: one in Barrio de San Pedro with a fine portal; one in Barrio de Santa María, amid the Baroque mansions, where they had enough *pesetas* to remodel the church and give it some fancy *retablos*. In nearby **Santa María de Mave**, the monastery founded in 1208 has a fine portal, an octagonal lantern and some Renaissance murals in one of its three apses; the monastery building itself has been converted into a charming hotel (*see* opposite). The church in **Olleros de Pisuerga** to the west is some 300 years older, a rare example of a Spanish church carved into the living rock.

Aguilar de Campóo

Set in the green mountain valley of the Río Pisuerga and next to a large man-made lake, Aguilar de Campóo is a picturesque town of cookie-bakers and leaning, medieval houses with big bold coats of arms, founded in the 10th century during the Reconquista resettlement scheme. The Aguilar, or eagle, of its name refers to its rocky limestone outcrop, its eagle's nest, crowned by a ruined but still mighty five-towered **castle** built in the 11th century. At the foot of the castle, the **Hermitage of Santa Cecilia** was founded in 1041, and has a fine 12th-century tower and excellent capitals: one shows the Massacre of the Innocents, by 11th-century knights in fishscale armour. The town walls were built in the 1300s by Pedro I of Castile; one of the surviving six gates has an inscription in Hebrew and Spanish, a unique souvenir of Aguilar's once sizeable Jewish population. On the arcaded Plaza de España, Charles V once spent a week at the **Palacio de los Marqueses**; the Gothic **Colegiata de San Miguel** has the Renaissance mausoleum of the marquises of Aguilar and a **museum** full of tombs, *retablos* and sculptures. Another square is named after Aguilar sailor Juan Martín.

Two kilometres west of Aguilar, the Cistercian monastery of **Santa María la Real** (1213) has more excellent capitals and a good cloister; in 1988 it won a Europa Nostra award for its restoration and now shelters a **Museo del Románico**, with plenty of information on, and a unique collection of, models of the region's churches. Tradition has it that Bernardo de Carpio is buried in a cave nearby; offended by Charlemagne's invasion of Spain in the *Chanson de Roland*, Castilian troubadours invented Bernardo as their own hero, a doughty warrior who along with the Castilians joined up with the Saracens and personally slew Roland, the brutish Frank invader. But after the battle of Roncesvalles Bernardo was betrayed by his own king and joined the Moors for good.

Hermitage of Santa Cecilia
get the key in the casa rectoral

Colegiata museum
open June and 1st half Oct Fri–Sun 10.30–1.30 and 5–8; winter daily 12–1, other times call t 97 912 26 88

Museo del Románico
open July–Aug daily 10.30–2 and 4–8; Sept–June Tues–Fri 4–7, Sat and Sun 10.30–2 and 4.30–7.30; adm

Romanesque Routes North of Aguilar

The road directly north of Aguilar takes in more Romanesque charmers: the 12th-century church at **Matalbaniega**, with two decorated portals, carved modillions and caryatids. **Cillamayor**'s Romanesque church has a funerary hypogeum; at **Revilla de Santullán**, the church has a handsome portal with 15 figures, sitting at desks like members of the board, and other sculptures that verge on the pornographic. Further along, **Valberzoso's** church has 15th-century frescoes; the village of **Brañosera** claims to be one of Spain's oldest municipalities, with its charter dating back to 824; its Romanesque church has a good 12th-century portal. **Salcedillo's** church also has a 12th-century portal; medieval **Villanueva de la Torre** has a 14th-century tower and church. **San Cebrián de Mudá**'s 12th-century church has Renaissance paintings and murals.

West of Aguilar, **Cervera de Pisuerga** was once an important frontier settlement, but has retired to its meadows and old family manors, proud of its recently restored 16th-century Gothic church, **Santa María del Castillo**, built on the medieval citadel, with a fine Hispano-Flemish *retablo* by Felipe de Vigarni and a beautiful painting of the *Adoration of the Magi* by Juan de Flandres, both in the Capilla de Santa Ana.

Three kilometres away, at **Ruesga**, there's a *parador* from which to enjoy the huge views across the mountains. At the northernmost point of Palencia province, **San Salvador de Cantamuda** is a graceful church with a pretty steeple and altar table. Southeast of Cervera de Pisuerga, **Perazancas de Ojeda** has a Romanesque parish church, and the 12th-century Lombard Romanesque hermitage of **San Pelayo** with contemporary murals.

Santa María del Castillo
open July–Sept daily 10–1 and 4–8; June Sat–Sun 10–1 and 4–8; rest of year call **t** *97 987 01 79; adm*

Where to Stay and Eat in the Románico Palentino

ⓘ **Aguilar de Campóo >**
Pza de España 30, **t** *97 912 36 41, www.aguilardecampoo.com*

ⓘ **Cervera de Pisuerga >>**
Plaza Modesto Lafuente 1, **t** *97 987 06 95*

Aguilar de Campóo ✉ 34800
★★★Valentin, Avda Generalísimo 21, **t** 97 912 21 25, *www.hotelvalentin.com* (€€). A classic mountain hotel with chintzy rooms, a pleasant garden and good restaurant.

★★Posada El Convento, in Santa María de Mave (12km from Aguilar de Campóo), **t** 97 912 36 11 (€€). Serene and part of a lovingly restored Benedictine monastery. Its restaurant (€€) is one of the best in the region.

Posada Santa María La Real, Avda de Cervera s/n, **t** 97 912 20 00, *www. posadasantamarialareal.com* (€€). Part of the 13th-century monastery

buildings have been transformed to house this charming *posada*, with a lovely garden.

Cortés Poza, C/ El Puente 39, **t** 97 912 30 55 (€€). Simple rooms and satisfying food awaits here: try the *caldereta de pescados y mariscos* (a huge seafood stew for two).

★★Villa de Aguilar, C/ José Antonio 15, **t** 97 912 22 25 (€). For those on a tighter budget; all rooms with bath.

Cervera de Pisuerga ✉ 34840
★★★Parador de Cervera Pisuerga, Ctra de Resoba, **t** 97 987 00 75, *cervera@ paradors.es* (€€€). On the edge of the Picos, this modern place is a plush spot for nature-lovers.

★★El Roble, General Mola 6, **t** 97 987 44 29, *www.hotelelroble.com* (€€). Stylish, modern hotel with well decorated rooms and a bright café-bar.

Along the Carrión River

West of Frómista, into the *campos góticos*, the Visigothic plains, the pilgrims' route continues to Carrión de los Condes, which occupies one of Old Castile's chief north–south arteries. Palencia and environs were more important in Roman and Visigothic times than now; among the things to see are two Roman villas and Spain's oldest dated church.

Back on the Pilgrim Track: Carrión de los Condes

West of Villalcázar de Sirga, Carrión de los Condes is named after the River Carrión and not for putrefying nobility, although it can't be denied that the Infantes or Counts of Carrión, who married the Cid's two daughters, were genuinely rotten villains; after picking up their big, glittering dowries, they beat their wives and tied them to oaks and left them for dead. The outraged Cid gathered up a posse, killed the counts, and found his daughters new, even more princely husbands. The wicked Infantes are buried in the lovely Renaissance cloister of **San Zoilo**, a Benedictine monastery that now also contains a luxury hotel by the river, founded in 1047, when the Emir of Córdoba sent the 4th-century relics of Zoilo to the Count of Carrión. The lower gallery of the cloister is the work of Juan de Badajoz, who began in 1537; the upper was added in 1604.

Over the 16th-century bridge from San Zoilo, the heart of Carrión has two worn 12th-century Romanesque churches that preserve interesting portals. **Santiago**, in the Plaza Mayor, has a fine Christ in Majesty and apostles and representatives of 22 medieval guilds, including an armourer, scholar, musicians, cooks, tailor, smith, soldiers bashing each other, and contortionists. On the edge of town, **Santa María del Camino** has a capital on the portal depicting the Tribute of 100 Maidens that the Castilians sent yearly to the Moors (probably because they had nothing else the Moors could possibly want); other figures are of Samson fighting the lion and women riding beasts. The interior is out of kilter, although whether it was done so intentionally (like Getaria, *see* pp.151–2) is hard to fathom; it could just be falling over. Lastly, the **Convent of Santa Clara** has a small museum, with religious art and a 17th-century organ. During the great days of the pilgrimage, the town produced two men of genius: Rabbi Shem Tov Ardutiel (Sem Tob), author of the *Danza General de la Muerte*, who died in 1370, and Íñigo López de Mendoza, the Marqués de Santillana, the Renaissance poet, not to be confused with the tycoon who bought the title (*see* p.203). Lastly, just off the road before the province of León, you can visit the 3rd-century AD **Roman villa** at **Quintanilla de la Cueza** for its colourful mosaic floors and the heating system or hypocausts, protected by a shelter; there's a small museum on the site.

San Zoilo
visiting times April–mid-Oct daily 10.30–2 and 4–8; mid-Oct–Mar Tues–Sun 1–2 and 4–6.30; now also contains a luxury hotel, see p.279

Santiago
information and tickets to church and museum from the church of Santa María; open summer daily 11–1.30 and 5–7.30; other times of the year call t 666 649 615

Convent of Santa Clara
open July–Aug Wed–Fri 9.30–1.30 and 4–6.30, Sat–Sun 9–2.30; Sept–June Mon–Fri 9.30–1.30 and 4–6.30, Sat–Sun 9–2.30

Roman villa
open April–mid-Oct 10–1.30 and 4.30–8; mid-Oct–Nov and Mar 10.30–1.30 and 4–6; closed Dec–Feb; adm

Getting along the Carrión River

There are frequent **trains** from Palencia to Burgos, Valladolid, Ávila, Madrid and Santander (via Frómista and Aguilar de Campóo); trains to León call at Paredes de Nava. Palencia's RENFE station is at Plaza de los Jardinillos, t 90 224 02 02.

Carrión de los Condes is connected by **bus** with Frómista and Palencia; there are at least two buses a day. Palencia's bus station is next to the train station, on Plaza de los Jardinillos, t 97 974 32 22.

South along the Carrión to Palencia

Paredes de Nava was the birthplace of two influential Castilian artists, painter Pedro Berruguete (d.1504) who worked in Urbino and introduced the Renaissance style to Spain as court painter to Ferdinand and Isabel, and his son Alonso (d. 1561), a pupil of Michelangelo, who brought Mannerism back with him and served

Museum
open July–mid-Oct daily 11–2 and 5–8; mid-Oct–mid-May daily 11–2 and 5–7; mid-May–June Sat–Sun 11–2 and 5–8

Santa María
open Tues–Sun 10.30–1.30 and 5–8

as court painter to Charles V, although sculpture was his real love.

A few of the Berruguetes' paintings, including a *retablo mayor* by Pedro, remain in **Santa Eulalia**. The adjacent **museum** has an impressive collection of works by other Renaissance masters (Gil de Siloé, Juan de Valmaseda, Juan de Flandes, Juan de Juni, among others) brought in from little churches in artsy Paredes de Nava. You'll find more paintings by Pedro Berruguete inside the church of **Santa María** in **Becerril de Campos**, 10km south.

Palencia

Once a thriving centre, Palencia remains one of the bigger wallflowers in the garden of Spain's provincial capitals; in 1185 Alfonso VIII made it the site of Spain's first university, though in 1239 it was removed to Salamanca. Charles V is partly responsible for Palencia's failure to thrive in later centuries, having not only sucked the city dry to pay the bribes he gave to be elected as Holy Roman Emperor, but also rubbed out the city's prospects and privileges in revenge for its leading role in the Comunero revolt.

Palencia cathedral
open mid-May–Sept Mon–Fri 10–1.30 and 4.30–7.30, Sat 10–5.30, Sun 11.15–1 and 4.30–8; Oct–mid-May Mon–Sat 8.45–1.30 and 4–6.30, Sun 11.15–1; adm to crypt and museum

The one thing they couldn't take away from Palencia is its Gothic **cathedral**, nicknamed *La Bella Desconocida* ('The Unknown Beauty'), in Plaza San Antolín. The exterior is magnificent; don't miss the gargoyles. Juan de Flandes' Renaissance *retablo mayor* is the prize in an interior that has remained more or less unchanged – a lack of Baroque curlicues and rolling eyeballs is a telltale sign of decline in a Spanish town. The oldest part of the crypt (673) is the only known surviving example of a Visigothic martyrium, built by King Wamba before he was shuttled off to a monastery (in the 7th century, the Visigothic kings lived in nearby Pampliega, a little village that time forgot). Among the **museum**'s highlights are an early *San Sebastián* by El Greco and a fine *Virgin and Child* by Pedro Berruguete. The clock in the transept has a lion and knight.

The bridge over the Carrión, the **Puentecillas**, is contemporary with the cathedral; 11th-century **San Miguel**, further south, is a fine little ogival Romanesque church, where the Cid married his

11

Old Castile and León | West from Burgos along the Pilgrim Route: Along the Carrión River

Museo de Palencia
*open July–Sept Tues–Sat
10–2 and 5–8, Sun 10–2;
Oct–June Tues–Sat 10–2
and 4–7, Sun 10–2*

Ximena. Around the corner, the **Museo de Palencia** occupies the 16th-century Casa del Cordón, containing archaeological souvenirs of Palencia's illustrious past. There are also some well-preserved mosaics. East of Calle Mayor, the 16th-century **Santa Clara** has a famous Cristo Yacente that elicited the comment from the ultra-pious Felipe II: 'If I had faith, I would believe that this was the real body of Christ.' Nearby, the 13th-century **Convento de San Francisco** has a magnificent *mudéjar* coffered ceiling in the sacristy.

**Museo de Historia
del Calzado**
*C/ Barrio y Mier 10;
open Mon–Wed and
Fri 10–2 and 4–8*

If you're feeling a little churched-out, Palencia offers something a bit different, in the shape of the privately run **Museo de Historia del Calzado** or **Iglesia de San Juan Bautista**, just off C/ Mayor, where Juan Carlos's personal cobbler displays pairs of His Majesty's shoes, along with other celebrities' footwear.

**Iglesia de San
Juan Bautista**
*open summer
Tues–Sun 10–1.30
and 5–8; winter
Tues–Sun 10.30–1.30
and 4–6; adm, free
on Wed to EU citizens*

Ten kilometres south of Palencia in the village of **Baños de Cerrato** (2km from Venta de Baños), the Visigothic King Recesvinto (he of the famous golden crown with dangling letters spelling his name) founded its own **Iglesia de San Juan Bautista** back in 661, the purest extant example of Visigothic architecture. Fretwork windows like impossible key holes and a carved doorway (and a belfry, added by restorers) relieve the simple stone exterior. Inside, the nave is divided by rows of horseshoe arches, and the capitals, the doorways and the apse are decorated with finely carved eight-pointed crosses (*croix pattées*), leaves, scallop shells, solar spirals and palms. Recesvinto's rather complex dedicatory inscription survives on the triumphal arch. In its use of pleasing, robust architectural volumes and the concentration of intricate detail in a few places, San Juan has been called 'the first Spanish church'. Recent excavations uncovered 58 7th-century tombs and the original plan of the church, with its three apses standing out separately like prongs on a fork; in the Middle Ages it was converted into a more ordinary rectangle. The Baños of its name refers to a nearby curative spring, closed in by two Visigothic arches and restored in 1941.

North of Carrión de los Condes: Saldaña and a Roman Villa

From Carrión de los Condes, the CL615 follows the River Carrión up to **Renedo de la Vega** and the ruins of the monastery of **Santa María de la Vega**, a *mudéjar* work of 1215; the parish church has a fine Renaissance cross. Further north, towards Lobera, a sign points

Villa of Olmeda
*www.dip-palencia.es;
open April–mid-Oct
Tues–Sun 10–1.30 and
4.30–8; mid-Oct–Mar
Tues–Sun 10.30–1 and
4–6; adm; includes adm
to Saldaña museum*

the way to **Pedrosa de la Vega** (1.5km), where the 3rd–4th-century Roman **Villa of Olmeda** was discovered in 1968 with its perfectly preserved polychrome mosaic floors, including not only geometric designs, but also mythological and hunting scenes. Nearby, in the pretty medieval village of **Saldaña**, the church of **San Pedro** houses finds from the ongoing excavations.

Where to Stay and Eat along the Carrión River

★ Palencia >>

ⓘ Carrión de
los Condes >
*Plaza Santa María,
t 97 988 09 32; open
weekends only May and
June, daily July, August
and Easter Week*

Carrión de los Condes ✉ 34120

***San Zoilo**, C/ Obispo Souto, t 97 988
00 49, *www.sanzoilo.com* (€€€–€€).
Monastery (*see* p.276) with attractive
rooms (the nicest are in the original
building) and a decent restaurant.

****Estrella del Bajo Carrión**, Ctra
Palencia-Riaño, Km 29 (south of
Carrión in Villoldo), t 97 982 70 05,
www.estrellabajocarrion.com (€€).
A comfortable, modern hotel with a
garden; the restaurant (€€) is good.

***Hs La Corte**, C/ Santa María 34, t 97
988 01 38, *www.hostallacorte.com* (€).
Rooms with or without bath along
with a decent restaurant.

Convento de Santa Clara, C/ Sta Clara
1, t 97 988 0134 (€). Austere convent
rooms with baths.

ⓘ Palencia >
provincial office:
*Plaza Abilio Calderón
s/n, t 97 971 51 30*

municipal office:
*C/ Mayor 105,
t 97 974 00 68*

Palencia ✉ 34000

***Rey Sancho de Castilla**, Avenida
Ponce de León, t 97 972 53 00, *www.
reysancho.com* (€€€). Modern hotel

offering swimming, tennis, football
and activities for children.

*****Palencia**, Avda de Cuba 25, t 97
916 57 01, *www.ac-hotels.com* (€€€).
Stylish, modern hotel on the
outskirts of town.

***Castilla Vieja**, Avda Casado del
Alisal 26, t 97 974 90 44, *castilla
viejareservas@mundivia.es* (€€€).
Similar to the Rey Sancho but with
no pool, this is a sound choice with a
good restaurant.

Asador La Encina, C/ Casañé 2,
t 97 971 09 36, *www.palenciadigital.
com/encina* (€€). Traditional Castilian
dishes such as suckling pig, hearty
stews, wild mushrooms plus fish.
Their tortilla has been awarded the
prize for the best in Spain. *Closed Sun
eve and 1st 2 wks Aug.*

La Fragata, C/ Pedro Fernández del
Pulgar 4–6, t 97 974 95 91 (€€–€).
Delicious, affordable contemporary
cuisine in a slick modern restaurant in
an old building.

Aparicio, C/ Gaspar Arroyo 6, t 97 974
12 39 (€). Local favourite; good range
of tapas and *raciones*.

Saldaña's ruined 11th-century castle was the residence of Doña
Urraca, sister and advisor of Alfonso VI; the 15th-century Gothic **San
Miguel** has a *retablo* attributed to Gil de Siloé and effigy tombs of
the Counts of Saldaña. The holy of holies in these parts is an 8th-
century statue of the Virgin in the **Ermita de la Virgen del Valle**.

West to León

The Camino de Santiago continues its flat way towards León,
imperceptibly rising as it crosses 236km of the largest province in
Castile. Framed by the Cordillera Cantábrica to the north and the
lower, softer Montes de León to the west, the province was a
refuge for Mozarabs from Andalucía in the first days of the
Reconquista, and what remains of their monasteries are among
the finest monuments along the whole road.

Sahagún and its *Mudéjar* Bricks

Sahagún started out as the site of a Roman villa and an early
Christian basilica dedicated to San Facundo, a martyred legionary.
During the 12th century, when it was the seventh official stop of
the *Codex Calixtinus*, it had a population of 12,000 and artificially
concentrated so much wealth in the middle of nowhere that it

Getting to Sagahún

Sahagún is reached by **trains** between Palencia and León and by **buses** between León and Carrión.

subsequently earned the nickname 'the Las Vegas of the Middle Ages'. Today a mere 3,000 souls try to fill up the dusty Plaza Mayor, the darkened old porticoes and forlorn houses.

Sahagún's rise and fall went hand in hand with that of Spain's most powerful Benedictine abbey, San Benito. In 904, the old Roman road had just begun its transformation into the pilgrims' way when the site was purchased by Alfonso III the Great of Asturias for a community of Mozarab refugees from Andalucía. Although it was twice burned by the Moors, the seeds of its future glory were sown in the 11th century when Sancho III of Castile snatched León, the inheritance of his brother Alfonso, and locked Alfonso up in the abbey. He was about to tear out Alfonso's eyes for good measure when their sister Urraca intervened. Urraca managed to save his eyes by promising nasty Sancho to become a nun. With both siblings locked away, Sancho felt safe on the throne. But Alfonso made a secret pact with the abbot of San Benito, who helped him escape and take refuge with the Moors in Toledo.

In 1072 Sancho was assassinated and Alfonso was crowned king of Castile and León. Like Henry VIII, Alfonso VI married his way through six wives; those from Aquitaine and Burgundy put him into contact with Cluny – the great promoter of the Santiago pilgrimage. Never forgetting the help he received at Sahagún, the king refounded San Benito in 1080 under the new Cluniac reforms and made his personal confessor, Bernard de Sédirac (the future primate of Spain), its first abbot. Alfonso poured money into the abbey, gave it vast estates and founded a huge pilgrims' hospital. In its heyday San Benito even minted its own coins; in 1534 its theological school had the status of a university. Philip II brought it low by moving the school to Navarra's Monasterio de Irache in 1596 and constraining the abbey to pay nearly all its rents to the crown.

In the 18th century two fires finished off what remained, leaving only a 17th-century portal by Felipe Berrojo, now a decorative city gate at the west end of town, an ungainly clock tower and the adjacent ruins of the 12th-century Gothic **Capilla de San Mancio** with its brick arches. Smaller bits of San Benito are in the museum in the **Real Monasterio de San Benito de Sahagún**: the tombs of Alfonso VI and some of his wives and the great silver custodia by master Enrique de Arfe, which makes appearances only for Corpus Christi although the nuns will show it if you ask (especially with a donation). They also run a pilgrims' *hostal*.

What Sahagún never had was a ready supply of building stone, which led the craftsmen who immigrated here from the Moorish

Real Monasterio de San Benito de Sahagún
open Easter–Oct Tues–Sat 9.45–12.45 and 4–6.35; closed Nov–Easter; adm

San Tirso
open June–Sept 10–2 and 4.30–8; Oct–May 11–2 and 4–6

lands to develop an architecture in brick, a medium that permitted new decorative patterns and delicacy. The first example, **San Tirso**, was built near the monastery in the first decade of the 12th century, with its squat, tapering skyscraper tower rising out of three round apses; recent restoration work unearthed two sculpted Mozarab imposts with floral reliefs from the original monastery. **San Lorenzo** is just a little later and more obviously Moorish in design, but has suffered more changes over time, its interior redone in the 18th century (the chapel has Renaissance reliefs by Juan de Juni); both churches have porticoes along their sides for the famous markets Sahagún held in its boom period. In 1259 the Franciscans founded another monastery and the much-damaged **Santuario de La Peregrina**, just outside the town on the N620, the third and latest *mudéjar* church, applying the new brick techniques to Gothic; inside, bits of original stucco work survive.

Santuario de La Peregrina
closed for restoration until at least 2009 – call t 98 778 21 17 to check

Near the medieval bridge that crosses the Río Cea stands a grove of poplars. According to the *Codex Calixtinus*, these are the lances of Charlemagne's paladins who, awaiting battle with the Moor Aigolando, planted them in the ground before going to sleep. Overnight some of the lances took root and flowered, a sign of impending martyrdom. Thinking to spare the men whose lances had taken root, Charlemagne let them stay in camp when he went off to fight the Moors. But when he returned, victorious, he found that all the men he had left behind had been massacred by a Moorish raiding party.

Five kilometres south, on the Cea's bank, two sisters founded **San Pedro de las Dueñas** in the 10th century, which has a Renaissance crucifix by Gregorio Fernández and 18 top-notch Romanesque capitals from the church's 1109 rebuilding, begun in stone and continued in brick by *mudéjar* craftsmen. Another road from Sahagún, the LE613, leads in 6km to the mighty, well-preserved 16th-century castle (private) at **Grajal de Campos**.

San Miguel de Escalada

After Sahagún the pedestrian *camino* parts from the highway, to meet again at **Mansilla de las Mulas** on the River Esla, which has preserved only the atmospheric ruins of its 12th-century walls, monasteries and *hostales*. Nearby, between Villamoros and Villasbariego, **Lancia** started out as an *oppidum* (fortified settlement) of the Astures; in 25 BC they were soundly defeated by the Romans after a fierce resistance: a few ruins remain and to this day farmers uncover antiquities in the surrounding fields.

This was the new frontier back in the early days of the Reconquista, when the kings of Oviedo had just added León to their title. Among the first pioneers on the scene were Abad Adefonso and his companions, refugees from Córdoba, who in 913

San Miguel de Escalada
just before Mansilla, take the road northeast 8km; open April–Sept Tues–Sat 10.30–1.45 and 4.30–8, Sun 10–1.45; Oct–Mar Tues–Sat 10.30–1.15 and 4.30–6, Sun 10.30–1.15

founded the beautiful church of **San Miguel de Escalada**. The site, a gentle hill overlooking a valley, previously had a Palaeochristian church dedicated to the archangel. A lovely portico of horseshoe arches, an *ajímez* window and a heavy 11th-century tower mark the exterior, while the interior is proof in golden limestone that the Cordobans never forgot the classic symmetrical Roman basilica form and its proportions. Delicate horseshoe arches divide the three aisles, and separate the transept and triple apse from the main body of the basilica (like the Byzantines, the Mozarab liturgy called for a screen between the holy precinct and the parishioners). The capitals have simple palmette designs; luxuriant floral and geometric reliefs with lions and peacocks eating grapes decorate the chancels and friezes; over the door you can make out the highly elaborate if faint dedicatory inscription. The ceiling, a later *mudéjar* addition, bears the arms of León and Castile.

Valencia de Don Juan

Southwest of Mansilla, **Valencia de Don Juan** was named after its first duke, son of Alfonso the Wise, and is worth a detour for a theatrical 15th-century **castle** that rises from the banks of the Río Esla and is featured on all León's tourist brochures, with its massive walls (on one side only, like a stage set) broken by a series of turrets and crenellations. The surrounding Esla *vega* is one of the most fertile swaths of the province, producer of Valdevimbre-Los Oteros, a light, fruity rosé wine with an orangeish rose colour, fermented in curious bunker-like *bodegas*. Its gentle sparkle comes from a technique called *madreo*. Only small quantities are produced; hunt down a bottle in Valencia de Don Juan or Villamañán to the west.

(i) **Valencia de Don Juan >>**
Avda Carlos Pinilla, t 98 775 07 01, www.aytovalenciade donjuan.org; open July–Sept only

Where to Stay and Eat West to Léon

Sahagún ✉ 24320

**Hs La Codorniz, Arco s/n 97, t 98 778 02 76 (€€–€). One of the smarter choices, with a good restaurant.

Hostal El Ruedo II, Plaza Mayor 1, t 98 778 18 34, www.restauranteelruedo. com (€€–€). Four double bedrooms with bathrooms, each decorated in bright but pastel colours. The €10 *menú del día* is also a good bargain.

*Hospedería Monástica, C/ Mayor 12, t 98 778 01 50 (€). In summer, the Benedictine nuns at San Pedro de las Dueñas (5km from Sahagún) offer tasty meals at this place over the weekends.

Fonda Asturiana, C /Lesmes Franco 12, t 98 778 00 73 (€). Colourful place with good food. Get there early, as it only seats 12.

Valencia de Don Juan ✉ 24200

**Hs El Palacio, C/ Palacio 3, t 98 775 04 74, www.hostalelpalacio.com (€€). This charming little inn, decorated with antiques and a document saying that King Philip III once slept here (in the bed of the missus) is the oldest house in town. Run by Asturians, it also has an excellent *sidrería* and good home cooking. *Open Easter–mid-Sept.*

**Villegas II, C/ Palacio 17, t 98 775 01 61 (€€). Family hotel with just five rooms and a garden, in the centre of town.

León

⭐ **León**

León tuvo veintecuatro reyes antes que Castilla leyes

(León had 24 kings before Castile even had laws)

Radiant under the famous spires of its cathedral, León is a singularly happy city of clean boulevards shaded by horse-chestnut trees – one of the few places in Spain to achieve *urbanización* with grace and elegance. Part of the credit for this must go to its hyperactive City Hall (Ayuntamiento), which blankets the city with posters depicting itself as a friendly lion, advising the Leonese to ride the bus, recycle their glass and not blaspheme in front of the children. The founding of a university has given the old city a transfusion of young blood and keeps the bars full.

History

Although the lion has long been the city's symbol, its name actually comes from Legio Septima Gemina, the Roman Seventh Legion, established here in AD 68 when Galba built a fort to guard the plain and the Roman road from Zaragoza. Reconquered from the Moors in the 850s by Ordoño I of Asturias (850–66), León changed hands several times more before King Ordoño II (914–24) moved his capital here. Even then, factionalism in the royal family left the city weak and prey to Moorish re-reconquests; in 981 al-Mansur grabbed it and his son reoccupied it from 996 until Alfonso V's victory at the Battle of Calatañazor in 1002. After this last Moorish hurrah, León, rebuilt and refortified, reconquered Castile. But just as León eclipsed Asturias, Castile – first a county, then a separate kingdom – eclipsed León. In 1252, under Ferdinand III 'el Santo', the on-again, off-again union of the two kingdoms was finalized. Castile never looked back, but for León, then one of the largest cities in Spain, the marriage spelt nothing but decline and marginalization: the nobles went off to the court in Burgos and the people left to settle the new frontiers gained by the Reconquista.

Into this vacuum of power and influence stepped the Church: the pilgrims' road became the chief source of income. Medieval pilgrims eagerly looked forward to León, with its Hilton of a *hostal*, where they could shake the dust off their wide-brimmed hats and catch their breath for the last leg of their journey. Broken and crushed during the Comunero revolt against Charles V, León sank into oblivion until the invention of the railway made its mines viable once again. These in turn declined, leaving León its share of modern autonomy atavists who, remembering the good old days of the 10th and 11th centuries, preach '*León sin Castilla*' ('León without Castile'). As yet their movement has little support.

León cathedral
www.catedraldeleon. org; open July–Sept Mon–Sat 8.30–1.30 and 4–8, Sun 8.30–2.30 and 5–8; Oct–June Mon–Sat 8.30–1.30 and 4–7, Sun and hols 8.30–2.30 and 5–7; free, guided visits depart 12pm Tues–Sat and 4pm Mon–Sat from the tourist office; adm to cloister and museum

The Cathedral

The Spaniards call this the most splendid articulation of French Gothic in Spain *La Pulchra Leonina* ('Belle of León'), a cathedral so remarkable that it would stand out even in France for its daring

León

to MUSAC

N

200 metres
200 yards

QUEVEDO

PUENTE DE
SAN MARCOS

Hospital de
San Marcos

PLAZA
SAN MARCOS

LUIS S. CARMOÑA

AVENIDA PADRE ISLA

AVENIDA SUERO DE QUIÑONES

PASEO DE SALAMANCA

Río

JUAN DE BADAJOZ

GRAN VÍA DE SAN MARCOS

LUCAS DE TUY

JUAN MADRAZO

RAMIRO VALBUENA

PASEO CONDESA DE SAGASTA

Jardines de la Condesa

COLÓN

LUCAS DE TUY

MERCADO
DE COLÓN

ROA DE LA VEGA

Gobierno
Civil

Bernesga

PASEO DE SALAMANCA

ROA DE LA VEGA

COLÓN

PLAZA
DE LA
INMACULADA

JULIO DE CAMP

GRAN VÍA DE SAN

AVENIDA DE ASTORGA

PASEO CONDESA DE SAGASTA

AVENIDA DE ROMA

ALCÁZAR DE TOLEDO

SAN AGUSTÍN

ALFONSO V

RENFE
Train
Station

AVENIDA DE PALENCIA

GLORIETA
GUZMÁN
EL BUENO

AVENIDA DE ORDOÑO II

GIL Y CARRASCO

REPÚBLICA ARGENTINA

MODESTO LAFUENTE

PLAZA
PÍCARA
JUSTINA

BURGO NUEVO

PLAZA
CORTES
LEONESAS

Parque
Bomberos

PASEO INGENIERO SÁENZ DE MIERA

Parque Infantil

Río Bernesga

AVENIDA FACULTAD DE VETERINARIA

BERNARDO DEL CARPIO

REPÚBLICA

VILLA DE BENAVENTE

ARGENTINA

GARCÍA I

Bus
Station

AVENIDA DE LANCIA

PLAZA
FERNANDO
MERINO

AVENIDA DE LANCIA

Rectorado
Universidad

Jardines
de
Papalaguinda

ANTONIO VALBUENA

COVADONGA

Jardín
San
Francisco

FEVE Train Station

FEDERICO ECHEVARRÍA

AVENIDA ÁLVARO LÓPEZ NÚÑEZ

BENEFICENCIA

MAMÉS

AVENIDA DE NOCEDO

LOS OSORIOS

SAN JUAN DE SAHAGÚN

PLAZA PADRE SEVERINO IBÁÑEZ

CONCHA ESPINA

PALOMERA

SANTA TERESA DE JESÚS

RENUEVA

AVENIDA RAMÓN Y CAJAL

PLAZA ESPOLÓN

CARRERAS

Medieval walls

PLAZA SANTO MARTINO

PLAZA SAN ALVITO

PLAZA VIZCONDE

SAN JUAN DE LA CRUZ

AVENIDA DE LOS CUBOS

Basilica Real de San Isidoro

PABLO FLÓREZ

SERRANOS

Santa Marina la Real

PLAZA SAN LORENZO

CAMPO

AVENIDA PADRE ISLA

AVENIDA RAMÓN Y CAJAL

PLAZA SAN ISIDORO

SAN

SAN PELAYO

PABLO FLÓREZ

CARDENAL LANDÁZURI

Medieval walls

SAN MARCOS

CID

Jardines del Cid

PLAZA OMAÑA

LÓPEZ CASTRILLÓN

Catedral

PLAZA SANTO DOMINGO

Los Botines

PLAZA SAN MARCELO

Palacio de los Guzmanes

PLAZA REGIA

PLAZA PUERTA OBISPO

CALLE ANCHA

AVENIDA JOSÉ MARÍA

REGIDORES

CONDE

LUNA

POZO

Ayuntamiento

AVENIDA DE LA INDEPENDENCIA

CALLE DE LA RÚA

MERCADO CONDE LUNA

Palacio de los Condes de Luna

AZABACHERÍA

MARIANO DOMÍNGUEZ BERRUETA

Antiguo Consistorio

PLAZA MAYOR

SAN PABLO

SAN MATEO

GENERAL LAFUENTE

CAÑO BADILLO

VÍCTOR DE LOS RÍOS

SAN JUAN XXIII

SANTA NONIA

PLAZA DE SANMARTÍN

San Martín

PLAZA DON GUTIERRE

CORTA LOS CASTAÑONES

PLAZA SALVADOR DEL NIDO

DAOIZ

SAN

SAN FRANCISCO

PLAZA SANTA MARÍA DEL CAMINO

Nuestra Señora del Mercado

PLAZA CAÑO DE SANTA ANA

SANTO TIRSO

CERCAS

CANTAREROS

SAN JUAN XXIII

PLAZA SAN FRANCISCO

Convento de San Francisco

CERCAS

CERCAS

Getting to and around León

By Train

The RENFE station is at Avda de Astorga 11 (t 90 224 02 02 for the centralized information and timetable service, and to make reservations for any RENFE trains). There are frequent trains to Burgos, Palencia, Medina del Campo, Madrid, Astorga, Ponferrada, Ourense and Lugo; regular trains depart for Oviedo and Gijón nine times a day, travelling through some magnificent mountain scenery and at least 500 tunnels.

The **Transcantábrico** makes the journey to Santiago de Compostela from May to October (plus holidays the rest of the year). It's a 7-day trip, which costs from €2,300. Info at *www.transcantabrico.feve.es*. There are also regular FEVE trains from León to Bilbao (journey time 7½ hrs), which take in the scenery of the Picos de Europa. More information from the FEVE station, Avda Padre Isla 48, t 98 727 12 10, *www.feve.es*.

By Bus

Buses (t 98 721 10 00) depart from the bus terminal just south of the RENFE station, on Pso Ingeniero Sáenz de Miera, for the villages in the province and for Oviedo, Burgos, Santander, Salamanca and Madrid.

and superb walls of stained glass. A similar amount of glass caused Beauvais, its closest rival in window-acreage, to collapse, a disaster León has managed to avert so far by increasing support to the walls and by maintaining a continual campaign to keep it vertical in the face of subsidence; expect some scaffolding. Although Calahorra in La Rioja claims the most storks' nests, León comes in a close second with some 100 families, to the extent that droppings on the stone have become a problem.

The first church was built by Ordoño II, who donated part of his estates for the construction of Santa María de la Regla. It was twice destroyed before 1204, when Alfonso IX began a new church of warm golden stone in unheard-of dimensions, modelled on the soaring Gothic cathedrals of Chartres and Reims. His successor, Ferdinand III, worried by the expense, tried to limit its size, but the Leonese responded by putting up their own money for the construction. The cathedral was more or less completed by the 15th century – the date of the openwork tower of the west façade by Joosken van Utrecht, linked rather oddly to the main body of the cathedral with visible buttresses. Outstanding 13th-century sculptures decorate the north, south, and especially the **west portal** with its three finely carved tympana – the one in the centre illustrates a lively scene of the Last Judgement, the devils boiling the sinners. In between the doors a pillar with a statue of Solomon was where the king or his representative sat in judgement.

The exterior, however, pales before the soaring **interior**, stripped of its Baroque frosting, leaving it bare and breathtaking, especially when the sun streams in, igniting the 19,400 sq ft of vivid greens, reds and golds of the richest stained glass imaginable. The oldest glass, in the chapels around the apse and the great rose window of the 12 Apostles, dates from the 13th century; the latest is 19th-century and made by Spanish artists. If you can draw your eyes away from the soaring walls of glass, note the **choir** in the centre of the nave, set behind an ornate triumphal arch of a façade and embellished with 15th-century alabaster carvings by Juan de Badajoz the elder; its midsection of glass was added fairly recently so you can see straight through to the altar, swimming in reflections of the windows. The *retablo mayor* contains an excellent Renaissance painting *Christ's Burial* by Nicolás Francés. The chapels in the ambulatory house beautiful Gothic tombs, and there's an altar to Nuestra Señora del Dado, at which a disgruntled gambler allegedly once flung his dice, hitting the Christ Child on the nose and making it bleed.

Cathedral museum and cloister
open July–Sept Mon–Fri 9.30–2 and 4–7.30, Sat 9.30–2 and 4–7; Oct–June Mon–Sat 9.30–1.30 and 4–7; adm; guided visits to museum available

Through the Plateresque Puerta del Dado, the **cathedral museum and cloister** has one of the largest collections of Romanesque Virgin Marys in Europe; also a *Crucifixion* by Juan de Juni and a Mozarabic Bible. The cloister was damaged in the 14th century and reworked with classical motifs by Juan de Badajoz the elder.

Around the Cathedral: The Barrio Húmedo

Alongside the cathedral run León's **walls**, built by Alfonso XI in 1324 over the Roman and early medieval fortifications; nearly half of the original 80 bastions remain intact. To the east extend the narrow lanes of the old town, where so many Leonese come to wet their whistles that everyone calls it the **Barrio Húmedo**, the 'Humid Quarter'. The elegant **Old Consistorio** (1677) presides in the arcaded **Plaza Mayor**, where Roman walls have been unearthed. A tower here belonged to the Ponce family, one of whom went to Florida seeking the Fountain of Youth; the adjacent **Plaza de San Martín** is the most humid corner of the humid quarter. By the market in Regidores, another famous family, the Quiñoneses, had their 14th-century **Palace of the Condes de Luna**, of which only the tower and façade remain. The best church is Romanesque **Nuestra Señora del Mercado** in the serene and lovely Plaza Santa María del Camino.

Nuestra Señora del Mercado
open daily 11–12 and 7–8

From the cathedral, busy Calle Ancha (the old Roman *decumanus*) leads up to Plaza de Botines and Plaza San Marcelo, where you suddenly come upon **Los Botines** ('The Spats'), León's version of Sleeping Beauty's castle. Antoni Gaudí's most conventional work, it was built in 1891 – 'in a moment of doubt', according to one of his biographers – as a private residence, with turrets, swirling Gaudí-esque ironwork and a statue of St George (patron of Gaudí's native Catalunya) overhanging the door, where, by the look on the dragon's face, the saint is scratching him in just the right spot.

Palacio de los Guzmanes
now the provincial Diputación, open for free guided visits daily 9–3, ask within

Two fine Renaissance palaces (and two incongruous modern sculptures) share the *plazas*: the arcaded **Ayuntamiento** and the **Palacio de los Guzmanes**, with a sumptuous façade designed by Rodrigo de Hontañón in 1559. Plaza Santo Domingo holds the **Museo de León**, with a small but prize collection: the 11th-century ivory Carrizo crucifix, enamels from Limoges, a Mozarab cross given

Museo de León
www.turismo.iranon.org/museodeleon; open July–Sept Mon–Sat 10–2 and 5–8, Sun 10–2; Oct–June Tues–Sat 10–2 and 4–7, Sun 10–2; adm

by King Ramiro II in 940 to Santiago de Peñalba, the Corullón calvary, three pairs of beautiful capitals from the first Mozarab church at Sahagún, made by the same craftsmen as at Escalada, medieval weapons of the Roman Seventh Legion, portraits of the knights of Santiago, and artefacts discovered in a Punic necropolis near the Maragato village of Santa Colomba de Somoza – a key discovery in unravelling the origins of the Maragatos (*see* p.294).

San Isidoro and the Panteón de los Reyes

Real Colegiata de San Isidoro de León
www.sanisidorodeleon. org; open July–Aug Mon–Sat 9–8, Sun 9–2; Sept–June Mon–Sat 10–1.15 and 4–6.30; church free, adm to museum and pantheon which are visited by guided tour only

If León's cathedral is one of the best in Spain, the city can claim a similar pedestal for the Romanesque frescoes in its **Real Colegiata de San Isidoro de León**, north of Plaza de Botines in Plaza San Isidoro. Founded in the 9th century, razed to the ground by the iconoclast al-Mansur, it was rebuilt by Ferdinand I, the first to unify León and Castile in 1037 and the first to call himself 'King of the Spains'. In 1063 León bagged the relics of St Isidoro of Seville, that 6th-century, encyclopedia-writing Visigothic nobleman and doctor of the Church whose bones, upon hearing of the Reconquista, started to speak, asking to be transferred to Christian territory. These chattering bones must have driven the Moors in Seville crazy, so they packed them off to León; the basilica was at once rededicated to him, enlarged and given its lofty bell tower. Once here, the gentle Isidoro, like a half-dozen other saints along the road, was conscripted into Reconquista duty; you can see him over the side door, on horseback in his bishop's gear, whacking the Moor with John Wayne gusto. Specifically, he helped Alfonso VIII reconquer Baeza, and to this day a confraternity from Baeza, in theory, maintains a 24-hour vigil by his relics in the church.

The façade has two entrances; the church is entered through the right-hand, 11th-century Puerta del Perdón topped by a tympanum sculpted with the Descent from the Cross, the Three Marys and the Ascension. This is the first Door of Pardon along the Camino de Santiago; if a pilgrim was too ill or weak to carry on, they could touch the door and receive the same indulgence and absolution as someone who had walked all the way to Compostela. The barrel-vaulted interior with its foiled arches, desecrated by Soult's French army in the Peninsular War, is something of a heavily restored disappointment; of the 12th-century original only the transept capitals and chapel remain.

The more ornate Puerta del Cordero, its tympanum carved with the Sacrifice of Isaac, leads into the original narthex of the church, the **Panteón de San Isidoro**, founded by Ferdinand I to house his simple stone sarcophagus and those of his descendants (now visitors enter on the guided tour via a tiny stone spiral staircase). Its two small groin-vaulted chambers are supported by elaborately carved capitals (Daniel in the Lions' Den and the Resurrection of

Lazarus), and the ceiling and walls are covered with extraordinary vivid frescoes from the 12th century, among the best-preserved Romanesque paintings anywhere still in their original setting. Stylistically similar to the 5th-century frescoes and mosaics in Santa Costanza (which all the pilgrims on their way to Rome would have visited), Christ Pantocrator and the Evangelists, with human bodies and animal heads (Luke looks like the Minotaur) reign over scenes of the shepherds, the Flight into Egypt, the Last Supper, the Tears of St Peter, the Seven Cities and Seven Lamps of the Apocalypse. Best of all, there's an allegory of the months, starting with the two-headed Janus, Roman god of the door, who looks both backward and ahead at the 'hinge' of the old and new years.

Although the French desecrated the tombs and burned the library, they somehow missed the treasures displayed in the **museum** on the first floor, which originally formed part of Ferdinand I's palace: St Isidoro's original silver reliquary, the gem-studded chalice of Doña Urraca (made from two Roman cups), and lovely Mozarab caskets covered with ivories and enamels. The library, rebuilt in the 16th century by Juan de Badajoz, has an illuminated Bible of 960 that somehow escaped the French firebugs.

The Hospital de San Marcos and MUSAC

León's third great monument lies at the end of the garden along the riverside Paseo Condesa de Sagasta. The **Hospital de San Marcos** was built in 1173 as headquarters for the Order of the Knights of Santiago, charged with the pilgrims' protection; at their hospital the weary, blistered pilgrim could rest and prepare for the rigours ahead. In 1514, when the powerful knights were more devoted to their own pleasure and status, they set about rebuilding their headquarters thanks to an enormous donation by Ferdinand the Catholic – something of a pay-off for electing him to the post of Grand Master and surrendering their semi-autonomy to the Crown. Over the 16th to 18th centuries the monastery was given its superb 330ft Plateresque façade, first designed by Pedro de Larrea but altered by many hands afterwards, including those of Juan de Badajoz the younger; its frieze of busts, niches (the statues were never completed), swags and garlands, scallop shells, pinnacles, and intricate lacy reliefs culminating in the portal topped by Santiago Matamoros and the arms of Charles V, who inherited the title of Grand Master from his grandfather Ferdinand. Used after 1837 as a barracks, the building went quickly to rack and ruin and was several times condemned by the city until 1961, when the government purchased it and invested a fortune to create Spain's most beautiful luxury hotel. Non-guests as usual can partake at the bar, and visit the upper choir of the adjacent church of **San Marcos** with its cockleshell façade as part of daily guided

Hospital de San Marcos museum
open July–Sept Mon–Sat 10–2 and 5–8, Sun 10–2; Oct–June Tues–Sat 10–2 and 4–7, Sun 10–2

MUSAC
Avda de los Reyes Leoneses 24, www.musac.es; open Tues–Sun 10–3 and 4–9; buses 7, 11,12

ⓘ **Leon** >
Plaza de Regla 4, t 98 723 70 82, www.aytoleon.com

⭐ **Parador San Marcos** >

⭐ **La Posada Regia** >

tours (ask in the *parador*). The chapterhouse and sacristy are by Juan de Badajoz the younger. The Hospital houses a new **museum** dedicated to the cult of Santiago and the pilgrim's road.

To prove it isn't a city stuck in the past, León established the glossy **MUSAC** (Museo de Arte Contempóraneo de Castilla y León) in a remarkable block of multicoloured cubes north of here. There is a good programme of temporary exhibitions: check the website.

Facilities in León

The **post office** is on Jardín de San Francisco; the **Locutório La Rúa**, C/ de la Rua 8, has public telephone and **Internet** facilities.

Where to Stay in León

León ✉ 24000

*****Parador San Marcos, Plaza San Marcos 7, **t** 98 723 73 00, *leon@ parador.es* (€€€€€–€€€€, concessions for over-65s). This is not only Spain's best hotel, it is a veritable antiques museum. There are less expensive rooms in the modern building behind, with views over the river and pretty gardens.

****Alfonso V, C/ Padre Isla 1, **t** 98 722 09 00, *www.hotelalfonsov.com* (€€€€). Despite the austere exterior, this relatively new hotel is well equipped and decorated in severe, classic style.

****NH Plaza Mayor, Plaza Mayor 15, **t** 98 734 43 57 (€€€). Part of a reliable chain, this is a crisp, modern hotel behind a neoclassical façade in the Barrio Húmedo. Excellent facilities.

***La Posada Regia, C/ Regidores 9–11, **t** 98 721 31 73, *www.regialeon.com* (€€€). Perhaps the most charming choice in the old city, this lovely inn has original wooden beams, quirky works of art, a great restaurant and delightful staff.

***Quindós, Gran Vía de San Marcos 38, **t** 98 723 62 00, *www.hotelquindos. com* (€€€–€€). Situated in the new part of town, very modern and arty; comes with excellent service.

***París, C/ Ancha 18, **t** 98 723 86 00, *www.hotelparisleon.com* (€€€–€€). A good little hotel with all the usual facilities, including internet; close to the cathedral. Good weekend deals.

Hs Boccalino, Plaza San Isidoro 9, **t 98 720 30 60, *Boccalino_3@hotmail. com* (€€). Sunny rooms in a peaceful location overlooking the Real Basílica de San Isidoro; the restaurant downstairs serves decent Italian food.

*Hs Gúzman El Bueno, C/ López Castrillon 6, **t** 98 723 64 12, *jabghostguzman@hotmail.com* (€) One of the best inexpensive choices in León – brightly painted rooms with bath in a restored old house, around the corner from Los Botínes.

*Hostal Casco Antiguo, C/ Cardenal Landázuri, 11, **t** 98 707 40 00, *www. vivaleon.com/inicio_hostal_casco_ antiguo_leon.htm* (€). How many *hostals* can boast a mix of Roman remains and medieval burial ground in their cellar? (Can be viewed by guests). This *casona Leonesa* has been elegantly updated. Unbeatable at the price.

*Pensión Blanca, C/ Villafranca 2, **t** 98 725 19 91, *pensionblanca@ono.com* (€). Excellent new budget option, in a turn-of-the-20th-century building with bright, modern rooms and Internet access.

Eating Out in León

León is famous for sweetbreads and black puddings (*morcilla*), game dishes and garlic soup with trout. In the Barrio Húmedo, Plaza San Martín is the bopping headquarters for bars, tapas and inexpensive restaurants.

Vivaldi, C/ Platerías 4, **t** 98 726 07 60, *www.vivaldi.com* (€€). Award-winning, elaborate cuisine plus marvellous wine list at what is generally considered the finest restaurant in the region (*menú degustación* €35).

Bodega Regia, C/ Regidores 9–11, **t** 98 721 31 73 (€€). Specializes in well-cooked traditional dishes at reasonable prices. *Closed Sun, plus second 2 wks Jan and first 2 wks Sept.*

El Faisán Dorado, C/ Cantareros 2, **t** 98 725 66 09 (€€). Has a good name for Mediterranean rice dishes, including paella and *fideuás*, along with classic Castilian fare; good wine list. *Closed Sun eve and Mon plus 2 wks Sept.*

Restaurante Zuloaga, Sierra Pambley 3, **t** 98 723 78 14 (€€). Fabulous must-see former palace skilfully redesigned as bar and restaurant with an interior courtyard. *Menú del día* €10. Come for a drink at least.

Adonías Pozo, C/ Santa Nonia 16, **t** 98 720 67 68 (€€). Elegantly decorated in *hacienda* style, this fine restaurant specializes in fish but also serves local meat dishes. Traditional favourites like *merluza en salsa verde* are cooked to perfection, or try swordfish *a la brasa*. *Menú degustación* €39. *Closed Sun.*

Casa Pozo, Plaza San Marcelo 15 (near the Ayuntamiento), **t** 98 722 30 39 (€€–€). Specializes in both trout and salmon. *Closed Sun eve.*

Palacio Jabalquinto, C/ Juan de Arfe, **t** 98 721 53 22, *www.palaciojabalquinto. com* (€). Refined cuisine and stylish surroundings in a 17th-century palace in the Barrio Húmedo. *Menú degustación* €39. *Closed Sun eve and Mon.*

El Besugo, C/ Azabachería 10, **t** 98 725 69 95 (€). An old-fashioned spot with good tapas and *raciones* including delicious grilled sardines. The slightly pricer restaurant upstairs serves classic Leonese dishes like roast lamb.

La Competencia, C/ Conde Rebolledo 17, just off Plaza San Martín, **t** 98 721 23 12 (€). Very popular for good pizza. There are three more Competencias in town.

El Gaucho, C/ Plegarías 16 (€). Just off Plaza San Martín, the *patatas bravas* at this bar are worth stopping off for.

Mesón El Llar, Plaza San Martín 9 (€). One of the very best tapas bars on the popular Plaza San Martín; try the delicious potatoes with aïoli.

El Nuevo Racimo de Oro, Plaza San Martín 8, **t** 98 721 47 67 (€). Great Leonese cuisine is served in this 12th-century building; there's a good bar as well and plenty of atmosphere.

La Poveda, C/ Ramiro Valbuena 9, **t** 98 722 71 55 (€). Track this place down for home cooking at the best price. *Closed Sun.*

La Ruta Jacobea, C/ del Cid, **t** 98 723 28 07 (€). *Campo*-style brick and stone bar fronting restaurant specialising in innovative seafood, like *sopa de truta* (trout soup). *Closed Sun.*

North of León

> **Cueva de Valporquero**
> *www.cuevade valporquero.org; open June–Sept 10–2 and 3.30–7; Mar–May and Oct–Dec 10–5; adm; bring non-skid shoes and a jacket*

Northern León encompasses the southern slopes of the Cordillera Cantábrica and the Picos de Europa and one of Spain's best caves, the **Cueva de Valporquero**, 46km from León through the spectacular gorges of the Torio river. The caves have no prehistoric art, but 4km of colourful galleries with little lakes, esplanades, a stalactite 'cemetery', and a chamber of wonders. Another beauty spot is the **Puerto de Pajares** (4,525ft), the lofty pass in the Cordillera Cantábrica used since antiquity as the main gate between León and Oviedo. The Leonese gateway to the Picos de Europa is **Riaño**, from where you can visit the **Valle de Valdeón** and **Valle de Sajambre** (*see* pp.215–16).

West of León

Two distinct regions fill the area between León and Galicia: between Astorga and Ponferrada is **La Maragatería**, the homeland

Getting around West of Léon

RENFE **trains** link Astorga and Ponferrada with León, Lugo and beyond, four times a day – although note that for Astorga the station is a long hike, while **buses** go to the centre. Astorga is the point of departure of buses for La Maragatería; Ponferrada for El Bierzo; and León for the villages in the south. The Cueva de Valporquero is accessible only by **car**, although there are often excursions organized from León.

ALSA has frequent **buses** to Cacabelos and Villafranca del Bierzo from León and Ponferrada; a less regular service calls in at Villafranca on the way to Galicia. AUPSA serve Vega de Espinareda from Ponferrada and Cacabelos. To continue into Los Ancares from here you'll need to have transport, hitch, or take a **taxi**.

of the Maragatos, one of Spain's marginal peoples; and west of Ponferrada is **El Bierzo**, a unique mountainous region, with some of the province's prettiest wooded valleys, distorted and eroded by mining and a favourite abode for 10th-century hermits.

Along the Pilgrimage Road to Hospital de Órbigo

On the N120, not far from the industrial sprawl west of León, is, for better or worse, the only modern chapel along the Camino de Santiago: **La Virgen del Camino**, a concrete box built in 1961 by Brother Coello de Portugal which houses a much-venerated 16th-century statue of the Virgin, set in a Baroque *retablo*; the stained-glass workshop at Chartres produced the ugly windows and Catalan sculptor Subirachs contributed the weird emaciated bronze figures of the Virgin and the Apostles that cover the front. One of the bridges the pilgrims crossed, 13th-century Puente del Paso Honros, still stands parallel to the N120, 23km west of León.

Astorga, Gaudí and the Maragatos

Astúrica Augusta was an important administrative centre for the Romans, close to the mines and a main station along their *Vía de la Plata*, the 'Silver Road' that ran down to Zamora and Seville and across to Galicia, to transport the gold of the Bierzo, the silver of Galicia and the copper of Asturias. Like León, Astorga had its own bishopric by the 3rd century; like León it was important in the Middle Ages because of the pilgrimage. It has declined genteelly ever since, helped along by a bit of sacking in the Peninsular War.

The best way to approach Astorga is to circle the centre, still belted by half of its robust Roman-medieval **walls**, and enter on the

Catedral de Santa María
open summer daily 9.30–12 and 4.30–6; winter 9–12 and 5–6

northwest side of town, where the **Catedral de Santa María** and Bishop's Palace looming over the walls make a startling impression. Begun in 1451, the cathedral was not completed until the 18th century, with too many cooks along the way; even the colour of the stone in the towers doesn't match. The façade with its flying buttresses between the towers was inspired by the cathedral in León, only here the ornamentation on the façade is floridly Baroque: intricate garlands, cherubs, columns with plump rings of vegetation and reliefs of the Descent from the Cross, the Adulterous Woman, and the Expulsion of the Merchants from the

Temple. The interior suffers from a clammy ecclesiastical anomie, with all the interest concentrated in the *retablo mayor*, in marble high relief, by Gaspar Becerra (1520–70), an Andalucian who studied with Michelangelo. Off the neglected, classical cloister, the

Museo de la Catedral houses some fine medieval pieces. Before leaving, look at the top of the cathedral apse, decorated with the figure of a Maragato named Pero Mato, who fought with Santiago at the legendary battle of Clavijo in 844.

Astorga seemed like a dusty, declining nowhere to Juan Bautista Grau y Vallespinós when he arrived as its new bishop. In 1887, hoping to give his see a dynamic jump start into the 20th century, he commissioned the most imaginative architect he knew, his good friend and fellow Catalan, Antoni Gaudí of Barcelona, to build him a new **Palacio Episcopal**. The rest of Astorga had deep reservations about the Modernista fairytale castle that began to sprout on the edge of town and, once the bishop died in 1893, the public's hostility to the project burst open so violently that Gaudí quit and refused ever to return to Astorga. Without his input, this pale asymmetrical castle (completed only in 1963), lacks the extraordinary detail and colour that characterize the works of Gaudí, who usually designed everything down to the furniture. Instead of a bishop, the palace now houses the **Museo de los Caminos**, a collection of pilgrimage paraphernalia. For a hint of Gaudí's intentions, don't miss the magnificent atmospheric throne room with its discreet stained glass and chapels.

The only Maragatos you're likely to notice, other than those carved into the cathedral apse (*see* above), are the two figures, Zancudo and Colasa, who bang the hour atop the attractive 17th-century **Ayuntamiento** at the east end of Astorga; in front of it you can descend into the Roman slaves' prison, the **Ergástula**, where the Maragatos' ancestors languished. The top two floors have been converted to house the **Museo Romano**; inside are ceramics and

Museo de la Catedral

open summer daily 10–2 and 4–8; winter daily 11–2 and 3.30–6.30; adm, combined adm with Museo de los Caminos available

Museo de los Caminos

open summer Tues–Sat 10–2 and 4–8, Sun 10–2; adm

Museo Romano

Plaza de San Bartolomé 2; open Tues–Sat 11–2 and 5–8, Sun 11–2, combined adm with Museo de Chocolate

Museo de Chocolate

*C/ José María Goy 5
open Tues–Sat 11–2 and
5–8, Sun 11–2; adm,
combined adm with
Museo Romano*

❸ Villages of the Maragatos

bronze artefacts from archaeological sites around Astorga, and some spectacular murals from the 2nd century BC. In Plaza Roma you'll find ruins of Roman houses, some with pretty mosaics. The tourist office organizes a walking tour.

Chocoholics will be more interested in the **Museo de Chocolate**, a thinly veiled excuse to sell some of Astorga's finest product. If you're buying, the dark chocolate is tooth-rottingly delicious.

West of Astorga: Villages of the Maragatería

The mostly ruined villages of the Maragatería have been in decline ever since the railway took over the Maragatos' ancestral occupation, but **Castrillo de los Polvazares** (6km from Astorga, just off the Camino de Santiago) has been restored to the verge of being twee, with old stone houses now mostly holiday homes, a score of roadside crosses and a main cobbled street built wide for mule trains. Further west, only a handful of people remain at **Santa Catalina de Somoza**, with its monument to a Maragato musician, while, up from El Ganso ('The Goose'), down-at-heel **Rabanal del Camino** was the ninth stop on the pilgrimage in the *Codex Calixtinus*, a spot safeguarded by the Templars: now only a few people remain to tend its little Romanesque church.

Maragato Mysteries

Astorga is the 'capital' of the Maragatos, who have lived here and in the villages to the west for as long as anyone can remember. Until the 19th century, they were muleteers and carriers, transporting nearly all the goods between Castile and Galicia, a line of work forced on them by their stubborn, almost uncultivatable land; their name has been traced back to the Latin *mercator*, or merchant. Grave and dry in manner, their honesty and industry were proverbial and no one hesitated to trust them with huge sums of money. Until recently they still wore their ancient costumes: huge slouched hats, very broad-bottomed breeches called *zaraguelles* (from the Arabic word for kilts) and red garters for the men; for the women, a crescent-shaped cap covered with a mantle and heavy earrings. They kept very much to themselves, marrying only other Maragatos. Twice a year, at Corpus Christi and the Ascension, they would gather in Astorga, and at exactly 2pm all would begin a dance called 'El Canizo', finishing at exactly 3; if any non-Maragatos attempted to join in, the dance would stop immediately. In the kitchen, they are known for their cakes called *mantecadas* (available in every Astorga pastry shop) and for the odd custom of eating their Maragato stew backwards: first they would eat the meat, then the vegetables, then the soup.

Who were the Maragatos? Common beliefs that they were Celts, Visigoths or Berbers, who came over in the 8th century and managed to hold on to this enclave after converting to Christianity, have been called into question by Dr Julio Carro, who in the late 1950s discovered a Punic necropolis near the village of Santa Colomba de Somoza, west of Astorga – hardly where you'd expect to find one, because the Phoenicians were sailors and León isn't exactly on the coast. Among the finds were figurines nearly identical to those found at Punic sites in Ibiza and dressed in a style very similar to the Maragatos. Carro's conclusion, based on his discoveries and on Maragato cultural traditions, was that the Maragatos were descended from Phoenicians and Iberians enslaved by the Romans to work the gold mines of El Bierzo. The Maragatos themselves agree, and to thank Carro for discovering their true origins they put up a stone plaque to him in the village of Quintanilla de Somoza. These days the Maragato traditions and insularity have practically vanished, although you can still recognize a Maragata at once by her lime-green stretch slacks and horn-rimmed glasses.

Where to Stay and Eat in Astorga

(i) Astorga >
Plaza Mayor s/n,
t 98 761 68 38,
www.ayuntamientode
astorga.com

(★) Viejo
Molino Cela >

(★) Guts Muths >>

Astorga ✉ 24700

Viejo Molino Cela, Nistal (5km from Astorga), t 98 760 05 02, *www.viejo molinocela.com* (€€€). A lovely riverside mill, exquisitely converted into a romantic rural hotel with a garden with white geese and elegant dining room (*guests only, book*).

***HR Gaudí**, Pza Eduardo de Castro 6, t 98 761 56 54 (€€). A comfortable and elegant choice, across from the Palacio Episcopal; its good, moderately priced restaurant with a fancy marble floor has Maragato dishes and fish.

****Hostal Gallego**, Avda Ponferrada 78, t 98 761 54 50 (€€). Rooms in a new building on the way out of town.

****Hs La Peseta**, Pza San Bartolomé 3, t 98 761 72 75 (€€–€). Central, and boasting that it has the best restaurant (€€) in Astorga; you can sample the generous wines of El

Bierzo with heaped plates of hake baked with rosemary or ox stew. *2 wks Closed 2 wks Jan and 2 wks Oct; restaurant closed Sun eve and Tues.*

Serrano, C/ Portería 2, t 98 761 78 66 (€€). Has an unusually good selection of salads and exotic treats like *langostinos al whiskey*, along with more typically Castilian meat dishes. *Closed Mon eve, last 2 wks June.*

Guts Muths, C/ Matanzas s/n, Santiago Millas, t 98 769 11 23, *www.guts-muths.com* (€€). There can't be many places in the world called Guts Muths, and there are certainly few places to stay that can claim to be as characterful. A cosy living room and succulent stews in the restaurant help to ward off night-time chills.

Casa Maragata I, C/ Húsar Tiburcio 2, t 98 761 88 80 (€). Dedicated purely to serving the local staple *cocido de maragato* in its *menú del día*. There is an equally good branch at Redentonstas 6. *Closed eves, last week in June and first week of July.*

After Rabanal, pilgrims tackled the wild Montes de León, climbing up to now-abandoned **Foncebadón**. Just beyond, at the top of the 4,935ft pass, stands the spindly **Iron Cross**, planted by a pilgrim untold years ago. Later pilgrims have added, one by one, the huge mound of slate stones at its foot. To the left rises **El Teleno** (7,179ft), one of the two holy mountains of the Celts in El Bierzo.

El Bierzo

In the old days the Romans dug for gold in these hills; the modern Leonese extract the iron and cobalt. El Bierzo has bleak mining towns, lovely mountain scenery, vineyards, orchards and tobacco fields, charming villages that time forgot, and ancient hermitages. Its inhabitants feel closer to their neighbours in Galicia than to León, and make half-serious murmurs about autonomy. After the Iron Cross the pilgrims' road descends into the fertile valleys of El Bierzo by way of **Manjarín**, another abandoned hamlet, and **Acebo**, with its still flowing pilgrims' Fountain of the Trout along its one street. From Acebo it's 5km south to **Compludo**, a tiny isolated hamlet, where San Fructuoso, the first holy man in El Bierzo, founded his first monastery in 614. Although this is now long gone, San Fructuoso's forge, the remarkable **Herrería de Compludo** (now a national monument) still works as well as it did in the 7th century, using the stream to turn its great wheel.

Ponferrada

Both the easy A6 and the dramatic, lonely (but well-signed) pilgrims' track over the Montes de León lead to Ponferrada. It is the largest town of El Bierzo, and sums up the region's split personality, part of it mine-blackened, slag-heaped and shabby, the other half medievally pretty. The town's name comes from a long-gone bridge with iron balustrades, erected over the Río Sil for the pilgrims by the local 11th-century pontifex, Bishop Osmundo.

Castillo de los Templarios
open May–Sept Tues–Sat 10.30–2 and 5–9; Oct–April Tues–Sat, 10.30–2 and 4–6; adm

On the east bank of the Río Sil stands Ponferrada's proudest monument, the 12th-century **Castillo de los Templarios**, its triple ramparts built to defend the pilgrims from the Moors; its fairytale gate and towers were added later, in 1340. In 1811 the French went out of their way to vandalize it, resulting in heavy restoration. Here and there you can see Templar crosses and *taus* carved on the walls. While building the castle, the Templars discovered a statue of the Virgin in the heart of a holm oak tree, now enshrined in the **Basilica de Nuestra Señora de la Encina** (1577), with a good *retablo mayor* by the school of Gregorio Fernández. Elsewhere in the old town, look for the medieval gate, the **Puerta del Reloj**, and the early 17th-century **Ayuntamiento**. Nearby is the **Museo del Bierz**, which displays bronzes retrieved from the mountain *castros* in Los Ancares and the original workings of Ponferrada's clock tower. Sitting on a hill, 2km south on the Madrid road, the minute church of **Santo Tomás de las Ollas** ('St Tom of the Pots' – there used to be a pottery workshop next door) is a curious Mozarabic church built by the monks of San Pedro de Montes, with horseshoe arches and, best of all, an elliptical 10-sided apse encircled with blind arcading.

Museo del Bierzo
open summer Tues–Sat 11–2 and 5–8.30, Sun 11–2; winter Tues–Sat 11–2 and 4–7; adm

Into the Valley of Silence

South of Ponferrada, the Oza river winds through the beautiful **Valle del Silencio** where, from the 7th century to the 10th, hermits took up their abode under the dramatic white flanks of Monte Aquiana, a mountain sacred to the Celts. Most of the hermits were Visigoths from Andalucía, come to spread the writings of San Isidoro of Seville. One of these was San Fructuoso, founder of the monastery of **San Pedro de Monte** in the village of **Montes**. To get there, take the road to San Esteban de Valdueza for 8km, then turn left for 14km on a narrow, hairpinning road that follows the River

---

DO El Bierzo

After Ponferrada the pilgrimage route enters the Valley of Bierzo, the bed of a dried-up lake, surrounded by a ring of mountains and crisscrossed by trout streams. Its microclimate is warm and damp, with few frosts – ideal for cultivating vines, both on steep slopes and on the riverbanks. The finest, DO El Bierzo reds, are made entirely from the native Mencía grape and have a personality all their own, although this is diluted when Prieto Picudo and Garnacha are added. The less interesting whites are made from Malvasia and Valenciana. Three of the top producers are Valdeobispo, Casar de Valdaiga and Palacio de Arganza (try their Almena del Bierzo).

Oza; at the end of the road, it's a steep 500m walk up. Reinhabited in 890 by St Genadio of Andalucía and his monks, the ruins are mostly 12th century, although Genadio's 919 dedication is still embedded in the wall and some of the original Asturian-style capitals are intact. Despite an 18th-century restoration, the whole complex is on the verge of collapse. The real jewel of El Bierzo, the recently restored little Mozarabic church of **Santiago de Peñalba**, is a bit farther on in a spectacular setting at the head of the valley. Founded by St Genadio and dedicated in 913, its perfect proportions are reminiscent of Palaeochristian basilicas in Africa, as is its shape: rectangular with three cupolas and two apses rather oddly facing one another. The rough stone and slate exterior doesn't prepare you for the refinement and fine craftsmanship inside. A track leads up to the hermit's cave of **San Genadio** for the magnificent view down onto the church and its tower, surrounded by a huddle of slate roofs.

Santiago de Peñalba

take the left turning over the river, and leave your car at the entrance of the little medieval hamlet; open April–Sept Tues–Sat 10.30–1.45 and 4.30–8, Sun 10–1.45; Oct–Mar Tues–Sat 10.30–1.15 and 4.30–6, Sun 10.30–1.15

Fifteen kilometres southwest of Ponferrada, the ruined **Castillo de Cornatel** was built in the 12th century by Ferdinand II to protect the pilgrim route between Ponferrada and Villafranca del Bierzo. The castle itself looks more impressive from the valley than it does close up, but its dominant position affords wonderful sunset views across the Lago de Carucedo to the mountains of Galicia.

Just beyond, **Carucedo** is the point of departure for an unusual journey through an ancient ecological disaster, **Las Médulas**. In the 1st century AD, the Romans noted the soft red soil was sprinkled with gold and minium (or red lead, used for painting), but to extract it meant sifting through thousands of tons of earth. Some 60,000 slaves were brought in to dig a complex network of galleries, wells, dams and canals to erode the soil. The work was gruelling and dangerous, and thousands died over the next two centuries in moving an estimated 300 million tons of earth to extract 90 tons of gold. Whole hills collapsed, and new ones of left-over tailings were piled up by the slaves, leaving behind a landscape like a row of jagged red spinal cords – or *medullas*. There's a natural balcony over Las Médulas from Orellán; from the village of Las Médulas, 4km from Carucedo, you can take a stroll (bring sturdy shoes) past the ancient canals, galleries, rock needles and surreal caves – a natural disaster perhaps, but a strangely beautiful one. It was recognized as a World Heritage Site in 1998.

Northwest of Ponferrada: the Ancares Leoneses

North of Ponferrada, a lonely road heads north to Vega de Espinareda and the beautiful, densely forested, mountainous **Ancares Leoneses**, now under the jurisdiction of the Reserva Nacional. Although sections are reserved for hunting, the park also protects a number of endangered species – a few brown bears,

Iberian wolves, roe deer and capercaillie – as well as a dying way of life in its 27 remote mountain hamlets, with their traditional *pallozas*, straw-topped round stone huts first built by the Celts.

Nestled snugly at the confluence of three valleys, **Vega de Espinareda** is the modern metropolis of Los Ancares; many of the emigrants from tiny mountain villages get their first taste of urban life here. The action is centred around a narrow pedestrian **Puente Romano**, but Vega's proudest monument is the ruined 16th-century **Monasterio de San Andrés**, on the western outskirts of town, founded in 923 by El Bierzo's home-grown saint, San Genadio. The attached church, built in 1778 in neoclassical style, contains a 13th-century crucifix, while behind the monastery the Fuente de la Vida offers a lifetime of good health to anyone who drinks seven draughts of its water.

North and west of Vega the Ancares begin in earnest, rising steeply above the villages of **Valle de Finolledo** and **San Martín**, before dropping smoothly into the wide green valley of **Burbia**, and, simultaneously, into the Middle Ages. The majority of the people here continue to live in rough stone huts, tend their rows of beans, herd sheep through the dirt streets, and regale visitors at great length with intimate family histories. From Burbia a dirt track leads to the abandoned village of **Campo del Agua**, which preserves the best collection of straw-roofed *pallozas* anywhere in Los Ancares. Serious hikers can tackle the full-day ascent of 5,880ft **Pico de los Tres Obispos**, one of the tallest mountains in the region.

More *pallozas* can be found in the next valley to the west, **Valle de los Ancares**, although there's no direct way across the mountains other than to walk (take LE712 north from Vega if you're driving). The best-preserved are in **Balouta**, and include what is believed to be the only permanently inhabited example in León. Roads lead onwards from Balouta through gorgeous mountain scenery to the Galician village of **Doiras**, from where it's possible to descend back into León via Balboa, or press on west to the main NVI, or the fast A6 highway, at Becerreá.

Further east, the **Castro de Chano** is a superbly preserved Celtiberian hill fort, just outside Peranzanes in the Valle de Fornela. The *castro* consists of 13 circular turrets, spectacularly positioned on a long spur, and is considered so valuable that access is restricted to archaeologists and dignitaries; a **replica** has been constructed nearby to satisfy lesser mortals.

*Castro de Chano
replica
open July–mid-Oct
Tues–Sun 10.30–1 and
4–7; closed winter
except for outside*

Carracedo

Cacabelos, 12km west of Ponferrada, was another important stop on the *camino*, although these days it's best known for its wines and its **Santuario de las Angustias**, where there's a famous scene of baby Jesus floating on a cloud playing cards with St Anthony. Don't

Santa María de Carracedo
open summer Tues–Sun 10–2 and 5–8; winter Tues–Sun 10–2 and 4–6; adm

miss a brief detour 3km south to the **Monastery of Santa María de Carracedo**, founded in 990 in a pastoral setting, this time by Bermudo II the Gouty of León. In 1138 it came under the patronage of Doña Sancha, sister of Alfonso VII, who built a new church and monastery. At the end of the 18th century the monks decided it was time for a change and began a large neoclassical church. It was only partially finished in 1811 when the French marched through and effectively put an end to the project, leaving half of a new church and much of the old intact, pieced together, restored and roofed over for the monastery's 1,000th birthday. By the church are the remains of a little **palace** built by Alfonso IX in the early 1200s to house his wife and two daughters when the pope annulled his marriage. The claims of the princesses to the throne were a reason behind the union of León and Castile declared by Ferdinand III el Santo – Alfonso IX's son from his second marriage.

Villafranca del Bierzo

The *Codex Calixtinus'* 10th stop on the Camino de Santiago, Villafranca del Bierzo, is one of the most attractive small towns along the whole road, embraced on all sides by mountains, built at the confluence of the Burbia and Valcarce rivers. As its name suggests, the town was founded by the French in the 11th century and in its heyday it had eight monasteries and six pilgrims' hospitals; today it makes wine and lodges visitors to the region.

On the hill where pilgrims entered Villafranca is the preserved 16th-century **Castillo de Villafranca** (private, no admission) and the 12th-century **Santiago**, a simple Romanesque church but an important one, with the second Puerta del Perdón along the road. Pilgrims too weary or ill to continue had only to touch the door to achieve the same indulgences as they would at Compostela. Some then keeled over dead and were buried in the adjacent cemetery. All of the church's unfortunately eroded decoration is concentrated around the Puerta del Perdón. The pilgrims would descend from the church and castle to walk along wide, atmospheric **Calle del Agua**, 'Water Street', lined with blazoned 16th- and 17th-century palaces with iron balconies that often looked over a real street of water, so frequently has the Burbia flooded it. The Plaza Mayor was set higher up away from danger, and near this you'll find the 13th-century church of **San Francisco**, all that remains of a monastery founded by St Francis himself during his pilgrimage. It has a magnificent 15th-century *mudéjar artesonado* ceiling. Down on the banks of the Burbia, the **Colegiata de Santa María** stands on the site of the 11th-century monastery founded by the monks of Cluny. It fell into ruins and was rebuilt from scratch in 1544 to designs by Rodrigo Gil de Hontañón. Construction continued into the 18th century, when the money ran out, leaving the nave cut short and

Colegiata de Santa María
open Mar–Oct daily 10–2 and 4–7; Nov–Feb Sat and Sun 10–2 and 4–7; the tourist office organizes guided visits at weekends

the west façade closed by a simple wall, although what was completed of the part-Gothic and part-Renaissance interior is uncommonly grand.

Just to the south of Villafranca, the 13th-century **San Juan de San Fiz** was built over a Roman cistern; the walls can still be seen under the raised presbytery. **Corullón** has two more lovely Romanesque churches: San Esteban and the recently restored San Miguel. Corullón's ivy-smothered castle affords a lovely view of the Bierzo valley. West of Villafranca, the pilgrims' road passes through the narrow valley of the Valcarce dotted with tiny villages. At **Herrerías**, with its old Hospital de los Ingleses (English Hostel), the road and pilgrims' route divide; the latter, rising to the pass at Cebreiro and hence into Galicia, was as dangerous and dreaded as it is beautiful.

Where to Stay and Eat in El Bierzo

(i) **Ponferrada >**
C/ Gil y Carrasco 4,
t 98 742 42 36,
www.ponferrada.org

(i) **Villafranca del Bierzo >>**
Avda Diaz Ovelar 10,
t 98 754 00 28,
www.villafrancadel
bierzo.org

Ponferrada ✉ 24400

****Temple Ponferrada, Avda de Portugal 2, t 98 741 00 58, www.templehotels.com (€€€). The largest, best-endowed hotel in town, in a pseudo-Templar castle; it can be noisy.

Taberna los Arcos, Plaza del Ayuntamiento 4, t 98 740 90 01, www.hotelbierzoplaza.com (€€€–€€). A converted 17th-century bodega is the setting for this charming restaurant with smart modern **rooms** above.

***Bérgidum, Avda de la Plata 4, t 98 740 15 12, www.hotelbergidum.com (€€). A modern, central place.

**Hotel El Castillo, Avda del Castillo 115, t 98 745 62 27, www.hotel-elcastillo.com (€€). Castle-gaze from your room at this modern marble-clad hotel across the way.

*Hs La Madrileña, Avda A López Peláez 4, t 98 741 28 57 (€). Basic but clean; rooms with shared bath for €24.

La Fonda, Pza Ayuntamiento 10, t 98 742 57 94 (€€–€). Uses local ingredients to create interesting dishes. Closed Sun eve.

Las Cuadras, Tras la Cava 2, t 98 741 93 73 (€). Located right by the castle walls and serving tasty tapas and fish.

(i) **Vega de Espinareda >**
Casa Consistorial,
Avenida de Ancores,
t 98 756 86 19

Vega de Espinareda ✉ 24430

Casa Rural Valle de Ancares, Pereda de Ancares (30km north), t 98 756 86 19 (€). A few comfortably rustic rooms in a traditional house, with heavy

wooden shutters. Meals are served, and mountain bikes can be rented.

HR Piñera, C/ La Conchera 18, t 98 756 46 12, www.hotelpinera.com (€). Pleasant and modern, it makes a good base for exploring the valleys – the owners can help to arrange 4WD rental. Next door, **El Jardín serves a reasonable menú del día.

Villafranca del Bierzo ✉ 24500

*Hospederia Convento San Nicolás El Real, C/ Travesía San Nicolás 4, t 98 754 04 83, www.hospederiasannicolas.com (€€). Occupies the wonderful old convent; the guest areas have been remodelled to modern standards, but original frescoes and paintings remain in the halls. A restaurant serves food with a religious theme. Open only at weekends during winter.

*Hs Casa Méndez, C/ Espíritu Santo 1, t 98 754 24 08 (€). Family-run with good home cooking, to go with its well-priced rooms with bath.

*Hs Comercio, C/ Puente Nuevo 2, t 98 754 00 08 (€). Offers few luxuries but plenty of character – this rambling old mansion can't have changed much since the 15th century. The huge, high-ceilinged rooms may have seen better days, but this is still the best bargain in town. Shared bath.

La Escalinata, Plaza de Prim 4, t 98 754 07 06 (€€). Bright décor and friendly service accompany a menu of ever-changing delights, in a lovely location opposite the castle. Open daily July–Sept; Oct–June Fri eve, Sat–Sun lunchtimes.

Galicia

If Asturias is Spain's Wales, then Galicia is in many ways its Ireland, for many years so far removed from the mainstream of Spanish life and history that it might just as well have been an island. Here the Celtic invaders of 1000 BC found their cosiest niche, in the same kind of rainswept, green land facing the setting sun that their brethren had settled farther north in Brittany and Cornwall. The Moors left no mark in Galicia, having been expelled in the 8th century by the kings of Asturias – who promptly turned their attention to the richer spoils of the south.

12

Don't miss

① The pilgrimage site at the end of the world
Santiago de Compostela p.315

② Rugged cliffs
Costa da Morte p.336

③ Glass balconies in a maritime 'Crystal City'
A Coruña p.331

④ Spectacular seafood
Vigo p.353

⑤ A lovely granite border town
Tui p.352

See map overleaf

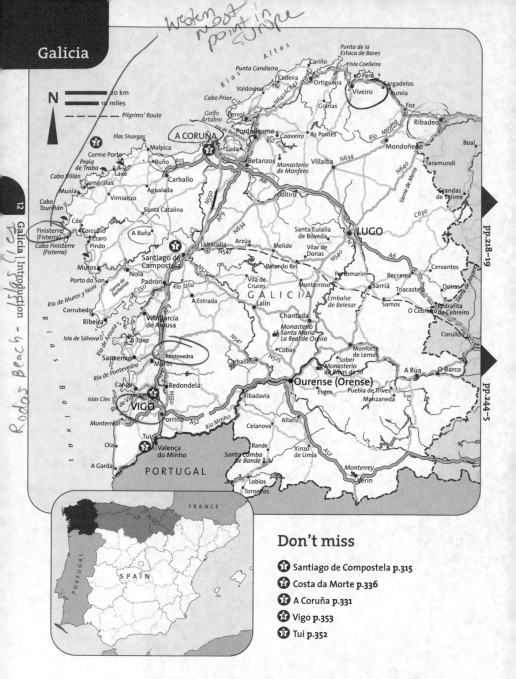

Galicia

[handwritten: western most point in Europe]

[handwritten left margin: Rodas Beach - Islas Cies]

Map labels: to km / 10 miles / Pilgrims' Route

N

Don't miss

1 Santiago de Compostela p.315
2 Costa da Morte p.336
3 A Coruña p.331
4 Vigo p.353
5 Tui p.352

pp.218-19
pp.244-5

While the rest of the north expanded into the newly won lands of the Reconquista, the Galicians, or Gallegos, were hemmed in by Portugal and forced to turn inwards, dividing their land into ever smaller holdings with every generation. Famines were common and, as soon as the New World was discovered, they emigrated in droves – there are more Gallegos in Buenos Aires alone than in all of Galicia. Even today Galicia is one of the poorest regions in Spain. Yet few places in Spain have such a lasting charm. The coastline is pierced by a dozen estuaries, or *rías*, wild and scenic in the north, and, in the south, sheltering serene beaches (Galicia has some 772 of these) and tiny coves, perfect for the smuggling that has long been a mainstay of the economy. Rivers in deep, narrow valleys with fantasy names – the Éo, the Ulla, the Lor, the Sil and Jallas – spill down wild mountains on their way to the sea. Bright green gardens cover every inch of cultivatable land, although a third of the acreage is wasted by the granite walls each Gallego has erected around his own little plot. Each farm, however small, has a sturdy, self-sufficient air, with its cow and conical hayrack, its trellis of vines (producing excellent white wines similar to Portugal's 'green' wines) and tiny plots of turnips, peppers, maize, cabbage, peas and Spain's finest potatoes. Many cottages have granaries (*hórreos*), monumental pieces of granite set up on pillars to protect the grain from rodents and damp, with window-like vents to permit air to circulate, topped by a gabled roof with crosses. Early travellers mistook them for hermitages.

Because of the endless division of land, much of Galicia is covered higgledy-piggledy with farms and houses in some 31,000 'villages' (most with populations of 100–200), sprinkled with the showy bungalows of the *Americanos* who made fortunes in Argentina. Many older houses, especially in A Coruña, have balconies closed in by glass 'crystal galleries', adorned with white mullions. Another distinctive feature of Galicia is the sculpted granite crosses at the crossroads. Some seem to have guided pilgrims, or marked out the high roads, or fulfilled vows, or perhaps even served the same geomantic organization as Neolithic menhirs and dolmens, only carved into Christian forms. In the Rías Baixas, especially along the rivers leading into them, you'll see the stately manor country villas the Gallegos call *pazos*, from the Roman *palatio*.

Galicia's language, Gallego, is chock-full of 'x's (pronounced 'sh') and closely related to Portuguese, and spoken by a greater percentage of the population than Basque or Catalan are in their respective regions. Even García Lorca penned verses in Gallego, inspired by the language of Alfonso the Wise's masterpiece the *Cantigas de Santa María* and the evocative poetry, reminiscent of Emily Dickinson's, by Rosalía de Castro (1837–85), especially her *Cantares Gallegos*. Rosalía was a key figure in the *Rexurdimento* (literary renaissance), inspired by the Catalans and, like theirs, a forerunner of Spain's nationalist movements. However, Gallego is in decline among young people, while regional langauges are on the rise in Euskadi and Catalunya (where 90 per cent of 18–29-year-olds speak them).

Culturally, Galicia has always looked to its ancient roots. The national instrument, the *gaita*, is very similar to Breton or Irish bagpipes, and Gallegos like nothing better than to blow it at festivals. Celtic influences are also strong in Galicia's festivals (many associated with death, witches and evil spirits); you can buy a 400-page book that lists every one of them. Irish immigrants in the 16th century introduced lace-making (*camarinhas*), still done by older women all along the coast.

In November 2002, the Bahamas-registered oil tanker, *Prestige*, ran into heavy seas off Cape Fisterra in Galicia. The 3,000-tonne oil spill devastated wildlife in the region and the fishing industry along a 400km stretch of coast was entirely shut down. After a massive (and ongoing) two billion-euro clean-up Galicia now boasts more Blue Flag beaches than ever before, but the long-term effects of the disaster remain a cause for concern. The Galician fishing industry is still in crisis, and the highly toxic chemicals in oil (polyaromatic hydrocarbons) are expected to affect plankton and the eggs of fish and shellfish, causing a knock-on effect in the food chain, for up to ten years. Don't let this put you off trying Galician cuisine (*see* pp.48–9): strict food controls are in place, and Galician seafood is considered by some to be the best in the world.

The Coast West of Asturias: As Mariñas de Lugo

In the Spanish drive to leave no coast unchristened, this wild Atlantic-thundered northernmost stretch of Galicia is known as As Mariñas de Lugo after the provincial capital Lugo. It surrenders every so often to admit sandy beaches decorated with storm-chiselled cliffs and rocks; until very recently, deplorably slow roads conspired to keep it a secret.

As Mariñas de Lugo

Getting along the Coast West of Asturias

Besides **buses** originating from Lugo, Gijón and A Coruña, the slow FEVE **train** from Oviedo to Gijón goes along the coast to Ferrol, stopping at Ribadeo, Foz, Burela, Viveiro, Covas, O Barqueiro and Ortigueira. See *www.feve.es.*

Ribadeo and Foz

Galician *rías*, or estuaries, are usually named after their largest towns. The first *ría* west of Asturias, **Ribadeo**, is named after a piquant old fishing town that staggers up to a dusty main **Praza de España**, where palm trees and the delightfully eclectic **Casa Morena** of 1905 lend it a lost Californian air. The 18th-century town hall was built as the home of the Marqués de Sargadelos, a liberal-minded reformer and philanthropist who was tied to the tail of a horse and dragged to his death for his beliefs. The hermitage atop **Monte de Santa Cruz**, 2km south of Ribadeo on LU133, offers splendid views of the Galician-Asturian coastline, guarded by a folksy monument to the Galician bagpiper; in early August Santa Cruz pipers from across Galicia gather here in an ear-splitting *eisteddfod*, the *Xira a Santa Cruz*. West, the tiny lobster-fishing village of **Rinlo** is the gateway to the sandy beach known either as the **Praia del Castro** or **As Catedrais**, after its rock formations in the sea. Other pretty beaches dwarfed by towering cliffs, **Praia de Rapadoira** and **Praia de Llas**, lie further west by **Foz**, an industrial fishing port at the mouth of the Río Masma. Only a lonely pile of stones, the **Peña do Altar**, recalls Foz's Celtiberian origins.

Inland: Mondoñedo

If Foz is no prize, Mondoñedo, 18km to the south up the Masma valley, offers some consolation. Mondoñedo was founded in 1117, when the diocese of San Martín de Mondoñedo (*see* overleaf) was relocated inland; it received a second boost in its fortunes in the 15th century, when it became capital of its own little province, a distinction that lasted until 1834 and witnessed the construction of many proud houses of provincial barons, some with the glassed-in balconies or *solanas* typical of Galicia. Mondoñedo's granite **cathedral** was begun in 1219, and when the time came to add a Baroque façade it was done with surgical discretion, preserving the Romanesque portal and Gothic rose window in harmonious blind arches. The interior is still late Romanesque and decorated with remarkable 14th-century frescoes of the Massacre of the Innocents; there's a wonderful organ with trumpets (1710), and a painted Gothic statue known as the *Virgen Inglesa*, brought over from St Paul's in London for safekeeping during the Reformation.

The 17th-century cloister's **Museo Diocesano** displays paintings from Seville, furniture, and fancy liturgical bric-a-brac. The cathedral square is Mondoñedo's best, particularly colourful

Museo Diocesano
open summer daily 11–1 and 4.15–6.30; winter daily 10–1 and 4.15–6.45; adm

12

Galicia | The Coast West of Asturias: As Mariñas de Lugo

during the Sunday morning market, and there's a pretty *alameda* before the Baroque church **Os Remedios**, decorated with grand Churrigueresque *retablos*, 'that sculpture of emblazoned tripes' as Pritchett calls it, and lots of candles, too, for the remedies in its name are said usually to be granted. Between Mondoñedo and Foz, the Benedictine **Monasterio de Vilanova de Lourenzá** dates from the 10th century, but became wealthy enough in the 17th and 18th centuries to finance a major rebuilding programme so ambitious that the fancy façade of the church by granite wizard Fernando de las Casas y Novoa was never quite finished. The graceful interior gives the lie to the idea that Spanish Baroque means dark, gloomy and heavy. Don't miss the exquisitely carved altarpiece in the sacristy (1680); in the chapel of Santa María de Valdeflores you can make a wish while stroking the bones of the monastery's founder.

Monasterio de Vilanova de Lourenzá
open 15 June–15 Sept Mon–Fri 11–1 and 4–7, Sat 11–1; mid-Sept–mid-June call t 98 212 21 04 to arrange visit; adm

Las Rías Altas: West of Foz to Viveiro, O Barqueiro and Ortigueira

From Foz, a brief inland detour will take you to the impressive, mightily buttressed 11th-century **San Martín de Mondoñedo**, a rare Romanesque church left untampered with over the centuries, mainly because it was abandoned by its parishioners, leaving intact and uncovered fine 13th-century murals and the original capitals and the tomb of San Gonzalo, who sank a Norman fleet with a single prayer. Heading west on the coast, you can pay your respects to the **Citanía de Fazouro**, a well-preserved Celtic *castro*; the similar Castro do Chan, near the pretty fishing port of **Burela**, yielded the unique golden torques in the Lugo museum.

San Martín de Mondoñedo
open 10–1 and 4–8

Just inland, **Sargadelos** had one of Spain's earliest ironworks and a famous Royal Ceramics factory, which closed in 1860, but re-opened in 1970 as the **Antigua Fábrica de Cerámica de Sargadelos**, making traditional blue and white jugs and avant-garde works.

Antigua Fábrica de Cerámica de Sargadelos
call t 98 255 78 41 for opening hours; see www.sargadelos.com for information on the ceramics courses held in summer

Beyond Cervo and Sargadelos, the Rías Altas, or Upper Estuaries, begin in earnest, offering some of the best wild and windy coastal scenery in Iberia. Fragrant eucalyptus groves dot the coast around **Viveiro**, at the head of its lovely *ría*. Viveiro is the choice place to stay in the Rías Altas, sheltered by its partly ruined medieval walls from the ravages of the Atlantic, automobiles, and time itself. In the 18th century it imported linen from the Baltic in exchange for Galician agricultural goods but these days its outer fishing port Celeiro, on the opposite side of the estuary, deals mostly in sardines. Three medieval gates survive, along with the fancy **Puerta de Carlos V** (1548) on Avenida Galicia, erected to curry favour with Charles V. Inside, the narrow lanes and pretty Praza de Pastor Díaz are paved in granite and lined with medieval houses sucking in light through their *solanas*, while the austere but pure 12th-century Romanesque **Santa María del Campo** provides a town centrepiece. Viveiro has some ravishing beaches: the sand plain of **Covas** sweeping out to a treetop rock 'castle', **O Faro** facing the ocean, and **Xilloi** and **Ares** near Celeiro, where legend has it an ancient city sank into the sea for refusing to hear the preaching of St James. You can get a good overview from the *mirador* atop **San Roque**, the mountain just behind Viveiro. To the west, the rugged **Isla Coelleira** – 'Rabbit Island' – has been forlorn and desolate ever since the Templars, who took refuge there from the pope's pogrom, were massacred one night in 1307 by the lord of Viveiro.

The next estuary west, the Ría do Barqueiro, provides a magnificent setting for the hamlet of **Vicedo** and its pretty azalea gardens, the wide beach at **Arealonga** and, over the *ría*, **O Barqueiro**, a picture-postcard amphitheatre of white, slate-roofed houses round a lobster port, in a landscape of piney fjords. A road leads down the *ría* to more beaches and to the tiny fishing hamlet and curling sandy beach of **Bares**, the northernmost settlement in Spain, marked by a lighthouse and blocks of walls from the days when it was a port for Phoenician ships en route to tin mines in Cornwall.

The next estuary, Ría de Santa María de Ortigueira, takes a veritable network of rivers. **Ortigueira** on the pine-wooded east bank is a peaceful, unremarkable town (except during its July Festival del Mundo Celta) with narrow streets running down to the waterfront. On the west bank of the *ría* (cross at Mera), the long toes of the Sierra de Capelada extend to Cape Ortegal, where the fishing village of **Cariño** is the last to look over the Cantabrian sea.

**Festival del
Mundo Celta**
*www.festivalde
ortigueira.com*

Cliffs, Lizards and Cedeira

West of Cariño the road takes in spectacular views of the 2,008ft cliffs of the **Garita de Herbeira** en route to the village and tiny sanctuary of **San Andrés de Teixido**, perched on savage, wave-battered cliffs. Wild horses roam here, and pilgrims flow in year-round for, as the saying goes, '*A San Andrés de Teixido, vaí de morto o que no foi de vivo*' ('If you don't go while alive, you'll go dead') – reincarnated as a lizard or toad, creatures that are never harmed in the village. On 8 September, the dead are given a formal invitation to the festival, when colourful, archaic dough figures are baked to be consumed before Mass, and pilgrims who over the past year had a close brush with the Grim Reaper are carried to the church in coffins. Buy an amulet or *santera* of the saint, or enquire about San Andrés' famous love herb, which was consumed after Mass as a prelude to a general orgy. A corniche road continues to the lovely town and port of **Cedeira**, which marks a series of stunning beaches, dunes and lagoons that stretch all the way to Ferrol. The Ría de Cedeira is lined with beauty spots: the lofty **Mirador de Peña Edrosa**, the lighthouse at **Punta Candelaria** and, to the west, the gorgeous setting of the hermitage of **San Antonio de Corveiro**.

12

Galicia | The Coast West of Asturias: As Mariñas de Lugo

Markets on the Coast West of Asturias

Mondoñedo: Thurs and Sun.

Foz: Tues.

Viveiro: Mon, Thurs and Sat

Cedeira: daily fish market; food market Wed and Sat.

(★) **Pazo da Trave** >>

Where to Stay and Eat on the Coast West of Asturias

(i) **Ribadeo** >
*Praza de España,
t 98 212 86 89,
www.ribadeo.org*

(i) **Viveiro**
*Avda Ramón Canosa,
t 98 256 08 79*

(★) **Nito** >>

Ribadeo ✉ 27700

****Parador de Ribadeo**, C/ Amador Fernández, t 98 212 88 25, *ribadeo@parador.es* (€€€€). Lacks atmosphere but comfortable and in a scenic spot overlooking the *ría*; the restaurant offers the day's catch.

***Hotel Balastrera**, C/ Carlos III, t 98 212 00 21, *www.balastrera.com* (€€€–€€). A delightful blue and white *indiano* villa with pretty rooms, garden and excellent restaurant.

Huerta de Ove, Ctra Santa Cruz, t 98 212 87 15, *www.huertadeove.com* (€€). The beaches west towards Foz are well supplied with campsites, but if you prefer a *casa de campo* this is charming, with gardens and pool.

***Hs Galicia**, C/ Virgen del Camino 1, t 98 212 87 77 (€). The cheapest decent place in Ribadeo.

San Miguel, Puerto Deportivo s/n, t 98 212 97 17 (€€). Dine on wonderful fresh seafood overlooking the port.

Mondoñedo ✉ 27740

***Montero II**, C/ Lence Santer 8 (across from the cathedral), t 98 252 10 41 (€). Old-fashioned, characterful place decorated with antiques.

***Hostel Restaurante Padornelo**, C/ Buenos Aires 1, t 98 252 18 92 (€). Small, simple rooms with bath.

Viveiro ✉ 27850

****Ego**, Praia de Area (3km from the centre), t 98 256 09 07, *info@hotelego.com* (€€€€). Modern, overlooking the beach, comfortable, and contains the region's best restaurant (*see* below).

Pazo da Trave, C/ A. Trave s/n, Galdo, t 98 259 81 63, *www.pazodatrave.com* (€€€). A luxurious 15th-century stately home in the countryside, with pools, gardens and an excellent dining room, which serves marine exotica (restaurant open to the public).

****Las Sirenas**, Sacido Coras, t 98 256 02 00, *chlassirenas@mixmail.com* (€€€). Among a clutch of hotels along Covas beach, this one is smart and offers rooms, flats and studios sleeping up to four. *Open all year.*

****Orfeo**, C/ J. García Navia Castrillón 2, t 98 256 21 01, *www.hotel-orfeo.com* (€€). Respectable, if characterless, rooms near the centre.

***Hotel Alameda**, C/ Brieiro 67, Área (4km from Viveiro), t 98 255 10 88 (€€). New beachside hotel, good for kids.

Nito (in the Hotel Ego), Praia de Áreas, t 98 256 09 87 (€€€–€€). This attractive and welcoming hotel-restaurant offers fresh seafood prepared to traditional local recipes and is justly famous throughout the region.

O Muro, C/ Margarita Pardo de Cela 28, t 98 256 08 23 (€€). Just inside the old walls, serving up steaming plates of *pulpo* and grilled fish and meat. Great lunch menu for under €10.

El Laurel, C/ Melintón Cortiñas, t 98 256 00 23 (€€–€). Try the dining room tucked behind this friendly wine bar for more excellent seafood.

The Galician Interior: The Road to Santiago

Pilgrims who made it as far as Villafranca del Bierzo (*see* p.299) had to gird their loins for one last trial: the Puerto Pedrafita in the Sierra de Ancares. This is Galicia at its wildest, driest and bleakest, deceptively covered with blooms in the spring, but the haunt of werewolves and witches in the evening – a zone apart, bound in

Getting around on the Road to Santiago

Lugo and the junction at Monforte de Lemos are linked by **train** to León, A Coruña, Ourense and Vigo, with speedy Talgos to Zaragoza, Barcelona, Bilbao and Irún. Lugo's station is on Pza Conde de Fontao, **t** 98 222 21 41. There's a RENFE office at Praza Maior 27, **t** 90 224 02 02. Lugo's **bus** station is on Praza de Constitución, **t** 98 222 39 85; buses from Lugo to León pass through Becerreá and Pedrafita.

---

dreams and legends. The regional government, the Xunta de Galicia, has restored the atmospheric old *camino francés* and put yellow scallop-shell markers every 500m. The *camino* itself rarely coincides with the highways, making this last leg of the journey especially pleasant for walkers; to maintain the medieval mood, Galicia's fierce sheepdogs are still in place with medieval sheepdog attitudes, just asking for a buffet from a stout pilgrim's staff.

O Cebreiro, Os Ancares, and the Pilgrim's Road

After Villafranca, the *camino* (and the road) pass through the narrow valley of the River Valcarce, ascending to the 3,609ft pass at **Pedrafita**, the boundary between León and Galicia. Here, in 1809, Sir John Moore's troops – fleeing to A Coruña, with Marshal Soult's terrible army in hot pursuit – nearly rebelled. Discipline had vanished in Villafranca, where the soldiers had sacked, raped and looted the homes of their Spanish allies; at Pedrafita and at **O Cebreiro**, another 650ft up, hundreds of men froze to death. Such was their haste that the soldiers threw thousands of pounds in gold – the army's pay – over the cliff, along with hundreds of horses, while the women and children camp followers were abandoned in the icy wilderness. It was one of the blackest pages in the history of the British army, and it was almost miraculous that Moore was able to restore order and continue to the coast. Today O Cebreiro has a huge car park to allow everyone to enjoy the views and have a look at the village's Celtic *pallozas*, oval stone huts topped with conical straw roofs where man and beast lived side by side. Two have been set aside as a Spartan pilgrim's refuge, while another pair house a small **ethnographic museum**.

O Cebreiro ethnographic museum
open Tues–Sat 11–2 and 3–6

A Benedictine monastery, **Santa María del Cebreiro**, contemporary with the Asturian churches of the 9th century (*see* p.231), was built over an old Celtic temple (note the carved stone re-used in the entrance). Pilgrims never failed to pay their respects in its squat slate church, where one of the greatest miracles of the road took place: in the late 13th century an old priest, tired of celebrating Mass for just one shepherd in the winter, was grumbling away during the Transfiguration when he and his parishioner were astonished to see the host transformed into flesh and the wine into blood. The chalice in which this miracle happened is a fine example of Romanesque goldwork and displayed in the right aisle; legend identifies it with the Holy Grail, left here by a pilgrim; next

12 Galicia | The Galician Interior: The Road to Santiago

to it in the case are the miraculous paten and a silver reliquary for the blood and flesh donated by Ferdinand V and Isabel I in 1489.

O Cebreiro and the mighty mountains to the north form part of the **Reserva Nacional de Os Ancares**, part refuge of the rare capercaillie (especially around Degrada) and part hunting reserve of roebuck and boar. Several of the tiny villages lost in the range also have *pallozas*, a few still inhabited by die-hards – **Villarello**, **Cervantes**, **Doiras** and, best of all, **Piornedo**, at the top of a twisting mountain road. **Becerreá**, on the Lugo road, is the main base for excursions into Os Ancares. From O Cebreiro, the *camino* ascends vertiginously to **O Poio** pass (4,387ft), but from here it's all downhill through mountain meadows, chestnut groves and tiny hamlets, where most of the pilgrims' chapels and *hostales* have survived only in name. The exception, **Triacastela**, huddled under an old *castro*, still has its Romanesque church of Santiago, with a simple Baroque tower, and by the River Ouribio a pilgrims' fountain and monument. During the construction of the cathedral of Santiago at Compostela, every medieval pilgrim would pick up a chunk of limestone in the quarries outside Triacastela, and carry it 100km to the Castañeda kilns to be melted into mortar. Modern pilgrims sometimes continue the custom, but now that the cathedral is finished they leave their stone atop Monte de Gozo.

At **San Xil**, the *camino* splits, the right branch heading prettily over hill and dale, while the other, longer one passes down the wooded Ouribio valley to the huge Benedictine **Abadía de San Xulián** at Samos, where the hospitable old monks seem glad to see visitors. Founded in 655, abandoned with the arrival of the Moors but rebuilt a few years later, the abbey had a famous library in the Middle Ages. The intellectual tradition continued in the 1700s, when Samos was the home of Padre Feijóo, the 'Spanish Voltaire', a major figure in the Spanish Enlightenment. The tiny slate chapel of San Salvador is from the 9th century, but the medieval monastery burned down in the 16th century and so did its replacement in 1951, leading to the reconstruction of the two cloisters, one late Gothic and the other, larger, very strict and buttoned-down Spanish Baroque. In the centre flows the lovely Fountain of the Nereids, said to be the work of Velázquez.

The two branches of the *camino* meet in **Sarria**, a cement-making town on the rail line. In its quietly aloof medieval core there's a ruined castle, the little Romanesque church of San Salvador and a pilgrims' hostel in the **Convento de los Mercedarios**, where the church has Isabelline Gothic frills. Ten kilometres west, **Portomarín** was a pilgrims' halt protected by the Templars, but even they couldn't have fended off the waters of the Minho, when the river was dammed in the 1960s to form the Embalse de Belesar, submerging the medieval bridge and village. Old Portomarín's

Abadía de San Xulián
adm by guided tour only, tours every 30mins Mon–Sat 10–12.30 and 4.30–6.30, Sun 12.30–1.30 and 4.30–6.30; adm

porticoed main street plan was salvaged in a new Portomarín, along with the pretty façade of **San Pedro** and the Romanesque tower church of **San Nicolás**. The latter has a rose window like a telephone dial and Romanesque portals so fine that they were long attributed to Master Mateo, one decorated with the 24 Elders playing their *rebecs* and the other with the Annunciation; step inside to see the single-aisled interior. The adjacent monument is to the electrical engineer who helped the villagers with their request to relocate rather than simply receive an indemnity for their property. And they continue to do what they've always done best: supply Galicia with excellent *aguardiente* – firewater which they not only distil but drain during the nightly *marcha*.

The Last Leg of the *Camino*

At **Vilar de Donas**, 'Ladyville' (just off the pilgrim's road, 15km west of Portomarín), the 13th-century granite church of **San Salvador** merits a detour. From the exterior you can see the ruined Gothic cloister of the long-gone monastery and the pretty Romanesque-Gothic portal, decorated with reading and praying monks; inside, the tall granite walls are emerald-green from the damp, while those in the rounded apse are embellished with 15th-century paintings: of the Resurrection, Annunciation, the queen of heaven and the noble ladies who gave their name to the village. The altar stone is carved with the miracle at O Cebreiro, with Jesus in person emerging out of the chalice; the 15th-century baldachin in the transept is one of the few to survive intact in Galicia. San Salvador was once the seat of the Knights of Santiago in Galicia (note the crossed swords, the symbol of the order, on the tombs).

If it weren't for the proximity of Santiago itself, the last two days' march along the *camino* would be disappointing, especially for the modern pilgrim. The *Codex Calixtino* advised pilgrims to say the rosary at **Palas do Rei**, the penultimate stop. The old road passes over a medieval bridge at **Furelos**, before arriving in **Melide**, where the church of Sancti Spiritus decorates the endearing Praza do Convento, and the roadside cross, marking the geographic centre of Galicia, is one of the oldest. Just outside Melide, you'll find a dolmen, the **Pedra de Raposo**, and the crumbling church of Santa María with 15th-century murals in the apse. **Arzúa** was the traditional last overnight stop, 30km (19 miles) from Compostela.

These days Santiago's airport is the dominant feature of **Labacolla** ('Wash Arse'), 8km from Compostela, where 'for the love of the Apostle' the pilgrims bathed in the stream flowing by the church. Sentries were posted to ensure they did this, as much against lice as for the sensibilities of St James. Another 5km would take them up to the now rather desolate hill (Km.717 along the *autopista*) of **Monte del Gozo** or Mountjoy, and the tremendous, long-awaited sight of the towers of Santiago. The first member of each pilgrimage band to sight the cathedral towers was called the 'King', a proud title that was passed down as a surname; if yours is King, Leroy or Rey, chances are you had a sharp-eyed ancestor. These days you barely make them out; Santiago's sprawl and traffic make the last few kilometres a hellish welcome to a heavenly goal.

Lugo: a Detour off the *Camino*

Many pilgrims made the detour to Lugo, the capital of Spain's poorest province but happily dozing away in retirement on the banks of the Minho after a career of some consequence. Its Celtic name *lug* means either the sun god or sacred forest, and when the Romans took it over in the 2nd century AD they renamed it Lucus Augusti, made it the capital of the province of Gallaecia and endowed it with a remarkable dark slate corset of walls, the best-preserved ancient fortifications in Spain, just over 2km long and 28ft high and interspersed with 85 rounded towers. For all that, Lugo was grabbed by the Suevi in the 5th century, the Visigoths in 585, and the Moors in the 8th century. The bastions now defend historic Lugo from its own modern sprawl.

Four ancient gates (and six modern ones) pierce the dark fastness of Lugo's fortifications. Pilgrims would enter the southern Santiago gate to visit Lugo's **cathedral**, built in 1177 and encased in a Baroque skin that offers a modest prelude to the great façade and three towers at Santiago de Compostela. On the west front, note the figure of Lugo's patron San Froilán with his wolf: the story goes that the saint was travelling with a well-laden mule when a ferocious wolf ambushed him and killed the mule. The angry saint scolded until the beast repented and agreed to bear the mule's load himself. Only the north, 14th-century, Gothic portal survived the Baroquers, with its fine Romanesque Christ in Majesty and a capital carved with a Last Supper. Inside there are fittings from every century: a Romanesque chapel and another from 1735, lavish and Baroque in the shape of a rounded Greek cross, dedicated to the Virgen de los Ojos Grandes, 'Our Lady of the Big Eyes', designed by Fernando de las Casas, master of the Obradoiro façade at Compostela. Glass protects a beautiful walnut *coro* carved with a proto Art Nouveau flair by Francisco Moure (1590–1621). The Renaissance *retablo mayor* survives in two bits, filling the transepts; there's a pretty Baroque cloister off the south transept. Since the miracle of O Cebreiro, the cathedral has had the rare privilege of *manifestado* (having the Host on permanent display).

Next to the cathedral, elegant Praza Santa María holds the handsome 17th-century **Bishop's Palace**, built in the style of a typical *Gallego pazo*. Just west, **Praza do Campo** with its fountain was the Roman forum; Lugo's medieval neighbourhood, **La Tinería**, extends here around Rúa Cruz and Rúa Nova. Just north of Prazo do Campo, the formal **Alameda Gardens** give onto the Praza Maior, site of Lugo's rococo **Ayuntamiento**. Rúa da Raiña heads north to busy Praza de Santo Domingo, dominated by an eagle on a column, dedicated to Augustus. The square has two Gothic churches: 14th-century **Santo Domingo** and 16th-century, *mudéjar*-influenced **San Francisco**, formerly part of a 12th-century monastery founded by St Francis on his return from pilgrimage to Santiago. The delicate cloister and refectory house the interesting **Provincial Museum** containing Celtic and Roman finds, including the biggest collection of sundials in Galicia, ceramics and folk art; if you like what you see, don't miss the Sargadelos shop in the square.

Provincial Museum
open July–Aug Mon–Fri 11–2 and 5–8, Sat 10–2; Sept–June Mon–Fri 10.30–2 and 4.30–8.30, Sun 11–2

Lugo's beauty spots are along the Río Minho, the most beautiful of Galicia's rivers; in the **Parque Rosalía de Castro**, outside the Santiago gate and popular during the evening *paseo*, the *mirador* has magnificent views of the valley. Nearby are the brick vaults of the **Termas Romanas**, or Roman hot baths, now part of a hotel-spa.

Santa Eulalia de Bóveda, and a Mystery

Some 16km southwest of Lugo (take the Ourense road for 4km, then bear right to Friol and follow the signs) is the extraordinary 4th-century subterranean chapel of **Santa Eulalia de Bóveda**, built over a Celtic temple as a Roman nymphaeum, and later used as a mausoleum. Discovered in 1962, steps lead down to what must have been an antechamber. A horseshoe arch with reliefs of female dancers on one side and the healing of a man on the other leads into a vaulted room with a shallow pool (perhaps used for immersion baptisms by the early Christians), decorated with colourful, winsome murals of birds and trees, dated 4th and 8th century – just predating the pre-Romanesque churches of Asturias. The columns by the pool were found nearby and re-erected; under the pavement, a drainage system kept the water clear. The only similar known building is in the Ukraine, and just as mysterious.

Santa Eulalia de Bóveda
open for guided tours in Spanish, summer Tues–Sat 11–2 and 4.30–8.30, Sun 11–2; winter Tues–Sat 10.30–2 and 3.30–5, Sun 11–2

Heresy, Galician Style

According to popular belief, the right wall of Santa Eulalia once contained the tomb of Galicia's first 'saint', Prisciliano, whose doctrines, a syncretism of old Celtic and Christian beliefs, attracted many followers in Galicia and León but upset the Church. For one thing, Prisciliano believed works of the spirit obliterated sexual differences, and that monks and nuns should live together. His followers walked barefoot to stay in contact with the earth's forces, were vegetarians, did sun-worshipping on the side and retreated to hermitages in the holy mountains of the Celts. The council of Zaragoza (380) interdicted him, and, when that had no effect, the bishop of Triers had him beheaded five years later – making Prisciliano one of the first holy men to be martyred by the Church instead of by the Romans. His death only increased the popularity of what became known as Priscilianism in Galicia until the early 9th century, when, by an extraordinary coincidence, the head and body of St James were discovered in Santiago. Galician nationalists know they really belonged to Prisciliano…

Sobrado dos Monxes
open Mon–Sat 10–1 and 4.30–7, Sun 12.15–1 and 4.30–7; adm

Another rewarding excursion from Lugo and a popular detour for pilgrims is northwest to the ruins of **Sobrado dos Monxes**, Galicia's greatest monastery, founded by the Cistercians in 1142. Although the original building (by an architect from Clairvaux specially sent over by St Bernard) hasn't survived, efforts are being made with government funds to preserve the massive towered Baroque church, the lovely, if rotting, choir stalls and the monumental, ogival kitchen; also intact are the 13th-century chapel dedicated to the Magdalen, a sacristy (1571) by Juan de Herrera, a 12th-century chapterhouse or Sala Capitular, and three 17th- and 18th-century cloisters. The monks now run a livestock-breeding centre and their own milk business as well as a basic pilgrim's *hostal*.

A Detour South: Monforte de Lemos

If you're driving, consider a detour south to **Monforte de Lemos**, dominated by a homage tower, all that remains of the medieval castle of the counts of Lemos. It had two important monasteries: Benedictine **San Vicente del Pino**, founded in the 10th century, with a late Romanesque church sheltering a 15th-century statue of St Anne; and, near the medieval bridge, the huge 16th-century Jesuit **Colegio de la Compañía**, inspired by the geometric Baroque of Herrera. Look in the chapel for a Renaissance *retablo* in walnut carved with the Life of the Virgin by de Moure, two El Grecos and a lovely triptych attributed to Hugo van der Goes. The area south of here towards the River Sil contains the vineyards of Amandi, one of Galicia's finest reds, grown in a village named, of all things, **Sober**.

Where to Stay and Eat on the Road to Santiago

O Cebreiro and Becerreá ✉ 27600

**Hs Piornedo, in Cervantes, t 98 216 15 87 (€€). A stone building with lovely views over the mountain.

**Hs San Giraldo de Aurillac, near the *pallozas*, t 98 236 71 25 (€€). Now a *mesón* and *hostal* in a former convent founded by French monks.

**Hs Rivera, Piornedo de Ancares, t 98 236 01 85 (€). Roadside *hostal* outside Becerreá, with café, pool and parking.

*Hs Herbón, G Jiménez 8, in Becerreá, t 98 236 01 34, *www.pensionhostal herbon.com* (€). Basic and clean.

Casa Catuxa, Ouselle (6.5km from Becerreá), t 98 236 03 15 (€). A lovely old stone house offering simple B&B.

Sarriá ✉ 27600

***NH Alfonso IX, Rua do Peregrino 29, t 98 253 00 05, *www.nh-hoteles.es* (€€). Modern chain hotel, well placed for the old town.

Casa A Rectoral de Goián, C/ Cabezares 8, t 98 253 3813, *www.rectoraldegoian. com* (€€). An 18th-century rectory houses this tranquil rural hotel, with gardens, restaurant and delicious breakfasts. It's 10km from Sarriá.

Casa Nova de Rente, Barbadelo, t 98 218 78 54 (€). Simple rooms in an old stone house in lovely countryside; a cheap home-cooked dinner is available on request. Camping area.

Lugo ✉ 27000

Although Lugo boasts of quirky delicacies such as pancakes with pig's blood, it also has good seafood restaurants. Ask the tourist office about the tapas competition usually held in Sept.

ⓘ Lugo >>
Praza Maior 27, t 98 223 13 61, www. concellodelugo.org

****Gran Hotel Lugo**, Avda Ramón Ferreiro 21, t 98 222 41 52, *www.gh-hoteles.com* (€€€). Top of the scale: a pool, piano bar, spa and a good seafood restaurant (**Os Marisqueiros**).

***Méndez Núñez**, C/ de la Reina 1, t 98 223 07 11, *www.hotelmendeznunez.com* (€€). Large, comfortable and well located within the walls; recently renovated rooms.

****Hs Mar de Plata**, Ronda Muralla 5, t 98 222 89 10 (€). You can have a view of the walls here – one of several budget choices just outside the walls, not far from the bus station.

****Hs San Roque**, Praza Comandante Manso 11, t 98 222 27 00 (€). One of the better budget choices outside the walls, in a quiet location set back from the main road.

***España**, Rúa Vilalba 2, t 98 223 15 40 (€). Good-value rooms with views over to the cathedral, private bath and TV.

***Hs Parames**, Rúa do Progreso 28, t 98 222 62 51, *hparames@wanadoo.es* (€). Decent and central, with a popular restaurant.

Casa Grande de Nadela, Nadela (6km from Lugo), t 98 230 59 15, *www.casagrandedenadela.com* (*restaurant and hotel* €€). One of the area's best restaurants, serving elaborate contemporary cuisine. It also has ten very comfortable guest rooms.

Campos, Rúa Nova 4, t 98 222 97 43, *www.restaurantecampos.com* (€€). For traditional Gallego sucking-pig, octopus and seasonal game dishes.

Mesón de Alberto, Rúa da Cruz, t 98 222 83 10, *www.mesondealberto.com* (€€). The best in town: classic and modern Galician dishes. Good tapas at the bar downstairs. *Closed Sun.*

Restaurante La Barra, San Marcos 27, t 98 225 29 20, *www.restaurantela barra.com* (€€). Mouthwatering meat and fish dishes in an Art Deco-meets-Starbucks ambience.

Verruga, Rúa da Cruz 12, t 98 222 95 72, *www.verruga.es* (€). Seafood restaurant with a good value lunch *menú. Closed Sun eve and Mon.*

Pulperia Palmira, Praza Comandante Manso 17, t 98 225 39 22 (€). Share a table and feast on octopus at this basic but friendly *comedor*.

Villalba ✉ 27400

***Parador Condes de Villalba**, Valeriano Valdesuso, t 98 251 00 11, *vilalba@parador.es* (€€€). A crenellated fortress with 3m-thick walls and slit windows. Book early for one of the six rooms in the old tower. The modern annexe is comfortable. Baronial dining in the restaurant.

***Villamartín**, Avda Tierra Llana, t 98 251 12 15, *www.hotelvillamartin.net* (€€). For half as much, you could check into this modern, functional place complete with disco.

Monforte de Lemos ✉ 27400

****Parador de Monforte de Lemos**, Praza Luis de Góngora, t 98 241 84 84, *monforte@parador.es* (€€€). Plush *parador*, with a fine restaurant, formerly an 11th-century monastery and the 16th-century palace of the Counts of Lerma. *Closed 7 Jan–mid-Feb.*

****Hs Río**, Rúa da Baramonde 30 (near the centre), t 98 240 18 50 (€). Basic but fine.

O Grelo, Campo da Virxe s/n, t 98 240 47 01 (€€). Delicious Gallego cuisine.

Castroverde ✉ 49110

Pazo de Vilabade, t 98 231 30 00, *www.elpazo.com* (€€). One of the nicest *pazos* in Galicia, with antiques and a lovely garden.

Santiago de Compostela

⭐ Santiago de Compostela

The original European tourist destination, Santiago de Compostela still comes up with the goods. Not only does it boast a great cathedral where pilgrims are promised 50 per cent off their time in Purgatory, but the moss-stained Baroque city is pure granite magic, a rich grey palette of a hundred moods crowned with curlicues. Any tendency towards atrophy into a Euro-tourist

12 Galicia | Santiago de Compostela

CORR DAS ARREPENTIDAS

DO CARME DE ABAIXO

RÚA DE ENTREGALERAS

RÚA DE GALERAS

RÚA POZA DE BAR

CRUZEIRO DO GAIO

CAMPO DAS HORTAS

RÚA DAS CARRETAS

AV DE COMPOSTELA

RÚA DAS HORTAS

Hospital Real/
Hostal de los
Reyes Católicos
H

San Fructuoso †

RÚA DE SAN FRANCISCO

Pazo de
Gelmírez/
Xelmírez

RÚA DO POMBAL

Carballeira de Santa Susana

Pazo
de Rajoy

PRAZA DO OBRADOIRO

RÚA DA TRINDADE

RÚA DE RAJOY

Colegio de
San Jerónimo

Cathedral

✠

Santa Susana

CAMPO DE SAN CLEMENTE

TRAVESÍA DE FONSECA

Colegio
Mayor de
Fonseca

PRAZA DAS
PRATERÍAS

AV DE RODRIGO DE PADRÓN

Colegio de S.
Clemenzo

Post Office ✉

RÚA DA RAINA

ℹ

RÚA DE GELMÍREZ

Oficina
do
Peregrino

Iglesia del Pilar

AVENIDA DE FIGUEROA

ℹ

RÚA DO FRANCO

RÚA DO VILAR

RÚA NOVA

AV DE ROSALÍA DE CASTRO

CARREIRA DO CONDE

RÚA DA SENRA

PRAZO
TOURAL

Santa María
Salomé †

RÚA DA CALDERERÍA

PRAZO
DE GALICIA

RÚA DAS ORFAS

RÚA XENERAL PARDIÑAS

RÚA DE MONTERO RÍOS

PRAZA DE
GALICIA

FONTE DE SANTO ANTONIO

CONCEPCIÓN ARENAL

RÚA DO PATIO DE MADRES

Convento de las
Mercedarias

†

✠ Train Station

RÚA DE GARCÍA BLANCO

↓ Santa María
del Sar

Convento de
San Francisco

AVENIDA DE XOAN XXIII

RÚA DOS CASTIÑEIROS

RÚA DOS XASMINS

RÚE DOS LOUREIROS

COSTA VELLA

RÚA DE SAN ROQUE

Convento
de Santa
Clara

San Martín
Pinario

PRAZA
SAN MARTÍN

RÚA DE SANTA CRISTINA

PRAZINA DE
SAN ROQUE

Convento de San
Martín Pinario

Museo das
Peregrinaciones

RÚA DE RAMÓN DEL VALLE - INCLÁN

APRILARES

PRAZA DE SAN
MIGUEL

PRAZA DA
IMMACULADA

SAN XOAN

CAMPAS DE

Casa da
Troya

RÚA DE TROYA

RUELA DE XERUSALEN

San
Miguel
dos Agros

RÚA DA ALGALIA DE ARRIBA

RÚA DA ALGALIA DE ABAIXO

RÚA DAS RODAS

Casa de la
Parra

RÚA DA AZABACHERÍA

Iglesia de
las Ánimas

Convento de Santo
Domingo de
Bonaval/Museo do
Pobo Galego

PRAZA DA
QUINTANA

Convento de
San Paio de
Antelares
(Museo de
Arte Sacra

PRAZA DE
CERVANTES

RUELA DAS ANIMAS

RÚA DE SAN BIEITO

Ayuntamiento
Antiguo

RÚA DAS CASAS REAIS

PORTO
DO
CAMIÑO

SAN DOMINGOS

RÚA DA CONGA

RÚA TRAVESA

Santa María
do Camino

RÚA DE BONAVAL

RÚA DE GELMÍREZ

RÚA DO PREGUNTOIRO

PRAZA DE SAN
AGOSTIÑO

PRAZA DE ABASTOS

RÚA DA VIRXE DA CERCA

RÚA DE SAN PEDRO

RÚA DO MEDIO

RÚA DA CALDERERÍA

PRAZA DE
SAN PEDRO

TRAVESA DA UNIVERSIDADE

University

RÚA DA VIRXE DA CERCA

N

100 metres
100 yards

CALZADA DE SAN PEDRO

RÚA DAS TROMPAS

BELVÍS

COSTIÑA DE S·ANTONIO

RÚA DOPEXIGO DE ABAIXO

RÚA DOPEXIGO DE ARRIBA

Monasterio
de Belvís

RÚA DE BELVÍS

CALZADA DE S·ANTONIO

Getting to and around Santiago de Compostela

By Air

Santiago's airport, t 98 154 75 00, *www.aena.es*, is at Labacolla, 11km to the east. It has regular flights to Barcelona, Madrid, Seville, Santa Cruz de Tenerife, Bilbao, Santander and San Sebastián, as well as direct flights to London, Paris, Dublin, Rome and Frankfurt. Iberia's office is at Gral. Pardiñas 36, t 90 240 05 00, *www.iberia.com*; there are buses to the airport from the bus station roughly every 60– 90 mins, t 98 154 24 16. Airport taxi stand t 98 159 15 75.

By Train and Bus

Santiago's **train station** is a 15-minute walk from the centre at the end of Rúa do Hórreo, t 981 52 02 02, with daily connections to Madrid, Ourense, A Coruña, Vigo, Zamora and other points. More inconveniently, the **bus station** is way out on Rúa de Rodríguez de Viguri, t 98 154 24 16, north of the old centre; city bus nos. 5 and 10 link it to Praza de Galicia. **Buses** go to nearly all points in Galicia, especially the Rías Altas.

See the rain on the streets, a moan of glass and stone, See in the failing wind The dust and ashes of your sea.

Federico García Lorca

museum shrine is thwarted by the university, which keeps the ancient streets and especially the bars full of life year-round and fuels the raw *urbanización* that engulfs the perimeters, swelling the population to more than 90,000.

Expect rain – the city, the 'Urinal of Spain', never fails gently to remind you that the showers are good for granite, fostering the elegant patina on its monuments and the micro-gardens that sprout out of the stone, an appropriate flourish to the Competelan Baroque of Simón Rodríguez and Fernando de Casas y Novoa with its 'vegetative impulse of verticality'. But on a cold winter's twilight you may see it stripped as bare as García Lorca did.

History

The story goes that in the year 813, a bright star led Pelayo, a hermit shepherd of Iria Flavia (Padrón), to the forgotten tomb of St James the Greater, the legendary Apostle of Spain. The place was named Compostela, a corruption of the Latin *campus stellae* or 'field of the star', although some say that Pelayo's discovery merely happened in the Roman cemetery, or *compostum*, where bodies decomposed. This theory was given a boost in the late 1940s when excavations in the cathedral's foundation revealed Roman graves over a Celtic *castro*. Of course apostles don't compost like everyone else, and the remains of James were just what Christian Spain required at the dawn of the Reconquista. Local bishop Theodomir confirmed the authenticity and built a chapel; in 829 Alfonso II the Chaste of Asturias built a much larger chapel over the tomb. So many pilgrims began to arrive that an even larger church was needed, and supplied by Alfonso III the Great in 896. This fell to al-Mansur and his Moorish armies when they swept through in 997; al-Mansur took the bells as a souvenir for the Great Mosque at Córdoba, where they were turned upside down to hold oil, but he left the Apostle's tomb alone, awed by the fearless piety of a single monk, who knelt there and prayed during the battle.

Some time in these early days James, the humble fisherman with a voice of thunder, was given a new posthumous role as Santiago Matamoros, a fierce Moor-thumping *Generalísimo*, the hero of the entirely apocryphal Battle of Clavijo of 844. This legend was 'confirmed' in a 12th-century document known as the *Privilegio de los Votos de Santiago*, purporting to be by Ramiro I of Asturias, the grateful victor of Clavijo, vowing a tax in perpetuity to the saint's church in Compostela (a tax imposed in Spain until 1834).

After al-Mansur, church and town were soon rebuilt, this time with walls. In 1075, thanks to the new tax, the present cathedral was begun, to accommodate the massive flow of pilgrims from all over Europe. By 1104, Compostela was made an archbishopric, under the feisty Diego Gelmírez; in 1189, Alexander III decreed it a Holy City, on a par with Jerusalem and Rome. In 1236, Ferdinand III the Saint brought back Santiago's bells from the Great Mosque. In 1589, with Drake (a pirate and, worse, a Protestant) ravaging the coast, Santiago was tucked away for safekeeping but, in a fit of amnesia, no one could remember where. Still, the pilgrims came, and only in the 19th century, when numbers declined drastically, did a cathedral workman stumble across the most important relics in Spain (1879). How to make sure they were genuine? An authenticated apostolic bone chip from Pistoia was sent over, and it fitted the notch in the skull like a hand in a glove.

On years when 25 July, Santiago's feast day, happens to land on a Sunday, a Holy Year is proclaimed and the city launches into a year's worth of festivities. The last one was in 2004, when hundreds of thousands of visitors enjoyed music, dance and street activities celebrating all things Gallego. For the next one, you'll have to wait until 2010. Santiago de Compostela was also named European City of Culture for the year 2000. The city gained some significant public works out of the deal, including a new communications port on Monte Pedroso designed by Norman Foster, and a generous park by the architect J.P. Kleihues.

Praza do Obradoiro

All roads in Compostela lead up to the towering granite magnet of the cathedral of Santiago, the town's *raison d'être* and culmination of the pilgrim's journey. Approach it from the huge Praza do Obradoiro, the 'Square of Works', also known as Praza de España, where for centuries the cathedral's stonemasons liberated the soul of Galicia's stone and made it sing and blaze like a Baroque bonfire. In the rain and mists, at morning or sunset or the heat of the day, the cathedral façade changes its tune; it cries out for a new Monet to paint its moods or, perhaps even better, a composer.

Before going in, pause for a look over the Praza do Obradoiro itself, where a colourful carnival of pilgrims, students, Gallegos holding demonstrations, vendors of postcards and plastic birds with flapping wings all play out their roles before a prize collection of civic monuments, erected over the last six centuries. Left, and adjacent to the cathedral, the rather plain **Pazo de Gelmírez** was built in the 12th and 13th centuries by the two archbishops whose worldly aplomb helped make Santiago great: Diego Gelmírez, the first to hold the job, who received a licence to mint money when he oversaw the forgery of the *Votos de Santiago* and used the funds to build the cathedral, and Arias, reputedly 'one of the great ecclesiastical pirates of 13th-century Spain'. They didn't build their own palace as well as they might have: new walls had to be added between the 16th and 18th centuries to keep it from collapsing. Although the upper section is still the archbishop's palace, you can visit the lower **medieval rooms**, especially the huge Romanesque dining hall, where the corbels under the vaults are carved with delicious scenes of a medieval feast, complete with musicians; one trencherman is tucking into an *empanada*. For sublime close-up views of the cathedral spires and across the whole city, the cathedral's **rooftop** has recently been opened to visitors.

Archbishop's Palace medieval rooms
adm included with Museo da Catedral ticket, see below, same opening times

Cathedral rooftop
access through the left door in the Pazo de Gelmírez; open Tues–Sun 10–2 and 4–8 by guided tour only; adm exp

Continuing around the square, the Plateresque **Hospital Real** (1501–9) was built for poor pilgrims by Ferdinand and Isabel with the booty from taking Granada in 1492. Based by Enrique de Egas on Filarete's design for the Ospedale Maggiore in Milan, its façade, typical of Plateresque, concentrates its embellishments in a few key spots, in its long Baroque balconies added in 1678 and in the crowded triumphal Gothic Renaissance altarpiece of a doorway. The building was used as a hospital until 1953, when it was converted into a five-star *parador*: at least have a drink down in the bar and try to visit the four courtyards and late Gothic chapel.

Tucked at the bottom of the stairway to the left of the hospital, the little church of **San Fructuoso** by Lucus Caaveiro (1757) is a good introduction to Compostela's special Baroque and its fondness for heavy geometrical forms. The enormous 18th-century **Pazo de Rajoy**, designed as a seminary and now the town hall, is pure Parisian neoclassicism, by French architect Charles Lemaur; on top note the proud figure of Santiago Matamoros.

Next, the 16th-century **Colegio de San Jerónimo** was founded as a university, where priests learnt languages to hear the pilgrims' confessions; classes were held just behind in the **Colegio Mayor de Fonseca**, built by Juan de Álava (1546) around a peaceful cloister with a beautiful *mudéjar* ceiling; the college is used as a library.

The Cathedral of Santiago

Back to that Baroque firecracker, the Obradoiro façade of the cathedral, where the two towers shoot like huge flames to heaven. On the right, the **Tower of the Bells** was built by José Peña de Toro in the 1600s, while the left-hand one was added by Fernando Casas y Novoa in the 1750s, when he tackled the main façade. A lively triple-ramp stair leads to a pair of doors, arranged to form a cross in stonework; stacked above are two calm windows in a shallow arch like the eye of a hurricane just before the front peaks in a flickering crest of granite fire. At the foot of the steps a door leads into the delightful **crypt of Master Mateo** or 'Catedral Vieja', built by the great master builder to distribute the weight of his Romanesque façade, but so elaborately, with ancient columns, capitals, and fine sculpture under the vaults, that people used to think this was the first cathedral.

Crypt of Master Mateo
open May–Oct Mon–Sat 10–1.30 and 4–7.30, Sun 10–1.30; Nov–April Mon–Sat 11–1 and 4–6, Sun 11–1 and 4–6.30; adm; keep your ticket for the treasury, cloister, museum and Pazo de Gelmírez

Inside the Cathedral: the Pórtico de la Gloria

Perhaps the most startling surprise awaits just within the busy Baroque doors up the staircase, where the original 12th-century façade of the cathedral survives perfectly intact. This is the sublime **Pórtico de la Gloria**, the greatest single piece of Romanesque sculpture, anywhere. Sculpted in warm brown granite between 1168 and 1188 by Master Mateo (dated and signed on the lintel of the central arch) its three doorways are dedicated to the Triumph of the Apocalypse, a theme that decorated many churches along the *camino*, but here, at the very end of the road, it reaches an apogee of joy and mirth, full of movement, life and rhythm; if the end of the world is like this, you want to be there. Nearly all the 200 or so figures are smiling or laughing, beginning with St James himself, welcoming you from his perch on the central pillar, carved with the Tree of Jesse; so many pilgrims have touched the pillar while bending to kiss the base in thanksgiving that the stone has five worn indentations from their fingers. It was originally brightly painted, and traces of a 17th-century touch-up remain.

Above St James in the central arch, Christ in Majesty appears 'like jasper and carnelian' according to the text in *Revelations*, raising both hands in blessing, surrounded by the four Evangelists, Apostles and angels. 'And round the throne was a rainbow that looked like an emerald', an ogival rainbow of musicians – the 24 Elders of the Apocalypse (plus a few stand-ins), each with a different instrument on his lap. On the two side pillars, apostles and prophets chat pleasantly, among them the famous laughing Daniel, who is said to owe his good humour to the loveliness of Queen Esther, whom he eyes across the way. The door on the right is dedicated to heaven and hell, mostly, and depicts children suffering the torments of the damned with their parents – on the surface a powerful psychological trick to make parents toe the line – while the scenes above the left door are more elusive and food for all kinds of interpretations; note the benign portrayal of Jews waiting for the Messiah and the twins, recalling the tradition that

*Thou shield
of that faith
which in Spain
we revere*

*Thou Scourge
of each foeman
who dares to
draw near*

*Whom the
Son of the God
whom the
elements tames,*

*Called Child of
the Thunder,
Immortal
Saint James!*

Pilgrims' hymn,
translated by
George Burrows

St James was Jesus' mortal twin (*see* p.347). After drinking in this eloquent draught of medieval happiness, pilgrims – then as now – lined up behind the central pillar before the curly-haired figure of Master Mateo, who is humbly kneeling to offer the cathedral to God; his nickname, '*O Santo dos Croques*', 'Saint-Bump-on-the-Head', comes from the millions who have bowed their heads to touch Mateo's in the hope that some of his genius would rub off.

The **Romanesque interior** of the cathedral is essentially as Master Mateo left it, a long, majestic, barrel-vaulted nave lined with galleries; it takes a while to get used to the gloom, the cathedral's Baroque additions blocking out much of the light that once poured through an unusual nine-sided rose window over the Pórtico de la Gloria. The huge, silver high altar glimmers, visible since the 1940s when the enclosed Baroque choir was removed. Of the chapels along the nave the most important is the first on the right, the 16th-century **reliquary chapel** and **Royal Pantheon**. Next on the right is the cathedral **treasury**, aglitter with the silver hammer used to pound open the Holy Door in Holy Years, silver scallop shells, a score of other religious trappings and a 16th-century monstrance with scenes from the lives of Jesus and St James.

Actually, when you get close up, the glow-in-the-dark 17th-century **high altar**, lavishly covered with Mexican silver, turns out to be a piece of tomfoolery, its cast of characters borrowed from a giant's Christmas tree. On top Santiago Matamoros cuts down the Moors. Just over the altar itself sits a stiff idol, a 12th-century statue of Santiago, patron saint of Spain, his clothes and throne later tricked out lavishly by a Mexican archbishop. The thing to do is climb the narrow stairway behind the altar, kiss the statue's robe and receive a holy card (for the certificate of indulgence, the *compostellana*, pilgrims should apply with their documents to the *Oficina arzobispal*, in the back of the cathedral). Below the altar you can pay your respects to the saint's bones in the 19th-century silver crypt; the outer, rounded wall here survives from Alfonso III's 9th-century church, while the inner wall is believed to be Roman.

In front of the high altar, notice the ropes and pulleys suspended from the octagonal dome or *cimborio*, from which, on high feast days, the ***botafumeiro***, the world's largest censer, is suspended and swung with terrifying force across the entire length of the transept in a comet-like arc of perfumed smoke and sparks. Weighing in at 119lb, the *botafumeiro* is a smaller brass version of the original silver model made in 1602 and pilfered by Napoleon's troops: it takes eight men, the *tiraboleiros*, to swing it on a system invented in the Middle Ages. Don't miss it if you're in town on a holy day, and try not to think about the time when Catherine of Aragón attended Mass and the *botafumeiro* broke loose and flew out of the window. The *botafumeiro* sweetened the air in the cathedral, where many medieval pilgrims slept at night (until a few behaved scandalously and doors were added to the previously wide-open Pórtico de la Gloria); others say the *botafumeiro* was invented as a public relations gimmick to upstage the pilgrimage to Rome.

The ten **chapels** radiating like petals from the ambulatory are all worth a look, especially the one straight behind the altar, the Romanesque **Capilla de San Salvador**, where pilgrims received Communion. Off the north transept, a doorway topped with a 13th-century relief of the Magi leads into the church-sized three-aisled Romanesque **Capilla de la Corticela**.

Cloister/Cathedral Museum
single adm ticket; see crypt for times

Off the south transept, a 16th-century Gothic-vaulted **cloister** big enough for a football match was designed by Juan de Álava and Gil de Hontañón to replace Master Mateo's Romanesque original, and holds the **Cathedral Museum** and **Library**. The highlight here is a faithful but incomplete restoration of Master Mateo's original granite *coro*, torn down in the overenthusiastic spring-clean of the late 16th century. The carvings show the new Zion descending from heaven, but the computer-designed modern facsimiles can't match the delicacy of the few original pieces that survive.

Elsewhere, the museum has an illuminated 12th-century *Codex Calixtinus*, while the library contains the *botafumeiro* when it's not in use. The archaeological section is of special interest for the fragments of Master Mateo's cloister, while the lavish 18th-century **Sala Capitular** contains some of the cathedral's impressive collection of tapestries, some remarkably insipid even if designed by the likes of Rubens and Goya. There are pretty views from the gallery off the upper rooms across the Praza do Obradoiro.

Around the Cathedral

Although low-key after the Obradoiro façade, the cathedral's other entrances each deserve a look. Heading anticlockwise from the Pazo de Gelmírez, you'll come first to the split-level **Praza das Praterías**, named after the silversmiths whose shops once filled the arcades of this jewel-like square. The double **Puerta de las Praterías** is the only one to remain essentially unchanged from the Romanesque cathedral. Some of the figures were salvaged from the demolished French door and the cathedral's Romanesque stone choir. Locals use the doors as a short cut across town, as their ancestors did in the Middle Ages, when cathedrals were covered public squares as much as religious shrines. From here you can gaze up the cathedral's highest tower, the ornament-laden 260ft **Berenguel** designed by Galician humanist Domingo de Andrade in the 1710s to hold the town clock. The *praza*'s geometric Baroque **chapterhouse** and fountain were designed by Fernández Sarela.

Continuing past the bulk of the Berenguel is the enclosed **Praza da Quintana**, an inviting place to sit on the steps and linger; the

12 Galicia | Santiago de Compostela

The Gallop to the Scallop

The very first thing a medieval pilgrim did upon arriving in the city was stop in the Barrio de los Conchieros, buy a scallop, eat it (this is where French pilgrims learned to make *coquilles St-Jacques*, after all) and stick the shell on the turned-up brim of his or her hat – visible proof that they had made it at last; strict laws forbade the selling of scallops anywhere else along the *camino*. By the 16th century, the real shell was replaced by a fancy souvenir replica, either in silver or in jet (*see* below).

The scallop, that tasty bivalve that thrives in the *rías* of Galicia, has been associated with the Santiago pilgrimage since the early Middle Ages. In Compostela, as usual, they can explain it with a miracle: a young Gallego, on the eve of his wedding, was spirited into the sea by his wayward horse and believed drowned, although in truth the horse was running along the waves to meet the stone boat bringing the body of St James to Galicia. When the bridegroom returned, escorting the boat, his body was covered with an armour of milk-white shells, so amazing the locals that they converted at once to the new faith. Its Spanish name, *venera*, calls up associations with the vagina and Venus, the goddess of love, who was born of the seafoam and surfed ashore on a giant scallop shell. For pilgrims, the shell also symbolized the end of the journey, the resurrection and unity in the world – the sea from which it came, the earth in its stony hardness, and the sun in its radiant lines. It's hard to think of another symbol so polyvalent, embracing sex, death, dinner and spiritual wholeness – not to mention a multinational company peddling the Diesel or Unleaded souls of the dead dinosaurs that fuel the way.

upper level is named 'of the living' and the lower 'of the dead', recalling the Roman cemetery that once occupied the spot. In the Middle Ages this was the square of cheap food, ladled out from the stalls. Alongside the square runs the stern façade of the **Convento de San Paio de Antelares**, 'Pelayo before the Altars', containing a **Museo de Arte Sacra**, where the Virgin holds the Child in one hand and thumps a devil with the other. The cloistered nuns keep up the square's culinary tradition with their famous almond and coconut tarts. In the lower square is the **Puerta Santa**, opened only during a Holy Year, or Año Xacobeo, when St James' Day – 25 July – falls on a Sunday. The doorway of 1611 consists of 24 compartments, each pigeonholing a carved figure from the Romanesque choir, which may have been the work of Master Mateo. In the upper level of the square, the handsome 17th-century **Casa de la Parra** is one of the prettiest in Santiago, decorated with stylized bunches of grapes.

Museo de Arte Sacra

entrance at rear, open April–Dec Mon–Sat 10.30–1.30 and 4–7; adm

The north façade faces **Praza de la Azabachería** ('of the Jet-makers'), where pilgrims bought souvenirs such as a little black figure of St James with you praying at his feet. The use of jet (hard black polished lignite) is said to be in memory of a local coal-worker, Contolay, who helped St Francis of Assisi on his pilgrimage. Two jet-makers are still in business, although they now specialize in jewellery and works of art: **Regueira**, at Azabachería 9, and **Mayer**, Platerías 6. In the Middle Ages, the square was the favourite rendezvous for French pilgrims.

Another attraction in Praza de la Azabachería was the chance for destitute pilgrims to hang their rags on an **iron cross**, the *crus d'os farrapos*, and pick up new clothes from the Benedictines around the corner at **San Martín Pinario**. San Martín, one of the most venerable monastic institutions in the city, was founded in 912 as the special protector of the Apostle's tomb. In the 1400s, the two other Benedictine houses in Santiago joined San Martín to form an institution powerful enough to challenge the Inquisition. In spite of complaints that it would compete with the cathedral, they commissioned an elaborate top-heavy façade by Gabriel Casas in the 18th century; note on top the monks' vocation reflected in the statue of St Martin of Tours sharing his cloak with a poor man. Inside, the vast **Claustro de la Portería** with its elegant fountain was completed by Casas' more famous follower, Casas y Novoa, while just beyond is an extraordinary, floating 17th-century staircase with Aztec decorations under a Baroque dome. Beyond, the huge barrel-vaulted **church** is the stage for Casas y Novoa's *retablo mayor*, one of the most over-ripe pieces of flummery ever produced, a feverish blast of intricate gilded detail. Casas y Novoa was also responsible for the **Capilla del Socorro** on the right side of the nave, and the rather more restrained sacristy; the elaborate 17th-century choir stalls are also well worth a look. The stately, colonnaded 18th-century façade facing Praza San Martín grows like an altarpiece above a sunken Baroque staircase designed by a Dominican named Manuel de los Mártires, all granite ribbons squirming below the level of the pavement.

In Praza San Miguel (in front of Praza San Martín) the 14th-century Gothic Pazo de Don Pedro contains the **Museo das Peregrinacións**; opposite, **San Miguel dos Agros** is another product of Santiago's 18th-century boom. But for a real eyeful of local Baroque continue along to Rúa da Algalía de Arriba and walk north to Rúa de San Roque, where the startling façade of **Santa Clara** by Simón Rodríguez almost jumps out at you, its fat, abstract volutes culminating in a trio of huge cylinders that look as if they could roll off the roof any second, altogether more 1930s in effect than 1730s.

Museo das Peregrinacións
www.mdperegrinacions.com; open Tues–Fri 10–8, Sat 10.30–1.30 and 5–8, Sun and hols 10.30–1.30; adm

Elsewhere in Santiago

Like any natural, organic medieval city, Santiago is a delight to wander in, its narrow, arcaded streets and intimate squares paved with granite flagstones, lined with old palaces, churches, and monasteries, tinged with green and gold from moss and lichens.

The founders of the two great mendicant orders of the 13th century both made pilgrimages and personally founded monasteries. In 1214, St Francis founded the **Convento de San Francisco**, in Rúa Campiño de San Francisco, northeast of the Hospital de los Reyes Católicos; the Benedictines were impressed enough with Francis' preaching to give him the land, in return for an annual basket of fish. Rebuilt in the 18th century, the convent has a fine granite cross sculpted by Caaveiro with scenes of Francis' life. St Dominic's rather larger **Convento de Santo Domingo de Bonaval**, founded during his pilgrimage in 1220, is due east on the Puerto del

Camino at the end of Rúa das Casas Reais. Behind the Baroque façade hides a handsome Gothic church from the 1300s and the Chapel of the Pantheon of Illustrious Gallegos, last resting-place of poet Rosalía de Castro and the caricaturist Castelao (d. 1950), the Goya of the Civil War. The convent and cloister house the **Museo do Pobo Galego** with a collection of folk items and rural tools, though most memorable of all is the triple spiral staircase, a stunning architectural *tour de force* by Domingo de Andrade, where three different, unsupported granite stairways interlace almost as if by magic in a single tower, each leading to different doors.

Museo do Pobo Galego
open Tues–Sat 10–2 and 4–8, Sun 11–2

Off the Azabachería, Rúa de Troya is named after the venerable **Casa-Museo da Troia**, base for the local *tunas*, not fish but bands of student minstrels in capes and ribbons, who play Galician-Celtic music around the Praza da Immaculada. The Azabachería leads into Praza Cervantes and a street called Preguntoiro ('Questioning') after all the pilgrims who asked for directions here. This curves around to arcaded Rúa Nova, site of the little church of **Santa María Salomé** with a Romanesque door under a Gothic arcade. Parallel extends **Rúa do Vilar**, Santiago's delightful, arcaded main shopping street, where the **Casa do Dean** has a fine Baroque portal; at the Confitería Mora (No.60), pick up a delicious *tarta de Compostela*, made with chocolate bumps in honour of the Santo dos Croques.

Casa-Museo da Troia
open Easter–end-Sept Tues–Sat 11–2 and 4–8, Sun 11–2; adm

For the classic view of Santiago's towers and roofs, walk along the **Paseo da Ferradura** just east of the cathedral, a leafy 19th-century park where old men will take your photo with cameras nearly as old as themselves.

Santa María del Sar

After all the Baroque in the centre of Santiago, take a break at the Romanesque 12th-century Santa María del Sar, a mile south of the Convento de las Mercedarias, another stately Baroque confection. Set alone in its meadow, Santa María is an architectural jewel with a different slant – literally. The piers and arches along the high barrel-vaulted nave have leant backwards from time immemorial; although the common explanation for it is subsidence, it may have been done intentionally – like the campanile of Pisa or the leaning towers of Bologna, along with other pieces of crooked bravura of the same period. The buttresses were added after the Lisbon earthquake of 1755. Don't miss the remarkable carvings by Master Mateo along one gallery in the **cloister**.

Santa María del Mar cloister
open Mon–Sat 10–1 and 4–7, Sun 10–1

ⓘ Santiago de Compostela >
Municipal: Rúa de Vilar 63, t 98 155 51 29, www.santiago turismo.com

Tourist Information in Santiago de Compostela

Walking tours in Spanish (daily) and English (three times a week in summer) can be booked at the municipal tourist office (€8 per person). They offer a wide range of activities, from city audio guides to hop-on hop-off tourist bus tickets. Full info at **Santiago Reservas**, t 902 19 01 60, *www.santiagoreservas.com*.

ⓘ **Santiago de Compostela** >
Provincial: *Rúa de Vilar 43*, **t** *98 158 40 81*, *www.turgalicia.es*

Pilgrim Information Centre: *Rúa de Vilar 30–32*, **t** *98 157 20 04*, *www.archicompostela. org*

⭐ **Costa Vella** >>

⭐ **Palacio del Carmen** >

The **post office** is on Travesía de Fonseca, near the Praza do Obradoiro; a good central *ciber* is **Cyber Nova 50**, Rúa Nova 50.

There is a **market** from Monday to Saturday in the covered market in Praza de San Félix.

Where to Stay in Santiago de Compostela

Santiago ✉ 15705

Finding a place to stay at any price is easy; even during the high holy day of 25 July you may be met at the bus or train station by landladies luring you to their *hostales* or *casas particulares* for around €15 a head.

*****Hs de Los Reyes Católicos, Praza del Obradoiro, **t** 98 158 22 00, *santiago@parador.es* (€€€€€). Poor pilgrims used to stay in this magnificent 15th-century building, but since 1954 it has been the luxurious *nec plus ultra* of Spanish *hostales* and one of Europe's best hotels. Most rooms look onto one of four shady patios and the bridal suites have been enjoyed by VIPs from Franco on up – but it's probably the priciest *parador* in Spain.

*****Palacio del Carmen, Oblatas s/n, **t** 98 155 24 44, *www.ac-hotels.com* (€€€€). A much-restored convent outside the centre, but with every amenity including a heated pool, fine restaurant and gardens.

****Hesperia Compostela, Hórreo 1, **t** 98 158 57 00, *www.hesperia-compostela.com* (€€€€). A grand old granite hotel with a touch of class and all the comforts.

***Rua Villar, Rúa do Villar 8–10, **t** 98 151 98 58, *www.hotelruavillar.com* (€€€). A new hotel in an ancient building; the stone walls and wooden beams ooze charm, while the contemporary art and designer gadgets add pizzazz. Smaller rooms are moderate.

***Virxe da Cerca, Rúa Virxe da Cerca 27, **t** 90 240 58 58, *www.pousadasde compostela.com* (€€€). Stylish serenity and beautiful gardens in an 18th-century Jesuit residence. The extension is slightly cheaper.

Hotel Airas Nunes, Rúa do Vilar 17, **t 90 240 58 58 (€€€). An elegant *pousada* in an early 18th-century building. The interior is fabulous, all honey-coloured stone with warm fabrics and finishing touches.

Hotel Sino, Algalia de Abaixo 5, **t 98 155 44 36, *www.sino-compostela.com* (€€€). The historic buildings have been nicely restored. Gourmet restaurant.

*As Artes, Trav. de Dos Puertas 2, **t** 98 155 52 54, *www.asartes.com* (€€€). A charming old stone house, with seven individually decorated rooms. It's next to the *parador*, a stone's throw from the cathedral, and extras include a massage room and tiny sauna.

Hotel San Clemente, Rúa San Clemente 28, **t 90 240 58 58 (€€€–€€). Another listed building with original stone and polished wood interior. Parking is available next door.

Hotel Rosa Rosae, Calle la Rosa, 7, **t** 98 152 83 00, *www.rosarosae.com* (€€). A new, stylish place with friendly service. Close to the airport bus.

Costa Vella, Rúa Porta da Peña 17, **t 98 158 36 37, *www.costavella.com* (€€). A beautiful, very peaceful place, located on a traffic-free street above the Convento de San Francisco. It's worth paying more for a sunny room overlooking the city; part of Santiago's old walls can be seen in the lovely garden. Their glossy new sister hotel, **Altair** (€€€), is nearby, with chic urban décor, wifi and café-bar.

Libredón Hostal, Praza de Fonseca 5, **t 98 157 65 20 (€€), *www.libredon barbantes.com*. Good views of the square and *palacio* from sparkling pine and white rooms.

Hs Mapoula, Entremurallas 10, **t 98 158 01 24, *www.mapoula.com* (€). Just inside the *casco viejo*, this *hostal* has nice airy rooms with baths.

Hs Suso, Rúa del Vilar 65, **t 98 158 66 11 (€). Located on Santiago's prettiest street, this pilgrims' favourite is run by a jovial fellow who knows everything and probably has something to do with the tasty tapas in the excellent bar downstairs.

*Pension Moure, Laureles 6, **t** 98 158 38 67 (€). Perfectly located, this peaceful *pensión* offers functional rooms with or without bath; those with private terraces enjoy wonderful views across the city.

*Hotel Oca Avenida, Fonte de San Antonio 5, t 98 157 80 07 (€). Provides character and comfort, with polished wooden floors in a restored 18th-century house.

*Hs La Estela, Raxoi 1 (by cathedral), t 98 158 27 96, hostelestella@yahoo.es (€). A friendly, charming hostal, with a lovely patina of age.

*Pensión da Estrela, Praza San Martín Pinario 5, t 98 157 69 24, www.pensiondaestrela.com (€). A simple, immaculate pensión: book early for a room with views over the old city.

Eating Out in Santiago de Compostela

Eating in Santiago is a pleasure – competition is keen and the food has to be good to succeed. Rúa do Hórreo has the biggest concentration of restaurants – one window of tempting seafood after another.

Casa Roberto, San Xulián de Sales 17, t 98 151 17 69 (€€€). For a special treat, drive out 8km to Vedra in the Valle de Ulla, where Roberto prepares some of the most delicious, imaginative dishes in all Galicia in a lovely country villa. Closed Sun eve and first 2 wks Aug.

Tacita d'Juan, Rúa Hórreo 31, t 98 156 32 55 (€€€). Offers nouvelle cuisine made from fresh Galician ingredients. Closed Sun and 3 wks Aug.

Don Gaiferos, Rúa Nova 23, t 98 158 38 94 (€€€–€€). For tradition mixed with international, seasonal dishes, try this beautiful vaulted dining room. Closed eves Sun and Mon, except in summer, closed fortnight Jan.

Toñi Vicente, Rúa Rosalía de Castro 24, t 98 159 41 00 (€€€–€€). Toñi Vicente's breathtakingly original take on Gallego cuisine has picked up awards and accolades from all quarters of the cookery world. Try the lubina braseada en fondo de buey (grilled sea bass on a bed of ox), or the delicious mango ravioli. Closed Sun, 2nd weekend in Sept and in mid-Dec–early Jan.

Casa Marcelo, Rúa Hortas 1, t 98 155 85 80, www.casamarcelo.net (€€€–€€). An utterly charming restaurant on a pretty old street, serving exquisite cuisine from the hand of master chef Marcelo Tejedor. There are no menus:

the daily offerings vary according to what's in season and Tejedor's remarkable imagination. The menú de degustación is a very reasonable €33. Closed Sun–Tues.

Moncho Vilas, Avda de Villagarcía 21 (on the outskirts), t 98 159 83 87, www.monchovilas.com (€€). One of the classic eateries where an informal tapas bar serves delicious seafood and empanadas, while a dining room upstairs produces simple fresh food. Closed Sun eves and Mon.

Vilas, Rosalía de Castro 88, t 98 159 21 70 (€€; menu €18). Another brother runs this even better bastion of Gallego cuisine in a turn-of-the-20th-century house. Closed Sat eve and Sun.

Don Quijote, Rúa Galeras, 20, t 98 158 68 59, www.quijoterestaurante.com (€€). If you ever tire of Gallego cuisine, come here to sample some traditional Castilian staples like cochinillo at this well-established restaurant.

San Nicolás, Rúa Sar 1, t 98 157 07 92 (€€). A chic restaurant in an old converted factory, serving creative Gallego cuisine at reasonable prices.

Mejillonería Belgo, Rúa Travesa 22, t 98 158 72 35 (€). A big local favourite, serving Galician mussels from the owners' own mussel farm.

Casa Manolo, Rúa San Bieto, t 98 158 29 50 (€; menu €7). Roomy restaurant, where a colossal menu drags in the crowds every lunchtime and evening.

Bars and Nightlife in Santiago de Compostela

The area around Rúa Franco is the focus of the evening marcha.

Bodeguilla de San Roque, San Roque 3 (near Santa Clara). Serves good wine with plates of delicious tetilla cheese and ham, and home-made croquetas.

La Borriquita de Belém, San Paio. For jazz with your drinks, try this place, which is not far from the cathedral.

Café Casino, Rúa do Villar 35. This 150-year-old café provides sink-into sofas and armchairs, piles of newspapers and a vast sitting-room space for drinking coffees and cocktails.

Café Jacobus, Rúa Azevacheria 5. Claims the widest selection of exotic coffees, infusions, and sinful chocolate concoctions. One of a chain of three.

Café Literarios, Praza Quintana 1. With a perfect terrace at the top of the steps of this lovely square.

Casa das Crechas, Via Sacra 3, t 98 156 07 51. Live music and other happenings can be taken in here. When you can't eat or drink any more, you can dance it off.

Pub Modus Vivendi, 98 Praza Feixoo. One of the veterans in the Old Quarter's circuit that, faithful to its 1970 roots, likes to play funk and soul music. Occasional live music.

Dado Dada, Alfredo Brañas 19, t 98 159 15 74. Santiago's classic jazz joint, with occasional live gigs.

El Franco, Rúa Franco 28, t 98 158 12 34. A typical place to start the evening's revelry with your first *aperitivo*. Cheap Gallego favourites on the menu too.

Garigolo Café-Teatro, Praza Algalia de Arriba 1. All kinds of performances – film screenings, cabaret, theatre, etc. – take place in this relaxed gay-friendly café.

Liberty, Alfredo Brañas 6. A popular place with plenty of action.

Metate, Colexón de San Paio. If you are an *aficionado* of chocolate, don't miss the hot chocolate and chocolate cocktails at this former factory.

Tupperware Lounge Café, Frai Rosendo Salvado 28. A hip hang-out, with tongue-in-cheek retro décor.

Back to the *Rías*: Golfo Ártabro

Two of Galicia's most important ports, Ferrol and A Coruña, occupy either end of the 20km Golfo Ártabro, savagely bitten out of the northwest coast, with four teeth marking the four estuaries that flow into it. You can get there by dawdling west along the Rías Altas (*see* p.306) or by racing up the A9 motorway from Santiago.

Ferrol and Pontedeume

Plump on the big fat Ría de Betanzos, swollen by four rivers, the salty city of **Ferrol** was named after its lighthouse (*faro*) and counts some 80,000 souls, many of whom work for or depend on the Spanish navy. Gently, slowly, the port city has dropped the article 'El' from the front of its name and the 'del Caudillo' stuck on the back in honour of Francisco Franco, born here in 1892, son of a naval supply officer, who grew up to be the youngest general in Spanish history before his career as dictator, never losing his Gallego roots in his maddening stubbornness and inscrutability – earning himself the nickname 'the Sphinx without a secret'. Besides the enormous docks, navy yards and sailors' red-light gauntlet, Ferrol has a pretty enough medieval core, a large planned 18th-century geometric, neoclassical quarter, the legacy of Philip V who greatly boosted Ferrol's fortunes, and a modern quarter that looks like SimCity. The best thing is to just wander among the pretty houses with 'crystal galleries' and the casino and gardens. A pair of castles on the slender waist of the *ría* defend the naval base.

At the bottom of the estuary, 5km from Ferrol, **San Martín de Xubia** was founded as a monastery in the 9th century. It was the only one in Galicia adopted by Cluny (1113), but all that survives is the Cluniac church with its three apses and carved capitals.

Getting around the Golfo Ártabro

By Air

A Coruña's **airport** is 9km away at Alvedro, **t** 90 240 47 04, *www.aena.es*, with connections to Madrid, Barcelona and Seville. There's an airport bus to the main bus station (departures are timed to meet flights).

By Boat

Three boats daily ply the *ría* between Ferrol and A Coruña, arriving next to A Coruña's tourist office; from the same spot, summer-only launches go to Praia de Santa Cristina.

By Train

RENFE connects Ferrol and A Coruña with Pontedeume and the main junctions at Betanzos, Santiago, Lugo, Vigo, Padrón and Villagarcía de Arousa. In A Coruña the San Cristóbal station is a bit out of the way on Avda Joaquín Planelles, **t** 98 118 72 59 – best to take bus no.1 from the nearby bus station to the historic centre. There's also a RENFE travel office on Fontán 3, **t** 90 224 02 02.

In Ferrol, RENFE and FEVE share the same station, **t** 98 137 04 01.

A new **tourist train** was rolled out in the summer of 2007 from Ferrol to Cape Ortegal, carrying a total of 54 passengers, and only running in July and Aug. The trip can be taken either for the day (Sat) or the whole weekend. Price €39 (Sat), €98 (Sat and Sun). For tickets and more info, call Viajes PacoTel, **t** 98 136 9040, *eanca@viajespaco.com*, or Estación de Ferrol de FEVE, **t** 98 173 04 01, *amedina@feve.es*.

By Bus

A Coruña's bus station is on C/ Caballeros, **t** 98 118 43 35 (near the RENFE station), with connections to the Costa da Morte and all major points in Galicia; ALSA provide services to Madrid, León, and the Basque country. Ferrol's buses depart from next to the train station, **t** 98 132 47 51, and go to Betanzos, Viveiro, Foz, Ribadeo and Lugo.

South of Ferrol, the charming medieval town of **Pontedeume** was once the preserve of the Counts of Andrade, who built and collected the tolls from their great bridge over the Ría Eume, once supported by 58 arches; some 15 arches still remain, as well as a 14th-century palace and tower emblazoned with the family's huge crest. The tolls financed the Andrades' hunts; note the weathered stone boars standing guard by the bridge. The parish church, the late-Gothic Santiago, is a trove of minor art. There are a couple of **beaches** along the *ría* (the **Praia Perbes** is a good one) and, off the NVI to Betanzos, **San Miguel de Breamo** (1137), with its façade pierced by a window in the shape of an 11-point star and capitals to warm the cockles of any Romanesque diehard's heart.

If you have a car, two ruined monasteries beckon inland from Pontedeume, as much for their architecture as for their lovely settings. Up the Eume river, the Benedictine **Monasterio de Caaveiro** was founded in 934 by San Rosendo, who became a bishop at 18 and defended Compostela from the Normans and Saracens. Although renowned as a stickler for the rules, Rosendo could hardly have founded Caaveiro in a more evocative place. Twenty kilometres south of Pontedeume, the 12th-century Cistercian **Monasterio de Monfero** with its two cloisters is equally derelict, even if more recently rebuilt in the 17th century, unabashedly grandiose for its remote setting; only the church, with a chequerboard façade of granite and slate blocks, is still in use.

Betanzos

Betanzos

Rising steeply over the head of yet another small estuary, lovely Betanzos is a far more ancient place, a Celtic village that grew into the Roman port of Brigantium Flavium. It thrived into the 18th century, when the Mandeo and Mendo rivers washed in so much silt that they stole Betanzos' sea coast. Progress stopped, leaving a time capsule: houses and mansions of all sizes with wrought-iron balconies, or *solanas*, line the narrow lanes that wind up the hill from the harbour's medieval gates. Life revolves around the charming, monumental **Praza de García Hermanos**, its central ornament a statue of two Indianos and a replica of Versailles' Fountain of Diana. Most of the surrounding buildings are from the 18th century, including a neoclassical palace now used as the National Archives of Galicia; this runs a small but interesting historical **Museo das Mariñas**. The town's three attractive churches are just off the square: the 14th-century **Santa María del Azogue**; 15th-century **Santiago**, with a figure of Santiago Matamoros on the tympanum; and Gothic **San Francisco**, inspired by the basilica at Assisi and its door topped with a bizarre figure of a boar with a cross rising out of its back. Inside, don't miss the delightful 14th-century tomb of Fernán Pérez de Andrade O Boo (the Good), who paid for the church and whose sarcophagus, supported on the backs of a boar and a bear, is covered with hunting scenes, perhaps in the hope that there'd be plenty of game in heaven. Take time to walk along the Ría Mandeo, one of Galicia's prettiest *rías*.

Rather than take the NVI or the AP9/E1 motorway directly to A Coruña, follow the pretty scenery along the Ría de Betanzos up to the local resort of **Sada**, to see its boardwalk and **La Terraza**, the finest Modernista building in Galicia, designed by López Hernández, a curious pavilion made of glass and giant music stands. The road to A Coruña passes the **Pazo de Meirás**, residence of Galicia's greatest novelist, Countess Emilia Pardo Bazán, and later Franco, whose descendants still own it; further along, offshore on a wooded islet, the 17th-century **Castillo de Santa Cruz** once defended A Coruña.

Museo das Mariñas
open Mon–Fri 10–2 and 4–7, Sat 10.20–1; adm

A Coruña

 A Coruña

Occupying the length of the Ría da Coruña and the southwest fringe of the Golfo Ártabro, A Coruña is the liveliest city in Galicia, a big (pop. 243,000), exuberant, commercial capital with character to spare. Sprawling over a peninsula and attached to the mainland by a thin neck of land, it has windswept beaches facing the Atlantic and a magnificent sheltered harbour in the estuary that has made its fortune and paid for all of its hypnotic wall of windowed balconies or *solanas* that gave A Coruña its nickname, 'Crystal City'.

Philip II and the Invincible Armada

The pious royal bureaucrat Philip II had more than one bone to pick with Queen Elizabeth's England in the 1580s: Elizabeth had recently invented the Bloody Mary by lopping off the head of Mary Queen of Scots, Philip's favourite candidate for the English throne, and England was helping the Protestants of the Netherlands in their revolt against Spain; Spanish trade routes were threatened but, worst of all, Elizabeth had confirmed the country's Protestant orientation. To solve all his problems and force England back into the Catholic fold, Philip decided on what seemed to be a foolproof plan: to build up the biggest fleet of warships in Spanish history, and co-ordinate this invincible armada with an invasion of England by his army in the Netherlands. Francis Drake got wind of Philip's plans and in 1587 sailed into Cádiz 'to singe the king's beard' by burning the parked fleet and setting the invasion date back by a year. Finally, on 22 July 1588, an Armada of 130 enormous galleons, manned by 10,000 sailors and 19,000 soldiers, set sail from A Coruña.

After some difficult sea battles, England's first stroke of luck came when the Armada set anchor near Calais, where it was to meet with the invasion fleet from the Netherlands. Lord Howard sent fireships against the Armada, which panicked the Spaniards into breaking up their formation; soon after, on 8 August, in a battle that raged along the Channel, the quick English defeated the lumbering Armada at Gravelines. When the Spaniards tried to sail home to regroup, the English forced them home the long way around Scotland, where storms wreaked havoc; by the time the Invincible Armada limped back to Spain, only 76 half-wrecked galleons pulled into port, minus 15,000 soldiers. Although the war between England and Spain dragged on until 1604, the repercussions of the defeat of the Armada endured for centuries. Philip's treasury was empty, but in cocky Elizabethan England the party had just begun.

A Coruña's relationship with Britain goes back to its first settlers, Phoenician merchants who imported tin from Cornwall. The Romans called it Ardobicum Corunium, and tenuously associated it with Hercules, who performed one of his Twelve Labours (stealing the cattle of Geryon) in Cádiz on the other side of Spain and reputedly had a hand in building the lighthouse. The Suevians and the Moors took turns running the show until 1002; in the Middle Ages, English pilgrims to Santiago often landed here, among them Chaucer's Wife of Bath and his patron John of Gaunt. Some 200 years later it was Spain's turn to invade England; see box, above.

In the 'Groyne'

The classic view of A Coruña is of its harbour along Avenida de la Marina, lined with a solid wall of crystal galleries set in white balconies, a window cleaner's vision of hell. It is magical to sail into, just as Drake fearlessly did in 1589, swooping down in the night with 30 ships to rub salt in Philip's wounds. Only a young girl named María Pita stood in the way, not only raising the alarm to save the city but somehow swiping Drake's flag in the process. In gratitude A Coruña gave her name to its biggest, busiest square, Praza María Pita, where the bars under its porticoes stay packed until the wee hours of the morning. One side is taken up with the city hall, the eclectic Modernista **Palacio Municipal** (1907) by Pedro Mariño, decorated with symbols of A Coruña.

The older part of A Coruña – what old British seadogs called 'the Groyne' – begins at Praza María Pita, a labyrinth of winding streets

**Casa Museo
de Emilia
Pardo-Bazán**
*open Mon–Fri 10–2
and 4–7; closed Aug*

squeezed around a hill. Near the harbour at Rúa Tabernas 13, Countess Emilia Pardo Bazán was born in 1851; the mansion now houses the **Casa Museo de Emilia Pardo-Bazán**, a small museum dedicated to the novelist.

Nearby Rúa Santiago leads into little Praza A Fariña (or de Azcárraga), its bright flowerbeds covering the spot where gallows once stood. For pilgrims who sailed into A Coruña, the over-restored 12th-century Romanesque church of **Santiago** was their first stop; one door has a carving of Santiago Matamoros at Clavijo, another the Lamb of God; its 16th-century tower once defended the city from English pirates. The **Colegiata de Santa María del Campo**, begun in the 1210s and finished in the 1400s, stands at the top of the square. Its sculptors were star-struck: star decorations run along the roof and on the west façade; the triple portal has a carving of the Three Magi. Over the north door two angels stand by as someone seems to fall out of the sky with star symbols, or perhaps Ezekiel's wheel of fire, whirling up in the cosmos. Inside are some fine Romanesque tombs, polychrome statues and, just to the left of the altar, another star, carved on a capital.

Just down from here, the little Plazuela de Santa Bárbara is A Coruña's most charming, site of the **Convento de Santa Barbara** (1613), where cloistered Poor Clares live behind the portal. Behind this, the **Convento de Santo Domingo** has two excellent Baroque chapels from the 17th century, especially the Capilla de la Virgen del Rosario, sheltering the city's patroness.

Santo Domingo stands on the edge of the evocative little **Jardín de San Carlos**, set in the walls of the old fortress of San Carlos. It contains the granite tomb of Sir John Moore, who in 1809 led the routed, dispirited British army across Galicia with the French on his tail. At Elviña, just before A Coruña, he sent most of his troops ahead to board ships for home, just as Marshal Soult launched into a vicious attack; Moore managed to stall the French long enough for 15,000 of his men to embark under Soult's nose, an operation that has been called a precursor to Dunkirk. Casualties were high on both sides (Moore died pierced by a cannonball) and the British lost at Elviña, only to return under the Duke of Wellington.

Museo Militar
*open Mon–Sat 10–2
and 4–7, Sun and hols
10–2; adm*

Torre de Hércules
*open July and Aug
10–8.45; April–May
and June–Sept daily
10–6.45; Oct–Mar
daily 10–5.45; adm*

Just opposite, A Coruña's busy military history is remembered in the **Museo Militar** in the old church of San Francisco. From here, bus no.3 will take you out 2km to the northernmost tip of the peninsula and the 431ft **Torre de Hércules**, A Coruña's proudest symbol. Built in the 2nd century AD in the time of Trajan, it's the oldest continuous working Roman lighthouse, but with an external skin from 1791. Bring a pep pill: you'll have to climb the 242 steps to the top for the splendid view of the city and ocean. Within walking distance from the Jardín de San Carlos, the Paseo do Parrote leads out to **Castillo de San Antón**, last rebuilt in 1779. It now defends

Museo Arqueológico
open July–Aug Tues–Sat 10–9, Sun and hols 10–3; Sept–June Tues–Sat 10–7.30, Sun and hols 10–2.30; adm

Museo de Bellas Artes
open Tues–Fri 10–8, Sat 10–2 and 4.30–8, Sun 10–2; adm

Casa de las Ciencias
www.casaciencias.org; open July and Aug daily 1–9; Sept–June daily 10–7; adm, combined adm with Aquárium and Domus available

Domus
open summer daily 11–9, winter daily 10–7

Aquárium
www.casaciencias.org; open daily 10–9; adm with Domus and Casa de las Ciencias available

artefacts from the Iron Age, the Celtic *castros*, Romans, and Middle Ages in the **Museo Arqueológico**.

In the newer part of A Coruña (beyond Praza de María Pita) the ex-Maritime Consulate in Praza do Pintor Sotomayor (off the Rúa Panaderas) houses the **Museo de Bellas Artes**, with a collection of European paintings, sculptures, ceramics and coins dating from the 17th century. Near the **Mercado San Agustín**, the old Praza dos Ovos has been converted into a charmingly goofy square devoted to comedians. A completely different atmosphere reigns in spooky Praza de España a block up from the market, with its soldiers and monument to José Millán Astray, the one-armed, one-eyed psychopath who led the Spanish Foreign Legion and taught his troops to cry *'¡Viva la Muerte!'* in the Civil War. The **Casa de las Ciencias** in Parque de Santa Margarita has a planetarium and museum dedicated to the world of science, technology and nature. On the other side of the isthmus lie A Coruña's beaches: the **Praias de Ríazor** and **Orzán** fill up in summer and are backed the Paseo Marítimo. Heading up towards the headland, is the ultra-modern **Domus**, or **Museum of Man**, designed by Arata Isozaki to look like an upturned boat and dedicated to the human body. A little further up, just below the Torre de Hércules, is the immensely entertaining **Aquárium**, with a vast subterranean tank of wheeling fish, a pool with six friendly seals, and an Octopus Garden.

If the summertime crush along the city beaches is unappealing, there are quieter, cleaner and prettier strands are outside the city at **Santa Cristina**, **Bastiagueiro**, **Santa Cruz**, **Mera** and **Lorbe** (this last is the farthest from town, 16km away).

Markets on the Golfo Ártabro

(★) **Casa do Castelo de Andrade >>**

Pontedeume: Sat.
Betanzos: Tues, Thurs and Sat.
A Coruña: Mon–Fri (Mercado San Agustín).

Where to Stay and Eat on the Golfo Ártabro

(ⓘ) **Ferrol >**
Praza Camilo José Cela, t 98 131 11 79, www.ferrol-concello.es

(★) **Pazo Libunca >**

Ferrol ✉ 15400
****Pazo Libunca**, Lugar de Castro, Castro (10km from Ferrol), t 98 138 35 40, www.libunca.com (€€€). A small, romantic hotel in a sumptuous Modernista villa surrounded by gardens. Excellent restaurant (€€€).
***Parador do Ferrol**, Almirante Fernández Martín, t 98 135 67 20,

ferrol@parador.es (€€€). The ageing, nautically decorated rooms have handsome views over the *ría*.
Casa do Castelo de Andrade, Lugar do Castelo de Andrade s/n, 7km from Pontedeume, t 98 143 38 39, *www. casteloandrade.com* (€€€). Handsome stone mansion, with just ten elegant, individually decorated rooms (some with Jacuzzi) and a pretty garden.
***Pazo da Merced**, Camiño da Merced, Neda, t 98 138 22 00 (€€€–€€). If you're driving, this is a pretty little place to stay, a 17th- and 18th-century manor with *ría* views and a pool. *Closed Oct–Easter week.*
***Hotel Suizo**, Dolores 17, t 98 130 04 00, *www.hotelsuizo.net* (€€€–€€). In a Modernista building with a café.
O'Parrulo, Avda Catabois 401, t 98 131 86 53 (€€). A classic, serving delicious local seafood like grilled clams from

Pontedeume

Avda do Torreón 2,
t *98 143 02 70*

the *ría*, along with succulent meats. There's a garden in summer, and a good wine selection. *Closed Wed eve, Sun, first 2 wks Aug, second 2 wks Dec.*

Casa Rivera, Galiano 57, **t** 98 135 07 59 (€). A popular local favourite, with traditional dishes like *caldeirada de pescados* (a sturdy fish stew) and a great-value lunch *menú. Closed Sun.*

Pataquiña, Dolores 35, **t** 98 135 23 11 (€). Offers heaps of good, well-prepared Gallego specialities; try their *salsa Pataquiña,* a delectable mixture of shrimp and crab in brandy and garlic.

Sur, C/ Magdalena 50, **t** 98 135 08 70 (€). Traditional bar with great tapas and good wine.

Betanzos ✉ 15300

*Los Ángeles, Los Ángeles 11, **t** 98 177 15 11 (€€–€). Modest but well-equipped rooms, an excellent local restaurant downstairs and private parking.

La Casilla, Ctra de Castilla 90, **t** 98 177 01 61 (€€). Packs out, especially at weekends, with crowds enjoying the famous local tortilla. *Closed Sun eve, Mon (except July–Aug), 3 wks in Nov.*

Casanova, Pza García Hermanos 15, **t** 98 177 06 03 (€€). Rustically romantic; serves tasty salmon and lamprey dishes for the bold upstairs, with a lively tapas bar downstairs.

A Coruña >

Municipal: Rua Sol,
t *98 118 43 44, www. turismocoruna.com*

Regional: Avda de la Marina s/n, **t** *98 122 18 22, www.turgalicia.es*

A Coruña ✉ 15000

A Coruña fills up in the summer. The bar area around Rúa Franja and Praza María Pita goes on well into dawn when the fishing fleet pulls in and everyone watches the Muro, the auctioning of the catch. There are dozens of atmospheric cafés, *mesones,* and tapas bars on and around Rúa La Franja, heading off Praza María Pita.

*****Finisterre, Pso del Parrote 2, **t** 98 120 54 00, *www.hesperia-hotels.com* (€€€€€). The best-located and most luxurious hotel in A Coruña, overlooking the sea, with pools, tennis courts, a nursery, playground and a health and wellness centre.

***Riazor, Avda Pedro Barrié de la Maza 29, **t** 98 125 34 00, *www.riazor hotel.com* (€€€). A pleasant, less costly alternative, with a fine beachside location and modern rooms.

Sol, Sol 10, **t 98 121 00 19, *www. hostalsolcoruna.com* (€€€–€€).

Pleasant, welcoming *hostal* despite the disconcerting flashing sign.

Hotel Maycar, C/ San Andrés 159, **t 98 122 60 00, *www.hotelmaycar.com* (€€). This modern hotel is centrally located and offers excellent value for money. Parking available.

El Pescador, Avda Che Guevara 81c (Ctra Santa Cruz), **t 98 163 95 02, *www.hotelelpescadorgalicia.com* (€€). A pebble's throw from the sandy beach of Santa Cristina.

*Hs Centro Gallego, Rúa Estrella 2, **t** 98 122 22 36 (€€–€). One of the best budget options: central, welcoming and clean. All rooms with private bath.

Hs Alborán, Ruego de Agua 14, **t 98 122 25 62, *www.hostalalboran.com* (€). Near the main *praza* with adequate rooms, perhaps not as distinguished inside as they look from the outside.

*Hs Las Rias, San Andrés 141, **t** 98 122 68 79 (€). Functional and friendly, offering all the necessary facilities.

*Hs Palacio, Pza de Galicia 2, **t** 98 112 23 38, *www.hostalpalacio.com* (€). Clean and welcoming.

A La Brasa, Juan Flórez 38, **t** 98 127 07 27, *www.gasthof.es* (€€). True to its name, this place specializes in meat and fish sizzling from the grill; if there are two of you, order *punta trasera de ternera a la parrilla,* a huge dish of succulent steak with baked potatoes.

Coral, Callejón de la Estacada 9 (near the port), **t** 98 120 05 69 (€€). This is one of the best seafood places; exceptional, delicate shellfish dishes are served in a classy setting. *Closed Sun except mid-July–mid-Sept.*

Casa Pardo, Novoa Santos 15, **t** 98 128 00 21 (€€). Currently considered the best in town, this long-established place offers lovely seafood and grilled meats and is famous for monkfish dishes. It also has a stylish branch (where the son is chef) in the Domus, with wonderful views over the bay. *Closed Sun; 2nd fortnight June.*

La Penela, Praza María Pita 12, **t** 98 120 92 00 (€€). A reliable and popular place on the main square. *Closed Sun.*

Taberna Pil Pil, Pelamios 7, **t** 98 121 27 12 (€). A wonderful spot, with a well chosen wine list to accompany its tasty local dishes. Try the house speciality, *bacalao al pil-pil.*

West of A Coruña: A Costa da Morte

 Costa da Morte

Before tourism invented the Costa del Sol and the Costa Blanca, the Galicians dubbed this region down to Finisterre the 'Coast of Death' after its number of drownings, shipwrecks and ancient Celtic memories; from the end of the west, from the end of the Milky Way, Celtic warriors would sail out to their reward in the seven-towered castle of Arianhrod. The scenery along this wild land of the setting sun is romantic, the waves are dramatic and the beaches pale and inviting, but the water is icy cold.

Ría de Corme e Laxe

Heading west of A Coruña and Carballo, **Buño** is Galicia's traditional pottery town par excellence, manufacturing yellow and brown earthenware plates and crocks in the shape of pigs for as long as anyone can remember. The road north of Buño ends up at **Malpica**, where the granite cliffs west of A Coruña first relax their vigilance. A former whaling port, Malpica is partly sheltered by the windswept Sisargas islets, populated only by a large seabird nursery (*boteros*, marine taxis, will take you out for a small fee). Appropriately enough, the Costa da Morte has some fine dolmens, or Neolithic tombs, beginning with Malpica's **Pedra de Arca**. Malpica has a beach, pounded with surf, or you can head to the sheltered **Praia de Niñons**, passing by way of the romantic little ivy-shrouded castle known as the **Torres de Mens**, next to a tiny Romanesque chapel decorated with erotic figures.

Corme Porto, a picturesque fishing village to the west, has a reputation for being a law unto itself, a nest of resistance to Franco's *Guardia Civil* goons even into the 1950s, perhaps because they tried to get in the way of Corme's main industry: smuggling. Ask directions to the **Pedra da Serpe** at Gondomil, a snake carved in the stone believed to date from the Phoenicians and connected to the legend of St Adrian, the local St Patrick, who is said to have gathered all the snakes in Galicia here and given them a mighty kick into the ground, where they disappeared. It has a fine white beach and dunes and a more sheltered strand, the **Praia de Balarés** just before the medieval bridge to **Ponteceso**, birthplace of poet Eduardo Pondal (1835–1917). **Laxe**, a pleasant fishing village across the estuary from Corme, has a white beach, safe even for children; for something more remote, continue south along the coast past Pedreira to the enormous **Praia de Traba** (one of the worst affected beaches after the *Prestige* disaster, but now cleaned up). There's a 14th-century church dedicated to Santiago and two intriguing dolmens on the road to Bayo, 5km inland: signs point to the **Dolmen of Dombate**, with engravings of a ship inside on the right, and the **Pedra Cuberta**, another 1km south, with a 20ft chamber.

Getting around West of A Coruña

A Coruña and Santiago are the main bases for transport to the Costa da Morte, but **buses** are not very frequent. If you plan to visit more than one place in a day, study the bus schedules first. Carballo, 35km southwest of A Coruña, is the main bus junction for the coastal villages.

Ría de Camariñas

After some rugged coast, the rocks relent to admit another *ría* shared by the remote fishing hamlets of **Camariñas** and **Muxía**, both renowned for intricate bobbin lace (Camariñas has a little museum dedicated to the art). From small, white and increasingly trendy Camariñas you can walk 5km (3 miles) to **Cabo Villán** and its lighthouse, a wild piece of savage, torn coast, which makes you feel small and far away from civilization, although perhaps less so now that a set of experimental windmills have been erected to harness the wild winds that whip the cape. **Muxía** has always been a bit more important, as the proud escutcheons on the houses testify. It is also the holy city of the Costa da Morte, with its seaside sanctuary of **Nostra Señora de la Barca**, where the Virgin Mary herself is said to have sailed in a stone ship when Santiago was preaching in these parts (it wasn't her only Spanish holiday: she made a similar appearance riding a stone pillar in Zaragoza). Ship-shaped votive offerings dangle in the church. Parts of the Virgin's own magic boat may be seen around the church, including the hull, the Pedra de Abalar, which moves whenever someone free of sin stands on it. If you suffer from colic or gastritis, a walk under the stone keel, the Pedra dos Cadrises (the stone that looks like a stylized dinosaur) should fix you up nicely. Four kilometres from Muxía, in **Moraime**, the Benedictine church of **San Xián** (Julian) is mostly from the 12th century, but was founded in the 900s as a shelter for pilgrims; although humidity has destroyed most of the frescoes, 26 (again, two extra) Elders of the Apocalypse survive on the main portal. Inland, along the AC432, the 16th-century **Castillo de Vimianzo**, once home to the cruel Álvaro Pérez de Moscoso, has been restored to house a collection of paintings, photos and crafts.

Castillo de Vimianzo
open Tues–Sun 10–2 and 4–6.30

Ría de Corcubión and the End of the World

Further south, a byroad off the AC432 leads up to the lighthouse at **Cabo Touriñán**, where, as the plaque states, and notwith-standing Finisterre, you are standing on the westernmost point of continental Europe. Another branch of the road leads to the huge (and hugely exposed) beach, the **Praia do Rostro**, before continuing south to the little industrial port of **Cée**, defended by the 18th-century Castillo de Cardenal. Cée has practically merged with **Corcubión**, an old fishing village sprinkled with manor houses and *solanas*. The parish church has a curious statue of St Mark, brought from Venice by a ship that refused to budge until the saint was taken ashore. White beaches are sprinkled under the pines, among them **Praia Sardiñeiro** with a few bars and restaurants.

Finisterre (Fisterra)

Beyond lies the traditional westernmost point of Europe, the granite houses of Finisterre huddled on the rocks around the church of the miracle-working Christ of the Golden Beard, who came out of the sea. According to tradition, these same waters contain the city of Duyo (Dugium), which sank beneath the waves at the same time as Pompeii went under the lava; but sunken cities are a wide-ranging Celtic conceit, like Ys in Brittany, that hark back to the Hesperides, the Blessed Isles beyond the West.

Two kilometres beyond is **Cabo Finisterre** with its lighthouse, the World's End, where the Roman legions and pilgrims from Santiago came to gaze at the sun setting. Often at other times the cape is bleak and wrapped in fog, when it's easy to imagine wandering souls flitting along the savage coast before taking their last step into the Beyond. At the foot of the cape, pilgrims would visit the Romanesque church and the **Ara Solís**, evoking the mysteries of life, death and resurrection. For the best overviews, take the road up to **Vista Monte do Facho** where sterile women used to rub up against a menhir until an 18th-century bishop ordered it destroyed.

From **Cée**, the AC550 follows the coast around to **Ezaro**, a wild, picturesque place where massive granite boulders on **Mount Pindo** (1,968ft), 'the Celtic Olympus', have mysterious engravings and ruins of ancient shrines. Unable to erode an estuary of its own through the mountain, the Río Xallas instead tumbles down in a dozen shimmering waterfalls to the sea, polishing the multi-coloured stones as it flows over them. Some of its wild charm has been sacrificed to a hydroelectric plant, but a wander upstream reveals the tumbling Xallas in a more pristine state. South, beyond the cute granite port of **Pindo**, the dune-backed beach of **Carnota** is the longest in Galicia (it also holds a more gloomy record for drownings: even if you think you're a strong swimmer, beware). Carnota also claims Galicia's largest *hórreo*, about 100ft long and made entirely of granite. Although the surrounding valley is fertile, this 18th-century *hórreo* was moved here from elsewhere and extended to win the title, which doesn't seem quite fair.

Where to Stay and Eat West of A Coruña

The gastronomic prize of the the Death Coast is barnacles, or *percebes*, which cost a fortune; the people who gather them are washed away so often that they can't buy insurance.

(★) Hostal As Garzas >>

Malpica ✉ 15113

***Fonte de Fraile**, Praia de Canido s/n, t 98 172 07 32, *www.fontedofraile. com* (€€€–€€). A pretty seaside hotel on the beach, with Jacuzzi and café.

*Hostal As Garzas**, in Barizo, t 98 172 17 65 (€€–€). In a fine location, this also has a restaurant.

**Hs JB, Rueiro da Praia 3, by the beach, t 98 172 19 06 (€). Comfy, with a bar. *Open all year.*

*Hs Panchito, Pza Villar Amigo 6, t 98 172 03 07 (€). A good little *hostal* in the centre.

San Francisco, t 98 172 04 89 (€). Good for reasonable fresh seafood.

Camariñas ✉ 15123

4 Ventos, C/ Molino de Viento 71, t 98 173 60 64 (€€). Come here for confortable, basic rooms and a restaurant.

*Hs Scala, Paseo Marítimo 6, t 98 173 71 09 (€). On the seafront, with frilly rooms (some with terraces), and a friendly family.

Corcubión ✉ 15100

***Praia de Quenxe, Lg. Praia de Quenxe 43, Redonda, Corcubión, t 98 174 74 50 (€€), *www.hotelpraiaquenxe. es*. You couldn't be closer to the beach. With clean rooms and friendly service, this is a good deal at the price.

*HR Las Hortensias, Praia de Quenxe, t 98 174 64 68/61 25 (€€). A simple alternative on the beachfront.

Casa Lestón, Ctra Finisterre (at Sardiñeiro), t 98 174 35 99 (€€). Can't be beaten for fresh fish.

Finisterre/Fisterra ✉ 15155

**O Semáforo, Faro s/n, t 98 172 58 69 (€€€). The famous lighthouse at Cabo Finisterre is a delightful little hotel, where you can enjoy the spectacular sunsets.

**Insula Finesterrae, A Insula 76, t 98 171 22 11, *www.insulafinisterrae.com* (€€). Rusticity and contemporary style are combined in this charming hotel by the lighthouse. With pool.

*Finisterre, Federico Ávila 8, t 98 174 00 00, *www.finisterreae.com* (€). At the end of the world, this is a large, modern hotel. They also run the simple *hostal* opposite (€), with a good, lively restaurant.

*Hs Rivas, Ctra Faro, t 98 174 00 27 (€). Cheapest of all – but only just.

Pensión Casa Velay, C/ La Cerca 1, t 98 174 01 27 (€). Just off main square; good-value basic doubles with bath.

Tira do Cordel, Praia de San Roque s/n, t 98 174 06 97 (€€–€). Some of the best seafood on this stretch of coast, famous for *navajas a la plancha* (razor clams from the *ría*).

Los Tres Golpes, C/ Huertas 2, t 98 174 00 47 (€€–€). A good simple restaurant, serving excellent shellfish.

Into the Rías Baixas

The Lower Estuaries, or Rías Baixas/Bajas, almost at once have tamer, greener scenery than their wild cousins to the north; here the ocean is predictably warm enough to maintain a regular holiday trade. These less exposed, less continuously 'flushed' *rías* can, however, get a bit dirty if you swim in the innermost coves.

Muros to Vilagarcía

Ría de Muros e Noia

Under Monte Costiños on the north edge of the *ría*, **Muros** is a fine, old-fashioned granite town, with narrow, arcaded lanes, a market, and a fountain with a stone turtle, all stacked under its Gothic church. This contains a startling crucifix that was found in the sea, the Cristo de la Agonía, with long, flowing hair like that of his counterpart in Burgos; and a stone serpent coiled in the basin of the holy water stoup. There's a good beach at **Louro**, 'the golden', 1.6km from Muros on the tip of the cape. Inland, past Ponte-Outes,

Entines has the shrine of miracle-working San Campio. After
making the ritual walk round the crucifix (six times clockwise,
three times anti-clockwise) you can pay a visit to Campio, or so it
seems – the skeleton of an Christian martyr brought from Rome in
the 18th century by a bishop of Santiago has been lovingly covered
with wax and dressed in a centurion's costume and a garland so
that he looks as if he is sleeping.

To reach Noia, cross the medieval **Ponte Nafonso**, named after its
master builder who lies buried under the 14th-century cross at the
end, having laboured 30 years without seeing it completed. **Noia**
(or Noya) is full of legends, beginning with its name, after Noah,
whose dove is said to have found the olive branch here while his
ark came to rest on the holy Celtic mountain of Barbanza just
south. This local Mount Ararat is adorned with dolmens and in
Noia you can visit the mysterious cemetery next to the Gothic
Santa María a Nova (1327) where guildsmen between the 10th and
16th centuries left headstones carved with symbols more pagan
than Christian; some 200 have designs relating to the trades of the

Getting around from Muros to Vilagarcía

RENFE trains between A Coruña and Vigo pass through Padrón and Vilagarcía.
There are hourly **buses** (7am–9pm) from Santiago to Noia, from where connections can be made to Porto do Son and beyond. From Vilagarcía, buses leave for Isla de Arousa.

deceased. Others are a total enigma. Another church, the early 15th-century **San Martín**, has a good rose window carved into its fortress-like façade, and fine carvings on the portal; opposite, the **Pazo de Tapal** dates from the same period.

Often windy beaches and lagoons dot the coast of the *ría* south from Noia. The main village, **Porto do Son**, lies between the state-of-the-art defensive outpost of NATO atop Mount Iroite and its rather more picturesque Celtic equivalent at the **Castro de Baroña**, located on an outcrop over the sea. From **Oleiros** you can drive up to a pair of *miradors* (1,633ft) on the Montes Barbanza, for great views from Cabo Finisterre to Vigo on a clear day. Oleiros also has an exceptional dolmen, **Axeitos** – an enormous rock measuring nearly 172 sq ft, supported by eight smaller ones. At the tip of the headland, **Corrubedo** has a proud set of dunes, the highest in all Galicia, constantly sculpted by the wind.

Ría de Arousa to Pádron

The shore-hugging AC550 first runs into the Ría de Arousa, touristically the most developed of all Galicia's estuaries, although this hardly means anything remotely like Torremolinos or Benidorm. The first town you come to, **Santa Uxia** (or **Eugenia**) **de Ribeira** (often known simply as Ribeira), combines tourism with its status as Spain's top coastal and underwater fishing port. The remains of a Phoenician port are nearby at **Aguiño**, while further south the **Isla de Sálvora** is a haunt of mermaids; a 16th-century *hidalgo* married one, and gave birth to a dynasty named Mariños de Lobeira. Locally a whole science has evolved to distinguish mermaids in case of doubt: they have smooth soles on their feet and no belly buttons. The rest of this shore has quiet beaches.

At the head of the estuary, at the mouth of the blood-sucking lamprey-rich River Ulla, **Padrón** is the raggle-taggle capital of Galicia's favourite vegetable tapa, midget-green *pimientas de Padrón*, roasted in oil and salted and astonishingly tasty, although occasionally one packs the same wallop as a jalapeño. Padrón has plenty of legendary baggage to accompany its peppers: it is ancient Iria Flavia, the port where Santiago's disciples sailed with their precious cargo, anchoring their stone boat to a stone 'memorial pillar' (*pedrón*), now displayed under the altar in the 17th-century church of **Santiago**. The stone boat was met by a pagan queen, Lupa, who mockingly gave the Christians two wild bulls to transport the coffin. When yoked the bulls became peaceful oxen; astonished, Lupa converted at once and was baptized by St James himself, who popped out of his coffin in the ox cart to do the job. On the Carretera de Herbón on the fringes of town, the **Casa-Museo de Rosalía de Castro** was the home of Galicia's favourite poet Rosalía de Castro (1837–85), the illegitimate daughter of a priest, who unhappily married historian Manuel Murguía, had six children, wrote beautiful poetry in Gallego and died young of cancer. Another house nearby is covered from top to bottom in bleached scallop shells. The bridge over the Ulla to Puentecesures is attributed to Master Mateo.

Casa-Museo de Rosalía de Castro
open June–Sept Tues–Sat 10–2 and 4–8, Sun 10–1.30; Oct–May Tues–Sat 10–1.30 and 4–7, Sun 10–1.30; adm

Vilagarcía to Isla A Toxa

From Padrón the AC550 continues south past **Catoira** and the romantic remains of Alfonso V's Towers of the West, part of the front-line defences of Santiago against the Normans (and scene of the annual Fiesta Vikinga). The big town on the south bank is **Vilagarcía de Arousa**, the glossy base for Galicia's drug-smuggling barons. After a drink and a look at all the suspicious types in a fancypants café, perhaps the best thing to do is leave and drive up to the home of the pagan queen, **Castro Lupario**, atop **Monte Lobeira** (5km from Vilagarcía) for the extraordinary views, or visit the woodsy, sand-fringed **Isla de Arousa**, reputedly the chief drop-off point for Colombian cocaine in Europe.

All this nefarious underworld activity seems far away in charming **Cambados**, an atmospheric, noble town with plenty of old family crests and a lovely granite-paved square; note the

The Perfect Accompaniment to Fish

As if seafood-lovers didn't have enough to rave about in Galicia, the *rías* also supply Albariño, the ideal dry, fruity white wine to go with their heaving plates of *mariscos*. Cambados is the capital of Albariño, and the first Sunday of every August the lovely gardens of its *parador* hosts a wine festival.

Burgundian monks at the Cistercian monastery of Armenteira (*see* p.346) introduced Albariño vines in the 12th century and they thrived; if most other vineyards in dry hot Spain produce red wines, the humid Atlantic coast and sunnier sheltered slopes of the *rías* provide the ideal climate for aromatic whites. In 1988, the growing region DO Rías Baixas was given its demarcation status, divided into the subzones of O Rosal, Val do Salnés (around Cambados), Condado de Tea (which also produces some reds) and the Zona del Albariño. Like its cousin, Portuguese *vinho verde*, Albariño is ever so slightly sparkling, sending a gentle trail of bubbles to the top of your glass (for lots of suds, go for the Albariño del Palacio). Although usually best drunk as young as possible, Cambados' Albariño Fefiñanes is stored in oak barrels for a few months to give it more flavour. Other recommended Albariños are Lagar de Cervera, Castelo de Fornos (from Bodegas Chaves) and Martín Codax, from Valariño-Cambados. Nothing goes to waste: the stems, seeds, and other leftovers (*oruja*) are distilled into fiery *aguardiente*.

Galicia has two other demarcated wine regions: DO Ribeiro, the largest, is just west of Ourense, where production is dominated by the large Bodega Cooperativa do Ribeiro, producer of whites (light Viña Costeira, or the rare, celebrated Brandomín) and some reds; the newly popular Armandi and Telura reds come from Ribeiro's new Bodegas Lapatena. The third region, DO Valdeorras, is out east of Ourense and produces as many red wines as whites. The latter are of interest for their recent revival of the native godella grapes (Viña Guiran and Viña Abad are two leading labels). The best reds probably come from Bodegas Jesús Nazareno, with Valdoura its most reputed wine.

Italianate details on the balconies around the 17th-century Praza de Fefiñanes. The cemetery church, **Santa Mariña Dozo**, on Camino de la Pastora has carvings on its vault of the allegory of the man who ate his own excrement; if you know where that comes from, please drop us a line.

From Cambados, the AC550 circles down to the overblown family resort of **O Grove**, linked by a bridge to **Isla A Toxa** (de la Toja), a sand-rimmed, pine-clad islet that first became famous when a donkey left for dead was miraculously restored after a few days. Now adorned with a casino (one that Franco always turned a blind eye to), shell-coated church, spa, nouveau-riche estates, sports complex, nine-hole golf course and watched by security guards, A Toxa is designed for people with bags of money, leaving O Grove for those who don't, but know how to have a good time. There is also the excellent **Acquariumgalicia**.

Acquariumgalicia.
www.acquariumgalicia.
com; open April–Sept
daily 10–9; Oct–Mar
Fri–Sun and hols 10–8;
call for times on
other days; adm

An Excursion Inland: From Vilagarcía to the Manor of the Goose

From Vilagarcía, the N640 leads in 12km to the old spa town of **Caldas de Reis**, founded by the Romans. If you decide to forgo drinking the waters, which promise marriage within a year, at least take a walk through the charming *alameda* and botanical gardens. Farther along, 8km east of the centre of **A Estrada** (the largest rural municipality in Spain), you can visit the exterior of the most lavish country villa in all Galicia, the sumptuous 18th-century **Pazo da Oca** with its ancient trees, arcaded patio, pond and chapel.

Pazo da Oca
gardens open daily
9am–dusk; adm

Markets from Muros to Vilagarcía

Noia: Thurs.
Vilagarcía de Arousa: Tues and Sat.
Cambados: Thurs.

Where to Stay and Eat from Muros to Vilagarcía

Muros ✉ 15250
**Hs La Muradana, Avda Castelao 99, t 98 182 68 85, *www.hotelmuradana.com* (€). A good place to eat and sleep.
*Hs Ría de Muros, Rua Castelao 53, t 98 182 60 56 (€€). Good, charming owner and value for money. Popular with repeat guests, so call ahead.
*Convento Padres Franciscanos Muros, t 98 182 61 46 (€). The Franciscan brothers run an austere but atmospheric *hostal* (June–Sept).

Noia ✉ 15250
Pesquería del Tambre, Santa Maria de Roo (4km from Noia), t 98 105 16 20, *www.pesqueriadeltambre.com* (€€€). An unsual and charming rural hotel, in a cluster of Modernista buildings used a century ago to produce electricity. *Closed Jan–mid-Feb.*
**Hs Ceboleiro, Avda Galicia 15, t 98 182 44 97 (€€). Friendly, with a decent restaurant; meals at around €20–40.

Porto do Son ✉ 15250
*Hs Arnela II, Travesía 13 de Septiembre 4, t 98 176 73 44 (€). Modern and friendly, with baths in all rooms.

Padrón ✉ 15900
Casa Antiga do Monte, Boca do Monte, Lestrove, t 981 81 24 00, *www.susavilaocio.es* (€€€). An elegant stone hotel in charming grounds just

⭐ **La Casa Grande de Cornide** >

ⓘ **Cambados** >>
Praza do Concello,
t *98 652 07 86,*
www.concello-combados.com

ⓘ **Vilagarcía de Arousa** >
Avda Juan Carlos I, 37,
t *98 651 01 44*

ⓘ **O Grove** >>
Praza de O Corgo,
t *98 673 09 75,*
www.turismogrove.com

outside Padrón, with an 18th-century *hórreo* and stylishly decorated rooms. Also offers pool, gym and all kinds of outdoor activities.
La Casa Grande de Cornide, in Cornide, **t** 98 180 55 99, *www.casagrandede cornide.com* (€€€). A *pazo-hosteria* from the 18th century with suites, a library and a museum of Gallego painting.
***Escala, Pazos, **t** 98 181 13 12 (€€). The fanciest place in Padrón.
***Pensión Jardín, Salgado Araujo 3-1, **t** 98 181 09 50 (€). A sweet little stone house, with fussy but cosy rooms.
Hs Casa Cuco, Avda de Compostela 16, **t 98 181 05 11 (€). Of all the places to stay, this has the best name going; rooms with or without bath.
Casa Ramallo, C/ Castros in Rois, **t** 98 180 41 80 (€€). Don't miss this favourite restaurant of Spanish novelist and Nobel Prize-winner Camilo José Cela. Family-run and rustic. *Closed Mon.*
Chef Rivera, Enlace Parque 7, **t** 98 181 14 54 (€). The culinary star of Padrón, this is your chance to try José Rivera Casal's superb, seasonal dishes (if you're not squeamish, the lamprey *empanada* is exquisite) and a mix of traditional Gallego and international cuisine, meals at around €17. Also has 17 **rooms** (€€).

Vilagarcía de Arousa ✉ 15900
Prices here are over the odds.
****Pazo O Rial, O Rial 1, Ctra Vilagarcía-Cambados, **t** 98 650 70 11, *www.pazorial.com* (€€€). Set in a pine wood, this 17th-century *pazo* is sweet and quiet and near the sea, with a pool and satellite TV.
***Castelao, Arzobispo Lago 5, **t** 98 651 24 26, *www.hcastelao.com* (€€€). Comfortable doubles and apartments in the centre.
Hotel Playa Compostela, Av. Rosalía de Castro, 134, Carril–Vilagarcía, **t** 98 650 40 10, *www.galinor.es/playacompos tela/index-e.html* (€€€). This is a comfortable option along the Arousa estuary, with modern amenities like wi-fi, whirlpools and air-conditioning (not all rooms.) The second floor rooms have small verandas.
*Hs 82, Pza de la Constitución 13, **t** 98 650 62 22 (€). Small but more than

pleasant; and there are several others like it along the waterfront.
Loliña, Alameda 1 in Carril, **t** 98 650 12 81 (€€). The day's catch gets the home-cooked treatment here, served in a sun-baked courtyard. *Closed Sun eve, Mon and end Dec to 3rd week Jan.*

Cambados ✉ 36630
***Parador de Cambados, Paseo de Cervantes, **t** 98 654 22 50, *cambados@ parador.es* (€€€). Occupies an old country *pazo* (manor house) with a beautiful garden and a restaurant featuring seafood.
*Europa, Ourense 12, **t** 98 654 37 25 (€€). Simple, modern hotel with neat rooms with bath.
*El Duende, Ourense 10, **t** 98 654 30 75 (€). Offers a nice, cheaper alternative by the sea. With or without bath.
Pazos Feijoo, Rúa Curros Enríquez 1, **t** 98 654 29 10 (€). Spick'n'span *hostal* in the centre of town.
Maria José, Rúa San Gregorio 2, **t** 98 654 22 81 (€). Surrender to the tender loving culinary care of Maria José, who makes a mean *sopa de mariscos.*

Ribadumia ✉ 36980
Pazo Carrasqueira, in Sisán, **t** 98 671 00 32, *www.pazocarrasqueira.com* (€€€–€€). A lovely 18th-century manor, with nine comfortable rooms, and a pool and gardens.

O Grove/A Toxa ✉ 36980
*****Gran Hotel La Toja, Isla A Toxa, **t** 98 673 00 25, *www.granhotelhesperia-latoja.com* (€€€€). In summer, in a park setting, you can enjoy golf, tennis, a spa, and a heated pool, while rubbing shoulders with the likes of Julio Iglesias, all in a park setting.
****Louxo, **t** 90 246 46 45, *www.louxolatoja.com* (€€€€–€€€). For slightly less than at La Toja, you can bask here in almost as much luxury.
***Mar Atlántico, Pedras Negras San Vicente do Mar, **t** 98 673 80 61, *www.hotelmaratlantico.com* (€€€). On the other side of town; similarly well equipped, with tennis courts.
***Bosque Mar, Reboredo, **t** 98 673 10 55, *www.bosquemar.com* (€€€). In O Grove proper, a pleasant family place with a garden and a swimming pool.

La Lanzada, Praia de la Lanzada, t 98 674 32 32 (€€€). Has lovely views over the ocean from its breezy rooms. The **Nueva Lanzada** (€€€) nearby is more upmarket.

El Besugo, González Besada 102, t 98 673 02 11 (€€–€). On the road to A Toxa, offering simple, clean rooms with or without bath. *Closed Oct–April.*

Hs Isolino, Avda Castelao 30, t 98 673 02 36 (€). One of the best deals in town, offering good-value modern rooms at the heart of O Grove's night-time scene.

Beira Mar, Avda Beiramar 30, t 98 165 05 49 (€€€). Serves delicious oysters plucked straight from the *ría*, in elegantly modern surroundings with views of the port.

O Crisol, Rúa Hospitál 10, t 98 673 00 29 (€€€). A long-time favourite for its excellent seafood and fine service. *Closed Mon.*

Casa Pepe, Rúa Castelao 149, t 98 673 02 35 (€€). Slightly cheaper than O Crisol, though with a similar pedigree, again specializing in local seafood.

Posada del Mar, Rúa Castelao 202, t 98 673 01 06 (€€). Has fine views from its dining room and good seafood croquettes, now served by its third generation.

Caldas de Reis ✉ 36650

Acuña, Herrería 2, t 98 654 00 10 (€€–€). Attached to the spa, this hotel has a charming Modernista air, with *solanas* overhanging the river.

Sena, Juan Fuentes 99, t 98 654 05 96, *www.hotelsena.com* (€). A cheaper option just on the outskirts of the centre, with a decent restaurant.

Casa Baltar, Alhóndiga 9, t 98 654 00 41 (€). An attractive dining room with a lovely summer terrace serving surprisingly contemporary local cuisine.

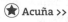 ⭐ **Acuña >>**

Ría de Pontevedra

Although nothing in the southern Rías Baixas is as tourist-orientated as the Ría de Arousa, the hotels of the Ría de Pontevedra fill up fast enough in the summer with vacationing Spaniards and Portuguese. The scenery is domesticated, green and pretty, while most of the beaches are safe even for the kids. Pontevedra, the provincial capital, is a handsome confection of granite, the best urban architecture in Galicia after Santiago itself.

The end of the Salnés peninsula, dividing the Arousa and Pontevedra estuaries, is occupied by the great sweep of the **Praia da Lanzada**, one of Galicia's finest beaches, the delight of wind-surfers and, in the old days, of family planners: hoping to get pregnant, women would flock to Lanzada and wade into the sea, lifting up their skirts and letting nine waves (one for each month of gestation) rush against them.

Nearby **Portonovo** and its neighbour **Sanxenxo** are jumping little resorts, with beaches like sugar and a Chamber of Commerce claim that they get more sun than the rest of Galicia; on summer evenings everyone for miles around descends on their clubs for a bop. Sanxenxo is also the departure point for ferries to the **Isla de Ons** (which, along with the Islas Cíes, the Isla Sálvora and the Isla Cortega forms part of the Parque Nacional de las Islas Atlánticas de Galicia), whose romantic gorse-covered hills and immaculate beaches suggest a lost Scilly Isle, stranded off Galicia. Aside from

Getting around the Ría de Pontevedra

In Pontevedra the RENFE **train station, t** 90 224 02 02, and **bus station, t** 98 685 24 08, are next to each other, but a long walk along Alféreces Provisionales; buses C1 and C2 can take you into town, except on Sundays. Frequent buses serve the main *ría* villages.

Up to eight **ferries** a day run from Portonovo and Sanxenxo to the Isla de Ons, from July to mid-September. Three boats make the longer journey out from Marin.

the gorgeous sand and crystalline water of **Praia de Melide**, the big attraction here is the **Buraco del Infierno**, a blowhole 16ft across and 130ft deep, through which the ocean explodes.

Continuing along the *ría*, pretty little **Combarro** has a famous view of its *hórreos* lined up along the shores of the *ría*. Roads from Sanxenxo or Combarro go up to the abandoned medieval **Monasterio de Armenteira**, where the Virgin favoured a monk named Ero: one morning, while listening to the song of a bird, he was granted a look into eternity. To him the ecstasy lasted but a few minutes, but upon returning to the monastery he found that centuries had passed (if the story sounds familiar *see* 'Leyre', in Navarra, p.102). The story is the subject of King Alfonso the Wise's *Cantiga CIII*, and of the carvings on the entrance to Armenteira. The rose window on the main façade of the church is believed to have been a mandala for meditation, the carved archivaults around the door are *mudéjar*, and the guardian will show you the unusual octagonal cupola inspired by Islamic architecture. Look for the peculiar masons' marks left on the walls.

Monasterio de Poio
www.mercedarios. com; although still home to a community of Mercedarian monks, it is open for visits April–Oct Mon–Sat 10–1.30 and 4.30–8, Sun 4.30–8; Nov–Mar Mon–Sat 10–1 and 4–6, Sun 4–6; adm; hostal open Easter–mid-Oct, t 98 677 00 00, hospederiamonasterio poio@terra.es

Just before Pontevedra, the **Monasterio de Poio** was founded in the 7th century by San Fructuoso, a member of the Visigothic royal family, who caused a sensation by walking across the water to the islet of Tambo to rescue a sinking boat. In the oldest part of the church is the tomb of yet another unorthodox Galician saint, Santa Trahamunda, whose body floated to Galicia in a stone boat from Córdoba; note her statue, clutching an Andalucían palm tree. The modern annexe is a *hostal* and the orchards contain an enormous 18th-century *hórreo* ever built – the monks say it's also the oldest.

Pontevedra

Pontevedra is nothing less than the perfect genteel granite Gallego town. Its streets are shaded with arcades, its squares marked with stone crosses. Ancient tradition states that it was first called Helenes, founded by Teucer (Teucro), who fought at Troy. *Teucro* means 'Trojan' in Castilian, and there is, in fact, a Teucro who fits the bill, a son of Scamander and a nephew of Priam, who is recorded as leading a band of Cretans to western Spain to found a colony. It's also significant that Teucro named the city after Helen, the sister of the twins Castor and Pollux, the favourite gods of Roman warriors. The cult of the warrior twins inspired the soldiers of the Reconquista in the apocryphal tradition that St James was the twin brother of Jesus. As if this weren't enough, Pontevedra (along with Mallorca, Barcelona and Corsica) also claims to be the birthplace of Columbus; there's a statue to him at the west end of the Alameda looking towards the ocean and the distant Americas.

Pontevedra's promising mythological progress was stymied back in the Middle Ages, when the Río Lérez silted up the port. By the time of Columbus, all the marine business had moved south to Vigo, leaving a compact, endearing and vibrant **Zona Monumental**, its showcases all within a stone's throw of the Praza da Peregrina. Here is the tall, twin-towered 18th-century **Virgen La Peregrina** church, built in the shape of a scallop, to house a statue of the city's patroness. It was one of the few instances where the Virgin had any role at all to play in the pilgrimages (Pontevedra lies on the *camino* from Portugal); in August her feast day is celebrated with folk dances and a procession of hundreds of revellers before a crowd so thick you can scarcely breathe.

Behind the Virgen La Peregrina, there's a lovely 16th-century fountain in a small garden and the 13th- and 14th-century church of **San Francisco** with some good tombs, while across the street arcaded **Praza da Ferrería** is a favourite hang-out for Pontevedrans. From here, Calle Pasantería descends to Pontevedra's most perfect little granite square, the **Praza da Leña**, with its granite porticoes and an ancient cross as its centrepiece. On one side two old houses have been joined to form the main body of the charming **Museo de Pontevedra**, which holds an excellent collection of jet figures from Santiago, Celtic goldwork, ancient headstones, paintings (by the likes of Zurbarán and Murillo) and works by the talented Gallego caricaturist Alfonso Castelao. The buildings are joined by an enchanting little stone courtyard, with trailing roses and ancient fountains. Almost next door, another section of the museum is housed in the Férnando López building, with a gallery of 19th-century painters, including works by Goya. The fourth section is the currently closed Sermiento, around the corner.

There are other pretty little squares tucked in the streets to the northwest, among them **Praza de Teucro** with its crystal galleries, named after the city's putative father. Just below, where Rúa Isabel II intersects with four other streets, there's a fine stone cross portraying Adam, Eve and the serpent – the numerous tapas bars in the vicinity are also tempting. Rúa Isabel II cuts across the Zona Monumental to the **Basílica de Santa María la Mayor**, constructed in the 16th century by the local Seafarers' Guild, with a Plateresque façade by Cornelis of Holland, with scenes of the Assumption and Death of the Virgin; two cannons still defend the church from incursions up the river. Inside there's a wooden Gothic *retablo* and some relief comic-strip-like carvings on the back wall. On the

Museo de Pontevedra
with three other locations around the town; open Tues–Sat summer 10–2.15 and 5–8.45, winter 10–1.30 and 4.30–8, closed Mon; adm; **Sermiento** *closed for restoration*

Convento de Santo Domingo
also part of the Museo de Pontevedra; open summer Tues–Sat 10–2.15 and 5–8.45; winter Tues–Sat 10–1.30 and 4.30–8, closed Mon

corner with Praza de España and the Alameda are the romantic, ivy-draped late 13th-century ruins of the **Convento de Santo Domingo**; the leafy Alameda and adjacent **Jardines de Vincenti** are favourite spots for the evening's *paseo*.

Out on a little promontory, a granite statue called the 'Emigrant's Wife', looking out forever across the *ría*, was put up by the people, for the people, honouring the earthy, independent, hardworking women who ran families and farms on their own for years.

Along the South Bank of the Ría de Pontevedra

If Pontevedra has a drawback it tends to be olfactory, a strong pong that wafts in when the wind's up from the massive paper mill to the south. Usually it doesn't hit you until you start down the *ría*, and usually it puts people off from exploring further; this coast, in spite of its garden charm and sandy coves, has scarcely any tourist facilities. Persevere. One of the chief curiosities is just past **Marín** and its naval academy, by the newish fishing hamlet and beach of **Mogor**: here are some of the most important **petroglyphs** in Spain, a labyrinth and spirals carved by the Celts. They inspired a local retiree to carve his own petroglyphs, some less than perfect spirals and symbols of God and Country.

Another 15km further south along the C550s you'll find **Bueu**, a sleepy fishing village with a couple or so *hostales*, a great base from which to explore the surrounding beaches (it's also one of the departure points for boats to the Isla de Ons). The sands continue 12km west, down towards the tip of the cape, **Hio**, site of Galicia's most elaborate stone crucifix, sculpted out of a single block of granite in the 19th century by José Cerviño of Pontevedra, with a Descent from the Cross and souls in Purgatory.

Tourist Information on the Ría de Pontevedra

(i) **Pontevedra >**
Gutiérrez Mellado s/n, t 98 685 08 14, www.concellopontevedra.es and www.riasbaixas.org

(i) **Sanxenxo >>**
Avda Generalisimo, t 98 672 02 85, www.sanxenxo.org

 Antigua Casa de Reis >>

As well as the **main tourist office**, Pontevedra's **tourist information booths** are located in the Alameda and the Jardines de Castro Sampedro. **Walking tours** (only in Spanish) are available during July, August and September.

Pontevedra's **post office** is on Hermanos Vázquez, down the road from the Capilla de la Peregrina.

Internet facilities are available at Santa Clara 2, just outside the *casco viejo*.

There is a **market** in Pontevedra in the Mercado by the river (*daily except Sunday*).

Where to Stay and Eat on the Ría de Pontevedra

Sanxenxo/Sangenjo ✉ 36000
There are scores of places to stay, but just try to get one in the summer without a reservation.

***Hotel Minso, Avda do Porto 1, t 98 672 01 50, *www.hotelminso.com* (€€€). Modern, central, and attractively renovated. *Closed Oct–Mar.*

***Rotilio, Arda del Puerto 7–9, t 98 672 02 00, *www.hotelrotilio.com* (€€€). Some of the best hotels are along Praia de Silgar, like this modern place (with superb seafood restaurant).

Antigua Casa de Reis, Reis 39, Padriñán (2km from Sanxenxo), t 98 669 05 50, *www.antiguacasadereis*.

com (€€€). A beautiful 19th-century stone house in lovely gardens, with rooms furnished with antiques, offering complete tranquillity. Wonderful breakfasts with home-made jam and a genuine welcome from the owners.

***Pazo el Revel, Revel 15, Villalonga (5km from Sanxenxo), t 98 674 30 00 (€€–€). An ivy-clad 18th-century *pazo*, with gardens, pool and restaurant.

*Hostal San Roque, Anebados 6, t 98 672 40 82 (€€–€). A good, central budget option – near the beach and the marina at Portonovo.

Pontevedra ✉ 36000

***Parador Casa do Barón, Barón 19, t 98 685 58 00, *pontevedra@parador. es* (€€€€–€€€). Sleep in an 11th-century Gallego *pazo* with a magnificent stone staircase and a garden.

***Virgen del Camino, Virgen del Camino, t 98 685 59 04, *www. hotelvirgendelcamino.com* (€€€). Modern, comfortable business hotel.

*Hotel Rúas, Sarmiento 37, t 98 684 64 16 (€€). Perfectly located in the Zona Monumental; has good rooms with bath, some with balconies overlooking the pretty Praza da Verdura.

*Comercio, Avda González Besada 3, t 98 685 12 17 (€€–€). Adequate and central; restaurant.

Pensión Casa Maruja, Avda Santa María 12, t 98 685 49 01 (€). Very, very basic and very, very cheap, but rooms have bath and TV.

Monasterio de Poio, 2km from Pontevedra, t 98 677 00 00 (€). The Mercedarian monks up here run a guesthouse (*see* p.346). *Closed mid-Oct–Easter.*

Casa Solla, Avenida Sineiro 7, San Salvador de Poio (2km out of town), t 98 687 28 84 (€€). One of the best and prettiest restaurants in Galicia; famous for its traditional recipes, freshest seafood and meat dishes and excellent service. *Closed Thurs and Sun eves, and all day Mon.*

Casa Filgueira, Praza da Lená 2, t 98 685 88 15 (€€). Eat and drink well at this charming restaurant and bar on the town's prettiest square. The award-winning wine selection is superb. *Closed Sun eve and Mon.*

Casa Román, Avda Augusto García Sánchez (south of the centre), t 98 684 35 60 (€€). Prides itself on select ingredients, especially shellfish. *Closed Sun eve and Mon (except Aug).*

Alameda de Doña Antonia, Soportales Herrería 4-1 (on the first floor), t 98 684 72 74 (€€). Has a well-deserved reputation for imaginative dishes – including duck breasts, baked honeyed lamb and seafood salads. *Closed Sun.*

Bar El Pitillo, Rúa Alta 3, t 98 687 23 22 (€). This popular spot is always full, and offers delicious simple meals cooked in garlic (try the heavenly *zamburiñas* (bay scallops), and mop up the sauce with fresh bread). Good local wines, too.

La Navarra, Princesa 13 (€). Evocative old *bodega* where locals help themselves to wine from the barrels, accompanied by thick slices of chorizo and cheese.

A Pegra Moura, Rúa San Nicolas. You can admire a small art exhibition with a tasty tapa in this modern new bar.

O Merlo, Santa María 4, t 98 684 43 43 (€). Great tapas. *Closed Mon.*

Ría de Vigo

The Ría de Vigo is the economic star of Galicia's estuaries: where all the others get narrower and shallower as they cut into land, the Ría de Vigo narrows at Rande (site of a huge suspension bridge), then widens again to form the sheltered inlet of San Simón, site of one of Europe's largest oyster beds. At the mouth of the estuary, the enchanting Cíes islets (part of the national park of Atlantic Islands, *see* p.345) protect the port from tempests off the Atlantic and enable mussel farmers to moor their wooden platforms or

Getting to and around the Ría de Vigo

By Air
Vigo's airport, t 98 626 82 00, *www.aena.es*, is 9km away, with flights to major Spanish cities and Lisbon.

By Bus and Train
There are plenty of buses, and several trains daily between Vigo and Pontevedra and beyond. A regular regional train plies between Vigo and A Coruña. The **train station** is at the top of Rúa Alfonso XIII, a 15min walk uphill from the port, t 90 224 02 02. **Buses** (to Tui, A Garda, Baiona, Pontevedra, O Grove, Vilagarcía, Santiago and A Coruña) depart frequently from the bus station near Praza de España, a few blocks from the train station; for information, t 98 637 34 11. Bus C4C links the centre with the bus station.

By Boat
On weekdays 6am–10pm and Sundays 9am–10.30pm, **ferries** (foot passengers only) sail every 30mins to Cangas, every hour to Moaña and up to 10 times daily from mid-June to mid-Sept to the Islas Cíes from Vigo's Estación Marítima near El Berbés (*port information t 98 622 52 72*). For the Cíes, buy your ticket early in the day so you can choose your return boat – the latest sailings fill up first. The islands are also accessible from Cangas and Baiona in summer.

bateas safely in the estuary, where the little molluscs incubate on long ropes suspended in the water. Vigo itself has grown to become the largest city in Galicia, with a population of 280,000.

The North Bank of the Ría and the Islas Cíes
From Hio (*see* p.348) the road crosses the dolmen-dotted promontory for the pleasant small resort of **Cangas**, stretching along the coast with a lively port in its centre and a pleasant beach at the end. In a pirate raid in the 17th century, nearly the entire male population was massacred, leaving the women, they say, to go mad, slowly; accused of witchcraft, they would meet on Areas Gordas beach on St John's Eve, and get into trouble; many ended up in the Inquisition's dungeons, including María Soliña, the subject of a famous Gallego nationalist song. Five kilometres east, **Moaña** is another if quieter resort in the Cangas mould, with an even better beach.

From Cangas, Vigo or Baiona the summer-only excursion to the two **Islas Cíes** (the third is off-limits as a bird sanctuary) is a delight. Linked by a lick of sand that forms a sheltered lagoon of calm crystal water, the islands offer a perfect lazy day out on the beach, with a couple of cafés and restaurants; or take a picnic and wander along the oceanside paths. As it is a national park, the only place to stay is a **campsite** with limited space; ring ahead to book, and buy a voucher in the booth at Vigo's port before getting your boat ticket.

Campsite
t 98 668 70 50 or t 98 643 83 58; open Easter week and summer only

Vigo
Nothing less than Spain's premier fishing port, bringing in more fish than anywhere in the world except Tokyo, Vigo occupies a privileged hillside spot that attracted both ancient Phoenician and Greek seamen. Its name comes from the Roman Vicus Spacorum,

but the city claims that its true founder was an early 12th-century troubadour, Martín Codax, who, as he describes in his most famous poem, liked to hang out with the boys where Vigo stands today and watch their lady-loves bathe in the estuary. The city's history is full of unwanted English visits: two by Sir Francis Drake (1585 and 1589) and in 1702, when the English surprised a joint Spanish and French treasure fleet just back from the New World, in the Battle of Rande. The English captured some of the ships but 11 were sunk or run aground near the tiny islets by the suspension bridge, the Puente de Rande; some sources say the silver had already been unloaded, but they haven't stopped treasure-seekers from looking.

Quiñones de León
www.museodevigo.com
; open Tues–Fri 10–8, Sat 5–8, Sun 10–1.30

Contemporary Art Museum
www.marcovigo.com; open Tues–Sat 11–9, Sun 11–3; adm

Museo da Mar de Galicia
open June–Sept Tues–Thurs 10–2 and 5–10, Fri–Sat 10–2 and 5–11.30, Sun 10–10; Oct–May Tues–Thurs 10–8, Fri–Sat 11am–11.30pm, Sun 10–9; adm

Zoo
open April–Oct daily 10–8.30; Nov–Feb daily 11–6.30; Mar daily 11–7.30; closed Mon in Mar and Nov; adm

For all that, there's not much to 'see' in Vigo beyond the fine views towards the sea, although the old part of town hugging the fishing port, the **Barrio del Berbés**, is thick with atmosphere and rough, cobbled streets. As in A Coruña, there's a lively fish auction by the waterside at the crack of dawn; if you've had a rough night you'll have no problem finding a dozen supremely fresh oysters on the half-shell from the fishwives along Rúa Teófilo Llorente or in the **Rúa da Pescadería** morning market. Look at the noblemen's palaces in López Puigcerver (**Calle Real**); from **Parque del Castro**, on top of the city, enjoy a great view of the *ría* from the modern monument to the Galeones de Rande.

The municipal museum **Quiñones de León** is in the 17th-century Pazo de Castrelos in the southwest of town, in the geometric gardens of the **Parque Quiñones de León**. The museum contains antique furniture and paintings by some of Galicia's most important artists, and funerary stelae from archaeological excavations around the city. Vigo also has a magnificent new **Contemporary Art Museum** on Rúa Príncipe. Overlooking the Ría at the Punta de Muíño, the sleek new **Museo da Mar de Galicia** offers an interesting glimpse into the region's maritime history. Vigo is home to Galicia's sole **zoo**, situated along the road to the airport.

South of Vigo to the Ría de Baiona

Vigo's main beaches, white **Praia de Canido** and **Praia Samil**, are just west and often crowded, but the main lure here is **Baiona** (Bayona), down the coast, one of Galicia's choice resorts, topped by the walls of the medieval **Castillo de Monterreal**. The grounds are occupied by a ravishing *parador*; fork out to tour the grounds and walls. The coast is embellished with little beaches of soft sand, namely **Ladeira**, **Santa María** and the magnificent crescent of **Praia América**. The latter was named after the fact that Baiona was the first place in Europe to learn that Columbus had discovered a New World, on 10 March 1493, when the little *Pinta* sailed into its port. A replica sits on a floating jetty in the harbour, complete with ship's cat, ropes of garlic, and dummy sailors.

Santa María
open Mon–Sat 9.30–
12.45 and 5.30–8.30,
Sun 9.30–1.30

The 13th-century church of **Santa María** is a good example of transitional architecture; more contemporary religious art is 1km south of town in the form of a huge granite sculpture of 1910, a sailors' *ex voto* to the **Virgen de la Roca**. Wild horses have a free rein in the hills here, rounded up once a year in a *rapa das Bestas*, or *curros*, when Gallego cowboys tame them, run a race or two, and let them go again. In **Oia**, 16km south along the pretty and wild coastline, there's a lonely 18th-century Baroque monastery, where the monks run a charming little *hostal*.

To the south, **A Guarda**, at the mouth of the Río Minho, may look more intriguing on the map than it does in reality, with its clutch of nouveaux-riches *americanos*' bungalows. However, a 40-minute walk (or shorter drive) up, in the excavated Celtic *castro* on **Monte Santa Tegra**, is one of Spain's most important *citanías*, or fortified hill settlements, inhabited from the 7th century BC up to the Roman period. It has over 100 houses, some reconstructed, others mere foundations, linked by cobbled lanes and encircled by walls.

From the top of Monte Santa Tegra there are fine views over the valley of the Minho into Portugal. Farther up there's a cromlech, or Neolithic stone circle, and at the very top a church with a small

Museum
open July–Sept
Tues–Sun 9.30–9;
Mar–June Tues–Sun
9.30–8; Oct–early Dec
Tues–Sun 10–7; adm

museum where you can find out about the strange carving discovered on the site, believed to be a map; if so, one of the oldest found in the West. The nearest beach is at **Camposancos**, 3km from A Guarda, overlooking the mouth of the wooded Río Minho, the frontier between Spain and Portugal.

Tui

⭐ Tui

From A Guarda the best thing to do is follow the course of the River Minho up to Tui (or Tuy, pronounced *twee*), a rare frontier town worth visiting in its own right. One of the seven ancient capitals of Galicia, Tui is picturesquely piled upon its acropolis; like Pontevedra, it claims to have been founded by wandering Greeks after the Trojan War. It was the capital of the Visigoth King Witiza in 700, and has seen many battles and border skirmishes with Portugal, defended by the walled city of Valença.

Tui's granite lanes and houses are crowned by the military profile of the **Catedral de Santa María** with its powerful walls and keep; until the 13th century it did double duty as Tui's castle. Construction began in 1120 but was not completed until much later; the stone has mellowed into a grey, vertical garden of wild flowers. There is a fine Romanesque porch and a portal from 1225, carved with the Adoration of the Magi by French-trained sculptors, one of the first and finest Gothic works in Galicia; be sure to note the lovely but strange coat of arms on the side wall, which has five stars and a crescent moon, said to symbolize the burning of the town by al-Mansur. The inside of the cathedral is also heavily fortified – against earthquakes – and contains the relics of San Telmo, also known as Pedro González of Astorga (confessor of King Saint Ferdinand of Castile), who also worked among the seafolk of Galicia in 1246. He is the patron saint of Spanish sailors, who confused his name with their first patron St Elmo (or Erasmus), who sends them his lucky fire to light upon their masts, igniting even their fingers without burning them. His tomb, accredited with miracles, oozes a vinegary gunk prized as a cure-all.

Among Tui's smaller churches are **Santo Domingo** (1415) – inside is a mix of Gothic and pre-Romanesque with finely carved effigies on the tombs and the stone pulpit – and the circular **San Telmo** (1803), the only example of Portuguese Baroque in Galicia.

In 30 minutes, you can walk from the centre of Tui to the lovely Portuguese walled town of **Valença do Minho**, crossing an iron bridge built by Gustave Eiffel. The views from Valença to Tui are lovely, as is Valença itself, blanketed in bright towels that Spaniards flock to buy. If it's hot, there are a couple of small river beaches.

Markets on the Ría de Vigo

Cangas: Fri.
Baiona: Mon.
Tui: Gallego/Portuguese market Thurs.

(i) **Cangas**
Paseo Castelao,
t 98 639 20 23

(i) **Vigo >**
Municipal: Rúa Teófilo
Llorente 5, t 98 622
47 57. www.turismo
devigo.org; also summer
booths in the city
centre; has a guide book
In English of walking
tours in the countryside

Regional: Rúa
Cánovas del Castillo (in
the port), t 98 643 05 76

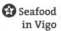 **Seafood in Vigo**

Where to Stay and Eat on the Ría de Vigo

Vigo ✉ 36200

Eating out is an excellent reason for staying in Vigo. To every kind of seafood and shellfish add the delicacies from the River Minho: salmon, lamprey and baby eels.

****Bahía de Vigo**, Canovas del Castillo 24, t 98 622 67 00 www.hotelbahiadevigo.com (€€€€€). A tall, modern block, with great views of the port and the *ría*; its restaurant, claimed to be the biggest *marisquería* in Spain, serves up colossal *parrilladas* of grilled seafood.

***Ensenada**, Alfonso XIII 7, t 98 644 74 40 (€€). Modern and in the centre with fine views across the bay.

Hs Puerta del Sol, Puerta del Sol 14, t 98 622 23 64, www.alojamientosvigo.com (€€). Stylish and charming, in a solid old stone building with glassed-in balconies in the upper floors. Also offers apartments.

Dinastía, Progreso 13, t 98 622 78 60, www.hotelspa.com (€). Excellent facilities: gym, Jacuzzi and TV.

*Hotel Águila**, C/ Victoria 6, t 98 643 13 98, www.hotelaguila.com (€). A change from Vigo's modern blocks, this pretty hotel is in an historic building by the Praza da Compostela.

Hs La Nueva Colegiata, Praza da Iglesia 2, t 98 622 09 52 (€). All rooms have bath, and double glazing to counter the wake-the-dead tolling of the bells across the *praza*.

El Mosquito, Pza da Pedra 4 (near the port), t 98 643 35 70 (€€€). For seafood or roast leg of lamb, the people's choice in Vigo is a classic place with a familiar atmosphere. *Closed Sun and 2nd fortnight in Aug.*

Síbaris, Avda Garcia Barbón 122, t 98 622 15 26 (€€€). Kudos for its first-rate land- and sea-cuisine in an upmarket, intimate setting. *Closed Sun.*

Timón Playa, Cánido 8, Corujo, t 98 649 08 15 (€€€). Perfectly prepared seafood, rice dishes and *empanadas* at this attractive beachfront restaurant, with views of the Cíes. *Closed Sun.*

El Castillo, Monte do Castro, t 98 642 11 11 (€€). Dine with a superb view; exquisitely grilled fish and meat. *Closed Sun eve and Mon.*

La Oca, Avda Purificación Saavedra 8, t 98 637 12 55 (€€). Award-winning

(i) **Tui ››**
*Edif. Área
Panorámica,
t 98 660 17 89*

(★) **Pazo da Touza ›**

cuisine at very reasonable prices, prepared with whatever's freshest at the Teis market nearby. *Book well ahead. Closed Mon eve, Tues eve, Sat eve and Sun eve and 3 wks Aug.*

Marisquería Bahía, Avda Cánovas Castillo, t 98 644 96 56, *www. marisqueriabahia.com* (€€–€). Another catch-of-the-day restaurant – but one of the best, with outside tables on seafood street and oysters hawked by fishermen's wives. *Closed Wed.*

Cocedero Bar La Piedra, Pescadería 3, t 98 643 12 04 (€). A classic in A Pedra, with stalls of oysters to eat on the street or on the terrace.

Baiona ✉ 36300

****Parador Conde de Gondomar, Monte Real, t 98 635 50 00, *baiona@ parador.es* (€€€€€–€€€€). Galicia's finest, housed in a modern reconstruction of a typical Galician *pazo* within the medieval walls of Monterreal, in a lovely park; it offers a pool, tennis, children's recreation area, and a short walk to the beach.

**Pazo de Mendoza, Elduayen 1, t 98 638 50 14, *www.pazodemendoza.es* (€€€). A tastefully restored 18th-century *casona*, with a restaurant (*expensive*) considered Baiona's finest, where the best Gallego traditions and ingredients are combined with the finest elements of *nouvelle* sensibility. The monumental *menú degustación* (€32) offers such delights as cuttlefish *brochette* in *Albariño tempura.*

Pazo da Touza, Rúa dos Pazos 119, Nigrán (8km from Baiona), t 98 636 69 89, *www.pazodatouza.com* (€€€). A beautiful 18th-century *pazo* set in orchards and gardens. Spacious rooms and wonderful breakfasts.

**Hs Tres Carabelas, Ventura Misa 61, t 98 635 54 41, *www.hoteltres carabelas.com* (€€). A fine old inn on a narrow cobbled lane right in the middle of town.

*Hs Mesón del Burgo, Barrio del Burgo, t 98 635 53 09 (€). One of a wide range of budget options, with sea views from most rooms.

Pedro Madruga, Ramón y Cajal 1, t 98 635 68 22 (€€€). Renowned as one of Baiona's finest *marisquerías*; its ample selection of (mostly live) crustaceous

goodies decorates an outside counter and provides pre-dinner entertainment for the crowds; *book in advance.*

O Moscón, Alférez Barreiro 2, t 98 635 50 08 (€€) One of the best around; known for its fine lobster (*bogavante*).

A Garda ✉ 01300

**Convento de San Benito, Pza de San Benito, t 98 661 11 66, *www.hotelsan benito.com* (€€). Set in a 16th-century monastery with a garden, antique-furnished rooms, and a collection of old *azulejos* in the cloister.

*Hs Martirrey, José Antonio 8, t 98 661 03 49 (€€). A harbourside *hostal* with rooms with or without bath.

*Pazo Santa Tecla, t 98 661 00 02 (€€–€). A delightful place near the top of Monte Tecla with views in every direction. *Open April–Sept.*

Marisquería Olga, Malteses 24, t 98 661 15 16 (€). Good fish soups and seafood wait at this friendly family-run *taberna. Closed Sun.*

Tui ✉ 36700

***Parador de Tui, Avda Portugal, t 98 660 03 00, *tui@parador.es* (€€€€). Overlooking the Minho, and located in a large reproduction of a typical Gallego *pazo* 1km below town, with a garden, tennis and pool; very refined.

Abadía do Pelouro Axeito, at Caldelas de Tui (12 km from Tui), t 98 662 90 24 (€€€). If you're looking for something special, this is a delightful rural hotel with rooms and apartments. With pool and bikes to rent.

*Hs San Telmo 91, Avda de la Concordia 88, t 98 660 30 11 (€). Basic cheapie, but all rooms have baths.

Hostal Cruceiro do Monte, Carretera de Baiona 23, t 98 660 09 53 (€). Simple and family-run, in a country setting; good home-cooked food.

O Novo Cabalo Furado, Pza do Concello, t 98 660 22 63 (€€). Good home cooking. *Closed Sun eve, Mon, Sun in summer, and 2nd 2 wks June.*

Jamonería, Pza do Concello, t 98 660 17 16 (€). Makes up for everyone else's marine obsession by serving *raciones* of ham and *queso de tetilla.*

Bodegón O Conde, Circus 9 (€). Tasty and inexpensive tapas.

Up the Minho to Ourense

Galicia's least known and only landlocked province is an introspective place, with more valleys, they say, than towns. The province is famous for wine (DO Valdeorras, DO Ribeiro, Verín and Monterrey), hot springs, and Julio Iglesias.

From Tui to Ribadavia

Both the train and road follow the wooded banks of the Minho, offering one more chance to cross into Portugal on the ferry from Salvaterra do Minho to the delightful walled city of Monção. To the east, past the first dam, the river becomes wider and more elegiac, around the start of the wine-growing region of Ribeiro. Ribeiro's charming 15th-century capital, **Ribadavia**, has the best-preserved Jewish *barrio* in Galicia; even after the expulsion of the Jews by the Catholic kings, many remained here, hidden with the help of the Christian population. Ribadavia has a beautiful **Praza Maior** and some interesting Romanesque churches: a tree grows out of the bell tower of the **Oliveira** church, **San Juan** has a 13th-century *cruceiro*, while the **Convento de Santo Domingo**, occasional residence of the kings of Galicia, has a fine Gothic church and a cloister. The **Museo Etnológico de Ribadavia** offers information on local wines and the ruined **Castillo de los Condes de Ribadavia** is an impressive pile of walls, gates, towers, and rock tombs.

Museo Etnológico de Ribadavia
open Tues–Sat 9.30–2.30 and 4–8, Sun 10–2; adm, except Sat pm and Sun

The Minho and its tributary, the Sil, are the 'holy rivers' of Galicia, their banks thick with churches and hermitages. South of Ribadavia, the village of **Celanova** is built around a vast **Praza Maior**, with a fountain in the middle (where you mustn't drink from the north spout, because of the risk of going mad) and a Cecil B. de Mille Baroque façade of 1681, pasted on the venerable Benedictine monastery of **San Salvador**. The church's Capilla Mayor holds a gargantuan *retablo* of 1697 and the choir is a masterpiece of Gothic carving. Although the monastery itself is occupied by a school, you can pick up the key to see the elegant Renaissance cloister, a Baroque cloister, and the garden at the back, the setting for the diminutive (25ft by 10ft) chapel of **San Miguel**, a Mozarabic jewel with a roof that looks like a Chinese hat.

An even older church is further south on the OU540 near **Bande**: the rural Visigothic chapel of **Santa Comba**, overlooking the reservoir of Limia. Built with a Byzantine plan around the year 700, Santa Comba is remarkably well preserved with its borrowed late Corinthian marble columns supporting a horseshoe arch. The rest of the decoration is quite sober, but there are traces of frescoes, including a man in the moon. A few kilometres further south around **Lobios** are monuments that predate Santa Comba; mono-lithic Roman *miliarios*, or milestones, standing from the days when this was the main Roman route between Astorga and the newly conquered territory of Gallaecia. The best can be found way up in the hills on the Portuguese frontier, south of **Torneiros**. The surrounding glacial valleys and granitic peaks are home to wolves and wild boar, and enjoy protection as a natural park.

East of Celanova (and south of Ourense just off the A52 motorway), the medieval town of **Allariz** is a monument in itself and site of two more Romanesque churches: **Santiago** with an unusual round apse and **San Esteban**, on the way to the ruins of the castle. The **Convento de Santa Clara** was founded in 1282 by Violante, the wife of Alfonso X, who is buried in the huge Baroque cloister. Between Allariz and Ourense, the ruined 12th-century **Santa Mariña das Aguas Santas** (a 15min walk from the village; bring a flashlight) has steps down to its crypt – actually a corridor dolmen.

Ourense (Orense)

Continuing up the Río Minho, Ourense greets visitors with a graceful **Ponte Romano**, its seven ogival arches striding over 100ft above the Minho. The footbridge was built by the Romans and rebuilt on the ancient piers in the 13th century. It's now been upstaged by a vast, modern bridge, built for the millennium.

Traffic is Ourense's day-in, day-out nightmare, funnelled down the discouraging main street, Rúa do Progreso, cut through the city in the 19th century. Equally discouraging *urbanizaciones* housing Ourense's 100,000 souls take up most of the rest of the space.

If you can find a place to park, or don't mind walking a mile in from the bus or train stations, you can see what first attracted the Romans: the steaming hot springs, *Aquae Urentes*, known by the Visigoths and Suevi as Warm Sea (hence *Ourense*). The main source, **As Burgas**, still steams out of the neoclassical fountain midway down Rúa do Progreso. The locals have invented many a use for the hot water – put a dead chicken in it, they say, and you can pluck it in two minutes. During 1386–7, when Ourense was John of Gaunt's capital when he tried to claim the throne of Castile, many Englishmen here had the first hot baths of their lives.

Up from here, the arcaded **Praza Maior** and its charming little annexe, **Praza de la Magdalena**, is Ourense's historic core and hub of its social life. The old episcopal palace in Praza Maior houses the

Museo Arqueológico Provincial
closed for renovation – call t 98 822 38 84

Museo Arqueológico Provincial, with a collection of finds spanning from the Neolithic era to the Bronze Age, as well as *retablos* and other bits of art salvaged from the province's numerous churches.

In the Praza Maior, the **cathedral** was begun in the 12th century and is entered through the Pórtico del Paraíso, a 13th-century (and rather naïve) brightly painted reproduction of Santiago's great Pórtico de la Gloria. The high altar contains the reliquary of

Getting to and around Ourense

Ourense is the main hub here, with **trains** to Santiago, Lugo, A Coruña, Vigo, Ribadavia, León and elsewhere. RENFE's Estación Empalme is across the river, t 90 224 02 02; tickets are also on sale at Rúa do Pasco 15, t 98 821 46 04. The **bus station** is 1km from the centre on the Vigo road, t 98 821 60 27, with frequent services to Vigo and all major points in Galicia.

Museo Catedraliceo
open July–Aug Mon–Sat 10–1 and 4–7; Sept–June Mon–Sat 12–1 and 4–7; adm

St Martin of Tours, while the florid Baroque chapel by Francisco Castro Canseco houses Ourense's oddest attraction, the Santísimo Cristo who, like the Christ of Burgos, has real hair and a beard and a wood and fabric body; according to legend it was made by Nicodemus and floated ashore near Finisterre. The **Museo Catedraliceo**, off the 12th-century cloister, has one of the first books printed in Galicia and the 'Treasure of San Rosendo' – rare 10th-century chesspieces carved from rock crystal.

Around Ourense

Oseira
guided visits only, April–Sept Mon–Sat 10, 11, 12, 3.30, 4.30, 5.30, 6.30, Sun 12.30, 3.30, 4.30, 5.30, 6.30; Oct–Mar same times except last visit 5.30; adm, guided visits only

From Ourense, take the N525 north to the turn-off to Cobas, and continue beyond to the monumental Cistercian monastery of **Oseira**, where Graham Greene spent time with his heretical thoughts on Catholicism and wrote *Monsignor Quixote* (1982). He came to the right spot; founded in 1137 by four hermits, Oseira was famous for monks who dabbled in alchemy and magic cures. The monastery façade has a gigantic Churrigueresque doorway and the odd crest of two bones with the tree of knowledge. The massive church dates from the 12th century, and has seven chapels around its altar, with the Virgen de la Leche, supposedly an alchemist's idol, in the main one. Don't miss the curious faces carved in the Claustro de los Medallones.

The most majestic scenery in these parts begins just east of Ourense, heading up the Minho along the N120, where the cliffs over the river rise ever steeper. At **San Esteban**, dominated by its Romanesque **Monasterio de Ribas de Sil**, the Sil flows into the Minho, and along the latter are wild gorges to walk along.

The nearly-as-dramatic OU536 east of Ourense goes up to **Esgos**, where a small by-road leads to the ruined monastery and church of **San Pedro de Rocas**, founded in 573 by followers of Prisciliano (*see* p.313), its three apses excavated in the rock. Abandoned in the Muslim invasion, the spot was rediscovered in the 10th century.

Manzaneda
www.manzaneda.com

The road continues to rise up higher and higher to **Puebla de Trives** (**Pobra de Trives**), where there's a ski resort, **Manzaneda**. If you're heading southeast from Ourense towards Bragança or Zamora, consider stopping in the old walled town of **Verín**, capital of the wine-growing Monterrey valley; high on one side of the valley looms the **Castle of Monterrey**, built in the 16th century, part of it converted into a *parador*. Try a bottle of Verín red – as long as you aren't driving; this Galician wine can pack 14 per cent alcohol.

Markets around Ourense

Ourense: 7th and 17th of month.
Allariz: 1st and 15th of month.
Ribadavia: 10th and 25th of month.
Verín: Wed and Fri.

Where to Stay and Eat around Ourense

ⓘ **Ribadavia** ›
Praza Maior 7,
t 98 847 12 75,
www.ribadavia.com

Ribadavia ✉ 32000

****Mosteiro de San Clodio**, Praza Eladio Rodríguez 1, Leiro (10km from Ribadavia) t 98 848 56 01, *www. eurostarshotels.com* (€€€). A beautiful, luxurious hotel in a lovingly restored 16th-century monastery; four-poster beds, gardens, pool and restaurant.

Hotel Rural Doña Blanca, San Clodio, Leiro (10km from Ribadavia) t 98 848 56 88, *www.hotelruraldonablanca.com* (€€€). A stylish fusion of old and new characterize this chic rural hotel in Leiro, with an outdoor pool for summer and tiny spa for winter.

***Pazo de Esposende**, t 98 849 18 91, *www.pazodeesposende.com* (€€€). This early 16th-century manor house with 10 doubles has been restored with simple elegance to cater for modern comforts including disabled facilities. Wine cellar stacked with local wines.

***Hs Oasis**, Ctra N 120, t 98 847 16 13 (€). Modern place a couple of km out of town, with pleasant rooms, views and a no-frills but perfectly acceptable budget restaurant.

***Hs Evencio**, Avda R. Valcárcel 30, t 98 847 10 45 (€). Has a swimming pool and garden to delight its guests.

Lobios ✉ 32868

****Lobios Caldaria**, Rio Caldo s/n, t 98 801 00 50, *www.caldaria.es* (€€€). Modern spa hotel, with all kinds of treatments and good amenities.

***Lusitano**, Ctra Concejal 312 (Mayeta Portela), lusitanohotel@terra.es, t 98 844 80 28 (€). This is the only other hotel in this area; all rooms with bath and breakfast included.

Ourense ✉ 32000

Ourense has plenty of business hotels but nothing with much charm.

ⓘ **Verín** ››
Casa del Escudo, t 98 841 16 14, www.verin.net

ⓘ **Ourense** ›
Municipal: Burgas 12, Bajo, t 98 836 60 64, www.ourense.es
Regional: Ponte Romana, t 98 837 20 20, www.turismourense.com

****Gran Hotel San Martín**, Curros Enríquez 1, t 98 837 18 11, *www.gh-hotels.com* (€€€€). Modern, business-orientated hotel with large, air-conditioned rooms in the centre.

****Eurostars Auriense**, El Cumial t 98 823 49 00, *www.hotel-auriense.com* (€€€). Another modern business hotel a few minutes from the centre, with pool, tennis and disco.

***Hotel Princess**, Avda de la Habana 4, t 98 826 95 38, *www.ga-hotels.com* (€€€). Central hotel off main square.

Martín Fierro (Casa Ovidio), Sáenz Díez 17, t 98 837 20 26, *www. restaurantemartinfierro.com* (€€). Choose one of three dining rooms and tuck in to the surf or turf delicacies from the grill, or try the tasty pilgrims' menu. *Closed Sun.*

San Miguel, San Miguel 12, t 98 822 12 45, *www.restaurante-sanmiguel.com* (€€). One of Ourense's best restaurants, specializing in seafood fresh from the coast, accompanied by Galicia's finest wines, served in the traditional *taza. Closed Tues.*

Pena Vixía, Hernán Cortés 29, t 98 824 69 69 (€€–€). A traditional *tasca*, which has been renovated and offers delicious gourmet tapas and *raciones*.

Puebla de Trives/Pobra de Trives ✉ 32600

***Casa Grande de Trives**, Marqués de Trives, t 98 833 20 66 (€€). Set in a lovely 18th-century building with seven rooms plus private chapel.

***Pazo Paradela**, Ctra de Barrio Km.2, t 98 833 07 14 (€€). Another, equally charming *pazo*, in a rural setting.

***As Maceiras**, Manzaneda (ski resort), t 98 833 00 34, *www. asmaceiras.net* (€€). Offers pool, sauna, gym, horse-riding. *Book.*

Verín ✉ 32600

***Parador de Verín**, 4km outside Verín, t 98 841 00 75, verin@parador.es (€€€). Part of the 16th-century Castle of Monterrey has been converted into this *parador*, with lovely views across the valley; its restaurant offers seafood and Gallego dishes.

***Dos Hermanas**, Avda de Sousas 106, t 98 841 02 80 (€). Literally a lower-range option, from where you can look up at the castle.

Language

Castellano, as Spanish is properly called, was the first modern language to have a grammar written for it. Among other European languages, Spanish is closest to Portuguese and Italian – and of course, Catalan and Gallego. Spanish, however, may have the simplest grammar of any Romance language, and if you know a little of any one of these, you will find much of the vocabulary looks familiar. It's quite easy to pick up a working knowledge of Spanish; but Spaniards speak colloquially and fast, sometimes leaving out half the consonants, so that expressing yourself may prove a little easier than understanding the replies. Spaniards will appreciate your efforts, though. Note that the Spaniards increasingly use the familiar *tú* instead of *usted* when addressing complete strangers.

For food and drink vocabulary, *see* pp.55–6.

Pronunciation

Pronunciation is phonetic but somewhat difficult for English speakers.

Vowels and Diphthongs

a short *a* as in 'pat'
e short *e* as in 'set'
i as *e* in 'be'
o between long *o* of 'note' and short *o* of 'hot'
u silent after *q* and in gue- and gui-; otherwise long *u* as in 'flute'
ü *w* sound, as in 'dwell'
y at end of word or meaning *and*, as i
ai, ay as *i* in 'side'
au as *ou* in 'sound'
ei, ey as *ey* in 'they'
oi, oy as *oy* in 'boy'

Consonants

c before the vowels *i* and *e*, it's a *castellano* tradition to pronounce it as *th*; many Spaniards and all Latin Americans pronounce it in this case as an *s*

ch like *ch* in 'church'
d often becomes *th*, or is almost silent, at end of word
g before *i* or *e*, pronounced as *j* (see below)
h silent
j the *ch* in 'loch' – a guttural, throat-clearing *h*
ll *y* or *ly* as in 'million'
ñ *ny* as in 'canyon' (the ~ is called a tilde)
q *k*
r usually rolled, which takes practice
v often pronounced as *b*
z *th*, but *s* in parts of Andalucía

Stress

If the word ends in a vowel, an *n* or an *s*, the stress falls on the penultimate syllable, otherwise it falls on the last syllable; exceptions to the rule are marked with an accent.

Useful Words and Phrases

yes/no *sí/no*
I don't know *No sé*
I don't understand Spanish *No entiendo español*
Do you speak English? *¿Habla usted inglés?*
Speak slowly *Hable despacio*
Can you help me? *¿Puede usted ayudarme?*
please *por favor*
thank you (very much) *(muchas) gracias*
you're welcome *de nada*
It doesn't matter *No importa/Es igual*
all right/OK *está bien/vale*
excuse me *perdóneme*
nothing *nada*
How do you do? *¿Cómo está usted?*
 or more familiarly *¿Cómo estás?, ¿Qué tal?*
Well, and you? *¿Bien, y usted?*
 or more familiarly *¿Bien, y tú?*
Hello *¡Hola!*
Goodbye *Adiós*
Good morning *Buenos días*
Good afternoon *Buenas tardes*
Good evening *Buenas noches*

What ...? *¿Qué ...?*
Who ...? *¿Quién ...?*
Where ...? *¿Dónde ...?*
When ...? *¿Cuándo ...?*
Why ...? *¿Por qué ...?*
How ...? *¿Cómo ...?*
How many? *¿Cuántos/Cuántas?*
I am sorry *Lo siento*
I am ill *No me siento bien*
Leave me alone *Déjeme en paz*
big *grande*
small *pequeño/pequeña*
hot *caliente*
cold *frío/fría*
toilet/toilets *servicios/aseos*
men *señores/hombres/caballeros*
women *señoras/damas*
exit *salida*
entrance *entrada*

Time and Days

What time is it? *¿Qué hora es?*
It is two o'clock *Son las dos*
... half past two *... las dos y media*
... a quarter past two *... las dos y cuarto*
... a quarter to three *... las tres menos cuarto*
noon/midnight *mediodía/medianoche*
month/week/day *mes/semana/día*
morning/afternoon *mañana/tarde*
evening *noche*
today/yesterday/tomorrow
  hoy/ayer/mañana
it is early/it is late *es temprano/es tarde*
Monday/Tuesday *lunes/martes*
Wednesday/Thursday *miércoles/jueves*
Friday/ Saturday *viernes/sábado*
Sunday *domingo*

Shopping and Sightseeing

What is that? *¿Qué es eso?*
I would like ... *Quisiera ... /Me gustaría ...*
Where is/are ...? *¿Dónde está/están ...?*
How much? *¿Cuánto/Cuánta?*
open/closed *abierto/cerrado*
cheap/expensive *barato/caro*
shop *tienda*
market *mercado*
tobacconist's *estanco*
beach *playa*
church *iglesia*
police station/policeman *comisaría/policía*

telephone *teléfono*
booking/box office *taquilla*
post office/stamp *correos/sello*
bank/money *banco/dinero*
Do you have any change? *¿Tiene cambio?*

Accommodation

Where is the hotel? *¿Dónde está el hotel?*
Do you have a room? *¿Tiene usted una
  habitación?*
Can I look at the room? *¿Podría ver la
  habitación?*
How much is the room per day/week?
  *¿Cuánto cuesta la habitación por día/
  semana?*
... with two beds *con dos camas*
... with double bed *con una cama grande*
... with a shower/bath *con ducha/baño*
... for one person/two people *para una
  persona/dos personas*
... for one night/ one week *una noche/
  una semana*

Transport and Tickets

bus/coach/train *autobús/autocar/tren*
bus/railway station *estación de autobuses/
  de ferrocarril*
bus stop *parada*
platform *andén*
ticket *billete*
I want to go to... *Deseo ir a.../Quiero ir a...*
Where is...? *¿Dónde está...?*
Do you stop at... ? *¿Para en... ?*
I want a (return/round-trip) ticket to...
  Quiero un billete (de ida y vuelta) a...
How much is the fare? *¿Cuánto cuesta el
  billete?*
rent *alquiler*
car/bicycle *coche/ bicicleta*
petrol (gasoline) *gasolina*
garage *garaje*
no parking *estacionamento prohibido*
give way/yield *ceda el paso*
here/there *aquí/allí*
close/far *cerca/lejos*
left/right *izquierda/derecha*
straight on *todo recto*
north (n./adj.) *norte/septentrional*
south (n./adj.) *sur/meridional*
east (n./adj.) *este/oriental*
west (n./adj.) *oeste/occidental*

Glossary

ajimez in Moorish architecture, an arched double window

alameda park or promenade

ayuntamiento city/town hall

azulejo painted glazed tiles, popular in Moorish and *mudéjar* work and later architecture

baldachin canopy on posts over an altar or throne

barrio city quarter or neighbourhood

bodega winery

Calvario Calvary, or outdoor Stations of the Cross

Castizo anything purely Spanish (from the Castilian point of view)

castrum Roman military camp

Churrigueresque florid Baroque style of the late 17th and early 18th centuries in the style of José Churriguera (1650–1725)

converso Jew who converted to Christianity

coro walled-in choir in the centre of a Spanish cathedral

corregidor royal magistrate

Cortes Spanish parliament

dolmen Neolithic funerary monument shaped like a table

DO *Denominación de Origen*, the Spanish equivalent of AOC for wine credentials

encierro running of the bulls

estación train station (RENFE)

Euskal Herria the Basque country

Euskera the Basque language

exte Basque house

frontón pelota court

fueros the exemptions or privileges of a region under medieval Spanish law

gaztelulaks earthen hilltop forts

hidalgo literally 'son of somebody' – the lowest level of the nobility, just good enough for a coat of arms

iglesia church

(torre del) homenaje the tallest tower of a fortification, sometimes detached from the wall (homage tower)

hórreo Asturian or Galician granary or corn crib

Isabelline Gothic late 15th-century style, roughly corresponding to the English Perpendicular

judería Jewish quarter

mercado market

mirador a scenic view point or belvedere

Modernista Art Nouveau

Morisco Muslims who submitted to Christianization to remain in Spain after the Reconquista

Mozarabic referring to Christians under Muslim rule in Moorish Spain

mudéjar Moorish-influenced architecture; Spain's 'National style' in the 12th to the 16th centuries

ogival pointed (arches)

oppidum pre-Roman town

país region or village

pallazo circular, conical-roofed shepherd's hut in Asturias and Galicia

pazo Galician manor house

Plateresque 16th-century style; heavily ornamented Gothic

playa beach

plaza de toros bullring

pronunciamiento military coup

reja iron grilles, either decorative ones in churches or those covering the exterior windows of buildings

retablo carved or painted altarpiece, often consisting of a number of scenes or sculptural ensembles

trinquete indoor *pelota* court

Transitional in northern Spanish churches, referring to the transition between Romanesque and Gothic

Further Reading

Atxaga, Bernardo, *Obabakoak* (Pantheon, 1993). Collection of stories by the best-known living Basque author.

Borrow, George, *The Bible in Spain* (various editions, first written in 1843). A jolly travel account by a preposterous Protestant Bible salesman in 19th-century Spain.

Brenan, Gerald, *Spanish Labyrinth* (Cambridge, 1943). Origins of the Civil War. *The Literature of the Spanish People* (Cambridge, 1976).

Carr, Raymond (editor), *Spain: A History* (OUP, 2000). Probably the best concise history of Spain available.

Casas, Penelope, *The Foods and Wines of Spain* (Penguin). The best Spanish cookbook in English, with great regional recipes.

Castro, Américo, *The Structure of Spanish History* (E. L. King, 1954). A remarkable interpretation of Spain's history, published in exile during the Franco years.

Collins, Roger, *The Basques* (Blackwell,1990). A good general introduction to the Basques.

Elliot, J. H., *Imperial Spain 1469–1714* (Pelican, 1983). Elegant proof that much of the best writing these days is in the field of history.

Ford, Richard, *Gatherings from Spain* (Everyman). A boiled-down version of the all-time classic travel-book *A Handbook for Travellers in Spain,* written in 1845. Hard to find but worth the trouble.

Hamilton, R. and Janet Perry, translators, *The Poem of the Cid* (Penguin).

Hemingway, Ernest, *The Sun Also Rises,* (*Fiesta* in the UK) (Arrow) and *Death in the Afternoon* (various editions). The former put Pamplona on the map, the latter is on bull-fighting.

Hooper, John, *The New Spaniards* (Penguin, 1995). A comprehensive and enjoyable account of modern Spanish life and politics.

Kurlansky, Mark, *The Basque History of the World* (Penguin Books, 2001). Wonderful, wide-ranging and *simpático* account of the Basques; history, cuisine and much more.

Lee, Laurie, *As I Walked Out One Midsummer Morning* and *A Rose for Winter.* Very well-written adventures of a young man in Spain in 1936, walking from Vigo to Málaga and his return 20 years later.

Lojendio, Louis, *Navarre Romaine* (Zodiaque, 1967). One of the excellent illustrated volumes in the French Zodiaque series on medieval art; other pertinent volumes for northern Spain are *Le Pré-Romaine Hispanique* (on the Visigoths and Asturian churches) and *Le Mozarabe.*

MacLaine, Shirley, *The Camino* (Simon & Schuster, 2000). The Hollywood star's spiritual memoir of her own pilgrimage to Santiago de Compostela.

Mitchell, David, *The Spanish Civil War* (Granada, 1982). Wonderful photographs.

Morris, Jan, *Spain* (Penguin, 1982). A little disappointing considering the author; careless generalizations and dubious ideas sustained by crystalline prose.

Mullins, Edwin, *The Pilgrimage to Santiago* (Secker & Warburg/Taplinger). Colourful and wide-ranging account of the journey.

Reilly, Bernard F., *The Medieval Spains* (Cambridge University Press, 1993). Dry but painstakingly detailed account of the origins of Spain.

Richardson, Paul, *Our Lady of the Sewers* (Abacus, 1999). An engaging collection of stories about almost forgotten corners and customs of Spain, including a description of Lekeitio's gruesome goose rodeo.

Thomas, Hugh, *The Spanish Civil War* (Penguin, 2003). The best general work.

Index

Cudillero
Santillana del Mar
Pontevedra
Vigo

Galicia 363

Islas Cíes

Main page references are in **bold**. Page references to maps are in *italics*.

About the Updater

Ali Qassim is of British birth but moved to Madrid, Spain when he was three months old. He first ventured to northern Spain in the mid-1990s to write for Canadian daily newspaper *The Globe and Mail* to write on topics ranging from Basque separatism to fishing disputes between Galicia and Canada. Even in those considerably greyer, pre-Guggenheim days, Bilbao distinguished itself for its *pinxtos* – perhaps the best in the country – although San Sebastian might argue otherwise.

Updater's acknowledgments: Ali would like to thank Josu Lauzirika for introducing him to the *pintxo* culture in Bilbao and to the warmth and hospitality of his family and friends; and thanks also to his parents for driving him to San Sebastian as a child and for their great enthusiasm for the Picos de Europa when they drove to the north all they way from the Alicante coast, many years later.

6th edition published 2008

Cadogan Guides is an imprint of
New Holland Publishers (UK) Ltd
London • Cape Town • Sydney • Auckland

New Holland Publishers (UK) Ltd	80 McKenzie Street	Unit 1, 66 Gibbes Street	218 Lake Road
Garfield House	Cape Town 8001	Chatswood, NSW 2067	Northcote
86–88 Edgware Road	South Africa	Australia	Auckland
London W2 2EA			New Zealand

cadogan@nhpub.co.uk
www.cadoganguides.com
t 44 (0)20 7724 7773

Distributed in the United States by Globe Pequot, Connecticut

Copyright © Dana Facaros and Michael Pauls 1996, 1999. 2001, 2003, 2006, 2008
© 2008 New Holland Publishers (UK) Ltd

Cover photographs: © O. Alamany/CORBIS and E. Vicens/CORBIS
Photo essay photographs © OLIVIA
Maps © Cadogan Guides, drawn by Maidenhead Cartographic Services Ltd
Cover and photo essay design: Sarah Gardner
Editor: Linda McQueen
Proofreading: Elspeth Anderson
Indexing: Isobel McLean

Printed in Italy by Legoprint
A catalogue record for this book is available from the British Library

ISBN: 978-1-86011-395-6

The author and publishers have made every effort to ensure the accuracy of the information in this book at the time of going to press. However, they cannot accept any responsibility for any loss, injury or inconvenience resulting from the use of information contained in this guide.

Please help us to keep this guide up to date. We have done our best to ensure that the information in this guide is correct at the time of going to press. But laws and regulations are constantly changing, and standards and prices fluctuate. We would be delighted to receive any comments. Authors of the best letters will receive a copy of the Cadogan Guide of their choice.

Northern Spain
touring atlas

Ria de Santa
Marta de
Ortigueira
Punta de la
Estaca de Bares
Porto de Bares
Porto do
Barqueiro
Ria del Barqueiro
Ria de Viveiro
Porto de Barqueiro
Isla Coelleira
Vicedo
Faro
Covas
Porto de Celeiro
Viveiro
Sargadelos
Burela
Grañas
Merille
Playa de Llas
Playa de Rapadoira
San Martin
Mondoñedo
Playa del Castro
Foz
Figueras
Tapia de
Casariego
Costa Verde
Playa de Bozo
Capo Vidio
Ribadeo
Castropol
Ortiguera
Navia
Luarca
Coana

Rio Masma
Mondoñedo
Boal
Rio Navia
Rio Negro

N634
Taramundi
Bárcena del
Monasterio
Navelgas
Salas
Villalba
Sierra de Meira
Grandas
de Salime
Berducedo
Obona
Tineo
Pola de Allande
Llamas del Mouro
Belmonte
de Miranda
ASTURIAS

N640
C630
Cangas
del Narcea

Santa Eulalia
de Bóveda
LUGO
Puerto del
Connio
Moal
Bosque de
Muniellos
C
a
n
t
á
b
r
i
c
a
Pola de
Somiedo

N540
A6
Becerrea
Cervantes
Balouta
Peranzanes
Villablino
Los
Bayos
Portomarin
Sarria
Triacastela
Samos
Doiras
Pedrafita
do Cebreiro
Cebreiro
Balboa
Burbia
Ancares
Leoneses
San Martin
de Moreda
Vega de
Espinareda
Valle de
Finolledo
Toreno
Sierra de Ancares
Rio Burbia
Rio Ancares
Rio León
Embalse
de Belesar
C630
L
e
ó
n

C
o
r
d
i
l
l
e
r
a
Villafranca
del Bierzo
Cacabelos
Corullón
Carracedo
Monforte
de Lemos
Sober
Monasterio
de Ribas de Sil
Esgos
A Rúa
O Barco
Rio Sil
Carucedo
Orellan
Las Médulas
San Estebán
Ponferrada
Montes
Acebo
Manjarin
Peñalba de
Santiago
Foncebadón
Rabanal del
Camino
Castrillo
de los
Polvazares
M
o
n
t
e
s
d
e
L
e
ó
n
Puebla de Trives
Manzaneda
El Teleno
A6
N120
Monterrei
Verin

2

4

Bay of Biscay

Costa Vasca

SAN SEBASTIÁN/
DONOSTIA

Monte Igueldo
Zarautz

Régil
Tolosa

Guipúzcoa

Beasain

Betelu

Sierra de Aralar
NA755
Santuario de
San Migel de Aralar

Altsasu

Baquedano

Zudaire

Estella

Monasterio
de Irache

Basílica de
San Gregorio

Los Arcos

Lodosa

Arnedo

Préjano

LA RIOJA

Cornago

Cervera del
Río Alhama

Inestrillas

Aguilar del
Río Alhama

NAVARRA

Fuenterrabia
Pasajes   Irún
Oiartzun   San Marcial
Bera

Lesaka   Etxalar

Parque Natural
Señorío de
Bertiz

Cabo
Higuer

Zugarramurdi   Urdazubi

Arizkun   Puerto
de Izpegui

Elizondo

Ituren
Zubieta

Leitza

Azpiroz

Huarte Arakil

N240

Lekunberri

Valcarlos

Orzanzurieta
Puerto   Roncesvalles
Ibañeta   Burguete   Orbaitzeta
Auritzberri   Sierra de Abodi
Ochagavia

Orhi

Pic d'Anie

PAMPLONA/
IRUÑA

Noam

N111

Puente la Reina
Cirauqui

Obanos

Santa Maria
de Eunate

Artajona

Tafalla

Olite

Ujué

Uroz
Artaiz

Agoitz

Lumbier

N240

Hoz de
Arbayún

Sierra de

Leyre

Yesa

Sangüesa   Javier

Navascues

Monasterio
de Leyre

Embalse de Yesa

Vidángoz

Valle de Salazar

Valle del Roncal

Isaba

Roncal

Burgui

Calahorra

A68

Rio Ebro

N232

Rio Cidacos

Alfaro

Corella

Cintruénigo
Fitero

Tudela

Cascante

Bárdenas

Reales

Rio Aragón

A68

Rio Ega

A15

N121

NA134

FRANCE

Pyrenees

N

20 km
10 miles
Pilgrims' Route